Hypnosis and Meditation

Hypnosis and Meditation

Towards an Integrative Science of Conscious Planes

Edited by

Amir Raz and Michael Lifshitz

OXFORD
UNIVERSITY PRESS

Great Clarendon Street, Oxford, OX2 6DP,
United Kingdom

Oxford University Press is a department of the University of Oxford.
It furthers the University's objective of excellence in research, scholarship,
and education by publishing worldwide. Oxford is a registered trade mark of
Oxford University Press in the UK and in certain other countries

© Oxford University Press 2016

Published in the United States of America by Oxford University Press
198 Madison Avenue, New York, NY 10016, United States of America

British Library Cataloguing in Publication Data

Data available

Library of Congress Control Number: 2015946404

ISBN 978–0–19–875910–2

Printed and bound by
CPI Group (UK) Ltd, Croydon, CR0 4YY

"I dedicate this book to all the special Stoomakrim in my nuclear as well as larger family — from young to old. Sharing is *stoomaker*ing."
-Amir Raz

"To all my guides, visible and invisible."
-Michael Lifshitz

Foreword

Janet Gyatso

Harvard Divinity School

This book excites me. It definitely makes me want to explore the interface of neurophysiology and meditation further, if not enter into its research myself. Each of these fields, already so rich and important on their own terms, shed new light on each other. I come at this volume as a historian of Buddhism but, even more so, I come at it as a mortal and imperfect human being, vitally interested in the potentials of meditative mindfulness and hypnosis for enhancing well-being. The comparison pursued in this book, between hypnosis and meditation, is particularly rich given the striking similarities—but also differences—between the two. Their study together has intriguing implications in medical, psychological, social, ethical, educational, and even business realms.

Both hypnosis and meditation have everything to do with suggestion. Both deploy repetitive techniques that mobilize one-pointed, immersive attention. Both suggest that mental exercises shaped by scientific, ethical, and historical knowledge can actually change our life, our capacities, our health. Both also raise foundational questions about the relation between mind and body, between subject and object, and between self and other. Both know the problems—on empirical and theoretical registers alike—when such pairs are polarized and bifurcated, and offer ways to bridge them.

Neuroscience contributes to our understanding of the history of these practices as well as their current-day use. It isolates empirically discernable operations of the brain, and also makes fine distinctions between cognitive and metacognitive processes, including executive monitoring, control, and overall orientation. These alert us not only to which elements of the brain's operation are triggered when we are hypnotized or meditating, but also how we might feel, and enhance, their specific effects. Analytical categories of mental function are also plentiful in Buddhist Abhidharma literature, where basic features of mind like intentionality, attention, discursive thought, agency, habituation, association, resolve, memory, conscientiousness, and so on are discussed at length for their role in meditative absorption. Buddhist meditation tradition provides a wide array of objects on which to focus, from the ubiquitous breath practice, which serves to bridge the autonomic and somatic nervous systems, to an array of intricate visualizations, such as one's own body as a decomposing corpse in order to evoke non-attachment, or scenarios involving our loved ones and enemies that evoke our compassion. In each case, we find detailed reflection on how particular objects of focus differently enable kinds of concentration. The potential contribution of such nuance to our understanding of hypnotic absorption is worthy of investigation.

Buddhist traditions also provide an array of ritual procedures that both precede and conclude any session of focused concentration. Once again, the repetitive practices in hypnotic induction would be ripe areas for comparison and further study. In Buddhist practice, rituals function to frame the main meditation in moral terms; they also ride on the repetitive patterns of intonation and movement to set in motion the attention-building exercises of the practice itself. Buddhist analyses insist on the integration of a moral frame into any concentration practice. They detail how the frame impacts the actual state of focused immersion, a point which I believe is crucial to appreciate if neuroscience is to really understand the full human experience, and potential use, of such states. While the scientific observation of the brain states helps clarify what they are physiologically, the Buddhist history of analysis shows in some detail how larger framing factors ineluctably impact the subjective quality and content of any induced state, whether meditative or hypnotic.

Buddhist lists of mental states and their concomitant factors are in service of a larger project to attain full moral perfection and liberation from suffering. While neuroscience and psychology demur before such lofty goals and are more interested in quotidian well-being, there is still a lot to learn from Buddhist phenomenologies of practice. One issue connected to the relation between the formal aspects of attentive concentration and the moral values these states induce is the long debate in Buddhist history on the distinction between "sudden" breakthroughs and the "gradual" sets of practices and prescriptive values that build the conditions for their occurrence. You find this issue everywhere, from discussions on the relationship between focused meditation (*śamatha*) and insight (*vipaśanā*), or again, between mindfulness (*smṛti*) and intelligence (*prajñā*), to the antinomian claims in Ch'an/Soen/Zen, Mahāmudrā, and Dzogchen that all one has to do is to do it, and everything else will fall into place. Yet virtually no Buddhist teacher or writer has been able to separate the moral frame from the practice entirely, and virtually all counsel the cultivation of both.

In the end, the high bar has always been the spontaneous appropriation of moral virtues as facilitated by intense habituated concentration, such that it becomes effortless, like the moment when learning to ride a bicycle suddenly clicks and one rides off on one's own. Thus, the main difference between all those traditions of meditation has really been about how to balance the two sides, which comes first, and how each feed the other. In fact, the question of where the fulcrum should be poised is still being worked through and shifted in modern, increasingly hybrid meditation circles around the world today.

The relation between the technicalities of immersive practice and the meanings we ascribe to it has large implications quite beyond either neuroscience or Buddhist soteriology. How do our internal voices, our expectations, and our imbibed values shape our experience? How hard is it to change them? Should we try to function without them altogether, as is sometimes suggested by practices that would simply build the muscle to focus, become immersed in simplicity and purity, and simply drop all expectations and distractions? Another question concerns the overarching watcher within subjective experience. When is that higher vantage beneficial and when might it be an obstacle, or even pathological? Is it actually possible to be immersed in something without having second-order awareness at all? Or is it best to try to merge the two, to be spontaneously mindful and focused on the one hand, and ethically aware and brilliantly open and creative on the other hand? And what about the value of spontaneity itself? Is "first thought" always "best thought"? Should our most immediate response be trusted and protected, or do alien forces inhabit even our first reactions? If we can de-automatize negative spontaneous states and reactions, can we also re-automatize good ones? The latter would seem to be germane to the study of hypnosis and its use in psychotherapy today.

All Buddhist traditions of meditation, be they schools that privilege the rhetoric of sudden spontaneity or not, have paid close attention to the social and psychological factors around concentration practice, both to enhance it and to weave it through with cultural value. In this, I have in mind not only the cultural conceptions of meditation, the motivations to enter onto such a path, and the resulting prestige that comes with being good at it. I am also thinking about the extended theoretical reflections on the way such factors in fact infiltrate the very nature of meditative experience. One has to do with the importance of the teacher–student relationship, whereby the student cultivates attitudes of respect and veneration that, in turn, affect their entire perspective on their own imminent immersion in mindfulness practice. Another side of that is how the teacher's care for one inculcates the critical confidence in one's own ability to practice mindfulness successfully.

A closely related idea would be the foundational matter of transmission and lineage as such. An elevated meditative experience or realization is seen, in its very nature, to participate in the enlightenment of the Buddha—or his surrogate, one's personal teacher—by virtue of a fundamental inter-subjectivity that is fundamentally auspicious and communicative. This adds to the texture of transference in that it mobilizes further transmission to others, such that a realization one has received through the teacher–student dynamic can only be authentic and real if there is someone else, another student, to receive it—and then pass it on again. Could it be that the relationship of the hypnotist with their patient also has intricately calibrated impact on the subject of hypnosis?

The present volume takes important steps towards articulating the many domains of neurological and psychological factors around focused hypnotic absorption. The promise I see for future, and even deeper, interdisciplinary collaboration between historians of Buddhist practice and scientists lies in the potential for collective recourse to the early texts. By that I mean not only the analytical ones like the Abhidharma enumerations of mental factors, but also, and especially, the personal ones like autobiographies and diaries by meditative retreatants. These exist in large numbers and are a key resource for a future phenomenology of the lived experience of the meditator. In the wake of the publication of volumes like the present one, the questions that scholars of meditation ask of those records will have to be reframed in light of the scientific intervention. That is a welcome development.

Foreword

Irving Kirsch

Harvard Medical School

I first met Amir Raz in 2000, when he travelled from New York to the University of Connecticut in Storrs to consult with me about a study he was planning. He proposed to use hypnotic suggestion to block the Stroop effect, an effect that is widely believed to be automatic and beyond voluntary control. I told him I did not think it would work, and he countered that he had pilot data suggesting it would. He was right, and the result was the seminal paper on the topic (Raz, Shapiro, Fan, & Posner, 2002). I then opined that he could obtain the same effect via suggestion without inducing hypnosis, and we collaborated on a replication in which we tested the effect of inducing hypnosis prior to giving the suggestion (Raz, Kirsch, Pollard, & Nitkin-Kaner, 2006). I turned out to be right about that one (phew!). Since then, I have followed Amir's work closely and with continued admiration. So it is with great pleasure that I accept the invitation from him and his very talented and productive graduate student, Michael Lifshitz, to write a foreword to this book on hypnosis and meditation.

Are hypnosis and meditation the same thing, similar but distinct, or entirely different? To answer that question, one has to separate the two fundamental components of hypnosis—the induction of a hypothesized trance state, and the administration of suggestions for altered experience and behavior. Close to a century of scientific research reveals that these two components of hypnosis are only loosely related. The induction of an altered state is not a prerequisite for subjective or behavioral responses to hypnotic suggestions. Indeed, it adds relatively little to the effects of suggestions (Braffman & Kirsch, 1999; Raz et al., 2006). So, let us look a little closer at each of these two components of hypnosis and consider how they might relate to meditation.

There are many kinds of suggestion. There is, for example, the kind of suggestion that occurs when people are given placebos (i.e., sham treatments with no physically active ingredients). There is the suggestion that something in the past happened differently than it actually did, often referred to as the misinformation effect. Also, there is the suggestion that a person intentionally do something, as when a waiter suggests that a customer try the fish that day. However, none of these are hypnotic suggestions. A hypnotic suggestion is a request to experience a clearly counterfactual state of affairs. The hypnotist might suggest that an arm has become heavy, as if weighted down by a pile of books; that an arm has become light, as if hoisted into the air by helium balloons attached to the wrist; that a hand has become numb and insensitive to pain, as if injected with novocaine; or that a black and white pattern will be seen as fully colored. The subject knows that there is no pile of books, that there are no balloons, that the hand has not been injected with anything, and that the pattern is in black and white, but nevertheless experiences heaviness, lightness, insensitivity to painful stimuli, and color in the black and white pattern. Furthermore, neuroimaging studies verify the reported changes in experience and that it can occur without the induction of hypnosis (e.g., McGeown et al., 2012).

So, the first question we can ask is whether meditation is related to hypnotic suggestion. I am not an expert in meditation, but I suspect that the answer is no. I have tried various forms of meditation but was never, during the process, given the kind of counterfactual suggestions that are characteristic of hypnosis.

The next question is whether there is a relationship between the hypnotic state (often referred to as "trance") and the meditative state. Are meditators in a trance? For that matter, are hypnotized subjects in a trance? Also, what is a trance anyway?

One key to understanding what the so-called hypnotic trance might be is a consideration of the diversity of procedures that have been used to induce it. Hypnosis has been induced by asking people to relax, to sleep, or to stay alert and wide awake. Although relaxation-based inductions are most common, relaxation is sometimes actively inhibited by having subjects vigorously peddle an exercise bicycle during the induction. Hypnosis (and its predecessor, mesmerism) has been induced by applying pressure to the forehead; by sounding gongs; by flashing lights; by having subjects touch magnetized rods, drink magnetized water, or stand under a magnetized tree. By and large, these various inductions seem to have the same, relatively small effect on responses to subsequent suggestions. The only common factor to these inductions is the subject's belief that it can produce the intended state. Furthermore, the nature of the state has varied substantially as a function of subjects' beliefs. Inductions used to produce convulsions in susceptible subjects, later to be replaced by the state of relaxation that is characteristically observed when hypnosis is induced (except, of course, when the induction is of the active, alert type). Whatever the hypnotic state is, it is clearly a product of suggestion.

Just as there are many types of hypnotic induction, so too there are a wide variety of meditation instructions and practices. Establishing the experiential and neurophysiological commonalities and differences between hypnotic inductions and mindfulness may require consideration of the type of hypnotic induction (e.g., relaxation versus active alert) and type of meditation, as well as the inclusion of control procedures (e.g., relaxation training). This volume provides a beginning toward that quest.

References

Braffman, W., & Kirsch, I. (1999). Imaginative suggestibility and hypnotizability: an empirical analysis. *Journal of Personality and Social Psychology*, **77**(3), 578–587.

McGeown, W. J., Venneri, A., Kirsch, I., Nocetti, L., Roberts, K., Foan, L., & Mazzoni, G. (2012). Suggested visual hallucination without hypnosis enhances activity in visual areas of the brain. *Consciousness and Cognition*, **21**, 100–116. doi: 10.1016/j.concog.2011.10.015

Raz, A., Kirsch, I., Pollard, J., & Nitkin-Kaner, Y. (2006). Suggestion reduces the Stroop effect. *Psychological Science*, **17**, 91–95.

Raz, A., Shapiro, T., Fan, J., & Posner, M. I. (2002). Hypnotic suggestion and the modulation of Stroop interference. *Archives of General Psychiatry*, **59**(12), 1155–1161.

Contents

Contributors

Jessica Baltman
Department of Psychology,
Binghamton University,
USA

Daniel Brown
Harvard Medical School, USA;
The Center for Integrative Psychotherapy,
USA

Etzel Cardeña
Department of Psychology,
Lund University, Sweden

Kalina Christoff
Department of Psychology,
University of British Columbia,
Canada

Michael H. Connors
Department of Cognitive Science,
Macquarie University,
Australia;
School of Psychiatry,
University of New South Wales,
Australia

Erin Courtice
Department of Psychology,
University of Ottawa,
Ottawa, Ontario, Canada

Quinton Deeley
Institute of Psychiatry,
King's College London,
UK

Zoltan Dienes
Sackler Centre for Consciousness Science,
University of Sussex,
UK

Victor Elinoff
Regional Clinical Research Inc.,
Binghamton,
USA

Norman A. S. Farb
Department of Psychology,
University of Toronto,
Canada

Leonardo Ferraro
Department of Cognitive Science,
University of Toronto,
Canada

Kieran C. R. Fox
Department of Psychology,
University of British Columbia,
Canada

Joshua A. Grant
Department of Social Neuroscience,
Max Planck Institute for Human Cognitive
and Brain Sciences,
Germany

Joseph P. Green
Department of Psychology,
Ohio State University at Lima,
USA

Anne Harrington
Department of History of Science,
Harvard University,
USA

Graham A. Jamieson
School of Behavioural, Cognitive,
and Social Sciences,
University of New England,
Australia

Thupten Jinpa
Department of Religious Studies,
McGill Institute of Tibetan Classics,
Canada

Yoona Kang
Annenberg School for Communication,
University of Pennsylvania,
USA

Michael Lifshitz
Integrated Program in Neuroscience,
McGill University,
Canada

Peter Lush
Sackler Centre for Consciousness Science,
University of Sussex,
UK

Steven Jay Lynn
Department of Psychology,
Binghamton University,
USA

Jelena Markovic
Department of Philosophy,
University of British Columbia,
Canada

William Jonathan McGeown
School of Psychological Sciences and Health,
University of Strathclyde, UK

Reed Maxwell
Department of Psychology,
Binghamton University,
USA

Benjamin W. Mooneyham
Department of Psychological
and Brain Sciences,
University of California, Santa Barbara,
USA

Peter Naish
Sackler Centre for Consciousness Science,
University of Sussex, UK

Ulrich Ott
Bender Institute of Neuroimaging,
Justus Liebig University Giessen,
Germany

Jim Parkinson
Sackler Centre for Consciousness Science,
University of Sussex, UK

Vince Polito
Department of Psychology and ARC Centre
of Excellence in Cognition and its Disorders,
Macquarie University,
Australia

Michael I. Posner
Department of Psychology,
University of Oregon,
USA

Amir Raz
Department of Psychiatry,
McGill University,
Canada;
Lady Davis Institute for Medical Research,
Canada

Ryan Scott
Sackler Centre for Consciousness Science,
University of Sussex, UK

Jonathan W. Schooler
Department of Psychological
and Brain Sciences,
University of California, Santa Barbara,
USA

Rebecca Semmens-Wheeler
Sackler Centre for Consciousness Science,
University of Sussex,
UK

David Spiegel
Department of Psychiatry and Behavioral
Sciences,
School of Medicine,
Stanford University,
USA

Yi-Yuan Tang
Department of Experimental Psychology,
Texas Tech University,
USA

Charles T. Tart
Department of Psychology,
University of California,
Davis CA,
and
Institute for Transpersonal Psychology,
Palo Alto CA,
USA

Evan Thompson
Department of Philosophy,
University of British Columbia,
Canada

Jason M. Thompson
University of California, San Francisco,
USA

Kálmán Tisza
Eötvös Loránd University,
Hungary

Tony Toneatto
Department of Psychiatry,
University of Toronto,
Canada

Samuel Veissière
Culture, Mind, and Brain Program,
Departments of Psychiatry and Anthropology,
McGill University,
Canada
Communication Studies,
Faculty of Humanities,
University of Johannesburg

John Vervaeke
Psychology Department and the Cognitive
Science Program at the University of Toronto,
Canada

Lynn C. Waelde
Pacific Graduate School of Psychology, Palo
Alto University, USA;
Department of Psychiatry
and Behavioral Sciences,
Stanford University School of Medicine,
USA

Michael D. Yapko
Clinical psychologist in private practice,
USA

Fadel Zeidan
Department of Neurobiology and Anatomy,
Wake Forest School of Medicine,
USA

Part 1

Introduction

Chapter 1

Contemplative experience in context
Hypnosis, meditation, and the transformation of consciousness

Michael Lifshitz

Abstract

This opening chapter introduces the theme of the book and discusses the potential value of bridging empirical studies of hypnosis and meditation. It offers a review of the different sections of the volume and synthesizes the overarching themes. Whereas numerous studies have documented the beneficial impact of hypnosis and meditation, few have harnessed these unique phenomena together, either clinically or as a means of illuminating cognitive questions. Yet, while historically and pragmatically distinct, hypnosis and meditation share much in the way of phenomenology, neurocognitive mechanisms, and potential therapeutic prospects. The marriage of these seemingly disparate yet overlapping contemplative practices promises to improve our scientific understanding of each, as well as unravel the underlying mechanisms. This chapter explores how crosstalk between the domains of hypnosis and meditation fosters novel approaches to self-regulation, binds subjective experience to brain science, and advances the empirical study of consciousness and cognition.

Introduction

The first time I sat down to meditate I was living in my parents' basement on the cusp of high school graduation. I had stumbled on an online meditation manual written by a respected Buddhist monk and was keen to try the simple instructions for myself. I crossed my legs on the floor and closed my eyes, resting my attention on the cool breeze passing in and out of my nose. Far from an experience of single-pointed concentration, it took just about two minutes before I grew restless and opened my eyes to keep reading. Yet, I knew I would be returning to this practice. During those two minutes, something shifted in my rapport with my own experience. A new relational space opened in my mind—a personal laboratory for exploring the movements of attention and consciousness from the inside out.

Three years later, I attended an undergraduate course on the varieties of attention taught by none other than Amir Raz, now my dear mentor and co-editor of this volume. A firm believer in the pedagogical value of direct experience, Amir devoted an entire lecture to a recording of the classic Harvard Group Scale of Hypnotic Susceptibility (Shor & Orne, 1962). As I focused on the drone of the recorded voice, my eyelids began to feel heavy and my attention drifted freely with the suggestions. When the voice proposed that my arm become a rigid metal bar and asked me to try to move it, my arm trembled but would not budge. Paradoxically, I felt as if I could have moved my arm if I had really needed to, and yet somehow it would not move. I experienced for the first time the peculiar sensation of my agency split in two—a phenomenon frequently addressed in the empirical literature on hypnotic dissociation (Woody & Sadler, 2008). As an avid meditator committed to examining the nuances of my experiential world, I was intrigued at how quickly and profoundly a few words of suggestion could alter this fundamental feature of my subjectivity.

Whereas most scholars and practitioners of hypnosis or meditation typically isolate their study to one technique or the other, my own empirical work and first-hand experiences have persistently shuttled me to the borders between these contemplative practices. Thus, the research path that began almost a decade ago in my parents' basement has led me to a sunny library, drafting the introduction to an academic volume bridging the realms of hypnosis and meditation. I am fortunate, through the graces of colleagues, teachers, and friends, to walk a path that merges my passion for exploring consciousness with an approach grounded in rigorous scholarship and empirical research. The vision for this book was shaped as much by late-night conversations on the front porch of the Mind and Life Summer Research Institute and practical workshops at the Society for Clinical and Experimental Hypnosis as by ongoing neuroimaging experiments and exploration of the scholarly literature. As a highly suggestible individual with a longstanding meditative practice, compiling the chapters in this volume has shifted how I approach my own daily investigation into the patterns of my experience. I hope it will do the same for you.

The evolving science of contemplative practice

Human beings have mobilized attention and suggestion to shape the stream of consciousness for millennia (Cardeña & Winkelman, 2011). In recent years, the evolving tools of cognitive research and clinical science have helped to illuminate the power of contemplative experience and highlight the remarkable flexibility of the human mind (Oakley & Halligan, 2013; Schmidt & Walach, 2014). While neuroscientists once viewed the brain as a static organ, recent empirical findings demonstrate that lived experience, from the thoughts we think to the cultures we live in, leave lasting imprints on our biology (May, 2011). Hypnosis and meditation offer powerful tools for observing and orchestrating the continuous remoulding of our bodies, brains, and minds (Lutz, Slagter, Dunne, & Davidson, 2008; Raz, 2011).

Research over the past decade has helped to demystify hypnosis and meditation, bringing these practices into the light of the scientific and clinical mainstream (Lifshitz & Raz, 2012). Contemplative experience has emerged from under a shroud of misconceptions at the fringes of academia to find a place on the front pages of our most hallowed scientific journals and popular news outlets. In only the last two years since we began work on this volume, mindfulness has featured as a cover story for *Time* magazine (Pickert, 2014) and a special issue of *American Psychologist* (Anderson, 2015), while both hypnosis and meditation have showcased separately as review articles in the prestigious scientific journal, *Nature Neuroscience* (Oakley & Halligan, 2013; Tang, Hölzel, & Posner, 2015). Publication counts in both fields continue to rise, with hundreds of new scientific papers appearing each year. Hospitals, schools, and corporations increasingly offer contemplative training to patients, students, and employees alike (Alderman, 2011; Bunting, 2014; Schumpeter, 2013). It would appear that Western culture as a whole—from scientists and clinicians to schoolteachers and chief executive officers—has opened its arms wide to the power of the contemplative mind.

Research and discussion surrounding hypnosis and meditation have often brought along a worrisome propensity toward oversimplifications and exaggerated claims. While we have come a long way from the colonial orientalism and animal magnetism of yore (Harrington, 2007), the situation today reflects many of the same old trappings. In the rapidly expanding field of mindfulness research, critical communities have begun to address concerns centering on the appropriation and dissemination of contemplative practices (North, 2014). Such critical voices, working from both within and outside the research community, highlight the potential risks of oversimplifying concepts, biasing research with a priori assumptions concerning efficacy, and appropriating practices and terminology from foreign traditions, most notably Buddhism (Farb, 2014; Kirmayer, 2015; Purser & Loy, 2013). The concerns are manifold. For example, how do we operationalize and examine complex culturally embedded practices without unfairly reducing them or overlooking crucial elements in the process? Given the current mindfulness vogue, how can researchers protect their findings from over-blown interpretation in both scientific and popular circles? In our excitement to apply mindfulness in secular settings from the hospital to the boardroom, are we watering down or mishandling teachings and practices from age-old traditions?

Bridging the domains of hypnosis and meditation

An integrative approach—addressing a gamut of related practices through a range of complementary scholarly and applied disciplines—can help to refine discussions, nuance terminology, bolster methodology, and highlight shades of meaning (Stehr & Weingart, 2000). Hypnosis and meditation overlap on many levels; however, few scholars have explored their complementary rapprochement (cf. Davidson & Goleman, 1977; Grant & Rainville, 2005; Halsband, Mueller, Hinterberger, & Strickner, 2009; Holroyd, 2003; Lynn, Das, Hallquist, & Williams, 2006; Spiegel, White, & Waelde, 2010; Otani, 2003; Yapko, 2011). Despite cultural and historical differences, hypnosis and meditation share common phenomenology, cognitive processes, and potential therapeutic merits (see Chapter 8 by Waelde, Thompson, & Spiegel). Yet, experts today typically study such practices separately, while hardly addressing points of intersection. This volume thus provides a synthesis of scholarly knowledge concerning the bridging of hypnosis and meditation.

Amir Raz and I have invited a diverse group of leading scientists, scholars, and practitioners to unravel the conceptual riches at the interface of hypnosis and meditation. In drawing together this distinguished group, we intend to shed light on consciousness research, including elements of attention, self-regulation, culture, neuroplasticity, and the relationship between brain and mind. At the heart of our vision lies a transdisciplinary approach bringing social, historical, and philosophical perspectives into dialog with contemporary advances in cognitive, neurobiological, and clinical science. In this chapter, I describe our vision for this present collection and discuss how the specific parts fit into a larger integrative approach to the science of self-regulation.

Definitions and divergences in fluctuating contexts

Hypnosis and meditation are blurry categories with diverging narratives. Rather than neatly delineating separate silos, these labels encompass a range of techniques and rituals emanating from diverse cultures, geographies, and worldviews (Johnson, 1982; Pintar & Lynn, 2008). Part 2 of this volume explores these nuances from a historical, anthropological, and philosophical perspective. The forms of meditation most popular today derive from millennia-old soteriological traditions of the Indian subcontinent and only recently gained prominence among clinical and research settings (Lutz, Dunne, & Davidson, 2007). Indeed, the science of meditation is still in its infancy. Only a few scattered accounts appeared in the empirical literature on meditation before the surge of research over the past decade (Harrington, 2007). Conversely, hypnosis as we understand it today emerged as a clinical tool in Western Europe and occupied a central position in prominent psychological and medical laboratories up until the second half of the twentieth century (Green, Laurence, & Lynn, 2014). Thus, the hypnosis literature provides a rich and largely untapped treasury of laboratory methods, empirical findings, and tractable theories probing the influence of attention and suggestion on consciousness and behavior (for an excellent overview of the empirical domain of hypnosis, see Kihlstrom, 2008).

While often overlooked, shifting contexts have tangible ramifications for the application and scientific understanding of contemplative practices. Hypnosis researchers have amassed a wealth of findings revealing how social variables such as culture, expectation, and motivation interact with cognitive styles and attention dynamics to co-create conscious experience (Benham, Woody, Wilson, & Nash, 2006; Lifshitz, Howells, & Raz, 2012; Lynn & Green, 2011). For example, hypnosis typically involves an induction procedure wherein the hypnotic guide encourages the participant to let go of everyday concerns and focus on responding to ensuing suggestions (Cardeña, 2014a). While researchers disagree as to the importance of the length and specific contents of the induction, merely labeling an intervention "hypnosis" appears to enhance reported depth and strengthen the influence of subsequent suggestions (Gandhi & Oakley, 2005). In short, the culture and context of hypnosis matters (Cardeña & Krippner, 2010; Kirmayer, 1992). Similarly, Buddhist traditions have long emphasized the importance of philosophical view and motivational framework in shaping the outcomes of meditative training. Right view and right intention constitute the first and second steps along the classic eightfold path toward enlightenment shared by all Buddhist traditions (Bodhi, 2011). Moreover, Mahayana Buddhists, including Zen and Tibetan practitioners, typically begin and end meditation sessions by formally affirming their intention through chant or prayer (Leighton, 2012).

Practitioners of meditation may dedicate thousands of hours to deepening and refining their motivation before ever crossing their legs to follow their breath (Zopa, 2012). While such attitudinal parameters have received comparatively little attention in mindfulness research (cf. Farb, 2012), at least two recent studies indicate that motivation and effort play an important role in fostering the cognitive improvement typically attributed to mindfulness training (Cardeña, Sjöstedt, & Marcusson-Clavertz, 2014; Jensen, Vangkilde, Frokjaer, & Hasselbalch, 2012). Such personal-level attitudes, moreover, reflect the larger and strikingly diverse sociocultural contexts through which we collectively enact contemplative experience. For example, cognitive anthropologist Samuel Veissière (see Chapter 5) presents an exploration of an online community of "tulpamancers" who adapt Tibetan Buddhist visualization practices to conjure imaginary sentient companions. Drawing on extensive Internet ethnography, he argues that joint attention and social interphenomenality shape our most private bodily experiences and sense of narrative self, both within and beyond contemplative contexts. Whenever we engage with meditative or hypnotic practices—whether to unravel cognitive processes, treat chronic pain, awaken wisdom and compassion, or invoke imaginary friends—we simultaneously engage with a historical milieu, a context of tradition, a framework of beliefs, and a network of expectations.

Researchers interested in either hypnosis or meditation have long wrestled with the challenge of fitting such multifaceted phenomena into concise definitions and coherent theoretical frameworks (e.g., Bishop et al., 2004; Cardeña, 2014a; Chiesa, 2013; Kirsch et al., 2011; Lutz et al., 2007; Schmidt, 2014; Wagstaff, 2014; Williams & Kabat-Zinn, 2011). In Chapter 2 of this book, historian of science Anne Harrington outlines how scholars throughout the twentieth century leveraged the monolithic concept of "trance" to make sense of complex behaviors such as hypnosis and meditation. Whereas researchers today largely eschew such catch-all reductionism, Harrington's piece points to parallel trends in contemporary practice and research. For example, scientists may propose a particular pattern of brain activity as a biological marker of a prototypical hypnotic or meditative state or trait (e.g., Brewer and Garisson, 2014; Hoeft et al., 2012). While this kind of approach can promote theoretical simplicity and help to distil complex traditions, it may also risk obscuring the profound heterogeneity among forms of meditation and hypnosis (Lifshitz, Campbell, & Raz, 2012; Terhune, Cardeña, & Lindgren, 2011). Furthermore, as Michael Connors and Vince Polito discuss at length in Chapter 10, doing good empirical work on these practices demands careful attention to a range of conceptual and methodological issues, from the role of individual differences to the choice of control conditions and the distinction between a procedure and its outcomes (see also Davidson, 2010; Grant, 2012).

If, for a moment, we set aside the tags of hypnosis and meditation and focus on parsing out the underlying phenomenological qualities, cognitive processes, brain signatures, and behavioral outcomes, we are left with a diverse assortment of practices that show broad family resemblances. Part 3 of this volume presents a breadth of perspectives directly juxtaposing the domains of hypnosis and meditation to highlight relevant intersections and divergences. Crucially, a given state or practice that we term "meditation" may overlap more with a certain form of "hypnosis" than with another variant of so-called meditation. Consider the popular notion of mindfulness. This term may conjure images of an individual sitting peacefully on a cushion with eyes closed, following the breath, letting go of thoughts, and engaging in non-judgmental awareness of the moment-to-moment stream of experiences. Yet, this widespread modern usage of the word differs from many traditional views. (For a range of perspectives on this topic, see the recent special issue of *Contemporary Buddhism*; Williams and Kabat-Zinn, 2011.)

The concept of mindfulness originates from a translation of the Pali *sati*—a technical term from the early canons of Indian Buddhism relating to the retention of awareness on a chosen object or theme (Analayo, 2003). In addition to the familiar practice of breath awareness, the original scripture on the foundations of mindfulness describes a range of techniques, including, to name but one striking example, imagining one's own body as a corpse progressing through ten vivid stages of decomposition. While largely absent from current discussions of mindfulness, such techniques play important roles in the originating traditions (see Chapter 3 by Thupten Jinpa and Chapter 4 by Quinton Deeley). Moreover, some oft-overlooked meditative practices—from intricate visualizations to the cultivation of positive mental states such as compassion—may appear more akin to forms of autosuggestion than to widespread notions of mindful breathing. Extending the domain of contemplative experience beyond the narrow confines of contemporary mindfulness practice promises to deepen the dialog between cognitive and clinical science and the rich lineages of hypnosis and meditation.

Illuminating self-regulation

Hypnosis and meditation are unique in their ability to profoundly impact a wide range of cognitive processes (Kihlstrom, 2014; Sedlmeier et al., 2012); as such, studying contemplative practices can shed light on fundamental features of human psychology. Part 4 of this volume focuses on unraveling the cognitive processes that underlie the transformative potential of hypnosis and meditation. A close cross-examination of these techniques serves both to clarify their intrinsic mechanisms and to refine understanding of a wide range of basic psychological processes from mind-wandering and meta-awareness to attention, absorption, delusion, suggestion, insight, and emotion (see Chapter 13 by Vervaeke & Ferraro and Chapter 14 by Ott; also, Cahn & Polich, 2013; Cardeña, 2014b; Hölzel et al., 2011; Landry, Appourchaux, & Raz, 2014; Lutz et al., 2008; Oakley & Halligan, 2013).

Hypnosis and meditation provide a means of regaining control over processes that are usually considered automatic and impervious to conscious will (Lifshitz, Aubert Bonn, Fischer, Kashem, & Raz, 2013). Chapter 11 by Kieran Fox and colleagues shows how examining the empirical nuances of de-automatization can clarify ongoing debates concerning the self-regulation of spontaneous thought. In recent years, a string of high-profile studies proposed a link between daydreaming and unhappiness (Killingsworth & Gilbert, 2010; Wilson et al., 2014; cf. Fox, Thompson, Andrews-Hanna, & Christoff, 2014), resurrecting a well-worn misinterpretation that construes meditation as a form of thought suppression (cf. Hurley, 2014). However, an accumulating science of mind-wandering reveals both costs (i.e., unwanted distraction from a task) and benefits (i.e., unprompted creative insight) of this pervasive habit (Smallwood & Andrews-Hanna, 2013). Moreover, this research trajectory is beginning to unravel the specific characteristics that make certain thoughts more or less pleasant and productive (e.g., past-oriented thinking appears linked to negative affect while prospective thought tends toward optimism; Smallwood & Schooler, 2014).

A close examination of meditative traditions shows that while certain forms of calming meditation may indeed quiet the discursive mind, these practices typically aim to facilitate a deeper first-person inquiry into the stream of conscious experience (Lodro, 1998; Thanissaro, 1997). Many practices strive not to stop thoughts but rather to promote a new attitude toward them—to experience the thoughts without clinging, like "clouds drifting through a clear sky" or "a thief passing through an empty house." Furthermore, active rational analysis and repeated verbal aspirations form the crux of many meditation techniques. Thus, similar to cognitive hypnosis therapy (Alladin, 2012), meditative practices appear to foster a degree of awareness of and choice over the frequency and type of thoughts we think, as well as promote a healthier relationship to those thoughts, rather than eradicate spontaneous thought altogether from daily life (Schooler et al., 2014). Cognitive psychology offers empirical tools for theorizing about and empirically probing into such contemplative mechanisms while simultaneously gleaning new insights for a general understanding of human psychology (see Chapter 12 by Mooneyham and Schooler).

Subjective experience and the brain

The advent of tools for imaging the living human brain was perhaps the most important factor in propelling the recent surge of scientific interest in contemplative practice (e.g., Kosslyn, Thompson, Constantini-Ferrando, Alpert, & Spiegel, 2000; Lazar et al., 2000; Lutz, Greischar, Rawlings, Ricard, & Davidson, 2004; Newberg et al., 2001; Rainville et al., 1999; Raz & Shapiro, 2002). While the brain seems to have eked its way into nearly every corner of this volume, Part 5 highlights chapters that specifically explore the interaction of contemplative experience with emerging views of brain structure and function. As cognitive neuroscience matures, methodological advances have refined knowledge of regional brain specialization (Shackman et al., 2011), opened avenues for exploring distributed cortical networks (Bressler & Menon, 2010), and fostered comprehensive models for guiding research (Park & Friston, 2013). Leveraging such methodological and theoretical advances, a rapidly growing contemplative neuroimaging literature is beginning to unravel how practices such as hypnosis and meditation influence a host of neural functions, from sensory processing to the sense of agency (Oakley & Halligan, 2013;

Tang & Posner, 2012). Moreover, examining distributed brain networks provides new avenues for comparison across diverse planes of consciousness (see Chapter 18 by McGeown; see also recent efforts contrasting connectivity profiles induced via distinct psychedelic substances—Roseman, Leech, Feilding, Nutt, & Carhart-Harris, 2014).

The chapters in Part 5 demonstrate how synthesizing the contemplative imaging literature can mutually enrich theories of cognitive neuroscience and brain regulation (e.g., see Chapter 16 by Tang and Posner). For example, chapter 17 by Graham Jamieson reframes findings concerning hypnosis and meditation in terms of an emerging "predictive coding" model of brain function. Whereas earlier theories construed self-regulation largely as a form of hierarchical top-down processing, this predictive coding approach highlights the dynamic reciprocal interplay between incoming sensory signals and ongoing cognitive-affective brain states (Todd, Cunningham, Anderson, & Thompson, 2012).

Hypnosis and meditation offer potent instruments for elucidating the relationship between subjective consciousness and objective brain function (Lifshitz, Cusumano, & Raz, 2013; Thompson, 2006). Yet, whereas scientists have access to a plethora of advanced methods for investigating brain and behavior, they face a dearth of techniques for the empirical analysis of phenomenology (Hasenkamp & Thompson, 2014). Integrating such phenomenological approaches with the tools of cognitive and brain science poses yet a further challenge (Varela, 1996). Throughout this volume, contributors repeatedly emphasize the imperative of developing methods for describing and operationalizing the nuances of lived experience (e.g., Chapter 9 by Tart and Chapter 15 by Cardeña). In Chapter 6, philosophers Jelena Markovic and Evan Thompson juxtapose hypnosis and meditation using an innovative neurophenomenological state-space model (Lutz, Jha, Dunne, & Saron, 2015) that plots contemplative practices along various experiential dimensions (e.g., meta-awareness, attentional aperture, and object orientation). This phenomenological neurocognitive matrix—a synthesis of traditional meditation manuals and cutting-edge findings from cognitive neuroscience—marks a major step forward from previous models that construed meditation along a single axis from concentrated to receptive attention (Lutz et al., 2008; for another recent approach to categorizing meditative states, see Schmidt, 2014).

Fine-grained phenomenological models will likely prove vital for an emerging wave of contemplative studies integrating experiential self-reports with the tools of brain science (Deeley et al., 2012; Hasenkamp, 2014). For example, a recent study leveraged a neurophenomenological approach to demonstrate that subjective ratings of hypnotic depth correlated with global connectivity changes in the electroencephalography signal. Furthermore, distinct patterns of connectivity tracked specific experiential dimensions (Cardeña, Jönsson, Terhune, & Marcusson-Clavertz, 2013). Another inventive study employed neurofeedback to relate meditative experience with activity in the posterior cingulate cortex—a major node of the default mode network associated with internal attention (Garrison, Scheinost, et al., 2013). Expert meditators focused on their breath while in an fMRI (functional magnetic resonance imaging) scanner as they viewed a graph that displayed real-time feedback from activity in their posterior cingulate. Following each meditation scan, participants described what aspect of their experience seemed most related to the displayed brain fluctuations. This approach allowed researchers to pinpoint the specific phenomenological quality most tightly linked to altered activity in the posterior cingulate cortex during meditation—namely, the quality of undistracted effortless awareness (Garrison, Santoyo, et al., 2013). Such studies illustrate how paying due attention to phenomenology can advance the cognitive neuroscience of contemplative experience and consciousness at large (Lutz & Thompson, 2003).

Therapeutic synthesis

Both hypnosis and meditation originated as instruments of self-awareness designed to ease suffering. Part 6 of this volume explores the therapeutic applications of hypnosis and meditation from a range of perspectives including cognitive neuroscience, personality theory, clinical intuition, psychoanalysis, and cognitive-behavioral therapy. As our understanding of the underlying mechanisms deepens, so does our ability to apply these practices in the treatment of a wide range of ailments, from chronic pain (Accardi et al., 2013; Chiesa & Serretti, 2011) to substance abuse (Brewer, Elwafi, & Davis, 2013; Lynn, Green, Accardi, & Cleere, 2010) and major depression (Lynn, Barnes, Deming, & Accardi, 2010; Segal, Williams, & Teasdale, 2012; Yapko, 2013). Moreover, recent findings highlight the impact of contemplative practice on health and physiology down to the level of gene expression and immune function (Jacobs et al., 2011; Kaliman et al., 2014; Kovács et al., 2008; Rosenkranz et al., 2013).

While researchers and practitioners have long utilized hypnosis and meditation to treat a similar range of conditions, variants of these practices likely operate through distinct mechanisms and thus cater best to different patients. Along these lines, Joshua Grant and Fadel Zeidan offer (in Chapter 21) a detailed neurobiological account revealing the unique and overlapping mechanisms that subserve hypnotic and meditative analgesia. From a more cognitive behavioral perspective, Norman Farb explores (in Chapter 20) the different aspects of personality targeted by mindfulness and hypnosis. Adopting a pragmatic approach to the bridging of hypnosis and meditation would likely help tailor interventions to specific individuals and foster integrative approaches to optimize healing (see Chapter 22 by Toneatto and Courtice; Alladin, 2014). In this respect, we are delighted to include contributions from active clinical researchers and therapists who have crossed the boundaries of tradition and begun synthesizing suggestion and mindfulness approaches to discover what helps real patients heal best (e.g., see Chapter 19 by Yapko and Chapter 23 by Lynn and colleagues).

Conclusion: toward an integrative science of conscious planes

The present collection rekindles a rich lineage of integrative research on contemplative experience (Cardeña & Winkelman, 2011; Erickson, 1965; Goleman & Davidson, 1979; Tart, 1972; Vaitl et al., 2005). One of my favorite stories from this colorful history concerns the little-known friendship and collaboration between Milton Erickson and Aldous Huxley. Erickson, arguably one of the most prominent hypnotists of the twentieth century, was famous for his ability to unlock latent insight in his patients through open-ended, non-directive suggestions. Huxley, on the other hand, was an intellectual with wide-ranging knowledge and first-hand experience of meditative techniques and psychedelic states (including his experiments with the mescaline cactus reported in *The Doors of Perception*). Less appreciated today is the fact that Huxley was also a gifted hypnotic subject; indeed, his ability to dissociate was so strong that, as a boy, he could simply ignore the school bullies until they left him alone. Putting Huxley's innate talent to good use, early in 1950, Erickson, serving the role of master hypnotist, guided him through a series of contemplative experiments probing the depths of internal space. Although sadly the bulk of their detailed notes perished in a California brush fire, the surviving documents report a meticulous exploration of diverse absorptions, dissociations, insights, time distortions, and mind–body phenomena (Erickson, 1965). To be sure, the scientific article that resulted from this rare crossing of minds hardly meets the hard-nosed criteria of contemporary behavioral psychology; nevertheless, these nascent explorations showcase empirical phenomenology in action and highlight the merits of uniting hypnosis and meditation to elucidate the boundaries of consciousness. Sixty-five years later, we have developed many new tools and nuanced theories for a science of consciousness—and still I cannot help but admire the open-minded spirit of these early pioneers.

I hope this book will serve to encourage a science of experience that takes integrative, cross-cultural, and phenomenological approaches seriously (for a pioneering example of such work, see Thompson, 2014). After all, human beings developed the remarkable powers of hypnosis and meditation not through brain imaging experiments or reaction time analysis but, rather, by adopting an empirical approach toward and from within their own subjective experience. Further exploring the profound pliancy of our minds will require linking subjective and sociocultural methodologies with the tools of behavioral and biological research, as well as building meaningful bridges to span the full range of contemplative practices (extending beyond hypnosis and meditation to encompass dreams, psychedelic states, prayer, and so on). I envision this book as a stride in that direction.

Cutting across disciplinary boundaries, the present collection offers a fresh outlook on contemplative research and practice. Synthesizing trailblazing neuroscientific findings with leading scholarship from the realms of cognitive science, phenomenology, psychiatry, history, religious studies, and anthropology, the chapters in this book illuminate empirical work on hypnosis and meditation to unravel underlying mechanisms and foster new therapeutic prospects. There is much work left undone, and with the 20/20 vision of hindsight I am compelled to point out at least a few things I would have done differently: I wish we had invited more contributions from underrepresented voices in these fields; I wish we had included more discussion of embodiment and movement-based practices such as Hatha Yoga and Tai Chi; and I wish we had focused more on compassion, altruism, and the ethical dimensions of contemplative experience. Alas, this book is but one step down a longer path.

My co-editor Amir Raz and I are indebted to our distinguished contributors for sharing their forward-thinking perspectives in a manner that is both scholarly and relevant to a wide audience spanning a range of expertise. Whether you are a seasoned specialist or a novice dipping your toes into the waters of contemplative practice, I would encourage you to scan through the table of contents, peruse the chapters, and explore the many complementary and, indeed, sometimes diverging, viewpoints herein. It is my sincere wish that this multifaceted collection will enrich the transformative potential at the heart of human experience with new theories, fresh awareness, and, with any luck, a deepening of wisdom and love.

References

Accardi, M. C., Hallquist, M. N., Jensen, M. P., Patterson, D. R., Lynn, S. J., & Montgomery, G. H. (2013). Clinical hypnosis for chronic pain in adults. *The Cochrane Library*.

Alderman, L. (2011, April 15). Using hypnosis to gain more control over your illness. *The New York Times*. Retrieved from http://www.nytimes.com

Alladin, A. (2012). Cognitive hypnotherapy: a new vision and strategy for research and practice. *American Journal of Clinical Hypnosis*, **54**(4), 249–262.

Alladin, A. (2014). Mindfulness-based hypnosis: blending science, beliefs, and wisdoms to catalyze healing. *American Journal of Clinical Hypnosis*, **56**(3), 285–302.

Analayo, B. (2003). *Satipatthana: the direct path to realization*. Birmingham, UK: Windhorse.

Anderson, M. (Ed.) (2015). The emergence of mindfulness in basic and clinical psychological science [Special issue]. *American Psychologist*, **70**(7).

Benham, G., Woody, E. Z., Wilson, K. S., & Nash, M. R. (2006). Expect the unexpected: ability, attitude, and responsiveness to hypnosis. *Journal of Personality and Social Psychology*, **91**(2), 342–350.

Bishop, S. R., Lau, M., Shapiro, S., Carlson, L., Anderson, N. D., Carmody, J., . . . Devins, G. (2004). Mindfulness: a proposed operational definition. *Clinical Psychology: Science and Practice*, **11**(3), 230–241.

Bodhi, B. (2011). *The noble eightfold path: way to the end of suffering*. Washington, USA: Pariyatti.

Bressler, S. L., & Menon, V. (2010). Large-scale brain networks in cognition: emerging methods and principles. *Trends in Cognitive Sciences*, **14**(6), 277–290.

Brewer, J. A., Elwafi, H. M., & Davis, J. H. (2013). Craving to quit: psychological models and neurobiological mechanisms of mindfulness training as treatment for addictions. *Psychology of Addictive Behaviors*, **27**(2), 366.

Brewer, J. A., & Garrison, K. A. (2014). The posterior cingulate cortex as a plausible mechanistic target of meditation: findings from neuroimaging. *Annals of the New York Academy of Sciences*, **1307**(1), 19–27.

Bunting, M. (2014, May 6). Why we will come to see mindfulness as mandatory. *The Guardian*. Retrieved from http://www.theguardian.com

Cahn, B. R., & Polich, J. (2013). Meditation states and traits. *Psychology of Consciousness: Theory, Research, and Practice*, **1**, 48–96.

Cardeña, E. (2014a). Spinning in circles. *The Journal of Mind–Body Regulation*, **2**(2), 121–123.

Cardeña, E. (2014b). Hypnos and psyche: how hypnosis has contributed to the study of consciousness. *Psychology of Consciousness: Theory, Research, and Practice*, **1**(2), 123.

Cardeña, E., Jönsson, P., Terhune, D. B., & Marcusson-Clavertz, D. (2013). The neurophenomenology of neutral hypnosis. *Cortex*, **49**(2), 375–385.

Cardeña, E., & Krippner, S. (2010). The cultural context of hypnosis. *Handbook of clinical hypnosis* (2nd ed.), pp. 743–771.

Cardeña, E., Sjöstedt, J. O., & Marcusson-Clavertz, D. (2014). Sustained attention and motivation in Zen meditators and non-meditators. *Mindfulness*, 1–6.

Cardeña, E., & Winkelman, M. (Eds.). (2011). *Altering consciousness: multidisciplinary perspectives*. Santa Barbara, CA: Praeger.

Chiesa, A. (2013). The difficulty of defining mindfulness: current thought and critical issues. *Mindfulness*, **4**(3), 255–268.

Chiesa, A., & Serretti, A. (2011). Mindfulness-based interventions for chronic pain: a systematic review of the evidence. *The Journal of Alternative and Complementary Medicine*, **17**(1), 83–93.

Davidson R. J. (2010). Empirical explorations of mindfulness: conceptual and methodological conundrums. *Emotion*, **10**, 8–11

Davidson, R. J., & Goleman, D. J. (1977). The role of attention in meditation and hypnosis: a psychobiological perspective on transformations of consciousness. *International Journal of Clinical and Experimental Hypnosis*, **25**(4), 291–308.

Deeley, Q., Oakley, D. A., Toone, B., Giampietro, V., Brammer, M. J., Williams, S. C., & Halligan, P. W. (2012). Modulating the default mode network using hypnosis. *International Journal of Clinical and Experimental Hypnosis*, **60**(2), 206–228.

Erickson, M. H. (1965). A special inquiry with Aldous Huxley into the nature and character of various states of consciousness. *American Journal of Clinical Hypnosis*, **8**(1), 14–33.

Farb, N. A. (2012). Mind your expectations: exploring the roles of suggestion and intention in mindfulness training. *The Journal of Mind–Body Regulation*, **2**(1), 27–42.

Farb, N. A. (2014). From retreat center to clinic to boardroom? Perils and promises of the modern mindfulness movement. *Religions*, **5**(4), 1062–1086.

Fox, K. C., Thompson, E., Andrews-Hanna, J. R., & Christoff, K. (2014). Is thinking really aversive? A commentary on Wilson et al.'s "Just think: the challenges of the disengaged mind." *Frontiers in Psychology*, **5**, 1427.

Gandhi, B., & Oakley, D. A. (2005). Does "hypnosis" by any other name smell as sweet? The efficacy of "hypnotic" inductions depends on the label "hypnosis." *Consciousness and Cognition*, **14**(2), 304–315.

Garrison, K. A., Santoyo, J. F., Davis, J. H., Thornhill IV, T. A., Kerr, C. E., & Brewer, J. A. (2013). Effortless awareness: using real time neurofeedback to investigate correlates of posterior cingulate cortex activity in meditators' self-report. *Frontiers in Human Neuroscience*, **7**.

Garrison, K. A., Scheinost, D., Worhunsky, P. D., Elwafi, H. M., Thornhill IV, T. A., Thompson, E., . . . Brewer, J. A. (2013). Real-time fMRI links subjective experience with brain activity during focused attention. *NeuroImage*, **81**, 110–118.

Goleman, D., & Davidson, R. J. (Eds.). (1979). *Consciousness, the brain, states of awareness, and alternate realities.* Ardent Media.

Grant, J. A. (2012). Towards a more meaningful comparison of meditation and hypnosis. *The Journal of Mind–Body Regulation*, **2**(1), 71–74.

Grant, J. A., & Rainville, P. (2005). Hypnosis and meditation: similar experiential changes and shared brain mechanisms. *Medical Hypotheses*, **65**(3), 625–626.

Green, J. P., Laurence, J. R., & Lynn, S. J. (2014). Hypnosis and psychotherapy: from Mesmer to mindfulness. *Psychology of Consciousness: Theory, Research, and Practice*, **1**(2), 199.

Halsband, U., Mueller, S., Hinterberger, T., & Strickner, S. (2009). Plasticity changes in the brain in hypnosis and meditation. *Contemporary Hypnosis*, **26**(4), 194–215.

Harrington, A. (2007). *The cure within: a history of mind–body medicine.* W.W. Norton & Company.

Hasenkamp, W. (2014). Using first-person reports during meditation to investigate basic cognitive experience. In S. Schmidt & H. Walach (Eds.), *Meditation–neuroscientific approaches and philosophical implications* (pp. 75–93). Springer International Publishing.

Hasenkamp, W., & Thompson, E. (2014). Examining subjective experience: advances in neurophenomenology. *Frontiers in Human Neuroscience*, **8**, 466.

Hoeft, F., Gabrieli, J. D., Whitfield-Gabrieli, S., Haas, B. W., Bammer, R., Menon, V., & Spiegel, D. (2012). Functional brain basis of hypnotizability. *Archives of General Psychiatry*, **69**(10), 1064–1072.

Holroyd, J. (2003). The science of meditation and the state of hypnosis. *American Journal of Clinical Hypnosis*, **46**(2), 109–128.

Hölzel, B. K., Lazar, S. W., Gard, T., Schuman-Olivier, Z., Vago, D. R., & Ott, U. (2011). How does mindfulness meditation work? Proposing mechanisms of action from a conceptual and neural perspective. *Perspectives on Psychological Science*, **6**(6), 537–559.

Hurley, D. (2014, January 14). Breathing in vs. spacing out. *The New York Times*. Retrieved from http://www.nytimes.com

Jacobs, T. L., Epel, E. S., Lin, J., Blackburn, E. H., Wolkowitz, O. M., Bridwell, D. A., . . . Saron, C. D. (2011). Intensive meditation training, immune cell telomerase activity, and psychological mediators. *Psychoneuroendocrinology*, **36**(5), 664–681.

Jensen, C. G., Vangkilde, S., Frokjaer, V., & Hasselbalch, S. G. (2012). Mindfulness training affects attention—Or is it attentional effort?. *Journal of Experimental Psychology: General*, **141**(1), 106.

Johnson, W. (1982). *Riding the ox home: history of meditation from shamanism to science.* London: Rider & Co.

Kaliman, P., Álvarez-López, M. J., Cosín-Tomás, M., Rosenkranz, M. A., Lutz, A., & Davidson, R. J. (2014). Rapid changes in histone deacetylases and inflammatory gene expression in expert meditators. *Psychoneuroendocrinology*, **40**, 96–107.

Kihlstrom, J. F. (2008). The domain of hypnosis, revisited. In M. Nash & A. Barnier (Eds.), *Oxford handbook of hypnosis* (pp. 21–52). Oxford: Oxford University Press.

Kihlstrom, J. F. (2014). Hypnosis and cognition. *Psychology of Consciousness: Theory, Research, and Practice*, **1**(2), 139–152.

Killingsworth, M. A., & Gilbert, D. T. (2010). A wandering mind is an unhappy mind. *Science*, **330**(6006), 932–932.

Kirmayer, L. J. (1992). Social constructions of hypnosis. *International Journal of Clinical and Experimental Hypnosis*, **40**(4), 276–300.

Kirmayer, L. J. (2015). Mindfulness in cultural context. *Transcultural psychiatry*, **52**(4), 447–469.

Kirsch, I., Cardeña, E., Derbyshire, S., Dienes, Z., Heap, M., Kallio, S., . . . Whalley, M. (2011). Definitions of hypnosis and hypnotizability and their relation to suggestion and suggestibility: a consensus statement. *Contemporary Hypnosis*, **28**(2), 107–115.

Kosslyn, S. M., Thompson, W. L., Costantini-Ferrando, M. F., Alpert, N. M., & Spiegel, D. (2000). Hypnotic visual illusion alters color processing in the brain. *American Journal of Psychiatry*, **157**(8), 1279–1284.

Kovács, Z. A., Puskás, L. G., Juhász, A., Rimanóczy, Á., Hackler Jr, L., Kátay, L., . . . Kálmán, J. (2008). Hypnosis upregulates the expression of immune-related genes in lymphocytes. *Psychotherapy and Psychosomatics*, **77**(4), 257–259.

Landry, M., Appourchaux, K., & Raz, A. (2014). Elucidating unconscious processing with instrumental hypnosis. *Frontiers in Psychology*, **5**.

Lazar, S. W., Bush, G., Gollub, R. L., Fricchione, G. L., Khalsa, G., & Benson, H. (2000). Functional brain mapping of the relaxation response and meditation. *Neuroreport*, **11**(7), 1581–1585.

Leighton, T. D. (2012). *Faces of compassion: classic Bodhisattva archetypes and their modern expression—an introduction to Mahayana Buddhism*. Wisdom Publications Inc.

Lifshitz, M., Aubert Bonn, N., Fischer, A., Kashem, I. F., & Raz, A. (2013). Using suggestion to modulate automatic processes: from Stroop to McGurk and beyond. *Cortex*, **49**(2), 463–473.

Lifshitz, M., Campbell, N. K., & Raz, A. (2012). Varieties of attention in hypnosis and meditation. *Consciousness and Cognition*, **21**(3), 1582–1585.

Lifshitz, M., Cusumano, E. P., & Raz, A. (2013). Hypnosis as neurophenomenology. *Frontiers in Human Neuroscience*, **7**.

Lifshitz, M., Howells, C., & Raz, A. (2012). Can expectation enhance response to suggestion? De-automatization illuminates a conundrum. *Consciousness and Cognition*, **21**(2), 1001–1008.

Lifshitz, M., & Raz, A. (2012). Hypnosis and meditation: vehicles of attention and suggestion. *The Journal of Mind–Body Regulation*, **2**(1), 3–11.

Lodro, G. G. (1998). *Calm abiding and special insight: achieving spiritual transformation through meditation*. Snow Lion Publications.

Lutz, A., Dunne, J.D., & Davidson, R.J. (2007). Meditation and the neuroscience of consciousness: an introduction. In P.D. Zelazo, M. Moscovitch, & E. Thompson (Eds.), *Cambridge handbook of consciousness* (pp. 499–554). Cambridge, UK: Cambridge University Press.

Lutz, A., Greischar, L. L., Rawlings, N. B., Ricard, M., & Davidson, R. J. (2004). Long-term meditators self-induce high-amplitude gamma synchrony during mental practice. *Proceedings of the National Academy of Sciences of the United States of America*, **101**(46), 16369–16373.

Lutz, A., Jha, A. P., Dunne, J. D., & Saron, C. D. (2015). Investigating the phenomenological matrix of mindfulness-related practices from a neurocognitive perspective. *American Psychologist*, **70**(7), 632–658.

Lutz, A., Slagter, H. A., Dunne, J. D., & Davidson, R. J. (2008). Attention regulation and monitoring in meditation. *Trends in Cognitive Sciences*, **12**(4), 163–169.

Lutz, A., & Thompson, E. (2003). Neurophenomenology integrating subjective experience and brain dynamics in the neuroscience of consciousness. *Journal of Consciousness Studies*, **10**(9–10), 31–52.

Lynn, S. J., Barnes, S., Deming, A., & Accardi, M. (2010). Hypnosis, rumination, and depression: catalyzing attention and mindfulness-based treatments. *International Journal of Clinical and Experimental Hypnosis*, **58**(2), 202–221

Lynn, S. J., Das, L. S., Hallquist, M. N., & Williams, J. C. (2006). Mindfulness, acceptance, and hypnosis: cognitive and clinical perspectives. *International Journal of Clinical and Experimental Hypnosis*, **54**(2), 143–166.

Lynn, S. J., & Green, J. P. (2011). The sociocognitive and dissociation theories of hypnosis: toward a rapprochement. *International Journal of Clinical and Experimental Hypnosis*, **59**(3), 277–293.

Lynn, S. J., Green, J. P., Accardi, M., & Cleere, C. (2010). Hypnosis and smoking cessation: the state of the science. *American Journal of Clinical Hypnosis*, **52**(3), 177–181.

May, A. (2011). Experience-dependent structural plasticity in the adult human brain. *Trends in Cognitive Sciences*, **15**(10), 475–482.

Newberg, A., Alavi, A., Baime, M., Pourdehnad, M., Santanna, J., & d'Aquili, E. (2001). The measurement of regional cerebral blood flow during the complex cognitive task of meditation: a preliminary SPECT study. *Psychiatry Research: Neuroimaging*, **106**(2), 113–122.

North, A. (2014, June 30). The mindfulness backlash. *The New York Times*. Retrieved from http://www.nytimes.com

Oakley, D. A., & Halligan, P. W. (2013). Hypnotic suggestion: opportunities for cognitive neuroscience. *Nature Reviews Neuroscience*, **14**(8), 565–576.

Otani, A. (2003). Eastern meditative techniques and hypnosis: a new synthesis. *American Journal of Clinical Hypnosis*, **46**(2), 97–108.

Park, H. J., & Friston, K. (2013). Structural and functional brain networks: from connections to cognition. *Science*, **342**(6158), 1238411.

Pickert, K. (2014, February). The mindful revolution. *Time*, **183**(4), 40–49.

Pintar, J., & Lynn, S. J. (2008). *Hypnosis: a brief history*. Oxford: Wiley-Blackwell.

Purser, R., & Loy, D. (2013). Beyond McMindfulness. *Huffington Post*. Retrieved from http://www.huffingtonpost.com

Rainville, P., Hofbauer, R., Paus, T., Duncan, G., Bushnell, M., & Price, D. (1999). Cerebral mechanisms of hypnotic induction and suggestion. *Journal of Cognitive Neuroscience*, **11**(1), 110–125.

Raz, A. (2011). Hypnosis: a twilight zone of the top-down variety: few have never heard of hypnosis but most know little about the potential of this mind–body regulation technique for advancing science. *Trends in Cognitive Sciences*, **15**(12), 555–557.

Raz, A., & Shapiro, T. (2002). Hypnosis and neuroscience: a cross talk between clinical and cognitive research. *Archives of General Psychiatry*, **59**(1), 85–90.

Roseman, L., Leech, R., Feilding, A., Nutt, D. J., & Carhart-Harris, R. L. (2014). The effects of psilocybin and MDMA on between-network resting state functional connectivity in healthy volunteers. *Frontiers in Human Neuroscience*, **8**.

Rosenkranz, M. A., Davidson, R. J., MacCoon, D. G., Sheridan, J. F., Kalin, N. H., & Lutz, A. (2013). A comparison of mindfulness-based stress reduction and an active control in modulation of neurogenic inflammation. *Brain, Behavior, and Immunity*, **27**, 174–184.

Schmidt, S. (2014). Opening up meditation for science: the development of a meditation classification system. In S. Schmidt & H. Walach (Eds.), *Meditation–neuroscientific approaches and philosophical implications* (pp. 137–152). Springer International Publishing.

Schmidt, S., & Walach, H. (Eds.). (2014). *Meditation–neuroscientific approaches and philosophical implications*. Springer International Publishing.

Schooler, J. W., Mrazek, M. D., Franklin, M. S., Baird, B., Mooneyham, B. W., Zedelius, C., & Broadway, J. M. (2014). The middle way: finding the balance between mindfulness and mind-wandering. *Psychology of Learning and Motivation*, **60**, 1–33.

Schumpeter. (2013, November 16). The mindfulness business. *The Economist*. Retrieved from http://www.economist.com

Sedlmeier, P., Eberth, J., Schwarz, M., Zimmermann, D., Haarig, F., Jaeger, S., & Kunze, S. (2012). The psychological effects of meditation: a meta-analysis. *Psychological Bulletin*, **138**(6), 1139.

Segal, Z. V., Williams, J. M. G., & Teasdale, J. D. (2012). *Mindfulness-based cognitive therapy for depression*. Guilford Press.

Shackman, A. J., Salomons, T. V., Slagter, H. A., Fox, A. S., Winter, J. J., & Davidson, R. J. (2011). The integration of negative affect, pain and cognitive control in the cingulate cortex. *Nature Reviews Neuroscience*, **12**(3), 154–167.

Shor, R. E., & Orne, E. C. (1962). *Harvard group scale of hypnotic susceptibility: Form A*. Palo Alto, California: Consulting Psychologists' Press.

Smallwood, J., & Andrews-Hanna, J. (2013). Not all minds that wander are lost: the importance of a balanced perspective on the mind-wandering state. *Frontiers in Psychology*, **4**.

Smallwood, J., & Schooler, J. W. (2014). The science of mind wandering: empirically navigating the stream of consciousness. *Annual Review of Psychology*.

Spiegel, D., White, M., & Waelde, L. C. (2010). Hypnosis, mindfulness meditation, and brain imaging. In D. Barrett (Ed.), *Hypnosis and hypnotherapy* (pp. 37–52). Santa Barbara: Greenwood Publishing Group.

Stehr, N., & Weingart, P. (Eds.). (2000). *Practising interdisciplinarity*. Toronto: University of Toronto Press.

Tang, Y. Y., Hölzel, B. K., & Posner, M. I. (2015). The neuroscience of mindfulness meditation. *Nature Reviews Neuroscience*, **16**(4), 213–225.

Tang, Y. Y., & Posner, M. I. (2012). Special issue on mindfulness neuroscience. *Social Cognitive and Affective Neuroscience*, **8**(1), 1–3.

Tart, C. T. (1972). States of consciousness and state-specific sciences. *Science*, **176**(4040), 1203–1210.

Terhune, D. B., Cardeña, E., & Lindgren, M. (2011). Dissociated control as a signature of typological variability in high hypnotic suggestibility. *Consciousness and cognition*, **20**(3), 727–736.

Thanissaro, B. (1997). One tool among many: the place of vipassana in Buddhist practice. *Access to Insight (Legacy Edition)*, March 8, 2011. Retrieved from http://www.accesstoinsight.org

Thompson, E. (2006). Neurophenomenology and contemplative experience. In P. Clayton & Z. Simpson (Eds.), *The Oxford handbook of religion and science* (pp. 226–235). Oxford University Press.

Thompson, E. (2014). *Waking, dreaming, being: self and consciousness in neuroscience, meditation, and philosophy*. New York City: Columbia University Press.

Todd, R. M., Cunningham, W. A., Anderson, A. K., & Thompson, E. (2012). Affect-biased attention as emotion regulation. *Trends in Cognitive Sciences*, **16**(7), 365–372.

Vaitl, D., Birbaumer, N., Gruzelier, J., Jamieson, G. A., Kotchoubey, B., Kübler, A., . . . Weiss, T. (2005). Psychobiology of altered states of consciousness. *Psychological Bulletin*, **131**(1), 98–127.

Varela, F. J. (1996). Neurophenomenology: a methodological remedy for the hard problem. *Journal of Consciousness Studies*, **3**, 330–349.

Wagstaff, G. F. (2014). On the centrality of the concept of an altered state to definitions of hypnosis. *The Journal of Mind–Body Regulation*, **2**(2), 90–108.

Williams, J. M. G., & Kabat-Zinn, J. (2011). Mindfulness: diverse perspectives on its meaning, origins, and multiple applications at the intersection of science and dharma. *Contemporary Buddhism*, **12**(01), 1–18.

Wilson, T. D., Reinhard, D. A., Westgate, E. C., Gilbert, D. T., Ellerbeck, N., Hahn, C., . . . Shaked, A. (2014). Just think: the challenges of the disengaged mind. *Science*, **345**(6192), 75–77.

Woody, E. Z., & Sadler, P. (2008). Dissociation theories of hypnosis. In M. Nash & A. Barnier (Eds.), *The Oxford handbook of hypnosis: theory, research, and practice* (pp. 81–110). Oxford: Oxford University Press.

Yapko, M. D. (2011). *Mindfulness and hypnosis: the power of suggestion to transform experience*. W.W. Norton & Company.

Yapko, M. D. (Ed.). (2013). *Hypnosis and treating depression: applications in clinical practice*. Routledge.

Zopa, L. R. (2012). *Bodhisattva attitude: how to dedicate your life to others* (Vol. 1). Lama Yeshe Wisdom Archive.

Part 2

Philosophical, historical, and cultural perspectives

Chapter 2

Thinking about trance over a century
The making of a set of impasses

Anne Harrington

Abstract

Despite differences in methods and (usually) goals, both hypnosis and meditation involve an unusual state of awareness, generally known as "trance." Yet, the idea of trance, as an object of scholarly and scientific study, turns out to have been marked, historically, by confusion and controversy. Is trance one thing or many things? A regression to a pathological, primitive state or ascent to an elevated state? Noisy or quiet? Biological or social? Meditation researchers, hypnosis researchers, and anthropologists (interested in phenomena like shamanism and spirit possession) have all, historically, struggled with questions like these in surprisingly similar ways. This chapter uses historical evidence to demonstrate this point, all with the end of suggesting that it could be enormously useful for these different communities to overcome their disciplinary isolation from one another, and see if there is a way in which they could make progress together.

Introduction

What is hypnosis? What is meditation? What do they have to do with each other? Historically, one answer has been more persistent than any other: despite differences in methods and (usually) goals, both hypnosis and meditation involve an unusual state of awareness, generally known as "trance."

What exactly is trance? Some people use the word as a kind of "not-in-Kansas-anymore" designation for anything off the map of prosaic consciousness, from the fog of terror to the contemplative stillness of meditating monks to the ecstatic energy of whirling dervishes. Others invoke etymology: the word trance comes from the Latin word *transire*, meaning *passage*. In one way or another, trance is supposed to involve a process in which a person passes from his or her everyday consciousness into some other kind of mental state, only to return to normal consciousness, generally in some way changed by the experience.

For our purposes, it turns out to be most helpful not to try to define trance from the outset but, rather, to map the ways in which generations of researchers (working within Western analytic frames of reference) have themselves historically understood and made use of the idea. When we do that, we discover two things. First, that trance, as an object of scholarly and scientific study, is a remarkably unstable concept, marked by confusion and controversy. What is the relationship between the trance phenomena experienced in non-Western cultures and the Western therapeutic practice called "hypnosis"? What again is the relationship between trance and meditation? Is trance one thing or many things? A regression to a primitive state or an elevated state? Noisy or quiet? Biological or social? Controversy and indecision reigns.

That fact may not be too surprising in itself, but the next fact may be more so. It turns out that meditation researchers, hypnosis researchers, and anthropologists interested in phenomena like shamanism and spirit possession have all, historically, struggled with similar unresolved issues over the nature of trance. Given this, would it not be useful for them to overcome their disciplinary isolation from one another, share their woes, and see if there is a way in which they could make progress together? Three brief historical excursions into the chief impasses that have bedeviled the efforts of each of these groups will make this point.

Impasse 1: Is trance a bad thing or a good thing?

The first impasse is also the most value-laden of the three. It is focused on the question: is trance a bad thing, a pathological state of consciousness? Or, on the contrary, is it a good thing, a potentially valuable path to human healing and human flourishing?

Pathological or health-enhancing? The case of hypnosis

The early history of hypnosis provides a first good entryway into the changing consensus on this question. The late eighteenth-century healing ritual known as animal magnetism, or mesmerism, was originally conceived as a strictly physical treatment designed to redress deficiencies or blockages in a patient's animal magnetism (an alleged previously unknown force in the human body). By the 1820s, however (and partly under the influence of Romantic-era philosophies), mesmerized patients were reliably falling into a strange state of consciousness called "magnetic sleep," in which they became unaware of their everyday surroundings, were deeply ("magnetically") attached to the mesmerist, and believed to be capable, with his guidance, of remarkable feats of self-healing, paranormal perception, and occult knowledge. Magnetic sleep was a trance state in all but name, and Romantic-era mesmerists were in no doubt about its health-enhancing nature.

Some people felt the mesmerists went too far, however. The 1840s saw the rechristening of animal magnetism as "hypnosis" (originally "neurhypnosis") by the Scottish surgeon, James Braid, which clearly laid out the terms of a more tempered approach to this special state of consciousness. No longer were we to suppose that this state opened up the mind to otherwise latent paranormal powers. Instead, we were invited to conceptualize trance as a kind of artificial sleep, a novel brain state involving heightened sensory awareness. This state was achieved, moreover, not through any special "magnetic" influence that the operator had on the subject, but, rather, through intense concentration on a single idea or object (such as a small mirror or watch). While there was nothing paranormal about it, hypnosis itself, as a state, was nevertheless "a very important, powerful, and extraordinary agent in the healing art," because the brain in this state of heightened sensitivity was able to respond to suggestions of healing in uniquely powerful ways (Braid, 1843, p. 11).

Because he emphasized the self-directed nature of hypnosis, Braid also made a connection to other kinds of phenomena, in ways that should interest us. The state of hypnosis, he said, was similar, if not identical, to the mental state aimed for by Hindu yogis, Zoroastrians, and the "Magi of Persia." In his words: "The eastern saints are all self-hypnotisers, adopting means essentially the same as those which I had recommended for similar purposes" (Braid, 2008, p. 137).

Meanwhile, other developments were afoot. In India, the surgeon James Esdaile successfully used the older practices of mesmerism (rather than Braid's hypnosis) as a means of anesthetizing a very large number of native patients undergoing surgery, and Braid himself affirmed the value of his results (Esdaile, 1856). In England, the physician John Elliotson also experimented with mesmerism as an anesthesia on patients in London hospitals, with some success (Elliotson, 1843). These developments were cut short by the introduction of chemical anesthesia in the late 1840s. There is evidence that at least some surgeons embraced chemical anesthesia in part because they had felt threatened by the vision of mesmerists in their operating theaters, interfering with their authority (Winter, 1998).

Mainstream medical interest in (hypnotic) trance then went underground for several decades. When, in the early 1880s, interest in this trance state was reignited, few were interested in its healing potential. Instead, the focus was on understanding trance as a pathological brain state marked by a reduced capacity for willful action and rational thinking. Its main benefit, in the eyes of many, lay in what it could teach medical science about the labile and degenerate nervous systems of patients suffering from hysteria. Some of the energy driving the new effort was fueled by anticlerical zeal within European medicine at the time. Instead of comparing hypnotized subjects to entranced "eastern saints," as Braid had done in the 1840s, a new generation of theorizers like Jean-Martin Charcot in Paris drew links between the trances of hypnosis and hysteria on the one side, and medieval descriptions of demonic possession and religious ecstasy on the other. All of this was undertaken with the goal of demonstrating that the saints and demoniacs of Catholic tradition were just undiagnosed cases of hysteria, whose experiences had no meaning outside of their pathology (Charcot & Richer, 1887; Goldstein, 1982).

By the early twentieth-century, Freudian psychoanalysis had emerged as a new powerful way for framing questions about the nature of trance, which gave a new spin to late nineteenth-century beliefs in its primitive, pathological nature. Freud did have some early interest in the therapeutic potential of hypnosis: he had originally used it as a tool for accessing his patients' repressed memories. However, he abandoned this technique because the use of hypnosis seemed to stir up such "archaic" emotional feelings in his patients. This fact, however, left him with a question: what was hypnosis anyway, and why did it have these powerful effects?

In his final set of reflections on the matter, presented in a book called *Group psychology and the analysis of the ego* (1920), Freud suggested that hypnosis was possible because human beings have inherited an unconscious inclination to surrender their will to the power of the powerful chieftain, god, or father. "The hypnotist," he wrote:

> . . . awakens in the subject a portion of his archaic inheritance which had also made him compliant towards his parents and which had experienced an individual re-animation in his relation to his father; what is thus awakened is the idea of a paramount and dangerous personality, towards whom only a passive-masochistic attitude is possible, to whom one's will has to be surrendered (Freud, 1920).

A decade later, prompted by conversations with the French biographer Romain Rolland (who was interested in Indian religious traditions), Freud also addressed the nature of trance states produced by meditative and yogic practices—specifically, the oft-reported "oceanic" feeling of "oneness with the universe." He proposed that these experiences had their roots in infantile experiences of subjective merging with the world, and especially with the mother (Harrison, 1979). They had no inherent higher spiritual meaning, and no particular therapeutic value.

In short, by the late 1920s, Freud had judged both hypnosis and meditation to involve regression to infantile states of mind. Hypnosis tapped into primitive instincts to do with submission to the authoritarian father, while mysticism tapped into primitive instincts to do with surrender to the "oceanic" embrace of the mother.

Pathological or health-enhancing? The case of religious trance

In these same years, anthropology—shaking itself (partially) loose from its nineteenth-century crude concerns with racial hierarchy and differences between civilized and savage societies, had begun to think about trance as well. The phenomena that concerned this discipline were not home-grown forms of trance like hypnosis, with a medical patina, but phenomena with religious significance like spirit possession and shamanism, present in "primitive" Native American, African, and Asian societies. A number began to follow the lead of the German-American anthropologist Franz Boas, who had insisted on the need to respect all practices in different cultures as meaning-making systems that needed to be understood in their own right (Boas, 1911, in Boas, 1989). His own reports of shamanism among the Kwatkiutl, therefore, did not address the question of the pathological nature (or not) of the associated trance states, but simply referred them to the local belief system and customs of that culture (Boas, 1897, in Boas, 1989).

Nevertheless, even after Boas, there remained a widespread tendency to mingle cultural analyses with medical judgments and to see (for example) shamanistic trance behaviors as evidence of undiagnosed schizophrenia (Noll, 1983; cf. Buckley, 1981). Spirit possession remained closely tied, in the thinking of many, to hysteria (e.g., Sargent, 1973). It might be possible to analyze the ways in which different societies made sense of trance in terms of their belief systems, but many outside those systems continued to regard the state as more pathological than not.

In 1965, the anthropologist Erika Bourguignon, however, perturbed this uneasy consensus by quietly insisting that trance was part of the general, healthy repertoire of human behaviors. Reviewing the literature on no less than 488 different cultures, she determined that some form of institutionalized altered state of consciousness was present in 90% of them. For the remaining 10%, there was simply insufficient evidence to be able to say for certain if trance was practiced (Bourguignon & Pettay, 1965). Based on these results, Bourguignon concluded that "the capacity to experience altered states of consciousness is a psychobiological capacity of the species, and thus universal," even though "its utility, institutionalization and patterning are, indeed, features of culture, and thus variable" (1973, p. 12). With her impressive statistical analysis, she directly challenged those who still believed trance experiences were marginal, deviant, or intrinsically pathological.

The 1960s would see the rise of new positive interest in the potential of certain kinds of trance (especially drug-induced varieties) to expand one's sense of reality. By the 1970s, experimentation with LSD was giving way to fascination with new kinds of meditative practices like "transcendental meditation" (TM) and Zen (see the section "Is 'trance' a special state or is it nothing special?"). Influential humanistic and transpersonal psychologists like Charles Tart and Arthur Deikman began insisting that everyday consciousness might be among the less interesting and valuable ways of engaging with reality (Tart, 1972; see also Chapter 9). Indeed, Deikman became well known for arguing that most people's everyday life was lived in a kind of "trance" and that practices like meditation contributed to greater awareness and awakening.

> So habitual is the trance of ordinary life that one could say that human beings are a race that sleeps and awakens, but does not awaken fully. Because half-awake is sufficient for the tasks we customarily do, few of us are aware of the dysfunction of our condition (Deikman, 1983).

It would be an exaggeration to say that the question as to whether trance is a good thing or a bad thing was resolved in the 1970s, but, by any measure, this was a good decade for people inclined to believe that trance states could contribute to human flourishing.

Impasse 2: Is trance a "special state" or is it nothing special?

At the same time, the 1970s were marked by a second unresolved controversy about the nature of trance, with a history that was at least as unstable as the one we have just reviewed.

Special brain state or nothing special? The case of hypnosis

The story here begins with late nineteenth-century attempts—already partly discussed—to investigate hypnosis as a special brain-state, probably of a pathological nature. Indeed, the Charcot school in Paris considered hypnosis a state of artificial hysteria, with fixed physiological stages, such as catalepsy and lethargy. For Charcot and his colleagues, in other words, hypnosis was a physiological state that followed internal laws, rather than a malleable psychological one that responded to suggestions from the hypnotist. In the mid 1880s, however, a rival of Charcot, Hippolyte Bernheim, challenged this perspective by a demonstration which pointed to quite a different conclusion: he could create all of Charcot's allegedly fixed physiological states in patients of his own but then, through something he called "the power of suggestion," he could change those states, or make them disappear (Bernheim, 1889/2006). Hypnosis seemed to be nothing more or less than what the operator, using suggestion, wanted it to be. Bernheim and others later went further and proposed that hypnosis (itself just a heightened state of receptivity to suggestion) was not even necessary for suggestion to work its powers on the mind and body. Waking suggestion in the absence of trance often seemed just as good.

For some late nineteenth-century hypnosis researchers, Bernheim's findings proved distinctly disturbing. It was hard to know how to study something that was apparently just a product of one's own commands. Maybe hypnosis was nothing more than submission to an authority figure, more a matter for politics and ethics than medicine. Partly in response, interest in hypnosis as a special trance state, with unique physiological or psychological characteristics, languished for some decades.

In the mid twentieth century, however, things took a new turn. As part of a belated effort to rekindle medical interest in hypnosis as a therapeutic tool (Pintar & Lynn, 2009), psychologist Ernest Hilgard argued that hypnosis, in fact, is a specific state—a "trance" state—that is categorically distinct from normal consciousness. However, to understand how it was, a new approach was needed. Hilgard found his new approach through his idea of the "hidden observer." He argued that, in hypnosis, there is a dissociation or splitting of awareness, different from anything seen in everyday life (the term "dissociation" was adopted from the French psychologist Pierre Janet). A person in a hypnotic state, for example, might say she feels no pain when an experimenter drives a pin into her arm, but it turns out that the "hidden observer" feels everything. Again, the person in a hypnotic state might become deaf or blind in response to a suggestion, but the "hidden observer" continues to hear and see and monitors everything (Hilgard, 1973, 1991). Hilgard's encouragement injunction to clinicians to reopen the case for seeing hypnosis as a "special state" encouraged other clinicians interested in hypnosis to develop a new, more united stance on this front, even if some of them pointed to other evidence for the special state theory of hypnosis than Hilgard had done (e.g., Crawford & Gruzelier, 1992; Spiegel & Spiegel, 1978/2008).

Not everyone was convinced. An alternative perspective, largely rooted in social psychology, had evidence of its own for concluding that, actually, all forms of so-called "hypnotic phenomena" could be accounted for using "constructs that [were] already an integral part of contemporary social psychology" (Spanos & Barber, 1974, p. 500). There was no need to posit the existence of a kind of trance-like "special state" to account for the phenomena observed in experimental and clinical settings. Psychologist Theodore Barber, for example, compared the behavior of stooges actively pretending to be hypnotized (simulators) and people presumably "really" hypnotized. He found that strongly motivated simulators were indistinguishable behaviorally from "really" hypnotized subjects. Social psychologists William Coe and Theodore Sarbin perhaps best summed up this new perspective when they argued that a hypnotized subject is like a dramatic actor who is highly absorbed in a given role. The hidden meaning of a hypnotic induction, they suggested, might be most appropriately phrased: "Please participate in a miniature drama" (Coe & Sarbin, 1991, p. 317; for more studies and analyses in this tradition, see Kirsch & Lynn, 1995; Sarbin & Coe, 1972; Spanos, 1991; Spanos & Chaves, 1970).

And so the battle lines were drawn. In 1992, in an essay pointedly entitled "Two hundred years of hypnosis research: Questions resolved? Questions unanswered!" Michael Dixon and Jean-Roch Laurence lamented the extent to which "research in hypnosis has essentially remained polarized, with separate schools adhering to basically the same theoretical perspectives that were established in the late 19th century": one camp persisted in arguing for the specific state-nature of hypnosis by proving that changes in cognitive (or, some insisted, brain) functioning occur, and the other camp persisted in arguing for the centrality of social role play, suggestion, and the demand characteristics of the hypnotic ritual (Dixon & Laurence, 1992, p. 40–44). It is true that, in a recent (2011) issue of the *International Journal of Clinical and Experimental Hypnosis,* psychologist Steven Jay Lynn and Joseph Green aimed to bring together the warring camps in an effort to find a path to "rapprochement." "Notions of unconscious processing and misattribution are not inconsistent with the concept of goal-directed action," they observed. Nevertheless, even they admitted that the project of reconciliation was still an unfinished one. "Complete rapprochement between competing theoretical camps," they admitted, may prove "elusive" (Lynn & Green, 2011).

Special brain state or nothing special? The case of meditation

Meanwhile, similar debates about the degree to which trance is a "special state" were going on in meditation research. In 1969, a graduate student at the University of California in Los Angeles, M. Robert Keith Wallace, decided to do his dissertation research on the physiological effects of a form of meditation derived from Hindu practices that had recently become widely popular in the United States and Europe—transcendental meditation, or TM. Taught by the Maharishi Mahesh Yogi from India, the claim of TM was that a mere 15–20 minutes of practice, twice a day, helped make a person's mind more peaceful, intelligent, and creative. Wallace recruited college students who had taken a course in TM, hooked them up to various measuring instruments, asked them to meditate, and found that, on average, they showed significant changes in their physiological state: reductions in oxygen consumption; reductions in resting heart rate; and changes in skin resistance (Harrington, 2007).

Most significantly, from Wallace's perspective, his subjects also showed significant changes in their brain waves—evidence, he believed, that their brains (and minds) were in a unique trance state. According to Wallace, electroencephalography (EEG) results showed a highly coherent pattern of brain-wave activity that he believed to be different from anything previously reported in the literature. The Maharishi and his followers had long claimed that TM practice produced a unique state of consciousness. Wallace, it seemed, had now proven them right. In 1970, Wallace announced his discovery of a "fourth major state of consciousness" in the flagship journal, *Science*:

> Physiologically, the state produced by transcendental meditation seems to be distinct from commonly encountered states of consciousness, such as wakefulness, sleep, and dreaming, and from altered states of consciousness, such as hypnosis and autosuggestion (Wallace, 1970).

The cardiologist Herbert Benson at Harvard Medical School disagreed. Benson had been interested for some time in the possibility that stress increased one's risk for heart disease, and was persuaded in the late 1960s to investigate TM as a potential strategy for stress reduction. When he first began studying TM practitioners, Benson had not known of Wallace's work, but upon discovering it, he proposed a collaboration. Wallace moved to Harvard, and he, Benson, and a third colleague, Archie F. Wilson, developed a new protocol to study their subjects. Blood pressure, heart rate, brain waves, rates of metabolism, and rates of breathing were all to be measured under two conditions: first, the subjects would be asked to sit quietly for 20 minutes; and second, they would be asked to sit quietly and meditate—repeat their mantra, etc.—for 20 minutes. The aim was to assess the distinctive contribution (if any) of meditation. "What we found," Benson later recalled, "was astounding. Through the simple act of changing their thought patterns, the subjects experienced decreases in their metabolism, breathing rate and brain wave frequency" (Benson, 2001).

At the same time, Benson was adamant that the changes in brain wave frequency in his meditating subjects were merely evidence that the practitioners were very relaxed; there was no reason to conclude from these data, he believed, that TM produced a "special state" of consciousness, with a unique brain signature. Benson's challenge to Wallace's EEG data infuriated the TM community, and helped trigger a series of studies in the 1970s aimed at resolving the issue, albeit with no clear outcome (e.g., AvRuskin, 1988; Corby, Roth, Zarcone, & Kopell, 1978; Delmonte, 1984; Elson, Hauri, & Conis, 1977; Fenwick, Donaldson, & Gillis, 1977; Morse, Martin, Furst, & Dubin, 1977). More recently, it has been claimed that the brain function of a few, very accomplished, meditators differs from anything seen in normal controls, especially in terms of their high frequency of gamma waves (Lutz, Greischar, Rawlings, Ricard, & Davidson, 2004) and their cerebral blood flow levels to certain brain areas associated with a state of waking rest (Brewer et al., 2011). No one has suggested, though, that these findings have resolved the controversy, or that we now have a reliable biomarker of the meditative trance state itself.

Impasse 3: Is trance "one thing" or is it "many things"?

Running alongside the continuing unresolved controversies about whether trance is or is not a good thing, and about whether trance is or is not a "special state" has been a third disagreement over whether trance is a single thing at all. Perhaps there is no such thing as "trance" as such. Perhaps there are only "trances"—a whole family of discrete phenomena, each of which requires investigation in its own right (cf. Aaronson, 1973).

Anthropologists in particular have pushed this perspective. Erica Bourguignon, for example, early introduced what became a widely accepted distinction in anthropology between two kinds of trance that she called "trance" and "possession-trance." For Bourguignon, "trance" was the term to be applied to certain altered states of consciousness that are experienced as being under voluntary control of the individual, whereas "possession-trance" was the term to be applied to other, distinctively different altered states of consciousness that were experienced as being largely involuntary (Bourguignon, 1973, 1989a).

Others within anthropology proposed alternative typologies. For example, in the early 1980s, anthropologists Larry Peters and Douglass Price-Williams proposed a distinction between "trance" and something they called "ecstasy" (Peters and Price-Williams, 1983). Trance, they suggested, was an altered state of consciousness involving voluntary mastery of the altered experience; it was commonly experienced during shamanistic practices and perhaps some experiences of Western hypnosis. Ecstasy, in contrast, was an experience of altered consciousness marked by a sense of loss of control; it was commonly experienced in certain kinds of possession rituals and ritual dance performances. Gilbert Rouget, well known for his analyses of the role played by music in trance, also differentiated trance from ecstasy, but (rather confusingly) focused on a quite different set of criteria for defining each. For Rouget, "ecstasy" was a state characterized by immobility, silence, and solitude (characteristic of various meditative traditions), while "trance" was an experience that he associated with music, movement, noise, and crowds (Rouget, 1985).

Some people who defended these various typologies, especially those within anthropology, also attempted to relate them to different hypothesized brain states. They suggested, for example, that some kinds of trance might be associated with the release of endorphins, facilitating resistance to pain. Others might be associated with the release of peptides such as oxytocin, facilitating feelings of attachment or affiliation (e.g., Wright, 1989). And some people came close to suggesting that there might be as many different kinds of trance as there were different cultural systems, because native explanatory systems of trance—the "rules" which dictate how trance feels and what it should look like—become instantiated in the experience itself (e.g., Bourguignon, 1989b).

In hypnosis research, a similar, if somewhat more muted, conversation was going on. Rather than talking about hypnosis as such, some said, the field needed to distinguish between self-hypnosis and hypnosis involving a hypnotist, or what was called hetero-hypnosis (Johnson, 1979); between cognitively oriented hypnosis and hypnosis with a strong emotional and relational dimension (Banyai, 1991); between the kind of hypnosis experienced by people with low susceptibility as opposed to that experienced by people with high susceptibility to trance (Brown, 1992; Woody, Bowers, & Oakman, 1992). Once people did that, the discipline would be on a much firmer basis for refining its understanding of the (likely varied) mechanisms and therapeutic potential of these practices.

Meditation researchers have also begun their own version of this conversation. As early as the late 1980s, the psychologist Daniel Goleman published a book that proposed a typology of different meditative states, and counted as many as 11 (Goleman, 1988/1996). Many laboratory studies that followed, however, often failed to engage with the implications of the fact that they might be dealing with a pluralistic set of traditions. Why should anyone have ever thought that practices as diverse as Sufi dancing, Tibetan tantric practices, and Taoist T'ai Chi could all just be subsumed under the same umbrella term "meditation"? One answer, a more recent generation of scholars have suggested, lies in the field's unfortunate continuing attachment to the early twentieth-century ideology of "perennialism." Perennialism has historically believed that, beneath their surface differences, all religions teach truths distilled from shared mystical insights (Huxley & Bradshaw, 1945). A more reasonable, if less romantic alternative, these scholars say, is to begin with difference as it presents itself in the lived traditions themselves. Instead of assuming that there is one mystical experience that is the same for everyone, we need to pay careful attention to nuanced differences in the introspective reports of different kinds of meditative states, and create a map of similarities and differences in experiences associated with different kinds of practices (e.g., Bitbol & Petitmengin, 2013). From there, one can begin to develop hypotheses about underlying shared and different brain mechanisms involved (e.g., Lutz, Slagter, Dunne, & Davidson, 2008; Liftshitz et al. 2014.).

Even as all these conversations proceed apace, some continue to defend an argument for unity. In anthropology, this defense has generally taken the form of suggesting that there is one mechanism underlying all different forms of trance, which is then differently patterned or strategically developed through different practices and in different cultural settings (e.g., De Rios and Winkelman, 1989; Winkelman, 2010, 2011). In hypnosis research, "dissociation" was, for a long time, a leading proposed cognitive mechanism thought to unite phenomena as apparently diverse as "conversion hysteria, hypnotic trance, mediumistic trance, multiple personality, fugue states, spirit possession states and highway hypnosis" (Ludwig, 1983). Most recently, though, attention here has turned to a network of brain regions that are active when the individual is in a state of wakeful rest, but not engaged with the outside world: the so-called "default mode network." Evidence has been gathered that this network is altered in certain meditative states (Brewer et al., 2011), in states of hypnosis (Deeley et al., 2012), and in the psychedelic state produced by drugs such as psilocybin used in traditional religious ceremonies (Carhart-Harris et al., 2012). These converging research efforts have led some researchers to wonder whether they have identified a candidate biomarker for trance, in general, that might also be sufficiently malleable to account for reported and observed differences in experience. Time may tell.

Conclusion

Hypnosis researchers, meditation researchers, and anthropologists have, historically, grappled with something called "trance." All three have inherited considerable confusion and controversy over what this entity might be, and even whether it is a useful construct at all. For much of the time, these research communities have largely argued about the issues in relative isolation from one another. If the respective fields now seek to begin new kinds of conversations and even collaborations, one useful starting point may be a reckoning of the role that trance—as an idea and an experience—has played in their respective research efforts over the years. In particular, they might usefully focus attention on the three persistent difficulties that have bedeviled research on trance: Is it or is it not a good thing? Is it or is it not a special state of consciousness? And, in the end, is it or is it not one thing at all? Why have these questions so persistently divided researchers in this field? What have been the distinctive contributions of different research traditions (hypnosis research, meditation research, cultural anthropology) to debates around these questions? The philosopher and essayist George Santayana is generally credited with the epithet, "Those who cannot remember the past are condemned to repeat it." In few fields does this seem more likely to be the case than this one.

References

Aaronson, B. S. (1973). ASCID trance, hypnotic trance, just trance. *American Journal of Clinical Hypnosis*, **16**(2), 110–117.

AvRuskin, T. (1988). Neurophysiology and the curative possession trance. *The Chinese Medical Anthropology Quarterly*, **2**(3), 286–302.

Banyai, E. (1991). Toward a social psychobiological model of hypnosis. In S. J. Lynn & J. W. Rhue (Eds.), *Theories of hypnosis: current models and perspectives*. New York: Guildford Press.

Benson, H. (2001). Mind–body pioneer—Mind/Body Medical Institute. *Psychology Today*

Bernheim, H. (2006). *Suggestive therapeutics: a treatise on the nature and uses of hypnotism*. Kessinger Publishing. (Original work published 1889)

Bitbol, M., & Petitmengin, C. (2013). A defense of introspection from within. *Constructivist Foundations*, **8**(3), 269–279.

Boas, F. (1989). *A Franz Boas reader: the shaping of American anthropology, 1883–1911*. Chicago: University of Chicago Press.

Bourguignon, E. (1973). *Religion, altered states of consciousness, and social change*. Ohio: The Ohio State University Press.

Bourguignon, E. (1989a). Trance and Shamanism: what's in a name? *Journal of Psychoactive Drugs*, **21**(1), 9–15.

Bourguignon, E. (1989b). Multiple personality, possession trance, and the psychic unity of mankind. *Ethos*, **17**(3), 371–384.

Bourguignon, E., & Pettay, L. (1965). Spirit possession, trance, and cross-cultural research. In *Proceedings of the 1964 Annual Spring Meeting of the American Ethnological Society*. Seattle: University of Washington Press.

Braid, J. (1843). *Neurypnology; or the rationale of nervous sleep, considered in relation with animal magnetism*. London: John Churchill.

Braid, J. (2008). *The discovery of hypnosis: the complete writings of James Braid, the father of hypnotherapy*. UK: CHH Ltd.

Brewer, J. A., Worhunsky, P. D., Gray, J. R., Tang, Y-Y., Weber, J., & Kober, H. (2011). Meditation experience is associated with differences in default mode network activity and connectivity. *Proceedings of the National Academy of Sciences*, **108**(50), 20254–20259.

Brown, D. P. (1992). Clinical hypnosis research since 1986. In E. Fromm & M. R. Nash (Eds.), *Contemporary hypnosis research* (pp. 427–458). New York: Guildford Press.

Buckley, P. (1981). Mystical experience and schizophrenia. *Schizophrenia Bulletin*, **7**(3), 516–521.

Carhart-Harris, R. L., Erritzoe, D., Williams, T., Stone, J. M., Reed, L. J., Colasanti, A., . . . David J. Nutta (2012). Neural correlates of the psychedelic state as determined by fMRI studies with psilocybin. *Proceedings of the National Academy of Sciences*, **109**(6), 2138–2143.

Charcot, J. M., & Richer, P. (1887). *Les démoniaques dans l'art*. Paris: Delahaye et Lecrosnier.

Coe, W., & Sarbin, T. R. (1991). Role theory: hypnosis from a dramaturgical and narrational. In S. J. Lynn & J. W. Rhue (Eds.), *Theories of hypnosis: current models and perspectives* (pp. 303–323). New York: The Guildford Press.

Corby, J. C., Roth, W. T., Zarcone, V. P., & Kopell, B. S. (1978). Psychophysiological correlates of Tantric yoga meditation. *Archives of General Psychiatry*, **35**, 571–577.

Crawford, H. J., & Gruzelier, J. H. (1992). A midstream view of the neuropsychophysiology of hypnosis: recent research and future directions. In E. Fromm & M. R. Nash (Eds.), *Contemporary hypnosis research* (pp. 227–266). New York: Guildford Press. Retrieved from http://psycnet.apa.org/psycinfo/1992-98303-009

De Rios, M. D., & Winkelman, M. (1989).Shamanism and altered states of consciousness: an introduction. *Journal of Psychoactive Drugs*, **21**(1), 1–7.

Deeley, Q., Oakley, D. A., Toone, B., Giampietro, V., Brammer, M. J., Williams, S. C. R., & Halligan, P. W. (2012). Modulating the default mode network using hypnosis. *The International Journal of Clinical and Experimental Hypnosis*, **60**(2), 206–228.

Deikman, A. J. (1983). *The observing self: mysticism and psychotherapy*. Beacon Press.

Delmonte, M. M. (1984). Electrocortical activity and related phenomenon associated with meditation practice: a literature review. *International Journal of Neuroscience*, **24**, 217–231.

Dixon, M., & Laurence, J-R. (1992). Two hundred years of hypnosis research: questions resolved? In E. Fromm & M. R. Nash (Eds.), *Contemporary hypnosis research* (pp. 34–66). New York: Guildford Press.

Elliotson, J. (1843). *Numerous cases of surgical operations without pain in the mesmeric state, with remarks upon the opposition . . . to the perception of the inestimable blessings of mesmerism*. H. Baillière.

Elson, B. B., Hauri, D., & Conis, D. (1977). Physiological changes in yoga meditation. *Psychophysiology*, **14**, 52–57.

Esdaile, J. (1856). *The introduction of mesmerism (with sanction of the government) into the public hospitals of India*. W. Kent.

Fenwick, P. B., Donaldson, S., & Gillis, L. (1977). Metabolic and EEG changes during TM: an explanation. *Biological Psychology*, **5**, 101–118.

Freud, S. (1975). *Group psychology and the analysis of the ego*. New York: W.W. Norton & Company. (Original work published 1920)

Goldstein, J. (1982). The hysteria diagnosis and the politics of anticlericalism in late nineteenth-century France. *The Journal of Modern History*, 209–239.

Goleman, D. (1996). *The meditative mind: the varieties of meditative experience*. G.P. Putnam & Sons. (Original work published 1988)

Harrington, A. (2007). *The cure within: a history of mind–body medicine*. New York: Norton.

Harrison, I. B. (1979). On Freud's view of the infant–mother relationship and of the oceanic feeling—some subjective influences. *Journal of the American Psychoanalytic Association*, **27**, 399–422.

Hilgard, E. R. (1973). A neurodissociation interpretation of pain reduction in hypnosis. *Psychological Review*, **80**, 396–411.

Hilgard, E. R. (1991). A neodissociation interpretation of hypnosis. In S. J. Lynn & J. W. Rhue (Eds.), *Theories of hypnosis: current models and perspectives* (pp. 83–104). New York, Guilford Press.

Huxley, A., & Bradshaw, D. (1945). *The perennial philosophy*. New York: Harper.

Johnson, L. S. (1979). Self-hypnosis: Behavioral and phenomenological comparisons with heterohypnosis. *The International Journal of Clinical and Experimental Hypnosis*, **27**(3), 240–264.

Kirsch, I., & Lynn, S. J. (1995). Altered state of hypnosis: changes in the theoretical landscape. *American Psychologist*, **50**(10), 846.

Lifshitz, M., Cusumano, E. P., & Raz, A. (2014). Meditation and hypnosis at the intersection between phenomenology and cognitive science. In *Meditation–neuroscientific approaches and philosophical implications* (pp. 211–226). Springer International Publishing.

Ludwig, A. M. (1983). The psychobiological functions of dissociation. *American Journal of Clinical Hypnosis*, **26**(2), 93–99.

Lutz, A., Greischar, L. L., Rawlings, N. B., Ricard, M., & Davidson, R. J. (2004). Long-term meditators self-induce high-amplitude gamma synchrony during mental practice. *Proceedings of the National Academy of Science, USA*, **101**(46), 16369–16373.

Lutz, A., Slagter, H. A., Dunne, J. D., & Davidson, R. J. (2008). Attention regulation and monitoring in meditation. *Trends in Cognitive Sciences*, **12**(4), 163–169.

Lynn, S. J., & Green, J. P. (2011). The sociocognitive and dissociation theories of hypnosis: toward a rapprochement. *International Journal of Clinical and Experimental Hypnosis*, **59**(3), 277–293.

Morse, D. R., Martin, J. S., Furst, M. L., & Dubin, L. L. (1977). A physiological and subjective evaluation of meditation, hypnosis, and relaxation. *Psychosomatic Medicine*, **39**(5), 304–324.

Noll, R. (1983). Shamanism and schizophrenia: a state-specific approach to the 'schizophrenia metaphor' of Shamanic states. *American Ethnologist*, 10(3), 443–459.

Peters, G., & Price Williams, D. (1983). Towards an experiential analysis of Shamanism. *American Ethnologist*, **7**, 398–418.

Pintar, J., & Lynn, S. J. (2009). *Hypnosis: a brief history*. John Wiley & Sons.

Rouget, G. (1985). *Music and trance: A theory of the relations between music and possession*. University of Chicago Press.

Sarbin, T. R., & Coe, W. C. (1972). *Hypnosis: a social psychological analysis of influence communication*. New York: Holt, Rinehart and Winston.

Sargent, W. (1973). *The mind possessed: a physiology of possession, mysticism, and faith healing*. London: Heinemann.

Spanos, N. (1991). A socio-cognitive approach to hypnosis. In S. J. Lynn & J. W. Rhue (Eds.), *Theories of hypnosis: current models and perspectives* (pp. 324–361). New York: The Guildford Press.

Spanos, N., & Chaves, J. (1970). Hypnosis research: a methodological critique of experiments. *The American Journal of Clinical Hypnosis*, **13**(2), 108–127.

Spanos, N. P., & Theodore, X. B. (1974). Toward a convergence in hypnosis research. *American Psychologist* **29**(7), 500.

Spiegel, H., & Spiegel, D. (2008). *Trance and treatment: clinical uses of hypnosis.* Arlington, VA: American Psychiatric Publishing. (Original work published 1978).

Tart, C. T. (1972). *Altered states of consciousness.* New York: Doubleday.

Wallace, R. K. (1970). Physiological effects of transcendental meditation. *Science,* **167**(3926), 1751–1754.

Winkelman, M. (2010). *Shamanism: a biopsychosocial paradigm of consciousness and healing.* Santa Barbara, California: Prager (ABC-CLIO).

Winkelman, M. (2011). A paradigm for understanding altered consciousness: the integrative mode of consciousness. In E. Cardena & M. Winkelman (Eds.), *Altering consciousness: multidisciplinary perspectives* (pp. 23–42). Santa Barbara, California: Prager (ABC-CLIO).

Winter, A. (1998). Mesmerism and the introduction of surgical anesthesia to Victorian England. *Engineering and Science,* **2**, 30–37.

Woody, E. Z., Bowers, K. S., & Oakman, J. M. (1992). A conceptual analysis of hypnotic responsiveness: experience, individual differences, and Contemporary hypnosis research. New York : Guilford Press, 1992, pp. 3–31.

Wright, P. A. (1989). The nature of the Shamanic state of consciousness: a review. *Journal of Psychoactive Drugs,* **21**(1), 25–33.

Chapter 3

Visualization as mental cultivation
Expanding our understanding of meditation

Thupten Jinpa

Abstract

There is, today, increasing awareness within the scientific world, as well as the larger public, about the benefits of meditation. Although the practices being studied may be derived from traditional Buddhist sources, there is little understanding, even among the researchers, of how meditation is conceived, what practices it consists of, and what role these practices play in the traditional Buddhist context. This chapter focuses on a specific form of visualization meditation popular in the Tibetan tradition, which primarily involves conscious creative imagining as a means of mental cultivation. Discussion of this practice serves to destabilize the popular conception of meditation as mere "unlearning" or "bare awareness"—a view that would indeed make meditation quite distinct from, and perhaps even irreconcilable with, hypnosis. In fact, meditation is akin to hypnosis in that it seeks to cultivate particular mind states (e.g., imagery, compassion) through specific modulations of attention and suggestion.

Introduction

In the summer of 2003, *TIME* magazine featured a cover story on the "Science of meditation," with the American actress Heather Graham sitting in a meditative pose on its cover. What appeared on the sidebar on that cover was quite telling. It read: "New Age mumbo jumbo? Not according to millions of Americans who meditate for health and wellbeing. Here is how it works." The ingenuity of this text is that, in few words, it accomplished three things. It acknowledged the potential initial skepticism of the general reader, through alluding to meditation's somewhat culturally alien roots; it then reassured the reader with the news that actually millions of fellow Americans already do it; and finally, it promised to explain how meditation works. This cover story of *TIME* can be seen as indicating a landmark shift in the wider cultural attitude towards meditation and its place within contemporary culture, at least in North America. In essence, the emerging new attitude that *TIME*'s cover story intended to convey was this: meditation is no longer one of those strange things that people do as a fad; it is something that millions of ordinary folks do, for their health and for their well-being. More importantly, now there is a serious science that backs up the benefits of meditation.

TIME's cover story leaves little doubt as to what its author saw as the main selling point about meditation; it is the "science of meditation"—more specifically, the numerous clinical studies on the effects of mindfulness. Although the scientific study of meditation predates the contemporary mindfulness movement (see Chapter 2), systematic clinical studies only began to take off after the emergence of secularized mindfulness practices, especially MBSR (Mindfulness-Based Stress Reduction) as developed by Jon Kabat-Zinn. The history of the evolution of modern mindfulness practice is a complex one, with some of its antecedents going back to early Theravada teachings as well as to a popular Buddhist meditation movement in Burma in the early twentieth century. This complex historical trajectory of modern mindfulness has been explored elsewhere (for a brief analysis of the evolution of modern mindfulness, see Sharf, 2000).

Whatever its origin, there is no denying that the story of mindfulness represents, to many, the best that can emerge from the meeting of contemplative tradition with modern science. Today, even a cursory glance on meditation research can reveal numerous clinical studies that have been conducted on the effects of mindfulness on a wide range of areas, from its effect on chronic pain to relief of stress, from treatment of depression to substance abuse, and from social anxiety to PTSD (post-traumatic stress disorder). Its outcomes on these kinds of important health measures seemed to have captured the attention of popular media as well as the imagination of the general public. Today, mindfulness has become part of the established lexicon of popular media, with people speaking of "mindful schools," "mindful leadership," "mindful parenting," and so on.

What might this rapid growth in the mindfulness movement, both within scientific research and the larger contemporary culture, entail for our understanding of meditation in general? How might this influence the scientific study of the nature and function of meditation practice? Can current popularity and success of mindfulness, aligned so closely to health outcome measures, ultimately become an obstacle for deeper scientific engagement with meditation? These are some of the questions I shall aim to address in this chapter. In the process, I shall also seek to expand our contemporary understanding of what meditation is, by calling attention to meditation's role within the larger vision of spiritual transformation, as understood by traditions such as Buddhism.

Are we speaking of states or processes?

One salient question vis-à-vis current "science of meditation," that has so far not received adequate critical attention, is what exactly do we mean by meditation, especially in the context of scientific research? What is the phenomenon that is being studied and measured? This lack of clarity regarding, to use technical scientific jargon, what the actual construct is, has been identified as a major shortcoming of the numerous meditation studies undertaken so far.[1] I am not speaking of the need to have an exact definition of meditation, nor am I suggesting that we should presuppose some kind of irreducible essence that all types and instances of meditations share in common. However, there needs to be some broad consensus on a set of characteristics that help us determine what constitutes meditation and what does not. There is also the need for greater critical awareness of the ways in which specific words like "meditation" and "mindfulness" come

---

[1] In 2007, the University of Alberta Evidence-based Practice Center produced an independent, peer-reviewed meta-analysis of the state of meditation research. This report was commissioned by the United States National Center for Complementary and Alternative Medicine (NCCAM). An important criticism of the report was how the current scientific research on meditation lacked "common theoretical perspective and is characterized by poor methodological quality." (See Ospina et al., 2007)

to acquire specific meanings and use, as a result of social and cultural forces. This is an area where the critical perspectives of humanities can be of great help.

Let us take the word "meditation", which is our focus here. The word itself is English and, with its Latin root, means generally, "to think, contemplate, and ponder." However, when we speak of the "science of meditation" or use the word meditation in contemporary culture and media, we do not use it in this original sense of the English term. Rather, we use it to refer to forms of spiritual practice associated more specifically with classical Indian traditions, especially Buddhism. In this second more popular usage, the term "meditation" covers a broad range of practices that include techniques to help calm the mind, focus our attention, enhance qualities like compassion, and bring greater integration of our values and aspirations with our desires and behavior, and so on. When used in this new sense, essentially, the English word "meditation" is being used to convey, at least from the classical Buddhist sources, two distinct but closely related Sanskrit terms—*dhyana* meaning "meditative absorptions" and *bhavana* meaning "mental cultivation." When referring to a state, the word "meditation" is being used to convey the sense of *dhyana*; in contrast, when the word is being used to refer to a practice and its associated processes, it conveys more the sense of the word *bhavana*. To complicate further, there is an additional Sanskrit term, *samadhi*— translated often as "concentration"—which tends to be rendered into English also as "meditation." Part of the lack of clarity about which the critics of the current science of meditation complain perhaps comes from researchers' conflation of these two senses of the term "meditation."

I shall not delve into the complex issue of the distinct meanings of these technical Buddhist terms and how the three might be interrelated. For our purpose, it is helpful to note that, in their traditional contexts, *dhyana* and *samadhi* are used mostly in describing meditative states, while the term *bhavana* is associated with practices and associated techniques.[2] Since *bhavana* is more specifically technique- and practice-oriented, descriptions of *bhavana* tend to be understandably more practical and specific. In contrast, descriptions of *dhyana* and *samadhi* tend to be more laden with doctrinal or metaphysical elements important to the specific tradition. A Hindu adept might attain a *samadhi* wherein he or she gains deep insight into their true self, *atman*, while a Buddhist adept might attain an insight that reveals the very absence of such an atman. It is no wonder, therefore, that the academic discussion of mystical experience has opened up an intense debate surrounding the question of whether or not it makes sense to speak of a state of oneness, which transcends specificity of tradition and culture.[3] Another methodological problem of taking a meditative state as the object of scientific study is the challenge of operationalizing the construct itself (see Chapter 10). Do we take the textual descriptions of the specific traditions of these states and attempt to identify the states by some kind of reverse inference, using, among other forms of data, brain-imaging results? Or, do we take the first-person reports of the adept as accurate accounts of mental states they are experiencing? The few attempts made so far at scientifically

---

[2] I am defining these Sanskrit terms according to the Indo-Tibetan Buddhist traditions. To make reading of the Sanskrit and Tibetan terms easier for non-specialists, I shall use easy phonetics throughout this chapter.

[3] This current debate on mysticism is broadly characterized as a contrast of two approaches to the scientific study of mystical experiences. The essentialist model views mystical experiences as being independent of socio-cultural contexts, while the contextualist approach understands mystical experiences as being embedded in the conceptual background of the mystic. It is primarily the writings of the Jewish thinker Steven Katz, including his *Mysticism and language* (Oxford University Press, 1992), and his contextualist interpretation of mysticism that opened the new wave of debates on the scientific study of mysticism.

studying the Buddhist *dhyana* states, for example, have shown serious limitations of this line of inquiry into scientifically understanding meditation.

What I see as a more fruitful approach in meditation research is to relate to meditation primarily in the second sense—that is, in the technical and practical sense conveyed by the Sanskrit term *bhavana*. Etymologically, the term connotes the notion of "cultivation," while its Tibetan equivalent *gom* (spelt *sgom*) carries the idea of developing "familiarity." Together, the Sanskrit and its Tibetan equivalent imply the idea of some kind of repetitive process of cultivating a familiarity, whether it is with respect to a habit, a way of seeing, or a way of being, grounded in a disciplined application of our mind. So, paying attention with conscious intention, sustaining that attention by constantly bringing back our mind, not letting our mind be swayed by automatic thought processes, and repetitively engaging in the chosen task are the characteristics we observe across the various practices that are traditionally referred to as meditations. Thus, in this sense of *bhavana*, meditation becomes something that we do. In contrast, in the sense of *dhyana*, meditation becomes something that we attain as a result.

Now, the advantage of focusing on meditation as a practice in the context of scientific study is quite evident. To begin with, the operationalization of what is being studied becomes more manageable. Although there will always be some gulf between what the person asserts he is doing, when doing meditation x, and what might be actually taking place, there is at least an explicit protocol of the practice that the person is supposed to be engaging in. Whether it is compassion meditation or mindfulness, the researchers will be able to examine the specific elements and steps that constitute the overall practice of the given meditation. This way of defining meditation is consonant with the approach, some have suggested, that would emphasize the particularities of the specific tradition's practices being studied (Lutz, Dunne, & Davidson, 2007). In addition, the study of meditation can then draw on therapeutic models, such as hypnosis and CBT (cognitive behavior therapy), which have a longer history of scientific research. In this respect, the detailed and concrete descriptions of the elements of a given meditation practice might also help develop hypotheses on the mechanisms of how specific effects might be occurring.

Given the broad definition of what meditation practice is, it is no surprise that in traditional sources, such as in the classical Buddhist texts, we find quite a diverse array of practices included in the category of meditation. For example, there is the meditation on impermanence, where the meditator takes the fundamental truth of the utterly transient nature of his life as *the object* of deep contemplation. Then, there is the meditation in the form of *cultivation* of positive mental qualities, such as compassion and loving kindness. Here, compassion and loving kindness are not so much the objects of meditation; rather, the person seeks to cultivate these qualities within his or her heart. There is also the practice of meditation as *imagined simulation*, such as where the person visualizes himself or herself as going through the various stages of the experience of dying. In addition, there is the meditation in the form of an *aspiration* where, for example, the meditator aspires to attain the enlightened attributes of the Buddha for the sake of bringing about the welfare of countless sentient beings. In general, the Tibetan Buddhist tradition subsumes the practice of meditation into two generic categories: absorptive meditation (*jog gom*) and discursive meditation (*che gom*), and the epitome of these two are "tranquil abiding" (*shamatha*) and "insight" (*vipasyana*). A seamless fusion of these two—*shamatha* and *vipasyana*—is understood to be the mark of true expertise in a meditator. Understanding this kind of diversity of meditation practices is crucial if we are to avoid the temptation of viewing meditation as constituting some kind of homogenous mental state, characterized primarily by absence of thought.

The role of meditation within its traditional context

Now, if we examine the role of meditation in its traditional context, we will be better able to appreciate why there is such diversity of practice under the rubric of meditation. Briefly put, meditation is part of the larger soteriological project of spiritual awakening, whereby we are enabled to bring home, powerfully, the insights and truths of the tradition. In plain English, meditation is what helps us to process and integrate the insights of the tradition into our own personal experience. This integration might take the negative form of dismantling our deep-seated notions of independence and selfhood, or the constructive role of giving insights into the nature and functions of the mental world. In both of these instances, what meditation does is to bring what was previously only a cognitive understanding, an idea, a belief, or even knowledge, to a point where it becomes part of our immediate and spontaneous knowledge. In this way, our knowledge directly impacts our behavior and attitudes—in short, the very way of our being in the world. In this way, meditation makes what was initially an effortful, deliberative, and often simulated activity into something that is characterized by effortlessness, immediacy, and spontaneity (for a neurocognitive account of such transformational processes, see Chapter 11).

In the Tibetan tradition, in particular, the role of meditation is often portrayed within the dynamic relationship of a trio—view, meditation, and action. View refers to the basic perception and attitudes we bring to the world, in our everyday engagement. It is our outlook, our worldview, which inevitably impacts the way we perceive our own selves and the world around us. One of the tasks of the spiritual aspirant is to engage with the insights of the tradition so that they inform our cognitive stance vis-à-vis reality. However, for these insights to have a real impact, so that they might shape our habits and behavior, they must be integrated into the very fabric of our personality, becoming almost second nature to us. This can only happen if we have integrated our perceptions, our attitudes, and our values through prolonged meditation practice. It is meditation that connects our intellectual knowledge and the desired change in our attitude and behavior. Meditation is, thus, the classical Indian tradition's answer to the perennial Greek question, "Why is it that our knowledge does not immediately translate into the appropriate action?"

Visualization as meditation—the case of deity-yoga practice

In the remaining part of this chapter, I would like to present the case of Tibetan deity-yoga (*lhai naljor*) practice, a form of Vajrayana meditation that is widespread in the Tibetan tradition, and examine what kinds of processes are involved in such meditations (for a description of the steps and elements of a Tibetan deity-yoga meditation, based on the popular meditation deity Vajrayogini, see Lopez, 2008). Let me briefly outline the basic structure of this kind of meditation and identify the key elements. The point of this is to offer a glimpse of the complexity of mental activity involved in a task that is an important element of formal meditation practice in the Indo-Tibetan tradition. The process involves not just emptying our mind of thoughts, but also an active, imaginative creation—not unlike a fiction—of our own virtual world and a new self within it. The practice involves applications of intention, attention, meta-awareness, and active imagining, with a high degree of suspension of ordinary thoughts and judgment.

Preliminaries

- ◆ You reaffirm your altruistic motive, especially in the context of the deity-yoga meditation.
- ◆ You then undergo a cleansing rite, including declaration and purification of any past known and unknown negative deeds.

◆ Finally, you invoke the inspirations of the great yogis that have been part of the lineage of the particular deity-yoga practice.

The Main Practice

◆ You dissociate from your ordinary everyday identity and all its attendant perceptions of the world, first by means of dissolving everything into a void. A more elaborate form of this meditation might actually involve imagining the process of dying, whereby your imagined death coincides with the dissolution of everything into emptiness. You then abide in this state of void for a while.

◆ From within this emptiness, you imagine the essence of your pure mind appearing in the shape of a specific colored letter standing upright in the empty space. The letter is made of light, symbolizing its insubstantial nature as well as its purity, unblemished by any conditioned ego identity. This is the arising of form from emptiness.

◆ In the third phase, you imagine the essence of your mind, represented in the form of a letter, emerging now into the full embodiment of an enlightened being—a meditation deity as described in the specific text of that particular practice. Not only do you arise into a full embodied being, but you do so within an entire world as well, traditionally envisioned as a *mandala*, a cosmic circle. At your heart is a letter, typically a character that has a long vowel as part of its form. A key part of this meditation is that you not only *perceive* yourself as an enlightened being with a particular form, but also *identify* yourself as such.

◆ Then, while as an enlightened being, you imagine engaging in all sorts of altruistic deeds, helping other sentient beings through your compassion and power.

◆ Still maintaining your perception and awareness of yourself as an enlightened deity, you engage in mantra repetition.

Throughout all these stages, the crucial point is to suspend your ordinary perceptions and personal identity. Your body is an enlightened form; your speech, a mantra; and your mind, the enlightened mind of the deity.

Concluding Practice

◆ In conclusion, you dissolve the entire imagined world back into emptiness. You do this in a gradual process, dissolving inwards from the outside—the entire world dissolves into the *mandala*, the aspects of the mandala dissolve into yourself, and you dissolve both from above and below into the letter at your heart. This letter, too, which has a complex form, progressively shrinks, finally dissolving into total emptiness. Then, you abide in this state of emptiness for a little while.

◆ Finally, before you end the meditation session, you imagine reappearing, ideally in a form that carries some resonance of that enlightened identity.

Typically, these kinds of meditations are undertaken on the basis of chanting of the *sadhana* text, a meditation text written in the form of a script. In monasteries, the deity-yoga meditations are often done in groups, where the chanting of the text is led by a chant master who is an expert in directing the pace as well as injecting the pauses within the chanting to allow the visualizations to be synchronized with the progression of the script. I remember being so impressed when I first had the opportunity to chant one of the main *sadhana* texts with the monks of the Gyuto Monastery, one of the two main tantric colleges of the dominant Geluk school.

From a functional perspective, the chanting of the text acts like auto-suggestion, while the immersion in the imagined scenarios enables suspension of one's everyday normal sense of self and the adoption of a different persona, not dissimilar to enactment or role playing. Since one deliberately assumes a new personal identity and deliberately confines one's perception to the imagined world, there is a narrowing of attention. However, unlike typical focused attention practice, such as *shamatha*, there is no retention of focus on a single object. However, with concentration, one follows the scenarios as they unfold in the process of "generating" oneself into an enlightened deity. We can see that this kind of meditation employs quite a large range of faculties and techniques. In addition to imagination/visualization, it requires concentration, attention, intention, identification, as well as suspension of our normal everyday awareness.

One important point to note regarding this type of meditation is the distinction drawn between *imagining* and *visualizing*, which is not so obvious. To visualize requires imagining, not vice versa. For example, when you imagine being an astronaut, say in a play, you can choose to visualize yourself as an astronaut. However, it is not necessary. You can simply pretend to be one, and act like one. Now, if you can visualize yourself as one, this will certainly make your task of imagining a lot easier. In deity-yoga meditation, too, what is essential is that you at least imagine assuming the appearance and identity of the specific enlightened deity. If you can visualize as such, this is of course even better.

Concluding points

In this chapter, I have aimed to draw attention to the problematic nature of the construct "meditation" in the context of the scientific research on meditation and conscious states more generally. I have argued that part of this problem comes from the manner in which the English word "meditation" is today used, both in scientific research as well as in popular culture. This usage involves the conflation of two distinct senses of the word "meditation", one as a state and the other as a practice or a process. I have argued that taking the second meaning of the word, as a practice, rather than as referring to a state, can bring greater clarity and efficiency to the scientific study of meditation. One important advantage of this approach is to bypass the issue of perennialism, whereby we feel compelled to somehow seek a unifying essence to all the diverse states of meditation. I have also argued how this practice- and technique-oriented definition of meditation is also more consonant with the role meditation is understood to play within its traditional context, at least in the Indo-Tibetan tradition I am familiar with. For when we understand the primary role of meditation in the larger project of spiritual practice, we will then appreciate the need for the diverse range of practices we see in these traditions. From the Buddhist tradition, for instance, the contemporary research world is familiar with mindfulness, compassion, and loving kindness meditations. However, there is still a vast array of practices that exist in the tradition's repertoire of meditation—deity-yoga, *chod* practice (see Chapter 4), emptiness meditation, physiologically oriented energy (*prana*) practices, and so on.

I have offered a brief outline of deity-yoga practice, which though widespread in the Tibetan tradition, is virtually unknown to the current science of meditation. The purpose of outlining this meditation is to illustrate the diversity of the practices that fall under the rubric of meditation, and how awareness of this diversity can help expand the horizons of meditation research. One striking feature of this Tibetan deity-yoga is the use of imagination in the sense of enactment, not dissimilar to a play, in meditation. As we broaden our understanding of what meditation is, such as through exposure to practices that are very different from typical mindfulness-type meditations, there is then the opportunity to bring to meditation research, perspectives and insights from other important fields of study, like hypnosis, that have a longer, more established history. This ability to bring perspectives from diverse fields will become increasingly important, especially as this research moves from simple study of the effects of meditation to understanding the underlying mechanisms.

References

Lopez, D. (2008). The meaning of meditation. In *Buddhism and science: a guide for the perplexed* (pp. 197–210). Chicago, IL; University of Chicago Press.

Lutz, A., Dunne, J. D., & Davidson, R. J. (2007). Meditation and the neuroscience of consciousness: an introduction. In P. D. Zelazo, M. Moscovitch, & E. Thompson (Eds.), *Cambridge handbook of consciousness* (pp. 499–554). Cambridge, England: Cambridge University Press.

Ospina, M. B., Bond, T. K., Karkhaneh, M., Tjosvold, L., Vandermeer, B., Liang, Y., . . . Klassen, T. P. (2007). *Meditation practices for health: state of the research. Evidence report/technology assessment no. 155.* Rockville, MD: Agency for Healthcare Research and Quality.

Sharf, R. H. (2000). The rhetoric of experience and the study of religion. *Journal of Consciousness Studies*, 7(11–12), 267–287.

Chapter 4

Transforming experience through the meditation and ritual of Chod
Insights from hypnosis research

Quinton Deeley

Abstract

Chod (Tibetan *gcod*), a ritual and meditation practice from the Tibetan Buddhist tradition, is associated with powerful transformations of experience that include the consumption of the practitioner's body by gods and demons in a deliberate act of self-offering. This practice is undertaken to realize Buddhist goals of compassion, non-attachment, and the direct recognition of non-self and the emptiness of phenomena. Practitioner accounts attest that these experiences of encounter with supernatural agents can be so vivid and realistic that they are terrifying. This raises the question of how the practice of Chod causes such powerful experiences of supernatural agents to arise. Chod's own account of how such experiences arise will be discussed in outline, before considering different perspectives from cognitive neuroscience and hypnosis research in particular. This leads to consideration of points of intersection as well as differences between the phenomena of Chod and hypnosis which resist their reduction to one another.

Introduction

This chapter discusses Chod (Tibetan *gcod*), a meditation practice from the Tibetan Buddhist tradition, which is associated with powerful transformations of experience that include the consumption of the practitioner's body by gods and demons in a deliberate act of self-offering. This practice is undertaken to realize Buddhist goals of compassion, non-attachment, and the direct recognition of non-self and the emptiness of phenomena. Practitioner accounts attest that these encounters with supernatural agents can be so vivid and realistic that they are terrifying. This raises the question of how the practice of Chod causes such powerful experiences of supernatural agents to arise. Indigenous Tibetan accounts of how such experiences arise are outlined, before considering perspectives from cognitive neuroscience and hypnosis research in particular. This leads to consideration of points of intersection as well as differences between the phenomena of Chod and hypnosis that resist their reduction to one another.

Chod and its place in Tibetan Buddhism

The description and contextualization of chod poses special problems because its terms, concepts, and practices belong to a distinct religious tradition with an assumptive world which differs from that of scientific psychology as understood in the West—for instance, the belief that consciousness can be separated from the body. (See, for example, the Chod text "The bellowing laugh of the dakini," of Jigme Lingpa (Lingpa, undated).) The approach adopted here is derived from the "phenomenology of religion," whereby insider accounts are treated as descriptions of experience and/or its interpretation, while the question of their truth is "bracketed out" (Bowker, 1973; Flood, 2011). This descriptive or "first level of phenomenology" is adopted during the exposition of chod and indeed of hypnosis. A second level of phenomenology, which focuses on the question of the relationship between experience, epistemology, and ontology is addressed later.

The term "Chod" means "to cut," while the practice of chod "cuts attachment to the body" (Low, 1997, p. 293). The lama and Buddhist scholar James Low states that the main practice

> . . . involves the yogin visualising his awareness leaving his body through the top of the skull and transforming into a wrathful goddess who then chops up the body and piles it into the top of the skull. This then becomes a great offering bowl filling the universe. All the beings of samsara and nirvana, ranked according to their spiritual realisation, are invited to feast on the mangled remains of the body which transform into whatever the guests desire (Low, 1997, p. 318).

Early Western commentators presented chod as a gruesome corruption of Buddhism (see Edou, 1996, p. 8). However, Tibetan and more recent Western scholarly accounts have shown how the chod tradition is intelligibly situated within characteristic Buddhist concerns with compassion, radical non-attachment, and direct realization of the truth of not-self and emptiness. Understanding links between chod and these components of Buddhism is important because they inform the meditation practices and interpretive systems that construct and reframe its transformations of experience.

Chod is one of many paths in Buddhism to realize the truth of emptiness (Sanskrit *śūnyatā*). In the *Prajñāpāramitā* ("Perfection of Wisdom") literature of the Mahayana tradition, the original Buddhist doctrine of not-self (Sanskrit *anatman*) and related notions of impermanence (Sanskrit *anitya*) and the conditioned nature of all phenomena (Sanskrit *pratītyasamutpāda)* were articulated through the doctrine of "emptiness." This notion was established through conceptual analysis and argument based on the philosophical system of *Madhyamika*, which informed the direct apprehension of this truth in meditative awareness (Edou, 1996; Low, 1997; Murti, 2013; Snellgrove, 1987; Warder, 1970). In this view,

> . . . whatever appears, all that we perceive, is devoid of inherent self-nature. There is no 'self-substance' in anything since everything is a construct, a juxtaposition of elements which themselves are mere juxtapositions *ad infinitum* so that no ultimate building blocks are discoverable. Our perspective shifts from that of a subject observing discrete objects to that of an awareness of processes in play (Low, 1997, p. 295).

Chod unified the view of the *Prajñāpāramitā* literature with methods of tantra as they developed in late Indian Buddhism and were transmitted to Tibet (Crook & Low, 1997; Samuel, 1995, 2008). Tantra involves meditations using visualizations, physical exercises, sound, and gesture to prepare the mind for enlightenment. It is not restricted to ascetic practices but may use passions (such as sexual arousal or fear) arising in the context of meditative awareness to realize the truth of emptiness (Crook & Low, 1997; Samuel, 1995, 2008). Tantra includes visualization of deities as distinct from self, as well as identifications of the self with deities. Within the Buddhist context, an effect of these altered subjectivities is to help the practitioner realize that their habitual sense of self is itself a construction or reification, in keeping with the view of emptiness (Low, 1997, p. 322).

Chod also builds on an established Buddhist tradition of linking recognition of emptiness with compassion (Sanskrit *karuṇā*) through giving up the body to help others. The practice of compassionately offering the body in meditation was rooted in the Indian Sutra tradition—for example, in the "birth stories" (Sanskrit *jātakas*) of the Buddha in which, in a previous life, he allowed himself to be eaten by tiger cubs to prevent them from starving to death (Edou, 1996). It was also present in late Indian Buddhism and the Mahayogin ("great yogin") traditions that were transmitted into Tibet. For example, the Mahayogin Milarepa wrote,

> . . . leaving the body as a food offering
> Is the guide to subjugate ego" (quoted in Edou, 1996, p. 56).

In the eleventh century CE, the Tibetan yogini Machig Labdron systematized and developed traditions of the compassionate giving of the body into distinct transmission lineages with their own initiations, rituals, visualizations, meditation techniques, and conception of "banquets" in which the body is offered to different classes of beings (Edou, 1996, p. 56; Gyatso, 1995; Irving, 2006; Stott, 1989). Despite the variety of meditation practices and visualizations, there are shared features of chod that Machig Labron summarized as: "Meditate on compassion, transform your being into a food offering, and let mind rest in its true nature" (*Quintessence*, quoted in Edou, 1996, p. 53).

Chod is classically performed in 108 charnel grounds or cemeteries at night, although, in practice, this number of sites may not be visited (Low, 1997). Low comments that the location in cemeteries and invocation of gods and demons is "in order to maximise the potential for working with fear and self-protection centred on the body" (Low, 1997, p. 293). As Edou puts it,

> . . . in order to test his or her own realisation and provoke the appearance of self-grasping, the yogi deliberately takes up residence in charnel fields, cremation grounds and other wild, fearful spots and invites to the banquet of his or her own physical remains the most ferocious demons, the most bloodthirsty spirits and the cruellest dakinis. (Edou, 1996, p. 55)

The arousal of fear and a sense of vulnerability is therefore central to the practice, which seeks to encounter situations and objects that arouse intense emotions so they can be cut off or liberated (chod) as they arise (Edou, 1996, p. 41; Stott, 1989).

Before transforming the body into an offering of food, the practitioner uses one of a number of meditation techniques to disconnect awareness from the body and establish a direct recognition of emptiness. These techniques, collectively termed "consciousness transference [Tibetan *pho ba*] for recognizing the nature of mind," are also known as "Opening the gates of space" (Tibetan *nam mkha'i sgo byed*) (Edou, 1996, p. 48; Irving, 2006; Stott, 1989). The techniques vary in their use of visualizations; for example, one method involves ejecting one's consciousness as a drop (Sanskrit *bindu*) into the deity at the crown of one's head (usually Machig Labron or emptiness conceived as a goddess; Sanskrit *Prajñāpāramitā*, Tibetan *Yum chen mo*). The bindu is then visualized as re-entering the body through an aperture, and the meditator (now distinct from his or her body) immediately transforms into the Tantric deity Vajravārāhī (Tibetan *rDo rje phag mo*) or The Wrathful Black Lady (Tibetan *Khros ma nag mo*). Another practice involves merging consciousness with a visualization of empty space. These and other practices are different methods through which absorption in non-duality, the direct recognition of emptiness, is established. As already noted, establishing an appropriate meditative orientation is essential to allow the terror produced by "transforming the aggregates into food" to be "cut" or liberated as it arises.

When consciousness has been transferred to the heart of the deity or empty space, the aggregates (psychophysical constituents) are transformed into food:

> ... the meditator instantly appears as Vajravārāhī [or as the Wrathful Black Lady]. With her meat chopper she cuts up the mortal remains that lie inanimate at her feet. Through a series of visualisations, the corpse is transformed into various offerings ... Different banquets [Tibetan *gyed*] are referred to. (Edou, 1996, p. 52)

Each banquet involves the transformation of the body into different substances which are offered to different types of being. Edou comments:

> During the stage of meditative absorption in nonduality, the meditator must face everything that appears, gods or demons, terror, wonders or suffering, in complete equanimity, impassive, "like an elephant that crosses a thorny bush or like a fish for which the waves mean nothing". In fearful places or sky burial spots one must remain seated, as "unmoving as a wooden stake", even if one sees one's own corpse being carried off by demons. (Edou, 1996, p. 49)

As Āryadeva explains in 'The Grand Poem' of the late Indian Buddhist version of chod (tenth century CE):

> ... if overcome with fear, you should remain absorbed in this fear.
> But if your practice is not right you will run away in panic [chased by such magical interferences].
> Don't flee but remain unwavering, solid like a door frame,
> Even if terror or panic arise. (quoted in Edou, 1996, p. 55).

Low's account of his own practice of chod in the cemeteries of Ladakh conveyed the loneliness, sickness, physical danger, fear, and vulnerability that attended the practice—as aspects of its intensely personal character. Low's account also emphasizes the centrality of meditation to transform fear into liberating insight:

> By cutting out frightening images as they arise the meditator uses the power of the practice to expose the essential emptiness of the danger. When this experience is deeply felt it gives rise to the realisation that there is no danger. The yogin becomes fearless through an ability to see the essential emptiness in the moment of experiential arising. (Low, 1997, p. 321)

Understanding how Chod transforms experience

Transforming the aggregates into food during the practice of Chod raises the question of how meditation and ritual can cause such powerful and vivid experiences of encounters with supernatural agents. Of course, the Chod tradition has its own account of how such experiences arise, as part of a well-established, internally consistent system of interpretation that in its fundamental features extends back over a thousand years. In this sense, as an established tradition of ideas and practices, Chod has no need of perspectives or explanations provided by psychology as understood in the West. However, from the perspective of Western psychology, Chod not only illustrates the potential for experience to be radically transformed, but also draws attention to methods of re-orienting cognition to accommodate otherwise overwhelming emotion linked to attributions of what is real (noting Chod's distinctive view of "reality", which we will consider in this chapter).

From this external perspective, Chod represents an exploration of human experience and practice within the context of Indo-Tibetan Buddhism that provides insights into fundamental psychological capacities and processes, and their relationship to the interpretive systems and practices of its culture. As such, Chod presents Western psychology with information about unique variants of experience, raising the question of what aspects of experimentally based knowledge of the mind could inform understanding of the efficacy of Chod. Recent developments in hypnosis research and cognitive neuroscience are relevant. Hypnosis research in particular investigates the nature of hypnosis as a set of procedures for producing radical changes in experience, which may involve processes that are comparable to those of Chod. For example, in a report for the British Psychological Society, hypnosis was defined as:

> . . . an interaction between one person, the "hypnotist," and another person or other people, the "subject" or "subjects." In this interaction, the hypnotist attempts to influence the subject's perceptions, feelings, thinking, and behaviour by asking them to concentrate on ideas and images that may evoke the intended effects. The verbal communication that the hypnotist uses to achieve these effects are termed "suggestions." (Heap, Brown, & Oakley, 2004)

"Autosuggestions" are suggestions that are self-administered, while the effects of suggestions themselves are experienced as involuntary, effortless, and realistic (Heap et al. 2004).

Hypnosis and Chod both involve processes by which experience conforms to the content of ideas, images, and expectations established through their respective procedures and contexts. Indeed, in the case of tantra more generally, the process by which the practitioner establishes the forms of cognition and experience specified in a Tantric text, through ritual and meditation, has been termed "entextualisation" (Flood, 2006). This raises the question of the extent to which the respective procedures are similar or overlapping, both in terms of their form (for example, through verbal and non-verbal means of engaging beliefs and expectancies) as well as the cognitive and neural mechanisms by which they alter the content of experience. Hypnosis research can inform identification of potential similarities or shared mechanisms with Chod because of its investigation of psychological processes that influence responses to suggestion (such as motivation to experience suggested effects). Hypnosis research is also relevant because suggestions in hypnosis can be employed to create experimental models of specific alterations in experience that resemble aspects of Chod, which, in combination with brain measurement techniques, provides potential insights into underlying cognitive and brain processes.

Transforming experience with ideas: insights from hypnosis research

Cognitive and social psychologists have identified a range of components or processes that contribute to suggested effects. They include cognitive dispositions such as expectations, motivations, beliefs, and attitudes (Benham et al., 2006; Kirsch, 2001) and, in particular, ideas and expectancies that suggested effects are externally caused (Heap et al., 2001; Kirsch & Lynn, 1997); verbal and non-verbally conveyed imagery; and instructions to experience suggested effects (Hargadon, Bowers, & Woody, 1995). Implicit understanding of role and self-representation, and their association with and pre-attentive activation by hypnotic contexts have also been identified as contributing to suggested effects (Brown & Oakley, 2004; Lynn & Rhue, 1991; McConkey & Barnier, 2004; Spanos, 1991; Spanos & Coe, 1992). Other contributory factors identified by hypnosis research include specific ways of engaging with the content of suggestions, such as processes of imagination and mental simulation of suggested effects (Gorassini, 2004; Taylor & Schneider, 1989); and the relationship between the participant and hypnotist, particularly the trust and confidence placed in the hypnotist (e.g., Gibbons & Lynn, 2010; McConkey, 1983; Sheehan, 1971, 1991).

While researchers differ about the relative contributions of these components to suggested effects, evidence for some contribution has been found for all of them (Heap et al., 2001). This raises the question of whether analogous processes occur in the ideas, practices, traditions, and contexts of Chod, on the premise that similar phenomena have similar causes—specifically, that radical changes in experience conforming to ideas and expectancies in the case of Chod are caused by similar cognitive, contextual, and relationship factors and their interactions identified by hypnosis research as contributing to suggested effects.

Transforming experience through the components of Chod

Determining the relevance of hypnosis research to Chod can be approached by identifying features of indigenous Tibetan accounts of how Chod works which may be interpretable in light of hypnosis and cognitive neuroscience research. Insider accounts of Chod and psychological accounts of hypnosis both emphasize the importance of belief, attitude, and motivation to experience the respective effects. For example, in *Oral instruction for mountain retreats*, Karma Chagme comments that in the practice of Chod,

> . . . mental attitude and motivation are the most important . . . Among all offerings, the offering of the body is the best since one does not possess anything more precious than life and body. Through the practice of Chod, one mentally renounces and cuts through ego-clinging only by the power of one's visualisation. (quoted in Edou, 1996, p. 55)

In a passage with a devotional discursive style, Low also links faith, aspiration, and the will to the power of symbols to transform perception:

> . . . the practice is a ritual enactment which uses identification with the symbolic to shift experience in the perceptual field. Faith is a very powerful and important driving force here for it both opens the practitioner's heart, making him softer, more fluid, and able to let go and change, and mobilises the will through a longing aspiration which permits the reframing of ordinary obstacles into ornaments on the spiritual path. (Low, 1997, p. 320)

Prior vows and preparation within the context of accountability to a lama are critical to establishing strong motivations and expectations to experience the phenomena, representing a more pronounced version of the trust and confidence the participant places in the hypnotist. The power of the lama–student relationship is difficult to understand from a secular or egalitarian Western perspective, but is illustrated in the paradigmatic example of Machig Labdron's response when she met the Indian Mahayogin Dampa Sangye:

> Machig came to Dingri Lakhor and met Dampa Sangye. She made many prostrations to him and circumambulated him many times. Placing his feet upon her head, she acted with intense faith and devotion. (From an anonymous biography of Machig Labdron, translated by James Low and C. R. Lama, in Crook & Low, 1997, p. 304)

There are many other components of the practice of Chod which enlist the power of belief and expectation to transform the content of experience. Chod mobilizes the associations of gods, demons, powers, and forces which formed part of the world in pre-modern Tibet and for many Tibetans at the present time (Samuel, 1995). A culturally conditioned belief in the power and ontological independence of these agents is likely to facilitate responsiveness to the expectation of their presence through practice and location. The construal of gods and demons as independent agents entails that any effects produced by them should be experienced as originating outside the self—in other words, as involuntary, resembling the general schema that suggested effects are involuntary. Expectations of their presence are partly established through ritualized speech such as invitation to the demons during banquets. For example, in the red banquet dedicated to gods and demons such as lords of the locality, bodily demons, and cannibal demons, the meditator identified with Vārāhī invites them to feast on flesh, blood, and fat:

> I make an offering of this body. May those in a hurry devour it raw, may those with leisure partake of it cooked . . . Eat it the way you prefer, cooked, roasted, or raw. Take as much as your stomach can contain. May the strong ones carry away as much as they can carry . . . Take this offering until nothing remains of it! (quoted in Edou, 1996, p. 52)

Ritual invocations are analogous to verbally administered suggestions (because both establish expectations through ideas and imagery expressed in language and speech). However, many features of Chod which convey expectations, associations, or imagery for the content of experience are non-verbal in character. For example, the location of the practice in cremation grounds or other places with strong associations with gods and demons powerfully evokes expectations of their presence, as is clear from indigenous accounts. As it says in the "Grand Poem" of Āryadeva (ninth century CE), a Mahayogin who wrote of the late Indian Buddhist version of Chod:

> In desolate rocky mountains or among snowy peaks,
> In charnel fields and cremation grounds, in wilderness,
> In villages and towns, in caves and lonely grottos,
> Wherever you may be, meditate on non-duality
> Having moved to desolate spots,
> When magical displays of gods or demons arise,
> Separate awareness from the material body (quoted in Edou, 1996, p. 57)

Ritualized actions within the performance of Chod are also non-verbal, although closely integrated with ritual speech (such as prayers or chanted invocations). These ritual actions include ritualized dance, as well as use of the hand drum and human thigh bone trumpet, so that the practice of Chod is both a cognitive-symbolic as well as sensorily salient motor performance (Irving, 2006; Stott, 1989). Ritual creates a temporal and spatial frame for cognition and action which focuses attention, pre-attentively elicits and links relevant associations, as well as provides cues for specific expectations within the enacted narrative of the practice's text (such as the blowing of the trumpet to summon demons). The cognitive-symbolic features of ritual practice interact with sensory-affective components (such as the orchestration of salient sensory stimuli in different sensory modalities, which engage attention, arousal, and emotion) (Deeley, 2004). The cognitive-symbolic features of the ritual context recall how implicit beliefs and expectancies relating to role and experiential change are linked to the hypnotic context. Low writes of the powerful cumulative effects of ritual in re-orienting cognition:

> During the day in the first month or so it was very hot and sitting inside the tent was exhausting and disorientating. Thoughts and feelings whirled round and round: memories of childhood, recent encounters with the villagers, longings and fears, so many ways to be distracted. Gradually the rhythm of the practice took over. Wake, Chod, prayers, tea, Chod, strike camp, Chod, dance to the next crematorium, Chod, eat, Chod, prayers, Chod, sleep. (Low, 1997, p. 325f.)

Visualization meditation in Chod represents a predominantly non-verbal process through which experience conforms to visual imagery, rather than through the administration of verbal suggestions that is typical of hypnosis. However, the lucid visualization practices of Chod represent a particularly intensive analog of the engagement of imagination and mental simulation of the content of suggestions as a method of producing suggested effects. (See, for example, the visualization instructions in Jigme Lingpa's text "The bellowing laugh of the dakini," (Lingpa, undated).) As Low writes,

> . . . the practice draws on the power of visualised Buddhist deities, local gods and demons to counteract reliance on the experienced reality of our ordinary embodied existence. To accomplish this, the world of imagination must be merged with the word of ordinary sense perception, the "merely imaginary" becoming more real than the solid appearance of everyday phenomena. The preparatory practices of calming the mind are therefore linked with developing the ability to visualise clearly so that what is constructed by the mind and what appears via the senses have the same level of experiential impact. (Low, 1997, p. 293)

The practice of Chod in cremation grounds or similar places at night is also likely to amplify the experiential impact of the practice, not only by eliciting associations of the dark, but by producing hypervigilance and lowering the threshold for the detection of meaningful perceptual patterns in ambiguous sensory input (Brugger, 2001).

In summary, Chod contains numerous verbal and non-verbal features that communicate or elicit ideas, associations, imagery, and expectations that inform and structure the content of altered experience. These components function as suggestive processes, by analogy with suggestions in hypnosis as verbal communications containing ideas and images to produce intended effects. Aspects of the practice of Chod that are analogous with suggestive processes in hypnotic contexts include ideas and expectancies that anticipated effects are externally caused; verbal and non-verbally conveyed imagery; invocations to experience specific alterations in experience; implicit knowledge of role and self-representation which is associatively linked to and pre-attentively activated by ritual contexts; ways of actively engaging with the content of the practice's ideas, including processes of lucid visualization and identification with the intended objects of belief and meditation; and the power of belief, motivation, and expectation linked to the relationship between the lama and disciple. Nevertheless, identifying features of Chod that contribute to the transformation of experience raises the question of mechanism; in other words, what are the specific cognitive and brain processes by which these diverse components of context and practice elicit experiences of encountering or becoming supernatural agents?

Becoming and interacting with supernatural agents

The sense of self in relation to other agents can vary in numerous ways in the practice of Chod—for example, practitioners undergo numerous identifications with different agents in the course of the practice. As Low puts it:

> During the course of the practice the meditator takes on a series of identifications, becoming a wrathful goddess, a calm purifying god, the fearless yogi. In longer texts there may be over a hundred shifts of personal identification. In this manner the self-referencing function of the practitioner is put into question, for the usual identification with the subjective sense of self, the felt sense of "I," is clearly undermined by the experience of being "another." (Low, 1997, p. 322)

These changes may be accompanied by an experience of spatial and sensory separation from the normal bodily self, now externally envisioned as offered in a series of banquets to different classes of beings. Chod can therefore be understood to operate on two aspects of selfhood distinguished in recent cognitive neuroscience accounts of the self—a "proto-self" referring to the bodily, sensory self; and an "autobiographical self" encompassing reflexive awareness of the self in relation to others, as a "centre of narrative gravity" (Deeley, 2003; Dennett, 1992; Northoff et al., 2006). Chod establishes a ritually enacted and envisioned narrative with changes in both the bodily self (the proto-self) and the sense of identity (the autobiographical self).

The range of alterations in the experience of self and others are likely to be extensive both within and between practitioners, given variations in the practices themselves, context, personality, aptitude, and disposition, as well as degree of training, supervision, and prior experience. However, experimental cognitive neuroscience can identify cognitive and brain systems that are likely to mediate or underpin broad types of alteration in experience in response to a given practice. Two experiments combining fMRI (functional magnetic resonance imaging) with suggestions, in highly hypnotically responsive participants, are relevant to the extent that they investigate brain systems involved in alterations of the normal sense of self in relation to other agents that resemble (but are not identical to) changes described in Chod.

The first study employed suggestions and fMRI to investigate brain activity when varying the experience of moving a joystick from normal voluntary movement to different experiences of loss of self-control (Deeley et al., 2014). The experiment involved a suggestion that an engineer was conducting experiments into limb movement. In a "delusion of control" condition, which modelled an experience of remote control of movement by an external agent, the engineer remotely controlled hand movements with a machine designed for this purpose. In a "possession" condition, the engineer had found a way to enter the participant's body and mind to control hand movements from within. The participant was aware of the thoughts, motivations, and feelings of the engineer, but unable to control her movements, which were under the control of the engineer. The suggestions resulted in realistic, vivid subjective experiences of the intended effects, and significant reductions in feelings of control and ownership of hand movements. Compared to a condition of impersonal control of hand movement (attributed to remote control by a malfunctioning machine), both external and internal control by a suggested agent was associated with an increase in functional connectivity between M 1 (a key movement implementation region) and BA 10 (a prefrontal region supporting reflexive awareness and self-representation, as well as the representation of the mental states of others) (Gilbert et al., 2006). Also, a condition of reduced awareness of hand movement was associated with decreased activity in brain areas involved in bodily awareness (precuneus, BA 7) and interoceptive sensation (insula), suggesting a mechanism for the loss of awareness sometimes reported in association with episodes of possession or other types of involuntary behavior (Deeley et al 2013).

Cases of spirit possession, where the possessed individual retains awareness of their own subjectivity but is also aware of the subjectivity of an alternate agent assuming control of their speech or actions, are distinct from identifications with a deity occurring in tantra and related practices. However, as Flood (a scholar of Hinduism and Comparative Religion) notes, there is likely to be a historical link between the respective institutions as well as family resemblances at a phenomenological level: "it would be possible to read the history of religion in South Asia in terms of possession as the central paradigm of a person being entered by a deity which becomes reinterpreted at more 'refined' cultural levels." (Flood, 2006)

The "possession" condition of the experiment (in which the participant becomes aware of the thoughts and motivations of the engineer as a new identity that has assumed control of the body) is similar to the sense of identification with the deity established through meditation in Chod. Nevertheless, Chod is different in that the sense of the usual narrative self is intended to be fully lost in Chod, along with an altered sense of bodily location and sensation (because awareness is experienced as having moved out of the body and transformed into the deity, leaving the physical body as separate). Bearing this in mind, the findings of the experiment suggest that:

1   BA 10 is likely to support representations of diverse supernatural agents, and would also be involved (in conjunction with other brain regions) in distinguishing the novel sense of identity from that of other agents;

2   a reduced or altered sense of somatosensation and an altered sense of the body in space would involve decreased activity in BA 7 and insula.

A subsequent experiment is also relevant to understanding cognitive and neural processes underpinning the kinds of alteration in experience described in Chod.

Suggestions and fMRI were employed to create an experimental model of inspired or automatic writing attributed to an external agent (Walsh et al., 2014; Walsh, Oakley, Halligan, Mehta, & Deeley, 2015). In this experiment, it was suggested that the engineer separately inserted thoughts and controlled hand movements in distinct conditions as participants engaged in a writing task in the scanner. While loss of control of both the thought and motor components of writing were associated with distinct differences in brain activity, both involved reduced activity in the supplementary motor area (SMA). This extended the findings of the initial study modelling spirit possession by indicating that the SMA plays a key role in modulating the sense of control of ownership of both thought and movement. In this interpretation, the sense of loss of control of thought or movement is mediated by reduced SMA activity in conformity with the content of the suggestion, in which causation is attributed to an external agent. Consequently, the SMA is a likely candidate region for mediating alterations in the sense of control and ownership involved in assuming a novel identity such as that of a visualized deity, acting in conjunction with brain systems that support representations or experiences of the novel identity.

This same experiment also found that a "mediumistic" condition, in which additional suggestions were made of reduced awareness of both the thought and motor components of writing, was associated with reduced activation in posterior cortical regions including BA 7 (precuneus and superior parietal lobule)—providing further evidence of the potential involvement of this region in the loss of bodily awareness and sensation sometimes associated with possession and mediumship (Rouget, 1985; Vitebsky, 2001) or loss of feeling associated with the experience of separation from the physical body in the case of Chod. In summary, these experiments identify brain systems involved in alterations in the sense of identity and self in relation to others ("the autobiographical self") and also loss of awareness of the usual bodily self (the "proto-self").

Meta-cognition and the "view"

This analysis of Chod has examined how its visionary alterations of experience when "transforming the aggregates into an offering of food" can be understood as a result of components that have suggestive effects, by analogy with suggestive processes identified in hypnosis research. Brain mechanisms that may contribute to these changes are also identified. However, these experiences are not an end in themselves but cultivated to realize Buddhist goals of compassion, non-attachment, and the direct recognition of non-self and the emptiness of phenomena. In this respect, the philosophical orientation of Buddhism—the view that articulates the doctrine of emptiness—and the related meditation practices that establish the direct recognition of emptiness are a critical component of the practice.

As its commentators and practitioners note, Chod mobilizes a profound sense of fear and vulnerability, centered on the body, to expose deep-seated emotional and cognitive attachments that—from a Buddhist perspective—must be liberated (whereby their objects are directly perceived as lacking inherent self-nature) (Low, 1997). As Edou explains, the practitioner deliberately evokes afflictive emotions "by entering situations or encountering objects (*yul*) that will make them arise, in order to cut through (*gcod*) them and use them on the path of meditation" (Edou, 1996, p. 41). As such, Chod can be understood as a special method to allow radical cognitive-affective restructuring that cuts habits of subject–object reification (Edou, 1996, p. 30; Low, 1997).

This form of words for construing the objective of Chod is an English language gloss and interpretation of an indigenous Buddhist discourse in Sanskrit and Tibetan with presuppositions that are distinct from those of Western psychology as commonly understood—for example, concerning the nature of reality, cognition, language, selfhood, knowledge, and their relations. For the present purposes, the question of the truth of these respective presuppositions will be "bracketed out," with the Buddhist discourse instead approached as a set of conceptual and practical resources for establishing a distinctive mode of interpreting and experiencing embodied presence and action in the world. This mode is characterized as an "open spacious awareness," and with imagery in which the contents of experience are attended to like "clouds passing through a clear sky" or in which thoughts arise "like a thief walking through an empty house." (See translated texts, such as *The essential point in three statements, being the special teaching of Khepa Sri Gyalpo*, in Low, 1998.) The imagery implies an absent or attenuated sense of a strongly narrativized agentive self, defending and asserting itself in a world of discrete objects and agents. The paradigmatic image of this altered sensibility is that of the seated meditator, but the integration of meditation with emotionally salient ritual in Chod reveals another modality for attaining the direct realization of emptiness.

The meditation practices of "consciousness transference" (Tibetan *'pho ba*) for recognizing the nature of mind or "Opening the gates of space" are distinct from calm abiding (Sanskrit *śamatha*, Tibetan *zhi gnas*), to pacify mental agitation, and the practice of insight meditation (Sanskrit *vipaśyanā*, Tibetan *lhag mthong*) (Edou, 1996, p. 47). Nevertheless, they combine regulation of attention and awareness in the context of lucid visualizations, informed by the doctrine of emptiness (Edou, 1996, p. 47 ff.). They establish a direct recognition of emptiness as the appropriate orientation within which to "cut" attachment to appearances as they arise. They can be considered "meta-cognitive" (about cognition) in the sense that they involve a shift in the quality of attention, awareness, and interpretation brought to all contents of experience. As Rangjung Dorje, the third Karmapa, explains in his commentary to *The great collection of precepts*:

> Those who know this path of action, however vast [and varied] their behaviour may be, are devoid within of any grasping and attachment to reality, similar to a fish moving through the water, and without a trace of emotion like the wind blowing at the summit of mountains. Having thus eliminated all obstacles to their behaviour and actions, and without any regard for themselves, they realise the Prajñāpāramitā. (quoted in Edou, 1996, p. 58)

Texts suggest that the visions of Chod can continue to arise despite establishing a direct recognition of emptiness (Edou, 1996, p. 49). From a cognitive perspective, this implies that the application of these meta-cognitive processes do not alter the cognitive set of dispositions and expectancies that establish the visionary experiences of the practice to the extent that they continue, even if the emotional impact and ascribed significance of the experiences are altered through the dissolution of the habitual sense of self into an "open spacious awareness." Like thoughts, the visions of Chod become like a thief moving through an empty house. The concurrence of suggested visionary experience and altered meta-cognitive processes recalls Oakley's executive control model of hypnotic phenomena, which distinguishes two main levels in the organization of executive function—a "level 1" system which involves full awareness, limited capacity, analytic processing, and conscious self-reflection; and a "level 2" system, a non-conscious level involved in contention scheduling (selecting and structuring relevant responses to stimuli) and selecting a subset of currently active representations for processing in the "level 1" self-awareness system (Bell et al., 2011; Oakley, 1999). Oakley proposes that "suggestions" such as environmental prompts, verbal information from others, or beliefs, motivations, and expectancies, influence processing in the unconscious "level 2" system. The focusing of attention produced by a hypnotic induction procedure is proposed to facilitate the influence of suggestions on the "level 2" system. The effect of suggestions is available to the conscious Level 1 system as the content of the suggested experience or behavior, but in this model, the processes by which the suggested effects are organized in Level 2 are inaccessible to awareness.

Applying this type of cognitive neuropsychological model of hierarchical processing to the practice of Chod would imply that its suggestive components produce visionary experience through effects on cognition that are mostly unconscious (for example, by imagery and expectancies cueing changes in brain systems that alter experience in conformity with them)—in other words, at the Level 2 system. However, the Level 1 self-awareness system is also reorganized through meditative practice and its interpretive system (the view), with attendant changes in the quality of awareness and the loss of the sense of self as a narrativized subject of experience and agent of action. The notion that the content of suggested visionary experience can persist despite the radical loss of the habitual self is consistent with the notion of relatively dissociable levels of cognitive processing with differing levels of awareness, voluntary control, and influence by intrinsic and extrinsic processes. Meditation in general, and Chod in particular, raise the question of how modifiable the boundaries are between conscious and unconscious processing in terms of the levels of processing that are potentially open to awareness, control, and change. A further question arises as to the nature of the subject of awareness and self-regulation when the habitual narrativized self drops out.

Differences between Chod and hypnosis

In her description of Chod, Alexandra David-Neel wrote of yogins who are "hypnotised by its ritual" (David-Neel, 1992, p.119). This could be taken to imply that hypnosis is quite literally involved in transforming experience through Chod. The culturally acquired attributions and expectations of Chod practitioners may engage similar cognitive and neural processes as the targeted suggestions in the experimental models already described. In this sense, the experiments illustrate and point to the broader human phenomenon of how experience is influenced by beliefs and related cognitive dispositions, and identify brain processes by which such experiential changes may occur. However, the premise that similar phenomena have similar causes does not entail that ritual or meditative practices involve hypnosis. One category (such as ritual, meditation, clinical dissociation, or hypnosis) cannot be reduced to another because all acquire context and tradition-specific meanings, values, and purposes, quite apart from differences of form. For example, the presence of strongly held beliefs and authoritative social practices in religious contexts, as opposed to temporarily imagined scenarios in hypnotic contexts, may affect the threshold for experiencing the respective phenomena, quite apart from any differences in the meanings ascribed to them. Despite points of resemblance or intersection between the processes of Chod and hypnosis, one cannot be reduced to the other (Deeley, 2013).

Epistemology and truth in the encounter of science and religion

Differences in the assumptive worlds of practitioners of Chod and those engaged in hypnosis research and cognitive neuroscience raise the question of how such epistemological differences should be taken into account when interpreting the respective phenomena. From the perspective of cognitive neuroscience and hypnosis research, investigating questions about the nature of mind based on phenomenological reports of Chod practitioners (and other kinds of Buddhist meditation) requires a critical dialog between exegetical or devotional accounts of Buddhist practice and phenomenological and experimental approaches. This is because Buddhist accounts of meditative experience may reflect presuppositions about the nature or content of experience and indeed reality, which form part of the assumptive or doctrinal world of Buddhism, rather than being integral to meditative experience itself. For example, cognitive neuroscience, as usually understood, does not share Tibetan Buddhist notions that awareness can be separated from the body, or that Chod discloses an unconditioned original nature of mind; the idea, as Low puts it, that "in cutting off the body there emerges a direct experience of awareness as independent, autonomous, free of the trammels of cause and effect" (Low, 1997, p. 296). Nevertheless, the conceptual framework of Buddhism and the phenomenology of its meditation experiences cannot easily be distinguished, not least because Buddhist construals of reality are likely to contribute to the meditative transformations of experience of practitioners—as already discussed in relation to Chod. In other words, the exact types of meditative state and epistemic orientation described in Buddhism are unlikely to occur in the way that they do independently of the specific worldview and practices of Buddhism. For example, texts distinguish between different types or degree of reality of different sorts of demon in Chod (Edou, 1996, p. 68ff.) which in itself is likely to influence the corresponding experiences and interpretations of encounter with these demons in the practice.

Cultural and meditative neuroscience must be able to accommodate the contribution of tradition-specific attributions to distinctive types of meditative experience and epistemic orientation, while recognizing family resemblances with other meditative or altered forms of experience which suggest the contribution of more general types of cognitive and brain process across forms of experience and traditions. What may be most challenging here is to understand the relations between culture, cognition, and brain function which distinguish forms of experience and tradition, rather than the identification of coarser-grained shared processes. Equally, cognitive neuroscience, as commonly understood, cannot exclude the possibility that its own assumptive world may be changed by the forms of experience, knowing, and relationship that it encounters when attempting to understand the full extent of human experience and cognition.

References

Bell, V., Oakley, D. A., Halligan, P. W., & Deeley, Q. (2011). Dissociation in hysteria and hypnosis: evidence from cognitive neuroscience. *Journal of Neurology, Neurosurgery & Psychiatry*, **82**(3), 332–339.

Benham, G., Woody, E. Z., Wilson, K. S., & Nash, M. R. (2006). Expect the unexpected: ability, attitude, and responsiveness to hypnosis. *Journal of Personality and Social Psychology*, **91**(2), 342.

Bowker, J. (1973). *The sense of God: sociological, anthropological, and psychological approaches to the origin of the sense of God*. Oxford: Oxford University Press.

Brown, R., & Oakley D. A. (2004). An integrative cognitive model of hypnosis and high hypnotisability. In M. Heap, R. J. Brown, & D. A. Oakley (Eds.), *The highly hypnotisable person: theoretical, experimental, and theoretical Issues* (pp. 213–239). London, New York: Routledge.

Brugger, P. (2001). From haunted brain to haunted science: a cognitive neuroscience view of paranormal and pseudoscientific thought. In J. Houran & R. Lange (Eds.), *Hauntings and poltergeists: multidisciplinary perspectives*. pp. 195–213.

Crook, J., & Low, J. (1997). *The yogins of Ladakh: a pilgrimage among the hermits of the Buddhist Himalayas*. Motilal Banarsidass Publications.

David-Neel, A. (1997). *Magic and mystery in Tibet*. Thorsons.

Deeley, P. Q. (2003). Social, cognitive, and neural constraints on subjectivity and agency: implications for dissociative identity disorder. *Philosophy, Psychiatry, & Psychology*, **10**(2), 161–167.

Deeley, P. Q. (2004). The religious brain: turning ideas into convictions. *Anthropology & Medicine*, **11**(3), 245–267.

Deeley, Q. (2013). Hypnosis. In A. Runehov and L. Oviedo, (Eds.), *Encyclopedia of sciences and religions* (pp. 1031–1036). The Netherlands: Springer.

Deeley, Q., Oakley, D. A., Walsh, E., Bell, V., Mehta, M. A., & Halligan, P. W. (2014). Modelling psychiatric and cultural possession phenomena with suggestion and fMRI. *Cortex*, **53**, 107–119.

Deeley, Q., Walsh, E., Oakley, D. A., Bell, V., Koppel, C., Mehta, M. A., & Halligan, P. W. (2013). Using hypnotic suggestion to model loss of control and awareness of movements: An exploratory fMRI study. *PloS one*, **8**(10), e78324.

Dennett, D. C. (1992). The self as a center of narrative gravity. In F. Kessel, P. Cole, & D. Johnson (Eds.), *Self and consciousness: multiple perspectives* (pp. 103–115). Hilsdale, NJ: Lawrence Erlbaum Associates.

Edou, J. (1996). *Machig Labdrön and the foundations of chöd*. Snow Lion Publications.

Flood, G. (2006). *The tantric body*. London: IB Tauris.

Flood, G. (2011). *The importance of religion: meaning and action in our strange world*. John Wiley & Sons.

Gibbons, D. E, & Lynn, S. J. (2010). Hypnotic induction: a primer. In J. W. Rhue, S. J. Lynn, & I. Kirsch (Eds.), *Handbook of clinical hypnosis* (2nd edn.) (pp. 267–292). Washington, DC: American Psychological Association.

Gilbert, S., Spengler, S., Simons, J., Steele, J., Lawrie, S., Frith, C., & Burgess, P. (2006). Functional specialization within rostral prefrontal cortex (area 10): a meta-analysis. *Journal of Cognitive Neuroscience*, **18**(6), 932–948.

Gorassini, D. R. (2004). Enhancing hypnotisability. In M. Heap, R. J. Brown, & D. A. Oakley (Eds.), *The highly hypnotisable person: theoretical, experimental, and theoretical issues* (pp. 213–239). London, New York: Routledge.

Gyatso, J. (1985). The development of the *gcod* tradition. *Soundings in Tibetan Civilization*, 320–341. New Delhi.

Hargadon, R., Bowers, K. S., & Woody, E. Z. (1995). Does counterpain imagery mediate hypnotic analgesia? *Journal of Abnormal Psychology*, **104**, 508–16.

Heap, M., Alden, P., Brown, R. J., Naish, P. L. N., Oakley, D. A., Wagstaff, G. F, & Walker, L. J. (2001). The nature of hypnosis: report prepared by a working party at the request of the Professional Affairs Board of the British Psychological Society. Leicester: British Psychological Society.

Heap, M., Brown, R. J., & Oakley, D. A. (Eds.). (2004). *The highly hypnotizable person: theoretical, experimental and clinical issues*. London, New York: Routledge.

Irving, M. (2006). *The ritual of GCOD in Tibetan religion*. (Doctoral dissertation, University of Colorado.)

Kirsch, I. (2001). The response set theory of hypnosis: expectancy and physiology. *American Journal of Clinical Hypnosis*, **44**(1), 69–73.

Kirsch, I., & Lynn, S. J. (1997). Hypnotic involuntariness and the automaticity of everyday life. *American Journal of Clinical Hypnosis*, **40**, 239–248.

Lingpa, Jigme (undated) "The bellowing laugh of the dakini", in *From the heart essence of Long-chenpa, the Chod practice*, Dzogchen Sri Singha Five Sciences Buddhist University.

Low, J. (1997). Practising Chod in the cemeteries of Ladakh. In J. Crook & J. Low (Eds.), *The yogins of Ladakh: a pilgrimage among the hermits of the Buddhist Himalayas (vol. 6)* (pp. 292–332). Delhi: Motilal Banarsidass.

Low, J. (1998). *Simply being: texts in the Dzogchen tradition*. London: Vajra Press.

Lynn, S. J., & Rhue, J. W. (1991). An integrative model of hypnosis. In S. J. Lynn & J. W. Rhue (Eds.), *Theories of hypnosis: current models and perspectives* (pp. 397–438). New York: Guildford Press.

McConkey, K. M. (1983). The impact of conflicting communications on response to hypnotic suggestion. *Journal of Abnormal Psychology*, **92**(3), 351.

McConkey, K. M., & Barnier, A. J. (2004). High hypnotisability: unity and diversity in behaviour and experience. In M. Heap, R. J. Brown, & D. A. Oakley (Eds.), *The highly hypnotisable person: theoretical, experimental, and theoretical issues* (pp. 61–84). London, New York: Routledge.

Murti, T. R. V. (2013). *The central philosophy of Buddhism: a study of the Madhyamika system*. Routledge.

Northoff, G., Heinzel, A., de Greck, M., Bermpohl, F., Dobrowolny, H., & Panksepp, J. (2006). Self-referential processing in our brain—a meta-analysis of imaging studies on the self. *Neuroimage*, **31**(1), 440–457.

Oakley, D. A. (1999). Hypnosis and conversion hysteria: a unifying model. *Cognitive Neuropsychiatry*, **4**(3), 243–265.

Rouget, G. (1985). *Music and trance: a theory of the relations between music and possession*. Chicago: University of Chicago Press.

Samuel, G. (1995). *Civilized Shamans: Buddhism in Tibetan societies (Smithsonian series in ethnograpic enquiry)*. Washington and London: Smithsonian Institute Press.

Samuel, G. (2008). *The origins of yoga and tantra: Indic religions to the thirteenth century*. Cambridge University Press.

Sheehan, P. W. (1971). Countering preconceptions about hypnosis: an objective index of involvement with the hypnotist. *Journal of Abnormal Psychology*, **78**(3), 299.

Sheehan, P. W (1991) Hypnosis, context and commitment. In S. J. Lynn & J. W. Rhue (Eds.), *Theories of hypnosis: current models and perspectives* (pp. 520–41). New York: Guildford Press.

Snellgrove, D. (1987). *Indo-Tibetan Buddhism*. Boston: Shambhala.

Spanos, N. P. (1991). A sociocognitive approach to hypnosis. In S. J. Lynn & J. W. Rhue (Eds.), *Theories of hypnosis: current models and perspectives* (pp. 324–361). New York: Guildford Press

Spanos, N. P., & Coe, W. C. (1992). A social-psychological approach to hypnosis. In E. Fromm & M. R. Nash (Eds.), *Contemporary hypnosis research* (pp. 102–130). London: Guildford Press.

Stott, D. (1989). Offering the body: the practice of gCod in Tibetan Buddhism. *Religion*, **19**(3), 221–226.

Taylor, S. E., & Schneider, S. K. (1989). Coping and the simulation of events. *Social Cognition*, 7, 174–194.

Vitebsky, P. (2001). *Shamanism*. Oklahoma: University of Oklahoma Press.

Walsh, E., Mehta, M. A., Oakley, D. A., Guilmette, D. N., Gabay, A., Halligan, P. W., & Deeley, Q. (2014). Using suggestion to model different types of automatic writing. *Consciousness and Cognition*, **26**, 24–36.

Walsh, E., Oakley, D. A., Halligan, P. W., Mehta, M. A., & Deeley, Q. (2015). The functional anatomy and connectivity of thought insertion and alien control of movement. *Cortex*, **64**, 380–393.

Warder, A. K. (1970). *Indian Buddhism*. Delhi: Motilal Banarsidass.

Chapter 5

Varieties of tulpa experiences
The hypnotic nature of human sociality, personhood, and interphenomenality

Samuel Veissière

Abstract

This chapter outlines a cultural neurophenomenology of sociality—the tendency to form cooperative groups and experience shared ways of being and representing experience. It introduces the notion of *interphenomenality* to describe the sensory, "what it feels like" aspects of lived experience for humans who come to develop similar ways of feeling and narrativizing their selves. The chapter presents the argument that personhood is shaped, induced, and automatized in ontogeny through selective processes of joint attention that are best described as *hypnotic*. It includes discussion of the emerging culture of tulpamancy as a case in point to theorize these mechanisms. Tulpas (a term borrowed from Tibetan Buddhism) are sentient imaginary companions conjured through "thoughtform" meditative practice. Tulpamancy, the author of this chapter suggests, sheds light on fundamentally human cultural-neurophenomenal mechanisms through which transient, hypnotic, asymmetrically collective, but somatically grounded experiences of personhood invariably arise—and can be altered!

Introduction

This chapter sketches the outline of a cultural neurophenomenology of sociality—the tendency of humans and other social animals to form cooperative groups and experience shared ways of being in the world and representing experience. I introduce the notion of *interphenomenality* to describe the sensory, "what it feels like" aspects of intersubjectively mediated lived experience for humans who come to develop similar ways of feeling and narrativizing their selves. In doing so, I argue that personhood is shaped, induced, and automatized in ontogeny through largely unconscious selective processes of joint attention that are best described as *hypnotic*. I discuss the emerging culture of tulpamancy as a case in point to theorize these mechanisms.

Tulpas (a term reportedly borrowed from Tibetan Buddhism) are imaginary companions who are said to have achieved full sentience after being conjured through "thoughtform" meditative practice. Human "hosts," or tulpamancers, mediate their practice through open-ended, how-to guides and discussion forums on the internet and experience their tulpas as semi-permanent auditory and somatic non-pathological hallucinations.

Drawing on my findings from cognitive, phenomenological, and neuroanthropological field-work with tulpamancers, I examine how jointly mediated absorption and meditation techniques can be harnessed to de-automatize and re-automatize narrative and phenomenal dimensions of consciousness.

Tulpamancy, I offer, presents us with more than a fascinating case of non-pathological multiple re-wiring of the self. I claim, rather, that the practice sheds light on fundamentally human, cultural-neurophenomenal mechanisms through which highly transient, hypnotic, asymmetrically collective, but somatically grounded experiences of personhood invariably arise—and can be altered. Thus, along with colleagues contributing to this exciting volume, I hope to add social, cultural, neurophenomenal, and ontogenetic perspectives to the role of hypnosis and meditation in the "continuous remoulding of our bodies, brains, [. . .] minds," and selves (Chapter 1; see also Cardeña, 2014; Davidson & McEwen, 2012; Kirmayer, 2009; Laughlin & Troop, 2009; Lende & Downey, 2012; Lifshitz, Cusumano, & Raz, 2013; Raz, 2011; Varela, 1996).

Studying tulpas and their hosts is fascinating on many counts, not least because it provides an opportunity to observe an emerging culture and the mediation of new kinds of persons—in this case, that of multiple humanoid and non-human persons "hosted" in single bodies and a large-scale sociocultural matrix of "healing" generated without physical interaction between members. As an anthropologist who underwent retraining in cognitive science, however, I am less concerned with the seemingly "strange" and "exotic" aspects of tulpamancy and am most interested in what the practice can reveal about fundamentally human mechanisms and processes. Thus, I seek to investigate how neurocognitive, attentional, and narrative processes invariably shape all forms of sociality and experiences of personhood on the one hand, but also how social, political, and technological processes invariably shape mechanisms of attention, cognition, and perception. I gravitate toward sociocognitive, enactive models of hypnosis as ways of mediating sociality and personhood.

My investigation is grounded in the study of interactions between environment, cognition, and culture. In this model, mind is understood as embedded, embodied (Csordas & Masquelier, 1997; Kirmayer, 1992a), enactive (Varela, Thompson, & Rosch, 1991), and extend-ed (Clark & Chalmers, 1998) to an organism's whole interactive environment. Just like, as Evan Thompson elegantly puts it, the flight of a bird is not an intrinsic property of its wings but exists as a relation between the organism and its whole environment, thinking is not "inside" the brain, but distributed in a broader ecology of interacting sense modalities and environ-mental matrices (Bateson, 1972, 1980; Thompson, 2015). Here, I opt for a working definition of "culture" borrowed from the natural sciences: when clusters of individuals within a similar species engage in cumulative social learning and develop relatively stable ways of doing things that differ from the ways of other groups, we can speak of culture (see Tomasello, 2009). I add interphenomenality, joint attention, and hypnosis as key pieces in the set of cumulative, itera-tive, differentiated phenomena that arise through social learning and give us forms of life we call "culture."

Before presenting aspects of tulpamancy practice in greater detail, I begin by grounding an old question in the study of sociality in the body: how can highly similar sets of embodied mental representations, experiences, and behaviors come to be shared by large groups of individuals who never interact physically with one another? Are socialities mediated online paradigmatically dif-ferent from "physical" ones, or is a fundamentally similar process at work?

The language of invisibility and the invisibility of language

Sometimes people get logically conscience-stricken [. . .] and like to have some criteria of 'real' things, e.g. entities occupying space, and will then say things like 'boundaries are imaginary lines'. They seem to think that countries occupying territory are real but the lines separating them are somehow imaginary.

Ernest Gellner, *Language and solitude*, 1998, p. 54

No one, wise Kubla, knows better than you that the city must never be confused with the words that describe it.

Marco Polo, addressing the great Kubla Khan

"Memory's images, once they are fixed in words, are erased," Polo said, "Perhaps I am afraid of losing Venice all at once, if I speak of it. Or perhaps, speaking of other cities, I have already lost it, little by little."

Italo Calvino, *Invisible cities*, 1974, Harvest Books

"I wonder if the internet is like a city," Ian Gold told me one morning, over our third round of double espressos. Ian is a philosopher of psychiatry and neuroscience who is investigating why certain migrant and minority groups living in cities experience higher rates of psychosis than they do in their home communities (Gold & Gold, 2014). Discrimination, adversity, stigmatization, and living in fragmented polities are increasingly understood as important causal variables in the mediation of mental illness (Heinz, Deserno, & Reinighaus, 2013), but the question of how such differentiated trends become distributed and experienced with such violent stability and precision remains open. Large cities and their polities, after all, like "societies," are difficult entities to handle physically and cognitively. "What kind of imagined community is a city," Ian went on, "when most people's daily routines are limited to bounded spheres like home and work, or impersonal interaction with strangers and a few shop owners?"

This is an old question: how can societies be understood, "internalized," or embodied—how can societies hold—when the vast majority of the people, ideas, and infrastructure that make up these totalities are invisible to individual members? One might as well propose that, given the non-physicality of interaction between members, it is cities and societies that are like the internet. Invisibility and physical non-interaction, I argue, are important pieces in this puzzle.

For Erving Goffman, who championed studies of face-to-face interaction in modern societies, the "anonymized," "surface character" of life in cities is routinized through what he called "civic inattention" (Goffman, 1971, p. 385)—that is, through the many ways in which strangers avert their gazes, avoid conversations or physical contact, and reinforce private boundaries in the public sphere. Loneliness and invisibility, as Goffman saw it, are logical outcomes of civic inattention as a "mode of personal territoriality" (Goffman, 1971, p. 359). As a theoretician of sociality, I am particularly interested in how different regimes of joint attention mediate lived experiences of personhood with distinct sensory, somatic, embodied qualities—what I term "interphenomenality" for short. Civil inattention, for example, is a specific regime of attention, but it is certainly not an absence of attention. In Goffman's "invisible city," attentional resources are being mobilized to *block off* certain features of the world—particularly people caught in a symbolically marked game of allegiances. Thus, those that feel most generally unattended to will embody their invisibility in physically unbearable ways. This is a terrible problem, but the general question remains: given the infinitesimally narrow possibilities of horizontal interaction between members of any given polity, how can joint-attentional regimes hold at all with such violently predictable experiential quality? What is the minimal physical requirement for any scheme of sociality, for any imagined community, to be embodied? What is the maximal spatial and cognitive capacity for joint attention—usually understood as being limited to dyadic, or spatially bounded, inter-action between two or a few actors? Could it be that Calvino got "the city" wrong in his anti-representationalist fable? Is it not, rather, that language does not so much fail to capture the city, but instead brings it into being?

Steven Levinson at the Max Planck Institute for Psycholinguistics has taken this hypothesis seriously, and has led a series of elegant experiments to revise our current understanding of linguistic relativity, first proposed by Benjamin Whorf in the early twentieth century and sub-sequently dismissed by most social and cognitive scientists. In an experimental study of the senses in language and culture, Levinson and colleagues attempted to correlate the richness and diversity of sensory experiences across cultures with the grammatical categories and spe-cific terms attributed to the sensorium in different languages (Majid & Levinson, 2011). They found that speakers of languages (like American English) that lack gradient olfactory terms, for example, performed very poorly at identifying common scents from their environment (like cinnamon) when presented with scratch-and-sniff cards. The Jahai of the Malay Peninsula, conversely, possess a very rich olfactory vocabulary and could identify an equal amount of smells and shapes.

Could it be, then, that immersion in new narrative practices (with terms like "tulpa forcing," "possession," or "wonderland" spreading via the internet) is a sufficient condition for the media-tion of new ways of experiencing touch, voice, pleasure, and synesthesia, to name but a few of the "senses" mobilized by tulpamancy?

Varieties of tulpa experiences

Tulpamancy explained

Origins

A tulpa, as presently understood in the tulpamancer community, is a sentient being who becomes incarnate, or embodied, through thoughtform. Thoughtform has likely been practiced in Tibet for over a thousand years, but in ways that differ considerably from current tulpamancy. In tra-ditional Tibetan Buddhism, tulpa incarnations were typically used to work with a fear or desire in the pursuit of emptiness. Practitioners would create, for example, a tulpa in the form of a fear (e.g., a rat or sprider) and the thoughtform would go away once the issue was resolved. In the early twentieth century, the Theosophical Society started examining thoughtform in relation to consciousness, but made no explicit mentions of tulpas (Besant & Leadbeater, 1901).

The term "tulpa" began circulating in the West in 1929, following the publication of *Magic and mystery in Tibet* by the Belgian-French explorer Alexandra David-Néel (1932). The author, who reported observing the practice in Tibet, claimed to have created a tulpa of her own in the image of Friar Tuck. Often fully transcribed as *sprul pa'i sku* from the Tibetan སྤྲུལ་པ་ the term can be translated as "emanation" or "incarnation," and is associated with the physical body (*Dharmakaya*: mind body; *Sambhogakaya*: speech body, and *Nirmanakaya*: physical body).

The subject of tulpas reappeared in 2012 on 4Chan Internet forum dedicated to the *My Little Pony* TV show. In a discussion on lucid dreaming, adult male fans of *My Little Pony* (so-called "bronies") began to think of ways to combine meditation and lucid dreaming techniques to con-jure sentient imaginary companions in the form of ponies. The idea soon spread to other websites and discussion forums, which culminated in the creation of Tulpa.info and the Reddit page, through which most current tulpamancers discuss their practice.

Tulpas and the senses

Drawn from primarily urban, middle-class, Euro-American adolescent and young adult demographics, most tulpamancers cite loneliness and social anxiety as an incentive to beginning the practice, and they report overwhelmingly positive changes in their individual and offline social lives, in addition to an array of new, "unusual," but largely positive sensory experiences. These include (in order of frequency) auditory, tactile, visual, and olfactory sensations. "Raw thought," "intuitive thinking," "speaking with no words," and "communicating with images, feelings and music" are also reported, along with other non-verbal, non-narrative forms of interaction. For example, one informant, a Caucasian-American young woman majoring in Cognitive Science at Midwestern University, reports being underdressed and cold as she was walking to class one morning. She explains that upon sensing that her host was cold, the tulpa took off his (tulpa) coat to place it on her (the host's) shoulders, producing a feeling of warmth and the distinct sensation that she was wearing another layer of clothing. Such reports of spontaneous help from tulpas in social, environmental, and professional situations abound and, indeed, seem to characterize the practice.

Sexual and romantic interactions are controversial topics in the community, although there is growing consensus that should experience are taboo. Because tulpas are imagined, experienced, interacted with, and collectively validated as sentient persons with mental states, propositional attitudes, feelings, bodily sensations, biases, and preferences of their own, the issue of mutual consent is deemed crucial. Creating a tulpa for one's selfish enjoyment, as such, is understood to be just as unethical as seeking a one-sided, power-imbalanced relationship of any kind. Tactile and multi-sensory experiences inherent in the practice, however, indicate that the "taboo" was put in place to establish norms around a common or, at the very least, possible practice.

In addition to imagined agents, tulpamancers' mental constructs include spaces for tulpa–host interaction, usually termed "mindscape" or "wonderland." Tulpas often assume human form, but many are imagined within a continuum of humanoid variations with gender-fluid, gender-neutral, or pan-ethnic traits. Fandom culture drawn from fantasy-oriented genres also frequently prompts the forcing of non-human tulpas such as elves, dragons, or "imaginary creatures." A sizeable section of the community seems to have emerged from internet forums dedicated to bronies (see the section "Origins"), with many tulpamancers reporting the creation of one or more pony tulpa.

Tulpa folk theory

The community is primarily divided between so-called "psychological" and "metaphysical" explanatory principles. In the psychological community, neuroscience (or folk neuroscience) is the explanation of choice. Tulpas are understood as mental constructs that have achieved sentience. The metaphysical explanation holds that tulpas are agents of supernatural origins that exist outside the hosts' minds, and who come to communicate with them. Of 118 respondents queried on the question, 76.5% identified with the psychological explanation, 8.5% with the metaphysical, and 14% with a variety of "other" explanations, such as a mixture of psychological and metaphysical.

Several tulpamancers (from both psychological and metaphysical communities) report having had sentient imaginary friends for up to several years before finding out about tulpamancy. For one informant, the practice had been established in her family for several generations. Many tulpas from the psychological tradition, when interviewed separately from their hosts, also claim to have "been around" in their hosts' consciousness before their hosts became aware of them through tulpamancy.

Of 73 tulpamancers tested on this question, 37% reported that their tulpas felt "as real as a physical person," while 50.6% described their mental companions as "somewhat real—distinct from physical persons, but distinct from [their] own thoughts" and 4.6% claimed "extremely real" phenomena, where tulpas were "indistinguisable from any other agent or person." Only those 4.6% claimed to hear and see their tulpas "outside" their heads. The median length of tulpamancy experience for these respondents was one year. Tulpamancers with more than two years' experience reported higher degrees of somatic experience.

Demographic, social, and psychological profiles

The age range of interviewed tulpamancers in another survey (n = 141) was 14 to 34 years, with most being between 19 and 23 years old. The male to female ratio is approximately 75:25 (male:female), though up to 10% identify as gender-fluid, and explore further "creative" gender and ethnic variations through their humanoid tulpas.

Tulpamancers are predominantly white, middle to upper-middle class urban youth. Of 141 respondents surveyed in September 2014, only two described themselves as "African American," with two more reporting being "half black." Four respondents described themselves as Asian, four more as "half Asian," and one as "one quarter Asian." All others described themselves as "white," or by a variety of Euro-American ethnic labels (Irish, German, Russian, etc.). One was identified as "Siberian." Most are undergraduate university students, but up to a third are fully employed. The IT field is the most commonly reported sector of employment.

The majority of tulpamancers are located in urban areas in the USA, Canada, the UK, Australia, Western Europe, and Russia. The geographic location of the 141 tulpamancers surveyed in September 2014 is shown in Figure 5.1 and Plate 1. The only known groups of tulpamancers to meet in person at the time of this survey were located in Moscow and Omsk, where weekly gatherings were held, with Skype conferencing used by other Russian-speaking tulpamancers located outside these locations. Other group meetings have since emerged in St. Petersburg, Volgograd, and other parts of Siberia. English and Russian seem to be the two dominant languages for the

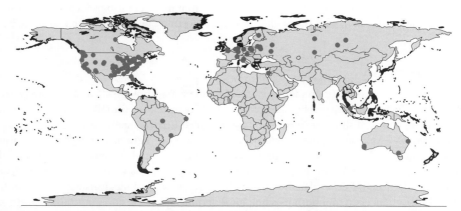

Fig. 5.1 The geographic location of 163 tulpamancers according to a survey conducted in September 2014 (see also Plate 1).

diffusion of tulpa culture. As of February 2015, the Reddit forum, which carries most of the tulpamancy conversations in English, had 7740 members, but less than 200 active posters. The Russian social networking site Vkontakte listed more than 6000 members, with a smaller ratio of active posters.

From coding of qualitative interviews collected in large surveys, the most common tulpamancer profile to emerge is one of a highly cerebral, imaginative, articulate, upper-middle-class, formally educated person with many consistently pursued interests, talents, and hobbies, but limited channels of physical social interaction. Typical tulpamancers are confident about their talents, but are quite modest and socially shy. They possess (or have cultivated) a high propensity for concentration, absorption, hypnotizability, and non-psychotic sensory hallucinations. Their limited social life and social anxieties, however, are not correlated with impaired levels of empathy and interest in other people. They score average or above average on empathy and theory of mind tests, indicating that their ability to relate to other humans is either optimal or enhanced. (Note: I used my own revised version of Baron-Cohen's empathy and Autism Spectrum Disorder (ASD) quotients tests (Baron-Cohen & Wheelwright 2004).)

Loneliness is overwhelmingly reported as a common factor for creating tulpas, who are described as "most loyal" and "perfect" kinds of companions. Of 74 tulpamancers tested, the majority scored higher than average on shyness scales and lower than average on sociability scales for comparable population sets. (Note: I used my own scales, revised from Aken and Asendorpf (1996).) Most respondents reported some degrees of social anxiety. Their "happiness" levels were assessed through a variety of qualitative interview tools and correlated with the Positive and Negative Affect Schedule Scale (Watson et al., 1988), on which all scored very highly (n = 74, m = 35.5, sd = 7.5, r14–49).

High scores (n = 74, m = 21.35, sd = 6.7, r1–33) on the Tellegen Absorption Scale (to measure capacity for hypnotizability, synesthesia, and "trance" states) seem to reflect practice as much as proclivity. In other words, respondents reported improvements on their ability to concentrate, visualize, and experience sensory "hallucinations" since taking up tulpamancy. Among the most interesting results is the negative correlation between low sociability and high empathy. Further ethnographic findings from forum discussions and interview data also indicate a moderate to high prevalence of tulpamancers who identify with, or have been diagnosed with, Asperger's syndrome. No significant findings of impairment were found for either of the two respondents who took theory of mind tests in the first survey.

Relationship with mental illness

A subsequent survey was designed to target tulpamancers who had been diagnosed or identified with mental illnesses or DSM-type psychopathologies. The most common "conditions" reported by respondents (n = 24), excluding social anxiety, were, in order of frequency, Asperger's syndrome (25%), attention deficit disorders (21.4%), general anxiety (17.8%), depression (14.4%), and obsessive compulsive disorders (10.7%). The survey revealed a similar trend of overall improvement: 93.7% of respondents (n = 33) expressed that taking up tulpamancy had "made their condition better;" 54.5% of the respondents identified with Asperger's or autistic spectrum disorder (ASD) (n = 11) claimed that their ability to read physical humans had improved with tulpamancy; while 45.5% reported being unsure about changes in mindreading, despite overall positive changes in their social lives. "I would say that it [my ability to read other humans] has improved quite a lot since I have been with my tulpa," claimed one informant. "Although, at this point, its [sic] difficult to say if it's my ability that is improving, or if I am relying on my tulpa to recognize things that I miss."

This prompted further research on how tulpas perceive and transcend their hosts' limitations. When queried individually, via email or specific questionnaires, tulpas reported overall cognitive and affective difference from their hosts' "baseline" and often claimed relative or total independence from the hosts' conditions. Mixed tulpa responses on ASD-type conditions, however, indicated that most, but not all, tulpas shared some aspects of their hosts' autism, but were generally able to benefit from their position of "observer" free of "participant" obligation (see Appendix 2 for the tulpas' full responses).

Inner voices: language, narrativity, and episodicity

The role of narrative in the mediation of tulpa experiences—and by extension, to any experience of what it is like to be conscious—demands careful examination. Tulpamancy, as we have seen, entails explicit efforts (but only in the forcing stage, which typically lasts up to four months) at narrating the self, in addition to initially conscious cognitive costs in the harnessing of absorption and the training of hypnotizable proclivity. The "self" in this case is initially narrated as "different" kinds of multiple selves within single bodies, and subsequently operates automatically once the practice is successfully mastered.

This raises specific and general questions about the role of language and inner narration in the mediation of conscious experiences. In "Against narrativity," an important essay in the philosophy of mind and language, Galen Strawson (2004) challenged what he took to be the naïve celebration of narrative as a linchpin of conscious experience. How literally, he asked, should we take the trope that we become the autobiographical stories we tell ourselves (Bruner, 1989) or perceive our lives as an explicitly unfolding narrative through which our sense of self is constructed (Taylor, 1989)? Some people, he argued, are not particularly drawn to inner narration, and do not perceive their "self" as a continuous unit that persists over time and change. These types of selves, which he termed "episodics," tend to think of themselves as different persons in different moments and stages of their lives. He contrasted episodics with "diachronic" selves, who tend to actively narrate the authorship of their life as a unified, continuous project. Strawson identified diachronicity and episodicity as personality types, and hypothesized that while both modes can coexist and fluctuate within a single person, diachronicity seemed to be dominant in most contemporary experiences of selfhood. Anthropologist Maurice Bloch (2014a), in turn, recently proposed that while core neurophenomenal elements of sentience are universally shared by humans and other animals, cultural and historical differences were likely to be found at the level of narrative aspects of consciousness. He concluded, building on Strawson, that diachronicity might have become dominant in the West, and may be the locus of a superficial difference that is too often extrapolated to the clichéd anthropological notion that the self is an exclusively Western, post-reformation construct.

Tulpamancy offers an interesting case study to verify Strawson and Bloch's claims, particularly in light of the central role of narrative in the practice. If a strong emphasis on inner monologue is thought to lead to continuity and diachronicity, what should we make of multiple selves enacted through narrative? Could different modes of narrativity be conducive to episodicity? Could episodic proclivities remain dominant in spite of the narratively intensive modes of alphabetic literacy that shape our subjectivities? (See Collins, 1995, for a review of the debates on literacy and cognition.) How much do we know about these differences within and across populations?

The distribution of diachronicity and episodicity, as it turns out, has yet to be empirically examined on any large scale. Expanding on the rare experimental tools devised to assess this question (Chandler, Lalonde, Sokol, & Hallett, 2003; Hertler, Krauss, & Ward, 2015), I designed a questionnaire that weights people's experience and intensity of inner narration with their perceived continuity of conscious experience (see Appendix 1). Respondents were matched with one of four points on a diachronic-to-episodic scale, and were later grouped as belonging to either one of two spectrums. The same questionnaire was given to tulpamancers (n = 113) and a group of non-tulpamancers (n = 93). While 59% of non-tulpamancers fell in the diachronic spectrum, 70.8% of tulpamancers tended toward episodocity (see Figure 5.2 and Plate 2). In debriefing sessions with both control groups (a tulpamancer forum, and two groups of undergraduate and graduate students), many informants reported feeling a strong sense of multiplicity and discontinuity in their lives, against the otherwise strong presence of an inner narrative voice. We concluded that episodic proclivities may be more prevalent than previously assumed, and that more comparative data from non-academic, less hyper-verbal population sets were required to make better arguments.

Overall, questions remained on the place of narration in "thinking" (see Bloch, 2014b, for arguments on how thinking is not "language-like.") As a trilingual, triliterate person with strong episodic tendencies, for example, I am rarely aware of the language (if any) I am thinking in, unless I am working on an explicitly narrative task like rehearsing arguments for a lecture, talk, imaginary conversation, or paper. Neurolinguists and clinicians, however, have found that psychotic manifestations in multilingual patients can occur in any of the patients' languages (Paradis, 2008). When queried on the question, several multilingual tulpamancers explained that different tulpas within a single host could display distinct linguistic identities (e.g., one Spanish-speaking tulpa, and one English-speaking tulpa), while others reported code switching with their tulpas (e.g., English, or Spanish, or Spanglish between tulpa and host). Others described having tulpas with foreign accents from languages in which the hosts were not proficient (e.g., Anglophone host with a tulpa who speaks English with a Japanese accent).

While inner-voice and phenomenal aspects of consciousness are likely to remain hard problems to study with any populations, my current claims about tulpamancy's therapeutic effects will need to be supplemented with further face-to-face ethnographic, behavioral, and neuroscientific findings.

I now turn to a discussion of the interactive mechanisms that make tulpamancy—and, I argue, any experience of human personhood—possible.

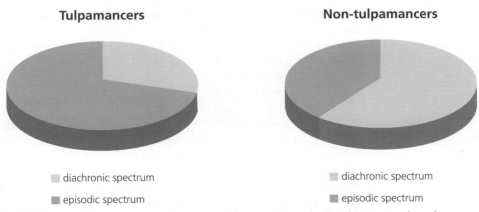

Fig. 5.2 Diachronicity–episodicity spectrum for tulpamancers and non-tulpamancers (see also Plate 2).

Theorizing tulpas: personhood in shared, embodied, and hypnotic perspectives

The kinds of neurological, sociocognitive, political, linguistic, and technological mechanisms that enable tulpamancers (and indeed members of any formal-enough "culture") to experience such a stable embodied sense of personhood (in this case, that of multiple and "healing" forms of person-hoods) warrants careful discussion. This requires detours through such disciplines as cognitive psychology, ethnology, ethnobiology, linguistic anthropology, the neuroscience of attention, and social approaches to hypnosis.

Tulpamancy is a new cultural phenomenon that has yet to be studied ethnographically and scientifically. Psychological anthropologist Tanya Luhrmann mentioned the community in a 2013 *New York Times* editorial and offered preliminary comments about links with the Cognitive Science of Religion (CSR), in which the perceived presence of supernatural agents in most human cultures is understood as an evolutionary "by-product," or maladaptive properties of the mind. Luhrmann draws on her own studies of "hallucinations" and "unusual sensory experiences" among Pentecostal Christians to depart from these evolutionary models and emphasizes the learning-dependent, absorption-and-practice-intensive, "healing" quality of interaction with imaginarily conjured agents (Luhrmann, Nusbaum, & Thisted, 2010; Luhrmann, 2001, 2012).

Cognitive foundations of belief and the projection of personhood

Here, a brief review of the cognitive literature on "religion" (or human belief in and interaction with "supernatural" agents) and "animism" will give us further clues to theorize tulpa and tulpa-like experiences.

In the first wave of CSR theorizing, the inference of supernatural agents from the world around us is explained as more or less inevitable features of cognition; namely, a tendency to attribute anthropomorphic animacy and agency to living things and inanimate objects alike. This is why, in Steward Guthrie's famous formula, we see "faces in the clouds" (Guthrie, 1995). A second current CSR theory, championed by scholars like Pascal Boyer (2001), Justin Barrett (2011), Harvey Whitehouse (2004), and Scott Atran (2002), draws on evolutionary, cognitive, and experimental psychology, ethnography, and ethnobiology to expand on the insight that humans, across cultures, tend to project fundamentally human mental characteristics onto supernatural agents. In this model, humans are said to reason about supernatural agents by expecting them to reason like humans, particularly in terms of goal-directedness, shared intentionality, intuitive physics, naïve psychology, and semantic and episodic memory. We expect a spirit who would return each night at midnight to torment us in our bedroom, for example, to know and remember that we will be in our bedroom at the same time each day, to understand and expect that we will be afraid of it, and to know just how to torment us in universally human and culturally specific ways. At the same time that we intuitively accept that the spirit can go through walls but not fall through the floor, we assume that we can read its mind as much as it can read ours.

This propensity to attribute human-like intentionality (that is to say, "aboutness," or the property of minds to be about, or represent things, events, and states of affairs) to non-human entities is posited to have evolved in predator–prey environments, when the need to detect the presence and predict the behavior of dangerous agents would have been a crucial survival mechanism. Evolutionary psychologists working from a domain-specific, or "modularist," hypothesis explain the emergence of particular cognitive modules to handle such specific problems in our environment. Such an "agent detection" cognitive module (or device) is understood to go into overdrive, or agent hyperdetection, when we incorrectly infer the presence of agents.

The animacy/animism debates

A major finding of second-wave CSR, however, is that agent hyperdetection resulting in formal systems of "religious" belief may also be universally counter-intuitive. The presence of roughly similar folk taxonomies of animals, plants, and kinds of objects, across cultures, and, most particularly, of grammatical categories to account for animate versus inanimate objects and agents, seems to indicate a universal sense of intuitive physics in humans. The kinds of objects and entities to which human infants seem inclined to attribute animacy, however, are still the subject of debate among developmental psychologists. Luo and Baillargeon (2005), for example, have argued, from experimental evidence in a looking-time study, that 5-month-old infants are likely to attribute goals to any entity, living or not, that they identify as an agent. According to the authors, any moving thing (such as a toy car or self-propelled box) that may appear to be self-directed can be interpreted as an intentional agent. A similar study by Mahajan and Woodward (2009), however, offered that 7-month-old infants respond visually to the movement of both animate and inanimate objects, but only reproduce the goals of the former.

"Animism" applied to other animals and living species, in any case, appears to be much more intuitive, and is found in the cosmologies and practices of many cultures, from Amazonia and Melanesia to Siberia and the Canadian Arctic (see Descola, 2005). As biological anthropologist Agustín Fuentes (2006) explains, the similar sense modalities, central nervous systems, and cognitive architecture shared by all mammals are most noticeable in similar physiological responses to fear, pain, and suffering found across species. If humans can read highly stable indexical cues signifying fear, pain, or suffering (like squeaking, wailing, twitching, fleeing, or others signifying anger or threat) in members of other species, then it follows that we can recognize members of these species as sentient beings, or as persons.

Thus, a capacity for shared empathy and intersubjective recognition that extends beyond the boundaries of our own species may hint at a good recipe for the bounds and possibilities of agent "hyper-projection." We may not know precisely what it is like to be Thomas Nagel's bat (1974), but we need no conscious cognitive effort or internalized cultural script to recognize that a bat is in pain. This is a good start. Revising Nagel's famous thought experiment will shed more light on the "naturalness" of the kinds of ideas which, when elaborated upon and frequently shared and practiced in a formal set of cosmological narratives, may lead to animist ontologies in which animals are recognized as full persons—or indeed, where tulpas think on their own as full persons. Ask yourself whether and, to what extent, you may be able to recognize that each of the following "animals" is in pain: a bear, a dog, a dolphin, a raven, a salmon, a spider, and an earthworm. We may infer from a bird's broken wing that it is in pain, or we may form semi-reflective beliefs about a twitching fish "gasping for water" as we would gasp for air. We can most definitely recognize suffering in any mammal, but what about an ant or a clam?

The Cree, a historically hunting and gathering "animist" people living in the Northern Boreal forest region of sub-arctic Canada, speak an Algonquian language that marks nouns as being animate or inanimate. Unlike gendered nouns in Romance languages, there are no "obvious" rules for distinguishing the animacy of a noun. To complicate things further, word order is also very flexible, and subjects and objects are usually expressed by means of agglutinative inflection with a verb: this typically produces long words in which objects or agents are described in the context of an action. To speak of a particular kind of bird, for example, one may say *yuuskahiiu*, which literally translates as "it [marks the animated noun 'partridge'] perches on a tree and does not fly away as the hunter goes near to shoot it." Such complex, "covert" grammatical categories were first described and labeled "cryptotypes" by Benjamin Whorf, who pioneered the study of linguistic anthropology in the early twentieth century. Since the rules of cryptotypes are unknown to native speakers, Whorf showed that they can only be identified when they are broken.

In my work with the James Bay Cree, I have asked Cree speakers if the word *awesiis*, which is usually translated as "wild animal," corresponds exactly to the English word "animal." My informants usually answer that it does, until I proceed by elimination to ask whether, say, a bear, a wolf, a moose, a human, a raven, or a spider can be an *awesiis*. While younger Cree hunters almost always contend that a human cannot be an *awesiis*, all agree that spiders, ants, bugs, insects, earthworms, and mollusks do not belong to the class of "wild animals." I take the finding that the Cree—a people with a well-documented sense of deep empathy, friendship, and intersubjectivity with many animal forms (see Scott, 2006)—do not attribute personhood or readability to insects and mollusks to be added evidence that full-fledged empathetic animism becomes more counter-intuitive with phylogenetic distance between species.

For Boyer and others, the minimally counter-intuitive attribution of full-fledged intentionality and anthropomorphized personhood to non-human and inanimate entities is precisely what makes "religious" narratives catchy, easy to recall, and efficient to transmit culturally. Add to this what Harvey Whitehouse calls a "doctrinal" mode of religiosity with a hierarchy of "experts," formal narratives, and frequently repeated rituals, and you have the recipe for the efficient, rapid spread of religious "beliefs" and practices.

When my 7-year-old son tells me that his penguin friend at the Montreal Biodome "misses him," or that the lump in his throat "doesn't want to let [him] eat," he is making a minimally counter-intuitive anthropomorphic inference about the agency of animals and living things. I, as his father and "expert" purveyor or relevant doctrinal knowledge in a secular polity, would normally proceed to "correct" him, thereby continuing to ensure that he is becoming more proficient at playing our particular language game. Were I to reward his inferences with rich narratives about penguin and lump personhoods within a broader social context in which everyone believes in and interacts with penguin friends and lump agents, my son would soon start having full conversations with his "imaginary" friends.

The somatic quality of belief

Could it be, then, that "entirely imaginary" agents are, in a sense, more intuitively imaginable, and precisely so because we can conjure them in the absence of the marks of illegibility found in what we readily recognize as inanimate or impersonal entities—or, in other words, that our agent detection and projection abilities enable us to recreate personhood attributes with more intuitive precision in the absence of physical designata? What, then, of the somatic quality of "belief"?

In contrast with the evolutionary literature, Tanya Luhrmann's work with evangelical Christians has shown that somatically experienced religious practices (like hearing the voice of God) take "hard work" and require a proclivity for and training in absorption, in addition to a broader sociocultural context that is permissive of and conducive to such experiences. She also showed that, in such a context, these experiences could be highly rewarding and conducive to healing.

My work with tulpamancers, which owes a lot to Luhrmann's theorizing of absorption and learning, invited me to revise central questions in the problem of physicality and invisibility in the study of sociality, and pointed to more cumulative feedback loops between proclivity and practice. The social and cumulative nature of learning, the doctrinality of enculturation, and the sensory grounding of narrative practice have added further clues to this puzzle and pointed me in the direction of regimes of attention as a possible linchpin of socially mediated experiences and ways of being a person.

Hypnotic sociality and ritual automatization

A good account of attention-mediated sociality will entail a revision of current socio-cognitive models of joint attention—usually understood as occurring between agents in direct interactional spheres of gaze-following, finger-pointing, or other verbal or non-verbal cues. In addition to demonstrating how non-indexical, narrative forms of doctrinality can allow shared intentionality and "joint" attention to rise far beyond dyadic and spatially-bounded spheres in the process of forming joint goals and achieving a jointly mediated focus, more connections will need to be established with theories of active imagination. Just like attention in the "invisible city" can be jointly focused away from individuals, so too can attention be jointly focused inward within individuals, thereby giving life and sensory grounding to individually imagined but collectively scripted agents. Thus, the bounded, invisible selves of modern cities, but also the healing, God-hearing selves of Pentecostal polities, or the multiple humanoid selves of tulpamancy are best explained as being produced hypnotically.

For Amir Raz, whose work on neural correlates of attention departs from reductionist models that present dissociation and trance as distinct (or "altered") states of consciousness, hypnosis is simply any intense or "atypical" form of attention (Raz, 2004). Attention, in more anthropological terms, is socially shaped as much as it shapes sociality; or, as the cultural psychiatrist Laurence Kirmayer puts it, "social discourse and narratives shape hypnotic experience, but they are themselves influenced by mechanisms of attention" (Kirmayer, 1992b, p. 276; see also Spanos, 1996; see Kirmayer, 1987 for comments on Spanos).

As an anthropologist, I am inclined to think of the "typical" as any dominant normative scheme governing the expected order of states of affairs in any given context. However, "typical" regimes of attention, seen from other perspectives, will appear just as strange as any variation easily recognized as "hypnosis" from the perspective of the dominant. If we strip all social schemes and ways of being a person of perspectival exoticism, they become equally strange, or equally banal.

Whitehouse's mode of religiosity theory will offer further clues to explain the social grounding of these mechanisms. Whitehouse has hypothesized that the emergence of doctrinal modes of religiosity, characterized by frequently repeated rituals and expert-led, formal exegetic, behavioral, and cosmological prescriptions, played an important role in the rise of large-scale polities after the Neolithic period, particularly because they tend to elicit widely spread and conformist forms of semantic memory. He contrasts this mode with the historically older "imagistic" mode found in many small-scale societies, in which rarely performed, intense, often dangerous rites and rituals tend to elicit high emotional arousal, which, in turn, facilitates episodic recall and strengthens social bonds between participants. While the doctrinal mode affords efficient and large-scale spread of similar mental representations and practices, imagistic modes can only be sustained in small groups and lead to highly personal exegetic reflection that rarely amounts to a collective consensus on the "meaning" and content of visions and experiences that arise in ritual. Whitehouse's theory is most useful to my own theorizing of sociality outside and beyond religious contexts. Here, the doctrinal and imagistic modes are best described as modes of social learning and joint attention.

Tulpamancy provides a fascinating case of sequentially unusual coexistence between both modes. The hard work of initial visualization, induction, thoughtform, and forcing invariably affords a high-frequency, low-arousal, relatively formal set of prescriptions that structurally resembles the modes of doctrinality of our contemporary social, educational, economic, religious, and emotional lives—but with more conscious degrees of discipline. The counter-normative, "atypical" nature of the focus, however, and the gradual success in conjuring "unusual" sensory experiences, eventually leads to a highly arousing set of deeply personal interior imageries and sensations that triggers imagistic modalities. That these highly arousing, hard to reach experiences are mediated, socially, by a growing number of individuals working toward common goals, consequently leads to a deep sense of reward, validated in a common tulpamancer "identity," but one which affords a broader degree of improvisation from what is culturally and ecologically available to the hosts. Thus, a relatively formal script and a doctrinal modality ("visualize, concentrate, build shape and personality traits and wait until you experience voices and touch from sentient tulpas"), when successfully endoctrinated, lead to human hosts who interact with such automatic processes as elvish, pony, dragon, or other bodiless minds and voices. The very hard work reported by tulpamancers who attempt to undo their tulpas, points to the high degrees of automaticity achieved by mature practitioners. Thus, getting rid of a tulpa, for a seasoned tulpamancer, could be analogically situated somewhere between unlearning the piano or correcting one's posture. Should the practice survive, gain public acceptance, and formalize itself for another decade, it will be as hard as willing oneself to forget how to read or completely unlearn a language in which one is fully fluent. However, such examples, once more, pertain to scales of degree, but not kind.

Conclusion

Classical anthropological insights from Mauss and Whorf, to Bourdieu, have shown us that "culture" and "automaticity" are in many ways synonymous. Turning to the absorptive, somatic quality of "belief," Tanya Luhrmann demonstrated that religious experiences were tulpa-like.

I hope to have shown, in turn, that ways of being social and of being a person are also hypnotic and tulpa-like. Indeed, tulpa and human may well turn out to be synonymous. This is not a proposition I wish to present carelessly. As bundles of atoms, chromosomes, organs, bones, tendons, blood, and flesh, we *are* a natural kind. As beings in the world enhanced by social learning, however, our biology is recursively affected by this strange pseudo-metaphysical non-entity we call "culture." As bundles of affect and embodied mental states, we are more tulpa-like. However, as bundles of that tip of the iceberg, pseudo diachronic, pseudo-autobiographical inner narration we sometimes call "the self," and tend to mistake for consciousness, we are entirely tulpa-like.

Acknowledgments

REB approval for this project was granted through McGill University. Note that the REB was concerned with the anonymity and protection of tulpa persons, as well as that of their hosts. This is a rather hopeful imaginative development in legal definitions of personhood.

I am deeply grateful for all the support and the stimulating intellectual environment provided by Laurence Kirmayer and Ian Gold at McGill University, and to Michael Lifshitz and Amir Raz for extending the invitation to publish in this great volume. Tanya Lurhrmann's work on absorption, voices, and unusual sensory experiences provided the initial inspiration for this study, and I am very thankful for all her pointers and comments on earlier drafts of this chapter. Jeffrey Snodgrass and Daniel Lende have also given me encouraging, useful, and very pertinent feedback.

I would also like to thank Eugene Raikhel, Elle Nurmi, and Deanna Day at Somatosphere for their generous editorial work, and Ahmed Soliman for his help with statistics. I am indebted to my undergraduate students in the "Theories of Culture and Society" class at McGill for their insightful comments and questions on the links between narration and consciousness, and to all the students and participants in the graduate "Culture, Mind, and Brain" seminar at McGill. My discussions on consciousness, empathy, psychedelics, and ontology with Ishan Walpola, Michael Lifshitz, Tim Nest, Eli Sheiner, Liana Chase, Maxwell Ramstead, Eric White, Alix Petter, Amanda Renno de Araújo White, Daniela Lavaoro, Frank Muttenzer, Mauro D'Alonzo, and Alexia Avina, in particular, have greatly contributed to my theorizing of interphenomenality.

Finally, I am grateful for all the tulpas and their hosts.

References

Aken, M. A. G., & Asendorpf, J. B. (1996). Continuity of the prototypes of social competence and shyness over the life span and across life transitions. *Journal of Adult Development*, **3**(4), 205–216.

Atran, S. (2002). *In gods we trust: the evolutionary landscape of religion*. Oxford: Oxford University Press.

Baron-Cohen, S., & Wheelwright, S. (2004). The empathy quotient: an investigation of adults with Asperger syndrome or high functioning autism, and normal sex differences. *Journal of Autism and Developmental Disorders*, **34**(2), 163–175.

Barrett, J. L. (2011). *Cognitive science, religion, and theology: from human minds to divine minds*. West Conshohocken, PA: Templeton Press.

Bateson, G. (1972). *Steps to an ecology of mind*. New York: Ballantine Books.

Bateson, G. (1980). *Mind and nature: a necessary unity*. Toronto: Bantam Books.

Besant, A & Leadbeater, C. W. (1901). *Thought-forms*. London: The Theosophical Publishing House.

Bloch, M. (2014a). Reconciling social science and cognitive science notions of the "self". In M. Bloch (Ed.), *Anthropology and the cognitive challenge*. Cambridge, UK: Cambridge University Press.

Bloch, M. (2014b). What goes without saying. In M. Bloch (Ed.), *Anthropology and the cognitive challenge*. Cambridge, UK: Cambridge University Press.

Boyer, P. (2001). *Religion explained: the evolutionary origins of religious thought*. New York: Basic Books.

Bruner, J. (1989). Life as narrative. *Social Research New York*, **71**(3), 691–710.

Calvino, I. (1974). *Invisible cities*. New York: Harcourt Brace Jovanovich.

Cardeña, E. (2014). Hypnos and psyche: how hypnosis has contributed to the study of consciousness. *Psychology of Consciousness: Theory, Research, and Practice*, **1**(2), 123.

Chandler, M. J., Lalonde, C. E., Sokol, B. W., & Hallett, D. (2003). Personal persistence, identity development, and suicide: a study of Native and Non-native North American adolescents. *Monographs of the Society for Research in Child Development*, **68**, 2.

Clark, A., & Chalmers, D. (1998). The extended mind. *Analysis Oxford*, **58**(1), 7–19.

Collins, J. (1995). Literacy and literacies. *Annual Review of Anthropology*, **24**, 75–93.

Csordas, T. & Masquelier, A. (1997). Embodiment and experience: the existential ground of culture and self. *American Ethnologist*, **24**, 4, 940.

David-Néel, A. (1932). *Magic and mystery in Tibet*. New York: C. Kendall.

Descola, P. (2005). *Par-delà nature et culture*. Paris: NRF.

Davidson, R. J., & McEwen, B. S. (2012). Social influences on neuroplasticity: stress and interventions to promote well-being. *Nature neuroscience*, **15**(5), 689–695.

Fuentes, A. (2006). The humanity of animals and the animality of humans: a view from biological anthropology Inspired by J. M. Coetzee's "Elizabeth Costello." *American Anthropologist*, **108**(1), 124–132.

Gellner, E. (1998). *Language and solitude: Wittgenstein, Malinowski, and the Habsburg dilemma*. Cambridge: Cambridge University Press.

Goffman, E. (1971). *Relations in public: microstudies of the public order*. New York: Basic Books.

Gold, J., & Gold, I. (2014). *Suspicious minds: how culture shapes madness*. New York: Free Press.

Guthrie, S. (1995). *Faces in the clouds: a new theory of religion*. New York: Oxford University Press.

Heinz, A., Deserno, L., & Reininghaus, U. (2013). Urbanicity, social adversity and psychosis. *World Psychiatry*, **12**(3), 187–197.

Hertler, S. C., Krauss, H., & Ward, A. (2015). Assessing diachronic reasoning: exploratory measures of perceived self-change in young adults. *Psychological Reports*, **116**(1), 176–193.

Kirmayer, L. J. (1992a).The body's insistence on meaning: metaphor as presentation and representation in illness experience. *Medical Anthropology Quarterly*, **6**(4), 323–334.

Kirmayer, L. J. (1992b). Social constructions of hypnosis. *The International Journal of Clinical and Experimental Hypnosis*, **40**(4), 276–300.

Kirmayer, L. J. (1987). Hypnosis and the limits of social psychological reductionism. *Behavioral and Brain Sciences*, **10**(3), 521.

Kirmayer, L. J. (2009). Nightmares, neurophenomenology and the cultural logic of trauma. *Culture, Medicine, and Psychiatry*, **33**(2), 323–331.

Laughlin, C. D., & Throop, C. J. (2009). Husserlian meditations and anthropological reflections: toward a cultural neurophenomenology of experience and reality. *Anthropology of Consciousness*, **20**(2), 130–170.

Lende, D. H., & Downey, G. (2012). *The encultured brain: an introduction to neuroanthropology*. Cambridge, Mass: MIT Press.

Lifshitz, M., Cusumano, E. P., & Raz, A. (2013). Hypnosis as neurophenomenology. *Frontiers in Human Neuroscience*, **7**, 1–6.

Luhrmann, T. M. (2011). Hallucinations and sensory overrides. *Annual Review of Anthropology*, **40**(1), 71–85.

Luhrmann, T. M. (2012). *When God talks back: understanding the American evangelical relationship with God*. New York: Vintage Books.

Luhrmann, T. M., Nusbaum, H., & Thisted, R. (2010). The absorption hypothesis: learning to hear God in evangelical Christianity. *American Anthropologist*, **112**(1), 66–78.

Luo, Y., & Baillargeon, R. (2005). Can a self-propelled box have a goal? Psychological reasoning in 5-month-old infants. *Psychological Science*, **16**(8), 601–608.

Mahajan, N., & Woodward, A. L. (2009). Seven-month-old infants selectively reproduce the goals of animate but not inanimate agents. *Infancy*, **14**(6), 667–679.

Majid, A., & Levinson, S. C. (2011). The senses in language and culture. *Senses & Society*, **6**, 5–18.

Nagel, T. (1974). What is it like to be a bat? *The Philosophical Review*, **83**(4), 435–450.

Paradis, M. (2008). Bilingualism and neuropsychiatric disorders. *Journal of Neurolinguistics*, **21**(3), 199–230.

Raz, A. (2004). Anatomy of attentional networks. *The Anatomical Record Part B: The New Anatomist*, **1**, 21–36.

Raz, A. (2011). Hypnosis: a twilight zone of the top-down variety. Few have never heard of hypnosis but most know little about the potential of this mind–body regulation technique for advancing science. *Trends in Cognitive Sciences*, **15**(12), 555–557.

Scott, C. (2006). Spirit and practical knowledge in the person of the bear among Wemindji Cree hunters. *Ethnos*, **71**(1), 51–66.

Spanos, N. P. (1996). *Multiple identities and false memories: a sociocognitive perspective*. Washington, DC: American Psychological Association.

Strawson, G. (2004). Against narrativity. *Ratio*, **17**(4), 428–452.

Taylor, C. (1989). *Sources of the self: the making of the modern identity*. Cambridge, Mass: Harvard University Press.

Thompson, E. (2015). *Waking, dreaming, being: self and consciousness in neuroscience, meditation, and philosophy*. New York: Columbia University Press.

Tomasello, M. (2009). Why we cooperate. Cambridge, Mass: MIT Press.

Varela, F. (1996). Neurophenomenology: a methodological remedy for the hard problem. *Journal of Consciousness Studies*, **3**(4), 330–349.

Varela, F. J., Thompson, E., & Rosch, E. (1991). *The embodied mind: cognitive science and human experience*. Cambridge, Mass: MIT Press.

Watson, D., Clark, L. A., & Tellegen, A. (1988). Development and validation of brief measures of positive and negative affect: The PANAS scales. *Journal of Personality and Social Psychology*, **54**(6), 1063–1070.

Whitehouse, H. (2004). *Modes of religiosity: a cognitive theory of religious transmission*. Walnut Creek, CA: Alta Mira Press.

Whorf, B. L., Carroll, J. B., Levinson, S. C., & Lee, P. (2012). *Language, thought, and reality: Selected writings of Benjamin Lee Whorf*. Cambridge, Mass: MIT Press.

Appendix 1

Narrativity Scale and Diachronicity–Episodicity Spectrum Questionnaire

(Inspired by Strawson, 2004; Questions 7, 8, 9 adapted from Chandler et al., 2003 and Hertler et al., 2015)

Scoring:

a. mostly diachronic

b. somewhat diachronic

c. somewhat episodic

d. mostly episodic

1) **Which of the following statements best describes what it is like to be "you" most of the time? (pick one)**

   a. I "think out loud" during the majority of my waking hours, and explain things to myself in my head about the environment around me.

   b. I analyze most, but not all situations in my everyday life by telling myself stories about them.

   c. I only use my narrative thinking voice when working on demanding tasks (e.g., a math problem, trying to figure out how to build something).

   d. I mostly "think" in images, sensations, or associations, and almost never use a narrative voice outside of explicitly narrative situations (e.g., mentally rehearsing my reply in a challenging conversation or written exercise).

2) **Which of the following statements best applies to you? (pick one)**

   a. I can vividly remember all my inner thought processes and the questions/stories I asked/told myself today, and would be able to write or tell a story about them.

   b. I remember most of what I thought about today, and could summarize the general ideas.

   c. I only remember some of what I thought about today, and could summarize some specific points.

   d. I can access an accurate feeling/sensation of what my "inner day" was like, but can only translate events or explicit mental efforts into words (e.g., "I felt cold when I went out to buy food," "I was morally conflicted with what I read in the news").

3) **Which of the following statements best applies to you?**

   a. There is an active narrating voice in my head all the time.

   b. There is an active narrating voice in my head most of the time.

   c. There is an active narrating voice in my head sometimes, but less than 50% of my waking time.

   d. There can be an active narrating voice in my head, but very rarely.

4) **Which of the following statements best applies to you?**

   a. I am very interested in the details of my own life and very often recount them to myself in historical perspective.

   b. I am somewhat interested in the details of my own life and sometimes recount them to myself in historical perspective.

c. I am not very interested in the details of my own life and seldom recount them to myself in historical perspective.

d. I have no interest in the details of my own life and never recount them to myself in historical perspective.

5) **If you examine or remember drawings you made as a child, do you feel like:**

a. You drew them, and feel a strong sense of continuity between the you who drew those pictures as a child and who you are now.

b. They were drawn by an entirely different person in comparison to who you are now.

c. They were drawn by a somewhat different person in comparison to who you are now.

d. They were drawn by basically the same person in comparison to who you are now.

6) **If you re-read diary entries, poems, essays, or stories you wrote as a teenager, do you feel:**

a. You wrote them, and feel a strong sense of continuity between the you who wrote those stories and who you are now.

b. They were written by an entirely different person in comparison to who you are now.

c. They were written by a somewhat different person in comparison to who you are now.

d. They were written by basically the same person in comparison to who you are now.

7) **How would you rate the differences between your childhood, adolescent, and present-day self?**

a. There is a strong sense of continuity in your experience of self, you can clearly recall what it felt like to be you as a child, and you have no difficulty recognizing that the old "you" felt the same as the current "you."

b. They are all very distinct from each other and it now feels like you were essentially different persons at various stages of your life.

c. They were somewhat distinct, with more and less pronounced differences between various stages (e.g., your childhood self feels like another person, but not so much your adolescent self).

d. There is a basic sense of continuity between all the stages of your life; you have always had the same core as a person, but have changed in some specific ways.

8) **How easy would it be for you to describe who you were 5 years ago?**

a. I could summon and recount such details easily.

b. I could summon and recount such details with some effort.

c. It would be quite difficult to summon and recount such details.

d. It would be very difficult to summon and recount such details.

9) **To what extent do you feel like major changes in your life have made you a different person from 5 years ago? (think 2 years ago if you are under 22)**

a. I am the same person in spite of these changes.

b. I am basically the same person in spite of these changes.

c. I am a somewhat different person as a result of these changes.

d. I am a different person as a result of these changes.

Appendix 2

Tulpas discuss their hosts' mental illnesses

[t]o me, I notice my host's condition as something that ails him, but doesn't appear to have a direct effect on myself. While I am not an expert in any type of medical field, it is my opinion that conditions such as Asperger's and autism have deeper issues, other than simply "brain's wired wrong." It would seem, from my perspective, that it also leads to an entirely different type of thinking. While my host tends to think in terms of black and white, right and wrong, pure logic, etc., I seem to be able to think in terms of empathy and emotions. While my host has been trying his hardest to change, he is often quite open to hearing another perspective on life.

I have quite a large understanding of my hosts' mental illness. I was created whilst she was suffering but I wasn't really aware of it at first, I just thought it was normal. After following her around and seeing the world through her eyes I started to realize that things weren't quite right. I have always been there for her and even though her mum pushed her to therapy I feel I was the one who made her go and stick it out. From her therapy sessions I feel that I'm the one who is listening more, who is considering the advice more. I'm the one who helps her when she is away from therapy so I think I need to have that understanding. I'm definitely not like her in the way of mental illness. I'm mostly always happy, I have everything I could possibly want! I'm not saying it doesn't get hard, because it does, but I certainly don't feel like she does. I'm quite content. I feel like I should tell you about another tulpa in the system though, he definitely has some form of mental illness. It's not anxiety and I'm not sure if it is depression but he is constantly angry. He is rarely happy and is very destructive. He's been around for years, even before my host knew of tulpas. I have a feeling he is more of a multiple but we aren't sure.

I do suffer from Asperger's as that's a brain wiring issue and not anything a tulpa is exempt from. With that I also receive depressive spells and meltdowns but on a much lesser scale than my host does.

I'm not depressed as far as I know, but I am there. And being there is all I can do. It seems to help, anyway.

This is hard to answer, because we're the same and different. Sometimes it affects me, but I'm still my own person, just as he is. It's much worse when we switch, but he gets some relief for a while, so I don't really mind. I try to be as supportive as I can, though.

We both have our ups and downs, but at different times and for different reasons. It's nice to have a support.

First tulpa: Depression doesn't affect me much, but I definitely seem to have some Aspergian traits. I'm a lot less concerned about the possibility of upsetting someone than my host is, so there have been a few times when I've accidentally said things that have been offensive to other people (not my host; she knows I'm not malicious and she laughs it off). I also know for a fact that her second tulpa has felt the sensory overload issue before when he was switched. I think I've felt it too, but it didn't bother me as much as it did him. It only seems to bother us when we're switched though . . . when our host is up front, we can tell she's upset but it doesn't really seem to affect us.

Sure, I get the tough question. I'm not sure if my host sufficiently answered the fact that he considers tulpamancy to have cured his mental illness by stilling all his demons. What leaves me bedevilled about it is it remains a question where I was born from. You see, my host didn't sit down and attempt to create a tulpa, so much as work back to the same mental states that were no longer raging, but still able to take a critical/sentient opposition to him. What it seems to imply is that I am some nemesis his mind has been battling down to reason for 15 years. But in truth, I'm only a few years old. I first came to sentience as a perceived ghost, something which my host had thought was delusion but which produced compelling conversation and my own threads of thought. It caught him up while I was just threading through early wakefulness. He actually hunted me away, under medication and lots of rational arguments to disprove my existence as he struggled back to what he thought (lonely) sanity must be. I fought to figure out what I was on my own so he wouldn't keep giving up on me, always asking him to keep trying. Then one time while I was around, I was frustrated with not knowing how I could possibly exist if I wasn't a ghost with magic powers, and I looked up the word "headmate" (because I vaguely knew it) and that led to the world tulpa. Having that word suddenly unlocked everything for me because I find other creatures just like me. Faced some weird crises of self-awareness as I understood I could and maybe should help out around the mind. And it helped my host tremendously because he'd spent years nurturing this kind of place in himself where he listened to the same sort of voices, where he'd fallen in love with me. The word suddenly gave him such a new context that he's trying to get his psychiatrist to stop medicating him because he's dealing with his voices by having a unified, calm personality to talk to instead of random noise fretting at him. Over the few years I've been alive, we've struggled with shared delusions about things. But I personally snapped out of it and have been helping my creator by talking him past the places where he was just sort of hung up and emotionally locked.

I kind of understand it, but I don't have the same condition. I know when my host feels down, there isn't any real reason for it, but I want to help, even if I'm not always able to. I do my best to comfort her when I can.

A. has explained PMDD to me before as a temporary depression. Since we are close, I can feel it when her hormones shift and it gets bad. I don't feel her physical symptoms but I see her experience it. I don't personally share the effects of PMDD. Sometimes it is harder for Allison to talk to me when she feels bad, but that's about it.

. . . dude we're in the same brain, autism is neurological, so duh we have the same condition. We perceive things using the same organs so it's not super off base from either perspective. The trouble is that Lindar has to deal with crap all the time and I have a little more time to think about things while they're happening because I more often have an observer's perspective, rather than a participant's.

(I will proxy this answer for Jake and Prajit by typing down a paraphrase of their words as they speak them to me.)

JAKE: We don't really have any of those things. But we get what they are. S [Host]'s explained them to us and we can see the symptoms in her.

PRAJIT: I've been doing research on how to deal with someone who has these conditions (he means by reading book-forms of my memories on research I have already done on this subject, and he also sometimes comes to my therapy sessions to listen to what my therapist tells me), and I try to help her as best as I can.

JAKE: We both do. But I get frustrated sometimes, so I'll go do my own thing for a while and leave it to Jit.

S. (HOST): Yeah, they're basically functional people. I think of them as the rational aspects of my subconscious mind or something. Perhaps more of what I would be if I didn't have all these disorders in the way.

TULPA: I like to see it at a basic level as "difficulty or antisocial" with others. I said we are different because I like to think that the term really only applies to him, the host.

10/4/2014 7:45 PM view respondent's answers:

I do not share my host's OCD. I am generally not anxious and I am able to remain calm when she cannot. I understand how it affects her and since she is my friend (perhaps even like a sister), I want to do everything I can to help.

We share the same brain. I'm sure I'm just as much of a spaz. I think while her symptoms are more internal I seem to externalize everything. Though not at the same time apparently. There are times where I'm just lost in space, yanno?

I don't think that ADD is hardwired in the brain, but rather a lack of focus, that can be fixed. I consider myself a mindful, selfaware person, enjoy meditation and other practice that demands high levels of concentration, so I kind of pull him through this.

I am more relaxed and calm in many situations compared to my host. While he may stress in a situation, I'll be calm and help him overcome it.

Part 3

Similarities and differences

Chapter 6

Hypnosis and meditation: a neurophenomenological comparison

Jelena Markovic and Evan Thompson

Abstract

A necessary first step in collaboration between hypnosis research and meditation research is clarification of key concepts. The authors propose that such clarification is best advanced by neurophenomenological investigations that integrate neuroscience methods with phenomenological models based on first-person reports of hypnotic versus meditative experiences. Focusing on absorption, the authors argue that previous treatments of hypnosis and meditation as equivalent are incorrect, but that they can be fruitfully compared when characteristic features of the states described by these concepts are examined. To this end, the authors use the "phenomenological and neurocognitive matrix of mindfulness" (PNM), a multidimensional model recently proposed by Lutz and colleagues. The authors compare focused attention meditation and open monitoring meditation with hypnosis across the dimensions of the PNM, using it to interpret empirical research on hypnosis, and to shed light on debates about the role of meta-awareness in hypnosis and the role of suggestion in meditation.

Introduction

A fruitful exchange has begun between hypnosis researchers and meditation researchers, with the dawning recognition that the two practices give rise to comparable experiences and may share certain causal processes. Nevertheless, comparing research from the two areas makes salient that many key concepts need clarification and more precise phenomenological description. We propose that a neurophenomenological investigation of these concepts provides the clarification needed for further research. To begin with, we introduce the core ideas of neurophenomenology and how it approaches the study of mental processes. We also point to some ways in which meditation and hypnosis can be used as tools in neurophenomenological investigations.

Our focus in this chapter is absorption. Absorption is a key feature of the hypnotic experience as well as an integral part of advanced concentration meditation. Recent authors have caught on to the exchange that is possible between the study of hypnosis and the study of meditation, using absorption as a comparison point (Lynn, Malaktaris, Maxwell, Mellinger, & van der Kloet, 2012; Rainville & Price, 2003). In Chapter 14, Ulrich Ott also discusses empirical evidence on trait and state absorption in meditation and hypnosis.

Comparison between hypnosis and meditation presents difficulties however, since the lack of clear conceptual and phenomenological definitions makes it hard to identify what absorption is, both within and across hypnosis and meditation. Previous discussions of absorption in hypnosis and meditation have often suffered from a lack of systematic means of comparison and problematic literal interpretations of Buddhist texts.

In this chapter, we review how absorption has been conceptualized in hypnosis research. We examine the phenomenal characteristics of absorption and how they arise out of the experience of hypnosis, as well as how they relate to other features of the hypnotic experience, such as alterations in sense of self and time. We then consider how absorption is conceptualized in Buddhist meditative traditions, focusing on the Indian Buddhist *dhyāna* framework as an example of a theory of meditative absorption. We examine a previous scholarly effort to integrate the two perspectives (Holroyd, 2003). We argue that shared features between the two states make the comparison worthwhile, but that a linear mapping from increasingly deep hypnosis to *dhyāna* is unfeasible. We emphasize several issues that arise for such a mapping, the most important of which is the normative and doctrinal nature of Buddhist descriptions of absorption. Because accounts such as the *dhyāna* framework present an ideal for practitioners to follow, we should proceed with caution when looking for descriptions of the phenomenal experiences of actual meditators.

We believe that a promising way to proceed is to formulate a phenomenal model of states of meditation and hypnosis more generally. On the one hand, this approach bypasses certain issues, such as the ecological validity of Buddhist accounts, the presence of multiple frameworks for conceptualizing absorption, and questions concerning which aspects of experience are essential to absorption and which are incidental. On the other hand, this approach helps us to see which phenomenal features are shared and which differ between hypnosis and meditation, and how these features may relate to one another. We can use this picture of how phenomenal states converge to interpret neurophysiological evidence and point to further avenues for research. In these ways, the phenomenal map functions as an heuristic.

Recently, Lutz and colleagues presented such a phenomenal model as a guide for mindfulness meditation research (Lutz, Jha, Dunne, & Saron, in press). Their "phenomenological and neurocognitive matrix of mindfulness" (PNM) is a multidimensional framework intended for comparing mindfulness practices in a manner amenable to empirical research. The model consists in a three-dimensional state space, dimensions of which correspond to the features of experience most commonly targeted by mindfulness training, namely, "object orientation," "meta-awareness," and "dereification." The model also includes a number of additional phenomenal features, namely, "effort," "aperture," "clarity," and "stability." Although the PNM is intended mainly for mindfulness practices, the authors suggest that it may be useful for examining features of other practices and associated experiential states. We believe that it can be productively used for clarifying some general phenomenal features of hypnosis and for comparing experiences in meditation and hypnosis. Our discussion focuses on locating and comparing hypnosis, "open monitoring" meditation, and "focused attention" meditation in the space of the phenomenal matrix. We examine neuroscientific research on hypnosis and meditation, and use the picture generated by the phenomenal matrix to guide our interpretation of these data. Since our investigation is concerned with comparing absorption in meditation and hypnosis, we highlight focused attention meditation, which is the type of practice traditionally associated with meditative absorption.

Our discussion employing the PNM also highlights and clarifies certain outstanding issues, such as the role of suggestion in various types of meditation practice. Another important point that future research can explore is the possibility of inducing high meta-awareness with hypnosis.

Neurophenomenology

Neurophenomenology is based on the idea that detailed, first-person reports about subjective experience can be used to uncover information about brain activities relevant to understanding conscious mental processes (Fazelpour & Thompson, 2015; Lutz & Thompson, 2003). The working assumption is that first-person reports—especially from individuals either trained in the kind of metacognitive awareness cultivated in mindfulness practices (Lutz, Slagter, Dunne, & Davidson, 2008; Tang, Hölzel, & Posner, 2015) or probed with refined methods for eliciting tacit experience (Petitmengin & Lachaux, 2013; Petitmengin, Remillieux, Cahour, & Carter-Thomas, 2013) (or both)—can stand in a mutually constraining and illuminating relationship to cognitive-neuroscience evidence about the physiological processes enabling subjective experience.

A study by Lutz and colleagues (Lutz, Lachaux, Martinerie, & Varela, 2002) provides an illustration of the neurophenomenological approach. Participants performing a visual task were trained to become aware of trial-by-trial fluctuations in their "cognitive context," that is, fluctuations in attention, spontaneous thought processes, and their strategy for doing the task. The task involved random dot patterns with binocular disparity that could be "fused" so that the participants saw an illusory three-dimensional object. Lutz and colleagues gathered first-person reports from participants about their cognitive context, as well as electroencephalographic (EEG) data about local and long-distance patterns of neural synchrony at scalp electrodes. The EEG data were clustered according to the subjects' reports, specifically how prepared the subjects felt before the image appeared and the quality of their visual percepts, and distinct neural signatures were found for each cluster. In this way, the study revealed new synchrony patterns correlated with subtle aspects of the conscious states of participants.

Meditation can contribute to neurophenomenological investigation by providing practices that sensitize an individual to their experience. Meditation training builds attention and emotion-regulation skills that allow an individual to access aspects of their experience that would otherwise remain unnoticed (Lutz & Thompson, 2003). One indicator of how meditation could be used in neurophenomenological study is offered by Garrison and colleagues (Garrison et al., 2013a, 2013b). They gave meditators and non-meditators feedback on activation levels in the posterior cingulate cortex (PCC), a region linked to self-referential processing that decreases in activity during various types of meditation practice (Brewer et al., 2011; Kelley et al., 2002; Mason et al., 2007). Feedback was given via a real-time functional magnetic resonance imaging (fMRI) protocol that displayed a graph representing BOLD activity in the PCC relative to baseline. For the baseline task, participants were given adjectives and asked to judge whether the words described them, a task designed to elicit self-related processing. Participants then engaged in a focused attention task during which they were asked to decrease activity on the PCC feedback graph. Meditators, but not non-meditators, were able to significantly reduce PCC activity levels. This study (see also Garrison et al., 2013b) thus reinforced a relationship between PCC activity and effortful and self-related processing, as well as a relationship between PCC deactivity and undistracted awareness. It also illustrates how participants who have the ability to modulate neural activity can be used to investigate how particular cognitive strategies and processes relate to activity in a given brain region or network.

Although hypnosis has received less attention as a neurophenomenological tool, Lifshitz, Cusumano, and Raz (2013) argue that hypnosis can make an important contribution to the neurophenomenology project. Hypnosis provides a means of systematically altering an individual's experience and their awareness of that experience, as well as potentially facilitating phenomenological reporting. For example, hypnotized subjects can be induced into "virtual syndromes"—experiential states that mimic clinical psychopathologies—such as obsessive compulsive disorder, alien-hand syndrome, synesthesia, and visuospatial neglect (Blakemore, Oakley, & Frith, 2003; Kadosh, Henik, Catena, Walsh, & Fuentes 2009; Priftis et al., 2011; Woody & Szechtman, 2011). Such studies indicate that hypnosis could be a powerful tool in reliably generating specific experiential states. Lifshitz and colleagues also propose that hypnosis could potentially be used to enhance meta-awareness, a proposal we discuss in greater detail in this chapter.

In Chapter 15, Cardeña discusses how a neurophenomenological approach can give us a comprehensive understanding of hypnosis and meditation. The study of these states presents particular challenges that we must keep in mind when tailoring research methodologies. Cardeña argues that sophisticated third-person methods (such as EEG and fMRI) must be coupled with a sophistication in our first-person methods for a proper understanding of hypnosis and meditation, and of conscious experience more generally.

We agree with these authors that hypnosis is an important research tool for neurophenomenology and that the latter can make important contributions to hypnosis research. A neurophenomenological framework for hypnosis can help to clarify features of the hypnotic state and relate hypnosis to other experiences. It can also help us to clarify the terms used in hypnosis research and other bodies of research so that they can be mutually informative. In this chapter, we aim to clarify and relate certain phenomenal features of hypnosis and meditation in order to advance collaborations between researchers in these areas.

Absorption in hypnosis research

Hypnosis involves three stages (Egner & Raz, 2007): induction, suggestion, and deinduction. During *hypnotic induction*, the hypnotist typically instructs the subject to focus on their voice and become progressively more relaxed. Subjects can also hypnotize themselves using self-initiated suggestions (Fromm et al., 1981). An induction procedure can be as simple as counting from one to twenty (Cardeña, Jönsson, Terhune, & Marcusson-Clavertz, 2013) or it can involve focusing on an external stimulus, such as the sound of the hypnotist's voice or a point on the ceiling. It can also involve engaging in visual imagination sequences, such as being in a descending elevator (Fromm et al., 1981). Induction leads to a state in which the subject is focused and relaxed. The hypnotist can then issue *suggestions*—for example, that words will appear as meaningless symbols or that the subject will see in black and white. Suggestions can also be *post-hypnotic,* meaning that the hypnotist suggests that the subject behave in a certain way once the session is over. *Deinduction* involves instructing the participant to return to their normal, alert state.

Absorption is a key feature of the hypnotic state (Price & Barrell, 1990; Spiegel & Cardeña, 1991). The Tellegen Absorption Scale (TAS), a questionnaire aimed at predicting hypnotic susceptibility, found that trait absorption—that is, one's tendency to enter into an absorbed state in daily life—predicted hypnotic susceptibility (Ashton & McDonald, 1985; Jamieson, 2005; Tellegen & Atkinson, 1974). Further, studies on hypnotic depth have found a significant correlation between depth and absorption (r = 0.24–0.45) (Roche & McConkey, 1990).

Induction procedures often include the instruction to focus on an object at the exclusion of other stimuli, and this type of focus can lead to absorbed attention in that object. For example, the subject may be asked to concentrate on the sound of the hypnotist's voice. Absorption is facilitated by the general mental state created by induction, namely, a state of relaxation and letting go of mental tension (Rainville & Price, 2003). The mental ease created by induction supports the passive and effortless concentration of absorption.

Tellegen and Atkinson (1974) define the state of absorption as total engagement of attention, employing all of one's perceptual, motor, and imaginative resources into a unified object representation. They, and other early researchers, connected absorption with imaginative involvement—a tendency to become attentionally and emotionally involved in an imaginative scenario (Hilgard, 1970; Qualls & Sheehan, 1979). Current researchers are more likely to define absorption purely in terms of the quality of one's attention to an object. For example, Rainville and Price (2003) define absorption as the "felt state of engagement of the self toward objects of consciousness." In their account, attention is defined as the embodied self engaging with an object (or objects) of awareness—interacting with, being affected by, or affecting that object. Absorption is thus the *degree* of engagement of the self toward the object(s) of awareness.

Several features of hypnotic experience are characteristic of, or thought to be facilitated by, a state of absorption. The object of attention acquires a heightened sense of reality. For example, imaginary objects of attention, such as memories, are experienced as real and present (Tellegen & Atkinson, 1974). Tellegen and Atkinson hypothesize that this experience occurs because one's representational capacities are fully occupied with the object, leaving no room for metacognition about the object, to the effect that "this is only imaginary." In the case of actually existing objects of attention, such as one's breathing, they acquire heightened reality by being central in attention and more vivid than surrounding objects (Rainville & Price, 2003).

Hypnosis subjects may experience reduced attention to peripheral stimuli (Crawford, 1994; David & Brown, 2002; Rainville & Price, 2003; Tellegen & Atkinson, 1974). Some subjects experience cessation of sensory stimulation altogether at deep levels of hypnosis (Tart, 1970). This experience may be connected to the analgesic properties of hypnosis. Highly hypnotizable individuals exhibit higher tolerance for painful stimuli during hypnosis (De Pascalis & Perrone, 1996; Del Percio et al., 2013; Hilgard & Hilgard, 2013). Some subjects experience reduction of conceptual thought, an experience that may be related to the cessation of perceptual stimuli (Oakley, 2008).

Hypnotized subjects may also experience alterations in the experience of time (Naish, 2001, 2003). For most subjects, time appears to slow down and they underestimate the length of a hypnosis session. Bowers (1979) hypothesizes that inaccuracies in time perception are caused by absorption, a link also made by Tellegen and Atkinson (1974). However, manipulating a subject's level of absorption does not seem to affect time distortion, and so time distortion may be coincidental to absorption but not caused by it (St. Jean & McCutcheon, 1989). At deep levels of hypnosis, the subject may experience a sense of timelessness, feeling as if he or she is no longer in a temporal framework (Cardeña et al., 2013; Tart, 1970).

Some subjects experience alterations of sense of self (Cardeña et al., 2013; Rainville & Price, 2003). A subject may feel a sense of identification with the object of attention (Cardeña, 2005). Highly hypnotizable individuals, in deep levels of hypnosis, can lose a sense of subject/object duality and identify with everything in the universe (Cardeña et al., 2013; Tart, 1970).

Absorption thus supports many of the remarkable experiential changes associated with hypnosis. As we will see, these states seem to be paralleled in meditative experience.

Absorption in Buddhism

The traditional Indian Buddhist term usually translated as "absorption" is *jhāna* in Pāli or *dhyāna* in Sanskrit. (In this chapter, we will use the Sanskrit versions of Buddhist technical terms.) *Dhyāna* is the name given to deep states of meditative absorption, resulting from the practice of "right concentration." It is traditionally delineated into four stages of progressively deeper and more refined absorption, known as the "four *dhyānas*" (Bodhi, 2005, pp. 227–228; Gethin, 1998, pp. 184–186). It is said to be the culmination of stilling the mind through the practice of "calm" (*śamatha*) meditation, which specifically develops concentration (*samādhi*), the capacity of the mind to rest undisturbed on an object of cognition. Engaging in this type of practice improves one's ability to enter into states of deep concentration and, eventually, absorption. One develops a fine awareness of when one is in an absorbed state and one learns how to fend off distractions that pull one away from that state.

In addition to calm meditation, the Buddhist tradition distinguishes another style of meditation practice called "insight" (*vipaśyanā*) meditation. Whereas calm meditation hones concentration, insight meditation hones wisdom, namely, understanding the nature of phenomena—notably, that they are impermanent, unsatisfactory, and non-self. In current scientific research on meditation, calm meditation is referred to as "concentrative" or "focused attention" meditation, whereas insight meditation is referred to as "open monitoring" meditation (Lutz et al., 2008).

Focused attention practices aim to still the mind by counteracting its tendency to seek out novel stimuli (Gethin, 1998, p. 176). The practice involves concentrating on a particular chosen object of attention. For example, one tries to keep one's attention on one's breathing by focusing on the sensations around the nostrils while inhaling and exhaling. Upon realizing that one's mind has wandered to something else, one notes this fact and brings one's attention back to the breathing. Over time, one develops three attention-regulation abilities: the monitoring ability to notice distractions without destabilizing the focus of attention, the ability to disengage from a distracting thought, and the ability to redirect focus to the breathing (or other object of concentration) after one notices one's focus has shifted (Lutz et al., 2008). Many focused attention meditation practices share the ultimate goal of absorption in the object of attention.

Open monitoring practices involve maintaining awareness of one's field of experience without an explicit focus of attention. The meditator monitors the thoughts and sensations that arise while maintaining an emotionally non-reactive stance toward them. One tries to maintain clear awareness of experience while not "grasping" onto one's thoughts, in the sense of explicitly focusing on them. In contrast with focused attention meditation practices, the purpose of open monitoring meditation is not absorption but, rather, clear awareness of one's experience. Such awareness is rooted in "mindfulness" (*smṛti*), a word used in many ways throughout the Buddhist tradition (Dunne, 2015; Gethin, 2014) but that generally refers to the presence of mind that allows for clear awareness of one's experience. In Anālayo's words: "Owing to such presence of mind, whatever one does or says will be clearly apprehended by the mind, and thus can be more easily remembered later on" (Anālayo, 2004, p. 48). By engaging in open monitoring meditation practices, one is said to learn to recognize one's habitual cognitive and emotional patterns (Lutz et al., 2008). In this sense, "insight" aims at cultivating wisdom, ridding the practitioner of the mental habits that are said to cause suffering.

There is debate about how the two styles of calm and insight meditation are related, with some schools viewing calm meditation as a prerequisite to insight meditation, and others seeing them as independent practices. Arguably, however, the two practices are meant to work in tandem (Anālayo, 2004, p. 87). Insight meditation allows the practitioner to take the right attitude to observed mental events and keeps calm meditation practice from becoming stagnant. Calm meditation allows the mind to be comfortable resting in the present moment and strengthens concentration so that the practitioner can do insight meditation more effectively. Together, the two practices build the mental qualities—ease and stability of present-moment awareness, and clear awareness of mental events—that are needed to clearly observe the arising and passing away of thoughts (Thanissaro, 1997).

Absorption is the culmination of concentration practice in calm meditation. Theravāda Buddhism, the branch of Buddhism based on the texts of the Pāli Canon (generally considered the oldest extant Buddhist texts), delineates four stages of *dhyāna*. The practitioner proceeds through the stages by focusing awareness on a single chosen object, and thereby building concentration (*samādhi*). Theravāda Buddhist texts, such as the Pāli *Nikāyas* (the collections of the Buddha's discourses) and the *Visuddhimagga (Path of Purification)* by the fifth-century CE philosopher Buddhaghoṣa, list many possible objects of meditation, depending on the stage of practice and the temperament of the practitioner. A common concentration object, especially favored by contemporary teachers, is the breath. When one sits down to practice, one brings one's attention to the object and tries to maintain this attention. Initially, one's mind will soon wander to other thoughts and sensations. At this stage, one's mind is said to be plagued by the "five hindrances" and to lack the "five limbs" of *dhyāna*. The five hindrances are (i) desire for pleasurable sensory objects, (ii) aversion or ill will, (iii) tiredness, (iv) restlessness, and (v) doubt. As one progresses in calm meditation practice, one lets go of the five hindrances and builds on the five limbs of *dhyāna*. These are (i) placing the attention on the object, (ii) examining the quality of the subjective state, (iii) joy, (iv) happiness, and (v) one-pointed focus wherein one's attention no longer strays to other objects (Gethin, 1998, pp. 184–186). At this point, the practitioner has reached the stage of "access consciousness," the precursor to *dhyāna*.

Access consciousness is not yet *dhyāna* because the limbs are still unstable. *Dhyāna* proper has four stages in which the practitioner refines the five limbs and abides in increasingly deeper stages of absorption. In the first stage of *dhyāna*, the five limbs are present, though the meditator has to exert effort to enter and stay in a state of concentration. In the second *dhyāna*, the practitioner can concentrate on the object without needing conscious placing of attention. After this, one experiences joy and then happiness, which arise and pass away in the third and fourth stages respectively. At the fourth stage, the meditator's mind is calm; one has moved beyond even happiness and entered into a state of profound equanimity. These four *dhyānas* are said to be followed by the "formless attainments," which are essentially refinements of the fourth *dhyāna* (Gethin, 1998, p. 185). These are specified as the experiences of (i) infinite space, (ii) infinite consciousness, (iii) nothingness, and (iv) neither perception nor non-perception.

Other Buddhist traditions provide different characterizations of absorption. For example, in the Tibetan tradition, calm meditation practice progresses through the "nine stages of calm abiding" (Asaṅga, Rahula, & Boin-Webb, 2001; Wallace, 1999). In the early stages, one is able to place one's attention on the object but cannot maintain it for more than a few minutes. Over the course of the nine stages, one is able to keep one's attentional focus for longer periods of time. Gradually, one stills one's mind while avoiding both excitation and laxity—hyperactivity of the mind versus sluggishness. The culmination of the practice is effortless one-pointed concentration.

Discussions of absorption as a culmination of focused attention meditation are also present in the non-Buddhist yoga tradition. In the yoga tradition expounded by Patañjali (Bryant, 2009), *dhyāna* is one of the "eight limbs" of yoga. The last three limbs, *dhārana, dhyāna*, and *samādhi*, describe a progression in concentrative or focused attention meditation. In the stage of *dhārana*—usually translated as "concentration"—one focuses attention on a specific object. Attention becomes stabilized and sustained continuously in the stage of *dhārana*. In *samādhi*, attention becomes unified with the object. This tradition also distinguishes two types of *samādhi*, one that involves concepts and one that is an objectless absorption devoid of concepts.

Relating hypnotic and meditative absorption

In both the hypnosis literature and Buddhist texts, absorption is a state of focused attention in which there is reduced awareness of or attention to peripheral stimuli, and due to which one may experience altered boundaries of the self and an altered perception of reality

(Pekala & Forbes, 1997). These experiences can include alterations in one's body image or even the sense that one's body has disappeared (Cardeña et al., 2013). Both practices can lead to cessation of speech and thought (Hilgard, 1968), as well as states in which one is unresponsive to external, even painful, stimuli (see Chapter 14). Deep states of hypnosis can parallel some experiences in deep states of meditation, such as loss of individual identity, sense of unification with all things, and experiences of emptiness or voidness (Cardeña et al., 2013; Erickson, 1965; Tart, 1970). Notably, studies investigating meditators using the TAS, created in the context of hypnosis research, have found that they have higher scores for absorption (Chapter 14; Davidson et al., 1976; Holzel & Ott, 2006).

It may seem that the two traditions are referring to the same absorption experience. Holroyd (2003) takes such a stance. He argues that the altered states referred to by the *dhyāna* framework are the same experiences that subjects have in deep hypnosis. Specifically, he argues that hypnotic induction leading to a deep state of hypnosis is akin to entering the four *dhyānas*. He makes this argument using both phenomenological and neurological data. For the phenomenological case, Holroyd discusses Cardeña's (2005) self-hypnosis study on hypnosis "virtuosos" (for more details on the procedure, see Cardeña, 2005 and Chapter 15). This study employed both concurrent and retrospective report. During hypnosis, participants provided depth ratings and were asked, "What are you experiencing?," approximately every 5 minutes. After hypnosis, participants were administered the Phenomenology of Consciousness Inventory (PCI) (Pekala, 1991; Pekala, Steinberg, & Kumar, 1986)—a questionnaire used to assess subjective experience—and a checklist of 189 consciousness-altering phenomena, such as differences in body image, sense of time, identity, and memory, as well as the level of depth at which they were experienced. These data were then compared to the data gathered by concurrent methods. The study used *neutral hypnosis*, meaning that no suggestions were given by the experimenter other than to become hypnotized (Cardeña et al., 2013; Kihlstrom & Edmonston, 1971).

During light hypnosis, subjects felt little more than relaxation. At medium hypnosis, subjects experienced alterations in body image, such as sensations of "floating" or "spinning," and they began to feel increasingly disconnected from the body and environment. In deep hypnosis, participants reported "free-floating" attention and greater control over their mental states. They also experienced vivid and spontaneous imagery, such as geometric patterns and synesthetic imagery. Interestingly, most participants reported both "brightness" or "flashes of light" and "great obscurity." Emotions during this state were mostly positive (including "love" and euphoric and bliss states), though some participants reported "fear."

Holroyd argues that the experiences had by hypnotized subjects as they moved from medium to deep hypnosis parallel those of meditators moving into deeper stages of *dhyāna*. First, in hypnosis, attention is initially focused on imagery at medium levels, and is then free-floating and absorbed at deep levels. He compares such attention with attention in meditation, which goes from active and concentrated in the first *dhyāna* to still and absorbed in the fourth *dhyāna*. Second, in hypnosis, emotions go from intensely positive at medium levels of hypnosis to absent at deep levels, in a way that seems to parallel the joy and bliss states of the second and third stages of *dhyāna* giving way to equanimity in the fourth *dhyāna*. Not mentioned by Holroyd, but also worth noting, is that experiences of light (which were reported by hypnotized subjects) are taken by some Theravāda Buddhist accounts as a sign that one has reached the initial stages of *dhyāna* (Lindahl, Kaplan, Winget, & Britton, 2013).

Holroyd discusses similarities between the deepest states of hypnosis and the fourth *dhyāna*. First, there seem to be parallels in the quality of attention. Holroyd takes the "free-floating" attention reported in the hypnosis case to be comparable to "attention focused on stillness," the attentional state of the fourth *dhyāna*. Second, thoughts may disappear in both deep hypnosis and meditative states. Third, there are similarities in self-experience. Both hypnotized subjects and meditators can dissociate from the body and lose a separate sense of self. Both can also experience non-duality and a feeling of being at one with all.

We agree that there are important similarities between the two cases and that hypnotized subjects may be experiencing some classic markers of *dhyāna*. Overall, the evidence seems promising for a comparison of absorption states between the two practices. Nevertheless, there are clear differences between the *dhyānas* and hypnotic absorption that make any one-to-one mapping unfeasible.

First, there is an asymmetry in the way that absorption is defined in the *dhyāna* framework versus hypnosis research. The *dhyānas* are specified according to both the content of one's experience and its attentional quality, whereas absorption in the hypnosis literature is specified primarily according to attentional quality. In the hypnosis case, although it is understood that engagement with an object forms the basis of the absorption experience (and hence its content) and that awareness of peripheral stimuli is reduced, there is no specification of the affective state of the subject, as there is in the case of the *dhyānas* (for example, rapture, happiness, and equanimity).

Second, absorption experiences in hypnosis and meditation differ in both content and attentional quality, with the result that the content of hypnotized subjects' experiences do not fit Holroyd's hypothesis that the four *dhyānas* map onto increasing depth of hypnosis. In one direction, Cardeña's study describes phenomena that seem similar to the deepest states of the "formless attainments" beyond the four *dhyānas*. For example, one participant said, "for a while I was just total nothing." Compare this report with a traditional description of the third "formless attainment:" "Through the total overcoming of the sphere of boundless consciousness, and with the idea 'Nothing is there,' he reaches the sphere of nothingness and abides therein" (Thera, 1952, p. 108). Some hypnotic subjects also appear to have experienced a degree of formlessness, as these reports suggest: "merging with pure light or energy and finding one's innermost core," and "I am not matter anymore . . . I'm just energy."

In the other direction, it is not clear whether the experiences of hypnotized subjects possess all of the characteristics of *dhyāna*. One issue worth investigating further is the presence of thoughts in states of absorption. Holroyd notes that thought can cease for hypnotized subjects at deep levels. This is corroborated by evidence that hypnosis results in reduced discursive thinking. Hypnotized subjects report fewer spontaneous thoughts and a reduction in the sense that their mind is cluttered with thoughts (Deeley et al., 2012). There is also an increase in sustained attention and self-reported absorption (Cardeña, 2005; Deeley et al., 2012; Rainville & Price, 2003). Within Buddhism, however, there is disagreement about whether conceptual thought is present in the first *dhyāna* (Anālayo, 2004). If even the first *dhyāna* is free of discursive thought, then the progression from medium to deep hypnosis will not proceed parallel to that of the four *dhyānas*, since Cardeña's subjects are still experiencing thoughts at medium levels. In addition, Holroyd compares self-described "free-floating" attention in deep states of hypnosis with the one-pointed attention of *dhyāna*. Yet "free-floating" seems to indicate a state of easy attention switching to various objects, which seems quite distinct from the focused attention of *dhyāna*. We would need more details about the attentional states of hypnotized subjects as well as meditators in order to compare them properly. Without such information, equivalence claims are not warranted.

The main obstacle to comparison is that although absorption in hypnotized subjects may share features with *dhyāna*, the subjects may not experience them in the progression of the *dhyāna* framework. It is also an open empirical question whether meditation practitioners experience absorption in this progressive way, or whether the progression framework needs to be understood as resulting from doctrinal and interpretative constraints. We take these points to mean not that absorption is incomparable between the two practices but rather that a linear, one-to-one mapping is not the best means of comparison.

In fact, such a comparison may not even be desirable. It is important to keep in mind when employing Buddhist texts for research purposes that textual descriptions of meditative states are highly normative. The *dhyāna* framework is not merely descriptive but also presents an ideal for the meditator to follow. One is meant to use this account as a guide and inspiration in one's practice. Moreover, the practice itself has a strong normative component, since the practitioner is aiming for liberation from suffering. A straightforward use of textual descriptions of *dhyāna* as a map of meditative experience glosses over the normative component of Buddhist textual descriptions. As just mentioned, the extent to which any meditator's own experiences follow the trajectory specified in the *dhyāna* framework remains an open question. Recall also that there are multiple interpretative frameworks for meditative absorption, and although there are many commonalities, there is no one way in which absorption is said to arise in meditation practice.

A better approach to comparison is to look at features of hypnosis and meditation more generally. We follow this approach in the rest of this chapter by using a phenomenal model proposed by Lutz and colleagues for the study of mindfulness practices (Lutz et al., in press). This approach maps experiences along certain characteristic dimensions, such as the degree of focus of attention or how vividly the contents of experience present themselves. Creating such a phenomenal state map involves determining the features that are central to each experience and that are most relevant for comparison. These features are then treated as dimensions along which we can map conscious states, in this case hypnosis and meditation. In what follows, we examine the "phenomenological and neurocognitive matrix of mindfulness" (PNM) model, proposed by Lutz and colleagues, and expand it to include hypnosis. We also suggest further dimensions for the model that are relevant to hypnosis in particular.

The phenomenological and neurocognitive matrix of mindfulness (PNM)

Lutz and colleagues created the PNM in order to provide an account of the possible range of mindfulness states that would be useful for empirical research (Lutz et al., in press). Instead of providing a unitary definition of mindfulness, they provide a phenomenal matrix (PM)—a family resemblance account that maps different practices and levels of expertise into a multidimensional phenomenal space. More specifically, the PM maps experiential states according to seven phenomenal features that are cultivated by mindfulness practices. Three of these—"object orientation," "dereification," and "meta-awareness"—are core features, insofar as they are targets of all styles of meditation practice and are useful for distinguishing between different practice styles. The four remaining dimensions—"aperture," "clarity," "stability," and "effort"—are secondary, in that they are important features of meditative experience but do not differentiate practice styles. These dimensions are derived from Buddhist texts but the authors note that empirical study needs to be done with practitioners in order to verify that textual descriptions of meditative states are phenomenologically accurate.

Lutz and colleagues have also formulated a neurocognitive framework for the PM, the phenomenological and neurocognitive matrix (PNM). The PNM describes how large-scale functional networks—such as the central executive network and the salience network, discussed in the section "The PNM networks"—underlie the features of the PM. In what follows, we outline the dimensions of the PM, provide a short description of the networks involved in the PNM, and, finally, discuss hypnosis within the framework of the PNM, comparing hypnotized individuals with meditators. The most relevant comparison for our purposes will be with focused attention meditation, because this style of practice specifically engenders absorption and its phenomenal profile is most akin to hypnosis. In our discussion, we make the assumption that conscious experience and neural activity change in systematic ways during hypnosis. We use "state" in a descriptive sense to refer to the phenomenal experiences associated with hypnosis (see Bell et al., 2011; Oakley, 1999). We make no claim to the effect that hypnosis is a distinct process (see Gruzelier, 2000; Wagstaff, 1998, 2000).

One challenge to keep in mind when looking at hypnosis is that the experience depends a lot on which suggestions are given to the participant. We try to avoid confounds, wherever possible, by referring to studies employing neutral induction, that is, induction that does not include suggestion.[1] A second large source of variability is individual differences. We attenuate this difficulty, to some extent, by referring to studies that use highly hypnotizable participants. There are several ways of classifying participants according to hypnotizability but most use a measure of suggestibility, with more suggestible individuals being classified as more hypnotizable. It is worth noting, however, that high hypnotizables also display variability in their experiences. Measures of hypnotizability that are sensitive to the particular response profile of an individual show that high hypnotizables do not have uniform response patterns to suggestion (Hilgard, 1979; McConkey & Barnier, 2004; Pekala et al., 1986; Terhune, Cardeña, & Lindgren, 2011).

Dimensions of the PM

Object orientation is the phenomenal sense that one's experience is directed toward a particular object (including objects of thought). This sense of directedness is not merely about the selection of an object in the sense of there being an object that is experienced more vividly than its surroundings. One's attention can also be directed toward an object that is not present and thus not available for selection. For example, when one looks for a friend in a crowd, one's attention is oriented to that person even when one cannot see them. Thus, object orientation includes a felt sense of attentional engagement with an object. Medium to low object orientation occurs in states of mind wandering, and very low object orientation occurs in expert open monitoring meditation, in which the practitioner observes the occurrence of thoughts but does not engage with them. Very high object orientation occurs in states of focused attention meditation but also in states of addictive craving, both of which have strong engagement with an object of awareness.

Meta-awareness: Lutz and colleagues present a particular view of meta-awareness that they relate to the Buddhist notion of *samprajanya*—usually translated as "clear knowing" (of experiential phenomena, especially one's mental states)—as well as to other Buddhist philosophical notions, such as "reflexive awareness" (*svasaṃvedana*). We use a definition more in line with current Western psychology. In this usage, "meta-awareness" refers to one's ability to access one's current contents of consciousness (Chin & Schooler, 2010). Low meta-awareness can occur in mind wandering (when a person is often unaware that their mind is wandering), and mind wandering can be interrupted with the return of meta-awareness. Low meta-awareness also occurs in states of craving, in which object orientation is high but the individual is unaware both of how the object appears to them and of their thoughts, feelings, and desires about the object. Meta-awareness is crucial to open monitoring meditation practice, because the ability to access

---

[1] It may be that hypnosis is never truly neutral. For instance, the same procedure increases suggestibility if subjects are told that it is hypnosis rather than relaxation (Gandhi & Oakley, 2005).

one's contents of consciousness is necessary for the moment-to-moment monitoring of one's experience characteristic of this style of practice. A focused attention meditator requires meta-awareness for detecting and disengaging from distractions, though at later stages, in which attention is absorbed by the object, meta-awareness may no longer be present.

Dereification is the degree to which thoughts are experienced as transient mental events rather than accurate depictions of reality. Dereification also cuts off the tendency to construct from thoughts a fixed and static representation of self. In cases of high reification, thoughts "present themselves as if the objects or situations they represent are occurring in the present moment" (Lutz et al., in press; see also Chambers, Gullone, & Allen, 2009; Hayes & Feldman, 2004; Papies, Barsalou, & Custers, 2012; Teasdale, 1999; Williams, 2010). These include experiences such as addictive craving, wherein the object acquires a solidity and permanence in thought, even resulting in an anticipatory physiological response.

In addition to the three dimensions of object orientation, meta-awareness, and dereification, which make up a three-dimensional state space model, Lutz and colleagues have identified a number of phenomenal qualities that can belong differentially to the experiential states mapped in this three-dimensional space.

Effort refers to how easy or difficult an experience feels to maintain. Focused attention meditation involves a high degree of effort at the novice level, but the effort diminishes as the practitioner gains experience. Open monitoring meditation aims to use less effort, as too much effort could encourage object selection.

Aperture refers to the scope of attention. In focused attention meditation, aperture is narrow, in the sense of being focused precisely on the target object. In open monitoring meditation, aperture is broad, extending to the entire field of conscious experience.

Clarity is the phenomenal vividness of the experience. Depressive rumination and craving can both have high clarity, since their objects typically appear salient and vivid. Clarity is said to be a feature of experts' experience in both focused attention and open monitoring styles of meditation.

Stability is the degree to which a quality of experience persists over time. This can occur even if the contents of experience are highly changeable. For example, an open monitoring meditator can observe the rapid flow of thoughts—an experience in which the content is continuously changing—while the quality of observing, including dereification and meta-awareness, stays constant. For both open monitoring and focused attention meditators, stability is middling at the novice level and high at expert levels.

The PNM networks

The *central executive network*, also called the dorsolateral or top-down attentional system (Corbetta & Shulman, 2002), includes the bilateral dorsolateral prefrontal cortex (PFC), ventrolateral PFC, dorsomedial PFC, and lateral parietal cortices. It is responsible for endogenous directing of attention as well as planning behavior and keeping information in working memory (Miller & Cohen, 2001; Seeley et al., 2007). Lutz and colleagues propose that the central executive network underlies object orientation because of its role in monitoring stimuli and maintaining attention.

The *salience network* is composed of the bilateral anterior insulae (aI) and dorsal anterior cingulate cortex (dACC), as well as subcortical structures involved in emotion, reward, and homeostasis. The salience network picks out salient stimuli in the environment using interoceptive and affective information. According to several models (Craig, 2009, 2010; Damasio & Dolan, 1999; Damasio, Everitt, & Bishop, 1996), the insulae, thalamus, and brainstem are responsible for creating a real-time representation of the bodily self using somatosensory signals. Because the salience network provides continuously updated information about the embodied self, Lutz and colleagues propose that it plays a central role in the meta-awareness dimension of the PNM. Open monitoring meditation may involve both the salience network and the monitoring and evaluative capacities of the central executive network.

The PNM: comparisons between hypnosis and meditation

Object orientation

Object orientation is a key dimension for absorption. Some definitions, like that of Rainville and Price (2003), identify absorption almost exclusively by its object-directedness.

The degree of object orientation in hypnosis is comparable to that of focused attention meditation experts and novices. Like focused attention meditation, hypnosis is characterized by focused attention and absorption in an object (Rainville & Price, 2003). Hypnotized individuals' object orientation seems stronger than that of focused attention novices because their attention is less frequently pulled away from its object.

Lutz and colleagues connect the object orientation dimension to central executive network activity because of this network's role in endogenous orienting, that is, voluntary directing of attention to a certain stimulus. Several studies demonstrate either increased central executive network activity in meditation (Hasenkamp, Wilson-Mendenhall, Duncan, & Barsalou, 2012) or increased activation of this network in attention tasks following meditation training (Jha, Krompinger, & Baime 2007; van den Hurk, Giommi, Gielen, Speckens, & Barendregt, 2010). In the hypnosis literature, studies show conflicting evidence regarding the role of executive attention (Semmens-Wheeler & Dienes, 2012). Some studies and theories of hypnosis claim that the executive attention system is more active in hypnosis (Crawford, 1994; Gruzelier, 1998; Rainville & Price, 2003; Woody & Bowers, 1994), whereas others claim that it is less active (Dietrich, 2003; Gruzelier, 2000; Hilgard, 1977; Kallio, Revonsuo, Hämäläinen, Markela, & Gruzelier, 2001). Interestingly, Rainville and Price (2003) found increased prefrontal cortex activation specifically associated with the absorption dimension of hypnotic experience. Perhaps conflicting results about central executive network activation can be explained by the degree of absorption present. Another potential resolution is to distinguish between different functions of executive processing (Lynn et al., 2012; to be discussed further in the section "Meta-awareness").

To further support their claim that endogenous attention orienting is the system underlying object orientation, Lutz and colleagues identify four functional markers of attention orienting and argue that meditation training improves their efficiency. These markers are improved task performance, greater neural activation to attended versus unattended stimuli, biasing activation of early perceptual neurons, and engagement of frontal and parietal cortices. Examining hypnosis in terms of functional markers is more difficult because the performance exhibited by participants could vary greatly depending on the suggestions given by the experimenter. Furthermore, many studies eschew placing participants in attentional tasks during hypnosis but rather test participants using post-hypnotic suggestion (e.g., Raz & Campbell, 2011). With regard to the first marker of improved performance, there is evidence that suggestion improves performance on tests of attentional orienting—namely, the Stroop and ANT (attention network test) (for a review, see Raz, 2005). Nevertheless, highly hypnotizable people differ at baseline on these tests, typically showing less efficient performance without suggestion (Dixon, Brunet, & Laurence, 1990; Dixon & Laurence, 1992; Raz, Shapiro, Fan, & Posner, 2002), though some studies show superior attentional performance and improved cognitive flexibility among highly susceptible individuals (see Crawford, 1994; Enea & Dafinoiu, 2013; Gruzelier, 1998).

We need a more detailed picture of attentional processes in hypnosis before we can say exactly where it fits in comparison with meditation. Particularly, the issue for future research is to determine the role of endogenous or executive attention and in what ways it may be present in hypnosis. This issue turns out to be complex, as discussed in the section "Meta-awareness."

Meta-awareness

Lutz and colleagues tie meta-awareness to the dynamic activity of both the central executive network and the salience network, and these networks remain important to our conception of meta-awareness as accessing the current contents of consciousness. The central executive network is involved due to its role in monitoring, maintaining, and integrating information; and the salience network is important due to its role in supporting the phenomenal sense of a bodily self through its moment-to-moment facilitation of feeling states.

It seems reasonable to suppose that hypnotized subjects have lower meta-awareness than focused attention meditators, whether novices or experts, given the suggestibility of hypnosis subjects. Meta-awareness is linked to executive control skills required for monitoring one's experience. Some theorists claim that a reduction or diversion of executive resources explains how hypnotized subjects can allow contradictions in their experience to go unquestioned (Kirsch & Lynn, 1998; Wagstaff, Heap, Oakley, & Brown, 2004; Woody & Bowers, 1994). For example, self-initiated movements can be experienced as automatic or subjects can maintain a hypnotically induced false belief in the face of contradictory evidence (e.g., Bryant & McConkey, 1989; Noble & McConkey, 1995).

Semmens-Wheeler and Dienes (2012) outline four ways in which the subjective experience of absorption could occur:

 (i)   One could be mind wandering and not notice it.

 (ii) One might be distracted by irrelevant thoughts but notice the distraction, using meta-awareness, and thereby disengage from them.

(iii) Irrelevant thoughts occur but one does not attend to them and is not distracted by them.

(iv)   One has single-pointed focus on the object of attention.

The first state is not genuine absorption because it is an illusion that results from inaccurate meta-representations of one's experience. Attention is not absorbed but it appears to be, or one believes that it is because meta-representations do not convey what is happening at the first-order level of experience. The authors advance the idea that a meditator experiences (iii) or (iv) because they train meta-awareness concurrently with absorbed attention and thus accurately represent themself as being in the absorbed state. They argue that hypnosis does not train or engage meta-awareness and thus may evince the earlier states of absorption, including perhaps the pseudo-absorption of (i). They support this claim with evidence that highly hypnotizable individuals have less accurate "higher-order thoughts"—meta-representations about their current experiences (Dienes, Beran, Brandl, Perner, & Proust, 2012).

In opposition to the aforementioned claim, Lifshitz, Cusumano, and Raz (2013) argue that hypnosis could be a useful shortcut method for generating meta-awareness in subjects without the need for years of practice (as in the meditative traditions). Meta-awareness requires maintaining openness to experience and overriding one's habitual tendency for conceptual elaboration. Lifshitz and colleagues argue that hypnotic suggestion is a plausible candidate as a tool for inducing meta-awareness, because it is capable of affecting attention and altering other processes typically thought to be automatic or unalterable via conscious control. As evidence that hypnosis can alter automatic processes, hypnotized subjects under suggestion to see the world in black and white reported seeing colored images in grayscale and had reduced activity in low-level brain regions associated with color processing (Kosslyn, Thompson, Costantini-Ferrando, Alpert, & Spiegel, 2000). As evidence that hypnosis can alter attentional processing, it is possible to reduce or even eliminate the Stroop effect with hypnosis (Augustinova & Ferrand, 2012; Parris, Dienes, & Hodgson, 2012; Raz & Campbell, 2011; Raz, Fan, & Posner 2006; Raz, Moreno-Íniguez, Martin, & Zhu, 2007; Raz et al., 2002, 2003). This finding is significant, because reading, once learned, is thought to be done automatically, and the robustness of the Stroop effect is a testament to how difficult it is to ignore linguistic stimuli. So, given that hypnotic suggestion is able to affect automatic and attentional processes, Lifshitz and colleagues argue that suggestion could also possibly induce meta-awareness.

An objection to the possibility of high meta-awareness in hypnosis subjects is that meta-awareness seems to conflict with suggestibility. That a subject is able to act and form beliefs that go against their previous beliefs and experience—for example, failing to recognize themself in the mirror—seems to indicate that they are not receptive to their entire field of experience in the manner characteristic of meta-awareness. There seems to be an element of self-deception in hypnosis that meta-awareness ought to eliminate. That hypnosis involves a degree of self-deception or inattentiveness is in line with dissociation and cold control theories of hypnosis, which posit that a hypnotic response consists in intending to perform a given action while being unaware of this intention (Dienes, Perner, & Jamieson, 2007; Hilgard, 1977; Spanos, 1986). Semmens-Wheeler and Dienes (2012) are working from a cold control framework when they argue that hypnotized subjects have inaccurate meta-representations. Although these authors tend to discuss meta-representations or higher-order thoughts (which are a type of meta-representation), we can see how a disparity between first- and second-order thoughts could be a problem for meta-awareness.

At the neuroscientific level, the issue of meta-awareness and hypnotic response hinges on executive control processing. High meta-awareness is thought to be the result of executive control activity, since executive regions are involved in endogenous attention and monitoring (Corbetta & Shulman, 2002; Ridderinkhof, van den Wildenberg, Segalowitz, & Carter, 2004). Previous research has found that activity in the dorsolateral PFC (dlPFC), a key region in top-down attention and executive control, distinguished between accurate and inaccurate higher-order thoughts. Lau and Passingham (2006) isolated two conditions in a perceptual discrimination task in which subjects were equally good at discriminating a masked shape but differed in the accuracy of their higher-order thoughts. Increased activity in the dlPFC was correlated with accurate higher-order thoughts. Further, an experimental study that disrupted dlPFC activity with transcranial magnetic stimulation (TMS) found that TMS interfered with subjects' awareness of seeing in a case where first-order perception was held constant (Rounis, Maniscalco, Rothwell, Passingham, & Lau, 2010).

It would seem that executive network activity would block suggestion because of its function as a monitoring process, and some hypnosis researchers have argued along the lines that hypnosis increases suggestibility because it reduces executive control function (Dietrich, 2003; Gruzelier, 1998, 2006). This reduction contrasts with meditation, which is meant to improve executive control function. Research on meditation typically finds increased central executive network activity in meditators—albeit with experience-related differences, which we discuss in the section "Dereification"). Neurophysiological evidence about executive activity in hypnosis is mixed. Studies finding increased activity in central executive network regions, such as the prefrontal cortex (e.g., Rainville & Price, 2003), might support the claim that hypnosis subjects possess high meta-awareness.

Relevant to this debate are EEG studies finding increased theta activity in the frontal cortex during hypnosis, as well as at baseline for highly hypnotizable participants (Crawford, Burrows, & Stanley, 2001; Crawford & Gruzelier, 1992; Graffin, Ray, & Lundy, 1995; Holroyd, 2003). This pattern of activity has been found in tasks requiring focused attention and effort (Crawford, 1994; Schacter, 1977), although some authors (e.g., Holroyd, 2003) argue that high frontal theta activity is indicative of cortical inhibition and a *reduction* in executive processing. Dienes and Hutton (2013) conducted an experimental study in which the dlPFC was disrupted in hypnosis subjects using low-frequency, repetitive transcranial magnetic stimulation (rTMS). They found that impairing dlPFC activity with rTMS enhanced the hypnosis response. This finding supports the view that hypnosis involves impaired meta-representations. Additionally, in Chapter 7, Dienes and colleagues defend the claim that hypnosis involves inaccurate metacognitions, that is, inaccurate second-order thoughts about one's first-order state. They characterize mindfulness as enhanced metacognition and argue for a tension between mindfulness and hypnotic response.

One way of resolving the issue about meta-awareness in hypnosis is presented by Lynn and colleagues (2012). They differentiate the monitoring and control functions of the executive system, claiming that the two do not always appear in tandem: "in hypnosis, there may be a decoupling between brain regions associated with monitoring and cognitive control" (see Egner, Jamieson, & Gruzelier, 2005; see also Sadler & Woody, 2006; Woody & Sadler, 2008). Cognitive control is the "flexible management of response processes" (Egner et al., 2005), whereas the monitoring function has the role of monitoring response conflicts that may arise, such as when one has to override a habitual response to a stimulus (Botvinick, Cohen, & Carter, 2004). Egner and colleagues (2005) found a decoupling between activity in the anterior cingulate cortex (ACC) and the lateral frontal cortex (LFC) (a region that includes the dorsolateral PFC). The ACC is thought to be responsible for conflict monitoring, whereas the LFC is a region responsible for cognitive control. These regions are *more* coupled during meditation (Brewer et al., 2011). Such a pattern of activity opens up the explanation that, in hypnosis, there is monitoring of the situation—and thus the subject may have high meta-awareness—but monitoring is decoupled from executive processing, so that suggestions are still followed.

The decoupling explanation also offers an interesting way of looking at guided meditation. Lynn and colleagues (2012) posit that decoupling between control and monitoring regions may be the product of the hypnotist "taking the lead" or, in a sense, standing in for the executive processing of the hypnotized subject (Lynn, Rhue, & Weekes, 1990). Such an effect may also be behind the empirical findings we see in guided meditation. Several studies of guided meditation have shown reduced executive control processing, which contrasts with the increased central executive network activity seen in unguided meditation (Cahn & Polich, 2006). These findings suggest the possibility that hypnotic suggestion (on a looser definition of hypnosis; see Lynn et al., 2012) may be a key mechanism behind guided meditation. Future research could investigate this possibility in greater detail.

Further along this line, we can consider the differing roles that suggestion plays in meditation versus hypnosis. Mindfulness practice instruction often involves suggestions that encourage meta-awareness and dereification, such as the following (which is often a part of focused attention meditation instruction): "Should you find yourself judging, simply remind yourself to return to observing or just following your breathing." Hypnosis participants, however, are encouraged to become absorbed and experientially involved in their experience (Lynn et al., 2012). So, there is an empirical question about whether hypnosis could also achieve increases in dereification and meta-awareness if the content of suggestion was similar to that of meditation instructions. Given the richness and complexity of meditation practice, future research could look at the extent to which different elements of the practice—such as training, suggestion, and individual differences—affect the dimensions of phenomenal experience seen in meditators.

Dereification

A dereified stance toward one's experience treats the contents of experience strictly as mental contents rather than as accurate depictions of reality. Dereification is closely related to meta-awareness, since awareness of one's experience is part of what allows one to take a dereified stance toward it. For this reason, we believe that meta-awareness is necessary for dereification. It follows that the two dimensions of meta-awareness and dereification cannot be orthogonal, as they are presented in the PNM. Nevertheless, the notion of dereification gets at something important and distinct from meta-awareness. Dereification refers to the more affective components of decentering or disidentifying from thoughts. When they are dereified, thoughts are not only monitored but also disconnected from elaborative processing, and their affective consequences are altered. They no longer carry the same impact.

All meditation styles probably train dereification to some degree but a paradigm case of low dereification occurs in open monitoring meditation in which one is taught to observe thoughts as passing and insubstantial phenomena. Focused attention meditation also includes noting one's thoughts when attention is distracted from the object of focus, a technique that trains dereification. Initially, dereification is effortful and consciously cultivated, but it eventually becomes habitual through repeated practice.

It is difficult to judge the degree of dereification in hypnosis, since no specific data are available on the topic. It is plausible, however, that hypnotized subjects have lower dereification than both focused attention meditation experts and novices. Focused attention meditation novices try to maintain enough emotional distance from their experience to concentrate on their object of attention, whereas hypnotized subjects are not under the same constraints. Additionally, early researchers of hypnosis related high hypnotizability to one's tendency to become emotionally involved in imaginary scenarios (Hilgard, 1979, 1970; Tellegen & Atkinson, 1974). It is not clear to what extent current researchers hold this view.

Lutz and colleagues believe that meditators' high level of dereification is evinced by their responses to forms of suffering, such as pain, social threat, and depression. With dereification, the sensory aspects of pain, for instance, become detached from its affective and personal significance. Thus, meditators show reduced activation in the central executive network and affective regions, such as the amygdala. They also show improved pain tolerance and reduced pain anticipation, even though their sensory activation to painful stimuli is increased relative to non-meditators (Grant, Courtemanche, & Rainville, 2011; Lutz, McFarlin, Perlman, Salomons, & Davidson, 2013).

Studies have shown that hypnosis can be an effective means of attenuating pain (Derbyshire, Whalley, & Oakley, 2009). Attenuation may occur through differential activity in the ACC and insulae, which indicates that the salience network may be involved in pain perception (Baron Short et al., 2010; Kupers, Faymonville, & Laureys, 2005; Rainville, Duncan, Price, Carrier, & Bushnell, 1997; Spiegel, White, & Waelde, 2010). Pain intensity may also be modulated by the central executive network, due to involvement of the dorsolateral PFC (Lorenz, Minoshima, & Casey, 2003).

That hypnosis can attenuate pain means that it has the potential to induce high dereification (though there are other paths to pain attenuation such as distraction; see Chapter 21). The discussion of meta-awareness in this chapter is also relevant. If hypnotized subjects are capable of exhibiting meta-awareness, then they may be capable of dereification as well. That hypnotized subjects can have emotional experiences similar to those of meditators, including experiences of equanimity, is promising evidence in this regard.

Effort

The hypnotized person exerts a low degree of effort, perhaps comparable to that of the focused attention meditation expert. According to Rainville and Price (2003), the state of focused attention achieved in hypnosis requires effort at the beginning of the session but then becomes passive and relatively effortless. Other authors also note the felt sense of effortlessness in hypnosis (e.g., Lifshitz et al., 2013). In Buddhist texts, the state of the focused attention expert is said to be effortless (Wallace, 1999). It is an empirical question whether this is the case or whether effortlessness is a normative ideal. Some attempts to address this issue have found that focused attention meditation experts have reduced dorsolateral PFC activity compared to novices and mid-level practitioners (Brefczynski-Lewis, Lutz, Schaefer, Levinson, & Davidson, 2007). According to the authors, these data support the claim that meditation experts are in an effortless state, although it is not clear that reduced dorsolateral PFC activity can be straightforwardly taken to indicate reduced effort (for related studies see Barch et al., 1997; Braver et al., 1997; Frith, Friston, Liddle, & Frackowiak, 1991; Levy & Goldman-Rakic, 2000; Petrides, 2000).

Aperture

The aperture of a hypnosis state may be small—comparable to that of a focused attention meditation state—since attention is thought to be object-focused in hypnosis, and both focused attention meditation and hypnosis are conducive to absorption (Rainville & Price, 2003). Some research indicates that hypnotized subjects are less responsive to irrelevant stimuli, a finding that supports this hypothesis (Fehr & Stern, 1967). Nevertheless, there are reasons to think that hypnosis results in more diffuse attention than does focused attention meditation. For instance, hypnotized subjects report their state as having "free-floating" attention (Cardeña, 2005).

Lutz and colleagues highlight the differences in aperture between focused attention and open monitoring meditators using differences in performance on a global-to-local attention task. This task measures speed of spatial attention allocation to a global pattern versus a local detail (Navon, 1977). It reveals a global precedence effect, meaning that most individuals are faster at detecting global targets than local ones. Focused attention meditators are able to override this preference and respond faster to local features. Other research has shown that both open monitoring and focused attention meditators disengage attention more quickly than controls from the global level. Studies of hypnotized subjects using this same task have found that highly hypnotizable people show the same effect as focused attention meditators during hypnosis, though they show a global precedence effect when not hypnotized (Enea & Dafiniou, 2013). (Note that this study used mood induction rather than neutral hypnosis. Subjects were asked to recall autobiographical events that made them feel either "happy and optimistic" or "sad and pessimistic" in order to induce either a positive or negative affect respectively.) The global-to-local attention task is an interesting way of studying spatial attention in the context of the PNM, though given that control participants already show a bias toward the global level, it is not clear whether the task is measuring aperture or some higher-order ability along the lines of attention switching or cognitive flexibility.

Clarity

Lutz and colleagues treat "clarity" as referring to both phenomenal vividness and the vividness of visual experiences. Given this notion of clarity, hypnotized individuals will score highly on the clarity dimension. Hypnosis is often accompanied by vivid visual imagery (Cardeña, 2005; Cardeña et al., 2013). Highly hypnotizable people also report more vivid imagery overall than low hypnotizables (Crawford, 1989; Hilgard, 1970; Sheehan, Fromm, & Shor, 1979; Tellegen &

Atkinson, 1974). Some studies show that hypnosis enhances vividness of imagery (Erickson, 1952), though others show mixed or no results (Coe, St. Jean, & Burger, 1980; Starker, 1974). More broadly, it is a hallmark of hypnosis to experience suggested states in a vivid and detailed manner regardless of sense modality. For instance, the Stanford Hypnotic Susceptibility Scale includes measures on auditory and taste experience, such as hearing a buzzing mosquito or having a sweet taste in one's mouth (Weitzenhoffer & Hilgard, 1962). Thus, we expect hypnosis to result in a clearer and more vivid overall experience.

Stability

The hypnotized subject's state is more stable than that of a focused attention novice because the former does not have to bring their attention back to its object when the mind wanders. Also, the hypnotized subject is more likely to experience absorption (Deeley et al., 2012; Rainville & Price, 2003), which is a stable attentional state. Rainville and Price (2003) report absorption-specific increases in the ACC which is part of the central executive network, indicating that this network may be involved in maintaining stability. The relationship between subjects in deep hypnosis and expert focused attention meditators on this dimension is not clear. The two states may be comparable or, if attention is more variable in deep hypnosis (Cardeña, 2005; Fromm et al., 1981), hypnosis may be less stable than focused attention.

Lessons for comparison

The PNM provides a useful framework for comparing hypnosis to focused attention meditation. Both states are high in object orientation, which is what gives each state the propensity toward absorption. Nevertheless, there is conflicting evidence regarding object orientation in the hypnosis case, since the hypnosis subject experiences more changing contents and free-floating attention. Further research could look to placing hypnosis subjects on this dimension, perhaps by examining performance on tasks involving endogenous attentional orienting (Lutz et al., in press).

Focused attention meditators and hypnosis subjects differ insofar as meditation involves more stability and effort. Effort is a particularly interesting dimension, given that in hypnosis, similar ratings can be obtained on other dimensions key to meditation training but with reduced effort, even at the novice level.

An important lesson that arises from comparing hypnosis and meditation using the PNM is that several features that have been thought of as uniquely meditative are also features of hypnosis. States with high object orientation, narrow aperture, and perhaps even high meta-awareness can be brought about by other interventions besides meditation, namely, by hypnosis.

Meta-awareness and dereification, in particular, are dimensions that need further study in hypnosis. Future research could look at how to separate out meta-awareness from cognitive control at the behavioral level in hypnosis, in order to better assess hypnotized subjects on that dimension. Additionally, it is not clear what is the typical aperture of a hypnosis state. When subjects describe having free-floating attention as well as absorption, is their state one with a narrow aperture whose object is ever-changing, or one with a wide aperture but high engagement with a particular object?

A further question is the causal role of these dimensions in hypnotic experience. For instance, is a state low in object orientation or effort more conducive to generating hypnotic experience? Future research could investigate such causal links.

Additional potential features

There are additional relevant features that could be incorporated into future efforts at mapping hypnosis experiences. These features could be used to compare hypnosis with states such as dreaming and mind wandering. They would also provide us with a more fine-grained method of examining hypnosis, since they are dimensions along which hypnosis participants differ. Research along these lines could examine whether these differences are systematic and what their neural, behavioral, and personality correlates are. The following are some examples based on the research of Pekala and Forbes (1997).

Dialoguing: This is the amount of discursive thought present as part of an experience. High dialoguing occurs in mind wandering and rumination as well as intentional goal-directed thought. Low dialoguing occurs in expert focused attention meditation. Hypnosis subjects differ in the extent to which they experience discursive thought (Pekala & Forbes, 1997).

Imagery: The PM includes clarity of visual experiences, but a useful measure for hypnosis research is the amount of visualization present in the experience. Examples of low imagery states include watching television and some instances of problem solving. High visualization states occur in hypnosis as well as some forms of meditation.

Rationality: This is the degree to which thoughts seem coherent and rational. Dream states are low in rationality, whereas goal-directed thinking is high in rationality. Hypnotic suggestions can reduce the rationality of thoughts and induce agnosia. For example, hypnotized participants in one study were induced to not recognize their faces in the mirror (Connors, Cox, Barnier, Langdon, & Coltheart, 2012). Some subjects experience reduced rationality during deep states of neutral hypnosis (Cardeña, 2005; Pekala et al., 1986).

Control: This is the extent to which one feels able to direct the experience. High control would often be coextensive with high rationality as well as high meta-awareness, though there are notable counter-examples. Mind wandering can be low in control, though it is relatively high in rationality. Lucid dreams can be high in meta-awareness while being low in control, that is, one is aware of one's state as a dream state but unable to change its contents or one's own reactions. Similarly, hypnosis, if Lynn and colleagues (2012) are correct, can have high meta-awareness but low control.

Conclusion

In this chapter, we aimed to contribute to the collaborative efforts between hypnosis and meditation researchers by mapping hypnosis into a phenomenal state space derived from meditation research (Lutz et al., in press). We examined how an absorbed state is instantiated in hypnosis versus meditation, finding key differences in effort and stability, and finding similarities in the object orientation of both experiences. We also tried to address difficult questions about the presence of meta-awareness in hypnosis. Overall, it is interesting to note that features of meditation are present in other states, and future research could examine how various factors, such as suggestion, practice, and individual differences, contribute to different dimensions of meditative experience.

We focused specifically on absorption and, to that end, we reviewed notions of absorption in hypnosis research literature as well as in traditional Indian Buddhist thought. We examined a recent attempt to integrate the two perspectives but argued that differences in the way that absorption is conceptualized in hypnosis and meditation literature preclude a direct comparison. We thus took a step back and examined hypnosis and meditation states more generally, along the dimensions of Lutz and colleagues' PNM of mindfulness. Central issues that arose were the contribution of suggestion to meditation practice and the possibility of engendering meta-awareness in hypnosis participants. We also noted some features of hypnotic experience that could be employed by future phenomenal state mapping.

Being able to see hypnosis and meditation experiences along the dimensions of the PNM has helped to clarify subtle ways in which the two types of experience differ and has pointed out gaps in our knowledge of these experiences. The PNM illustrates a broader approach of using phenomenological features as dimensions for comparing different conscious states. We believe that a state space framework systematizes first-person reports of experience in a manner useful to experimental neurophenomenological research. We have used it as a neurophenomenological tool for comparing hypnosis and meditation, though the phenomenal state space approach can also be applied to other states. As one example, it may be interesting to look at mind wandering using this framework. The framework may provide a way of distinguishing between mind wandering and related states such as rumination—for example, rumination seems higher in object orientation and more stable—as well as a way of distinguishing subtypes of mind wandering such as tuning out versus zoning out (marked by the presence and absence of meta-awareness, respectively).

References

Anālayo, B. (2004). *Sattipatthana: the direct path to realization*. Windhorse Publications.

Asaṅga, R. W., & Boin-Webb, S. (2001). *Abhidharmasamuccaya: the compendium of the higher teaching*. Jain Publishing Company.

Ashton, M. A., & McDonald, R. D. (1985). Effects of hypnosis on verbal and non-verbal creativity. *International Journal of Clinical and Experimental Hypnosis*, **33**(1), 15–26.

Augustinova, M., & Ferrand, L. (2012). Suggestion does not de-automatize word reading: evidence from the semantically based Stroop task. *Psychonomic Bulletin & Review*, **19**(3), 521–527.

Barch, D. M., Braver, T. S., Nystrom, L. E., Forman, S. D., Noll, D. C., & Cohen, J. D. (1997). Dissociating working memory from task difficulty in human prefrontal cortex. *Neuropsychologia*, **35**(10), 1373–1380.

Baron Short, E., Kose, S., Mu, Q., Borckardt, J., Newberg, A., George, M. S., & Kozel, F. A. (2010). Regional brain activation during meditation shows time and practice effects: an exploratory fMRI study. *Evidence-Based Complementary and Alternative Medicine*, **7**(1). doi: 10.1093/ecam/nem163

Bell, V., Oakley, D. A., Halligan, P. W., & Deeley, Q. (2011). Dissociation in hysteria and hypnosis: evidence from cognitive neuroscience. *Journal of Neurology, Neurosurgery & Psychiatry*, **82**(3), 332–339.

Blakemore, S.-J., Oakley, D. A., & Frith, C. (2003). Delusions of alien control in the normal brain. *Neuropsychologia*, **41**(8), 1058–1067.

Bodhi, B. (2005). *In the Buddha's words. An anthology of discourses from the Pāli Canon*. Wisdom Publications.

Botvinick, M. M., Cohen, J. D., & Carter, C. S. (2004). Conflict monitoring and anterior cingulate cortex: an update. *Trends in Cognitive Science*, **8**(12), 539–546.

Bowers, K. S. (1979). Time distortion and hypnotic ability: underestimating the duration of hypnosis. *Journal of Abnormal Psychology*, **88**(4), 435.

Braver, T. S., Cohen, J. D., Nystrom, L. E., Jonides, J., Smith, E. E., & Noll, D. C. (1997). A parametric study of prefrontal cortex involvement in human working memory. *Neuroimage*, **5**(1), 49–62.

Brefczynski-Lewis, J., Lutz, A., Schaefer, H., Levinson, D., & Davidson, R. (2007). Neural correlates of attentional expertise in long-term meditation practitioners. *Proceedings of the National Academy of Sciences*, **104**(27), 11483–11488.

Brewer, J. A., Worhunsky, P. D., Gray, J. R., Tang, Y.-Y., Weber, J., & Kober, H. (2011). Meditation experience is associated with differences in default mode network activity and connectivity. *Proceedings of the National Academy of Sciences*, **108**(50), 20254–20259.

Bryant, E. (2009) *The Yoga Sūtras of Patañjali*. New York: North Point Press.

Bryant, R. A., & McConkey, K. M. (1989). Hypnotic blindness, awareness, and attribution. *Journal of Abnormal Psychology*, **98**(4), 443.

Cahn, B. R., & Polich, J. (2006). Meditation states and traits: EEG, ERP, and neuroimaging studies. *Psychological Bulletin*, **132**(2), 180–211. doi: 10.1037/0033-2909.132.2.180

Cardeña, E. (2005). The phenomenology of deep hypnosis: quiescent and physically active. *International Journal of Clinical and Experimental Hypnosis*, **53**(1), 37–59.

Cardeña, E., Jönsson, P., Terhune, D. B., & Marcusson-Clavertz, D. (2013). The neurophenomenology of neutral hypnosis. *Cortex*, **49**(2), 375–385.

Chambers, R., Gullone, E., & Allen, N. B. (2009). Mindful emotion regulation: an integrative review. *Clinical Psychology Review*, **29**(6), 560–572.

Chin, J. M., & Schooler, J. W. (2010) Meta-awareness. In W. P. Banks (Ed.), *Encyclopedia of consciousness*, **volume 2** (pp. 33–41). Oxford: Oxford University Press.

Coe, W. C., St. Jean, R. L., & Burger, J. M. (1980). Hypnosis and the enhancement of visual imagery. *International Journal of Clinical and Experimental Hypnosis*, **28**(3), 225–243.

Connors, M. H., Cox, R. E., Barnier, A. J., Langdon, R., & Coltheart, M. (2012). Mirror agnosia and the mirrored-self misidentification delusion: a hypnotic analogue. *Cognitive Neuropsychiatry*, **17**(3), 197–226.

Corbetta, M., & Shulman, G. L. (2002). Control of goal-directed and stimulus-driven attention in the brain. *Nature Reviews Neuroscience*, **3**(3), 201–215. doi: 10.1038/nrn755

Craig, A. (2009). How do you feel—now? The anterior insula and human awareness. Nature Reviews Neuroscience, **10**(1), 59–70.

Craig, A. (2010). Once an island, now the focus of attention. *Brain Structure and Function*, **214**(5), 395–396.

Crawford, H. (1989). Cognitive and physiological flexibility: multiple pathways to hypnotic responsiveness. In V.A. Gheorghiu, P. Netter, M. Eysenck, & R. Rosenthal (Eds.) *Suggestion and suggestibility: Theory and Research* (pp. 155–167). Berlin: Springer-Verlag.

Crawford, H. J. (1994). Brain dynamics and hypnosis: attentional and disattentional processes. *International Journal of Clinical and Experimental Hypnosis*, **42**(3), 204–232.

Crawford, H. J., Burrows, G., & Stanley, R. (2001). Neuropsychophysiology of hypnosis: towards an understanding of how hypnotic interventions work. In G. D. Burrows, R. O. Stanley, & P. B. Bloom (Eds.), *International handbook of clinical hypnosis* (pp. 61–84). Chichester, UK: John Wiley & Sons.

Crawford, H. J., & Gruzelier, J. H. (1992). A midstream view of the neuropsychophysiology of hypnosis: recent research and future directions. In E. Fromm, M.R. Nash (Eds.), *Contemporary hypnosis research* (pp. 227–266). New York: Guilford Press.

Damasio, A., & Dolan, R. J. (1999). The feeling of what happens. *Nature*, **401**(6756), 847–847.

Damasio, A. R., Everitt, B., & Bishop, D. (1996). The somatic marker hypothesis and the possible functions of the prefrontal cortex [and discussion]. *Philosophical Transactions of the Royal Society of London, Series B: Biological Sciences*, **351**(1346), 1413–1420.

David, D., & Brown, R. J. (2002). Suggestibility and negative priming: two replication studies. *International Journal of Clinical and Experimental Hypnosis*, **50**(3), 215–228.

Davidson, R. J., Goleman, D. J., & Schwartz, G. E. (1976). Attentional and affective concomitants of meditation: a cross-sectional study. *Journal of Abnormal Psychology*, **85**(2), 235.

De Pascalis, V., & Perrone, M. (1996). EEG asymmetry and heart rate during experience of hypnotic analgesia in high and low hypnotizables. *International Journal of Psychophysiology*, **21**(2), 163–175.

Deeley, Q., Oakley, D. A., Toone, B., Giampietro, V., Brammer, M. J., Williams, S. C., & Halligan, P. W. (2012). Modulating the default mode network using hypnosis. *International Journal of Clinical and Experimental Hypnosis*, **60**(2), 206–228.

Del Percio, C., Triggiani, A. I., Marzano, N., De Rosas, M., Valenzano, A., Petito, A., . . . Babiloni, C. (2013). Subjects' hypnotizability level affects somatosensory evoked potentials to non-painful and painful stimuli. *Clinical Neurophysiology*, **124**(7), 1448–1455.

Derbyshire, S. W., Whalley, M. G., & Oakley, D. A. (2009). Fibromyalgia pain and its modulation by hypnotic and non-hypnotic suggestion: an fMRI analysis. *European Journal of Pain*, **13**(5), 542–550.

Dienes, Z., & Hutton, S. (2013). Understanding hypnosis metacognitively: rTMS applied to left DLPFC increases hypnotic suggestibility. *Cortex*, **49**(2), 386–392.

Dienes, Z., Beran, M., Brandl, J. L., Perner, J., & Proust, J. (2012). Is hypnotic responding the strategic relinquishment of metacognition? In M. J. Beran, J. Brandl, J. Perner, & J. Proust (Eds.), *Foundations of Metacognition* (pp. 267–277). Oxford: Oxford University Press.

Dienes, Z., Perner, J., & Jamieson, G. (2007). Executive control without conscious awareness: the cold control theory. In G. A. Jamieson (Ed.), *Hypnosis and conscious states: the cognitive neuroscience perspective* (pp. 293–314). Oxford: Oxford University Press.

Dietrich, A. (2003). Functional neuroanatomy of altered states of consciousness: the transient hypofrontality hypothesis. *Consciousness and Cognition*, **12**(2), 231–256.

Dixon, M., Brunet, A., & Laurence, J.-R. (1990). Hypnotizability and automaticity: toward a parallel distributed processing model of hypnotic responding. *Journal of Abnormal Psychology*, **99**(4), 336.

Dixon, M., & Laurence, J.-R. (1992). Hypnotic susceptibility and verbal automaticity: automatic and strategic processing differences in the Stroop color-naming task. *Journal of Abnormal Psychology*, **101**(2), 344.

Dunne, J. (2015) Buddhist styles of mindfulness: a heuristic approach. In B. Ostafin, B. Meier, & M. Robinson (Eds.), *Handbook of mindfulness and self-regulation*. New York: Springer-Verlag.

Egner, T., Jamieson, G., & Gruzelier, J. (2005). Hypnosis decouples cognitive control from conflict monitoring processes of the frontal lobe. *Neuroimage*, **27**(4), 969–978.

Egner, T., & Raz, A. (2007). Cognitive control processes and hypnosis. In G. A. Jamieson (Ed.), *Hypnosis and conscious states: the cognitive neuroscience perspective* (pp. 29–50). Oxford: Oxford University Press.

Enea, V., & Dafinoiu, I. (2013). Flexibility in processing visual information: effects of mood and hypnosis. *International Journal of Clinical and Experimental Hypnosis*, **61**(1), 55–70. doi: 10.1080/00207144.2013.729435

Erickson, M. H. (1952). Deep hypnosis and its induction. In L.M. LeCron (Ed.), *Experimental hypnosis* (pp. 70–114). New York: Macmillan.

Erickson, M. H. (1965). A special inquiry with Aldous Huxley into the nature and character of various states of consciousness. *American Journal of Clinical Hypnosis*, **8**(1), 14–33.

Fazelpour, S., & Thompson, E. (2015). The Kantian brain: brain dynamics from a neurophenomenological perspective. *Current Opinion in Neurobiology*, **31**, 223–229.

Fehr, F. S., & Stern, J. A. (1967). The effect of hypnosis on attention to relevant and irrelevant stimuli. *International Journal of Clinical and Experimental Hypnosis*, **15**(3), 134–143. doi: 10.1080/00207146708407519

Frith, C. D., Friston, K., Liddle, P., & Frackowiak, R. (1991). Willed action and the prefrontal cortex in man: a study with PET. *Proceedings of the Royal Society of London. Series B: Biological Sciences*, **244**(1311), 241–246.

Fromm, E., Brown, D. P., Hurt, S. W., Oberlander, J. Z., Boxer, A. M., & Pfeifer, G. (1981). The phenomena and characteristics of self-hypnosis. *International Journal of Clinical and Experimental Hypnosis*, **29**(3), 189–246.

Gandhi, B., & Oakley, D. A. (2005). Does "hypnosis" by any other name smell as sweet? The efficacy of "hypnotic" inductions depends on the label "hypnosis." *Consciousness and Cognition*, **14**(2), 304–315.

Garrison, K. A., Santoyo, J. F., Davis, J. H., Thornhill IV, T. A., Kerr, C. E., & Brewer, J. A. (2013a). Effortless awareness: using real time neurofeedback to investigate correlates of posterior cingulate cortex activity in meditators' self-report. *Frontiers in Human Neuroscience*, 7, 440.

Garrison, K. A., Scheinost, D., Worhunsky, P. D., Elwafi, H. M., Thornhill IV, T. A., Thompson, E., . . . Brewer, J. A. (2013b) Real-time fMRI links subjective experience with brain activity during focused attention. *Neuroimage*, **81**, 110–118.

Gethin, R. (1998). *The foundations of Buddhism*. Oxford University Press.

Gethin, R. (2014). Buddhist conceptualizations of mindfulness. In K. W. Brown, J. D. Creswell, & R. M. Ryan (Eds.), *Handbook of mindfulness* (pp. 9–39). New York: Guilford Press.

Graffin, N. F., Ray, W. J., & Lundy, R. (1995). EEG concomitants of hypnosis and hypnotic susceptibility. *Journal of Abnormal Psychology*, **104**(1), 123.

Grant, J. A., Courtemanche, J., & Rainville, P. (2011). A non-elaborative mental stance and decoupling of executive and pain-related cortices predicts low pain sensitivity in Zen meditators. *Pain*, **152**(1), 150–156.

Gruzelier, J. (1998). A working model of the neurophysiology of hypnosis: a review of evidence. *Contemporary Hypnosis*, **15**(1), 3–21.

Gruzelier, J. H. (2000). Redefining hypnosis: theory, methods and integration. *Contemporary Hypnosis*, **17**(2), 51–70.

Gruzelier, J. H. (2006). Frontal functions, connectivity and neural efficiency underpinning hypnosis and hypnotic susceptibility. *Contemporary Hypnosis*, **23**(1), 15–32.

Hasenkamp, W., Wilson-Mendenhall, C. D., Duncan, E., & Barsalou, L. W. (2012). Mind wandering and attention during focused meditation: a fine-grained temporal analysis of fluctuating cognitive states. *Neuroimage*, **59**(1), 750–760.

Hayes, A. M., & Feldman, G. (2004). Clarifying the construct of mindfulness in the context of emotion regulation and the process of change in therapy. *Clinical Psychology*, **11**(3), 255–262.

Hilgard, E. (1979). Divided consciousness in hypnosis: the implications of the hidden observer. In E. Fromm & R. E. Shor (Eds.), *Hypnosis: developments in research and new perspectives* (pp. 45–79). New York: Aldine.

Hilgard, E. R. (1968). *The experience of hypnosis*. Harvest Books.

Hilgard, E. R. (1977). *Divided consciousness: multiple controls in human thought and action*. New York: Wiley.

Hilgard, E. R., & Hilgard, J. R. (2013). *Hypnosis in the relief of pain*. Routledge.

Hilgard, J. R. (1970). *Personality and hypnosis: a study of imaginative involvement*. Chicago: University of Chicago Press.

Holroyd, J. (2003). The science of meditation and the state of hypnosis. *American Journal of Clinical Hypnosis*, **46**(2), 109–128.

Hölzel, B., & Ott, U. (2006). Relationships between meditation depth, absorption, meditation practice, and mindfulness: a latent variable approach. *Journal of Transpersonal Psychology*, **38**(2), 179–199.

Jamieson, G. (2005). The modified Tellegen absorption scale: a clearer window on the structure and meaning of absorption. *Australian Journal of Clinical and Experimental Hypnosis*, **33**, 119–139.

Jha, A. P., Krompinger, J., & Baime, M. J. (2007). Mindfulness training modifies subsystems of attention. *Cognitive, Affective, & Behavioral Neuroscience*, **7**(2), 109–119.

Kadosh, R. C., Henik, A., Catena, A., Walsh, V., & Fuentes, L. J. (2009). Induced cross-modal synaesthetic experience without abnormal neuronal connections. *Psychological Science*, **20**(2), 258–265.

Kallio, S., Revonsuo, A., Hämäläinen, H., Markela, J., & Gruzelier, J. (2001). Anterior brain functions and hypnosis: a test of the frontal hypothesis. *International Journal of Clinical and Experimental Hypnosis*, **49**(2), 95–108.

Kelley, W. M., Macrae, C. N., Wyland, C. L., Caglar, S., Inati, S., & Heatherton, T. F. (2002). Finding the self? An event-related fMRI study. *Journal of Cognitive Neuroscience*, **14**(5), 785–794.

Kihlstrom, J. F., & Edmonston Jr. W. E. (1971). Alterations in consciousness in neutral hypnosis: distortions in semantic space. *American Journal of Clinical Hypnosis*, **13**(4), 243–248.

Kirsch, I., & Lynn, S. J. (1998). Dissociation theories of hypnosis. *Psychological Bulletin*, **123**(1), 100.

Kosslyn, S. M., Thompson, W. L., Costantini-Ferrando, M. F., Alpert, N. M., & Spiegel, D. (2000). Hypnotic visual illusion alters color processing in the brain. *American Journal of Psychiatry*, **157**(8), 1279–1284.

Kupers, R., Faymonville, M.-E., & Laureys, S. (2005). The cognitive modulation of pain: hypnosis- and placebo-induced analgesia. *Progress in Brain Research*, **150**, 251–600.

Lau, H. C., & Passingham, R. E. (2006). Relative blindsight in normal observers and the neural correlate of visual consciousness. *Proceedings of the National Academy of Sciences*, **103**(49), 18763–18768.

Levy, R., & Goldman-Rakic, P. S. (2000). Segregation of working memory functions within the dorsolateral prefrontal cortex. In W. X. Schneider, A. M. Owen, & J. Duncan (Eds.), *Executive control and the frontal lobe: current issues* (pp. 23–32). Berlin: Springer-Verlag.

Lifshitz, M., Cusumano, E. P., & Raz, A. (2013). Hypnosis as neurophenomenology. *Frontiers in Human Neuroscience*, **7**, 469. doi: 10.3389/fnhum.2013.00469

Lindahl, J. R., Kaplan, C. T., Winget, E. M., & Britton, W. B. (2013). A phenomenology of meditation-induced light experiences: traditional Buddhist and neurobiological perspectives. *Frontiers in Psychology*, **4**, 937.

Lorenz, J., Minoshima, S., & Casey, K. (2003). Keeping pain out of mind: the role of the dorsolateral prefrontal cortex in pain modulation. *Brain*, **126**(5), 1079–1091.

Lutz, A., Jha, A. P., Dunne, J. D., & Saron, C. (in press). Investigating the phenomenological and neuro-cognitive matrix of mindfulness-related practices. *American Psychologist*.

Lutz, A., Lachaux, J.-P., Martinerie, J., & Varela, F. J. (2002). Guiding the study of brain dynamics by using first-person data: synchrony patterns correlate with ongoing conscious states during a simple visual task. *Proceedings of the National Academy of Sciences USA*, **99**(3), 1586–1591. doi: 10.1073/pnas.032658199

Lutz, A., McFarlin, D. R., Perlman, D. M., Salomons, T. V., & Davidson, R. J. (2013). Altered anterior insula activation during anticipation and experience of painful stimuli in expert meditators. *Neuroimage*, **64**, 538–546.

Lutz, A., Slagter, H. A., Dunne, J. D., & Davidson, R. J. (2008). Attention regulation and monitoring in meditation. *Trends in Cognitive Sciences*, **12**, 163–169.

Lutz, A., & Thompson, E. (2003). Neurophenomenology integrating subjective experience and brain dynamics in the neuroscience of consciousness. *Journal of Consciousness Studies*, **10**(9–10), 31–52.

Lynn, S., Malaktaris, A., Maxwell, R., Mellinger, D. I., & van der Kloet, D. (2012). Do hypnosis and mindfulness practices inhabit a common domain? Implications for research, clinical practice, and forensic science. *The Journal of Mind–Body Regulation*, **2**(1), 12–26.

Lynn, S. J., Rhue, J. W., & Weekes, J. R. (1990). Hypnotic involuntariness: a social cognitive analysis. *Psychological Review*, **97**(2), 169.

Mason, M. F., Norton, M. I., Van Horn, J. D., Wegner, D. M., Grafton, S. T., & Macrae, C. N. (2007). Wandering minds: the default network and stimulus-independent thought. *Science*, **315**(5810), 393–395.

McConkey, K., & Barnier, A. (2004). High hypnotisability: unity and diversity in behaviour and experience. In M. Heap, R. J. Brown, & D. A. Oakley (Eds.), *The highly hypnotizable person: theoretical, experimental and clinical issues* (pp. 61–84). London/New York: Routledge.

Miller, E. K., & Cohen, J. D. (2001). An integrative theory of prefrontal cortex function. *Annual Review of Neuroscience*, **24**(1), 167–202.

Naish, P. (2001). Hypnotic time perceptions: Busy beaver or tardy timekeeper?. *Contemporary Hypnosis*, **18**(2), 87–99.

Naish, P. (2003). The production of hypnotic time-distortion: Determining the necessary conditions. *Contemporary Hypnosis*, **20**(1), 3–15.

Navon, D. (1977). Forest before trees: the precedence of global features in visual perception. *Cognitive Psychology*, **9**(3), 353–383.

Noble, J., & McConkey, K. M. (1995). Hypnotic sex change: creating and challenging a delusion in the laboratory. *Journal of Abnormal Psychology*, **104**(1), 69.

Oakley, D. A. (1999). Hypnosis and conversion hysteria: a unifying model. *Cognitive Neuropsychiatry*, **4**(3), 243–265.

Oakley, D. A. (2008). Hypnosis, trance and suggestion: evidence from neuroimaging. In M. R. Nash & A. J. Barnier (Eds.), *The Oxford handbook of hypnosis: theory, research and practice* (pp. 365–392). Oxford: Oxford University Press.

Papies, E. K., Barsalou, L. W., & Custers, R. (2012). Mindful attention prevents mindless impulses. *Social Psychological and Personality Science*, **3**(3), 291–299.

Parris, B., Dienes, Z., & Hodgson, T. L. (2012). Temporal constraints of the post-hypnotic word blindness suggestion on Stroop task performance. *Journal of Experimental Psychology*, **38**(4), 833–837.

Pekala, R. J. (1991). The phenomenology of consciousness inventory. In *Quantifying consciousness: An empirical approach* (pp. 127–143). Springer.

Pekala, R. J., & Forbes, E. J. (1997). Types of hypnotically (un)susceptible individuals as a function of phenomenological experience: towards a typology of hypnotic types. *American Journal of Clinical Hypnosis*, **39**(3), 212–224.

Pekala, R. J., Steinberg, J., & Kumar, V. (1986). Measurement of phenomenological experience: Phenomenology of Consciousness Inventory. *Perceptual and Motor Skills*, **63**(2), 983–989.

Petitmengin, C., & Lachaux, J.-P. (2013). Microcognitive science: bridging experiential and neuronal microdynamics. *Frontiers in Human Neuroscience*, **7**, 617. doi: 10.3389/fnhum.2013.00617

Petitmengin, C., Remillieux, A., Cahour, C., & Carter-Thomas, S. (2013). A gap in Nisbett and Wilson's findings? A first-person access to our cognitive processes. *Consciousness and Cognition*, **22**, 654–669.

Petrides, M. (2000). The role of the mid-dorsolateral prefrontal cortex in working memory. In W. X. Schneider, A. M. Owen, & J. Duncan (Eds.), *Executive control and the frontal lobe: current issues* (pp. 44–54). Berlin: Springer-Verlag.

Price, D., & Barrell, J. (1990). The structure of the hypnotic state: a self-directed experiential study. In J.J. Barrell (Ed.) *The experiential method: exploring the human experience* (pp. 85–97). Acton, MA: Copely Publishing.

Priftis, K., Schiff, S., Tikhonoff, V., Giordano, N., Amodio, P., Umiltà, C., & Casiglia, E. (2011). Hypnosis meets neuropsychology: simulating visuospatial neglect in healthy participants. *Neuropsychologia*, **49**(12), 3346–3350.

Qualls, P. J., & Sheehan, P. W. (1979). Capacity for absorption and relaxation during electromyograph biofeedback and no-feedback conditions. *Journal of Abnormal Psychology*, **88**(6), 652.

Rainville, P., Duncan, G. H., Price, D. D., Carrier, B., & Bushnell, M. C. (1997). Pain affect encoded in human anterior cingulate but not somatosensory cortex. *Science*, **277**(5328), 968–971.

Rainville, P., & Price, D. D. (2003). Hypnosis phenomenology and the neurobiology of consciousness. *International Journal of Clinical and Experimental Hypnosis*, **51**(2), 105–129.

Raz, A. (2005). Attention and hypnosis: neural substrates and genetic associations of two converging processes. *International Journal of Clinical and Experimental Hypnosis*, **53**(3), 237–258. doi: 10.1080/00207140590961295

Raz, A., & Campbell, N. K. (2011). Can suggestion obviate reading? Supplementing primary Stroop evidence with exploratory negative priming analyses. *Consciousness and Cognition*, **20**(2), 312–320. doi: 10.1016/j.concog.2009.09.013

Raz, A., Fan, J., & Posner, M. I. (2006). Neuroimaging and genetic associations of attentional and hypnotic processes. *Journal of Physiology (Paris)*, **99**(4–6), 483–491. doi: 10.1016/j.jphysparis.2006.03.003

Raz, A., Landzberg, K. S., Schweizer, H. R., Zephrani, Z. R., Shapiro, T., Fan, J., & Posner, M. I. (2003). Posthypnotic suggestion and the modulation of Stroop interference under cycloplegia. *Consciousness and Cognition*, **12**(3), 332–346.

Raz, A., Moreno-Íniguez, M., Martin, L., & Zhu, H. (2007). Suggestion overrides the Stroop effect in highly hypnotizable individuals. *Consciousness and Cognition*, **16**(2), 331–338.

Raz, A., Shapiro, T., Fan, J., & Posner, M. I. (2002). Hypnotic suggestion and the modulation of Stroop interference. *Archives of General Psychiatry*, **59**(12), 1155–1161.

Ridderinkhof, K. R., van den Wildenberg, W. P., Segalowitz, S. J., & Carter, C. S. (2004). Neurocognitive mechanisms of cognitive control: the role of prefrontal cortex in action selection, response inhibition, performance monitoring, and reward-based learning. *Brain and Cognition*, **56**(2), 129–140.

Roche, S. M., & McConkey, K. M. (1990). Absorption: nature, assessment, and correlates. *Journal of Personality and Social Psychology*, **59**(1), 91.

Rounis, E., Maniscalco, B., Rothwell, J. C., Passingham, R. E., & Lau, H. (2010). Theta-burst transcranial magnetic stimulation to the prefrontal cortex impairs metacognitive visual awareness. *Cognitive Neuroscience*, **1**(3), 165–175.

Sadler, P., & Woody, E. Z. (2006). Does the more vivid imagery of high hypnotizables depend on greater cognitive effort? A test of dissociation and social-cognitive theories of hypnosis. *International Journal of Clinical and Experimental Hypnosis*, **54**(4), 372–391.

Schacter, D. L. (1977). EEG theta waves and psychological phenomena: a review and analysis. *Biological Psychology*, **5**(1), 47–82.

Seeley, W. W., Menon, V., Schatzberg, A. F., Keller, J., Glover, G. H., Kenna, H., . . . Greicius, M. D. (2007). Dissociable intrinsic connectivity networks for salience processing and executive control. *The Journal of Neuroscience*, **27**(9), 2349–2356.

Semmens-Wheeler, R., & Dienes, Z. (2012). The contrasting role of higher order awareness in hypnosis and meditation. *The Journal of Mind–Body Regulation*, **2**(1), 43–57.

Sheehan, P. W., Fromm, E., & Shor, R. (1979). Hypnosis and the processes of imagination. In E. Fromm & R. E. Shor (Eds.), *Hypnosis: developments in research and new perspectives* (2nd edn.). New York: Aldine.

Spanos, N. P. (1986). Hypnotic behavior: a social-psychological interpretation of amnesia, analgesia, and "trance logic." *Behavioral and Brain Sciences*, **9**(03), 449–467.

Spiegel, D., & Cardena, E. (1991). Disintegrated experience: the dissociative disorders revisited. *Journal of Abnormal Psychology*, **100**(3), 366.

Spiegel, D., White, M., & Waelde, L. C. (2010). Hypnosis, mindfulness, meditation, and brain imaging. In D. Barrett (Ed.), *Hypnosis and Hypnotherapy*, 37–52. Praeger.

St. Jean, R., & McCutcheon, N. (1989). Does absorption mediate hypnotic time perception? *British Journal of Experimental and Clinical Hypnosis*, **6**, 171–176.

Starker, S. (1974). Effects of hypnotic induction upon visual imagery. *The Journal of Nervous and Mental Disease*, **159**(6), 433–437.

Tang, Y-Y., Hölzel, B. K., and Posner, M. I. (2015). The neuroscience of mindfulness meditation. *Nature Reviews Neuroscience*, **16**, 213–225.

Tart, C. T. (1970). Transpersonal potentialities of deep hypnosis. *Journal of Transpersonal Psychology*, **2**(1), 27–40.

Teasdale, J. D. (1999). Metacognition, mindfulness and the modification of mood disorders. *Clinical Psychology & Psychotherapy*, **6**(2), 146–155.

Tellegen, A., & Atkinson, G. (1974). Openness to absorbing and self-altering experiences ("absorption"), a trait related to hypnotic susceptibility. *Journal of Abnormal Psychology*, **83**(3), 268.

Terhune, D. B., Cardeña, E., & Lindgren, M. (2011). Dissociated control as a signature of typological variability in high hypnotic suggestibility. *Consciousness and Cognition*, **20**(3), 727–736.

Thanissaro, B. (1997). One tool among many: the place of Vipassana in Buddhist practice. *Access to Insight (Legacy Edition)*, 8 March 2011, http://www.accesstoinsight.org/lib/authors/thanissaro/onetool.html.

Thera, N. (1952). *The Buddha's path to deliverance*. Kandy, Sri Lanka: Buddhist Publication Society.

van den Hurk, P. A., Giommi, F., Gielen, S. C., Speckens, A. E., & Barendregt, H. P. (2010). Greater efficiency in attentional processing related to mindfulness meditation. *The Quarterly Journal of Experimental Psychology*, **63**(6), 1168–1180.

Wagstaff, G. F. (1998). The semantics and physiology of hypnosis as an altered state: towards a definition of hypnosis. *Contemporary Hypnosis*, **15**(3), 149–165.

Wagstaff, G. F. (2000). On the physiological redefinition of hypnosis: a reply to Gruzelier. *Contemporary Hypnosis*, **17**(4), 154–162.

Wagstaff, G. F., Heap, M., Oakley, D., & Brown, R. (2004). High hypnotizability in a sociocognitive framework. In M. Heap, R. J. Brown, & D. A. Oakley (Eds.), *The highly hypnotizable person: theoretical, experimental and clinical issues* (pp. 85–114). London/New York: Routledge.

Wallace, B. A. (1999) The Buddhist tradition of Samatha: methods for refining and examining consciousness. *Journal of Consciousness Studies*, **6**(2–3), 175–187.

Weitzenhoffer, A. M., & Hilgard, E. R. (1962). *Stanford Hypnotic Susceptibility Scale, form C (*volume 27*).* Palo Alto, CA: Consulting Psychologists' Press.

Williams, J. M. G. (2010). Mindfulness and psychological process. *Emotion*, **10**(1), 1–7.

Woody, E. Z., & Bowers, K. S. (1994). A frontal assault on dissociated control. In S. J. Lynn & J. W. Rhue (Eds.), *Dissociation: theoretical and research perspectives*. New York: Guilford Press.

Woody, E. Z., & Sadler, P. (2008). Dissociation theories of hypnosis. In M. R. Nash & A. J. Barnier (Eds.), *The Oxford handbook of hypnosis: theory, research and practice* (pp. 81–110). Oxford: Oxford University Press.

Woody, E., & Szechtman, H. (2011). Using hypnosis to develop and test models of psychopathology. *The Journal of Mind–Body Regulation*, **1**(1).

Zeidan, F., & Grant, J. A. Meditative and hypnotic analgesia: different directions, same road? In A. Raz & M. Lifshitz (Eds.), *Hypnosis and meditation: towards an integrative science of conscious plane*. New York: Oxford University Press.

Chapter 7

Hypnosis as self-deception; meditation as self-insight

Zoltan Dienes, Peter Lush, Rebecca Semmens-Wheeler, Jim Parkinson, Ryan Scott, and Peter Naish

Abstract

Although meditation and hypnosis appear to be similar, both in skills demanded (e.g., imaginative involvement) and in their use as therapies, this chapter argues that the two are essentially different. Whereas mindfulness meditation aims to develop accurate meta-awareness, the hypnotic experience results from a lack of awareness of intentions; hypnosis is effectively a form of self-deception. The claim is supported by reviewing evidence that (a) meditators are not very hypnotizable; (b) highly hypnotizable people become aware of their intentions especially late while meditators have awareness especially early; and (c) meditators show particularly strong intentional binding but highly hypnotizable people do not. We suggest that one path to high hypnotizability is hypofrontality.

Introduction

A theme among many theories of hypnosis is that hypnotic response is a form of strategic self-deception about what mental state one is in (e.g., Dienes & Perner, 2007; Hilgard, 1977; Spanos, 1986). By contrast, a theme for many meditation practices, Buddhist as well as some non-Buddhist, is that they involve and cultivate mindfulness; and mindfulness, where it succeeds, involves being aware of the mental states one is in. Thus, by this argument, hypnotic response implies a lack of mindfulness, at least for those particular mental states about which one is strategically deceived. This chapter will consider the argument, its strengths and weaknesses, and present new empirical evidence for a tension between hypnotic response and mindfulness.

The chapter relies on a distinction between first-order and second-order mental states (e.g., Carruthers, 2000; Proust, 2012; Rosenthal, 2005). A mental state is, in part, individuated by its content; thus, the thought that "clouds pass through the sky" is different from the thought that "I will make it to the valley tonight, Zeus be willing" because the contents are different. If the content of a mental state refers only to the world (e.g., "clouds pass through the sky"), the mental state is a first-order state. If the content refers to a first- order mental state that one is in (e.g., the thought that "I *see* that clouds pass through the sky"), it is a second-order state, a type of metacognitive state. We will now apply this distinction first to hypnosis and then to mindfulness in order to relate the two.

The nature of hypnosis

Hypnotic response appears to involve what would normally be clearly intentional motor or cognitive actions in the service of the subject, such as lifting an arm, imagining an elephant, or acting like a child (White, 1941)—but where the experience is that of the action being involuntary, or the imagination being perceptual, or the pretense being belief (see Oakley & Halligan, 2013 for an overview). One theoretical response is to argue that the resemblance of these motor and cognitive actions to intentional actions is illusory; the action is not intentional in the first place. For example, response expectancy theory (Kirsch, 1985) asserts that the expectation that an experience or response will happen is the sufficient psychological cause of the response or experience (cf. also Naish, 1986). Intentions are not needed as causes, only expectations. Similarly, Woody and Sadler (2008) postulate a breakdown in executive functioning during hypnotic response so that actions occur relatively automatically.

The correct theory of hypnotic response is not settled (see Nash & Barnier, 2008 for a theoretical review). Thus, another class of theories has explained the compelling subjective experiences metacognitively. That is, the subject does intend to act, imagine, or pretend, but they are not aware of that intention (e.g., Hilgard, 1977; Kihlstrom, 1997; Kirsch & Lynn, 1998a; Lynn, Rhue, & Weekes, 1990; Spanos, 1986). In other words, the first-order state of intending may be entirely normal; what makes the experience distinctively hypnotic is that the person forms an inaccurate higher-order thought (HOT) to the effect that they are not intending, despite sustained reflection on the volitional nature of the action. Dienes (2012) describes the common component of the latter type of theories as "cold control" in that the theories involve executive control without accurate higher-order thoughts (control without accurate HOTs). Cold control theory is simple in that it asserts that the unique aspect of an action that makes it hypnotic is purely metacognitive, a strategic lack of awareness. While further tests are needed (e.g., Dienes & Semmens-Wheeler, 2012), we take as evidence for cold control, the findings that expectations often fail to fully predict hypnotic response (e.g., Benham, Woody, Wilson, & Nash, 2006; Semmens-Wheeler, Dienes, & Duka, 2013) and that hypnotic response can involve executive tasks, such as overcoming prepotent responses (e.g., Lifshitz, Bonn, Fischer, Kashem, & Raz, 2013; Raz, Kirsch, Pollard, & Nitkin Kaner, 2006; Spanos, Radtke, & Dubreuil, 1982; Wyzenbeek & Bryant, 2012) (see Dienes, 2012, for further evidence for cold control).

Here, we see what predictions follow from cold control theory. That is, we will take a hypnotic response to be a strategic self-deception; specifically, the intentional performing of a motor or cognitive action while actively maintaining the higher-order thought that the action is not intentional. Thus, not all responses in a hypnotic context (clinical or academic) are hypnotic responses; not all hypnotherapy involves hypnotic response; and not all suggestion or influence is hypnotic (Tasso & Perez, 2008). To be hypnotic, the subject must create an altered experience of volition or reality in accord with the requirements of the situation by strategic self-deception (Dienes, 2012). Such an approach defines a psychological mechanism that may operate even when the context is not considered hypnotic (e.g., during spirit possession; Dienes & Perner, 2007), and whether or not any formal induction is used (cf. Kirsch et al., 2011).

The nature of mindfulness

Now, we consider the relevance of the first-order/second-order distinction to mindfulness. Gotama, the historical founder of the Buddhist tradition, developed a means of cultivating mindfulness about 2500 years ago, defining it by painting a picture in metaphors and contexts in the Pali Suttas, not by giving necessary and sufficient conditions. For our purposes, the picture is quite clear enough, and as relevant to the Buddhist tradition as to the secular use of mindfulness (Kabat-Zinn, 2013; Peacock, 2014). In one metaphor, mindfulness was personified by Gotama as a gatekeeper, guarding the sense doors of a house, letting in only wholesome mental reactions (Analayo, 2003, pp. 53–57). That is, in this metaphor, mindfulness considers mental states with respect to their mental state properties (i.e., mindfulness as a second-order mental state). This impression is reinforced by the later Milanda Panha in which mindfulness is likened to the King's advisor reminding the King of what is beneficial—so that the meditator knows what mental qualities to pursue and what can be let go (Gethin, 2013).

Mindfulness is also defined by the practices said to cultivate it and, most specifically, by the four foundations of mindfulness (Analayo, 2003). While the first foundation involves awareness of one's own and others' bodies in, at least part, their physical form (i.e., first- order mindfulness), the remaining foundations concern, exclusively, awareness of mental states (second-order mindfulness). The fourth foundation also includes, specifically, awareness of volitions. In sum, mindfulness involves cultivating accurate awareness of mental states (cf. Hargus, Crane, Barnhofer, & Williams, 2010; Teasdale et al., 2002). Keng, Smoski, and Robins (2011) in effect draw on a first/second order distinction in arguing that

> . . . in early Buddhist teachings, mindfulness refers rather specifically to an introspective awareness with regard to one's physical and psychological processes and experiences. This is in contrast to certain Western conceptualizations of mindfulness, which view mindfulness as a form of awareness that encompasses all forms of objects . . . in Buddhist teachings, mindfulness more fundamentally has to do with observing one's perception of and reactions toward sensory objects than focusing on features of the . . . objects themselves (p. 1042).

Here, we bring up some differences between mindfulness and hypnosis concerning the specific sort of awareness that the second-order state involves. The nature of the awareness involved in mindfulness is also revealed by metaphor: according to the Suttas, being mindful is like a cowherd able to sit under a tree and watch his cows from a distance; another metaphor involves watching from a tower (Analayo, 2003, pp. 53–57). These metaphors indicate how the aim is not to get so close to mental states as to be sucked into the content, while at the same time still remaining aware of them. To do this, mindfulness involves considering mental states as vehicles or carriers of content (e.g., noticing how mental states arise and pass) (Aronson, 2004). Thus, mindfulness requires being neither so distanced from a mental state that it is dissociated (unwatched, unconscious) nor so close that one is engrossed in it without awareness of its vehicle properties (the content automatically taken for real); hypnosis may involve either of these extremes (Kihlstrom, 2007; Wilson & Barber, 1982). Another metaphor for mindfulness describes carrying a bowl brimming with oil, where one drop must not be spilt, despite the commotion of a crowd watching a beautiful girl singing and dancing and a man with a sword ready to cut off one's head if a single drop is spilt (Analayo, 2003, p. 122). That is, mindfulness is performed with steadiness and equanimity (cf. Olendzki, 2013); hence the description sometimes given of "non-judgmental." Other attitudes compatible with mindfulness are joy and compassion (Olendzki, 2013). By contrast, the attitude one takes to any worldly or mental state in hypnosis is whatever is suggested, including anger (Houghton, Calvert, Jackson, Cooper, & Whorwell, 2002), anxiety (France, 2013), and aversion (e.g., Raij, Numminen, Närvänen, Hiltunen, & Hari, 2009; Rainville et al., 1999)[1].

---

[1] Anger, aversion, and anxiety may be the objects of mindfulness; however, these objects would not be regarded with anger, aversion, or anxiety, if they were being regarded mindfully.

In summary, while meditation and hypnosis have invited at least cursory comparison over the decades (e.g., Davidson & Goleman, 1977; Grant & Rainville, 2005), and their similarities and differences in many respects remain intriguing (e.g., Dumont, Martin, Broer, 2012; Liftshitz, Campbell, & Raz, 2012; Lynn, Malaktaris, Maxwell, Mellinger, & van der Kloet, 2012), here we focus on what we conjecture to be key to each: hypnotic response is centrally a (strategic) failure of metacognition while meditation, as a practice of mindfulness, is centrally an enhancement of metacognition (see Semmens-Wheeler & Dienes, 2012). We will discuss implications of this position that we have begun to explore: a tension between mindfulness and hypnotic response; relations between the time when one becomes aware of intentions, on the one hand, and both hypnotizability and experience with meditation, on the other; and the effect of manipulations (such as alcohol) that make a person more mindless on hypnotic response.

Mindfulness and hypnotic response in tension: correlational studies

We will first describe studies looking at correlations between mindfulness and hypnotic response to argue for a tension between the two; then at how responses that look hypnotic do occur in the Buddhist literature, to raise doubts about that tension; then a new study phrasing hypnotic suggestions in a Buddhist way to more severely test the claimed low hypnotisability of meditators. Finally, we comment on how we could establish a causal relation between mindfulness and hypnotic response by going beyond correlational studies.

Hypnotic response in mindful people

Semmens-Wheeler (2013) looked at two methods of assessing a negative relation between mindfulness and hypnotic response. The first method was with established questionnaires assessing the degree of mindfulness in everyday life (see Baer, 2013, for a review of measuring mindfulness by questionnaires; and Grossman & Van Dam, 2013, for criticisms). The second method used experienced meditators who had cultivated mindfulness. Semmens-Wheeler found that people high on a standard measure of hypnotizability (as assessed by Waterloo Stanford Group Scale of Hypnotic Susceptibility (WSGS:C), Bowers, 1993) differed on questionnaire measures of mindfulness (Brown & Ryan's Mindful Attention Awareness Scale (MAAS), 2003, and Baer, Smith, & Allen's Kentucky Inventory of Mindfulness Skills (KIMS), 2004)[2]. That is, on average, the more hypnotizable a person, the less self-ratedly mindful they were in everyday life.

Semmens-Wheeler (2013) compared scores of 12 expert meditators on the WSGS:C with scores of over 500 screened participants in the University of Sussex database; the meditators passed on average 3 out of 12 suggestions, and were less susceptible than the average of all subjects in the database combined (5.5 suggestions). On average, the meditators would be classified as "lows."

----

[2] Lows had a mean score of 1.9 and highs of 9.8 on the WSGS:C. Lows scored 3.52 and highs 3.28 on the MAAS $t(47) = 2.22$, $p = 0.031$; and lows scored 3.13 and highs 2.97 on the KIMS, $t(50) = 1.84$, $p = 0.07$. The means for the mindfulness scales are expressed in terms of the average rating per item. The MAAS is on a 1–6 scale and the KIMS on a 1–5 scale with end points in both cases being "always" and "never." Consistent with our results, Black and Green (2014) recently found a negative correlation between Frewen et al.'s (2008, 2011) Meditation Breath Attention Scores (MBAS) and the Harvard Group Scale of Hypnotic Susceptibility (HGSHS:A), $r = -0.29$, p < 0.05. On the other hand, Black and Green did not find any significant correlations between HGSHS:A and the Five Factor Mindfulness Questionnaire (FFMQ, overall or with any of the five factor scores), overall $r = 0.03$ (N = 77).

(See Semmens-Wheeler & Dienes, 2012, for a review of previous work on meditation and hypnosis.) However, the tendency for meditators to be less hypnotizable than non-meditators may simply result from poor attitudes or low expectations on the part of meditators about hypnosis, perhaps reflecting attitudes derived from their religious traditions. On the other hand, attitudes towards hypnosis, as measured by the Attitudes Toward Hypnosis Scale (Spanos, Brett, Menary, & Cross, 1987), were similar between meditators and non-meditators, and the difference between meditators and non-meditators in hypnotic response remained as large after controlling for this measure of attitudes. Moreover, meditators and non-meditators were similar in their expectancy to respond hypnotically, and the differences in hypnotic response between meditators and non-meditators remained after controlling for expectancy. We wished to test these alternative explanations of the low hypnotizability of meditators more thoroughly. In particular, does indicating degree of agreement to the 14 questions of the Spanos et al. (1987) questionnaire sensitively measure all relevant attitudes to hypnosis by which meditators may differ from non-meditators? We tried another approach.

Hypnotic response in Buddhist literature

The context defined explicitly as hypnosis in our culture is just one context in which the same psychological mechanisms underlying hypnotic response operate (cf. Cardeña, van Duijl, Weiner, & Terhune, 2009). Hypnotic response occurs when a person strategically alters their sense of volition or reality; for example, by having intentional actions experienced as involuntary or imagination experienced as perception (Dienes & Perner, 2007). While Buddhism requires mindfulness in all meditation, some practices in Buddhist traditions seem hypnotic. For example, many of the Mahayana scriptures appear to have been derived from visions taken as actual communications from Buddha (Williams, 2009). Further, selected Tibetan monks may at times be taken over by spirits (e.g., Pehar Gyalpo), where the monk acts as an oracle, speaking not by his own volition, according to his own phenomenology (Ellingson, 1998)[3].

Consider also the visualizations practiced in tantric Buddhism (e.g., Chapter 3; Williams & Tribe, 2000; Yeshe, 1998). In one set of exercises, an inner body is imagined with energy channels, having prescribed colors, channels, Sanskrit markings, and energy flows. The language used in formulating instructions in these exercises often presents these processes and structures as objective, as something perceived rather than imagined, especially as the exercises progress. For example, ". . . see the navel and secret chakras. Then look up and see the throat, crown, and brow chakras" (Yeshe, 1998, p. 109); "meditate in this way until you are completely familiar with your channels and chakras. Eventually you will know exactly where everything is, just as you know where everything is in your purse" (Yeshe, 1998, p. 110). The Dalai Lama, referring to the channels, commented "And if you actually direct your mind, your awareness to these points, you find there really is a special kind of response, suggesting that there is something there, that this is not simply fiction" (Hayward & Varela, 1992, p. 79). Similar comments can be made about deity tantra, where one imagines one is a deity, and the process of imagination becomes more convincing with time: "when visualizing him or herself as the deity . . . the practitioner, when seen through the eyes of awakened perception, *is* the deity" (Williams & Tribe, 2000, p. 225); "Do not merely pretend to be the deity. Have the inner conviction that you are the deity" (Yeshe, 1998, p. 79).

---

[3] Not all monks are accomplished meditators (Dreyfus, 2003; Gombrich, 2006) and we are not clear if the State Oracle of Tibet who channels Pehar is an experienced meditator or not. Nonetheless, the succeeding examples are of apparent hypnotic responses combined with meditation.

Being convinced one is a deity resembles, for example, the hypnotic suggestion to be another person (e.g., of a different gender; Burn, Barnier, & McConkey, 2001). Of course, the interpretation of these practices depends on whether or not the energy channels are imagination, and whether or not people really become deities.

Tantra is not alone in presenting experiences that appear hypnotic, even if tantra especially emphasizes exercises rich in imaginative involvement (Kozhevnikov, Louchakova, Josipovic, & Motes, 2009). A rather different Buddhist tradition from tantra is the Theravada one (Gombrich, 2006; for a discussion of the contrast with tantra, see e.g., Gombrich, 1996, Chapter V). In describing the experiences of concentration meditation in a Theravada tradition, Snyder and Rasmussen (2009) say "Next, direct the wisdom eye to the bones of your own skeleton . . . look for colour variation, breaks, and cracks in the bones" (p. 86) which resembles, for example, a hypnotic suggestion to see through X-ray spectacles. Snyder and Rasmussen refer to perceiving one as having a crystal body that glows with a brilliant light, just as with a hypnotic hallucination. It is not just modern-day practitioners, but also the canonical literature of Theravada that provides examples of apparently hypnotic responses. In the Pali suttas, the powers that may be experienced include making multiple copies of oneself, recollecting past lives, flying through the air (even to the sun), and perceiving things far away (e.g., Bodhi, 2005, p. 274; see also Nanamoli, 1999, Chapter XII)[4].

If at least some of these examples are taken as hypnotic (i.e., strategic self-deception about intentions in order to further one's goals), then they indicate that extensive training in mindfulness is consistent with a degree of hypnotic response (and in Semmens-Wheeler, 2013, meditators showed some responsiveness, on average). In addition, some hypnotic-like suggestions exist in certain modern mindfulness exercises (Chapter 19; Lynn et al., 2012; Yapko, 2011), also indicating some mutual compatibility. How should cold control theory accommodate these observations? On the one hand, the examples could be seen as demonstrating how different practices in a single tradition can coexist even though they develop opposite tendencies (just as meditations emphasizing mindfulness versus compassion, both key practices within the Buddhist traditions, may have opposite effects on the amygdala response to emotional images; Desbordes et al., 2012). On the other hand, these examples may indicate that there is no tension at all between mindfulness and hypnotic response, contrary to cold control theory. Maybe the poor hypnotizability of long-term meditators reflects merely that the traditional hypnotic context is not one where it is clear to practitioners that their hypnotic skills are relevant. What may be needed is to place hypnotic response into a Buddhist context so that an understanding of the relevance of their hypnotic capacities to the task is made clear. Then, on this account, long-term meditators may respond no worse than average to imaginative tasks presented not as hypnotic but as Buddhist exercises[5].

---

[4] It is not clear how many meditators have these canonical supernatural experiences, or indeed if, historically, the description of such experiences entered into the canon purely for propaganda reasons, when competing with other Indian religions.

[5] A further response is to argue that the examples listed are not cases of hypnosis or cold control at all. Perhaps one might accept that, for example, the energy channels are no more the product of the imagination than is the outside world itself—and on the idealism and "non-duality" that often goes with tantric traditions, though not typically Theravadan ones, the distinction between imagination and perception takes on a certain subtlety; contrast Hamilton (2000), Gombrich (2009), and Siderits (2007). Nonetheless, whatever the personal metaphysics of the practitioner, if the experience of the energy channels is phenomenologically one of being aware of what is there, a good case for the use of cold control can be made.

Hypnotic suggestions phrased in a Buddhist way

We formulated a task context that aimed to present standard hypnotic suggestions as Buddhist exercises, or at least as exercises relatively consistent with Buddhist beliefs (the preamble was about the same length as a standard hypnotic induction; see Appendix 1 for the "Buddhist-friendly" and standard hypnotic preamble/induction). For example, the Buddhist preamble emphasized how the skillful use of attention can make the mind pliable, how thoughts automatically condition further mental states and actions, how imagination can act as a seed for bringing about experiences, how advanced practitioners can create dreams at any time, and how there is a not a self to author actions. Through statements such as these, it was hoped to motivate the experience of actions as involuntary and imagination as perception.

Andreea Avram, for her Honors final-year project at the University of Sussex, recruited 14 mindfulness meditators from Buddhist centers around Brighton, who had been practicing regular mindfulness meditation for at least 5 years; 14 non-meditators were recruited matched for age and gender. Half of each group was randomly assigned either to a normal hypnosis session or to a "Buddhist-friendly" version with the same suggestions (rephrased to remove reference to hypnosis). Each session started with the preamble; then expectation ratings were taken for each upcoming suggestion; then an induction and the suggestions were delivered[6]. Ten suggestions were used from the WSGS:C (Bowers, 1993), excluding the age regression and post-hypnotic suggestions. Suggestions were scored according to both the scoring criteria of the WSGS:C and to a subjective rating taken immediately after each suggestion[7].

Now, to summarize predictions. If we have succeeded in motivating the tasks as Buddhist friendly, the meditators' expectations should improve for the Buddhist-friendly rather than the traditional suggestions. Ideally, the expectations should become at least as great as those for non-meditators. If there is a genuine contradiction between a tendency to mindfulness and hypnotic response, then meditators should nonetheless remain less responsive than non-meditators, even though we have strived to make the suggestions Buddhist friendly.

The expectations for meditators were low, though somewhat higher for the Buddhist- friendly version (mean = 0.9 out of a maximum of 5, SE = 0.19) compared to the standard hypnosis version (mean = 0.4, SE = 0.09), $t(12) = 2.52$, $p = 0.027$. The preamble increased the motivations of meditators somewhat. For non-meditators, the mean expectation for the Buddhist-friendly version was 1.5 (SE = 0.13) and for the standard hypnosis version was 1.8 (SE = 0.36). The interaction of script type with group was significant, $F(1, 24) = 4.37$, $p = 0.047$. Thus, the Buddhist-friendly script differentially impacted the expectations of meditators and non-meditators. Nonetheless, we were not entirely successful: non-meditators still had higher expectations for an imaginative response than meditators, even for just the Buddhist-friendly script, and by a large margin, $t(12) = 2.77$, $p = 0.017$.

We now turn from expectations to the actual effects. For meditators, changing the context from standard to Buddhist-friendly increased the subjective experience of hypnotic response, from 0.1

---

[6] An example expectation rating is: "If you were to imagine that you hear and feel a mosquito, and you attended clearly to this idea, how strongly do you expect that you would have some sensation of hearing or feeling a mosquito on you? On a scale from 0 to 5, say 0 if you know you will not feel any such sensation, 5 if you are completely certain you will feel some sensation of a mosquito being there, and any number in between depending on how strongly you expect you would feel some sensation."

[7] An example subjective rating was: "On a scale from 0 to 5, how strongly you felt the sensation of a mosquito being there, in either sound or touch, where 0 means you felt no sensation and 5 means you felt by any means as if there actually was a mosquito there."

(SE = 0.6) (out of 5) to 0.5 (SE = 0.11), t(12) = 2.89, p = 0.014. The corresponding scores for non-meditators were both considerably greater, 1.9 (SE = 0.42) and 2.0 (SE = 0.47) respectively. Thus, despite the mild modulation of meditators' responses, meditators remained substantially less responsive than non-meditators, no matter what the script, F(1, 24) = 26.09, p < 0.001.

In summary, we at least replicated the low hypnotic response of meditators versus non-meditators (cf. Semmens-Wheeler, 2013), despite trying to make the suggestions more Buddhist-friendly. However, we did not succeed in making the suggestions highly plausible as Buddhist exercises. Future research could depart from the content of standard hypnotic suggestions to make the suggestions more distinctively Buddhist and, thus, more severely test our conjecture. We hope others may be tempted to take up this task. Perhaps using meditators with extensive experience in both tantra and mindfulness would prove revealing about the value of extensive experience in finessing the combination of mindfulness and cold control in precise ways. However, for the time being, the conjecture that meditators who cultivate mindfulness do not respond very well hypnotically survives.

A key problem with the preceding studies is that they are correlational. The acid test is what happens to hypnotic response after a mindfulness intervention to which participants are randomly assigned. Working with Clara Strauss and Kate Cavanagh, who have developed online mindfulness interventions (e.g., Cavanagh et al., 2013), we have established two types of online mindfulness interventions, based on the distinction between first-order and second-order mental states. Thus, if a key aspect of mindfulness is accurately and non-reactively being aware, then one could be mindful of the world (first order) or else mindful of one's mental states (second order). In one intervention we have developed, *mindfulness of the world*, meditations, and exercises concern exclusively present-centered awareness of the physical world[8]. In another matched intervention, *mindfulness of mental states*, meditations, and exercises concern exclusively awareness of one's mental states (including sensations, thoughts, and intentions). If one can, in a couple of weeks, cultivate mindfulness of the world without developing much mindfulness of mental states, and vice versa, then the mindfulness of mental states intervention should, according to cold control, reduce hypnotic response more than the mindfulness of the world intervention, which may have an effect little different from a waiting-list control. So far, this remains a prediction we make in advance of data collection[9,10].

---

[8] Dunne (2013, p. 77) traces a focus on present-centered awareness in Buddhism to the seventh-century scholar Dharmakirti.

[9] Interestingly, the Stoics developed mindfulness practices where the first order and second order are conceptually separated as different endeavors. A defining part of Stoicism, from the beginning with Zeno of Citium (fl. 300BC), was the tranquil, detached assessment of mental impressions so as not to accept their content automatically (e.g., Graver, 2007) (i.e., second-order mindfulness). Acceptance of fate, including the world as it is, was always part of Stoic (though not Buddhist) principles (Bobzien, 2001), and at least by the time of Seneca (fl. AD50), we have the beautiful articulation of the value of present-moment awareness of the world (e.g., Davie, 2007) (i.e., first-order mindfulness). Thus, in traditional terms, first-order mindfulness was part of Stoic physics and second-order mindfulness was part of Stoic ethics (cf. Sellars, 2013). Or, in Hadot's (2001) turn of phrase (in analyzing the work of the Stoic emperor Marcus Aurelius, fl. AD150), the *discipline of assent* concerns accurately and non-reactively assessing mental states (second-order mindfulness) while the *discipline of desire* concerns tranquil and joyous acceptance of the present worldly state of affairs (first- order mindfulness). Mindfulness practices in Stoicism and Buddhism may have developed independently, as they are presented in distinctive ways, but see McEvilley (2006).

[10] The distinction between these two types of mindfulness practice may prove useful for other research as well (e.g., into impulsivity).

Mindfulness meditation promotes awareness of intentions

Dreyfus (2013) laments that the absence of mindfulness

> ... is glaring in the considerable literature concerning the awareness of intentions, their role in action and the degree to which they play causal roles. I am deeply struck by the fact that I have never seen the idea of mindfulness mentioned in this context or heard about its use in relevant experiments. And yet, I would think that mindfulness practitioners would be ideal subjects for such experiments and discussions, since they are supposed to have the ability to pay close attention to their bodily and mental states. Hence, they should be able to distinguish more carefully their own intentions and the degree to which those precede their actions or fail to do so. (p. 53)

Indeed, if mindfulness makes one more readily aware of intentions, it should impair cold control, which is the argument of this chapter. We attempted to directly test this conjecture by use of the Libet task (Libet, Gleason, Wright, & Pearl, 1983), in which people make a spontaneous movement and then indicate when they were aware of either the movement itself or else the intention or urge to make the movement.

Haggard, Cartledge, Dafydd, and Oakley (2004) were the first to apply the Libet paradigm to a hypnotic context. They were interested in awareness of the timing of the movement of the finger itself. They showed that the subjective timing for an ideomotor action (i.e., an action suggested to feel involuntary) was more similar to a passive movement than a fully voluntary one. Semmens-Wheeler (2013) followed up the research, comparing highly hypnotizable subjects with low hypnotizable simulators, as well as with experienced meditators, in terms of their awareness of when they voluntarily moved their finger. Overall, the mean timings did not differ significantly across groups[11]. What is crucial for current concerns, though, is not awareness of when the finger moved but awareness of the timing of intentions.

Lush, Dienes, and Naish (submitted) focused on this crucial aspect of cold control theory: awareness of the timing of intentions. Participants rested their hand in an apparatus that enabled the pressure of one finger to complete a circuit. They were asked to lift their finger (so breaking the circuit) at any time of their choosing. The apparatus included a clock with a hand that completed a single revolution every 2400 ms. Participants used the clock position to indicate the time that they had first experienced their immediate intention to move, while the apparatus itself logged the time when the finger actually moved. There were four groups of participants. Three groups were selected from the University of Sussex hypnosis screening database. Specifically, there were 7 high, 19 low, and 20 medium hypnotizable subjects (as determined by the WSGS:C). For the fourth group, 11 meditators were recruited from Buddhist centers in Brighton; they had a mean of 13 years of meditation experience and 15 hours per month of meditation.

Comparing the declared "intention time" with the actual moment of lifting, Lush et al. found highly hypnotizable people gave significantly later timings (+119 ms, SE = 22 ms) than either mediums (+5 ms, SE = 23 ms) or lows (–25 ms, SE = 25 ms). Meditators (–66 ms, SE = 12 ms) responded even earlier than mediums (or highs). While meditators and lows did not differ significantly in mean timings, the meditators were highly consistent: their variance in timings

---

[11] Though Bayesian analyses indicated that the null findings were not sensitive. Subjective timings for simulators, meditators, and reals were –29 (SE = 25 ms), 5 (SE = 36 ms), and +56 (SE = 43 ms) for voluntary movements, where a negative number indicates the estimated time of the movement occurred prior to the movement. Semmens-Wheeler (2013) found that reals had significantly greater (later) timing errors for ideomotor actions than simulators, suggesting that the findings of Haggard, Cartledge, Dafydd, and Oakley (2004) were not due to demand characteristics.

(SD = 46 ms) was significantly lower than that of lows (SD = 113 ms). Interestingly, if, post hoc, the meditators were split according to meditation experience (more than 9 years), the 7 meditators in the more experienced group had a standard deviation of only 10 ms in the stated timing of their intention—a remarkably consistent estimate.

In summary, we confirmed predictions. Hypnotizability is associated with a delayed awareness of intending to make a voluntary movement; conversely, mindfulness meditation experience is associated with an early awareness. Explaining the results requires making a first order/second order distinction. The first-order intention will be a continuously evolving neural event which may (Libet et al., 1983) or may not (Schurger, Sitta, & Dehaene, 2012) be related to the readiness potential that precedes the movement by some hundreds of milliseconds. Our second-order concepts are unlikely, in general, to be as fine-grained as the first-order states themselves (contrast Miller & Schwarz, 2014), if only because we evolve or learn for any capacity to be just good enough. For example, for visual perception, Overgaard and Sørensen (2004) found that just four categories of clarity were sufficient and natural for participants to introspect the clarity of first-order states.

Our awareness of the formation of an intention will depend on how fine-grained our relevant mental state concepts are. At least some highs may have coarse categories of the nature of first-order intentions—and intentions thus remain unconscious for longer compared to mediums (because the intentional state has to continuously develop for longer until it can be detected by the application of a relatively coarse concept). Indeed, for these highs, it may be just the natural propensity of intentions to remain unconscious a bit longer that enables them to strategically render the intentions unconscious altogether, thus creating illusions of involuntariness. Conversely, meditators, through training, may have fine-grained mental state concepts, enabling them to catch intentions sooner. Indeed, watching mental states arise and pass is crucial to Buddhist meditation. It would be surprising if such extensive experience did not fine-tune the metacognitive processes engaged. (There is also another possibility that we could not fully evaluate from debriefing participants: the meditators may have learned a theory about the timing of intentions through their tradition, and this theory influenced awareness of intentions in a top–down way.)

We have recently explored another relation between intentions and timing. Haggard, Clark, and Kalogeras (2002) were the first to demonstrate intentional binding, using a procedure that followed an action by a contingent outcome, such as a bell ringing. The task of the subject was to estimate the duration of the time lapse between action and outcome. That estimate was shorter if the action was intentional rather than externally caused (e.g., by transcranial magnetic stimulation). The degree of intentional binding, as measured by the change in time estimation, seems related, in part, to the subjective sense of agency in causing the external event (Ebert & Wegner, 2010). Thus, intentional binding seems linked to metacognition, and not just the presence of an intention. However, intentional binding is not a measure of the timing of awareness of intentions, but an implicit measure sensitive to cues for whether intentions are causally relevant to an external outcome (Moore & Haggard, 2008). It is thus hard to make clear predictions for what differences our varying groups of participants may show in intentional binding.

Lush, Parkinson, & Dienes (submitted) tested high, medium, and low hypnotizable groups and experienced meditators on intentional binding with a voluntary movement[12]. They did

---

[12] The study is a prelude to investigating ideomotor action and intentional binding, and displaced robotic agency, with meditators and groups of different hypnotizability, together with Pedro Da Gama, Axel Cleeremans, and Patrick Haggard.

not find an effect of hypnotizability, but meditators had stronger intentional binding than the other groups. One explanation may be that meditators were able to attend to the task more consistently than non-meditators (cf. e.g., Lutz et al., 2009; Tan, Dienes, Jansari, & Goh, 2014, for positive effects of meditation on attention tasks; cf. e.g., Dienes et al., 2009; Kallio, Revonsuo, Hämäläinen, Markela, & Gruzelier, 2001, for the weak relation of hypnotizability, overall, to performance on various attention tasks). However, there was no difference between meditators and non-meditators in within-participant variability in RTs, implying the same consistency of paying attention between groups.

Intentional binding is comprised of two components, and meditators showed a stronger effect with one of those components. Specifically, intentional binding consists of (i) the estimate of the time of the action moving toward the outcome, and (ii) the estimate of the time of the outcome moving toward the action. For meditators, the timing of the outcome was shifted strongly toward the action; the evidence for a difference in the converse shift of the action toward the tone was insensitive. According to one model of intentional binding (Waszak, Cardoso-Leite, & Hughes, 2012), the outcome component of intentional binding is due to more quickly perceiving an outcome that is highly predicted from the action. It may be that constant practice in being mindful of intentions and their consequences led to stronger predictive models for meditators than non-meditators (compare the fourth foundation of mindfulness, which explicitly includes practice in being mindful of intentions, and also the first foundation of being mindful of bodily actions; Gunaratana, 2012, Chapter 2). Interestingly, the stronger intentional binding of meditators compared to non-meditators is a case where mindfulness training is associated with less accurate judgments (of the tone as being sooner than it actually was). In any case, whatever the explanation, even if highs did not behave in the opposite way to meditators, they also did not behave like them on this task.

Mindless hypnotic response

The final type of evidence concerning the relation between mindfulness and hypnotic response considers what happens to hypnotic response if metacognition is experimentally impaired. Rounis, Maniscalco, Rothwell, Passingham, and Lau (2010) found that rTMS (repetitive transcranial magnetic stimulation) to the left dorsolateral prefrontal cortex (DLPFC) reduced awareness of seeing shapes when overall first-order awareness was controlled. That is, the DLPFC may be involved in maintaining accurate higher-order thoughts, so disrupting it reduces the accuracy of awareness of mental states. Dienes and Hutton (2013) reasoned that if it were harder to have accurate higher-order thoughts, it would be easier to respond hypnotically, according to cold control theory. Dienes and Hutton applied rTMS to the left DLPFC or to a control site, the vertex, in counterbalanced order. Subjects were given four hypnotic suggestions by a hypnotist blind to the site stimulated. Subjects rated their subjective response on a 0–5 scale. Stimulation of the DLPFC increased hypnotic response overall (by about a third of a rating point), as predicted[13].

Sayette, Reichle, and Schooler (2009) showed that alcohol also reduces metacognition (specifically, the awareness that one's mind has wandered). Thus, with a similar logic to Dienes and Hutton (2013), Semmens-Wheeler et al. (2013) administered real or placebo alcohol to participants who were given nine hypnotic suggestions, which were also rated on a 0–5 subjective response scale. As predicted, the participants who had alcohol rather than placebo were more responsive to hypnotic suggestion (by 0.8 of a rating point).

---

[13] A direct replication of this study is in progress by Max Coltheart, Amanda Barnier, and Rochelle Cox at Macquarie University.

In both these studies, an insult was delivered to the prefrontal cortex, an insult calculated to reduce metacognition, but one that would have had other effects as well. Other evidence useful for putting the results in context is that there is little consistent relation between frontal task performance generally, such as attentional or inhibitory tasks, and hypnotic response (e.g., Dienes et al., 2009). Further, there is evidence that hypnotic response actively involves executive processes (Crawford, Knebel, & Vendemia, 1998; see Kirsch & Lynn, 1998b, for a review of conflicting behavioral studies up to that time; for more recent work, see Naish, 2014; Tobis & Kihlstrom, 2010; Wyzenbeek & Bryant, 2012). Thus, the conjecture that it is specifically the disruption of metacognition that made the insult effective remains viable.

While the effect of rTMS to the left DLPFC on meditation has not been tested, meditation has been associated with increased activity in the left DLPFC (e.g., Brefczynski-Lewis, Lutz, Schaefer, Levinson, & Davidson, 2007; Newberg et al., 2001). Sayette et al.'s (2009) finding that alcohol increases mind wandering while reducing one's awareness that one's mind has wandered clearly shows alcohol reduces mindfulness.

One further recent study is relevant. "Ego depletion" is a manipulation that briefly disrupts later executive functioning by performing an initial difficult, rather than easy, inhibitory task. For a while after the "depletion," self-control is impaired (cf. Baumeister, Bratslavsky, Muraven, & Tice, 1998, and Kurzban, Duckworth, Kable, & Myers, 2013, for different theoretical accounts). In unpublished studies, Ryan Scott has not yet found an effect of ego depletion on metacognition in a learning or a perception context. What would the effect of ego depletion be on hypnotic response? Scott, Williamson, and Dienes (in preparation) gave participants either a difficult or easy Stroop task (the ego depletion manipulation) and then four hypnotic suggestions. Depletion *reduced* hypnotic response (by about half a point on the equivalent of a 0–5 scale). The reduction in hypnotic response is consistent with evidence that hypnotic responding uses executive resources (e.g., Wyzenbeek & Bryant, 2012). In summary, hypnotic response is not about having impaired executive function in general. We speculate that hypnotic response is specifically related to metacognition.

Conclusion

In this chapter, first we have argued that according to cold control theory, mindfulness and hypnotic response involve a tension, and then, we have reviewed new relevant studies conducted since our last opinion piece on this topic (Semmens-Wheeler & Dienes, 2012). Specifically, we replicated the low hypnotizability of experienced meditators; found that highs had an especially late awareness of intentions and meditators, an especially early awareness; and found that whereas disruptions of frontal function (with alcohol, TMS to the DLPFC) known to impair metacognition enhanced hypnotic response, disruptions that are not shown to impair metacognition (ego depletion) impaired hypnotic response. We conclude that it may be hard to be mindless about an intention if one's general tendency is to be mindful. One route to high hypnotizability may be to avoid chronic mindfulness.

Researchers have previously postulated that there are multiple pathways to high hypnotizability or multiple ways of being highly hypnotizable (Barber, 1999; Hilgard, 1979; Sheehan & McConkey, 1982; Terhune & Brugger, 2011). Sometimes, a distinction is made that is relevant to this chapter. Barber's three-dimensional theory of high hypnotizability distinguished amnesic subjects, who spontaneously tend to forget life events, from subjects who are extremely motivated and have strong expectations about their ability to respond hypnotically. (The remaining category of high hypnotic responder was fantasy-prone.) The Pali word for mindfulness is *sati*, which means literally "to remember" (Gethin, 2013); amnesic subjects are not mindful. Yet there is no reason to think highly motivated subjects are, in themselves, mindless. Crucially, Terhune, Cardeña, & Lindgren (2011)) showed that high hypnotizables can be separated into high and low dissociating groups (as assessed by the Dissociative Experiences Scale, DES) which differ in their performance on executive tasks and the conditions under which they mind wander (see also Marcusson-Clavertz, Terhune, & Cardeña, 2012; Terhune & Brugger, 2011). Note that the DES is negatively correlated with mindfulness ($r = -0.3$, as measured by the FFMQ; de Bruin, Topper, Muskens, Bögel, & Kamphuis, 2012). Thus, one possibility is that there are two ways of implementing cold control—the mindless and the mindful.

Dienes (2012) distinguished HOT coupling from HOT control: HOT coupling is the general tendency to have accurate higher-order thoughts (i.e., for HOTs to be accurately coupled to first-order states); HOT control is the ability to have accurate HOTs or not, according to plan. One way of being highly hypnotizable is by having low HOT coupling in general (mindless). However, maybe highly mindful people can respond hypnotically if they have high HOT control. Note though that our meditators have not been highs. Could they be trained to be highs with, for example, the Carleton Skills Training Package for modifying hypnotic susceptibility (Bertrand, Stam, & Radtke, 1993)? This is a matter for future research.

While we argue that there is a tension between hypnosis and mindfulness, there remains plenty of room for exploring the role of demand characteristics and suggestion in meditation (see Chapters 10 and 19). Our own data show that suggestion can, to some degree, coexist with high levels of mindfulness. For example, according to one tradition (Buddhaghosa, 2003), when a person concentrates on the breath or other object for an extended period, a sign of concentration being established is the arising of a visual image (the "nimitta"), as if by itself, which then becomes the focus of concentration (see e.g., Shankman, 2008). Not everyone comes to see the nimitta. Is there a relation between those that see it and hypnotizability? While cold control theory argues against suggestion playing a key role in meditation, that surely means we should explore just what role suggestion does play.

One way of criticizing the approach in this chapter concerning the relation between hypnosis and meditation is to argue that either or both of hypnosis or meditation have not been properly characterized. For example, it could be argued that the essence of hypnosis is not cold control but the weakening of the conceptual role of a unified enduring self (cf. Hilgard, 1977; Kihlstrom, 1997), and that is also the point of Buddhist meditation (Collins, 1982), so the two are similar (see Chapter 20). Or it could be argued that the essence of hypnosis is executive disruption (Woody & Sadler, 2008) and the essence of meditation is attentional regulation (cf. Lutz, Slagter, Dunne, & Davidson, 2008), so the two are different (but not precisely in the respect that cold control dictates). Or it could be argued that the essence of both hypnosis and meditation is expectation and suggestion; this could make them similar (Chapter 19; Yapko, 2011) or different, because the content of those expectations and suggestions are different in radical ways, resulting in them working differently (Farb, 2012). Or the essence of both hypnosis and meditation may be a reduction in the operation of interoceptive prediction error signals (within a predictive coding framework) (see Chapter 17), so the two are similar.

Both hypnosis and meditation are rich phenomena. We hope we have shown the value of taking cold control and mindfulness as respectively central to each because of the experiments motivated through this approach and, thus, the preliminary evidence we have been able to present in this chapter.

Acknowledgment

This research was supported by Interuniversity Attraction Poles Program of the Belgian Federal Science Policy Office (grant 7/33) and by the Sackler Centre for Consciousness Science.

References

Analayo (2003). *Satipatthana: the direct path to realization*. Cambridge: Windhorse Publications.

Aronson, H. B. (2004). *Buddhist practice on Western ground: reconciling Eastern ideals and Western psychology*. London: Shambala.

Baer, R. A. (2013). Measuring mindfulness. In J. M. G. Williams & J. Kabat-Zinn (Eds.), *Mindfulness: diverse perspectives on its meaning, origins and applications* (pp. 241–261). London: Routledge.

Baer, R. A., Smith, G. T., & Allen, K. B. (2004). Assessment of mindfulness by self-report: The Kentucky Inventory of Mindfulness Skills. *Assessment*, **11**(3), 191–206.

Barber, T. X. (1999). Hypnosis: a mature view. *Contemporary Hypnosis*, **16**, 123–127.

Baumeister, R. F., Bratslavsky, E., Muraven, M., & Tice, D. M. (1998). Ego depletion: is the active self a limited resource? *Journal of Personality and Social Psychology*, **74**, 1252–1265.

Benham, G., Woody, Z., Wilson, K. S., & Nash, M. R. (2006). Expect the unexpected: ability, attitude, and responsiveness to hypnosis. *Journal of Personality and Social Psychology*, **91**, 342–350.

Bertrand, L. D., Stam, H. J., & Radtke, H. L. (1993). The Carleton Skills Training Package for modifying hypnotic susceptibility—a replication and extension: a brief communication. *International Journal of Clinical and Experimental Hypnosis*, **41**, 6–14.

Black, K. N., & Green, J. P. (2014). *Examining hypnotizability, meditation-attentional focus, and performance solving anagrams*. Paper presented at the annual convention of the American Psychological Association, Washington DC, August 2014.

Bobzien, S. (2001). *Determinism and freedom in Stoic philosophy*. Oxford: Oxford University Press.

Bodhi, B. (2005). *In the Buddha's words: an anthology of discourses from the Pali Canon (teachings of the Buddha)*. Massachusetts: Wisdom Publications.

Bowers, K. S. (1993). The Waterloo-Stanford Group C (WSGC) Scale of Hypnotic Suggestibility: normative and comparative data. *International Journal of Clinical and Experimental Hypnosis*, **41**, 35–46.

Brefczynski-Lewis, J. A., Lutz, A., Schaefer, H. S., Levinson, D. B., & Davidson, R. J. (2007). Neural correlates of attentional expertise in long-term meditation practitioners. *Proceedings of the National Academy of Sciences*, **104**, 11483–11488.

Brown, K. W., & Ryan, R. M. (2003). The benefits of being present: mindfulness and its role in psychological well-being. *Journal of Personality and Social Psychology*, **84**(4), 822–848.

Buddhaghosa, B. (translated by B. Nanamoli) (2003). *The path of purification: Visuddhimagga*. Onalaska, USA: Pariyatti Press.

Burn, C., Barnier, A. J., & McConkey, K. M. (2001). Information processing during hypnotically suggested sex change. *International Journal of Clinical and Experimental Hypnosis*, **49**, 231–242.

Cardeña, E., van Duijl, M., Weiner, L., & Terhune, D. (2009). Possession/trance phenomena. In P. Dell & J. O'Neill (Eds.), *Dissociation and the dissociative disorders: DSM-V and beyond* (pp. 171–181). Routledge.

Carruthers, P. (2000). *Phenomenal consciousness: a naturalistic theory*. Cambridge University Press.

Cavanagh, K., Strauss, C., Cicconi, F., Griffiths, N., Wyper, A., & Jones, F. (2013). A randomised controlled trial of a brief online mindfulness-based intervention. *Behaviour Research and Therapy*, **51**, 573–578.

Collins, S. (1982). *Selfless persons*. Cambridge: Cambridge University Press.

Crawford, H. J., Knebel, T., & Vendemia, J. M. C. (1998). The nature of hypnotic analgesia: neurophysiological foundations and evidence. *Contemporary Hypnosis*, **15**, 24–35.

Davidson, R. J., & Goleman, D. J. (1977). The role of attention in meditation and hypnosis: a psychobiological perspective on transformations of consciousness. *International Journal of Clinical and Experimental Hypnosis*, **25**, 291–308.

Davie, J. (2007). *Seneca: dialogues and essays*. Oxford: Oxford University Press.

de Bruin, E. I., Topper, M., Muskens, J. G. A. M., Bögel, S. M., & Kamphuis, J. H. (2012). Psychometric properties of the Five Facets Mindfulness Questionnaire (FFMQ) in a meditating and a non-meditating sample. *Assessment*, **19**, 187–197.

Desbordes, G., Negi, L. T., Pace, T. W. W., Wallace, B. A., Raison, C. L., & Schwartz, E. L. (2012). Effects of mindful-attention and compassion meditation training on amygdala response to emotional stimuli in an ordinary, non-meditative state. *Frontiers in Human Neuroscience*, **6**, 292. doi: 10.3389/fnhum.2012.00292

Dienes, Z. (2012). Is hypnotic responding the strategic relinquishment of metacognition? In M. Beran, J. L. Brandl, J. Perner, & J. Proust (Eds.), *The foundations of metacognition* (pp. 267–278). Oxford: Oxford University Press.

Dienes, Z., Brown, E., Hutton, S., Kirsch, I., Mazzoni, G., & Wright, D. B. (2009). Hypnotic suggestibility, cognitive inhibition, and dissociation. *Consciousness and Cognition*, **18**, 837–847.

Dienes, Z., & Hutton, S. (2013). Understanding hypnosis metacognitively: rTMS applied to left DLPFC increases hypnotic suggestibility. *Cortex*, **49**, 386–392.

Dienes, Z., & Perner, J. (2007). The cold control theory of hypnosis. In G. Jamieson (Ed.), *Hypnosis and conscious states: the cognitive neuroscience perspective* (pp. 293–314). Oxford: Oxford University Press.

Dienes, Z., & Semmens-Wheeler, R. (2012). Response to Terhune: testing cold control theory. *Journal of Mind–Body Regulation*, **2**(1), 169–171.

Dreyfus, G. (2003). *The sounds of two hands clapping: the education of a Tibetan Buddhist monk*. Berkeley: University of California Press.

Dreyfus, G. (2013). Is mindfulness present-centred and non-judgmental? A discussion of the cognitive dimensions of mindfulness. In J. M. G. Williams & J. Kabat-Zinn (Eds.), *Mindfulness: diverse perspectives on its meaning, origins and applications* (pp. 41–54). London: Routledge.

Dumont, L., Martin, C., & Broer, I. (2012). Functional neuroimaging studies of hypnosis and meditation: a comparative perspective. *The Journal of Mind–Body Regulation*, **2**, 58–70.

Dunne, J. (2013). Towards an understanding of non-dual mindfulness. In J. M. G. Williams & J. Kabat-Zinn (Eds.), *Mindfulness: diverse perspectives on its meaning, origins and applications* (pp. 71–88). London: Routledge.

Ebert, J. P., & Wegner, D. M. (2010). Time warp: authorship shapes the perceived time of actions and events. *Consciousness and Cognition*, **19**, 481–489.

Ellingson, T. (1998). Arrow and mirror: interactive consciousness, ethnography, and the Tibetan State Oracle's trance. *Anthropology and Humanism*, **23**, 51–76.

Farb, N. A. S. (2012). Mind your expectations: exploring the roles of suggestion and intention in mindfulness training. *Journal of Mind–Body Regulation*, **2**, 27–42.

France, K. L. (2013). *Hypnotic induction of unconscious anxiety: a new perspective*. Unpublished Masters dissertation, University of Sussex.

Frewen, P. A., Evans, E., Maraj, N., Dozois, D. J. A., & Partridge, K. (2008). Letting go: mindfulness and negative automatic thinking. *Cognitive Therapy and Research*, **32**, 758–774.

Frewen, P. A., Lundberg, E., Mackinley, J., & Wrath, A. (2011). Assessment of response to mindfulness meditation: Meditation Breath Attention scores in association with subjective measures of state and trait mindfulness and difficulty letting go of depressive cognition. *Mindfulness*, **2**(4), 254–269.

Gethin, R. (2013). On some definitions of mindfulness. In J. M. G. Williams & J. Kabat-Zinn (Eds.), *Mindfulness: diverse perspectives on its meaning, origins and applications* (pp. 263–280). London: Routledge.

Gombrich, R. F. (1996). *How Buddhism began: the conditioned genesis of the early teachings*. School of Oriental and African Studies, London: Munshiram Manoharlal Publishers.

Gombrich, R. F. (2006). *Theravada Buddhism: a social history from ancient Benares to modern Colombo (The library of religious beliefs and practices)*. London: Routledge.

Gombrich, R. (2009). *What the Buddha thought (Oxford Centre for Buddhist Studies monographs)*. Sheffield: Equinox Press.

Grant, J. A., & Rainville, P. (2005). Hypnosis and meditation: similar experiential changes and shared brain mechanisms. *Medical Hypotheses*, **65**, 625–626.

Graver, M. R. (2007). *Stoicism and emotion*. Chicago: University of Chicago Press.

Grossman, P., & Van Dam, N. T. (2013). Mindfulness by any other name . . .: trials and tribulations of sati in Western psychology and science. In J. M. G. Williams & J. Kabat-Zinn (Eds.), *Mindfulness: diverse perspectives on its meaning, origins and applications* (pp. 219–239). London: Routledge.

Gunaratana, B. H. (2012). *The four foundations of mindfulness in plain English*. Massachusetts: Wisdom Publications.

Hadot, P. (2001). *The inner citadel: the meditations of Marcus Aurelius*. Cambridge, MA: Harvard University Press.

Haggard, P., Clark, S., & Kalogeras, J. (2002). Voluntary action and conscious awareness. *Nature Neuroscience*, **5**, 382–385.

Haggard, P., Cartledge, P., Dafydd, M., & Oakley, D. A. (2004). Anomalous control: when free-will is not conscious. *Consciousness and Cognition* **13**, 646–654.

Hamilton, S. (2000). *Early Buddhism: a new approach: the I of the beholder*. London: Routledge.

Hargus, E., Crane, C., Barnhofer, T., & Williams, J. M. G. (2010). Effects of mindfulness on meta-awareness and specificity of describing prodromal symptoms in suicidal depression. *Emotion*, **10**, 34–42.

Haywood, J. W., & Varela, F. J. (Eds.) (1992). *Gentle bridges: conversations with the Dalai Lama on the sciences of mind*. London: Shambala.

Hilgard, E. R. (1977). *Divided consciousness: multiple controls in human thought and action*. New York: Wiley-Interscience.

Hilgard, J. R. (1979). *Personality and hypnosis: a study of imaginative involvement* (2nd edn.). Chicago: University of Chicago Press.

Houghton, L. A., Calvert, E. L., Jackson, N. A., Cooper, P., & Whorwell, P. J. (2002). Visceral sensation and emotion: a study using hypnosis. *Gut*, **51**, 701–704.

Kabat-Zinn, J. (2013). Some reflections on the origins of MBSR, skilful means, and the trouble with maps. In J. M. G. Williams & J. Kabat-Zinn (Eds.), *Mindfulness: diverse perspectives on its meaning, origins and applications* (pp. 281–306). London: Routledge.

Kallio S., Revonsuo A., Hämäläinen H., Markela J., & Gruzelier J. (2001). Anterior brain functions and hypnosis: a test of the frontal hypothesis. *International Journal of Clinical and Experimental Hypnosis*, **49**, 95–108.

Keng, S. L., Smoski, M. J., & Robins, C. J. (2011). Effects of mindfulness on psychological health: a review of empirical studies. *Clinical Psychology Review*, **31**, 1041–1056.

Kihlstrom, J. F. (1997). Consciousness and me-ness. In J. Cohen and J. Schooler (Eds.), *Scientific approaches to consciousness* (pp. 451–468). Mahwah, NJ: Lawrence Erlbaum Associates, Inc.

Kihlstrom, J. F. (2007). Consciousness in hypnosis. In P. D. Zelazo, M. Moscovitch, & E. Thompson (Eds.), *Cambridge handbook of consciousness* (pp. 445–479). Cambridge: Cambridge University Press.

Kirsch, I. (1985).Response expectancy as a determinant of experience and behaviour. *American Psychologist*, **40**, 1189–1202.

Kirsch, I., Cardeña, E., Derbyshire, S., Dienes, Z., Heap, M., Kallio, S., . . . Whalley, M. (2011). Definitions of hypnosis and hypnotizability and their relation to suggestion and suggestibility: a consensus statement. *Contemporary Hypnosis and Integrative Therapy*, **28**(2), 107–111.

Kirsch, I., & Lynn, S. J. (1998a). Social-cognitive alternatives to dissociation theories of hypnotic involuntariness. *Review of General Psychology*, **2**, 66–80.

Kirsch, I., & Lynn, S. J. (1998b). Dissociation theories of hypnosis. *Psychological Bulletin*, **123**, 100–115.

Kozhevnikov, M., Louchakova, O., Josipovic, Z., & Motes, M. A. (2009). The enhancement of visuospatial processing efficiency through Buddhist deity meditation. *Psychological Science*, **20** (5), 645–653.

Kurzban, R., Duckworth, A., Kable, J. W., & Myers, J. (2013). An opportunity cost model of subjective effort and task performance. *Behavioural and Brain Sciences*, **36**, 661–679.

Libet, B., Gleason, C. A., Wright, E. W., & Pearl, D. K. (1983). Time of conscious intention to act in relation to onset of cerebral activity (readiness-potential). The unconscious initiation of a freely voluntary act. *Brain*, **106**, 623–642.

Lifshitz, M., Bonn, N. A., Fischer, A., Kashem, I. F., & Raz, A. (2013). Using suggestion to modulate automatic processes: from Stroop to McGurk and beyond. *Cortex*, **49**, 463–473.

Liftshitz, M., Campbell, N., & Raz, A. (2012). Varieties of attention in hypnosis and meditation. *Consciousness and Cognition*, **21**, 1582–1585.

Lutz, A., Slagter, H. A., Dunne, J. D., & Davidson, R. J. (2008). Attention regulation and monitoring in meditation. *Trends in Cognitive Sciences*, **12**, 163–169.

Lutz, A., Slagter, H., Rawlings, N. B., Francis, A. D., Greischar, L. L., & Davidson, R. J. (2009). Mental training enhances attentional stability: neural and behavioral evidence. *Journal of Neuroscience*, **29**, 13418–13427.

Lynn, S. J., Malaktaris, A., Maxwell, R., Mellinger, D. I., & van der Kloet, D. (2012). Do hypnosis and mindfulness practices inhabit a common domain? Implications for research, clinical practice, and forensic science. *The Journal of Mind–Body Regulation*, **2**, 12–26.

Lynn, S. J., Rhue, J. W., & Weekes, J. R. (1990). Hypnotic involuntariness: a social cognitive analysis. *Psychological Review*, **97**, 169–184.

Marcusson-Clavertz, D., Terhune, D., & Cardeña, E. (2012). Individual differences and state effects on mind-wandering: hypnotizability, dissociation, and sensory homogenization. *Consciousness and Cognition*, **21**, 1097–1108.

McEvilley, T. (2006). *The shape of ancient thought*. New York: Allworth Press.

Miller, J., & Schwarz, W. (2014). Brain signals do not demonstrate unconscious decision making: an interpretation based on graded conscious awareness. *Consciousness and Cognition*, **24**, 12–21.

Moore, J., & Haggard, P. (2008). Awareness of action: inference and prediction. *Consciousness and Cognition*, **17**, 136–114.

Naish, P. L. N. (1986). Hypnosis and signal detection: an information processing account. In P. L. N. Naish (Ed.), *What is hypnosis?* (pp. 121–144). Milton Keynes, UK: Open University Press.

Naish, P. L. N. (2014). Inhibition and disinhibition in hypnosis. *Contemporary Hypnosis and Integrative Therapy*, **30**, 135–141.

Nanamoli, B. (translator) (1999). *Visuddhimagga: the path of purification*. Onalaska: Pariyati Publishing.

Nash, M., & Barnier, A. (Eds.) (2008). *The Oxford handbook of hypnosis: theory, research, and practice*. Oxford: Oxford University Press.

Newberg, A. B., Alavi, A., Baime, M., Pourdehnad, M., Santanna, J., & d'Aquili, E. G. (2001). The measurement of regional cerebral blood flow during the complex cognitive task of meditation: a preliminary SPECT study. *Psychiatry Research: Neuroimaging*, **106**, 113–122.

Oakley, D. A., & Halligan, P. W. (2013). Hypnotic suggestion: opportunities for cognitive neuroscience. *Nature Reviews Neuroscience*, **14**, 565–576.

Olendzki, A. (2013). The construction of mindfulness. In J. M. G. Williams & J. Kabat-Zinn (Eds.), *Mindfulness: diverse perspectives on its meaning, origins and applications* (pp. 55–70). London: Routledge.

Overgaard, M., & Sørensen, T. A. (2004). Introspection distinct from first order experiences. *Journal of Consciousness Studies*, **11** (7–8), 77–95.

Peacock, J. (2014). *Sati* or mindfulness? Bridging the divide. In M. Bazzano (Ed.), *After mindfulness: new perspectives on psychology and meditation* (pp. 3–22). Hampshire: Palgrave Macmillan.

Proust, J. (2012). *Philosophy of metacognition: mental agency and self-awareness*. Oxford: Oxford University Press.

Raij, T. T., Numminen, J., Närvänen, S., Hiltunen, J., & Hari, R. (2009). Strength of prefrontal activation predicts intensity of suggestion-induced pain. *Human Brain Mapping*, **30**, 2890–2897.

Rainville, P., Hofbauer, R. K., Paus, T., Duncan, G. H., Bushnell, M. C., & Price, D. D. (1999). Cerebral mechanisms of hypnotic induction and suggestion. *Journal of Cognitive Neuroscience*, *11*, 110–125.

Raz, A., Kirsch, I., Pollard, J., & Nitkin Kaner, Y. (2006). Suggestion reduces the Stroop effect. *Psychological Science*, **17**, 91–95.

Rosenthal, D. (2005). *Consciousness and mind*. Oxford: Oxford University Press.

Rounis, E., Maniscalco, B., Rothwell, J., Passingham, R. E., & Lau, H. (2010). Theta-burst transcranial magnetic stimulation to the prefrontal cortex impairs metacognitive visual awareness. *Cognitive Neuroscience*, **1**, 165–175.

Sayette, A. M., Reichle, E. D., & Schooler, J. W. (2009). Lost in the sauce: the effects of alcohol on mind wandering? *Psychological Science*, **20**, 747–752.

Schurger, A., Sitta, J. D., & Dehaene, S. (2012). An accumulator model for spontaneous neural activity prior to self-initiated movement. *Proceedings of the National Academy of Science*, **109**, 16776–16777.

Sellars, J. (2013). *Stoicism*. California: University of California Press.

Semmens-Wheeler, R. (2013). *The contrasting role of higher order awareness in hypnosis and meditation*. Unpublished PhD Thesis, University of Sussex.

Semmens-Wheeler, R., & Dienes, Z. (2012). The contrasting role of higher order awareness in hypnosis and meditation. *Journal of Mind–Body Regulation*, *2*(1), 43–57.

Semmens-Wheeler, R., Dienes, Z., & Duka, T. (2013). Alcohol increases hypnotic susceptibility. *Consciousness and Cognition*, **22** (3), 1082–1091.

Shankman, R. (2008). *The experience of Samadhi: an in-depth exploration of Buddhist meditation*. London: Shambhala.

Sheehan, P. W., & McConkey, K. M. (1982). *Hypnosis and experience: the exploration of phenomena and processes*. Hillsdale, NJ: Erlbaum.

Siderits, M. (2007). *Buddhism as philosophy: an introduction*. Surrey: Ashgate.

Snyder, S., & Rassmusen, T. (2009). *Practicing the Jhanas: traditional concentration meditation*. Boston: Shambhala Publications.

Spanos, N. (1986). Hypnotic behaviour: a social–psychological interpretation of amnesia, analgesia, and "trance logic." *Behavioural and Brain Sciences*, **9**, 449–502.

Spanos, N. P., Brett, P. J., Menary, E. P., & Cross, W. P. (1987). A measure of attitudes toward hypnosis: relationships with absorption and hypnotic suggestibility. *American Journal of Clinical Hypnosis*, *30*(2),139–150.

Spanos, N. P., Radtke, H. L., & Dubreuil, D. L. (1982). Episodic and semantic memory in post-hypnotic amnesia: a re-evaluation. *Journal of Personality and Social psychology*, **43**, 565–573.

Tan, L. F., Dienes, Z., Jansari, A., & Goh, S. Y. (2014). Effect of mindfulness meditation on brain–computer interface performance. *Consciousness and Cognition*, **23**, 12–21.

Tasso, A. F., & Perez, N. A. (2008). Parsing everyday suggestibility: what does it tell us about hypnosis? In M. Nash & A. Barnier (Eds.), *The Oxford handbook of hypnosis: theory, research, and practice* (pp. 283–310). Oxford: Oxford University Press.

Teasdale, J. D., Moore, R. G., Hayhurst, H., Pope, M., Williams, S., & Segal, Z. V. (2002). Metacognitive awareness and prevention of relapse in depression: empirical evidence. *Journal of Consulting and Clinical Psychology*, **70**, 275–287.

Terhune, D. B., & Brugger, P. (2011). Doing better by getting worse: posthypnotic amnesia improves random number generation. *PLoS ONE*, **6**(12), e29206. doi:10.1371/journal.pone.0029206

Terhune, B., Cardeña, E., & Lindgren, M. (2011). Dissociative tendencies and individual differences in high hypnotic suggestibility. *Cognitive Neuropsychiatry*, **16**, 113–135.

Tobis, I., & Kihlstrom, J. F. (2010). Allocation of attentional resources in posthypnotic responding. *International Journal of Clinical and Experimental Hypnosis*, **58**, 367–382.

Waszak, F., Cardoso-Leite, P., & Hughes, G. (2012). Action effect anticipation: neurophysiological basis and functional consequences. *Neuroscience and Biobehavioral Reviews*, **36**(2), 943–959.

White, R. W. (1941). A preface to a theory of hypnotism. *Journal of Abnormal and Social Psychology*, **36**, 477–505.

Williams, P. (2009). *Mahayana Buddhism: the doctrinal foundations* (2nd edn.). London: Routledge.

Williams, P., & Tribe, A. (2000). *Buddhist thought: a complete introduction to the Indian tradition*. London: Routledge.

Wilson, S. C., & Barber, T. X. (1982). The fantasy-prone personality: implications for understanding imagery, hypnosis, and parapsychological phenomena. In A. A. Sheik (Ed.), *Imagery: current research theory and application* (pp. 340–390). New York: Wiley.

Woody, E., Z., & Sadler, P. (2008). Dissociation theories of hypnosis. In M. Nash & A. Barnier (Eds.), *The Oxford handbook of hypnosis: theory, research, and practice* (pp. 81–110). Oxford: Oxford University Press.

Wyzenbeek, M., & Bryant, R. A. (2012). The cognitive demands of hypnotic response. *International Journal of Clinical and Experimental Hypnosis*, **60**, 67–80.

Yapko, M. D. (2011). *Mindfulness and hypnosis: the power of suggestion to transform experience*. New York, NY: Norton.

Yeshe, T. (1998). *The bliss of inner fire: heart practice of the six Yogas of Naropa*. Massachusetts: Wisdom Publications.

Appendix 1
Buddhist-friendly preamble

We will explore some exercises involving attention, concentration, how the skillful use of attention may be associated with a pliable mind. Scientific research supports the experience of meditators that learning the skillful use of attention makes a real difference to how the mind works. We are interested in how attention changes our experiences. For example, we are interested in how strongly attending to an idea, such as a movement, may make that movement automatically happen. Of course, if your sustained imagination makes your arm move, you could stop the movement anytime, if you wished, just by changing your attention and imagination. Your mind is pliable and responds to your thoughts, each state conditioned on the previous. But if you are willing to play the game, you could keep the movement happening, seemingly by itself, if you attend in the right way. Similarly, when we create an image in our imagination, and concentrate on it, we create a seed for the imagination becoming real. By imagining a feeling in a clear way, we can make the feeling actually happen. Imagining us being compassionate in all directions, helps make us compassionate. Tantric Buddhist practices make particular use of this principle; imagining the embodiment of an ideal in a sustained way, helps us achieve the ideal. We are interested in exploring this principle on a small scale, seeing how imagining, say, a feeling of heaviness could make your hand heavy.

Maybe, for example, you can imagine a subtle body within your own body, an inner body with many channels of energy flow of its own. We will try flowing some inner energy in your limbs and seeing its effect on the physical body.

What is the difference between imagination and reality? Is reality a dream? You may know the answer better than me! But our perception of reality is constructed, just as a dream is. In dream yoga, skilled adepts learn to control their dreams. Some people can produce a dream, any time of the day, just by intending it. I wonder if you can produce dream-like experiences by the way you attend and imagine.

We often impute a "self," a thinker, a controller, an author of our mental states. Yet, in agreement with the arguments of Gotama 2500 years ago, who perhaps first proposed the thesis, there seems not to be a self to be found above and beyond our mental and physical constituents. Thus, while we may think "I intended my arm to move," for example, this imputation is not necessary. Consider thinking about your arm moving, and then your arm moving. There is an idea of movement. Then there may be movement conditioned by the idea. But we need not think "I made my arm move." In effect, one may be aware of an idea of one's hand moving down, and aware of the arm thereby moving down, and thus aware of the arm moving without oneself having to intend it. Our behaviors happen because of mental states that condition them; a self is not needed. I wonder if you will notice this or not in the exercises that we will perform.

Do you have any questions? For any exercise you do not wish to perform, that is OK, just tell me. All exercises will involve clear awareness of your environment, should you wish that, and of your body and your mind, just as you wish. The exercises are about regulation of attention and imagination. We will now describe each one first before we actually try them. Let's begin!

1. Now, please seat yourself comfortably and rest your hands in your lap. That's right. Rest your hands in your lap. Now close your eyes and just focus on my voice. We will begin by being aware of our body, and making our attention pliable, flexible. You have shown your willingness by coming here today, and so I am assuming that your presence here means that you want to experience all that

you can. Pay close attention to my words, and let happen whatever you feel is going to take place. Just let yourself go. Pay close attention to what I tell you to think about; if your mind wanders, that will be okay; just bring your thoughts back to my words. Nothing will be done to embarrass you.

2. Now take it easy and just let yourself relax. Whatever you experience is all right. Just let yourself experience whatever happens and keep focusing on my words. You will find that you can relax, but at the same time sit up comfortably in your chair with little effort. You will be able to shift your position to make yourself comfortable as needed, without it disturbing you. Now starting with your right foot, be aware of your foot . . . the muscles of your right leg . . . now be aware of your left foot . . . the muscles of your left leg . . . be aware of your right hand . . . your right forearm . . . upper arm . . . and shoulder . . . that's right . . . now your left hand . . . and forearm . . . and upper arm . . . and shoulder . . . be aware of your chest . . . your neck . . . now scan your head from bottom to top . . .

All right then, now we will begin the exercises.

Standard preamble

1. Now, please seat yourself comfortably and rest your hands in your lap. That's right. Rest your hands in your lap. Now close your eyes and just focus on my voice. I am about to help you to relax, and meanwhile I will give you some instructions that will help you to gradually enter a state of hypnosis. You can become hypnotized if you are willing to do what I tell you to, and if you concentrate on what I say. You have already shown your willingness by coming here today, and so I am assuming that your presence here means that you want to experience all that you can. Pay close attention to my words, and let happen whatever you feel is going to take place. Just let yourself go. Pay close attention to what I tell you to think about; if your mind wanders, that will be okay; just bring your thoughts back to my words, and you can easily experience more of what it's like to be hypnotized.

Hypnosis is perfectly normal and natural, and follows from the conditions of attention and suggestion we are using together. It is chiefly a matter of focusing sharply on some particular thing. Sometimes you experience something very much like hypnosis when driving along a straight highway and you are oblivious to the landmarks along the road. What is important here today is your willingness to go along with the ideas I suggest and to let happen whatever is about to happen. Nothing will be done to embarrass you.

2. Now take it easy and just let yourself relax. Whatever you experience is all right. Just let yourself experience whatever happens and keep focusing on my words. You will find that you can relax completely, but at the same time sit up comfortably in your chair with little effort. You will be able to shift your position to make yourself comfortable as needed, without it disturbing you. For now, just relax more and more. As you think of relaxing, your muscles will actually begin to relax. Starting with your right foot, relax the muscles of your right leg . . . now the muscles of your left leg . . . just relax all over . . . relax your right hand . . . your forearm . . . upper arm . . . and shoulder . . . that's right . . . now your left hand . . . and forearm . . . and upper arm . . . and shoulder . . . relax your neck, and chest . . . more and more relaxed . . . completely relaxed . . . completely relaxed.

3. As you become relaxed, your body will feel deeply at ease . . . comfortably heavy. You will begin to have this pleasant feeling of heaviness and comfort in your legs and feet . . . in your hands and arms . . . throughout your body . . . as though you were settling deep into the chair. Your body feels comfortable and heavy . . . your eyelids feel heavy too, heavy and tired. You are beginning to feel very relaxed and comfortable. You are breathing freely and deeply, freely and deeply. You are becoming more and more deeply and comfortably relaxed.

4. You now feel very relaxed, but you are going to become even more relaxed. You feel pleasantly, deeply relaxed and very comfortable as you continue to hear my voice. Just let your thoughts dwell on what I'm saying. You are going to become even more relaxed and comfortable. Soon you will be deeply hypnotized, but you will have no trouble hearing me. You will remain deeply hypnotized until I tell you to awaken later on. Soon I shall begin to count from one to twenty. As I count, you will feel yourself going down further and further into a deeply relaxed, a deeply hypnotized state . . . but you will be able to do all sorts of things I ask you to do without waking up . . . one . . . you are going to become more deeply relaxed and hypnotized . . . two . . . down, down deeper, and deeper . . . three . . . four . . . more and more deeply hypnotized . . . five . . . six . . . seven . . . you are sinking deeper and deeper into hypnosis. Nothing will disturb you . . . just let your thoughts focus on my voice and those things I tell you to think of. You are finding it easy just to listen to the things I tell you. Eight . . . nine, ten . . . halfway there . . . always deeper . . . eleven . . . twelve . . . thirteen . . . fourteen . . . fifteen . . . although deeply hypnotized you can hear me clearly. You will always hear me distinctly, no matter how deeply hypnotized you become. Sixteen . . . seventeen . . . eighteen . . . deeply hypnotized. Nothing will disturb you. You are going to experience many things that I will tell you to experience . . . nineteen . . . twenty. Deeply hypnotized now! You will not wake up until I tell you to. You will wish to remain relaxed and hypnotized and to have the experiences I describe to you.

Even though you are deeply relaxed and hypnotized, I want you to realize that you will be able to write, to move, and even to open your eyes if I ask you to do so, and still remain just as hypnotized and comfortable as you are now. It will not disturb you at all to open your eyes, move about, and write things. You will remain hypnotized until I tell you otherwise. All right, then . . .

Chapter 8

Hypnosis and mindfulness: experiential and neurophysiological relationships

Jason M. Thompson, Lynn C. Waelde,
Kálmán Tisza, and David Spiegel

Abstract

The neural and phenomenological overlap between hypnosis and mindfulness is reviewed in this chapter. The historical emergence of hypnosis and mindfulness in their respective applications to modern medicine and psychology are discussed. Hypnosis is defined as a form of effortless, absorbed awareness with a present moment focus in which imaginative or visual percepts are often prominent. Mindfulness is specified as a broad construct that encompasses an array of meditative practices, the states of awareness supported by those practices, and an enduring trait derived from long-term practice. The overlap between hypnosis and mindfulness is discussed in terms of their respective positions along four dimensions: effort, attention, continuity of awareness, and agency. Experiential and neurophysiological points of comparison are considered in relation to those four dimensions. In conclusion, hypnosis and mindfulness are proposed to be unique states of consciousness with overlapping, yet distinct, experiential and neurophysiological features.

Introduction

Hypnosis and mindfulness have often been compared and contrasted. It has frequently been argued that they are synonymous: that, for example, mindfulness might be construed as a form of self-hypnosis. Points of comparison between these two techniques are indeed striking, despite their evident contrasts in historical origin. Both involve notable changes in subjective awareness that overlap with the experience of relaxation. Both have increasingly been used as components of clinical interventions, especially in the treatment of chronic pain and psychiatric disorders such as anxiety and depression. Both have been shown to involve changes in neural network connectivity and to overlap with the neurophysiological mechanisms of dissociative processes. At the same time, hypnosis and mindfulness differ in regard to their historical origins, cultural context, and phenomenology.

The extent of the neurological and physiological overlap between these two states is an unresolved question. The endeavor to specify the overlap and differences is motivated by two objectives: first, elucidating the characteristics of the overlap may serve to illuminate features of core neuropsychological, emotional, and nociceptive processes which they modify in subtly contrasting ways, the clarification of which may prove beneficial to psychology, neuroscience, and medicine. Second, specificity about the overlap may prove useful in determining mechanisms and the relative strengths and weaknesses of both techniques in clinical intervention.

The following critical review pursues the foregoing objectives through an analysis of the relationships between hypnosis and mindfulness in historical, conceptual, and theoretical terms, and with regard to salient points of comparison and contrast on both experiential and neurophysiological levels.

Historical origins

Hypnosis and mindfulness emerge from distinct historical and conceptual foundations. An instructive comparison can be made in terms of each technique's respective theoretical and practical position in regard to the phenomenon of human suffering. The word "hypnosis" is derived from the ancient Greek *hypnos*, meaning sleep (Halsband, Mueller, Hinterberger, & Strickner, 2009). Hypnosis originated in the European psychotherapeutic tradition and is the oldest Western psychological treatment (Ellenberger, 1970). Freud used hypnosis in treatment and incorporated several hypnotic techniques (e.g., suggestion) in early psychoanalysis (Breuer & Freud, 1936). Freud considered the hypnotist/patient relationship as analogous to the parent/child relationship, and hypnosis as a form of regression (Bonshtein, 2012). His early ideas regarding transference derived from intense emotional reactions of patients in hypnosis, and he conceived of hypnosis as acting via transference mobilization (Freud, 1925). Indeed, he set hypnosis aside, moved his chair behind the couch, and began asking patients to free associate with eyes open instead, after one patient emerged from a hypnotic trance and threw her arms around his neck.

Early theoretical paradigms conceptualized hypnosis either with an emphasis on the interpersonal power of the hypnotist or in terms of hypnotic susceptibility as a sign of weakness or mental illness (Charcot, 1889). Later models placed less emphasis on the hypnotist and more on the hypnotic subject (Bernheim, 1957). This approach eventually led to the development of empirical hypnotizability scales (Hilgard & Hilgard, 1979; Spiegel & Spiegel, 2004). Other models described hypnosis as a form of behavior shaped or even constructed by social expectancies (Vandenberg, 1998). Subsequent to the Second World War, hypnosis increasingly moved into the mainstream, partly as a result of the clinical experience of doctors who discovered its utility in the treatment of trauma (Kardiner & Spiegel, 1947; Spiegel, 1981 2007). Behavioristic and social constructivist models of hypnosis subsequently shifted to the margins as discoveries in psychoneuroimmunology and then neuroscience identified physiological markers of hypnosis and hypnotizability (Hoeft et al., 2012), and hypnosis increasingly came to be identified as clinically effective for conditions that were otherwise difficult to treat, such as pain and somatization (Butler, Symons, Henderson, Shortliffe, & Spiegel, 2005; Butler et al., 2009; Lang et al., 2000; Weisberg, 2008).

Like hypnosis, mindfulness emerged from origins outside of Western medicine and science, but has lately become a topic of increasing empirical interest. In contrast with the European origins of hypnosis, mindfulness originated in the Eastern contemplative traditions of Vedic philosophy and Buddhism. Although the conceptual intricacies of these historically expansive traditions are beyond the scope of this chapter, one dimension of the pragmatic essence of both Vedic philosophy and Buddhism that can be highlighted is their emphasis on the benefit of enhancing the capacity for present-tense sensory-cognitive awareness as a means of overcoming the inevitable hardships of human existence.

Thomas William Rhys Davids (as cited in Bodhi, 2000) coined the English word "mindfulness" in 1881 as a translation of the Pali noun *sati*. Mindfulness as a term in contemporary usage typically denotes either the practice of mindfulness meditation or other practices intended to induce a state of enhanced attention to the present moment (e.g., mindful walking). A number of increasingly popular psychological interventions, such as acceptance and commitment therapy (Hayes, Strosahl, & Wilson, 1999) feature mindfulness exercises as a treatment component. Mindfulness has thus acquired a meaning in modern secular usage that is, for the most part, divested of the metaphysical and ethical frameworks in which meditative practices were construed in their Eastern contemplative origins. The term has come to denote a type of intensified attentional capacity and state (Nash & Newberg, 2013) which appears to be effective both in reducing forms of psychological distress such as anxiety and depression, and in ameliorating stress experienced by people coping with chronic medical conditions (Goyal et al., 2014). Mindfulness has been taught to a wide range of clinical and non-clinical populations, across diverse demographic groups, with evidence of beneficial impacts even after relatively short periods of training.

In summary, like hypnosis, mindfulness is a state of consciousness involving shifts in attentional focus that appears to be relatively easy to acquire as a baseline skill (albeit very difficult to master) and which can be applied to therapeutic aims. In consideration of the historical trajectory linking their respective origins and current clinical application overall, hypnosis and mindfulness emerged from culturally distinct foundations but have come to be applied to similar clinical objectives with comparable therapeutic outcomes.

Conceptual and theoretical relationships

The extent to which attention and related neurocognitive factors represent the most salient explanatory level in theoretical accounts bridging hypnosis and meditation has been a subject of separate theoretical debates within these two fields that in some ways echo each other. The parallels between those debates are illuminating in terms of the similarities between hypnosis and mindfulness. In the hypnosis literature, neurocognitive models have come to dominate sociocognitive models. Hypnosis in neurocognitive terms has been proposed to be a state of consciousness that can be induced independent of any special interpersonal or social environment (Lynn & Green, 2011). The neurocognitive-dominant model in this regard departs from historically older models that emphasized the interpersonal power of the hypnotist. Contemporary theoretical accounts of hypnosis that include interpersonal, social, or attachment factors are relatively sparsely represented in the literature. Empirical evidence has tended to support the dissociated control theory in preference to the social cognitive theory (Sadler & Woody, 2006), though one recent multifactorial conceptualization of hypnosis proposed an integration of social expectancy, neurocognitive, and trait factors (Hammond, 2005).

An important development in the establishment of hypnosis as an acceptable integrative medicine intervention was the emergence of evidence indicating cognitive and neurophysiological markers that differentiate highly hypnotizable individuals from those with a low susceptibility to hypnosis (Hasegawa & Jamieson, 2002; Hoeft et al., 2012). The differential activation of the anterior cingulate cortex (ACC) in hypnosis, relative to rest, supported the conceptualization of hypnosis as a distinct state of consciousness (Lynn & Green, 2011). High hypnotizables have been shown to demonstrate a reduced level of Stroop interference in comparison with lows following post-hypnotic suggestion (Raz, Shapiro, Fan, & Posner, 2002). Highs differ from lows in terms of EEG (electroencephalography) phase synchronization in frontal regions (Baghdadi & Nasrabadi, 2012), and demonstrate a higher proportion of occipital alpha than lows (Halsband et al., 2009).

The decoupling of frontal control and cognitive systems in hypnosis has been proposed as a key marker of the hypnotic state (Egner, Jamieson, & Gruzelier, 2005).

The history of empirical mindfulness paradigms has similar features to the foregoing (for an examination of historical connections, see Chapter 2). Pioneers of the scientific study of meditation examined whether meditation was distinct from relaxation or early stage sleep. EEG studies commencing in the 1960s provided preliminary support for mindfulness as a distinct state of awareness (Kasamatsu & Hirai, 1966). Following the emergence of fMRI (functional magnetic resonance imaging) in the early 1990s, an explosion of interest in identifying neural correlates of meditation followed. Straightforward conclusions from the several hundred studies conducted since are rendered elusive as a consequence of the significant degree of heterogeneity across studies in sample sizes, population characteristics, neural regions of interest, types of meditation, and levels of meditation experience (Lutz, Slagter, Dunne, & Davidson, 2008). In general terms, however, meditation has been shown to be associated with changes in structures and networks that support attention and emotion regulation (Eberth & Sedlmeier, 2012; Goyal et al., 2014). In the minimal degree to which head-to-head comparisons have been conducted, meditation has in turn been distinguished from hypnosis, for instance in terms of EEG signature (Halsband et al., 2009).

A comparable increasing emphasis on neurocognitive factors similarly characterizes the historical course of the mindfulness literature in its assimilation of Eastern contemplative sources by Western psychological and medical science. Mindfulness is typically described in a Western context as a state in which enhanced present-moment attention facilitates a state of awareness in which cognitive and sensory percepts are experienced from a more detached, less self-identified position. While this aspect of the modern conceptualization of mindfulness accords with classical descriptions, aspects of those descriptions that stress social factors as necessary features of development in mindfulness practice have yet to be recapitulated in modern empirical investigations. For example, the requisite degree of mindfulness training of mindfulness teachers, and the role of mindfulness-oriented communities in producing therapeutic benefits and supporting and nurturing a sustained commitment to mindfulness practice, are questions that have yet to be answered in the literature (Waelde, Thompson, Robinson, & Iwanicki, in submission).

In summary, mindfulness, like hypnosis, has come to be theorized almost entirely in neurocognitive terms, thereby perhaps solidifying the outward impression of the two techniques' apparent mutual resemblance. It may, however, be premature to infer from the absence of evidence regarding the role of social factors in mindfulness that this amounts to evidence that social factors are unimportant. Elucidating social factors involved in mindfulness, including the student–teacher relationship so strongly emphasized in both Vedic and Buddhist traditions (Feuerstein, 1998), could enrich our understanding of mindfulness, highlight important differences between mindfulness and hypnosis, and broaden the neurocognitive framework in which these practices are now construed.

Experiential and neurophysiological relationships

An important consideration in the evaluation of experiential parallels between hypnosis and mindfulness is the limited extent to which head-to-head comparisons have been conducted involving subjects with comparable levels of practice in both techniques. A significant degree of epistemological caution is consequently warranted in the endeavor to infer similarities or contrasts between subjective states to which neither party has mutual access, outside the limited extant evidence base of direct phenomenological comparison studies. That said, five dimensions of experiential comparison appear pertinent to the present review: effort, attention, continuity of awareness, imagery, and agency.

Effort: trait versus practice

One experiential feature common to both is a state of relaxed effortless absorption (see Chapter 14). Both hypnosis and mindfulness are marked by shifts in degree of arousal distinguished by patterns of cortical electrical activity (Dunn, Hartigan, & Mikulas, 1999; Fenwick et al., 1977; Halsband et al., 2009).

One point of departure is the level of initial effort required to induce these effortless states. Reports of hypnosis typically describe the capacity of the hypnotic subject to experience a state of awareness often richly imbued with imaginative characteristics in which the subject immerses with a feeling of involuntary, effortless engagement (Bowers, 1982–1983). Effortlessness and engagement similarly characterize reports of the experience of mindfulness, although the intensity of those features appears to correspond with experience level (Brefczynski-Lewis, Lutz, Schaefer, Levinson, & Davidson, 2007).

The effect of repeated practice on the degree of effortlessness and engagement appears to be more a feature of mindfulness than hypnosis. Whereas hypnotic engagement seems to be almost entirely a function of trait differences in hypnotizability, mindfulness engagement appears to be a function of repeated practice over months or years. More recent research has, however, questioned this neat dichotomy between the trait-like quality of the hypnotic profile and the practice-based nature of mindfulness. One study found that the degree of mindfulness engagement was moderated by neural differences in an empathy task at baseline (Mascaro, Rilling, Negi, & Raison, 2013). Such trait differences represent a key methodological concern regarding the inferences derived from experimental observation of the distinctive neurological characteristics of expert meditators, because it is not clear if meditation or pre-existing trait differences caused those characteristics (Fox et al., 2014). Equally, some evidence exists of the capacity of hypnotic subjects to become increasingly adept in self-hypnosis (Spiegel & Spiegel, 2004).

In summary, the capacities for hypnosis and mindfulness are both contingent upon trait and practice, though trait differences are more salient in the former, and practice duration in the latter.

Attention: narrow versus broad

A key experiential feature of both hypnosis and mindfulness is an alteration of attention, specifically an intensification of present-moment focus and a feeling of absorption. An early head-to-head comparison between transcendental meditation and hypnosis found that meditation and hypnosis were similar in terms of their impact on attention, though hypnosis appeared to require less effort to manage distractions (Brown, Forte, Rich, & Epstein, 1982). The role of the dorsal anterior cingulate cortex (dACC) and dorsolateral prefrontal cortex (DLPFC), structures associated with conflict monitoring, has been noted in both hypnosis and mindfulness in this regard (Halsband et al., 2009). Connectivity enhancements between the DLPFC and the salience network have been reported as greater in highly hypnotizable subjects relative to lows (Hoeft et al., 2012). Both meditation and hypnosis involve enhanced activation of interoceptive structures, specifically the dACC, DLPFC, and the frontoinsular cortex (Hoeft et al., 2012; Melloni et al., 2013).

Changes in attention appear to be accompanied in both hypnosis and mindfulness by changes in executive control and the default mode network (DMN). A study of high hypnotizables in a resting state found greater connectivity, relative to low hypnotizables, between the DLPFC and the salience network, and greater coactivation of the executive and salience networks (Hoeft et al., 2012).

Meditation has similarly been shown to enhance executive control (Teper & Inzlicht, 2013), perhaps especially so in novice meditators, who may recruit areas of the prefrontal cortex to enhance emotion regulation in a "top-down" fashion (Chiesa, Seretti, & Jakobsen, 2013). Self-reported hypnotic depth has been shown to correlate inversely with DMN activity (Deeley et al., 2012); meditation has similarly been associated with attenuated DMN connectivity (Taylor et al., 2013).

Hypnosis appears to overlap phenomenologically, in terms of absorption, more closely with concentrative ("focused attention") meditative techniques (Lutz et al., 2008) that involve a narrowing of attention on a meditative object such as the breath or a body part, though the degree of narrowing in focused attention forms of meditation may not be equivalent to that achieved in hypnotic states. Receptive ("open monitoring") meditative techniques, by contrast, involve an expansion rather than narrowing of attentional focus and, in this sense, diverge from hypnosis (Harrer, 2009). Another difference is that hypnosis typically involves induction by a hypnotist, whereas mindfulness is typically self-induced (Bell, Oakley, Halligan, & Deeley, 2011). This polarity between the hetero-suggestive nature of hypnosis versus the auto-suggestive nature of mindfulness breaks down in consideration of the counter-examples of self-hypnosis (Spiegel & Spiegel, 2004) and guided meditation (see Chapter 19). It could therefore be hypothesized that self-hypnosis is very close to meditation and guided meditation close to hetero-hypnosis; further empirical investigation of this question is warranted.

The impact of meditation-induced attentional changes has been proposed as a core mechanism of mindfulness-based clinical intervention, in which distressing cognitions diminish in emotional valence through decentering or cognitive diffusion (Carmody, Baer, Lykins, & Olendzki, 2009; Hayes, Luoma, Bond, Masuda, & Lillis, 2006). The resultant quality of equanimity has been proposed as a particularly important feature of mindfulness (Desbordes et al., 2014). The treatment mechanism of hypnosis for clinical disorders such as depression has been proposed in an analogous form characterized by an experience in which the subject is directed to expand awareness beyond symptoms (Alladin, 2010), though it is not clear whether this benefit derives from distraction or a decentered perceptual stance.

The impact of attentional changes in both hypnosis and mindfulness has been proposed as a key component of each technique's clinical utility in analgesia. Both hypnosis and mindfulness are effective forms of analgesia (Feldman, 2004; Zeidan, Grant, Brown, McHaffie, & Coghill, 2012). Brain structures involved in hypnosis overlap with those structures involved in pain processing (Feldman, 2004; Rainville, Duncan, Price, Carrier, & Bushnell, 1997; Rainville, Hofbauer, Bushnell, Duncan, & Price, 2002). The role of hypnosis in reducing pain unpleasantness is related to its impact on the primary somatosensory cortices (Spiegel & Spiegel, 2004). The analgesic use of hypnosis derives from its capacity to facilitate the top-down frontal regulation of limbic activity, thereby overriding the automatic processes involved in pain perception (Feldman, 2004; Rainville et al., 1997). Mindfulness has been proposed to function using similar mechanisms (Lutz, McFarlin, Perlman, Salomons, & Davidson, 2013; Zeidan et al., 2012), though these effects may depend on enhanced self-regulatory capacity developed with practice (Evans, Eisenlohr-Moul, Button, Baer, & Segerstrom, 2014). Both hypnosis and mindfulness overlap with placebo responsivity (Benedetti, Mayberg, Wager, Stohler, & Zubieta, 2005; Chiesa & Serretti, 2010; Wager, Atlas, Leotti, & Rilling, 2011), although the extent of this overlap has yet to be clarified (see Chapter 21).

Continuity of awareness: dissociation versus integration

The respective overlap between hypnosis and meditation with dissociative processes provides an especially useful way of differentiating the two states. Dissociation was originally defined as a narrowing of the field of consciousness (Janet, 1920). The term has subsequently become understood to comprise a range of "disruptions and fragmentations of the usually integrated functions of consciousness, memory, identity, body awareness, and perception of the self and environment" (Lanius, Brand, Vermetten, Frewen, & Spiegel, 2012, p. 701).

Dissociation can be a response to traumatic environments such as war zones or childhood abuse, although the term also encompasses non-pathological interruptions in awareness such as day-dreaming (Butler, 2006). Neurophysiologically, dissociation appears to involve a process of emotional hyperregulation, entailing excessive cortical inhibition of traumatic memories (Lanius et al., 2010).

Dissociation overlaps with hypnosis in that the latter similarly involves a state in which events appear to unfold with a sense of involuntary automaticity to which the subject is an outside observer (Zeig, 1980). Hypnosis has thus been described as "dissociation in a structured setting" (Vermetten & Bremner, 2004, p. 285). The foregoing experience of automaticity has been attributed to the disaggregation of the executive system into two parts, only one of which is available to conscious awareness, thereby creating an experience of ostensibly involuntary compliance with a hypnotic suggestion (Hilgard, 1965), or to reduced cognition as a result of attenuated frontal lobe activity (Bowers, 1992). The extent of the hypnosis/dissociation overlap is underscored by the strong correlation between hypnotizability and both dissociative identity disorder (Bliss, 1983) and post-traumatic stress disorder (PTSD) symptom severity in Vietnam combat veterans (Stutman & Bliss, 1985), and by the role of exaggerated corticolimbic inhibition in conversion disorders (Bell et al., 2011). In summary, dissociation and hypnosis both involve a fragmentation of awareness.

Mindfulness would appear to function as the direct opposite of the foregoing (see Chapter 7). That is, where hypnosis involves a dissociative discontinuity of consciousness, mindfulness involves its integration. Mindfulness and dissociation can thus be understood to exist as the twin opposing poles of an awareness spectrum (Corrigan, 2002). Intriguingly, in one neurological respect, the two states appear quite similar: mindfulness shares with dissociation an increased level of corticolimbic inhibition. Indeed, evidence that long-term meditation practice tends to enhance cortical control of limbic emotional processes (Sperduti, Martinelli, & Piolino, 2012) is often invoked as a proposed mechanism for the efficacy of mindfulness-based interventions (Chiesa & Serretti, 2010).

However, this apparent neurophysiological overlap is starkly belied by clinical and phenomenological observation: whereas dissociation involves an amnestic exclusion of attention and a lack of integration of thought, mindfulness involves a directed quality of attention and a deidentification from fixed thoughts (Waelde, 2004). Indeed, it is precisely because the aim of many forms of meditation is to cultivate present-moment attention that meditation can be usefully employed as an intervention for trauma-related dissociation (Waelde, 2015). A possible caveat to this argument might be advanced from the small case-study literature of traumatized individuals who have inadvertently co-opted meditation as an avoidance mechanism, and for whom the experience of "mindfulness" is, in objective terms, more likely dissociative than mindful (Brown, 2009; Cashwell, Glosoff, & Hammond, 2010; Engler, 2003).

Such counterexamples aside, mindfulness, in principle, diverges from hypnosis in that while hypnosis is dissociative, mindfulness is integrative.

Imagery: prominent versus minimal

The role of visual imagery is a prominent feature of hypnosis. Indeed, hypnosis has been defined as controlled imagination (Nogrady, McConkey, & Perry, 1985), although hypnotizability and imagery ability are uncorrelated (Kogon et al., 1998). Imagery is, similarly, a feature of some forms of meditation, in particular Tibetan Buddhist meditation (Wallace, 1993; see Chapters 3 and 4), but is not a central aspect of other meditative traditions such as Zen or Vipassana. The role of visual imagery in hypnosis encompasses both visual imagination and the image of the subject's body. Suggestibility, or the use of imagination, is a prominent feature of hypnosis, in contrast to many forms of meditation that direct the meditator to let go of reified conceptualizations of experience and attend to the reality of phenomenological experience as it actually presents itself (Harrer, 2009).

Suggestibility, a hallmark of hypnotic trance, is central to the technique's clinical use. Hypnotic trance has been observed to function both as a natural response to trauma and as a trauma treatment. Hypnosis has been used in trauma treatment to access disturbing memories in a technique with close ostensible parallels to exposure treatment (Poon, 2009). Hypnotic states can mimic the phenomenology of conversion disorders and their prefrontal neurocognitive mechanisms (Bell et al., 2011); indeed, the utility of hypnosis as a means of inducing transient laboratory analogs of psychopathological states has led to the development of some novel studies in which hypnosis is used to create and study clinical syndromes, such as mirrored self-misidentification (Connors, Barnier, Coltheart, Cox, & Langdon, 2012) and other disorders (Nash & Wong, 2011). By contrast, suggestibility is typically absent from accounts of the treatment mechanisms of mindfulness-based interventions. The impact of mindfulness on emotion regulation has instead been theorized as the outcome of shifts in top-down and/or bottom-up regulation of limbic-based emotional dysregulation (Chiesa et al., 2013). However, the use of suggestibility in hypnosis does come close to overlapping conceptually with meditative forms that involve visualization of oneself as being transformed by meditation on a deity (Landaw & Weber, 1993; see also Chapter 3).

Visual components are common in hypnotherapy; for example, a focus on positive imagery or an imaginative exercise in which the therapist invites a depressed patient to picture a "door of forgiveness" (Alladin, 2010) or to enhance self-efficacy by exerting the imagination to conceive a non-depressed version of the hypnotic subject (Yapko, 2010). Some meditation techniques include directions to focus on an imagined visual object such as the image of white light; Tibetan Buddhist meditation can involve very complex visualizations that take years to fully realize through repeated practice (Kozhevnikov, Louchakova, Josipovic, & Motes, 2009; Landaw & Weber, 1993). Several other meditation forms, however, are based primarily on somatosensory rather than visual awareness (e.g., concentration on the breath); while open monitoring forms (e.g., Vipassana and Zen) involve the endeavor to develop a non-discriminative attitude to any sensory or cognitive percept that spontaneously arises, irrespective of modality.

In terms of neural markers, one PET (positron emission tomography) study showed that the hypnotic illusion of color activated neural regions involved in actual visual color perception (Kosslyn, Thompson, Costantini-Ferrando, Alpert, & Spiegel, 2000). In summary, imagery is a prominent feature of hypnosis but a minimal feature of mindfulness.

Agency: hidden observer versus no self

An important difference between hypnosis and mindfulness concerns their respective impact on the experience of agency and selfhood. Hilgard and colleagues reported that the experience of hypnotic analgesia featured the possibility for subjects of identifying a "hidden observer" who was capable of registering the experimentally induced pain despite its subjective absence in the hypnotic state (Hilgard, Morgan, & MacDonald, 1975). Some meditative states differ from hypnosis in this regard in that they involve an experience in which the subjective sense of first-person perspective or selfhood is significantly reduced, at times even to the point where the practitioner experiences a non-dualistic merger between the perceiving awareness and perceptual content (Austin, 1999, 2009; Josipovic, 2014). It has been suggested that the current taxonomy of meditative forms in the empirical literature, which involves a bifurcation between focused attention and open monitoring forms (Lutz et al., 2008), does not capture the non-dualistic dimension of some meditative experience, and that further research could thus profitably investigate the establishment of a non-duality scale to complement the present two-part taxonomy (Josipovic, 2010). The foregoing non-dualistic attenuation of separate selfhood is, by contrast, typically absent from reports of hypnotic states.

The impact of meditation on self networks has been proposed as a unifying framework to account for the impact of mindfulness on emotional dysregulation and its enhancement of compassion and ethical behavior (Vago & Silbersweig, 2012). Hypnosis has been used, clinically, to help depressed patients create a more positive identity (Yapko, 2010). Hypnosis has been proposed as a form of "self-referential thinking"; in contrast to meditation, which has been described as a state in which the separate self recedes from view and perceptual contents unfold in the absence of a witness (Brown et al., 1982).

One model proposed to describe the changes in agency in hypnosis differentiates two types of agency—pre-reflective and reflective—suggesting that the latter form recedes in hypnosis (Polito, Barnier, & Woody, 2013). This claim parallels evidence that meditation decouples two dissociable forms of self network—narrative and experiential (Dor-Ziderman, Berkovich-Ohana, Glicksohn, & Goldstein, 2013; Farb et al., 2007; Vago & Silbersweig, 2012; see also Chapter 20).

In summary, while both hypnosis and mindfulness involve intensified present- moment awareness, an impact on time perception and body awareness, and a feeling of effortlessness, they differ in the experience of agency. Hypnosis also involves powerful focal concentration that emphasizes intense awareness of the content of thought or perception in space, but may therefore decontextualize it temporally (e.g., hypnotic age regression) (Spiegel & Spiegel, 2004). In the absence of well-designed phenomenological comparisons, it is hard to strictly differentiate the respective changes in agency. A review of the literature indicates that hypnosis shares with some forms of mindfulness an experience of a "hidden observer" that witnesses perceptual content without involvement in that content. However, the full scope of meditative phenomenology may extend upon a non-dualistic spectrum, at the far point of which the witnessing awareness is further attenuated.

Conclusion

Hypnosis and mindfulness are neurocognitive and experiential phenomena that closely overlap in regard to their impact upon effort, attention, dissociation, imagination, and agency. Hypnosis and focused attention meditation share an experience of narrow absorbed attention marked by changes in executive control and alterations in default mode network activation. Visual imagery is a prominent feature of hypnosis but absent from mindfulness, with the exception of visualization-based meditation forms. A quality of effortlessness characterizes hypnosis and the experience of expert, but not novice, meditators. Hypnotizability and mindfulness are both traits, though the latter appears more contingent upon training than the former. The attenuation of an observing awareness appears to be common to both hypnosis and mindfulness, though the degree of attenuation may extend further on a non-dualistic spectrum in some forms of meditation.

In synthesis, it can be theorized that the hypnotic state replicates or closely parallels a form of hetero-induced focused attention mindfulness, with prominent visual elements and a moderate attenuation of agency. Mindfulness can, in turn, be theorized as a form of self-hypnosis, perhaps for beginners more than experienced meditators, insofar as novice meditators mirror a hypnotic top-down regulation of attention. At the same time, hypnosis and mindfulness can be broadly differentiated in terms of their positions on opposite ends, respectively, of the five dimensions of effort (trait versus practice), attention (narrow versus broad), awareness (dissociative versus integrative), visualization (prominent versus minimal), and agency (hidden observer versus no self). That is, hypnosis and mindfulness are unique states of consciousness with overlapping, yet distinct, experiential and neurophysiological features.

References

Alladin, A. (2010). Evidence-based hypnotherapy for depression. *International Journal of Clinical and Experimental Hypnosis*, **2**, 165–185. doi: 10.1080/00207140903523194

Austin, J. (1999). *Zen and the brain: toward an understanding of meditation and consciousness*. Cambridge, MA: MIT Press.

Austin, J. (2009). *Selfless insight: Zen and the meditative transformations of consciousness*. Cambridge, MA: MIT Press.

Baghdadi, G., & Nasrabadi, A. M. (2012). EEG phase synchronization during hypnosis induction. *Journal of Medical Engineering and Technology*, **36**(4), 222–229. doi: 10.3109/03091902.2012.668262

Bell, V., Oakley, D. A., Halligan, P. W., & Deeley, Q. (2011). Dissociation in hysteria and hypnosis: evidence from cognitive neuroscience. *Journal of Neurology, Neurosurgery and Psychiatry*, **82**(3), 332–339. doi: 10.1136/jnnp.2009.199158

Benedetti, F., Mayberg, H. S., Wager, T. D., Stohler, C. S., & Zubieta, J. K. (2005). Neurobiological mechanisms of the placebo effect. *Journal of Neuroscience*, **25**(45), 10390–10402. doi: 10.1523/JNEUROSCI.3458–05.2005

Bernheim, H. H. (1957). *Suggestive therapeutics; a treatise on the nature and uses of hypnotism*. Oxford, UK: Associated Booksellers.

Bliss, E. L. (1983). Multiple personalities, related disorders and hypnosis. *American Journal of Clinical Hypnosis*, **26**(2), 114–123. doi:10.1080/00029157.1983.10404151

Bodhi, B. (2000). *A comprehensive manual of Adhidhamma*. Seattle: BPS Pariyatti.

Bonshtein, U. (2012). Relational hypnosis. *International Journal of Clinical and Experimental Hypnosis*, **60**(4), 397–415. doi: 10.1080/00207144.2012.700613

Bowers, K. S. (1992). Imagination and dissociation in hypnotic responding. *International Journal of Clinical and Experimental Hypnosis*, **40**, 253–275.

Bowers, P. G. (1982–1983). On not trying so hard: effortless experiencing and its correlates. *Imagination, Cognition and Personality*, **2**, 3–13.

Brefczynski-Lewis, J. A., Lutz, A., Schaefer, H. S., Levinson, D. B., & Davidson, R. J. (2007). Neural correlates of attentional expertise in long-term meditation practitioners. *Proceedings of the National Academy of Sciences USA*, **104**(27), 11483–11488. doi: 10.1073/pnas.0606552104

Breuer, J. J., & Freud, S. S. (1936). Studies in hysteria. *Nervous and Mental Disorders Monograph Series*, **61**, ix.

Brown, C. (2009, April 26). Enlightenment therapy. *The New York Times*. Retrieved from http://www.nytimes.com

Brown, D., Forte, M., Rich, P., & Epstein, G. (1982). Phenomenological differences among self-hypnosis, mindfulness meditation, and imaging. *Imagination, Cognition and Personality*, **2**(4), 291–309.

Butler, L. D. (2006). Normative dissociation. *Psychiatric Clinics of North America*, **29**(1), 45–62. doi:10.1016/j.psc.2005.10.004

Butler, L. D., Koopman, C., Neri, E., Giese-Davis, J., Palesh, O., Thorne-Yocam, K. A., Spiegel, D. (2009). Effects of supportive-expressive group therapy on pain in women with metastatic breast cancer. *Health Psychology*, **28**(5), 579–587. doi: 2009–14439-009 [pii] 10.1037/a0016124

Butler, L. D., Symons, B. K., Henderson, S. L., Shortliffe, L. D., & Spiegel, D. (2005). Hypnosis reduces distress and duration of an invasive medical procedure for children. *Pediatrics*, **115**(1), 77–85.

Carmody, J., Baer, R. A., Lykins, E. B., & Olendzki, N. (2009). An empirical study of the mechanisms of mindfulness in a mindfulness-based stress reduction program. *Journal of Clinical Psychology*, **65**(6), 613–626. doi:10.1002/jclp.20579

Cashwell, C. S., Glosoff, H. L., & Hammond, C. (2010). Spiritual bypass: a preliminary investigation. *Counseling and Values*, **54**, 162–174.

Charcot, J. M. (1889). *Clinical lectures on diseases of the nervous system* (translated by Savill, T.). Retrieved from: http://books.google.com/books?id=DwQJAAAAIAAJ&pg=PP1#v=onepage&q&f=false

Chiesa, A., & Serretti, A. (2010). A systematic review of neurobiological and clinical features of mindfulness meditations. *Psychological Medicine*, **40**(8), 1239–1252. doi: 10.1017/S0033291709991747

Chiesa, A., Serretti, A., & Jakobsen, J. C. (2013). Mindfulness: top-down or bottom-up emotion regulation strategy? *Clinical Psychology Review*, **33**(1), 82–96. doi: 10.1016/j.cpr.2012.10.006

Connors, M. H., Barnier, A. J., Coltheart, M., Cox, R. E., & Langdon, R. (2012). Mirrored-self misidentification in the hypnosis laboratory: recreating the delusion from its component factors. *Cognitive Neuropsychiatry*, **17**(2), 151–176. doi: 10.1080/13546805.2011.582287

Corrigan, F. M. (2002). Mindfulness, dissociation, EMDR and the anterior cingulate cortex: a hypothesis. *Contemporary Hypnosis*, **19**, 8–17. doi:10.1002/ch.235

Deeley, Q., Oakley, D. A., Toone, B., Giampietro, V., Brammer, M. J., Williams, S. C., & Halligan, P. W. (2012). Modulating the default mode network using hypnosis. *International Journal of Clinical and Experimental Hypnosis*, **60**(2), 206–228. doi: 10.1080/00207144.2012.648070

Desbordes, G., Gard, T., Hoge, E. A., Hölzel, B. K., Kerr, C., Lazar, S. W., . . . Vago, D. R. (2014). Moving beyond mindfulness: defining equanimity as an outcome measure in meditation and contemplative research. *Mindfulness*, **6**(2), 356–372. doi:10.1007/s12671-013-0269-8

Dor-Ziderman, Y., Berkovich-Ohana, A., Glicksohn, J., & Goldstein, A. (2013). Mindfulness-induced selflessness: a MEG neurophenomenological study. *Frontiers in Human Neuroscience*, **7**, 582. doi: 10.3389/fnhum.2013.00582

Dunn, B. R., Hartigan, J. A., & Mikulas, W. L. (1999). Concentration and mindfulness meditations: unique forms of consciousness? *Applied Psychophysiology and Biofeedback*, **24**(3), 147–165.

Eberth, J., & Sedlmeier, P. (2012). The effects of mindfulness meditation: a meta-analysis. *Mindfulness*, **3**(3), 174–189. doi:10.1007/s12671-012-0101-x

Egner, T., Jamieson, G., & Gruzelier, J. (2005). Hypnosis decouples cognitive control from conflict monitoring processes of the frontal lobe. *Neuroimage*, **27**(4), 969–978.

Ellenberger, H. F. (1970). *The discovery of the unconscious: the history and evolution of dynamic psychiatry*. New York: Basic Books, Inc.

Engler.J (2003). Being somebody and being nobody: a re-examination of the understanding of self in psychoanalysis and Buddhism. In J. Safran (Ed.), *Psychoanalysis and Buddhism: an unfolding dialogue* (pp. 35–79). Boston: Wisdom Publications.

Evans, D. R., Eisenlohr-Moul, T. A., Button, D. F., Baer, R. A., & Segerstrom, S. C. (2014). Self-regulatory deficits associated with unpracticed mindfulness strategies for coping with acute pain. *Journal of Applied Social Psychology*, **44**(1), 23–30. doi:10.1111/jasp.12196

Farb, N. A., Segal, Z. V., Mayberg, H., Bean, J., McKeon, D., Fatima, Z., & Anderson, A. K. (2007). Attending to the present: mindfulness meditation reveals distinct neural modes of self-reference. *Social Cognitive and Affective Neuroscience*, **2**(4), 313–322. doi: 10.1093/scan/nsm030

Feldman, J. B. (2004). The neurobiology of pain, affect and hypnosis. *American Journal of Clinical Hypnosis*, **46**(3), 187–200.

Fenwick, P. B., Donaldson, S., Gillis, L., Bushman, J., Fenton, G. W., Perry, I., . . . Serafinowicz, H. (1977). Metabolic and EEG changes during transcendental meditation: an explanation. *Biological Psychology*, **5**(2), 101–118.

Feuerstein, G. (1998). *The yoga tradition: its history, literature, philosophy and practice*. Chino Valle, AZ: Holm Press.

Fox, K. C. R., Nijeboer, S., Dixon, M. L., Floman, J. L., Ellamil, M., Rumak, S. P., . . . Christoff, K. (2014). Is meditation associated with altered brain structure? A systematic review and meta-analysis of morphometric neuroimaging in meditation practitioners. *Neuroscience and Biobehavioral Reviews*, **43**, 48–73. doi:10.1016/j.neubiorev.2014.03.016

Freud, S. (1925). *An autobiographical study (vol. XX)* (translated by J. Strachey & A. Freud). London: Hogarth Press.

Goyal, M., Singh, S., Sibinga, E., Gould, N., Rowland-Seymour, A., Sharma, R., & . . . Haythornthwaite, J. (2014). Meditation programs for psychological stress and well-being: a systematic review and meta-analysis. *JAMA Internal Medicine*, **174**(3), 357–368. doi:10.1001/jamainternmed.2013.13018

Halsband, U., Mueller, S., Hinterberger, T., & Strickner, S. (2009). Plasticity changes in the brain in hypnosis and meditation. *Contemporary Hypnosis*, **26**(4), 194–215. doi:10.1002/ch.386

Hammond, D. (2005). An integrative, multi-factor conceptualization of hypnosis. *American Journal of Clinical Hypnosis*, **48**(2–3), 131–135. doi:10.1080/00029157.2005.10401508

Harrer, M. E. (2009). Mindfulness and the mindful therapist: possible contributions to hypnosis. *Contemporary Hypnosis*, **26**(4), 234–244. doi:10.1002/ch.388

Hasegawa, H., & Jamieson, G. A. (2002). Conceptual issues in hypnosis research: explanations, definitions and the state/non-state debate. *Contemporary Hypnosis*, **19**(3), 103.

Hayes, S. C., Luoma, J. B., Bond, F. W., Masuda, A., & Lillis, J. (2006). Acceptance and commitment therapy: model, processes and outcomes. *Behavior Research and Therapy*, **44**(1), 1–25. doi:10.1016/j.brat.2005.06.006

Hayes, S. C., Strosahl, K. D., & Wilson, K. G. (1999). *Acceptance and commitment therapy: an experiential approach to behavior change*. New York, NY: Guilford Press.

Hilgard, E. R. (1965). *Hypnotic susceptibility*. New York: Harcourt, Brace & World.

Hilgard, E. R., Morgan, A. H., & Macdonald, H. (1975). Pain and dissociation in the cold pressor test: a study of hypnotic analgesia with "hidden reports" through automatic key pressing and automatic talking. *Journal of Abnormal Psychology*, **84**(3), 280–289. doi:10.1037/h0076654

Hilgard, J. R., & Hilgard, E. R. (1979). Assessing hypnotic responsiveness in a clinical setting: a multi-item clinical scale and its advantages over single-item scales. *International Journal of Clinical and Experimental Hypnosis*, **27**(2), 134–150. doi:10.1080/00207147908407553

Hoeft, F., Gabrieli, J. D., Whitfield-Gabrieli, S., Haas, B. W., Bammer, R., Menon, V., & Spiegel, D. (2012). Functional brain basis of hypnotizability. *Archives of General Psychiatry*, **69**(10), 1064–1072. doi: 10.1001/archgenpsychiatry.2011.2190

Janet, P. P. (1920). *The major symptoms of hysteria* (2nd edn.). Oxford, UK: Macmillan.

Josipovic, Z. (2010). Duality and nonduality in meditation research. *Consciousness and Cognition*, **19**(4), 1119–1121. doi:10.1016/j.concog.2010.03.016

Josipovic, Z. (2014). Neural correlates of nondual awareness in meditation. *Annals of the New York Academy of Sciences*, **1307**, 9–18.

Kardiner, A, & Spiegel, H. (1947). *War stress and neurotic illness*. New York: Hoeber.

Kasamatsu, A., & Hirai, T. (1966). An electroencephalographic study on the Zen meditation (Zazen). *Folia Psychiatrica et Neurologica Japonica*, **20**(4), 315–336.

Kogon, M., Jasiukaitis, P., Berardi, A., Gupta, M., Kosslyn, S., & Spiegel, D. (1998). Imagery and hypnotizability revisited. *International Journal of Clinical and Experimental Hypnosis*, **46**(4), 363–370.

Kosslyn, S. M., Thompson, W. L., Costantini-Ferrando, M. F., Alpert, N. M., & Spiegel, D. (2000). Hypnotic visual illusion alters color processing in the brain. *American Journal of Psychiatry*, **157**(8), 1279–1284.

Kozhevnikov, M., Louchakova, O., Josipovic, Z., & Motes, M. A. (2009). The enhancement of visuospatial processing efficiency through Buddhist deity meditation. *Psychological Science*, **20**(5), 645–653.

Landaw, J., & Weber, J. (1993). *Images of enlightenment: Tibetan art in practice*. Ithaca, NY: Snow Lion Publications.

Lang, E. V., Benotsch, E. G., Fick, L. J., Lutgendord, S., Berbaum, M. L., Berbaum, K. S., & Spiegel, D. (2000). Adjunctive non-pharmacological analgesia for invasive medical procedures: a randomised trial. *The Lancet*, **355**, 1486–1490.

Lanius, R. A., Brand, B., Vermetten, E., Frewen, P. A., & Spiegel, D. (2012). The dissociative subtype of posttraumatic stress disorder: rationale, clinical and neurobiological evidence, and implications. *Depression and Anxiety*, **29**(8), 701–708.doi:10.1002/da.21889

Lanius, R. A., Vermetten, E., Loewenstein, R. J., Brand, B., Schmahl, C., Bremner, J. D., & Spiegel, D. (2010). Emotion modulation in PTSD: clinical and neurobiological evidence for a dissociative subtype. *American Journal of Psychiatry*, **167**, 640–647. doi:10.1176/appi.ajp.2009.09081168

Lutz, A., McFarlin, D. R., Perlman, D. M., Salomons, T. V., & Davidson, R. J. (2013). Altered anterior insula activation during anticipation and experience of painful stimuli in expert meditators. *Neuroimage*, **64**, 538–546. doi: 10.1016/j.neuroimage.2012.09.030

Lutz, A., Slagter, H. A., Dunne, J. D., & Davidson, R. J. (2008). Attention regulation and monitoring in meditation. *Trends in Cognitive Sciences*, **12**(4), 163–169. doi: 10.1016/j.tics.2008.01.005

Lynn, S. J., & Green, J. P. (2011). The sociocognitive and dissociation theories of hypnosis: toward a rapprochement. *International Journal of Clinical and Experimental Hypnosis*, **59**(3), 277–293. doi: 10.1080/00207144.2011.570652

Mascaro, J. S., Rilling, J. K., Negi, L. T., & Raison, C. L. (2013). Pre-existing brain function predicts subsequent practice of mindfulness and compassion meditation. *Neuroimage*, **69**, 35–42. doi: 10.1016/j.neuroimage.2012.12.021

Melloni, M., Sedeño, L., Couto, B., Reynoso, M., Gelormini, C., Favaloro, R., . . . Ibanez, A. (2013). Preliminary evidence about the effects of meditation on interoceptive sensitivity and social cognition. *Behavioral and Brain Functions*, **9**, 47. doi:10.1186/1744-9081-9-47

Nash, J. D., & Newberg, A. (2013). Toward a unifying taxonomy and definition for meditation. *Frontiers in Psychology*, **4**, 1–18. doi:10.3389/fpsyg.2013.00806

Nash, M. R., & Wong, A. (2011). Hypnosis in the laboratory creates a window on psychopathology. *International Journal of Clinical and Experimental Hypnosis*, **59**(4), 469–476. doi:10.1080/00207144.2011.594752

Nogrady, H., McConkey, K. M., & Perry, C. (1985). Enhancing visual memory: trying hypnosis, trying imagination, trying again. *Journal of Abnormal Psychology*, **94**, 195–204.

Polito, V., Barnier, A. J., & Woody, E. Z. (2013). Developing the sense of agency rating scale (SOARS): an empirical measure of agency disruption in hypnosis. *Consciousness and Cognition*, **22**(3), 684–696. doi: 10.1016/j.concog.2013.04.003

Poon, M. W. (2009). Hypnosis for complex trauma survivors: four case studies. *American Journal of Clinical Hypnosis*, **51**(3), 263–271.

Rainville, P., Duncan, G. H., Price, D. D., Carrier, B., & Bushnell, M. C. (1997). Pain affect encoded in human anterior cingulate but not somatosensory cortex. *Science*, **277**, 968–971.

Rainville, P., Hofbauer, R. K., Bushnell, M. C., Duncan, G. H., & Price, D. D. (2002). Hypnosis modulates activity in brain structures involved in the regulation of consciousness. *Journal of Cognitive Neuroscience*, **14**(6), 887–901.

Raz, A., Shapiro, T., Fan, J., & Posner, M. I. (2002). Hypnotic suggestion and the modulation of stroop interference. *Archives of General Psychiatry*, **59**(12), 1155–1161.

Sadler, P., & Woody, E. Z. (2006). Does the more vivid imagery of high hypnotizables depend on greater cognitive effort? A test of dissociation and social-cognitive theories of hypnosis. *International Journal of Clinical and Experimental Hypnosis*, **54**(4), 372–391. doi: 10.1080/00207140600856715

Sperduti, M., Martinelli, P., & Piolino, P. (2012). A neurocognitive model of meditation based on activation likelihood estimation (ALE) meta-analysis. *Consciousness and Cognition*, **21**, 269–276. doi:10.1016/j.concog.2011.09.019

Spiegel, D. (1981). Vietnam grief work using hypnosis. *American Journal of Clinical Hypnosis*, 24(1), 33–40.

Spiegel, H. (2007). The neural trance: a new look at hypnosis. *International Journal of Clinical and Experimental Hypnosis*, **55**(4), 387–410. doi: 781772265 [pii]

Spiegel, H, & Spiegel, D. (2004). *Trance and treatment: clinical uses of hypnosis*. Washington DC: American Psychiatric Publishing.

Stutman, R. K., & Bliss, E. L. (1985). Posttraumatic stress disorder, hypnotizability, and imagery. *The American Journal of Psychiatry*, **142**(6), 741–743.

Taylor, V. A., Daneault, V., Grant, J., Scavone, G., Breton, E., Roffe-Vidal, S., . . . Beauregard, M. (2013). Impact of meditation training on the default mode network during a restful state. *Social Cognitive and Affective Neuroscience*, **8**(1), 4–14. doi: 10.1093/scan/nsr087

Teper, R., & Inzlicht, M. (2013). Meditation, mindfulness and executive control: the importance of emotional acceptance and brain-based performance monitoring. *Social Cognitive and Affective Neuroscience*, **8**(1), 85–92. doi: 10.1093/scan/nss045 doi:10.1016/j.concog.2010.01.007

Vago, D. R., & Silbersweig, D. A. (2012). Self-awareness, self-regulation, and self-transcendence (S-ART): a framework for understanding the neurobiological mechanisms of mindfulness. *Frontiers in Human Neuroscience*, **6**, 296. doi: 10.3389/fnhum.2012.00296

Vandenberg, B. (1998). Hypnosis and human development: interpersonal influence of intrapersonal processes. *Child Development*, 69(1), 262–267.

Vermetten, E., & Bremner, J. (2004). Functional brain imaging and the induction of traumatic recall: a cross-correlational review between neuroimaging and hypnosis. *International Journal of Clinical and Experimental Hypnosis*, **52**(3), 280–312. doi:10.1080/0020714049052352

Waelde, L. C. (2004). Dissociation and meditation. *Journal of Trauma and Dissociation*, 5, 147–162. doi:10.1300/J229v05n02_08

Waelde, L. C. (2015). Mindfulness and meditation for trauma-related dissociation. In V. Follette, J. Briere, J. Hopper, D. Rozelle, & D. Rome (Eds.), *Mindfulness-oriented interventions for trauma: integrating contemplative practices* (pp. 301–313). New York, NY: Guilford Press.

Waelde, L. C., Thompson, J. M., Robinson, A., & Iwanicki, S. (in submission). *Trauma therapists' training, personal practice, and clinical applications of mindfulness and meditation*.

Wager, T. D., Atlas, L. Y., Leotti, L. A., & Rilling, J. K. (2011). Predicting individual differences in placebo analgesia: contributions of brain activity during anticipation and pain experience. *Journal of Neuroscience*, **31**(2), 439–452. doi: 10.1523/JNEUROSCI.3420–3410.2011

Wallace, B. A. (1993). *Tibetan Buddhism from the ground up*. Boston: Wisdom Publications.

Weisberg, M. B. (2008). 50 years of hypnosis in medicine and clinical health psychology: a synthesis of cultural crosscurrents. *American Journal of Clinical Hypnosis*, **51**(1), 13–27.

Yapko, M. D. (2010). Hypnosis in the treatment of depression: an overdue approach for encouraging skillful mood management. *International Journal of Clinical and Experimental Hypnosis*, **58**(2), 137–146. doi: 10.1080/00207140903523137

Zeidan, F., Grant, J. A., Brown, C. A., McHaffie, J. G., & Coghill, R. C. (2012). Mindfulness meditation-related pain relief: evidence for unique brain mechanisms in the regulation of pain. *Neuroscience Letters*, **520**(2), 165–173. doi: 10.1016/j.neulet.2012.03.082

Zeig, J. K. (1980). Symptom prescription and Ericksonian principles of hypnosis and psychotherapy. *American Journal of Clinical Hypnosis*, **23**(1), 16–22.

Chapter 9

Meditation: some kind of (self-)hypnosis?

A deeper look

Charles T. Tart

Abstract

This chapter aims to offer some answers to the question of the relationship between meditation and hypnosis, because the author believes little seems to have been done since the crude equation of the two decades ago. The chapter clarifies the psychological nature of both hypnosis and meditation, and provides some general methodological points about studying and using altered states of consciousness (ASCs). In the process, a clear definition of what is meant by hypnosis and meditation for this discussion is included. The chapter deals with the traditional use of meditation for spiritual growth purposes, about which the current blossoming of research has not revealed much. The chapter aims to distil, in an accessible, informal manner, the author's overall understanding, gathered over more than 50 years of studying a wide variety of ASCs and spiritual systems, as well as a decade of work in experimental hypnosis.

Introduction

All through my career, I have frequently been asked about the relationship between meditation and hypnosis, and I suspect practically all of us involved with hypnosis have also had to deal with variations of that question. The standard answer, the old answer—which has been around at least 50 years, and probably a lot longer—put forward by Western psychological and psychiatric authorities, was that meditation was some form of self-induced hypnosis. I am going to focus on comparing meditation with hypnosis per se, and not look at the "self" part of self-hypnosis, partly for lack of space, and partly because our knowledge of self-hypnosis is much less than that of hypnosis in general.

Until the rising popularity of meditation in our culture, beginning in the last decade or so, when we thought of meditation we visualized, and still often visualize, something like a Hindu yogi, sitting in a cross-legged, full lotus posture, doing something mysterious called "meditating." This was probably the idea of meditation held by most of those who explained it as some form of hypnosis. Sometimes explicitly, often implicitly, meditation was thought to be something done by foreigners, and there was probably something "schizoid" about it. If you hear strong cultural ethnocentrism and prejudice in that view, there was plenty of it. Throughout my career, I have always been amazed at how insensitive we psychologists are to our cultural biases (for a deeper discussion of these historical biases in the study of hypnosis and meditation, see Chapter 2 by Anne Harrington).

I think that attempting to explain meditation as hypnosis was partly a genuine attempt to make objective, scientific sense of it, given what (little) was known about meditation, and partly an attempt to explain meditation *away*. We have to remember that the general cultural background when these explanations were first put forward was that of the British conquest of India, of the West "civilizing" the East and trying to bring its people up to what we believed was our advanced level. Historically, from what I have read, Westerners were first fascinated by the apparent mental science of the East, especially what they found in India. However, normally, people refuse to give too much status to those they are conquering, so we had a cultural need to subrate their knowledge as inferior to our knowledge, to explain it *away*, while appearing to be scientific as part of our own exalted self-image. Thus, we arrived at the equation *meditation = hypnosis*, or, to elaborate on some of the implications, meditation was *nothing but* a form of (self)- hypnosis. This equation was made with the implicit assumption that we thoroughly understood hypnosis and self-hypnosis—an assumption which I think we can seriously question, even today. Also, there was another negative quality implicit in that equation, namely, the popular (if erroneous) association of hypnotizability with gullibility, with having some kind of weak will.

What I am going to try to do in this chapter is to suggest some better answers to the question of the relationship between meditation and hypnosis, because I do not think much has been done since the crude equation of the two. I want to clarify the psychological nature of both hypnosis and meditation, and make some general methodological points about studying and using altered states of consciousness (ASCs). I will define, more clearly, what I mean by hypnosis and meditation for the purposes of this chapter's comparisons. Note that I am not dealing here with the recent explosion of what I might call "meditation light" as merely a popular technique for stress reduction, although it is very useful, or the recent neurophysiological studies of meditation. I am dealing with the traditional use of meditation for spiritual growth purposes, and, as much as I find the current blossoming of research fascinating, it has not revealed much about the deep objectives and possible results of such practices. I also feel attempts to explain meditation away as nothing but brain states is scientifically inadequate, as detailed elsewhere (Tart, 2009).

Why can I add something? I started with just as little knowledge as our predecessors, but I did have an intensive research background in modern hypnosis, which widened into some understanding of ASCs in general. In particular, as I studied the exotic forms of consciousness, the altered states, I developed a sensitivity to how much we take for granted about our ordinary, "normal" consciousness, and how little we actually know about it. On the meditation side, I have a strong theoretical and scientific interest in the nature of "meditation," plus some decades of personal experience, the "inside" of meditation, and have had instruction in meditation from a variety of teachers. My experience is especially strong in how to do meditation incorrectly and, thus, the various difficulties of "meditation," as I do not have a natural talent for it! So while I have been meditating in various ways for many years, I do not consider myself particularly adept at it, but, on the other hand, compared to people who have not studied and practiced meditation extensively, I have sufficient understanding of it that one of my recent books, *Mind science: meditation training for practical people*, is a useful guide to how to meditate, especially for people of a rational and/or scientific temperament.[1] In addition, I teach an online workshop on meditation and mindfulness in everyday life, several times a year (www.GlideWing.com), as well as, until my recent retirement, a classroom-based graduate course at Sofia University (www.Sofia.edu, formerly the Institute of Transpersonal Psychology).

Comparing hypnosis and meditation: three major problems

Ambiguity of terms

The first problem lies in the ambiguity of the terms "hypnosis" and "meditation." Both terms have been used to cover such a variety of mental practices and resultant altered states, by various people, that anything that is described as hypnosis by one authority might well be described as meditation by another authority, and vice versa. Ambiguity increases even further when a teacher is leading a guided meditation. A primary characteristic of meditation practice is that the meditator does all the work, but in hypnosis, a subject is relatively passive and lets the hypnotist do the guiding, the work.

As an example of loose usage of the terms, when I first became interested in meditation in the early 1960s, I looked it up in an authoritative psychological dictionary, and I found it was defined as "serious thinking." In one way I was pleased with this, since, having done a lot of thinking in my life, did not that mean I must already be an accomplished meditator? On the other hand, it is ridiculously general to define meditation as simply serious thinking, although some kinds of directed thinking are indeed called meditation in some spiritual systems and in general linguistic usage. So, the caveat from this first problem is that anything I say about meditation and hypnosis can be contradicted from people's experience in the way these terms are used by people or from authoritative literature! However, the specific picture I give here should, I hope, be useful for scientific research and application.

State-specific knowledge

The second problem is that of what I have named *state-specific knowledge*. I do not have space to go into that in any detail here, but I have made the point elsewhere (Tart, 1972, 1975) that various ASCs have useful points and drawbacks, strengths and weaknesses, and have specific kinds of knowledge and understandings that can only really be understood, appreciated, and worked with adequately *within* that ASC. This is certainly true for some potential outcomes of some kinds of meditation, although I am not sure how true it is for hypnosis. Because of this, I long ago (Tart, 1972; updated in Tart, 1998b) proposed that we create *state-specific sciences*, each unique to a particular ASC.[2] What

---

[1] Many teachers have patiently taught me various aspects of meditative practices, but I want to particularly acknowledge and thank lama Tarthang Tulku, Shinzen Young, lama Sogyal Rinpoche, and lama Tsoknyi Rinpoche.

[2] There are also important questions, raised in Tart (1972 and 1998d), as to whether the traditional spiritual systems that practice meditation are state-specific *sciences* or state-specific *technologies*—sciences in that basic questions are an important focus of inquiry, with foundational aspects of the practice system open to question and revision, versus technologies in that the foundational ideas about the practice are not questioned and are taken as faith, although there can be technical inquiry about how to best practice within the system. Some of the current neurophysiological research on meditation, for example, is an application of state-specific (makes good sense in "normal" consciousness) technology to explain meditation in mainstream, physicalistic science terms, rather than questioning the validity of that metaphysical and epistemological approach from, say, a meditative perspective.

we need to remember for our purposes here is that some of the most important aspects of meditation probably cannot really be comprehended within our ordinary state of consciousness, and fuller understanding will require our ordinary state knowledge to be supplemented with appropriate state-specific knowledge.

Unquestioning acceptance of the "normal" state

The third problem is the widespread, implicit assumption that the everyday state of consciousness we find ourselves in is "normal," is "just there naturally," and is "inherently superior to all ASCs." That is, we assume that the everyday knowledge base we work from and its thinking processes, the state of ordinary consciousness that we are presumably in while reading this, is sound, is well understood, and is inherently superior to mental functioning in all other states. While there is some truth in this assumption, there is a lot of blindness in it, and it leads to a great deal of arrogance and culture boundedness, especially to the degree that it remains implicit and, so, unexamined. I cannot do much more in this brief space than make that assumption conscious and explicit, but it will often give us trouble in dealing with hypnosis and meditation, and other ASCs.

Background to meditation and hypnosis comparison

As some background to start a comparison of meditation and hypnosis, I would first wrestle with an aspect of that third assumption, that ordinary consciousness is just there, is "natural." More than half a century of doing research has convinced me that ordinary consciousness is an *active construction*, it is not simply there. It is an active, *semi-arbitrary* construction, the habitual "shape" and "style" of which is very much determined by personal history and the culture one is raised in, as well as basic biologically determined qualities. Right now, even if you think you are in a relatively calm state, just reading this, in point of fact your mind is working quite hard to create and maintain the state we think of as ordinary consciousness. However, we are so used to doing this work, and it is so automatized that we almost never notice how much work we are doing. Indeed, one of the most interesting aspects of some meditative states that produce mental quiet is that, for the first time, you acquire a baseline from which you can see how incredibly active ordinary consciousness is.

Again, I can only touch on this for lack of space, but my *States of consciousness* (Tart, 1975) goes into considerable detail. If you are curious, you can also read some of the accounts by scientists of their ASC experiences on my The Archives of Scientists' Transcendent Experiences (TASTE) website (www.issc-taste.org), or technical journal articles on my main website (blog.paradigm-sys.com) (articles on my systems approach to states of consciousness that will elaborate these points). The bottom line for us here is that ordinary consciousness is not just there (and it is not necessarily inherently superior), but it is a semi-arbitrary construction and a very active system. Indeed, I long ago gave up using the phrases "normal consciousness" or "ordinary consciousness" in other than casual communications, and coined the term *consensus consciousness* when I want to be more technically and psychologically precise. Consensus consciousness was developed and induced over many years, and the "induction procedure" for it, if we can call ordinary development that, is far more powerful and thorough that anything we ever do with hypnosis. A detailed analysis of this induction procedure is presented in Chapter 10, "Consensus trance: the sleep of everyday life" in my book, *Waking up* (Tart, 1986). I will use the term "consensus consciousness" from now on to refer to the state in which we spend most of our time.

Systems approach to consciousness

Figure 9.1 is an overview of my systems approach to consciousness, which has been guiding my research and understanding of consciousness in general and of ASCs for most of my career. The details shown are not important for our purposes here, so just glance at it. This approach is both reductionistic and analytic on the one hand, and allows for emergent system properties from the activities of the psychological subsystems and processes on the other hand. The psychological subsystems shown are nothing absolute but, rather, pragmatic representations of the major areas of psychological functioning that we need to understand in order to make sense of both ASCs and consensus consciousness, given our current level of understanding.[3] Some of those subsystems include things such as *exteroception*, our senses for taking in information about the external world, *interception*, our sensing of our body and internal processes, *input processing*, to account for the enormous amount of largely automated processing that goes on before sensory perceptions reach consciousness.

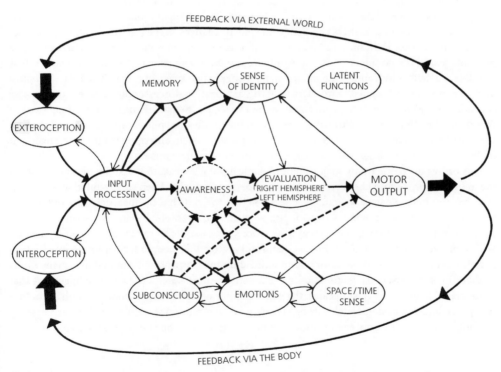

Fig. 9.1 Tart's systems approach to consciousness: major subsystems and information flow.

---

[3] Those inclined may speculate on how these psychological functions correlate with or are at least partially based in brain functions. Always a fascinating quest, this is not necessary for our current emphasis on the psychology of consciousness, meditation, and hypnosis.

Figure 9.1 represents the subsystems interacting in a particular way (arrows showing major information flow routes) to illustrate a fact of importance to us here, namely, that *any state of consciousness is stabilized*, and stabilized by multiple forces or processes. Consensus consciousness, for example, is stabilized by various kinds of feedback control. When various aspects of psychological functioning start to get too far from their normative range in which they function and help maintain the overall state, active correction measures are applied, *feedback stabilization*. Also, and especially important for our discussion, consensus consciousness (or any state of consciousness) is stabilized by what I called *loading stabilization*: our basic awareness is used up, absorbed, as it were, so it is not free to go in directions which might destabilize the state of consciousness you are currently in. The constant thinking which is a hallmark of ordinary consciousness, for example, thinking which runs along familiar lines and which leads to familiar, "normal" emotions and actions, uses up most of our awareness capacity and so stabilizes consensus consciousness. Similarly, consciousness is loaded by receiving lots of familiar sensory inputs from our exteroceptors, and lots of familiar bodily inputs from our interoceptors. Interfering with the stabilization processes is one of the primary ways we work to induce an altered state.

Figure 9.2 shows, in diagrammatic form, the pattern process of induction of any altered state. The baseline state is here represented as a pile of various shaped objects, representing subsystems and processes, a pile whose "shape" is stable in the ordinary gravitational field, to represent the fact that a state of consciousness can persist in spite of changes in the environment. If there were a sudden loud noise right now, for example, you might experience a momentary startle, but you probably would not go into an ASC—it would be very poor engineering to have any state be that unstable. To deliberately induce an *altered* state, we apply two kinds of forces. The first, *disruptive forces*, are primarily designed to interfere with the stabilization processes of the baseline state. The second, *patterning forces*, are primarily designed to shape the nature of the desired new state.[4] Figure 9.2 shows an unstable, transition period in the middle, the pile coming apart, and then, in the fourth panel, a new "shape" of consciousness, the new system emerging from a rearrangement of the subsystems of consciousness—*if* the induction procedure works.

This brings us to one of my major methodological points: we cannot assume that just because the induction procedure has been presented to a person that it has been successful, that an altered state has resulted. We have to actually assess whether the ASC has been successfully induced, is present. Saying that someone is in a meditative state, for example, because they sat down in a certain position and were given certain instructions is an excellent way to introduce major noise and error variance into meditation research. It mixes together people for whom the meditation practice did not work with those for whom it did and those for whom it resulted in varying kinds of alterations in consciousness functioning. The same caution applies to hypnosis: to assume that someone is "hypnotized" just because the experimenter or therapist has gone through an induction procedure can be completely wrong. This kind of assumption was often made in experimental studies, and has introduced enormous amounts of noise into our knowledge of hypnosis.[5]

---

[4] Sometimes, the same psychological or physical procedure can be both a disruptive and a patterning force.

[5] Throughout my career, many investigators have had high hopes that we will soon have reliable physiological indicators of whether a person is hypnotized, and to what degree, and whether someone is in a certain meditative ASC or not. Such a development will be very useful if it happens, but it may not. You can measure variations in the speed of an automobile engine, for example, but that tells you very little of what the driver is thinking about. I would not delay or abandon development of more useful psychological/experiential indicators based on the hope of physiological indicators.

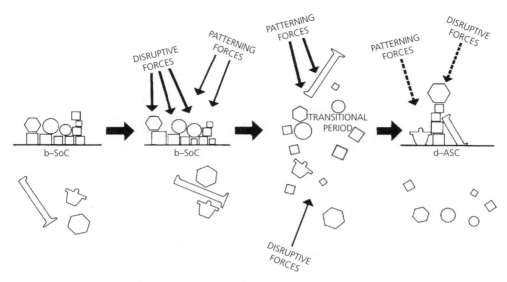

Fig. 9.2 Induction of an altered state of consciousness (ASC).

Looking at induction this way, it is important to realize that a *formal induction technique*, designed to induce an altered state, *never works in isolation*. For example, sometimes when I am lecturing to students about ASC induction, I stand in front of the blackboard, saying nothing, and start drawing a large circle with chalk, going over and over the circle, around and around. When I finally tell the students I am showing them one of the world's most powerful techniques for inducing an ASC, they look at me blankly. However, if you were an Eskimo, this is a traditional induction method for producing a shamanistic ASC, a state (or states) that, when the induction works, is very powerful.

Even techniques we think of as primarily physiological are strongly affected by their social, psychological, and expectational context. In looking at the old literature on the use of marijuana in medicine around the beginning of the twentieth century, for instance, active extracts of it were used in a wide variety of doses for a wide variety of ailments, but the patients almost never spoke to their physicians of any ASC resulting from this marijuana use. They took the medicine the doctor gave them to get rid of their cough or ease their pain, and if their minds started feeling funny, they shrugged those effects off and got on with lives. Physiological effects that were the results of the drug ingestion occurred, but unless combined with appropriate psychological forces, had little or no effect on consciousness.

To elaborate on the importance of context in meditation or hypnosis, Figure 9.3 shows various factors that may affect the outcome of any particular meditation or hypnosis session. This figure is adapted from my phenomenological study of marijuana intoxication (Tart, 1971), substituting a drawing of a yogi meditating for a user smoking marijuana that was in the earlier study. In both cases, if you do not know the nature and intensity of these various contextual factors, you probably cannot understand whether an ASC occurs as a result of the induction practice and its nature.

To repeat and emphasize, the *context* of induction technique is always important. You approach an induction technique as a member of a particular historical culture, and you approach it with

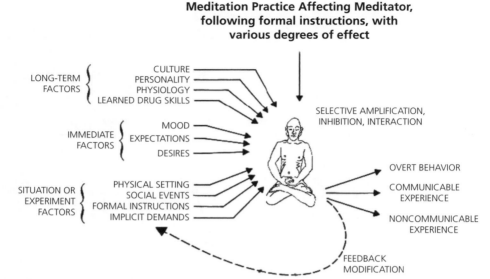

Fig. 9.3 Factors affecting induction and nature of meditative and hypnotic states.

your *consensus* consciousness. That is, the assumptions and values of your culture are deeply embedded in the various automated functionings of your everyday consciousness. You have immediate expectations of what the induction technique will do to you, and you have expectations about the long-term consequences of having the technique applied. Indeed, I would say that in many cases, *the largely implicit expectational context will have a lot more to do with what happens in an experiment or practical application of hypnosis or meditation than the specific induction procedure or specific instructions given.* I stress this because, historically, in our insecurity as the young science of psychology, in our wanting to be "real scientists," our wanting to be "objective," we often trivialized our research, looking at the easy external aspects of behavior but ignoring what was important, what was unique to developing a psychology, a science of the psyche, of the mind. I sometimes envy my colleagues in the "easy" sciences, like physics or chemistry, where their mood or their subject matter's "mood" (objects do not come into the lab in moods, people do) has no effect on experimental outcomes. However, we deal in psychology and it is a hard science, a difficult science, and that is just the way it is!

Having discussed background factors, you may wonder where I am going in the rest of this chapter. First, I am going to describe three states of consciousness, beginning with a kind of "pure" or "model" case of the hypnotic state, and then two models of the most common and fundamental types of meditative practices and states. Again, in the real world, there are many variations of these, all described as "hypnosis" or "meditation," so exceptions to what I describe will always exist, but, hopefully, my describing model states will focus our discussion. Second, I am going to look at the variability of the contexts in which hypnosis and meditation are used, to give us a more specific understanding of how different ASCs or phenomena within states might result from the effects of these contexts. Third, I am going to look at the qualities of these selected, model cases of hypnosis and meditative states and try to be fairly specific about major differences between them.

By the time we finish doing this, we will probably have lost the forest for the trees with all that detail, so I will back out and take a wider look at what I think is a general and deep difference between hypnosis and meditation. Hopefully, all this can guide research or applications and help us learn to give a much more sophisticated and useful answer to the question of the similarities and differences between meditation and hypnosis than the old equation that meditation is some kind of hypnosis.

Deep hypnosis: fading of the consensus reality orientation

The model of a hypnotic state I am going to focus on is one characterized by a general fading and harnessing of the important and pervasive activity of what I have called the consensus reality orientation (CRO). I was inspired to develop this concept by Ronald Shor's seminal work on three dimensions of hypnotic depth (Shor, 1959, 1962). Shor theorized about fading of the generalized reality orientation (GRO), all that knowledge about how things ordinarily should be that is instantly ready to inform and condition our perceptions, thoughts, feelings, and actions. This largely automated evaluative activity pervades and shapes consensus consciousness. As the GRO/CRO becomes relatively inactive with successful hypnotic induction, a suggestion to a deeply hypnotized person is perceived in isolation, as it were, rather than automatically evaluated (and probably devalued) as it might be in consensus consciousness. I have renamed this concept the *consensus* reality orientation, as a reminder that what is "normal" or "ordinary" for general consciousness for a particular culture can be very specific to that culture.

So, our idealized model of a deep hypnotic state is one of mental quiet and a heightened receptivity to suggestions that are not automatically evaluated by the subject's CRO. A suggestion given in an ordinary waking state that the subject's outstretched arm is very heavy and being pulled downward by a special force (e.g., in consensus consciousness) would likely be subjected to immediate CRO evaluation (perhaps along the lines of "Of course it's heavy, that's from muscle fatigue, what's the big deal?"), greatly weakening its effectiveness. In a deep hypnotic state, on the other hand, the CRO is relatively inactive, so the suggestion is simply accepted without questioning.

The CRO is also manifested in the constant background thinking and feeling—and remember that a lot of what we call "perception" is really a kind of automated thinking that can be influenced by the CRO—that goes on all the time in consensus consciousness. Everything we perceive and think about is subjected to automatic, often implicit questions like "What is it?", "How does it fit?", "What are normal values for this situation?", "What is in it for me?", "What should I do next?", "Should I approach or avoid it, embrace it or resist it?". This constant background activity of the CRO constitutes a major stabilizing activity, *loading stabilization*, as I spoke about in slightly different terms earlier.

When a subject is deeply hypnotized in the model sense I am defining here, Shor's trance dimension, they are awake and alert, and that alertness includes a particular sensitivity, a rapport, with the hypnotist. Otherwise, the subject's mind is quiet and idling until specifically stimulated. A typical answer to the question of "What are you thinking about?" addressed to a deeply hypnotized (in this sense) subject is "Nothing." The subject is highly suggestible, the suggested effect is experienced as experientially real. Shor, of course, postulated other important possible dimensions of hypnotic depth (role playing involvement and archetypal regression), but, for our model case here, we will consider a person to be deeply hypnotized in that the CRO is not active and he or she is highly suggestible.

Quieting (concentrative, shamatha) meditation

The first basic type of meditation I want to talk about I am going to call *quieting meditation*. It is also frequently referred to as *concentrative meditation*, and a technical Buddhist term for it is *shamatha meditation*. The basic practice is to mentally focus on a selected concentration point and *rest* the mind there. A traditional concentration point, for example, is the breath, either in terms of the movement of the belly or in terms of the warming and cooling sensations as air goes in and out of the nostrils. One is instructed to put attention there, to continually sense this focus point, and, if you discover that your mind has wandered, to gently bring it back to the focus point.

Our prejudice in Western psychology, going back to William James and perhaps earlier, has long been that it is impossible to do this kind of focus for more than a few seconds. That certainly seems to be the case in many peoples' ordinary experience, and was my own experience for a long time when I started to attempt this kind of quieting meditation—but remember, we "ordinary" people have never been trained to concentrate in this way. Concentrating in this way, for even a few seconds, is quite different from the constant, wandering mental activity characteristic of consensus consciousness, an activity that, as we have seen, also helps stabilize consensus consciousness. As one gets more skilled at this type of quieting meditation, thoughts and feelings become less "loud" and intrusive, less likely to grab attention and carry one away, less frequent, and intervals of mental quiet between thoughts can be experienced (and quietly enjoyed).

Why do quieting meditation? Importantly, learning to concentrate is an essential requirement for many other meditative actions. Further, an analogy to illustrate its value, and one that is commonly used in the East, is that our mind is like a pond of muddy water. There is a great treasure lying on the bottom of the pond, but gusty winds (our perceptions, thoughts, feelings, and reactions) are constantly agitating the water, keeping the mud stirred up and waves sloshing all over the surface, so we can see nothing but muddy water and wave-reflected flashes of outside light when we look at the surface. We cannot see what is in the depths, we do not know where to dive for the treasure. Quieting meditation amounts to an injunction to stop agitating the muddy water! If you can do this, the waves will quiet, the mud will eventually settle out, and you have the possibility of seeing the treasure hidden below the surface of the mind. I have often heard lama Sogyal Rinpoche note that, in Tibetan, there is a very beautiful, almost musical saying: "chu ma nyok na dang, sem ma chö na de." It means, roughly, "Water, if you don't stir it, will become clear; the mind, left unaltered, will find its own natural peace." Quieting meditation can produce a very peaceful state, highly valued in and of itself (although it is seen as a means to the higher end of enlightenment in most forms of Buddhism I am familiar with).

Table 9.1, compiled by me from a variety of sources, shows the degree to which quieting meditation can be refined.[6] It is best read from bottom to top. These are traditional Buddhist levels of concentrative meditation; what happens as one gets better at holding focus and reaches more and more subtle states. Again, I do not want the reader to get concerned about the details here. I am just trying to show that the people who have practiced quieting meditation for centuries have developed sophisticated and detailed typologies of what is possible with it.

....

[6] Note that I am, personally, not very skilled at quieting meditation, occasionally experiencing brief but not prolonged periods of mental quiet, so that might bias my characterizations of quieting meditation in Table 9.1. Plus the fact that the reported experiences are inherently difficult to communicate about in ordinary consciousness.

Table 9.1 Levels of quieting, concentrative meditation: ascending states of consciousness on Buddhist path of quieting meditation

8th jhana	Neither perception nor non-perception; equanimity and one-pointedness
7th jhana	Awareness of no-thingness; equanimity and one-pointedness
6th jhana	Objectless infinite consciousness; equanimity and one-pointedness
5th jhana	Consciousness of infinite space; equanimity and one-pointedness
4th jhana	Equanimity and one-pointedness; bliss; all feelings of bodily pleasure cease
3rd jhana	Feelings of bliss; one-pointedness and equanimity; rapture ceases
2nd jhana	Feelings of rapture, bliss, one-pointedness; no thought of primary object of concentration
1st jhana	Hindering thoughts, sensory perception, and awareness of painful bodily states all cease; initial and unbroken sustained attention to primary object of concentration; feelings of rapture, bliss, and one-pointedness
Access concentration state	Hindering thoughts overcome, other thoughts remain; awareness of sensory inputs and body states; primary object of concentration dominates thought; feelings of rapture, happiness, equanimity; initial and sustained thoughts of primary object; flashes of light or bodily lightness

As I said, in the West, we tend to think such sustained focus is not possible. We do not have a tradition of training people's minds this way. However, to illustrate what is possible, I recall a discussion several colleagues and I had with the prominent scholar and meditation teacher Alan Wallace, who had spent many years studying and practicing quieting meditation with Tibetan Buddhist teachers. He recounted an incident that happened when he was on a six-month solitary retreat, and was not supposed to leave his isolated meditation hut at all during that time. At one point he was so upset with his poor performance that he left his hut to see his teacher for more instruction. He found he could not keep his mind focused solely on a single point for more than two hours before a wandering thought finally intruded! The rest of us in this discussion had all practiced various forms of meditation to varying degrees, but, for us, a *minute* or two of complete focusing and quiet constituted a very good meditation session. So, Wallace could not understand why we all laughed so much when he complained that he could not do it for more than two hours at a time! He very seriously explained that the old monk in the next meditation hut could go for *six* hours at a time before having an interfering thought, and Alan was just trying to improve his practice.

Insight meditation

The second type of meditation I want to discuss here is often called *insight meditation*. The traditional Buddhist term for this is *vipassana*, and the term *opening up meditation* is sometimes used. The word "insight" is actually somewhat misleading for a Western audience, as we may think it involves specific psychological insights into causes of experience and behavior—"I have difficulty with my boss at work," for example, "because he is like my father in some ways and that activates unresolved issues with my father"—but vipassana is really insight in a very general sense of clearer perception of the *whole range* of mental activity. Perceiving an itch or pain with much greater clarity than normal is insight in this sense. (For a novel theoretical discussion of cognitive processes at work during insight practice, see Chapter 13.)

Rather than instructing the meditator to keep his or her mind fixed on a single point, as in quieting meditation, a wider range of phenomena, such as whatever the strongest sensation in the body at any particular moment is, is taken as the focus area. The meditator is instructed to pay clear attention to *exactly* what that feels like, moment by moment, without trying to control it. That is, vipassana, insight meditation is training in concentration (stay on the selected focus *range*, come back if you drift), insight (as clarity about what is being experienced), and *equanimity* (accept what happens without trying to force it in any particular direction). In consensus consciousness, we are constantly trying to control and edit our experience, to enhance things we like and get rid of things we do not like. In insight meditation, one learns to use clear, calm, concentrated attention to allow and follow whatever is happening. Concentration ability is automatically trained and required to maintain clarity and equanimity toward ongoing experience. While the range of focus might be restricted to say, body sensations during the learning stage, the range is eventually expanded to include *all* experience, as enlightenment requires clear perception of all experience.

Table 9.2 shows my compilation of levels of attainment possible through insight meditation in the Buddhist tradition.[7] As with Table 9.1, it is best read from bottom to top. Again, do not pay attention to the details; I just want you to see that in this 2500-year-old tradition, there has been considerable sophistication and elaboration of what is possible as a result of this kind of meditation.

Table 9.2 Ascending states of consciousness on Buddhist path of insight meditation

Nirodha	**Total cessation of deluded, samsaric consciousness**		
Effortless insight	Contemplation is quick, effortless, indefatigable; instantaneous knowledge of *anatta, anicca, dukkha*; cessation of pain, pervasive equanimity		
Realization	Realization of the dreadful, unsatisfactory, and wearisome nature of physical and mental phenomena; physical pain; arising of desire to escape these phenomena; perception of vanishing of mind objects; perception fast and flawless; disappearance of lights, rapture, etc.		
Pseudonirvana	Clear perception of the arising and passing of each successive mind moment, accompanied by various phenomena such as brilliant light, rapturous feelings, tranquility, devotion, energy, happiness, strong mindfulness, equanimity toward objects of contemplation, quick and clear perception, and attachment to these newly arisen states		
Stage of reflections	These processes seen as neither pleasant nor reliable; experience of *dukkha*, unsatisfactoriness; these processes are seen to arise and pass away at every moment of contemplation; experience of *anicca*, impermanence; these dual processes are seen as devoid of self; experience of *anatta*, not-self; awareness and its objects are perceived at every moment as distinct and separate processes		
Mindfulness	Mindfulness of body function, physical sensations, mental states, or mind objects		
Access concentration	Previous attainment of access concentration on path of concentration	**Bare insight**	Achievement of ability to notice all phenomena of mind to point where interfering thoughts do not seriously disturb practice

[7] As with my qualification of Table 9.1, be aware that I am not skilled at more than basic practice, so my compilations may not be completely accurate, as well as these experiences being inherently difficult to write about in ordinary consciousness.

I have outlined a model form of hypnosis and two model forms of meditation, so now let us start looking at these states in more detail. To summarize, when induction/practice is successful:

Deep) hypnosis = state of mental quiet and enhanced suggestibility, fading of the CRO

Quieting meditation = increasing mental quiet as meditator's skill at concentration increases, potentially leading to jhana ASCs

Insight meditation = increasing ability to observe ongoing experience with concentration, clarity, and equanimity, potentially leading to enlightenment

However again, I have to remind you, given the wide-ranging ways that people use the terms hypnosis and meditation, you will be able to find teachings and writings that contradict anything I write here! We need though some relatively fixed models, as the aforementioned, to begin to clarify our knowledge.

Variability of hypnosis and meditation context

As I mentioned earlier, there is a general cultural context within which the specific practices and expectations associated with hypnosis or meditation are carried out, and elements of context may modify what results from practice. Table 9.3 shows some of this general cultural context for consensus consciousness, the hypnotic state we are focusing on, and the two model kinds of meditation I have sketched out (quieting meditation and insight meditation).

For Westerners, our general context is that consensus consciousness is implicitly and often explicitly considered the best possible way for a mind to be organized, the best possible state for it to be in, indeed, the only "rational" state. The hypnotic state is regarded as an unusual, specialized state, an ASC. It is certainly not for normal, everyday use, although there can be specialized, therapeutic uses, and, given still widespread negative connotations of gullibility and the like, it is a state that is inferior to consensus consciousness. By contrast, in the Eastern and Buddhist context in which various forms of meditation are generally practiced, consensus consciousness is considered an inferior state, *maya* (Hindu) or *samsara* (Buddhist), both roughly translated as "illusion," a state of bondage in which we experience all sorts of unnecessary suffering as a result of ignorance of our true nature and habitual (karmic) processes that create unnecessary suffering. Getting out of consensus consciousness and into the altered states associated with meditation, leads to liberation. I will not elaborate on what liberation means, but it is the superior goal in this context.

Note the concept "refuge" listed in the first row of Table 9.3. Rather than ordinary, consensus-culture standards being the baseline of life, the reliable place for Buddhists practicing meditation to take refuge in is the Buddha, the Dharma, and the Sangha. That is, they try to take as their fundamental orientation and refuge, not ordinary life but

(a) people who have attained enlightenment, such as the historical Buddha,

(b) the Buddhist teachings on how to reach enlightenment or liberation, the Dharma, and

(c) the Sangha, the community of other practitioners/teachers who will give them support and guidance on their way to becoming Buddhas themselves.

Quite a different context from our ordinary one!

The next row in Table 9.3 deals with the expectations of immediate state qualities that are liable to be experienced in these four contexts. In consensus consciousness, we expect to be largely rational, controlled, adapted adequately to life, and generally realistic (although what is "real" can be very much determined by cultural, consensus- consciousness norms). When a Westerner agrees to be hypnotized, he or she generally expects to experience a passive, sleep-like state, with

Table 9.3 Contexts for consensus consciousness, hypnosis, quieting and insight meditation

Setting	Consensus consciousness (CC)	Hypnosis	Quieting meditation *shamatha* (on the breath)	Insight meditation *vipassana* (on flow of body sensations)
General cultural context	Best state, only rational state; "refuge" in cultural norms and goals	Unusual, specialized state; not for "normals;" inferior to CC	CC is inferior state of bondage; ASCs lead to liberation; refuge in Buddha, Dharma, and Sangha	CC is inferior state of bondage; ASCs lead to liberation; refuge in Buddha, Dharma, and Sangha
Expectations of immediate state qualities	Rational, controlled, adaptive, realistic	Passive, sleep-like state; loss of free will; suggestible; "subject" to will of hypnotist; unusual, but *transitory* experiences	Spiritual progress; escape from immediate suffering; relaxing and pleasant	Spiritual progress; escape from immediate suffering; often relaxing and pleasant, but unpleasant when material being worked through
Expectations of long-term state consequences	Happiness; acceptance; being "sane" and "normal"	In experiments, no long-term change; in therapy, getting better	Attainment of high spiritual states, *jhana* states	Attainment of highest states, enlightenment
Relationship expectations	Relative equality within social norms	Special rapport with hypnotist; power to hypnotist	Independence; unconditional happiness while in state	Independence; permanent unconditional happiness; compassion for all sentient beings
Moral/aspirational context	Normal morality	Normal morality	Aim of spiritual progress, moral life essential	Aim of spiritual progress, enlightenment, moral life essential

some loss of free will, and to become highly suggestible. He or she expects to become "subject" to the will of the hypnotist. Unusual experiences are considered likely to happen, but they are expected to be *transitory* experiences, not leaving any permanent effects. In the two meditative contexts, by contrast, spiritual progress is expected. Both in quieting and insight meditation, a meditation practitioner expects to escape from all immediate suffering, such as worrying or bodily tensions or pains, as well as to be creating a foundation for eventual total transcendence of suffering, and some experiences in meditation may be important insights into the nature of self and reality that are necessary to attain enlightenment.

The third row in Table 9.3 deals with the expectations about long-term consequences that might result from these states. In Western culture, we expect to find happiness and acceptance as a result of being in and operating effectively in consensus consciousness. After all, that is the "sane" and "normal" state to be in, and other people in consensus consciousness will reward us for being in a similar state of consciousness and thus being able to attain goals valued in our culture. We do not expect long-term consequences from hypnosis if we are subjects in an experiment, although we might certainly hope for long-term, positive changes along the lines of getting "better" (more "sane" and "normal") if the hypnosis is used in conjunction with psychotherapy.

In looking at the meditation context, we now have differences between quieting meditation and insight meditation. In traditional Buddhist practice, quieting meditation will allow the attainment of high spiritual states considered of great value, the *jhana* states, but that is not considered the ultimate goal. Insight meditation (which is predicated on having a certain skill level, *access concentration*, acquired in quieting meditation to begin with) allows the possibility of the highest attainment, full enlightenment, by deeper understanding of one's fundamental nature. That is, the meditator becomes a Buddha, him or herself, and no longer experiences unnecessary suffering.

The penultimate row in Table 9.3 deals with relationship expectations. In consensus consciousness, we expect a relative equality of relationships with other people, within established hierarchies and social norms. Much of the fulfillment of life is expected to come from interpersonal relationships. When we are hypnotized, we expect to sometimes have special rapport with the hypnotist, and for the hypnotist to have considerable, but temporary, power over us. In the meditation context, however, relationships are expected to be quite different. In both cases, independence from *needing* social relationships is expected. It is not that one will not have or care for social relationships—indeed, one may have much higher-quality ones—but that the accomplished meditator is no longer desperately *needy* for the support that they offer.[8]

In quieting meditation, for example, if one attains the jhana states, one experiences *unconditional* happiness. That is, these ASCs are inherently happy, to various degrees, without depending on any outside conditions, including other people, being some particular way. However, when one comes out of the jhana states induced by quieting meditation, one returns to being one's ordinary

---

8 The role of the meditation teacher in Buddhism is quite variable and complex. At one extreme, as usually found in Theravada Buddhism, the teacher is a spiritual friend who shows you how to practice, but the outcome depends on your own efforts. In some forms of Vajrayana Buddhism, at the other extreme, the teacher is the master or guru, and the highest enlightenment can only come when, through his or her realization, you are introduced to the ultimate nature of mind. As mentioned briefly already, the situation becomes confusing when a meditation practice is "guided" by an authority figure, especially a teacher or a master, as it is unclear how much of such guidance constitutes the induction and construction of a hypnotic-like state and how much a matter of the meditator doing all the work, only getting directional instructions from the guiding person.

self again, subject to conditional happiness: that is, you are happy when you get what you want and avoid what you do not want, and unhappy when you cannot do this. When the insights into one's true nature are deep enough, in insight meditation, this can lead to permanent, unconditional happiness. That is, there is a permanent change in the meditator, permeating all of his or her life. The deep causes of suffering are understood and abandoned; an end of suffering is not just something associated with being in a special meditative state.

It is very important to note that this realization, liberation, enlightenment, also includes deep realization of an inherent compassion toward *all* sentient beings, so one's relationships naturally change in the direction of helping other sentient beings to be happy.[9] It is not a moral injunction that you *should* be kind to others or else, but rather, it is a change, as I understand it, based on a deep realization of our interconnectedness, such that being kind to others is the only sensible thing to do.

Finally in Table 9.3 is a very important contextual variable that I tend to take for granted, so seldom do I think of it consciously—namely, the moral/aspirational context. In ordinary life or in hypnosis for experimental or therapeutic applications, our usual aspiration is to live a normal life, as defined by our culture and particular philosophy of life or religion, and this is usually implicit. I have never, for the many experimental subjects I have dealt with in my years of hypnosis research, asked them about their moral or religious or spiritual convictions. It was taken for granted that they were normal, and that I, as hypnotist, was normal. In meditation contexts, by contrast, it is usually explicitly, as well as habitually implicitly, assumed that normal life is badly lacking in what is important and that the aspiration of learning and practicing various forms of meditation is spiritual progress, becoming freer of ordinary limitations and delusions and gaining spiritual insights that lead toward enlightenment. Just looking at the details of meditation practice per se in these contexts is not sufficient to understand what might occur, as these moral/aspirational contexts are active as background factors, shaping potential results of specific practices. For example, we Westerners are fascinated by meditation practice as being something exotic, but Buddhism lists meditation as two of eight basic life practices designed to promote spiritual progress, namely right view, right intention, right speech, right action, right livelihood, right effort, right mindfulness, and right concentration.

Qualities of (model) hypnotic and meditative states

Starting with the principle that the context of the induction technique and the expectations surrounding it can lead to quite different effects, we have looked at some of the big differences in contexts of consensus consciousness, our model hypnotic state, and two model meditation techniques (quieting meditation and insight meditation). Now, let us look at a variety of the specific differences that can actually occur. In Table 9.4, I have organized these by the major subsystems of my systems approach to states of consciousness (Tart, 1975), so we have some structure.

Exteroception

The first row in Table 9.4 shows effects for *exteroception*, the sense organs and hardwired processes that keep us in touch with our external environment. In consensus consciousness, there is

---

[9] Since the ultimate happiness is becoming enlightened through insight meditation, in addition to specific acts to benefit others, teaching them how to master insight meditation becomes the greatest gift possible. Full Buddhist enlightenment is thus said to consist of the development of both wisdom and compassion.

Table 9.4 Effects of four states/practices on basic subsystems of consciousness

Psychological subsystem qualities	Consensus consciousness	Hypnosis	Quieting meditation *shamatha* (on the breath)	Insight meditation *vipassana* (on flow of body sensations)
Exteroception	Active; scanning; very variable	Narrowed and intensified by suggestion	Usually diminished or absent	Minimal; not attended to except for internal correlates
Interoception	Active; very variable	Narrowed and/or intensified by suggestion; and/or absent	Fixed and/or enhanced	Especially active; clear
Input processing	Very active; implicit	Narrowed and controlled by suggestion	Strong focus and conscious control	Less active; may become explicit; more conscious control
Memory	Very active; implicit and explicit	Minimal unless suggested, then enhanced	Not used, so inactive, ignored; present focus; if memories rise, ignored as distractions	Not used, so inactive, ignored; present focus; if memories rise, ignored as distractions or allowed to flow without attachment
Sense of identity	Ordinary **Me!**	Largely dormant; suggested identities strong	Fades, potentially to nothing, no "thing"	Fades, potentially to nothing, no "thing;" plus flashes of insight into deeper identity
Evaluation and decision making	Active; implicit as well as explicit	Passive unless suggestions to activate; under hypnotist's control	Dormant except for task focus; conscious control	Dormant except for task focus and maintenance of equanimity; conscious control
Subconscious	Implicit; inferred from behavior and self-report	Perhaps more accessible via suggestions	Inactive?	Sometimes insights
Space/time creation	Very active but implicit; we think we just perceive space and time	Malleable by suggestion	Fades; timelessness	Fades; timelessness; insights into the constitution of perceptions concerning space and time
Psychological subsystem qualities	Consensus consciousness	Hypnosis	Quieting meditation *shamatha* (on the breath)	Insight meditation *vipassana* (on flow of body sensations)
Motor output	Usually active	None except for suggested activity	Usually none	Usually none
Awareness	**Me!** and **My!** world	Simple awareness; readiness unless specific suggestions shape, then malleable	Task effort → absorption → *jhana* states	Task effort → clarity → insight into true nature → enlightenment

generally active scanning of the environment, although the level of that can be variable. When you are reading a book, you are scanning a lot less than when you are taking a walk or participating in a conversation, for example. In deep hypnosis, exteroception is both narrowed and intensified. Narrowed in the sense that there is very little, if any, conscious active scanning of the environment unless specifically suggested, but, if there is specific suggestion calling for it, the experienced intensity of this exteroception will go up.[10]

In our model of quieting meditation, where, you recall, the meditator is focused on some sensation like the breath, exteroception is greatly diminished and, when advanced meditative states (jhanas) develop, exteroception is absent as far as experience is concerned. The meditator is in some ASC with little or no experienced sensory input; their body has been, as it were, temporarily left behind. In insight meditation, we have some variability. Generally, exteroception is minimal if one is attending to, say, the exact moment-by-moment quality of varying body sensations. However, exteroception is not actively blocked. The meditator is not deaf, so, for example, he or she will hear sounds. My experience, and that of some other meditators, is that external sounds will often have specific bodily effects, a synesthetic tactile sensation triggered by the sound, for example, so there may be some exteroception in this way.

Interoception

The second row of Table 9.4 deals with *interoception*. Again, this is moderately active although largely implicit in consensus consciousness. We keep track of our bodies and what we are doing with them. In hypnosis, interoception is typically quite narrowed in that the subject generally sits still, and so most interoceptors physiologically adapt out.[11] If movements are suggested, or suggestions given that the subject pay attention to internal, bodily processes, they can be intensified in perception. Suggestions that one's arm is so light it is floating upward, for example, can result in feeling lightness, as well as one's arm seeming to move by itself. Contrarily, with appropriate suggestions for analgesia, interoception can be totally removed from the consciousness of the deep hypnotic state, such that stimuli that would normally be perceived as quite intense or painful are not consciously perceived at all.

In quieting meditation, interoception is firmly fixed on the focus point and that specific focus is usually enhanced. If the meditator is following the movement of the belly in the course of breathing, for instance, he or she will try to keep this the only interoceptive sensation, and so qualities of this sensation, perhaps varying from moment to moment, will be sensed that normally are not a part of consciousness. The meditators sense their bodies more than normal, although in a specialized way. In insight meditation, deliberately focused on whatever the strongest body sensation is at any particular moment, for example, interoception is usually much more intense than it normally is. The meditator may not only sense qualities of internal sensations not normally detected, but, as a result of developing equanimity, be able to do things like deal with pain much more effectively than usual: the pain is likely to be experienced as a varying *sensation*, rather than

---

[10] I am focusing on the conscious experience of hypnotized subjects here, but there is probably a more implicit awareness of the environment that is responsible for the great sensitivity of subjects to cues about what is expected of them, other than the formal, verbal suggestions.

[11] Much of this bodily stillness may be an effect of the typical use of sleep analogies in inducing hypnosis, rather than being absolutely necessary to induce and maintain a hypnotic state (see work on active-alert inductions, e.g., Banyai & Hilgard, 1976).

reacted to as *suffering* (for a detailed review comparing recent studies on hypnotic and meditative analgesia, see Chapter 21).

Input processing

One of the most important subsystems of consciousness is what I have called *input processing*. I am sure this is actually a variety of specialized subsystems, some hardwired physiological subsystems, some psychologically programmed subsystems, lumped together here for convenience. These are the physiological and psychological mechanisms that take in a vast amount of exteroceptive and interoceptive input, screen it for what is relevant to the person, abstract it, modify it, add to it, and then deliver the much less rich, but more meaningful percepts that constitute perception to awareness. This process is very active in consensus consciousness, but it is implicit; it is generally not a conscious process at all. We do not know we are doing this enormous amount of abstracting, processing, and fabrication. We feel as if we are simply perceiving the world as it is.

Input processing can be highly narrowed or broadened in overall bandwidth, and certainly focused by suggestion in the hypnotic state. It can be narrowed in the sense that only certain exteroceptive or interoceptive stimuli, as suggested, will be perceived at all, or the nature of the construction/fabrication process can be changed so that a stimulus is perceived in a different way than it normally would be. Giving a subject something unpleasant to smell after you have suggested that you will give them something pleasant, and the subject perceives a pleasant smell, is an example of controlling input processing through hypnotic suggestion.

In quieting meditation, there is some *conscious* control over input processing in order to maintain a focus on the object of meditation, the breath in our example. This can become a case of far more conscious control being exerted over what is experienced than in consensus consciousness.[12] In insight meditation, input processing may become less active in the sense that, say, exteroceptive input is not having deliberate attention paid to it if the focus range is specified as internal body sensations, but, on the other hand, more control is being exerted over interoceptive input in that the meditator strives to maintain clarity and equanimity within the desired range of experience. In consensus consciousness, a pleasant or unpleasant stimulus usually activates all sorts of reactions, and our consciousness becomes largely involved in the reactions, often losing touch with the actual stimuli. In insight meditation, the usual goal is to keep consciousness as close to the actual, ongoing stimulation as possible. Meditators sometimes also report insights into the nature of the normally implicit input processing subsystem (i.e., they see how they habitually alter or distort various kinds of stimuli).

Memory

The *memory subsystem*, shown in the fourth row of Table 9.4, is very active in consensus consciousness, both explicitly and implicitly. We frequently attempt to remember things, with various degrees of success, and various kinds of memory are the basis for much input processing: you cannot screen out or accentuate stimuli on the basis of relevance unless there are remembered criteria of relevance, even though this is usually done implicitly and automatically. In the hypnotic state, unless a person is asked to remember things, or given a suggestion for false memory, the memory subsystem is not consciously active: subjects do not engage in much remembering, except at the

---

[12] Note that usually this control is a matter of focusing more on the desired sensation, not a fighting with or active rejection of other sensations.

implicit level that is necessary for so many other actions. It is also possible to successfully suggest amnesia for the events of the hypnotic statement—amnesia which can instantly be eliminated by another suggestion.

In both kinds of meditation, except for possible implicit operations, conscious use of memory is largely inactive. There is a very strong focus on the present time, either in terms of the highly specific object of meditation in quieting meditation or on the larger range of focus in insight meditation. The meditator is interested in what a body sensation feels like *now*, and remembering what it felt like earlier or thinking about how it might feel in the future is a failure of present-time focus, so attention is brought back to the present. Insofar as memories arise, they are considered distractions and given little attention, unless the vipassana has a wider-range intention that includes spontaneously rising memories.

Sense of identity

Our *sense of identity subsystem*, outlined in the fifth row of Table 9.4, gives certain of our experiences a special **Me!** quality (represented here by emboldening "Me" and adding the exclamation point to show how important self is to self[13]) and consequent emotional charge. There is considerable implicit activity here, as well as explicit experiences of feeling more or less involved in one's personal identity, in consensus consciousness. The sense of identity function becomes largely dormant in the hypnotic state,[14] unless a specific suggestion is given, such as taking on another identity. In the quieting meditation state, the ordinary sense of **Me!** fades, potentially to the point where the meditator would report, in retrospect, that he or she had no particular identity at all, that he or she was nothing or, more precisely, no "thing."[15] In insight meditation, there is also this fading of one's ordinary identity, to the point of having no particular identity in consciousness, but there may also be insights into the nature of one's deeper identity (or lack of any permanent identity), as well as experience of non-duality, of identity with all things, not just an isolated self. This phenomenon is almost impossible to talk about in ordinary language, because ordinary language is constructed around physical things and ordinary identity.

Evaluation and decision making

The *evaluation and decision-making subsystem* refers to the many ways in which we decide what a situation or experience is about, its relevance to our needs, and what sort of actions we should take. We make numerous evaluations and decisions in consensus consciousness all the time, both implicitly as well as explicitly. In hypnosis, by contrast, this subsystem is generally passive. The subject has surrendered his or her normally very active evaluation and decision-making capacity to the suggestions of the hypnotist, and, unless there are suggestions that require evaluation and decision making, this subsystem will remain largely passive.

---

[13] In some of my other writings, I use **ME!** (**M**ind **E**mbodied), with the exclamation point to emphasize the importance given to sense of self.

[14] Note that in hypnosis that is much deeper than usually found in laboratory studies or clinical work, changes in identity can occur similar to those found in insight meditation. See Tart (1970) for an example of this.

[15] This leads us toward the issue of the insight of emptiness, a foundation of enlightenment in Buddhism, which is too complex to go into here, especially because of the unintended and unfortunate nihilistic connotations that have resulted from translating the Eastern language terms as "emptiness."

In both kinds of meditation, the evaluation and decision-making subsystem is dormant except for maintaining task focus, keeping the processes of the mind under conscious control—"This is a distraction from my goal. What's the best way to have it fade away?" for example. In quieting meditation, this is a matter of making sure that one keeps attention focused on the object of meditation and does not drift off into *thinking about* the focus object instead of actually *sensing* it. In insight meditation, one similarly keeps attention focused on the desired range of objects of meditation and, in addition to monitoring that one does not drift off into thoughts about the objects of focus instead of actually sensing them, one deliberately maintains an attitude of equanimity toward the range of focused objects.

Subconscious

The *subconscious* or *unconscious subsystem*, in the seventh row of Table 9.4, is one of the most mysterious processes. In consensus consciousness, the subconscious is a theoretical inference: we see intelligent, coordinated behavior along with a lack of relevant conscious experience, and so postulate that some intelligent aspect of mind, outside of consciousness, is responsible for what we observe. Many investigators and therapists have argued that the subconscious is more accessible in hypnosis. Suggestions may activate it and/or make aspects of functioning that were normally unconscious, now conscious. It is hard to know what, if anything, happens to subconscious functioning in the two types of meditation. It is tempting to say it is inactive in quieting meditation, as, if this is done very successfully, there is little experience except that of the object of meditation. This is similar for the range of objects of meditation in insight meditation, although the spontaneous insights that can bubble up in this latter kind of meditation sometimes will cover material from what we would normally call the subconscious or unconscious. The way to tell how active the unconscious is in either type of meditation would be to have distracting thoughts and feelings reported to an outside observer who might then rate how much these express unconscious issues, based on in-depth psychological knowledge of a particular meditator. However, such reporting could seriously disrupt the meditation process.

Space/time creation

The *space/time subsystem* is responsible for the creation of our spatial and temporal framework for interacting with external and internal reality. The functioning of this subsystem is very active, but almost totally implicit in consensus consciousness. We think we simply *perceive* space and time. However, in the ASC of, say, nocturnal dreaming, events also happen in a space and time framework, but one that is entirely internally created and has no reference to external space and time. Dreaming nicely illustrates how the space/time subsystem creates space and time. In consensus consciousness, the space and time this subsystem creates must be highly coordinated with external space and time for adaptive behavior, leading to our feeling that we simply perceive real space and real time.

This subsystem is highly malleable to suggestion in hypnosis. Time can be made to seem to move faster or slower, space can become shallower or deeper, as in Aaronson's fascinating experiments in the 1960s (Aaronson, 1969). In both meditative states, the meditator is highly present-centered, and feelings of timelessness are often reported about the meditative states, so the space/time subsystem seems to become largely dormant.

Motor output

Motor output refers to our many ways of affecting the world, such as through obvious muscular movements and actions, to speech, and to some control over internal bodily processes. Motor output is highly active in consensus consciousness, but usually inactive in the hypnotic state unless some motor action is specifically suggested. Reducing or inactivating motor output is an important component in the induction of many altered states, for motor output per se is a familiar and massive activity that can act as a kind of loading stabilization, maintaining the baseline state of consciousness, and producing further exteroceptive input, as a consequence of one's effects on the world, that can also load and stabilize the baseline state of consciousness.

In the two kinds of meditation, the meditator generally sits very still for long periods of time, so familiar motor output is largely absent. To avoid misunderstanding, I should add, though, that if insight meditation leads to liberation, it does not mean that the person has to stay still for the rest of their life in order to enjoy the changes and benefits that have resulted from enlightenment!

Awareness

Finally, in the tenth row of Table 9.4, we have the most mysterious aspect of consciousness and one that I am not even sure should be called a subsystem as it is more fundamental than the others, namely, *basic awareness* or *pure awareness*. In my systems approach I distinguish between *basic awareness* and *consciousness*, the former being the most basic kind of knowledge that *something* is happening, the latter being the highly developed, articulated, often quite verbal *construction* that fills up so much of our ordinary experience.[16] Indeed, in consensus consciousness, it may not even make sense to a person to try to distinguish basic awareness from consciousness, but in both kinds of meditation, the meditator fairly quickly learns to recognize an immediate distinction between basic awareness, which is the larger "container" within which particular articulated kinds of consciousness manifest, and the particular sensations, thoughts, and emotions which are the content within the container. This container and contents analogy can only partially convey the difference, but it can be experienced.

Basic awareness in consensus consciousness is usually absorbed in perceptions, thoughts, and feelings having to do with **Me!** and **My!** and **My world!** and what should be done that benefits **Me!**. In the hypnotic state, the deeply hypnotized subject, not having been given specific suggestions, is probably experiencing something like basic or pure awareness. He or she is aware of various things that happen in the laboratory, but all the automatic elaborations/fabrications do not happen to him or her as they would in consensus consciousness, unless specific suggestions are given by the hypnotist to make these occur.[17]

In quieting meditation, the practice of staying focused leads to the absorption of basic awareness into the various jhana states. (That is my best understanding, extrapolating from textual sources and my own experience. However, please recall that I am not that accomplished in quieting meditation.) In insight meditation, the task effort of focusing leads to experiences of greater and greater clarity as to what one is experiencing, equanimity about it, and insights into one's true nature, which can ultimately lead to the state that we so inadequately call "enlightenment." As I mentioned earlier, we need state-specific knowledge here, which cannot really be conveyed in ordinary consciousness.

---

[16] I make this particular distinction between awareness and consciousness pretty consistently in my writings, but if the reader is confused, it is because others distinguish in different ways or use the terms synonymously.

[17] Note that if hypnosis is carried to extremely deep levels, beyond those usually seen in the laboratory or clinic, transpersonal experiences, including modifications of space and time perception, can occur (Tart, 1970).

I have presented much information, while at the same time feeling that I really needed to go into far more detail on each of the various points, citing supporting evidence, and so on, to make them really clear. However, that is just impossible in this limited space. I hope all the aforementioned will act as a stimulus to finding more precise knowledge and as suggestions for directions for further study and research. Even more so, I hope this discussion has increased researchers' sensitivity to the context and expectations surrounding both hypnosis and meditation, so that future research will be truly insightful, rather than shallow and spuriously "objective."

Given these definitions, delimitations, and considerations, obviously I think the equation *meditation = some kind of (self)-hypnosis* is quite inadequate. More specifically, hypnosis, defined here as a suggestible state in which the CRO has faded and a person experiences suggestions as experientially real, is not the same thing as quieting meditation.[18] Further, hypnosis is certainly not the same as insight meditation. The more adequate equations are: *quieting meditation ≠ (self)-hypnosis* and *insight meditation ≠ (self)-hypnosis*.

Now to conclude, let us back up and take a look at the forest again, after all these trees, this detail. I want to take a preliminary look at a powerful, general difference between hypnosis and the practice and outcomes of meditation.

Organizing thought versus transcending thought

Figure 9.4 (see also Plate 3) is designed to illustrate consensus consciousness as a very busy state. I have sketched a large, rectangular space filled with varying shades and intensities of **P**erceptions, **T**houghts, and **E**motions, with perceptions leading to thoughts, thoughts leading to emotions, emotions leading to perceptions, and so on. Although I have met a very few people who report

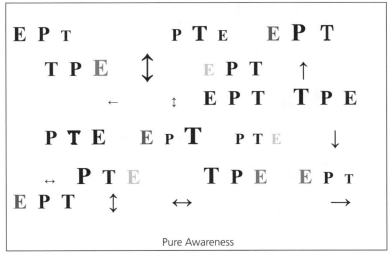

T = Thoughts;   P = Perceptions;   E = Emotions

Fig. 9.4 The busy state of ordinary consensus consciousness (see also Plate 3).

---

[18] There may be some similarities in mental quiet per se, but I do not know if there has been any direct comparison.

that sometimes they have periods of mental blankness during their ordinary state of consensus consciousness, for most of us (especially, I think, academics) consciousness is a never-ending, three-ring circus, and often a poorly controlled, poorly organized three-ring circus. Pure awareness, shown in light type to represent subtlety, is theoretically there as the container behind all this content, but generally not experienced as something distinct.

"Normal" consensus consciousness

In Figure 9.5, I have represented deep hypnosis as a strongly organized state of consciousness, not scattered all over mental space as consensus consciousness usually is. Recall that, for the model of hypnosis we are talking about, there is practically no thought, perception, or emotion unless suggested, and even that tends to be tightly organized and coherent, wholly absorbing basic awareness in its highly structured manifestation. I have sketched this in Figure 9.5 by putting the thoughts, perceptions, and emotions in a tight column, and drawn in a very heavy, unvarying typeface to show the high degree of organization that hypnotic suggestion can bring about. This illustrates one end of the general dimension I am talking about: the hypnotic state is very good for organizing and structuring thought processes, and consequent emotions and perceptions (see Chapter 11).

Deep, quiet hypnotic state

It is getting harder to represent things diagrammatically, but in Figure 9.6 I have shown a deep state of quieting meditation, where there is practically no thought, perception, or emotion, and yet this basic awareness, this pure awareness, which is largely implicit in consensus consciousness and hypnosis, is now experienced directly. This is sometimes described, in a way that is generally confusing to ordinary consciousness, as "emptiness" or "nothing." No "thing" is happening, but it is decidedly not a state of dullness! The meditator feels vividly awake and alive, even though there's no specific *content* of experience. One leading scholar of mystical experience (Forman,

T = Thoughts;   P = Perceptions;   E = Emotions

Fig. 9.5 Deep hypnosis as an organized state of consciousness.

Fig. 9.6 Deep state of quieting meditation.

1990, pp. 3–52) has described this as the "pure consciousness" experience. (Forman is using "consciousness" where I would use "awareness.")

I wish I could define the pure awareness experience more clearly, but description is very much a function of the verbal articulation and organization of consensus consciousness. So, while pure awareness can be experienced and understood in a state-specific way, and we can probably learn to describe it better (if not more adequately) than we do now, I have little hope that we can really learn to describe it in a completely sufficient way within consensus consciousness.

If you have not had direct experience of pure awareness, you might be wondering at this point, "What good is it?". Certainly, it is theoretically interesting as the source or container behind our more articulated consensus consciousness, but what else? Those who experience even a few seconds of it, in quieting or insight meditation, usually find it rewarding to do so, and frequently report an after-effect, a re-vitalization, a refreshing and deepening of ordinary experience. I will propose a computer analogy here to convey some of this.

We have all, unfortunately, had the experience of our computers locking up. Too much is going on, there's a conflict over sharing resources internally, and, finally, the whole machine locks. Older Windows users will recognize and flinch at the mention of the "blue screen of death!". Experiencing pure awareness is like hitting the reset button on an older (bio)computer (or "ctrl–alt–delete" on current Windows computers): the machine can reboot, all the clutter and conflict is gone, and we can now load the program we want and work effectively again. Since some problems in our lives are quite analogous to our (bio)computer locking up from overload, there are obviously great psychological advantages to being able to "hit reset" and bring, anew, our native resources to bear.

Also, as I have already mentioned briefly, some proficiency in quieting meditation is considered a basic foundation for the really successful practice of insight meditation.

Let us now look at the other end of this general dimension that I am speaking of— transcending thought (and consequent feelings). Not suppressing, but transcending. Imagine a spectrum with intense thoughts at one extreme and transcendence of thought into "something else" at the other

Fig. 9.7 Enlightenment: the end point of insight meditation.

extreme. In consensus consciousness, we are toward the thought end of that continuum, although thought is not always well organized. The hypnotic state allows for tighter control of thought; the meditative states take us in the direction of transcending thought altogether.

What is that transcendence? My final diagram, Figure 9.7, tries to illustrate the end point of insight meditation—enlightenment. This is the biggest challenge of all to represent diagrammatically, and you will see that I have either succeeded brilliantly, in a Zen manner, or bypassed the issue altogether by leaving the space entirely blank!

I would very briefly note, however, that while we tend to think of enlightenment as some mysterious state of consciousness, some exotic condition, in some Buddhisms, enlightenment is thought of as an altered state of *being* rather than simply of *consciousness*, and enlightened Buddhas[19] do not just lie around blissing out, they are usually very active and very effective in the world, carrying out their desire to help others.

Practical applications

So when is it best to meditate, and when is it best to (self-)hypnotize? Should you try to organize your thoughts and feelings through hypnosis or self-hypnosis (as well as all our less exotic ways of regulating our minds), or should you try to transcend thought altogether? To me, it is clear that this is not really an either/or question. There are certainly plenty of times when a better organization of our thoughts (and consequent feelings, perceptions, and actions) would be a great improvement in life, both in terms of personal happiness and effectiveness in leading a good life. However, thought is not life: it is a reflection *about* life. Fifty plus years of research and personal

[19] There has supposedly been many enlightened Buddhas over the centuries—Buddha is a generic term for someone who reaches enlightenment, not just one particular historical figure.

experience have made it very clear to me that we also need to learn to *transcend* thought, in order to touch something deeper in ourselves, and to work on realizing our full potential.

However, exactly how should we focus on the one end of the spectrum, and exactly how on the other? How far can we go in either direction on this general dimension of thought and transcendence? How can modern psychology make old meditation techniques more effective? They are very difficult for many people to learn, so understanding how to teach the skills more effectively would be a major advance. How can the old meditation traditions help us have a deeper, more effective psychology? Can we, as I have argued elsewhere (Tart, 1998a, 1998b), use training in meditation to give us the trained observers and high-quality introspective observations we need, so we really could have a science of psychology, of the *mind*, instead of feeling like we are a derivative enterprise, waiting for the neurologists to explain our field (away)? (For more discussion of the importance of phenomenological methods in the science of consciousness, see Chapters 8 and 15.)

As I said at the start of this chapter, these reflections are a work in process. I hope that they have been stimulating to you, and that you will help in furthering progress!

References

Aaronson, B. (1969). Hypnosis, depth perception, and psychedelic experience. In C. T. Tart (Ed.), *Altered states of consciousness: a book of readings* (pp. 315–323). New York: Wiley.

Banyai, E. I., & Hilgard, E. R. (1976). A comparison of active-alert hypnotic induction with traditional relaxation induction. *Journal of Abnormal Psychology*, **85**(2), 218.

Forman, R. (Ed.) (1990). *The problem of pure consciousness*. Oxford: Oxford University Press.

Shor, R. (1959). Hypnosis and the concept of the generalized reality orientation. *American Journal of Psychotherapy*, **13**, 582–602.

Shor, R. (1962). Three dimensions of hypnotic depth. *International Journal of Clinical and Experimental Hypnosis*, **10**, 23–38.

Tart, C. T. (1970). Transpersonal potentialities of deep hypnosis. *Journal of Transpersonal Psychology*, **2**, 27–40.

Tart, C. T. (1971). *On being stoned: a psychological study of marijuana intoxication*. Palo Alto, California: Science and Behavior Books.

Tart, C. T. (1972). States of consciousness and state-specific sciences. *Science*, **176**, 1203–1210

Tart, C. T. (1975). *States of consciousness*. New York: E. P. Dutton.

Tart, C. T. (1986). *Waking up: overcoming the obstacles to human potential*. Boston: Shambhala.

Tart, C. T. (1998a). *Altered states of consciousness—a thirty-year perspective*. Invited address, Divisions 12, 17, and 30, American Psychological Association, San Francisco, August 14.

Tart, C. T. (1998b). Investigating altered states of consciousness on their own terms: a proposal for the creation of state-specific sciences. *Ciencia e Cultura, Journal of the Brazilian Association for the Advancement of Science*. **50**, 2/3, 103–116.

Tart, C. T. (2009). *The end of materialism: how evidence of the paranormal is bringing science and spirit together*. Oakland, California: New Harbinger.

Chapter 10

Toward a science of internal experience
Conceptual and methodological issues in hypnosis and meditation research

Vince Polito and Michael H. Connors

Abstract
Hypnosis and meditation both involve private, subjective experiences. As a result, they can be difficult to investigate in empirical studies. This chapter discusses some of the theoretical and methodological challenges in conducting such research, and ways of addressing these. It focuses, in particular, on four conceptual issues in hypnosis research that the authors believe might also be useful in studying meditation. These are: distinguishing the procedures participants follow from their reported effects; separating participants' trait capacities and contextual influences; considering the interplay between cognitive and social processes; and controlling for demand characteristics. The chapter notes how awareness of these issues may enrich understanding of meditation and help guide research into subjective experience more broadly.

Introduction

Both hypnosis and meditation are complex practices with rich and diverse histories. Although it is not yet clear the degree to which the domains of these two techniques overlap, a key common strand is that both involve internal subjective experiences. This chapter explores theoretical and methodological challenges in investigating what are essentially private mental events and suggests conceptual distinctions that may facilitate a more rigorous empirical science of hypnosis and meditation. In particular, we discuss how a number of conceptual issues in hypnosis research might enrich the study of meditation.

Hypnosis has been a topic of investigation in Western science since the eighteenth century and has been a controversial field since its inception (Gauld, 1995). The history of hypnosis research has been characterized by vigorous debate as to the veracity, causes, effects, and practical applications of the phenomenon (Hilgard, 1977; Hull, 1933; McConkey, 2008; Sheehan & Perry, 1976). Despite considerable theoretical differences, broad agreement has emerged among researchers as to the elements of hypnotic phenomena that need to be explained (Hilgard, 1965, 1975; Kihlstrom, 1985, 2008), and commonly accepted best practices for conducting research and clinical work have developed (Lynn, Rhue, & Kirsch, 2010; Nash & Barnier, 2008). That is not to say that all researchers agree on definitional questions; however, there does exist within the field a shared scientific language to describe the phenomena of hypnosis and a general understanding of the range of positions that various theorists hold (Cox & Bryant, 2008; Lynn & Rhue, 1991; Woody & McConkey, 2003).

Meditation has followed a somewhat different trajectory. Meditative techniques were practiced for millennia prior to engagement with Western scientific frameworks (Lutz, Dunne, & Davidson, 2007). During that time, highly detailed accounts, instructions, and traditions developed around meditative practices. It is only in the last five decades that this field has been intensively investigated from the perspective of Western, empirical, psychological science. A considerable focus in the meditation research literature has been the influence that meditation has on psychological, neurophysiological, and individual difference variables. In a meta-analysis of the effects of meditation on a wide range of psychological outcome variables, Sedlmeier et al. (2012) found that meditation had a positive impact on emotionality, relationships, attention, and cognitive capacities. In addition, a growing body of evidence now suggests that meditation (like hypnosis) can be an effective adjunct to therapeutic interventions for conditions such as anxiety, depression, and pain (Baer, 2003; Goyal et al., 2014; Hofmann, Sawyer, Witt, & Oh, 2010; Smith, Richardson, Hoffman, & Pilkington, 2005). Meditation may also induce neurophysiological changes: a review by Fox et al. (2014) found evidence of significant neural changes in brain areas associated with meta-awareness, body awareness, memory consolidation, and emotion regulation.

In recent years, however, several researchers have provided thoughtful, reflective critiques of the meditation literature, highlighting potential confounds in empirical research due to inconsistencies in the ways that meditation is defined, operationalized, and measured (Davidson, 2010; Grossman, 2008, 2011; Sauer et al., 2013; Sedlmeier et al., 2012; Van Dam, Earleywine, & Borders, 2010). Similar challenges have been faced by hypnosis researchers, and it may be that some of the conceptual distinctions that have emerged in the hypnosis literature can also help clarify and refine research on meditation.

Useful concepts from hypnosis research

The complexity of these domains, multiplicity of techniques, individual differences, and varying timescales for effects present many potential confounds and confusions. A challenge for any science of hypnosis and meditation is to conceptualize the domain of these phenomena in a way that allows detailed, consistent empirical investigation. We discuss four concepts that we believe are important in hypnosis research and reflect on how they might also apply to meditation research.

Procedure and product

The first concept that we consider useful has been to make a clear distinction between two different ways that the term hypnosis can be understood: hypnosis-as-procedure and hypnosis-as-product (Barnier & Nash, 2008; Nash, 2005; Polito, Barnier, & McConkey, 2014). Hypnosis-as-procedure refers to the practical aspects of the hypnotic interaction—primarily what the hypnotist does. In a research setting, this usually consists of four phases: an introduction to the process that is about to occur, a hypnotic induction, a series of hypnotic suggestions, and then a deinduction. Hypnosis-as-product, in contrast, refers to the subjective, behavioral, and neurophysiological alterations in participants that result from this procedure—that is, the effects of hypnosis. Whereas hypnosis-as-procedure is what the hypnotist does in the hypnotic context, hypnosis-as-product is what the participant experiences (Barnier & Oakley, 2009).

The specific details of a hypnotic procedure can vary immensely (Woody & Barnier, 2008). Typically, an induction involves instructions for relaxation and focused attention, but inductions can also feature vigorous physical activity (Bányai & Hilgard, 1976), or can be entirely self-directed by the participant themselves (Shor & Easton, 1973). The hypnotic suggestions administered also vary considerably. For example, these can range from simple suggestions for ideomotor movements in the context of research on motor control (e.g., Galea, Woody, Szechtman, & Pierrynowski, 2010), to detailed suggestions for cognitive-perceptual restructuring oriented toward specific therapeutic goals in a clinical context (e.g., Nash, 2008; Oakley & Halligan, 2002).

A given hypnotic procedure will not necessarily lead to hypnosis-as-product, so it is important to assess the effects of hypnosis empirically. Researchers and practitioners pay a great deal of attention to assessing hypnosis-as-product (Barnier & McConkey, 2004; Sheehan & McConkey, 1982) and have developed a wide range of methodologies and assessment tools to understand and quantify participants' experiences. Here, we outline three ways this has been achieved.

First, hypnosis-as-product can be analyzed in terms of behavioral responses. The effects of hypnosis are essentially private subjective experiences but researchers often use behavior as an indirect indication of these subjective changes. Typically, specific criteria are established for passing each suggestion (Woody & Barnier, 2008). In the case of a suggestion for arm levitation, for example, this could be whether or not the participant raises their arm at least 30 centimeters. This approach is exemplified in standard measures of hypnotizability such as the Harvard Group Scale of Hypnotic Suggestibility, Form A (HGSHS:A; Shor & Orne, 1962; Weitzenhoffer & Hilgard, 1962) and the Stanford Scale of Hypnotic Suggestibility, Form C (SHSS:C; Weitzenhoffer & Hilgard, 1962).

Second, hypnosis-as-product can be assessed through direct reports of participants' subjective experiences. This can take a variety of forms. For example, some researchers have asked participants to give moment-to-moment, verbal ratings of the degree to which they feel they are experiencing the effects of suggestions (Laurence & Nadon, 1986). McConkey, Wende, and Barnier (1999) employed a more sophisticated methodology to assess moment-to-moment experience: they tracked participants' fluctuating experiences during a hypnosis session using a handheld dial device that participants continually updated. They found that, rather than hypnotic effects being "switched on" immediately in response to a hypnotic suggestion, phenomenal changes arose gradually and then faded away as each suggestion was administered, tested, and then cancelled.

Subjective experiences can also be assessed through retrospective ratings, after a hypnosis session has concluded. For example, Kirsch, Council, and Wickless (1990) and Kihlstrom (2002a) added additional items in the HGSHS:A, asking participants to rate the subjective involuntariness of their responses to the hypnotic suggestions; Bowers (1981) likewise included similar items with the SHSS:C. Researchers also have developed independent scales that can be used to retrospectively assess subjective experiences in hypnosis. One example is the Phenomenology of Consciousness Inventory (Pekala & Kumar, 1986), which surveys multiple dimensions of conscious experience and has shown that hypnotic responding is frequently associated with a subjective sense of dissociated control and attention to internal processes (Kumar, Pekala, & McCloskey, 1999). Another example is the recently developed Sense of Agency Rating Scale (Polito, Barnier, & Woody, 2013), which specifically assesses changes in agency during hypnosis. Findings with this latter scale have shown that the feeling of involuntariness typically associated with hypnotic responding is a multidimensional construct that varies over the time course of a hypnotic session (Polito, Barnier, Woody, & Connors, 2014).

More formal interviews after the hypnosis session provide another way of assessing subjective experience retrospectively. In contrast to quantitative measures, which necessarily tap a limited range of experiences, qualitative interviews allow for richer and more detailed accounts of hypnotic effects. A specific methodology for qualitative hypnosis research is the Experiential Analysis Technique (EAT; Sheehan & McConkey, 1982). The EAT is a semi-structured interview whereby, at the conclusion of a hypnosis experiment, participants watch video recordings of their responses during the session, with an independent experimenter. This experimenter stops the video at specific points and asks participants questions about their experiences during each segment of the recording. This can provide additional contextual information for quantitative data and highlight hypnotic effects that might otherwise have been missed (Barnier, Cox, Connors, Langdon, & Coltheart, 2011; Connors, Cox, Barnier, Langdon, & Coltheart, 2012).

Third, hypnosis-as-product can be inferred through neurophysiological measures. In recent years, there has been increasing interest in the neural correlates of hypnotic effects (Oakley & Halligan, 2013; Oakley, 2008; see also Chapter 18). Various changes in neural functioning have been shown to occur both in neutral hypnosis—that is, in the hypnotic context in the absence of any suggestions (Deeley et al., 2012; Rainville, Hofbauer, Bushnell, Duncan, & Price, 2002)—and in response to specific suggestions (e.g., Cojan, Archimi, Cheseaux, Waber, & Vuilleumier, 2013; Kosslyn, 2000). For example, research has identified distinct neural correlates of hypnotically suggested pain (Derbyshire, Whalley, & Oakley, 2009), hypnotic hallucinations (Szechtman, Kalogeras, Bowers, & Nahmias, 1998), and hypnotic paralysis (Halligan, Athwal, Oakley, & Frackowiak, 2000; for reviews, see Oakley, 2008; Oakley & Halligan, 2009).

Together, these various methods provide converging data on hypnosis-as-product (Cox & Bryant, 2008; Sheehan & Perry, 1976). By making a distinction between procedure and product, and recognizing that the former does not necessarily imply the latter (Kirsch, Mazzoni, & Montgomery, 2007), hypnosis researchers have developed a nuanced view of the elements that contribute to hypnosis. This perspective allows for a multiplicity of very different types of suggestions to be considered part of hypnosis-as-procedure. It also provides a range of tools for assessing the effects of these procedures in constructive ways.

Meditation research can be conceptualized in very similar terms: meditation-as-procedure can be thought of as the physical and cognitive practices that individuals perform, whereas meditation-as-product can be thought of as the phenomenological experiences, behavioral changes, and neurophysiological correlates that occur as a result of these mediation practices. In meditation research, this distinction, although recognized by some investigators (e.g., Rao, 2011), is generally less explicit than in hypnosis research. In fact, many meditation studies conflate procedure and product by simply reporting that participants performed some meditation procedure as evidence of product, without independently verifying whether or not the procedure actually led to any change in meditation-as-product (Nash & Newberg, 2013). Here, we briefly consider procedure and product in meditation separately and provide some suggestions for how clearer boundaries between these two elements might facilitate future meditation research.

There is unquestionably an enormous variety of practices that could be considered meditation-as-procedure (Walsh & Shapiro, 2006) and a great deal of effort in the meditation literature has been spent developing various categorization schemas to group different meditation traditions according to their features. For example, Shear (2006) distinguished techniques based on the specific mental faculties used (attention, feeling, reasoning, visualization, memory, bodily awareness); the manner in which those faculties were used (actively, passively, effortlessly, forcefully); and the objects to which these faculties were directed (thoughts, images, concepts, internal energy, aspect of the body, love, god). Walsh and Shapiro (2006) similarly categorized practices according to the type of attention involved, the relationship between the practice and other cognitive processes, and the goal of the practice. Whereas these taxonomies allow fine-grained analysis of differences across various techniques, probably the most popular schema has been a much simpler proposal by Lutz, Slagter, Dunne, and Davidson (2008). Inspired by traditional Buddhist meditation texts, Lutz et al. categorize practices into two broad categories: focused attention and open monitoring. These two categories may involve distinct psychological and neurological processes that account for much of the variation between techniques.

Meditation-as-product has received mixed attention. On the one hand, there has been considerable interest in identifying the neural correlates of various forms of meditation (e.g., Barnhofer, Chittka, Nightingale, Visser, & Crane, 2010; Manna et al., 2010; Vago & Silbersweig, 2012; Wang et al., 2011). Findings among these studies have varied; however, there is growing evidence that many forms of meditation are associated with power increases in theta and alpha bands, and increased activity in frontal and prefrontal areas (Cahn & Polich, 2006). In contrast, research into phenomenological experiences and behavioral changes associated with meditation have received much less attention. Although numerous studies have looked at the long-term effects of meditation (see Sedlmeier et al., 2012 for a comprehensive review), only a relatively small number of studies have investigated the direct subjective experience of meditation in a systematic way. In fact, very few non-neurophysiological methods have been developed for the assessment of meditation-as-product (notable exceptions include Lau et al., 2006; Levinson, Stoll, Kindy, Merry, & Davidson, 2014; Nash & Newberg, 2013). Because of the emphasis on long-term outcomes, the measures that have been developed have tended towards operationalizing the effects of meditation in terms of influences on other psychological constructs and characteristics, such as anxiety and stress, rather than in terms of the immediate phenomenological experience of meditation (Grossman & Van Dam, 2011). This lack of focus on the intrinsic features of meditative experience has meant that this aspect of meditation and mindfulness has remained poorly defined.

A common feature throughout the meditation research literature is for authors to offer a tentative interpretation of key terms and to call for increased specificity and convergence of definitions in the field (e.g., Awasthi, 2013; Bishop et al., 2004; Nash & Newberg, 2013). To progress beyond this definitional impasse, it may be useful for meditation research to incorporate similar methods to those used in hypnosis research.

Members of our research team (Polito et al., 2013) faced a similar set of challenges in developing the Sense of Agency Rating Scale (SOARS), a psychometric scale that assesses subjective sense of agency in hypnosis. Prior to the creation of this measure, there were many published accounts of altered agency associated with hypnosis but no agreed terminology or method for describing and assessing this construct. We compiled a comprehensive set of terms used in the literature to describe agency, constructed scale items based on these terms, and then asked participants to rate the degree to which each item matched their experiences in hypnosis. We performed factor analysis on participants' responses and refined this measure across multiple studies. This ultimately resulted in a validated, multifactorial measure of sense of agency that has informed a new theoretical account of subjective control in hypnosis (Polito, Barnier, Woody, & Connors, 2014).

A similar research strategy might be useful in developing a clearer account of meditation-as-product. This would likely involve a combination of self-report measures, qualitative interviews, and custom-designed scales to better characterize changes in subjective experience during meditation. In fact, there have been promising moves in this direction with calls for multimethod approaches and the emergence of new techniques such as neurophenomenology, which promises to systematically integrate phenomenological and neurophysiological data in meditation research (Garland & Gaylord, 2009; Mikulas, 2011; Sauer et al., 2013; see also Chapters 6 and 15).

Trait and state

The second concept that we consider useful has been to distinguish between individuals' capacities (i.e., trait effects) and contextual influences (i.e., state effects) in hypnosis. In the section "Procedure and product," we highlighted that a given hypnosis procedure should not be assumed to create any particular corresponding product (i.e., changes in subjective experience). Rather, hypnotic effects are strongly influenced by the interaction of state and trait variables.

One of the foundational findings of hypnosis research has been that individuals differ markedly in their capacity to experience hypnosis (Barnier, Cox, & McConkey, 2014). This capacity to respond to suggestions in the context of hypnosis is referred to as "hypnotizability", and is a stable trait that seems, for the most part, only very modestly related to other personality characteristics or cognitive capacities (Laurence, Beaulieu-Prèvost, & du Chènè, 2008). In hypnosis research, hypnotizability is assessed through standardized measures. These are almost exclusively "work-sample" scales that score participants' responses to hypnotic suggestions in terms of predefined behavioral criteria (Woody & Barnier, 2008). Whereas a variety of measures have been developed, the two most commonly used in a research setting are the HGSHS:A (Shor & Orne, 1962) and the SHSS:C (Weitzenhoffer & Hilgard, 1962). These have been described as the "gold standard" in hypnotizability research (Barnier & Oakley, 2009). Considerable data from studies conducted across multiple populations and cultures have reliably shown that approximately 15% of people are "high hypnotizable" (i.e., able to respond to all or most suggestions), 70–80% are "medium hypnotizable" (i.e., able to respond to some but not all suggestions), and 10–15% are "low hypnotizable" (i.e., able to respond to only a few suggestions) (Barnier & Oakley, 2009).

To control for the trait effects of hypnotizability, researchers sometimes pre-screen participants and then compare experimental groups of individuals with differing levels of hypnotic ability— for example, comparing the experiences of low and high hypnotizable participants (Woody & Barnier, 2008). In such a design, only high hypnotizable participants would be expected to respond hypnotically. The importance of controlling for individual differences has long been recognized as a key consideration in hypnosis research, with Bowers claiming that "an effect is not a classic suggestion effect unless it is correlated with hypnotic ability as standardly assessed" (as quoted in Woody & Barnier, 2008; see also Bowers, 1976). The importance of trait influences on hypnosis cannot be over-emphasized. Although some participants may comply with the perceived demands of the hypnotic context (as discussed in the "Demand characteristics" section), an individual can only be expected to experience genuine hypnotic effects if they have the personal capacity to do so.

In hypnosis, "state" variables refer to influences related to the hypnotic context and other factors that may vary over time. Important state variables in research include the nature of the hypnotic induction administered, environmental features (such as the location in which the hypnosis session is being conducted), and the tone of the hypnotist's voice. Many of these features mark the interaction as hypnotic, as opposed to being some other kind of social interaction. Systematically controlling for state influences in the context of research can be difficult as participants, particularly those who are experienced with hypnosis, may interpret suggestions as hypnotic cues regardless of any other situational factors (Cox & Bryant, 2008). One strategy has been to consider the hypnotic induction as a ritual marker of the hypnotic "state." This is problematic, as evidence suggests that some participants can experience marked changes in cognitive, perceptual, and physiological processes even in the absence of an induction (Bowers & Kelly, 1979; Polito, Barnier, Woody, & Connors, 2014; Raz, Kirsch, Pollard, & Nitkin-Kaner, 2006).

Nevertheless, a number of designs in hypnosis research attempt to (at least partially) control for state influences by testing participants of a similar level of hypnotizability and manipulating the impact of the induction. One commonly employed design has simply been to test high hypnotizable participants with and without a hypnotic induction (Orne, 1979). The assumption of such a design is that the induction interacts with other variables (e.g., traits, social cues, cognitive factors) to facilitate hypnosis. In response to questions around the specific importance of an induction for hypnosis to occur, alternative designs have compared a traditional induction to instructions for increased imagination (McConkey, Bryant, Bibb, & Kihlstrom, 1991), an obviously non-hypnotic task (mathematical puzzles; Connors et al., 2013; Nogrady, McConkey, & Perry, 1985), and task motivational instructions (Barber & Calverley, 1962). Variation in participants' responses and experiences across these different manipulations, although not perfectly isolating the role of the hypnotic "state," do highlight the impact of contextual factors on hypnotic effects.

Distinguishing between trait and state effects in hypnosis has allowed researchers to better understand how hypnotic phenomena relate to one another. Rather than simply viewing everything that happens in the hypnotic context as occurring due to a broad and monolithic concept of "hypnosis," recognizing the simultaneous influence of trait and state effects (and their interaction with other variables) has allowed a more nuanced view of the domain of hypnosis (Kihlstrom, 2003a). This clarity has encouraged research that integrates hypnosis with other fields, for example, guiding research into the relationship between hypnotizability and memory (Barnier, 2002; Kihlstrom, 2003b). It has also enabled researchers to form and investigate sophisticated research questions, for example, distinguishing between the neural correlates of hypnotizability, neutral hypnosis, and specific hypnotic suggestions (Oakley, 2008; Oakley & Halligan, 2013).

In meditation research, a similar distinction can be made between the influence of specific personal characteristics that are relatively stable over time—for example, an individual's inherent capacity for focused attention (trait)—and the influence of the specific meditative context and other variables that can fluctuate over time (state). Historically, throughout the meditation literature these two elements have often been confounded with one another and with other variables. Recently, however, a number of researchers have started to explicitly address these confounds. Awasthi (2013) reviewed a number of neurophysiological studies that did not properly account for trait or state effects and recommended clearer operational definitions of meditative effects as a way of improving future research. Similarly, Nash and Newberg (2013), Rao (2011), and Lutz et al. (2008) have emphasized the gradual development of meditative abilities (traits) and their impact on meditative states. These are important issues for future research in meditation.

Trait differences related to meditation have been most commonly conceptualized as "mindfulness" (Baer, 2003) and a number of measures have been developed to assess this construct. The most cited measure (according to Sauer et al., 2013) has been the Mindfulness Attention Awareness Scale (MAAS; Brown & Ryan, 2003). Other measures that have been used in meditation research include the Kentucky Inventory of Mindfulness Skills (KIMS; Baer, Smith, & Allen, 2004), the Freiburg Mindfulness Inventory (FMI; Walach, Buchheld, Buttenmüller, Kleinknecht, & Schmidt, 2006), and the Five Factors Mindfulness Questionnaire (FFMQ; Baer, Smith, Hopkins, Krietemeyer, & Toney, 2006). Whereas each of these measures claims to measure mindfulness, Grossman (2008) has argued that they are based on distinct theoretical concepts and noted that correlations between the measures are low. Inconsistencies between these various trait measures are necessarily related to the broader definitional difficulties across the domain of meditation outlined in the "Procedure and product" section.

An additional concern regarding the use of mindfulness measures is that trait effects have often been confounded with state effects. This is particularly the case, for example, in some early studies that compared the neural activity of inexperienced participants at rest with the neural activity of experienced practitioners during mediation (e.g., Banquet, 1973; Deepak, Manchanda, & Maheshwari, 1994; Khare & Nigam, 2000; for a review see Awasthi, 2013). Even in research designs without such an obvious confound, it is not always clear if differences between experts and novices reflect trait differences, such as pre-existing characteristics and acquired characteristics from long-term meditation, or state differences, such as the effect of the meditative context or experiential changes associated with a particular episode of meditation.

This issue could be addressed by adopting designs similar to those used in hypnosis; for example, by testing participants high in trait mindfulness inside and outside of the meditative context. A complication, however, is establishing how to define the meditative context. Although both hypnosis and meditation can take the form of either a social interaction (i.e., one person administers a procedure to another person) or a solitary exercise (i.e., an individual self-directs a procedure), meditation is most commonly self-directed. Meditation also tends not to follow a specific script and can take place in many different settings. A consequence of this is that, unlike hypnosis (which typically involves an observable induction procedure), there is often no obvious observable marker of the meditative context. This poses challenges for separating state and trait. One way of meeting these challenges might be to assess participants' moment-to-moment subjective experiences in different experimental conditions—for example, by repeatedly recording ratings of attention during a normal meditation procedure and during a relaxation control condition (Davidson, 2010).

A further issue relevant to the distinction between trait and state effects in meditation is the role of training. In hypnosis, although various attempts have been made to train low hypnotizable participants to respond to hypnosis, the results have been largely unconvincing. Although it is possible to train participants to emulate the outward physical behaviors of high hypnotizable participants (Gorassini & Spanos, 1986, 1999), there is little evidence that the training promotes genuine changes in subjective experience or that the effects of the training persist in other contexts or across time (Bates, 1992; Bowers & Davidson, 1991; for a review, see Barnier & McConkey, 2004). Hypnosis thus seems to reflect a relatively stable trait that is not easily modifiable. In contrast, the ability to meditate seems to implicitly require some level of practice and training (Tang et al., 2007). There is, for example, some evidence that meditative training can result in relatively stable changes to attention and mind wandering (Brewer et al., 2011).

Despite this, the nature of the relationship between meditation training and trait mindfulness is somewhat unclear, and there are a number of unresolved questions. For example, it is not clear if people have an inherent capacity for mindfulness or if this is an entirely learned skill (Grant, 2012). Likewise, it is not clear if the social and contextual cues of meditation training have a facilitatory effect on participants' practice, independent of trait mindfulness (Tang, Rothbart, & Posner, 2012). Even more critically, it is not clear if trait mindfulness is a single capacity or involves multiple distinct components (e.g., perhaps particular levels of training might correspond to specific meditative capacities; Grossman, 2011). Woody, Barnier, and McConkey (2005) have proposed a similar idea regarding hypnosis, arguing for a componential model of hypnotizability, whereby a generalized capacity for hypnosis explains much of the variation across participants, while additional specialized component abilities are required for specific hypnotic effects. Similarly, Terhune, Cardeña, and Lindgren (2011) have found evidence that there are distinct subtypes of high hypnotizable individuals capable of responding to different types of suggestions. A possible future direction for meditation research might be to investigate whether there are comparable general and specific mindfulness capabilities that vary across individuals, meditative practices, and levels of expertise.

Recent methodological and conceptual reviews of meditation research (e.g., Awasthi, 2013; Grossman, 2008; Mikulas, 2011; Sauer et al., 2013; see also Chapters 13 and 15) suggest growing awareness of these issues. The increasing focus on methodologies for quantifying trait mindfulness is particularly encouraging. Distinguishing between trait and state effects in meditation has the potential to improve our understanding of the way that different meditation phenomena relate to one another, and we suggest that the conceptual frameworks used in hypnosis research may be instructive in this goal. Improved conceptual clarity would likely lead to new and refined measures, which would in turn facilitate new research questions and hypotheses within the broader science of subjective experience.

Cognitive and social influences

The third concept that we consider useful has been an awareness of the interplay between cognitive and social processes. Hypnosis, by definition, involves cognitive changes in the context of a social interaction between the hypnotist and person being hypnotized (in the case of self-hypnosis, both roles are performed by the same person; Kihlstrom, 2008). As a result, hypnosis research has needed to examine both cognitive and social influences. An enduring debate is whether hypnosis can be understood as involving mainly social variables or cognitive changes. Although such a simple dichotomy is likely to be problematic (Kihlstrom, 2003a), various theorists have emphasized one over the other (e.g., Barnier, Dienes, & Mitchell, 2008; Lynn, Kirsch, & Hallquist, 2008).

In meditation research, much more focus has been placed on cognitive changes associated with meditation—either as state or trait—while largely ignoring the social context in which meditation occurs. Meditation, however, is traditionally engaged in for a particular spiritual purpose and within a particular cultural setting (Chiesa, 2013). It remains to be seen as to the extent to which meditation can be excised from this setting for the purposes of laboratory research or clinical intervention (Faure, 2012; MacCoon, MacLean, Davidson, Saron, & Lutz, 2014; Mitchell, 2002). It is likely, for example, that the particular beliefs a person holds, their motivations, and the social groups to which they belong influence their meditative practice (Sedlmeier et al., 2012). Neglecting this is likely to lead to an impoverished view of the phenomena.

This also has specific implications for research. Sedlmeier et al. (2012), for example, note that details about instructors, demographic background, participants' personality, and recruitment are often sparse in the literature. Research, instead, typically only reports the type of meditative practice undertaken and the duration of practice. Both these measures are problematic. Type of meditative practice is usually insufficient because of the heterogeneity within even simple meditative practices in terms of technique and the context in which it is engaged. A simple breath meditation, for example, can be done in many different ways and can be done simply to improve concentration or with a more soteriological goal (Gethin, 1998; Mitchell, 2002). Duration of practice is also problematic, showing only a very modest association ($r = 0.05$) with the effects of meditation in Sedlmeier et al.'s (2012) meta-analysis. Furthermore, there is evidence from other domains of expertise showing that training is necessary but not sufficient for expertise (Campitelli & Gobet, 2011; Hambrick et al., 2014). In particular, there are considerable differences between individuals in terms of the amount of practice required to achieve levels of expertise (Campitelli & Gobet, 2008), and pre-existing individual differences greatly influence final attainment (Campitelli & Gobet, 2011; Hambrick & Meinz, 2011).

Other general social variables may also influence meditative outcomes. Some authors have explained hypnosis in terms of factors that describe other complex social behavior, such as expectancies, attributions, beliefs, and relationships (Lynn et al., 2008). Although there has been considerable debate as to whether hypnosis can be entirely reduced to these factors, it is clear that these variables play an important role in hypnosis. There is evidence, for example, that increasing expectancy may lead to greater responsiveness from hypnotized participants (Lynn et al., 2008). It remains to be seen how these variables affect meditation. This is particularly relevant to the reliability of self-report measures of subjective experience in meditation, which might be especially affected by various socio-cognitive influences. This is an important area for future research.

Demand characteristics

The fourth concept that we consider useful is controlling demand characteristics. Whereas many general social factors are important to both hypnosis and meditation, the particular social setting of a laboratory experiment may also influences participants' responses. In particular, demand characteristics—features of the experimental situation that invite particular responses from participants—are an inescapable part of laboratory research (Kihlstrom, 2002b; Orne, 1959, 1979). These have been studied perhaps most intensely in hypnosis, due to skepticism and debate about the nature of hypnotic effects. In a hypnosis session, participants may alter their behavior in response to subtle pressure from the hypnotist to comply, their preconceptions of what hypnosis involves, and particular cues in the experimental setting, such as the wording of the suggestion and how it is tested. More broadly, in the act of hypnosis, both the hypnotist and the participant enter into an implicit arrangement with predefined social roles (Kihlstrom, 2002b). This complicity encourages participants to adjust their behavior to what they believe is required, and so undermines the ecological validity of the experiment.

In hypnosis research, demand characteristics are traditionally investigated using the real–simulator design developed by Orne (1962, 1979). In this design, genuinely hypnotized, high hypnotizable participants (reals) are compared to a quasi-control group of low hypnotizable participants instructed to fake hypnosis (simulators). The hypnotist remains blind as to which participants are in each group and administers a hypnotic induction and hypnotic suggestions to all participants. The rationale of this design is that if reals respond in the same way as simulators, it is not possible to rule out the possibility that reals are merely responding to social cues. If, however, reals respond differently to simulators, it is likely that their behavior is not simply due to situational cues. This design thus allows experimenters to investigate what social cues are available to participants and the likely impact of these cues on behavior (Sheehan & Perry, 1976).

Although such a design may not be useful for ongoing meditation research, it could provide important insights into the experimental cues that influence behavior. Participants, for example, are typically aware that they are taking part in a study on meditation and this, by itself, is likely to cue certain responses and behaviors (Lifshitz & Raz, 2012). For example, meditators are likely to complete questionnaires or answer questions in the context of being a meditator—rather than in terms of their other social roles and identities—and may be inclined to emphasize the benefits of meditation to provide what they believe the experimenter is looking for (Sauer et al., 2013). It is even possible that some neurophysiological characteristics could be affected by the unique social context of the experiment, in which the participant's identity as a meditator is highly salient and the participant is scrutinized in great detail (see, e.g., Campbell-Meiklejohn, Bach, Roepstorff, Dolan, & Frith, 2010; Mason, Dyer, & Norton, 2009; Zaki, Schirmer, & Mitchell, 2011, for evidence that social influence can affect neurophysiology).

Even without deploying complicated designs such as real–simulator studies, meditation research might benefit from a more explicit focus on assessing demand characteristics. For example, at the conclusion of a study, participants could be asked, by an independent interviewer, what they thought the experimenter was looking for and the extent to which they felt pressure to provide particular responses. In addition, questionnaires could include items to detect impression management and compliance—for example, including items that assess responses that one would not necessarily expect to change as a result of meditation (such as physical strength and abilities), as well as items that assess expectations around meditation and its effects on others. Research could also examine whether participants' responses vary depending upon the context in which they are assessed—whether in the laboratory or in other settings when other aspects of their identity are more salient—and in response to financial incentives (Jensen, Vangkilde, Frokjaer, & Hasselbalch, 2012).

Conclusion

We acknowledge that hypnosis and meditation differ in many important ways. These differences include, in particular, the goals of practice, the contexts in which they typically occur, the techniques involved (procedure), their effects (product), the role of individual differences, and their social, cultural, and historical backgrounds. There is also considerable heterogeneity within each tradition, and differences in how these techniques are practiced both in everyday settings and in the laboratory. Nevertheless, we believe that the various distinctions we have identified in hypnosis research can help to inform meditation research.

Research into both hypnosis and meditation is challenging precisely because both primarily involve alterations in subjective experience. Since it is not possible to directly observe these alterations, researchers must infer what these alterations involve using various methodologies. Both hypnosis and meditation have developed different methods for addressing this challenge. Whereas hypnosis research has focused on the various subjective, behavioral, and neurophysiological alterations that occur within a particular social interaction, meditation research has focused on changes associated with specific training and the development of expertise. Dialogue between these traditions may thus help to enrich each other, as well as to guide investigation into the nature of subjective experience more broadly.

References

Awasthi, B. (2013). Issues and perspectives in meditation research: in search for a definition. *Frontiers in Consciousness Research*, **3**, 613. doi:10.3389/fpsyg.2012.00613

Baer, R. A. (2003). Mindfulness training as a clinical intervention: a conceptual and empirical review. *Clinical Psychology: Science and Practice*, **10**(2), 125–143. doi:10.1093/clipsy.bpg015

Baer, R. A., Smith, G. T., & Allen, K. B. (2004). Assessment of mindfulness by self-report: the Kentucky Inventory of Mindfulness Skills. *Assessment*, **11**(3), 191–206. doi:10.1177/1073191104268029

Baer, R. A., Smith, G. T., Hopkins, J., Krietemeyer, J., & Toney, L. (2006). Using self-report assessment methods to explore facets of mindfulness. *Assessment*, **13**(1), 27–45.

Banquet, J.-P. (1973). Spectral analysis of the EEG in meditation. *Electroencephalography and Clinical Neurophysiology*, **35**(2), 143–151.

Bányai, E. I., & Hilgard, E. R. (1976). A comparison of active-alert hypnotic induction with traditional relaxation induction. *Journal of Abnormal Psychology*, **85**(2), 218–224. doi:10.1037/0021-843X.85.2.218

Barber, T. X., & Calverley, D. S. (1962). "Hypnotic behavior" as a function of task motivation. *Journal of Psychology*, **54**(2), 363–389.

Barnhofer, T., Chittka, T., Nightingale, H., Visser, C., & Crane, C. (2010). State effects of two forms of meditation on prefrontal EEG asymmetry in previously depressed individuals. *Mindfulness*, **1**(1), 21–27. doi:10.1007/s12671-010-0004-7

Barnier, A. J. (2002). Remembering and forgetting autobiographical events: instrumental uses of hypnosis. *Contemporary Hypnosis*, **19**(2), 51–61. doi:10.1002/ch.242

Barnier, A. J., Cox, R. E., Connors, M., Langdon, R., & Coltheart, M. (2011). A stranger in the looking glass: developing and challenging a hypnotic mirrored-self misidentification delusion. *International Journal of Clinical and Experimental Hypnosis*, **59**(1), 1. doi:10.1080/00207144.2011.522863

Barnier, A. J., Cox, R. E., & McConkey, K. M. (2014). The province of "highs": the high hypnotizable person in the science of hypnosis and in psychological science. *Psychology of Consciousness*, **1**(2), 168–183. doi:10.1037/cns0000018

Barnier, A. J., Dienes, Z., & Mitchell, C. (2008). How hypnosis happens: new cognitive theories of hypnotic responding. In M. R. Nash & A. J. Barnier (Eds.), *The Oxford handbook of hypnosis: theory, research and practice* (pp. 141–177). Oxford, UK: Oxford University Press.

Barnier, A. J., & McConkey, K. M. (2004). Defining and identifying the highly hypnotisable person. In M. Heap, R. J. Brown, & D. A. Oakley (Eds.), *The highly hypnotizable person: theoretical, experimental and clinical issues* (pp. 30–60). New York: Routledge.

Barnier, A. J., & Nash, M. R. (2008). Introduction: a roadmap for explanation, a working definition. In M. R. Nash & A. J. Barnier (Eds.), *The Oxford handbook of hypnosis: theory, research and practice* (pp. 1–18). Oxford: Oxford University Press.

Barnier, A. J., & Oakley, D. A. (2009). Hypnosis and suggestion. In W. P. Banks (Ed.), *Encyclopedia of consciousness* (pp. 351–368). Oxford, UK: Elsevier.

Bates, B. L. (1992). The effect of demands for honesty on the efficacy of the Carleton Skills-Training Program. *International Journal of Clinical and Experimental Hypnosis*, **40**(2), 88–102.

Bishop, S. R., Lau, M., Shapiro, S., Carlson, L., Anderson, N. D., Carmody, J., . . . Devins, G. (2004). Mindfulness: a proposed operational definition. *Clinical Psychology*, **11**(3), 230–241. doi:10.1093/clipsy. bph077

Bowers, K. S. (1976). *Hypnosis for the seriously curious*. Monterey, CA: Brooks/Cole.

Bowers, K. S. (1981). Do the Stanford scales tap the "classic suggestion effect"? *International Journal of Clinical and Experimental Hypnosis*, **29**(1), 42. doi:10.1080/00207148108409142

Bowers, K. S., & Davidson, T. M. (1991). A neodissociative critique of Spanos's social-psychological model of hypnosis. In S. J. Lynn & J. W. Rhue (Eds.), *Theories of hypnosis: current models and perspectives* (pp. 105–143). New York: Guilford Press. Retrieved from http://psycnet.apa.org/psycinfo/1991–98913-004

Bowers, K. S., & Kelly, P. (1979). Stress, disease, psychotherapy, and hypnosis. *Journal of Abnormal Psychology*, **88**(5), 490–505. doi:10.1037/0021-843X.88.5.490

Brewer, J. A., Worhunsky, P. D., Gray, J. R., Tang, Y.-Y., Weber, J., & Kober, H. (2011). Meditation experience is associated with differences in default mode network activity and connectivity. *Proceedings of the National Academy of Sciences*, **108**(50), 20254–20259. doi:10.1073/pnas.1112029108

Brown, K. W., & Ryan, R. M. (2003). The benefits of being present: mindfulness and its role in psychological well-being. *Journal of Personality and Social Psychology*, **84**(4), 822.

Cahn, B. R., & Polich, J. (2006). Meditation states and traits: EEG, ERP, and neuroimaging studies. *Psychological Bulletin*, **132**(2), 180.

Campbell-Meiklejohn, D. K., Bach, D. R., Roepstorff, A., Dolan, R. J., & Frith, C. D. (2010). How the opinion of others affects our valuation of objects. *Current Biology*, **20**(13), 1165–1170.

Campitelli, G., & Gobet, F. (2008). The role of practice in chess: a longitudinal study. *Learning and Individual Differences*, **18**(4), 446–458.

Campitelli, G., & Gobet, F. (2011). Deliberate practice necessary but not sufficient. *Current Directions in Psychological Science*, **20**(5), 280–285. doi:10.1177/0963721411421922

Chiesa, A. (2013). The difficulty of defining mindfulness: current thought and critical issues. *Mindfulness*, **4**(3), 255–268.

Cojan, Y., Archimi, A., Cheseaux, N., Waber, L., & Vuilleumier, P. (2013). Time-course of motor inhibition during hypnotic paralysis: EEG topographical and source analysis. *Cortex*, **49**(2), 423–436. doi:10.1016/j.cortex.2012.09.013

Connors, M. H., Barnier, A. J., Langdon, R., Cox, R. E., Polito, V., & Coltheart, M. (2013). A laboratory analogue of mirrored-self misidentification delusion: the role of hypnosis, suggestion, and demand characteristics. *Consciousness and Cognition*, **22**(4), 1510–1522. doi:10.1016/j.concog.2013.10.006

Connors, M. H., Cox, R. E., Barnier, A. J., Langdon, R., & Coltheart, M. (2012). Mirror agnosia and the mirrored-self misidentification delusion: a hypnotic analogue. *Cognitive Neuropsychiatry*, **17**(3), 197–226. doi:10.1080/13546805.2011.582770

Cox, R. E., & Bryant, R. A. (2008). Advances in hypnosis research: methods, designs and contributions of intrinsic and instrumental hypnosis. In M. R. Nash & A. J. Barnier (Eds.), *The Oxford handbook of hypnosis: theory, research and practice* (pp. 311–336). Oxford: Oxford University Press.

Davidson, R. J. (2010). Empirical explorations of mindfulness: conceptual and methodological conundrums. *Emotion*, **10**(1), 8–11. doi:10.1037/a0018480

Deeley, Q., Oakley, D. A., Toone, B., Giampietro, V., Brammer, M. J., Williams, S. C. R., & Halligan, P. W. (2012). Modulating the default mode network using hypnosis. *International Journal of Clinical and Experimental Hypnosis*, **60**(2), 206–228. doi:10.1080/00207144.2012.648070

Deepak, K. K., Manchanda, S. K., & Maheshwari, M. C. (1994). Meditation improves clinicoelectroencephalographic measures in drug-resistant epileptics. *Biofeedback and Self-regulation*, **19**(1), 25–40.

Derbyshire, S. W. G., Whalley, M. G., & Oakley, D. A. (2009). Fibromyalgia pain and its modulation by hypnotic and non-hypnotic suggestion: an fMRI analysis. *European Journal of Pain*, **13**(5), 542–550. doi:10.1016/j.ejpain.2008.06.010

Faure, B. (2012). A gray matter: another look at Buddhism and neuroscience. *Tricycle: The Buddhist Review*, **XXII**, 70–75.

Fox, K. C. R., Nijeboer, S., Dixon, M. L., Floman, J. L., Ellamil, M., Rumak, S. P., . . . Christoff, K. (2014). Is meditation associated with altered brain structure? A systematic review and meta-analysis of morphometric neuroimaging in meditation practitioners. *Neuroscience and Biobehavioral Reviews*, **43**, 48–73. doi:10.1016/j.neubiorev.2014.03.016

Galea, V., Woody, E. Z., Szechtman, H., & Pierrynowski, M. R. (2010). Motion in response to the hypnotic suggestion of arm rigidity: a window on underlying mechanisms. *International Journal of Clinical and Experimental Hypnosis*, **58**(3), 251–268.

Garland, E., & Gaylord, S. (2009). Envisioning a future contemplative science of mindfulness: fruitful methods and new content for the next wave of research. *Complementary Health Practice Review*, **14**(1), 3–9. doi:10.1177/1533210109333718

Gauld, A. (1995). *A history of hypnotism*. Cambridge, UK: Cambridge University Press.

Gethin, R. (1998). *The foundations of Buddhism*. Oxford: Oxford University Press.

Gorassini, D. R., & Spanos, N. P. (1986). A social-cognitive skills approach to the successful modification of hypnotic susceptibility. *Journal of Personality and Social Psychology*, **50**(5), 1004.

Gorassini, D. R., & Spanos, N. P. (1999). The Carleton Skill Training Program for modifying hypnotic suggestibility: original version and variations. In I. Kirsch, A. Capafons, E. Cardeña-Buelna, & S. Amigo (Eds.), *Clinical hypnosis and self-regulation: cognitive-behavioral perspectives* (pp. 141–177). Washington, DC: American Psychological Association.

Goyal, M., Singh, S., Sibinga, E. M. S., Gould, N. F., Rowland-Seymour, A., Sharma, R., . . . Haythornthwaite, J. A. (2014). Meditation programs for psychological stress and well-being: a systematic review and meta-analysis. *JAMA Internal Medicine*, **174**(3), 357–368. doi:10.1001/jamainternmed.2013.13018

Grant, J. A. (2012). Towards a more meaningful comparison of meditation and hypnosis. *Journal of Mind–Body Regulation*, **2**(1), 71–74.

Grossman, P. (2008). On measuring mindfulness in psychosomatic and psychological research. *Journal of Psychosomatic Research*, **64**(4), 405–408. doi:10.1016/j.jpsychores.2008.02.001

Grossman, P. (2011). Defining mindfulness by how poorly I think I pay attention during everyday awareness and other intractable problems for psychology's (re)invention of mindfulness: comment on Brown et al.(2011). *Psychological Assessment*, **23**(4), 1034–1040.

Grossman, P., & Van Dam, N. T. (2011). Mindfulness, by any other name . . . : trials and tribulations of sati in Western psychology and science. *Contemporary Buddhism*, **12**(1), 219–239. doi:10.1080/14639947.2011.564841

Halligan, P. W., Athwal, B. S., Oakley, D. A., & Frackowiak, R. S. (2000). Imaging hypnotic paralysis: implications for conversion hysteria. *The Lancet*, **355**(9208), 986–987. doi:10.1016/S0140-6736(00)99019-6

Hambrick, D. Z., & Meinz, E. J. (2011). Limits on the predictive power of domain-specific experience and knowledge in skilled performance. *Current Directions in Psychological Science*, **20**(5), 275–279.

Hambrick, D. Z., Oswald, F. L., Altmann, E. M., Meinz, E. J., Gobet, F., & Campitelli, G. (2014). Deliberate practice: is that all it takes to become an expert? *Intelligence*, **45**, 34–45. doi:10.1016/j.intell.2013.04.001

Hilgard, E. R. (1965). *Hypnotic susceptibility*. New York: Harcourt, Brace & World.

Hilgard, E. R. (1975). Hypnosis. *Annual Review of Psychology*, **26**(1), 19–44. doi:10.1146/annurev.ps.26.020175.000315

Hilgard, E. R. (1977). *Divided consciousness: multiple controls in human thought and action*. New York: Wiley and Sons.

Hofmann, S. G., Sawyer, A. T., Witt, A. A., & Oh, D. (2010). The effect of mindfulness-based therapy on anxiety and depression: a meta-analytic review. *Journal of Consulting and Clinical Psychology*, **78**(2), 169–183. doi:10.1037/a0018555

Hull, C. L. (1933). *Hypnosis and suggestibility*. New York: Appleton-Century Crofts.

Jensen, C. G., Vangkilde, S., Frokjaer, V., & Hasselbalch, S. G. (2012). Mindfulness training affects attention—or is it attentional effort? *Journal of Experimental Psychology*, **141**(1), 106.

Khare, K. C., & Nigam, S. K. (2000). A study of electroencephalogram in meditators. *Indian Journal of Physiology and Pharmacology*, **44**(2), 173–178.

Kihlstrom, J. F. (1985). Hypnosis. *Annual Review of Psychology*, **36**(1), 385–418. doi:10.1146/annurev.ps.36.020185.002125

Kihlstrom, J. F. (2002a). Measurement of involuntariness in hypnotic response. Retrieved March 11, 2012, from http://ist-socrates.berkeley.edu/~kihlstrm/PDFfiles/Hypnotizability/HGSHSAResponse1002.pdf

Kihlstrom, J. F. (2002b). Demand characteristics in the laboratory and the clinic: conversations and collaborations with subjects and patients. *Prevention and Treatment*, **5**, Article 36c.

Kihlstrom, J. F. (2003a). The fox, the hedgehog, and hypnosis. *International Journal of Clinical and Experimental Hypnosis*, **51**(2), 166–189. doi:10.1076/iceh.51.2.166.14611

Kihlstrom, J. F. (2003b). Hypnosis and memory. *Learning and memory* (2nd edn.) (pp. 240–242). Farmington Hills, MI: Macmillan Reference.

Kihlstrom, J. F. (2008). The domain of hypnosis, revisited. In M. R. Nash & A. J. Barnier (Eds.), *The Oxford handbook of hypnosis: theory, research and practice* (pp. 21–52). Oxford: Oxford University Press.

Kirsch, I., Council, J. R., & Wickless, C. (1990). Subjective scoring for the Harvard Group Scale of Hypnotic Susceptibility, Form A. *International Journal of Clinical and Experimental Hypnosis*, **38**(2), 112. doi:10.1080/00207149008414506

Kirsch, I., Mazzoni, G., & Montgomery, G. H. (2007). Remembrance of hypnosis past. *American Journal of Clinical Hypnosis*, **49**(3), 171–178.

Kosslyn, S. M. (2000). Hypnotic visual illusion alters color processing in the brain. *American Journal of Psychiatry*, **157**(8), 1279–1284. doi:10.1176/appi.ajp.157.8.1279

Kumar, V. K., Pekala, R. J., & McCloskey, M. M. (1999). Phenomenological state effects during hypnosis: a cross-validation of findings. *Contemporary Hypnosis*, **16**(1), 9–21. doi:10.1002/ch.145

Lau, M. A., Bishop, S. R., Segal, Z. V., Buis, T., Anderson, N. D., Carlson, L., . . . Devins, G. (2006). The Toronto Mindfulness Scale: development and validation. *Journal of Clinical Psychology*, **62**(12), 1445–1467. doi:10.1002/jclp.20326

Laurence, J.-R., Beaulieu-Prèvost, D., & du Chènè, T. (2008). Measuring and understanding individual differences in hypnotizability. In M. R. Nash & A. J. Barnier (Eds.), *The Oxford handbook of hypnosis: theory, research and practice* (pp. 225–253). Oxford: Oxford University Press.

Laurence, J.-R., & Nadon, R. (1986). Reports of hypnotic depth: are they more than mere words? *International Journal of Clinical and Experimental Hypnosis*, **34**(3), 215–233. doi:10.1080/00207148608406987

Levinson, D. B., Stoll, E. L., Kindy, S. D., Merry, H. L., & Davidson, R. J. (2014). A mind you can count on: validating breath counting as a behavioral measure of mindfulness. *Frontiers in Psychology*, **5**, 1202. doi:10.3389/fpsyg.2014.01202

Lifshitz, M., & Raz, A. (2012). Hypnosis and meditation: vehicles of attention and suggestion. *Journal of Mind–Body Regulation*, **2**(1), 3–11.

Lutz, A., Dunne, J. D., & Davidson, R. J. (2007). Meditation and the neuroscience of consciousness: an introduction. In P. Zelazo, M. Moscovitch, & E. Thompson (Eds.), *The Cambridge handbook of consciousness* (pp. 499–554). Cambridge, UK: Cambridge University Press.

Lutz, A., Slagter, H. A., Dunne, J. D., & Davidson, R. J. (2008). Attention regulation and monitoring in meditation. *Trends in Cognitive Sciences*, **12**(4), 163–169. doi:10.1016/j.tics.2008.01.005

Lynn, S. J., Kirsch, I., & Hallquist, M. N. (2008). Sociocognitive theories of hypnosis. In M. R. Nash & A. J. Barnier (Eds.), *The Oxford handbook of hypnosis: theory, research and practice*. Oxford: Oxford University Press.

Lynn, S. J., & Rhue, J. W. (1991). Hypnosis theories: themes, variations, and research directions. In S. J. Lynn & J. W. Rhue (Eds.), *Theories of hypnosis: current models and perspectives* (pp. 601–626). New York: Guilford Press.

Lynn, S. J., Rhue, J. W., & Kirsch, I. (Eds.). (2010). *Handbook of clinical hypnosis* (2nd revised edn.). Washington, DC:American Psychological Association.

MacCoon, D. G., MacLean, K. A., Davidson, R. J., Saron, C. D., & Lutz, A. (2014). No sustained attention differences in a longitudinal randomized trial comparing mindfulness based stress reduction versus active control. *PloS ONE*, **9**(6), e97551. doi:10.1371/journal.pone.0097551

Manna, A., Raffone, A., Perrucci, M. G., Nardo, D., Ferretti, A., Tartaro, A., . . . Romani, G. L. (2010). Neural correlates of focused attention and cognitive monitoring in meditation. *Brain Research Bulletin*, **82**(1–2), 46–56. doi:10.1016/j.brainresbull.2010.03.001

Mason, M. F., Dyer, R., & Norton, M. I. (2009). Neural mechanisms of social influence. *Organizational Behavior and Human Decision Processes*, **110**(2), 152–159.

McConkey, K. M. (2008). Generations and landscape of hypnosis: questions we've asked, questions we should ask. In M. R. Nash & A. J. Barnier (Eds.), *The Oxford handbook of hypnosis: theory, research and practice* (pp. 53–77). Oxford: Oxford University Press.

McConkey, K. M., Bryant, R. A., Bibb, B. C., & Kihlstrom, J. F. (1991). Trance logic in hypnosis and imagination. *Journal of Abnormal Psychology*, **100**(4), 464.

McConkey, K. M., Wende, V., & Barnier, A. J. (1999). Measuring change in the subjective experience of hypnosis. *International Journal of Clinical and Experimental Hypnosis*, **47**(1), 23. doi:10.1080/00207149908410020

Mikulas, W. L. (2011). Mindfulness: significant common confusions. *Mindfulness*, **2**(1), 1–7. doi:10.1007/s12671-010-0036-z

Mitchell, D. W. (2002). *Introducing the Buddhist experience*. New York, NY: Oxford University Press.

Nash, M. R. (2005). The importance of being earnest when crafting definitions: science and scientism are not the same thing. *International Journal of Clinical and Experimental Hypnosis*, **53**(3), 265–280. doi:10.1080/00207140590961934

Nash, M. R. (2008). Foundations of clinical hypnosis. In M. R. Nash & A. J. Barnier (Eds.), *The Oxford handbook of hypnosis: theory, research and practice* (pp. 487–502). Oxford: Oxford University Press.

Nash, M. R., & Barnier, A. J. (Eds.). (2008). *The Oxford handbook of hypnosis*. New York: Oxford University Press.

Nash, J. D., & Newberg, A. (2013). Toward a unifying taxonomy and definition for meditation. *Consciousness Research*, **4**, 806. doi:10.3389/fpsyg.2013.00806

Nogrady, H., McConkey, K. M., & Perry, C. (1985). Enhancing visual memory: trying hypnosis, trying imagination, and trying again. *Journal of Abnormal Psychology*, **94**(2), 195–204. doi:10.1037/0021–843X.94.2.195

Oakley, D. A. (2008). Hypnosis, trance and suggestion: evidence from neuroimaging. In M. R. Nash & A. J. Barnier (Eds.), *The Oxford handbook of hypnosis: theory, research and practice* (pp. 365–392). Oxford: Oxford University Press.

Oakley, D. A., & Halligan, P. W. (2002). Hypnotic mirrors and phantom pain: a single case study. *Contemporary Hypnosis*, **19**(2), 75–84. doi:10.1002/ch.244

Oakley, D. A., & Halligan, P. W. (2009). Hypnotic suggestion and cognitive neuroscience. *Trends in Cognitive Sciences*, **13**(6), 264–270. doi:10.1016/j.tics.2009.03.004

Oakley, D. A., & Halligan, P. W. (2013). Hypnotic suggestion: opportunities for cognitive neuroscience. *Nature Reviews Neuroscience*, **14**(8), 565–576. doi:10.1038/nrn3538

Orne, M. T. (1959). The nature of hypnosis: artifact and essence. *Journal of Abnormal and Social Psychology*, **58**(3), 277.

Orne, M. T. (1962). On the social psychology of the psychological experiment: with particular reference to demand characteristics and their implications. *American Psychologist*, **17**(11), 776.

Orne, M. T. (1979). On the simulating subject as a quasi-control group in hypnosis research: what, why, and how. In E. Fromm & R. E. Shor (Eds.), *Hypnosis: developments in research and new perspectives* (pp. 399–444). New York: Aldine.

Pekala, R. J., & Kumar, V. K. (1986). The differential organization of the structures of consciousness during hypnosis and a baseline condition. *Journal of Mind and Behavior*, **7**(4), 515–539.

Polito, V., Barnier, A. J., & McConkey, K. M. (2014). Defining hypnosis: process, product, and the value of tolerating ambiguity. *Journal of Mind–Body Regulation*, **2**(2), 118–120.

Polito, V., Barnier, A. J., & Woody, E. Z. (2013). Developing the Sense of Agency Rating Scale (SOARS): an empirical measure of agency disruption in hypnosis. *Consciousness and Cognition*, **22**(3), 684–696. doi:10.1016/j.concog.2013.04.003

Polito, V., Barnier, A. J., Woody, E. Z., & Connors, M. H. (2014). Measuring agency change across the domain of hypnosis. *Psychology of Consciousness*, **1**(1), 3–19. doi:10.1037/cns0000010

Rainville, P., Hofbauer, R. K., Bushnell, M. C., Duncan, G. H., & Price, D. D. (2002). Hypnosis modulates activity in brain structures involved in the regulation of consciousness. *Journal of Cognitive Neuroscience*, **14**(6), 887–901. doi:10.1162/089892902760191117

Rao, K. R. (2011). Applied yoga psychology studies of neurophysiology of meditation. *Journal of Consciousness Studies*, **18**(11–12), 11–12.

Raz, A., Kirsch, I., Pollard, J., & Nitkin-Kaner, Y. (2006). Suggestion reduces the Stroop effect. *Psychological Science*, **17**(2), 91–95. doi:10.1111/j.1467–9280.2006.01669.x

Sauer, S., Walach, H., Schmidt, S., Hinterberger, T., Lynch, S., Büssing, A., & Kohls, N. (2013). Assessment of mindfulness: review on state of the art. *Mindfulness*, **4**(1), 3–17. doi:10.1007/s12671-012-0122-5

Sedlmeier, P., Eberth, J., Schwarz, M., Zimmermann, D., Haarig, F., Jaeger, S., & Kunze, S. (2012). The psychological effects of meditation: a meta-analysis. *Psychological Bulletin*, **138**(6), 1139–1171. doi:10.1037/a0028168

Shear, J. (2006). Introduction. In J. Shear (Ed.), *The experience of meditation: experts introduce the major traditions* (pp. xiii–xxii). St. Paul, MN: Paragon House.

Sheehan, P. W., & McConkey, K. M. (1982). *Hypnosis and experience: the exploration of phenomena and process.* Hillsdale, NJ: Lawrence Erlbaum.

Sheehan, P. W., & Perry, C. (1976). *Methodologies of hypnosis: a critical appraisal of contemporary paradigms of hypnosis.* Hillsdale, NJ: Lawrence Erlbaum Associates.

Shor, R. E., & Easton, R. D. (1973). A preliminary report on research comparing self- and hetero-hypnosis. *American Journal of Clinical Hypnosis*, **16**(1), 37–44.

Shor, R. E., & Orne, E. C. (1962). *The Harvard Group Scale of Hypnotic Susceptibility, Form A*. Palo Alto, CA: Consulting Psychologists' Press.

Smith, J. E., Richardson, J., Hoffman, C., & Pilkington, K. (2005). Mindfulness-based stress reduction as supportive therapy in cancer care: systematic review. *Journal of Advanced Nursing*, **52**(3), 315–327. doi:10.1111/j.1365–2648.2005.03592.x

Szechtman, H., Kalogeras, J., Bowers, K. S., & Nahmias, C. (1998). Where the imaginal appears real: a positron emission tomography study of auditory hallucinations. *Proceedings of the National Academy of Sciences, USA*, **95**(4), 1956–1960.

Tang, Y.-Y., Ma, Y., Wang, J., Fan, Y., Feng, S., Lu, Q., . . . Posner, M. I. (2007). Short-term meditation training improves attention and self-regulation. *Proceedings of the National Academy of Sciences*, **104**(43), 17152–17156. doi:10.1073/pnas.0707678104

Tang, Y.-Y., Rothbart, M. K., & Posner, M. I. (2012). Neural correlates of establishing, maintaining, and switching brain states. *Trends in Cognitive Sciences*, **16**(6), 330–337. doi:10.1016/j.tics.2012.05.001

Terhune, D. B., Cardeña, E., & Lindgren, M. (2011). Dissociated control as a signature of typological variability in high hypnotic suggestibility. *Consciousness and Cognition*, **20**(3), 727–736. doi:10.1016/j.concog.2010.11.005

Vago, D. R., & Silbersweig, D. A. (2012). Self-awareness, self-regulation, and self-transcendence (S-ART): a framework for understanding the neurobiological mechanisms of mindfulness. *Frontiers in Human Neuroscience*, **6**, 296. doi:10.3389/fnhum.2012.00296

Van Dam, N. T., Earleywine, M., & Borders, A. (2010). Measuring mindfulness? An item response theory analysis of the Mindful Attention Awareness Scale. *Personality and Individual Differences*, **49**(7), 805–810. doi:10.1016/j.paid.2010.07.020

Walach, H., Buchheld, N., Buttenmüller, V., Kleinknecht, N., & Schmidt, S. (2006). Measuring mindfulness—the Freiburg Mindfulness Inventory (FMI). *Personality and Individual Differences*, **40**(8), 1543–1555.

Walsh, R., & Shapiro, S. L. (2006). The meeting of meditative disciplines and Western psychology: a mutually enriching dialogue. *American Psychologist*, **61**(3), 227–239. doi:10.1037/0003–066X.61.3.227

Wang, D. J. J., Rao, H., Korczykowski, M., Wintering, N., Pluta, J., Khalsa, D. S., & Newberg, A. B. (2011). Cerebral blood flow changes associated with different meditation practices and perceived depth of meditation. *Psychiatry Research: Neuroimaging*, **191**(1), 60–67. doi:10.1016/j.pscychresns.2010.09.011

Weitzenhoffer, A. M., & Hilgard, E. R. (1962). *Stanford Hypnotic Susceptibility Scale, Form C*. Palo Alto, CA: Consulting Psychologists' Press.

Woody, E. Z., & Barnier, A. J. (2008). Hypnosis scales for the twenty-first century: what do we need and how should we use them? In M. R. Nash & A. J. Barnier (Eds.), *The Oxford handbook of hypnosis: theory, research and practice* (pp. 255–281). Oxford: Oxford University Press.

Woody, E. Z., Barnier, A. J., & McConkey, K. M. (2005). Multiple hypnotizabilities: differentiating the building blocks of hypnotic response. *Psychological Assessment*, **17**(2), 200–211. doi:10.1037/1040–3590.17.2.200

Woody, E. Z., & McConkey, K. M. (2003). What we don't know about the brain and hypnosis, but need to: a view from the buckhorn inn. *International Journal of Clinical and Experimental Hypnosis*, **51**(3), 309–338. doi:10.1076/iceh.51.3.309.15523

Zaki, J., Schirmer, J., & Mitchell, J. P. (2011). Social influence modulates the neural computation of value. *Psychological Science*, **22**(7), 894–900.

Part 4

Cognitive mechanisms

Chapter 11

Increasing cognitive-emotional flexibility with meditation and hypnosis
The cognitive neuroscience of de-automatization

Kieran C. R. Fox, Yoona Kang, Michael Lifshitz, and Kalina Christoff

Abstract

Meditation and hypnosis both aim to facilitate cognitive-emotional flexibility, i.e., the "de-automatization" of thought and behavior. However, little research or theory has addressed how internal thought patterns might change after such interventions, even though alterations in the internal flow of consciousness may precede externally observable changes in behavior. This chapter outlines three mechanisms by which meditation or hypnosis might alter or reduce automatic associations and elaborations of spontaneous thought: by an overall reduction of the chaining of thoughts into an associative stream; by de-automatizing and diversifying the content of thought chains (i.e., increasing thought flexibility or variety); and, finally, by re-automatizing chains of thought along desired or valued paths (i.e., forming new, voluntarily chosen mental habits). The authors discuss behavioral and cognitive neuroscientific evidence demonstrating the influence of hypnosis and meditation on internal cognition and highlight the putative neurobiological basis, as well as potential benefits, of these forms of de-automatization.

Introduction

When left free and unconstrained, what do people think about of their own accord? Or rather, since the process of thought seems to be largely spontaneous and uncontrollable, what does the mind-brain think about of *its* own accord? Is there any possibility of increasing the flexibility and diversity of these spontaneous chains of thought? Although cognitive psychologists have been addressing this question for several decades now (e.g., Klinger, 2008; Singer, 1966; Singer & McCraven, 1961), cognitive and clinical neuroscientists are only just beginning to seriously apply scientific scrutiny to such "spontaneous" thought processes (Andrews-Hanna, Smallwood, & Spreng, 2014; Fox & Christoff, 2014, 2015; Fox, Spreng, Ellamil, Andrews-Hanna, & Christoff, 2015; Smallwood & Andrews-Hanna, 2013).

Spontaneous thought processes have been studied under various names, including day-dreaming, mind wandering, and stimulus-independent thought, although they are not always characterized by "spontaneity" per se. (For a discussion of terminology, see Christoff, 2012; Dixon, Fox, & Christoff, 2014; Fox & Christoff, 2014.) For the sake of simplicity, we use these terms more or less interchangeably in this chapter, wherein we focus not on nuances of terminology but, rather, on outlining what is known about the subjective content and neural basis of these spontaneous thought processes. Although the subjective *content* of spontaneous thought has been fairly well studied over the past few decades (e.g., Klinger, 2008; Singer, 1966; Singer & McCraven, 1961), and is now being addressed with large-scale studies utilizing experience sampling with thousands of participants (e.g., Killingsworth & Gilbert, 2010), we still know comparatively little about the cognitive *processes* underlying it. What seems intuitively apparent, however, is that most of our spontaneous thought is characterized by *automaticity*—our streams of thought flow quickly, without conscious effort, and along habitual, well-worn paths.

Spontaneous thought: phenomenological content, neural correlates, and cognitive automaticity

In this introductory section, we outline three main features central to an understanding of spontaneous thought processes: the *phenomenological content*, as reported by first-person reports from many studies over the past few decades; the preliminary understanding we have of the *neural correlates* of various spontaneous thought processes; and, finally, the evidence concerning the *cognitive automaticity* of most of our streams of thought. We then turn our attention to a number of ways that our automatized patterns of thought may be made more flexible and diverse, and present arguments for why such de-automatization might be beneficial.

Phenomenological content and neural correlates

First-person accounts reveal spontaneous thought to be a highly varied and complex phenomenon, drawing on all sensory modalities, reaching into the distant past and anticipated future, and spanning the intellectual gamut from escapist fantasy to scientific and artistic creativity (Andrews-Hanna, Reidler, Huang, & Buckner, 2010; Fox, Nijeboer, Solomonova, Domhoff, & Christoff, 2013; Fox, Thompson, Andrews-Hanna, & Christoff, 2014; Klinger, 1990, 2008, 2013; McMillan, Kaufman, & Singer, 2013; Smallwood & Andrews-Hanna, 2013). The cognitive neuroscientific study of spontaneous thought lags far behind this phenomenological work, but a general picture of brain activity contributing to the various forms of "mind wandering" is beginning to emerge, implicating a correspondingly wide range of brain regions (see Fox et al., 2015; see also Figure 11.1 and Plate 4).

The salient involvement of the medial prefrontal cortex, posterior cingulate cortex, and a swathe of lateral parietal lobe (including the temporoparietal junction and parts of the inferior parietal lobule) strongly parallels the core regions of the so-called "default mode" network of brain regions that are consistently recruited during the resting state (Buckner, Andrews-Hanna, & Schacter, 2008). The medial temporal lobe, critical to memory formation and recall, as well as prospection (imagining the future) (Addis, Pan, Vu, Laiser, & Schacter, 2009; Schacter, Addis, & Buckner, 2007), is also consistently recruited (Fox et al., 2015). Finally, there is strong evidence for recruitment of the lateral prefrontal cortex, dorsal anterior cingulate cortex, temporopolar cortex, and the insula during mind wandering—findings often neglected in both empirical and theoretical work on spontaneous thought (Fox et al., 2015).

Although the specific functional contributions and temporal dynamics of these various brain areas still remain poorly understood (Andrews-Hanna et al., 2014; Fox et al., 2015),

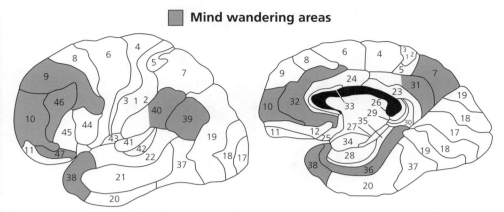

Fig. 11.1 Brain regions consistently recruited by various forms of spontaneous thought (see also Plate 4).

Approximate Brodmann areas (BAs) consistently recruited in functional neuroimaging studies of various spontaneous thought processes. Note the contribution of medial temporal lobe structures that may be involved in generating memories and imagined future scenarios (BA 36, 38), as well as lateral prefrontal cortex areas potentially underlying goal-directed planning and selection among various spontaneous thoughts.

Adapted from K. Brodmann, *Vergleichende Lokalisationslehre der Großhirnrinde in ihren Prinzipien dargestellt auf Grund des Zellenbaues*, Barth, Leipzig, Copyright © 1909.

some tentative steps have been made toward an understanding of these interrelationships. One preliminary conception put forth by our group divides spontaneous thought into roughly three stages (see Table 11.1), which preferentially (though not exclusively) recruit specific brain areas implicated in spontaneous thought in general (see Figures 11.1 and 11.2 and Plate 4). In the first *generative* stage, spontaneous thoughts arise of their own accord, via mechanisms as yet unknown. Medial temporal lobe structures, particularly the hippocampus and parahippocampus, seem likely sources of many of the memories and imagined future scenarios that form the basis for much of spontaneous conceptual thought (Addis et al., 2009; Ellamil, Dobson, Beeman, & Christoff, 2012; Ellamil et al., in preparation; Gelbard-Sagiv, Mukamel, Harel, Malach, & Fried, 2008), whereas the insula may contribute to higher-order, spontaneous "thoughts" about the visceral state of the body (Craig, 2004, 2009; Critchley, Wiens, Rotshtein, Öhman, & Dolan, 2004).

In the subsequent *elaborative* stage, initially isolated thoughts are associated to other thoughts, memories, and emotions, and may develop into a *stream* of thought that tends to follow habitual paths and tendencies. The medial prefrontal cortex (PFC), with its strong involvement in self-referential processing (D'Argembeau et al., 2007; Northoff et al., 2006), and the posterior cingulate cortex and temporopolar cortex, which are strongly tied to recall, elaboration, and processing of memory (Andrews-Hanna, Reidler, Sepulcre, Poulin, & Buckner, 2010; Christoff, 2013; Christoff, Ream, & Gabrieli, 2004; Svoboda, McKinnon, & Levine, 2006), seem likely to be involved in this elaborative process (Ellamil et al., in preparation; Farb et al., 2007).

A final *evaluative* or *executive* stage may sometimes occur, in which thoughts are monitored, directed, and possibly selected for their relevance to the self and long-term goals. The most likely players at this stage appear to be the dorsal anterior cingulate cortex, as well as the dorsolateral and

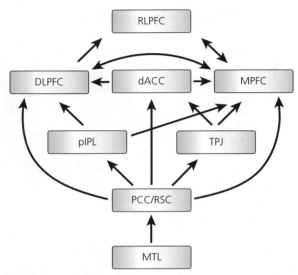

Fig. 11.2 A preliminary model of neural pathways underlying internally generated spontaneous thought.

A preliminary model suggests that many spontaneous thoughts may, at least in part,originate in the medial temporal lobe (MTL; especially hippocampus and parahippocampus) as either spontaneously recurring memories or imagined future scenarios (the *generation* stage; see Table 11.1), and are then elaborated upon by numerous other brain regions such as the posterior cingulate cortex (PCC; BA 31) and/or retrosplenial cortex (RSC), and medial prefrontal cortex (MPFC) in an *elaboration* stage. Finally, "higher" areas such as the dorsolateral prefrontal cortex (DLPFC; BA 9/46), rostrolateral prefrontal cortex (RLPFC; BA 10), and dorsal anterior cingulate cortex (dACC) may be recruited to evaluate, select among, and guide these streams of thought (the *evaluation* stage). Note that this model does not include occurrence of spontaneous thoughts related to the body's various interoceptive signals, or thoughts based directly on incoming stimuli from the external world; see Dixon et al. (2014) for such details. Unidirectional arrows are meant to indicate the primary direction of information flow, but all interregional connections should be considered reciprocal. pIPL: posterior inferior parietal lobule (BA 39/40); TPJ: temporoparietal junction (BA 39/40).

Adapted from *Neuropsychologia*, 62, Matthew L. Dixon, Kieran C.R. Fox, and Kalina Christoff, A framework for understanding the relationship between externally and internally directed cognition, pp. 321–30, doi:10.1016/j.neuropsychologia.20140.05.024, Copyright 2014, Elsevier. With permission from Elsevier.

rostrolateral prefrontal cortex—regions often recruited during spontaneous thought, metacognition, and top-down cognitive control (see Figure 11.1) (Andrews-Hanna et al., 2014; Christoff, Gordon, Smallwood, Smith, & Schooler, 2009; Fox & Christoff, 2014; Fox et al., 2015).

Cognitive automaticity

Still less studied than the phenomenological content and neural basis of spontaneous thoughts, is the degree to which they chain together into *streams* of thought, and the tendency of these streams to follow predictable, habitual paths—that is, the degree to which spontaneous thinking is characterized by "automaticity" (see the section "The automaticity of spontaneous thought: advantages and disadvantages"). Automaticity might characterize any or all stages of spontaneous thought (see Table 11.1 and Figure 11.2): we might predictably generate ideas of a certain nature; elaborate upon such ideas in a habitual fashion; or evaluate our own spontaneous thoughts and emotions in habitual, characteristic judgments and valuations.

Table 11.1 Three possible stages of spontaneous thought

Stage	Core contributing brain regions*
Generation Origination/creation of new thoughts and imagery; spontaneous recall of memories, or imagination of future scenarios; recombination of experiences in memory consolidation and reconsolidation	Medial temporal lobe (hippocampus, parahippocampus); posterior cingulate cortex; temporoparietal junction
Elaboration Spontaneously arising thought is spun out into a stream of associated thoughts and emotions	Medial prefrontal cortex; temporopolar cortex
Evaluation Spontaneous thoughts or streams of thought are judged and evaluated for their personal utility or emotional valence; possible guidance/steering of streams of thought by metacognitive brain areas	Lateral prefrontal cortex; dorsal anterior cingulate cortex

*Brain regions listed appear to show relatively greater contributions at a given stage, but the lists should by no means be considered definitive or mutually exclusive. See also Figure 11.2 for a graphical illustration of the regions involved and a preliminary model of the functional neuroanatomical flow of spontaneously arising thoughts through various brain areas.

When might such automaticity be helpful—and when harmful? Are there ways in which we can increase the flexibility and diversity of the cognitive and emotional aspects of our spontaneous thought? Practices geared toward changing both the content and process of spontaneous thought are as ancient as their scientific study is new—such techniques have existed for millennia and continue to be developed in modern clinical contexts. In this chapter, we discuss two such methods and highlight the cognitive neuroscientific evidence supporting their effectiveness: the ancient practices of meditation, and the comparably recent methods of clinical (i.e., "hypnotherapy") and experimental hypnosis.

Meditation and hypnotherapy both begin with the simple premise that patterns of everyday thought and behavior are suboptimal for virtually everyone, and can be improved to increase one's well-being. The problem is not only that we fail to live up to particular moral paragons endorsed by given people, societies, or religions; more importantly, we often even fail to think the way *we* want to think, feel the way we want to feel, and do the things we want to do. It seems that, in many ways, we are not free to choose our own actions, much less our own thoughts and feelings: a large, perhaps dominant, portion of our thinking and behavior is guided instead by habitual thought patterns, automatic behaviors, and default emotional reactions (which we collectively refer to here using the umbrella term "automaticity"—see the section "The automaticity of spontaneous thought: advantages and disadvantages"). On the milder end of the spectrum, this can lead to regrets, missed opportunities, biased opinions, and unfair treatment of ourselves and others; in its more pernicious forms, to self-destructive behaviors such as drug and alcohol addiction, clinical syndromes such as depression, anxiety, or post-traumatic stress disorder, and widespread societal issues such as racism and sexism. Both meditation and hypnotherapy, however, appear to offer systematic methods of de-automatizing these habitual thought patterns.

The automaticity of spontaneous thought: advantages and disadvantages

It seems then that many of our spontaneous thought processes are supported by heuristic routines that are processed automatically, outside of conscious awareness (Bargh & Chartrand, 1999). We use the term *automaticity* to refer to the process of effortlessly engaging in behaviors, or patterns of thinking, according to previously established associations, without conscious monitoring (cf. LaBerge & Samuels, 1974). Automaticity is usually a desired result of learning that reflects mastery and fluency, and can help lessen the self-regulatory burden by freeing up limited cognitive resources from tasks for which they are no longer needed (e.g., Bargh & Chartrand, 1999). Compared to deliberate cognitive processes, automatic processes are fast, relatively effortless, and tax few cognitive resources.

Although automaticity can therefore be a beneficial aspect of cognition, and is indeed a necessary part of life, automatized cognitive or emotional reactivity can also potentially lead to a wide range of detrimental outcomes. At the individual level, automatic reactivity to events may subserve maladaptive thought patterns prevalent in mental health disorders, such as lack of perceived control in anxiety disorders (Chorpita & Barlow, 1998), addiction (Forsyth, Parker, & Finlay, 2003), and negative rumination in depression (Nolen-Hoeksema, 1991). At the societal level, an often highly automatic and unconscious process of intergroup attitude formation and maintenance (Monteith, Zuwerink, & Devine, 1994) can activate negative and stereotypic associations, unconsciously influencing one's opinions of, and behavior toward, outgroup members of another race or economic class (Bargh, 1989; Fiske, Cuddy, & Glick, 2007; Gaertner & Dovidio, 2008).

Early efforts to de-automatize maladaptive mental habits were made in the field of clinical psychology. In the landmark analysis of depression, for instance, Beck (1967) characterized the disorder as involving automatic chains of irrational thoughts and established a therapeutic technique based on de-automatization. His attention-based cognitive therapy involves bringing attention to the largely automatic sequence of irrational thought patterns in order to break (i.e., de-automatize) them. The long-term aim is the replacement of old maladaptive mental habits with new, more adaptive ones (which we refer to as *re-automatization*; see the section "Re-automatization of spontaneous thought processes"). More recent findings further suggest that de-automatization of resistant mental habits is also possible in the social domain; for example, counter-stereotyping egalitarian goals can be preemptively activated to eliminate stereotyping tendencies (Moskowitz & Li, 2011).

Many of these studies and interventions aim only for short-term effects, however—a "proof of concept" that thought and behavior can be modified by interventions, rather than a large-scale overhaul of mental habits. There appear to be more thorough and systematic forms of de-automatization though that might prove more effective over the long term—namely, meditation training and hypnotic suggestion. The remainder of this chapter will explore various ways in which automatized patterns of thought and emotional reactivity can be made more flexible and diverse via these methods. We draw primarily on functional neuroimaging research that has begun to shed some light on the possible neural mechanisms underlying de-automatization, and appears to support the efficacy of meditation and hypnosis in altering these processes.

Recognizing and combating the automaticity of spontaneous thought processes: the benefits of meta-awareness

Although some unconscious methods of de-automatization have already been alluded to (e.g., Dasgupta & Greenwald, 2001; Moskowitz & Li, 2011; Sassenberg & Moskowitz, 2005), the first step in the conscious and systematic de-automatization of spontaneous thought processes is considered to be the *recognition* of thought's automaticity in the first place. Few of us even recognize how often we are mind wandering (Christoff et al., 2009; Fox & Christoff, 2015; Schooler et al., 2011), much less the true degree to which our thoughts and emotions simply follow well-trod paths. The experience of psychiatrist and neuroscientist Roger Walsh (1977), when he first began practicing meditation, exemplifies this realization:

> I was forced to recognize that what I had formerly believed to be my rational mind preoccupied with cognition, planning, problem solving, etc., actually comprised a frantic torrent of forceful, demanding, loud, and often unrelated thoughts and fantasies which filled an unbelievable proportion of consciousness even during purposive behavior. The incredible proportion of consciousness which this fantasy world occupied, my powerlessness to remove it for more than a few seconds, and my former state of mindlessness or ignorance of its existence, staggered me . . . Foremost among the implicit beliefs of orthodox Western psychology is the assumption that man spends most of his time reasoning and problem solving, and that only neurotics and other abnormals spend much time, outside of leisure, in fantasy. However, it is my impression that prolonged self-observation will show that at most times we are living almost in a dream world in which we skillfully and automatically yet unknowingly blend inputs from reality and fantasy in accordance with our needs and defenses . . . The subtlety, complexity, infinite range and number, and entrapping power of the fantasies which the mind creates seem impossible to comprehend, to differentiate from reality while in them, and even more so to describe to one who has not experienced them. (Walsh, 1977, p. 154)

Despite the pervasiveness of such automaticity, it is encouraging that a frank recognition of the power and frequency of automatic thought processes does not require years of self-observation: Walsh's (1977) insight is typically among the first realizations experienced by a beginning practitioner of meditation (Gunaratana, 2011). In some of our recent work (Fox & Christoff, 2014; Kang, Gruber, & Gray, 2013), we have discussed how metacognitive awareness of such habitual patterns of mind wandering might be a key element in breaking down these persistent chains of thinking, and re-orienting them towards desired and valued alternative patterns of thought. For instance, a recent fMRI (functional magnetic resonance imaging) study from our group compared brain activity during mind wandering both with, and in the absence of, meta-awareness of the fact that one was mind wandering (Christoff et al., 2009). We found that although very similar brain regions were activated in both cases (compared to periods when subjects were not mind wandering), numerous regions were significantly *less* active when meta-awareness was present than when it was absent (see Figure 11.3 and Plate 5; see also Table 3 in Christoff et al., 2009). When meta-awareness was present, significantly less brain activation was observed in numerous medial temporal lobe regions strongly implicated in long-term memory (Schacter et al., 2007) and the generation of spontaneous thoughts (Christoff et al., 2004; Fox et al., 2015); in downstream visual brain areas, such as the fusiform and lingual gyri, implicated in mental imagery and the imagined visual scenes accompanying dreaming (Domhoff & Fox, 2015; Fox et al., 2013; Solms, 1997); and in the medial prefrontal cortex, implicated in self-referential processing and the elaboration of streams of thought (see Figure 11.3). Recently, we have shown that these regions (among others) become increasingly active when one moves from externally directed thought, to daydreaming, to full-blown and immersive dream mentation (see Figure 3 in Fox et al., 2013; see also Domhoff and Fox, 2015).

One interpretation of these results is that meta-awareness during mind wandering dampens the *generative* and *elaborative* stages of spontaneous thought, either by reducing the

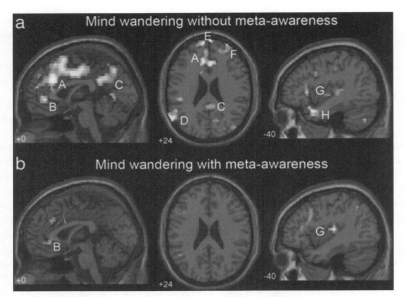

Fig. 11.3 Differences in brain activity between mind wandering with and without meta-awareness (see also Plate 5).

Although mind wandering both with (panel b) and without (panel a) meta-awareness recruits a similar set of brain regions, recruitment is much more widespread for the latter (panel a). This pattern may suggest that meta-awareness attenuates, or otherwise exerts selective pressure upon, the stream of spontaneous thought (Fox & Christoff, 2014).

Reproduced from Kalina Christoff, Alan M. Gordon, Jonathan Smallwood, Rachelle Smith, and Jonathan W. Schooler, Experience sampling during fMRI reveals default network and executive system contributions to mind wandering, *Proceedings of the National Academy of Sciences of the United States of America*, 106 (21), pp. 8719–8724, Figure 4, doi: 10.1073/pnas.0900234106, Copyright © 2009, The National Academy of Sciences.

quantity of thoughts by selectively choosing which thoughts are allowed to take shape (Fox & Christoff, 2014) or, perhaps, by preventing such deep immersion in these streams of thought (Fox et al., 2013). (Both notions are suggestive of a "non-elaborative" mental stance; see the section "Reducing the chaining of spontaneous thoughts: a non-elaborative mental stance"). The notion that meta-awareness is allowing only selective elaboration of certain streams of thought, or otherwise attenuating the intensity of daydreaming (Fox & Christoff, 2014; Schooler et al., 2011), is supported by behavioral studies which show that performance on externally directed tasks is significantly worse when meta-awareness of mind wandering is absent than when it is present (Smallwood, McSpadden, Luus, & Schooler, 2008; Smallwood, McSpadden, & Schooler, 2007). These performance deficits may therefore be due to greater elaboration of thoughts in the absence of meta-awareness, and/or a deeper immersion in streams of thought (see also the section "Reducing the chaining of spontaneous thoughts: a non-elaborative mental stance").

Once the occurrence (i.e., generation) of automatic spontaneous thought (Figure 11.4a) is recognized, there are several different ways in which the habitual course of the stream of thought might be changed (see Figure 11.4 and Table 11.2). Perhaps the simplest change (at least conceptually, but certainly not in practice) is a reduction of the chaining together of thoughts into associative streams (Figure 11.4b), by adopting what is sometimes referred to as a "non-elaborative" mental

Table 11.2 Overview of automatized and more flexible patterns of spontaneous thought

Cognitive process	Overview
Automatized spontaneous thought	The usual form of thought for most people, most of the time: thoughts are deeply immersive and reified, and chain together in habitual patterns, centering on particular topics. Original, creative thought and new patterns of emotional reactivity are relatively rare.
Meta-awareness/non-elaborative mental stance	Conscious awareness and/or monitoring of spontaneously arising thoughts either dampens the intensity and immersive nature of thoughts, or prevents them from chaining together into associative streams of thought beyond one's control.
De-automatized spontaneous thought	Thoughts are not necessarily less immersive or less liable to chain together into associative streams, but the pattern of these streams is now less rigid and habitual: the stream of thought is broader, more flexible, more likely to follow novel paths.
Re-automatized spontaneous thought	Patterns of thought are deliberately reformed along new paths that are "automatized" but intentionally chosen. Desirable or personally useful patterns of thinking that are at first difficult and resource-draining are cultivated to become automatic mental habits.

stance. Another possibility is the general "de-automatization" of thought patterns (Figure 11.4c), such that a given thought becomes likely to lead to a number of further thoughts—instead of always chaining together habitually with a particular subsequent idea. *Re*-automatization of spontaneous thought (Figure 11.4d), on the other hand, involves the voluntary reformation of thought associations along new, specific habitual paths.

In the following sections, we discuss each of these possibilities in turn. By these divisions, we do not in any way mean to imply that these processes necessarily, or even usually, occur linearly or in isolation—rather, we discuss each one separately for the sake of simplicity only (Figure 11.4). We examine what might be involved in each type of thought de-automatization, and present evidence from both behavioral research and functional neuroimaging that supports the capacity of meditation training and hypnotic suggestion to facilitate this increased cognitive and emotional flexibility.

Furthermore, any of these de-automatization processes (Table 11.2; Figure 11.4) might conceivably be applied at any of the three putative stages of spontaneous thought (see Table 11.1), but throughout this chapter, we discuss them largely in relation to the *elaboration* stage, both for the sake of simplicity and also because the bulk of the cognitive neuroscientific evidence bears on the elaborative stage. In theory, however, de-automatization processes might be just as relevant for altering the frequency and type of thoughts arising during the *generation* stage, for instance by biasing the very content of thought—or in altering one's habitual judgments of one's own thoughts during the *evaluation* stage. A more detailed discussion of these possibilities awaits future theoretical work.

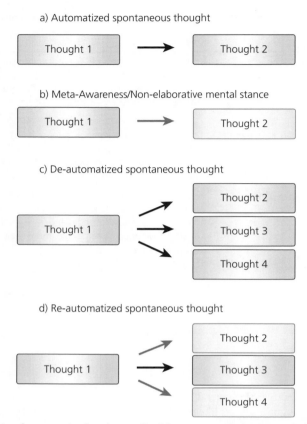

Fig. 11.4 Schematic of automatized and more flexible patterns of spontaneous thought.

A schematic illustration of typical automatized spontaneous thought processes, and various ways in which cognition and emotion might become more flexible and less habitual with meditation practice or hypnotherapy; see also Table 11.2. **(a)** Typical thought is highly automatized, in that once a given *Thought 1* has arisen (either spontaneously, seemingly without reason; or perhaps dependent on a particular stimulus or a prior thought drifting below the threshold of awareness), it tends, strongly, to lead to a particular *Thought 2* (indicated by a strong black arrow). **(b)** With the non-elaborative mental stance adopted, for instance, by mindfulness meditation practitioners, thoughts are less likely to chain together into streams; the chance that *Thought 1* leads automatically to any other *Thought 2* is reduced (indicated by the "noisy," speckled arrow). **(c)** With de-automatization, thoughts are not necessarily any less likely to chain into streams, but the automaticity of these streams has been reduced: the stream of thought is now more flexible (i.e., characterized by less rigidity and more variability). A given *Thought 1* is now likely to lead to any number of other thoughts. **(d)** With the re-automatization of thought, a particular habitual stream of thought is chosen and cultivated. With practice, training, or suggestion, a given *Thought 1* is now more likely to lead to *Thought 3*, but not other thoughts (e.g., *Thought 2* and *Thought 4*).

Reducing the chaining of spontaneous thoughts: a non-elaborative mental stance

Perhaps the simplest way (conceptually at least, but rarely so in practice) of changing the stream of spontaneous thought is to simply reduce the flow altogether. We refer to this reduction of the "chaining" of individual thoughts into an ongoing stream as a "non-elaborative" mental stance. A general goal of "quieting the mind" in this way is a central part of many meditation practices (e.g., Gunaratana, 2011; Iyengar, 2005).

There are numerous strategies for reducing the chaining of thoughts into elaborate and engrossing streams of fantasy, a major one being an increased focus on the sensory aspects of thoughts and perceptions (Fox et al., 2012; Kerr, Sacchet, Lazar, Moore, & Jones, 2013)—as opposed to allowing the mind to elaborate upon them with further thoughts about how they are related to one's self (e.g., Farb et al., 2007). For instance, one study of novices who underwent eight weeks of meditation training (Farb et al., 2007) subsequently presented them with various words (such as "cowardly," "envious," "cheerful," and "industrious") selected to spark self-related thinking about one's personality and behavior. In the first condition, "narrative" focus, participants were asked to dwell on the ideas evoked by these words: to think about whether and how each word related to their personality, what the words meant to them, and so on—in short, to engage in an elaborated stream of thoughts and judgments. In a second condition, "experiential" focus, they were asked to instead focus solely on whatever experience was evoked by the words in the present moment, whether it be thoughts, body sensations, or other mental events. Participants were asked to return their attention to the present moment if their thoughts started to run away with them—that is, to adopt a non-elaborative mental stance (Farb et al., 2007).

Compared to a wait-list control group with no meditation training, the meditation practitioners exhibited greater brain activity in several somatosensory and interoceptive brain regions during "experiential" versus "narrative" focus—and a corresponding decrease of activity in midline brain regions implicated in mind wandering (Figure 11.5 and Plate 6; Farb et al., 2007). Although this study did not directly address whether fewer thoughts were experienced when adopting a non-elaborative mental stance, it provided intriguing neural evidence that this might be the case (Figure 11.5).

Accumulating evidence supports the idea that mindfulness meditation can reduce the flow of thoughts: one recent study that involved two weeks of training in mindfulness meditation showed reduced self-reported rates of mind wandering in the mindfulness practitioners as compared to the control group (Mrazek, Franklin, Phillips, Baird, & Schooler, 2013). Another study instead examined long-term, expert meditation practitioners as compared to meditation-naïve control subjects (Brewer et al., 2011). Meditators self-reported less mind wandering during several forms of meditation practice and, concurrently, exhibited reduced brain activity in the same set of midline brain regions implicated in mind wandering as the aforementioned study (Farb et al., 2007).

Similar to certain forms of meditation, typical hypnotic induction procedures appear to quiet mental chatter, increase absorption, and alter activity within default mode regions associated with mind wandering. In one recent study, researchers induced hypnosis in an fMRI scanner and found that highly suggestible individuals showed reduced activity in classical default network regions including the right anterior cingulate gyrus, cortical midline structures of the left medial frontal gyrus, bilateral posterior cingulate cortices, and bilateral parahippocampal gyri (Deeley et al., 2012). These de-activations corresponded to self-reported increases in hypnotic depth and reductions in analytic thinking and mental chatter. An independent group showed similar dampening in default mode structures during hypnosis, albeit mostly restricted to the frontal components of this network (McGeown, Mazzoni, Venneri, & Kirsch, 2009). Furthermore, the degree of default mode dampening during the hypnotic induction predicted responsiveness to a subsequent hypnotic suggestion (Mazzoni, Venneri, McGeown, & Kirsch, 2013). Collectively, these data suggest that reductions in discursive thought and associated default mode activity may comprise a hallmark of hypnosis.

Although the aforementioned examples all suggest an *overall reduction* in the quantity of spontaneous thoughts with meditation and hypnosis, these experiments can only *suggest* reduced

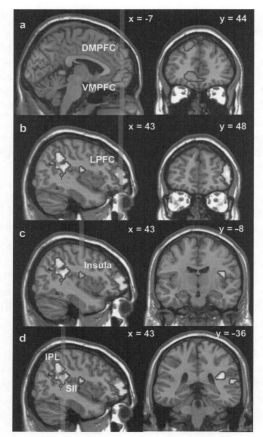

Fig. 11.5 Neural correlates of a non-elaborative mental stance after brief meditation training (see also Plate 6).

After mindfulness meditation training, subjects were presented with words (e.g., "cowardly," "envious," "cheerful," "industrious") selected to spark self-related thinking about one's personality and behavior. When subjects were instructed to focus simply on their present- moment experience and do their best not to elaborate on the thoughts sparked by these words, those who had undergone meditation training showed markedly different brain activity compared to controls. Meditators showed reduced brain activity in medial prefrontal cortex areas implicated in self-referential processing **(a)**, and simultaneous increases of activity in several areas related to processing body image and interoceptive sensations, including the insula **(c)**, inferior parietal lobule **(d)**, and secondary somatosensory cortices **(d)**. Increased activity was also apparent in lateral prefrontal cortex areas **(b)** implicated in metacognition and executive control, suggesting a heightened awareness of, and perhaps control over, spontaneously arising thoughts. These data support the notion that the adoption of a non-elaborative, present-centered mental stance, grounded in the body, can reduce our habitual elaboration of thoughts.

Reproduced from Norman A. S. Farb, Zindel V. Segal, Helen Mayberg, Jim Bean, Deborah McKeon, Zainab Fatima, and Adam K. Anderson, Attending to the present: mindfulness meditation reveals distinct neural modes of self-reference, *Social Cognitive and Affective Neuroscience*, 2 (4), pp. 313–322, Figure 3, doi: 10.1093/scan/nsm030 (c) 2007, by permission of Oxford University Press.

chaining of thoughts. A recent study from our group, however, has directly investigated chaining of thoughts in expert meditation practitioners, with the aim of differentiating the neural correlates of a single thought that arises and passes away, from one which develops into an ongoing stream of thought (Ellamil et al., in preparation).

To address this question, we had participants in the fMRI scanner indicate the arising of a thought by pressing a button—but beyond this, they also indicated whether a *single* thought had arisen and then passed away, or whether the first thought had been elaborated into a *chain* of

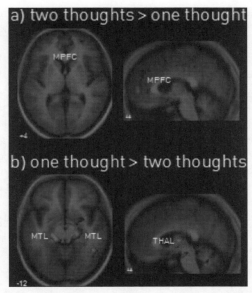

Fig. 11.6 Neural correlates of single transient thoughts versus further elaboration of thoughts (see also Plate 7).

Participants highly experienced in introspection (long-term meditation practitioners) engaged in a simple, ostensibly thought-free form of meditation and then indicated, by pressing a button, whenever a thought arose in their minds. Additionally, they indicated whether only a single thought had arisen and then passed away, or whether the generation of a given thought was followed by subsequent chaining of this thought with others into an elaborated stream of two or more thoughts. Comparing brain activation across these two conditions, our group found that the generation of a single thought (panel b) is preferentially dependent on memory centers of the medial temporal lobe (MTL) and sensory relay areas in the thalamus (THAL). In contrast, chaining of thoughts (panel a) into an elaborated stream more powerfully recruited medial prefrontal cortex (MPFC) areas strongly implicated in mind wandering and related forms of spontaneous thought.

Reprinted from Ellamil, M., Fox, K. C. R., Dixon, M. L., Todd, R. M., Thompson, E., & Christoff, K. (in preparation). Neural activity related to the specific content and chaining together of spontaneous thoughts. With permission from Fox, K. C. R.

two or more thoughts. We then compared neural activity associated with single versus chained thoughts and found that single spontaneous thoughts seem to arise dependent on recruitment of memory centers of the medial temporal lobe and also to recruit sensory relay centers of the thalamus (Figure 11.6b). However, similar to the results of the studies already mentioned (Brewer et al., 2011; Farb et al., 2007), the elaboration of individual thoughts into connected streams of thinking more strongly recruited brain areas such as the medial prefrontal cortex (Figure 11.6a).

Collectively, these studies (Brewer et al., 2011; Ellamil et al., in preparation; Farb et al., 2007) suggest that medial prefrontal cortex areas are involved in the automatized elaboration of thought streams, and that paying increased attention to present-moment experience (as taught in various meditation traditions, or as induced by hypnotic suggestion) can dampen activity in these areas, reduce the chaining of thoughts, and upregulate activity in brain areas related to exteroceptive and interoceptive body sensation.

De-automatization of spontaneous thinking: broadening the stream of thought

In contrast to a non-elaborative mental stance, which aims at reducing the chaining and quantity of thoughts (Figure 11.4b), the goal of de-automatization is to derail habitual patterns and thus broaden the thought stream. Instead of a narrow, prescribed course, with de-automatization, a given thought or stimulus may lead to any number of subsequent thoughts or emotional experiences (Figure 11.4c). With de-automatization, spontaneous thinking is not necessarily reduced, but greater flexibility and variety is now present (Figure 11.4c).

Hypnosis overrides automatic cognitive processes

In recent years, a growing body of cognitive neuroscience evidence has demonstrated that suggestion can swiftly override a wide range of deeply ingrained processes. Perhaps one of the most striking and well-known examples of de-automatization is a series of studies showing that suggestion can reduce, or in some cases even eliminate, the classic "Stroop" effect (Lifshitz, Aubert Bonn, Fischer, Kashem, & Raz, 2013; Raz, Fan, & Posner, 2005; Raz, Kirsch, Pollard, & Nitkin-Kaner, 2006; Raz, Moreno-Íniguez, Martin, & Zhu, 2007; Raz, Shapiro, Fan, & Posner, 2002). In the Stroop paradigm, incongruent trials—in which participants are asked to report the color of a word displayed in an incompatible font color (e.g., the word "blue" displayed in red font)—lead to conflict between two automatized cognitive reactions (i.e., reading basic words and perceiving color). Thus, incongruent trials are strongly associated with slower reaction times and greater activity in neural regions involved in cognitive conflict, such as the dorsal anterior cingulate cortex (Figure 11.7 and

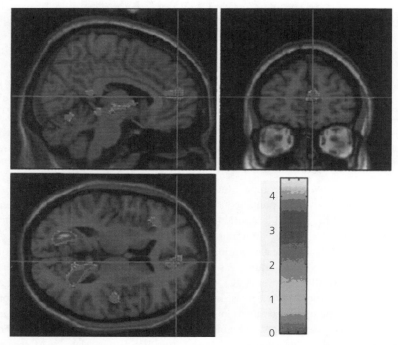

Fig. 11.7 Brain activations during Stroop task conflict are reduced by hypnotic suggestion (see also Plate 8).

Brain regions showing *less* activation, after hypnotic suggestion, during incongruent versus congruent trials on the Stroop task. Note, in particular, the reduced activity in the anterior cingulate cortex (under crosshairs), a region strongly implicated in conflict processing and resolution. Alongside behavioral results indicating less conflict, and equal performance, in the hypnotized condition, these fMRI findings suggest that hypnotic suggestion can reduce automatized cognitive reactions to perceptual stimuli.

Adapted from Amir Raz, Jin Fan, and Michael I. Posner, Hypnotic suggestion reduces conflict in the human brain, *Proceedings of the National Academy of Sciences of the United States of America*, 102 (28), pp. 9978–9983, Figure 1a, doi: 10.1073/pnas.0503064102, Copyright © 2005, The National Academy of Sciences.

Plate 8; Raz et al., 2005). Yet, Raz et al. (2002) showed that highly suggestible individuals can attenuate, or in some cases even abolish, this Stroop interference effect following a rapid and straightforward suggestion to perceive the stimulus words as meaningless symbols of a foreign language. Multiple studies from independent groups around the world have since replicated these initial findings (e.g., Augustinova & Ferrand, 2012; Casiglia et al., 2010; Parris, Dienes, Bate, & Gothard, 2013; Parris, Dienes, & Hodgson, 2012, 2013; Raz & Campbell, 2011; Raz et al., 2005, 2006, 2007).

Results from a seminal functional neuroimaging study (Raz et al., 2005) support the collective behavioral results. In the absence of suggestion, strong activations were seen throughout the brain in response to incongruent versus congruent Stroop trials, as might be expected by the conflicting automatic processes inherent to incongruent trials. Most notable during suggestion-free incongruent trials was significantly increased activation in the dorsal anterior cingulate cortex, known to have a critical role in both monitoring and resolving cognitive conflict (Figure 11.7; Raz et al., 2005). Following suggestion, however, this conflict was reduced both behaviorally and neurally: reaction time and accuracy were now comparable on congruent and incongruent trials, and significantly less brain activity occurred within the anterior cingulate cortex (Figure 11.7; Raz et al., 2005). Interested readers may wish to consult Lifshitz et al. (2013) for a fuller exposition of the putative mechanisms and interpretational issues surrounding these findings (see also Chapter 16).

A number of recent studies have extended the prospect of hypnotic de-automatization beyond Stroop interference to other deeply ingrained processes. In the realm of visual attention, suggestion improved performance on two classic paradigms probing involuntary response conflict: the Flanker (Iani, Ricci, Gherri, & Rubichi, 2006) and Simon (Iani, Ricci, Baroni, & Rubichi, 2009) tasks. Another study recently demonstrated that hypnosis could derail cross-modal perception in the classic McGurk effect—an auditory illusion crafted by presenting visual and auditory streams that are incongruent, demonstrating the influence of visual facial movements on auditory speech percepts (McGurk & MacDonald, 1976). So robust is the McGurk effect that people are typically unable to avoid the illusion even if they are aware of the audiovisual discrepancy (McGurk & MacDonald, 1976) and regardless of practice (Summerfield & McGrath, 1984). Yet, a simple suggestion for increased auditory acuity greatly reduced illusory speech percepts and improved correct audio identifications on the McGurk task (Déry, Campbell, Lifshitz, & Raz, 2014). Along similar lines, researchers were able to override cross-modal perceptual integration in a single, highly hypnotically suggestible face-color synesthete, eliciting concomitant alterations in her event-related potential (ERP) profile (Terhune, Cardeña, & Lindgren, 2010).

Thus, the potential for using suggestion to de-constrain habitual cognitive patterns seems to generalize beyond the Stroop effect and offers intriguing prospects for further cognitive and applied investigations, including in the realms of spontaneous thought and its disorders. For example, in Chapter 23, Lynn et al. offer an intriguing account of how suggestion-based de-automatization can translate to meaningful clinical outcomes related to craving and addiction.

Improving implicit intergroup attitudes

Outside of the laboratory, is there a possibility of de-automatizing spontaneous thought processes with direct relevance to everyday life? One such form of detrimental spontaneous thinking is the formation and maintenance of implicit intergroup attitudes. Implicit judgments against stigmatized social groups are often automatically activated without conscious awareness, and typically measured with response-latency techniques such as the Implicit Association Test (IAT; Greenwald, Poehlman, Uhlmann, & Banaji, 2009) to circumvent limitations of introspective self-reports.

While implicit intergroup attitudes are highly resistant to change due to their automatic and unconscious nature (Devine, 1989), recent findings suggest that de-automatization of such biases is possible through the practice of meditation (Kang, Gray, & Dovidio, 2013). In one study, loving-kindness meditation—a concentration practice that aims to establish a deep sense of positive interconnectedness to others (Salzberg, 2004)—improved automatic intergroup orientations. Specifically, participants who completed six weeks of loving-kindness meditation training showed reduced implicit bias toward members of two socially stigmatized outgroups, Black and homeless people, as measured by IATs (Kang, Gray, & Dovidio, 2013). Importantly, the reduction of implicit bias was not present in the closely matched active controls who attended a six-week loving-kindness group discussion course that aimed to understand and share ideas of loving-kindness and compassion in the absence of any actual meditation training. This suggests that mere conceptual understanding of compassion may be insufficient for the de-automatization of such deeply ingrained attitudes; actual practices such as meditation may be necessary.

Reducing the affective-elaborative component of pain

Yet another form of automatized thought that many would presumably like to reduce is the emotional and cognitive distress and yearning for cessation that tends to accompany physical discomfort and pain. (For a much more in-depth take on pain, hypnosis, and meditation, see Chapter 21). Aside from the purely sensory aspects of pain, nociception is ubiquitously attended by elaborative thoughts that relate the pain to the self, and by affective experiences involving distress and various other negative emotional valuations of the sensory experience (Grant, 2014; Grant, Courtemanche, & Rainville, 2011; Rainville, Duncan, Price, Carrier, & Bushnell, 1997).

Beyond these subsequent *elaborations* of painful stimuli, even the mere *expectation* or anticipation of pain can influence the subsequent amplitude of an actual pain experience. For instance, in one study, the mere expectation of a painful stimulus appeared to amplify the actual experience of unpleasantness in response to a normally innocuous stimulus, as indexed by increased brain responses within areas implicated in pain processing (Sawamoto et al., 2000).

These cognitive-emotional elaborations appear to be a habitual, spontaneous response to a painful sensation, rather than an intrinsic aspect of nociception itself (Grant, 2014). They appear to be dissociable from, and temporally subsequent to, the purely sensory aspects of pain—and what is more, they may contribute significantly to the subjectively experienced unpleasantness of nociceptive experience (Rainville et al., 1997). As physical pain and discomfort are an unavoidable part of everyday life, and a severe burden in clinical disorders such as neuropathic pain (Woolf & Mannion, 1999) and chronic migraine (Olesen et al., 2006), an intervention that reduces our habitual tendency to engage in negative cognitive-emotional valuation of nociceptive experience is of obvious benefit to healthy people, as well as those suffering from certain clinical conditions.

Numerous studies over the past few decades have shown that mindfulness meditation indeed appears to be effective for the relief of various forms of chronic pain (e.g., Kabat-Zinn, 1982; Kabat-Zinn, Lipworth, & Burney, 1985; Morone, Greco, & Weiner, 2008)—but what might be the cognitive-neural mechanisms of this change? A recent study using fMRI explored whether mindfulness meditation might reduce the habitual affective-elaborative component of pain, by exploring differences in brain activity between long-term Zen practitioners and meditation-naïve controls (Grant et al., 2011). In line with earlier studies showing that the same sample of Zen practitioners exhibits higher self-reported pain thresholds (Grant & Rainville, 2009) and increased cortical thickness in sensory pain areas (Grant, Courtemanche, Duerden, Duncan, & Rainville, 2010), the

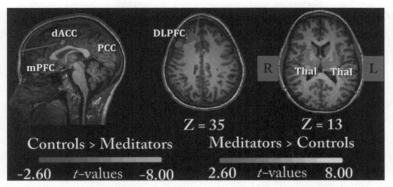

Fig. 11.8 Meditators show less affective-elaborative brain activation in response to pain (see also Plate 9).

In response to a painful thermal stimulus, long-term meditation practitioners showed greater brain activations in primary sensory pain areas, including the dorsal anterior cingulate cortex (dACC) and bilateral thalamus (Thal). In contrast, meditation-naïve controls showed greater activation in brain areas strongly implicated in elaborative and self-referential thought, including the medial prefrontal cortex (mPFC), posterior cingulate cortex (PCC), and dorsolateral prefrontal cortex (DLPFC). Z values indicate vertical position in stereotactic Talairach space.

Adapted from *Pain* 152 (1), Joshua A. Grant, Jérôme Courtemanche, and Pierre Rainville, A non-elaborative mental stance and decoupling of executive and pain-related cortices predicts low pain sensitivity in Zen meditators, pp. 150–156, doi:10.1016/j.pain.2010.10.006, © 2011, International Association for the Study of Pain.

researchers found that pain elicited greater brain activations in sensory pain areas in the meditators, including the thalamus, insula, and dorsal anterior cingulate cortex—suggesting that the meditators elaborated less on their pain, and instead focused more on its immediate sensory components (Figure 11.8 and Plate 9; Grant et al., 2011).

Further support for this interpretation came from the finding that functional connectivity (temporal correlation of activity patterns—Buckner, Krienen, & Yeo, 2013; Van Dijk et al., 2010) among the sensory pain areas was strengthened in the long-term meditation practitioners. On the other hand, functional connectivity between primary sensory pain areas and secondary affective-elaborative areas was increased in controls and decreased in long-term meditation practitioners (Grant et al., 2011), again supporting the idea that novices continued to elaborate upon their pain with further emotional and cognitive associations, whereas the meditators tended to remain focused on its purely sensory aspects. Intriguingly, the degree of this decoupling in meditation practitioners significantly predicted their lower pain sensitivity—offering perhaps the most convincing evidence for the aforementioned interpretations of the neuroimaging results.

Although the aforementioned study was not able to directly address the question of whether reduced cognitive-affective elaboration of the sensory pain experience was the *direct* cause of the observed lowered pain sensitivity and cortical decoupling, the results are nonetheless suggestive. (For a detailed analysis of the mechanisms underlying analgesia via mindfulness and hypnosis, see Chapter 21.) Note, too, that this example of reducing the affective-elaborative component of pain might also be considered an example of a "non-elaborative mental stance" (see the section "Reducing the chaining of spontaneous thought: a non-elaborative mental stance"). However, as noted in the section "Recognizing and combating the automaticity of spontaneous thought processes: the benefits of meta-awareness," we distinguish each sub-form of de-automatization (Table 11.2; Figure 11.4) largely for the sake of clarity—and not because of any strong demarcations between these various means of increasing cognitive-emotional flexibility.

Re-automatization of spontaneous thought processes

The philosopher P. D. Ouspensky aptly described the cognitive process we refer to here as *re-automatization*:

> We do not realize what enormous power lies in thinking . . . The power lies in the fact that, if we always think rightly about certain things, we can make it permanent—it grows into a permanent attitude . . . If you start from right thinking, then after some time you will educate in yourself the capacity for a different reaction. (Ouspensky, 1957, pp. 76–77)

As desirable as conscious, flexible thought patterns may be, automatization (as already noted) is beneficial in at least two respects: automatic behaviors and mental processes require fewer attentional resources and, relatedly, are faster (Moors & De Houwer, 2006). Therefore, altering patterns of spontaneous thought and emotion should not be considered solely a "negative" or reductive process: there is room, too, for constructive action in the creation of healthy, optimal habitual thinking that then effortlessly promotes one's well-being (Figure 11.4d).

This notion is familiar in meditation traditions: a practitioner engaging in loving-kindness meditation, for instance, might seek to change their usual habit of responding with irritation or anger to personally offensive stimuli, to a new pattern of responding with compassion and understanding instead. Similarly, practitioners of compassion meditation train themselves to respond to signs of others' pain and distress with compassion and a genuine desire to alleviate their suffering, instead of prior habitual reactive patterns of indifference or pity. An fMRI study (Lutz, Brefczynski-Lewis, Johnstone, & Davidson, 2008) in which participants were exposed to emotionally negative human vocalizations (i.e., sounds indicative of human pain and distress) found some evidence supporting the view that meditation might effect such re-automatization. Compared to control participants with no meditation experience, expert compassion meditation practitioners showed increased blood oxygen level dependent (BOLD) signal in the superior temporal sulcus, amygdala, and temporoparietal junction. These regions have been linked to auditory and emotional processing, as well as "theory of mind" (imagining the beliefs and intentions of others) and empathy (Völlm et al., 2006), suggesting, to the authors, not only enhanced processing of the sounds themselves but also increased compassionate responses in the meditators (Lutz et al., 2008). The long-term compassion meditation practitioners seemed to have successfully re-automatized their reactions to negative human vocalizations, such that their default response was no longer fear or worry, but rather compassionate concern.

Subsequent work supports the idea that brief meditation training can re-orient people from habitually selfish, to increasingly altruistic, behavior (Condon, Desbordes, Miller, & DeSteno, 2013; Weng et al., 2013), and might do so by altering neural function in the nucleus accumbens, which plays a major role in the neurochemical dopamine signaling that gives rise to our subjective sense of what feels fulfilling and rewarding (Weng et al., 2013).

Another meditation study suggestive of re-automatization divided participants into three groups: novice meditation practitioners, expert practitioners with approximately 19,000 hours of experience, and extremely advanced expert practitioners with an average of approximately 44,000 hours of experience (Brefczynski-Lewis, Lutz, Schaefer, Levinson, & Davidson, 2007). During a demanding, sustained attention task (typically very challenging for beginners), brain activity in attention networks showed an inverted U shape across the three groups: activity was highest in the expert meditators, and lower in both novices and the extremely advanced experts (Brefczynski-Lewis et al., 2007). This finding suggested, to the authors, that the expert meditators had learned to increase recruitment of these regions to consciously sustain attention in an effortful manner (which the novices could not do), but that in extremely advanced practitioners, this process had become relatively automatic and effortless, resulting in brain activity similar to that seen in novices (Brefczynski-Lewis et al., 2007). As noted in the section "The automaticity of spontaneous thought: advantages and disadvantages," "automaticity" denotes a process that has become essentially effortless with either continued practice or repeated exposure. This inverted U pattern of brain activation suggests that concentration meditation is initially difficult or almost impossible for those without training; with increased training, an effortful process of learning takes place, as suggested by greater brain activation; and, finally, sustained attention becomes ever more automatized with continued practice, resulting in minimal brain activation, comparable to that of novices.

In the realm of hypnosis, burgeoning research indicates that suggestion may be capable of shifting cognitive processes from effortful to automatic without extensive practice (Lifshitz et al., 2013). Preliminary support for this prospect comes from a study showing that a suggestion engendered digit-color synesthesia effects in highly hypnotizables by promoting perceptual integration across sensory modalities (Kadosh, Henik, Catena, Walsh, & Fuentes, 2009). More recently, two pilot experiments explored the prospects of rendering an effortful task easier in the realm of visual attention (Lifshitz et al., 2013). The first experiment involved the masked-diamond paradigm, in which participants identify the direction of moving geometric figures (e.g., clockwise, counter-clockwise) with invisible apexes. When a visual mask occludes the invisible apexes, motion detection is immediate and effortless; without the occluding masks, however, determining the direction of motion is extremely difficult for most people (see http://razlab.mcgill.ca/demomotrak.html). Pilot results show that highly suggestible, but not less suggestible, individuals were able to perform the task with remarkable accuracy following a suggestion to visualize the occluding masks, indicating that they could shift the difficult, almost intractable, task into the realm of automaticity. The second pilot experiment involved a classic visual search task, in which participants scan a display for a target item among distractors. Among highly suggestible individuals, a suggestion to see the target pop out effortlessly from the distractors significantly improved the efficiency of search.

These early findings support the prospect of using suggestion to render processes more automatic without extensive exposure or practice. Indeed, clinical hypnosis practitioners have been leveraging this potential for decades in helping patients replace undesired mental activities (e.g., negative ruminations in depression) with more wholesome cognitive processes (e.g., fostering optimistic outlooks) (Yapko, 2013).

Re-automatization, then, is similar to everyday automatized thought, in that it involves automatic, "habitual" routines. The main difference is that thought is now re-oriented toward goals and thinking patterns one approves of or desires. The aim, with training, is to more effortlessly think in ways that one deems right, good, or desirable. In many cases, it would seem ideal that good habits and patterns of thought would also become automatized and, therefore, relatively effortless and non-resource-draining.

Discussion and future directions

In this chapter, we have outlined numerous ways in which our patterns of thinking and feeling might be made more flexible via meditation training and hypnotic suggestion (Table 11.1; Figure 11.4). We have also touched on the results of some seminal studies that point toward a broad understanding of the functional neural correlates of these changes, as measured with neuroimaging tools such as fMRI. In this final section, we speculate on the neuroanatomical and molecular neurobiological changes that might underlie the functional neural plasticity associated with cognitive-emotional flexibility.

Do stable neuroanatomical changes accompany increased cognitive-emotional flexibility and functional neural plasticity?

Throughout this chapter, we have discussed cognitive-emotional flexibility, and functional neural plasticity, related to de-automatization, but we have not addressed potential neuro*anatomical* changes that might accompany these behavioral and functional differences. The cognitive and functional neural changes discussed throughout this chapter imply neuroanatomical alterations however—perhaps not just at the level of synapses, but potentially on a scale observable with non-invasive neuroimaging methods (Zatorre, Fields, & Johansen-Berg, 2012). In particular, it seems plausible that long-term, persistent engagement in hypnosis or meditation training might lead to structural brain plasticity subserving the more readily observable changes in behavior and brain activity. The study of these morphological brain differences in humans with non-invasive neuro-imaging methods is known as "morphometric" neuroimaging, and aims to characterize various structural aspects of the brain's gray and white matter (see, e.g., Draganski & May, 2008; May & Gaser, 2006; Zatorre et al., 2012).

To our knowledge, very little work has addressed the relationship between neuroanatomical structure and hypnosis (though for two seminal studies exploring neuroanatomical correlates of high hypnotic suggestibility, see Horton, Crawford, Harrington, & Downs, 2004; Huber, Lui, Duzzi, Pagnoni, & Porro, 2014). On the other hand, more than 20 studies have now investigated meditation practitioners using morphometric neuroimaging methods (for some seminal studies, see Grant et al., 2010; Holzel et al., 2008; Lazar et al., 2005; Pagnoni & Cekic, 2007).

Recently, some of us (Fox, Nijeboer, et al., 2014) undertook a comprehensive review and meta-analysis of these morphometric studies of meditation practitioners (Figure 11.9 and Plate 10). Among numerous intriguing differences in gray and white matter, some consistent meta-analytic clusters are of particular relevance to the preceding discussion of de-automatization. Consistent neuroanatomical differences were observed in the rostrolateral prefrontal cortex (Brodmann area 10), for instance (Figure 11.9, left panel), which is strongly implicated in meta-cognitive awareness and accuracy (Christoff & Gabrieli, 2000; Christoff, Ream, Geddes, & Gabrieli, 2003; Fleming & Dolan, 2012; Fleming, Dolan, & Frith, 2012; Fleming, Weil, Nagy, Dolan, & Rees, 2010; McCaig, Dixon, Keramatian, Liu, & Christoff, 2011). As we have already noted, meta-awareness of the automaticity of spontaneous thought patterns seems a prerequisite to any enduring change of these patterns (see the section "Recognizing and combating the automaticity of spontaneous thought processes: the benefits of meta-awareness"); structural plasticity in what is arguably the key meta-cognitive brain region might therefore support these changes.

Also of interest are meta-analytic differences in the insular cortex (Figure 11.9, left panel; Fox, Nijeboer, et al., 2014). Although the insula has been implicated in a wide variety of cognitive and emotional processes (Menon & Uddin, 2010; Singer, Critchley, & Preuschoff, 2009), its role in interoception (awareness of internal bodily sensations) is particularly prominent (Craig, 2004, 2009; Critchley et al., 2004). As discussed in the section "Reducing the chaining of spontaneous thought," a non-elaborative mental stance often involves increased focus on the immediate, present-centered sensations from within the body as a means of avoiding becoming ensnared in automatized streams of thought (Farb et al., 2007; Fox et al., 2012; Kerr et al., 2013). Structural differences in the insula might therefore play a role in the increased awareness of the body and present-moment experience cultivated by meditation practitioners (Farb, Segal, & Anderson, 2013a, 2013b; Farb et al., 2007; Fox et al., 2012; Kerr et al., 2013).

A further area of interest is the medial temporal lobe, particularly the hippocampus and par-ahippocampal cortex (Figure 11.9, right panel), which appear to exhibit altered structure in

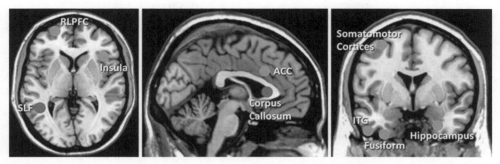

Fig. 11.9 Brain regions showing consistent structural differences in meditation practitioners (see also Plate 10).

Brain regions which show significant structural differences in meditation practitioners versus meditation-naïve controls, as measured via various morphometric neuroimaging techniques. Schematic results based on a meta-analysis of all morphometric neuroimaging studies of meditation practitioners. ACC: anterior cingulate cortex; ITG: inferior temporal gyrus; SLF: superior longitudinal fasciculus; RLPFC: rostrolateral prefrontal cortex.

Reprinted from *Neuroscience & Biobehavioral Reviews*, 43, Kieran C.R. Fox, Savannah Nijeboer, Matthew L. Dixon, James L. Floman, Melissa Ellamil, Samuel P. Rumak, Peter Sedlmeier, and Kalina Christoff, TIs meditation associated with altered brain structure? A systematic review and meta-analysis of morphometric neuroimaging in meditation practitioners, pp. 48–73, doi:10.1016/j.neubiorev.2014.03.016, Copyright 2014, Elsevier. With permission from Elsevier.

meditation practitioners (Fox, Nijeboer, et al., 2014). The well-established role of the medial temporal lobe in the consolidation of memory (Squire, 2004, 2009; Squire, Stark, & Clark, 2004) has more recently been complemented by recognition of its possible role in the *re*consolidation of memories that have been reactivated (Finnie & Nader, 2012; Nader, Schafe, & Le Doux, 2000; Schwabe, Nader, Wolf, Beaudry, & Pruessner, 2012). Structural differences in medial temporal lobe structures may therefore be related to the reorganization of memories themselves, and of one's habitual reactions to spontaneously arising recollections. A more detailed discussion of this possibility follows.

What is the molecular neurobiological basis of de-automatization?

Even with a basic model of various forms of de-automatization (Figure 11.4), and identification of some potential neuroanatomical correlates, the deeper mystery remains of what cellular and molecular neurobiological mechanisms might subserve the cognitive-emotional flexibility observable at a larger scale as functional and structural brain plasticity and cognitive de-automatization.

The emerging field of memory *reconsolidation* might speak to this issue. For decades, the general consensus was that after an initial period of consolidation, a memory was basically stable. A growing literature, however, supports the idea that *reactivated* memories again enter a labile state where their consolidation can be disturbed, and the memory thereby weakened (Duvarci & Nader, 2004; Duvarci, Nader, & LeDoux, 2005, 2008; Finnie & Nader, 2012; Nader et al., 2000; Schwabe et al., 2012). If memories are reactivated in some manner, a brief time window opens during which these memories can be tampered with, pharmacologically, and their subsequent consolidation reduced or potentially blocked entirely. We propose that if memories arise again spontaneously, during mind wandering for instance, they ought to enter a similarly labile state and be open to deconsolidation or reconsolidation at the molecular level.

A mechanistic account suggests that emotional enhancement of memory is one major route whereby such reconsolidation of memory might take place. As emotion (both positive and negative) enhances memory for many kinds of stimuli (Markovic, Anderson, & Todd, 2014), blocking the neurobiological pathways mediating this emotional modulation during the period of memory reactivation might prevent, or at least modulate, reconsolidation. Several studies, targeting a variety of possible neurobiological mechanisms (including mRNA (messenger ribonucleic acid) synthesis and protein synthesis) of emotionally modulated memory, have now shown such results, usually in relation to fear-related or otherwise negatively valenced memories (Duvarci & Nader, 2004; Duvarci et al., 2005; Duvarci, Nader, & LeDoux, 2008; Nader et al., 2000).

Many of these studies have been conducted in laboratory animals (rats in particular), inviting the question of how relevant such deconsolidation of fear memory might be for our own species. One intriguing study directly addresses this concern, however, by employing a pharmacological intervention in human subjects. By administering the drug propranolol, a β-adrenergic receptor antagonist, Kindt, Soeter, and Vervliet (2009) were able to demonstrate analogous fear memory deconsolidation effects in humans (Kindt et al., 2009). Another study followed up on these results by performing a similar experiment alongside acquisition of fMRI data: Schwabe et al. (2012) administered either propranolol, or a placebo, during the reactivation of previously acquired emotional or neutral material. Their findings supported the earlier propranolol study (Kindt et al., 2009) in showing impaired reconsolidation of emotional material in the propranolol, but not placebo, group (Schwabe et al., 2012). FMRI showed corresponding differential neural activity, during both reactivation and testing of the emotional memories, in the amygdala and hippocampus—two of the key brain structures involved in memory reconsolidation (Schwabe et al., 2012).

Due to the strong reliance of spontaneous thought processes upon memories (Andrews-Hanna, Reidler, Huang, et al., 2010; Fox et al., 2013; Klinger, 2008), the tendency of memories to chain together into an associated stream of thought (e.g., Ellamil et al., in preparation; Figure 11.6 and Plate 7), and the ubiquity of emotion in spontaneous thoughts (Fox et al., 2013; Fox, Thompson, et al., 2014), these results suggest the intriguing possibility that non-pharmacological interventions like meditation and hypnotherapy might be able to reduce the occurrence, emotional intensity, or chaining of thoughts and memories. Damping one's emotional reactivity to spontaneously arising thoughts and moment-to-moment experience, for instance (Feldman, Greeson, & Senville, 2010), might therefore lead to similar "deconsolidation" events at the molecular neurobiological level, preventing older patterns of thought from being reconsolidated and perpetuated. These ideas remain highly speculative, however, and await detailed future work.

Conclusion

The great neuroanatomist Santiago Ramón y Cajal once wrote, "The youthful brain is wonderfully pliable and, stimulated by the impulses of a strong will to do so, can greatly improve its organization by creating new associations between ideas and by refining the powers of judgment" (Ramon y Cajal, 2004, p. 23). We believe that the evidence reviewed here supports a similar conclusion for not-so-youthful adult brains as well. Under appropriate conditions and with effective techniques (for instance, training from a meditation instructor, or suggestion from a hypnotherapist), there appears to be an impressive degree of flexibility at both the cognitive and neural level.

Acknowledgments

The authors thank Dr. Norman A. S. Farb, Dr. Amir Raz, Dr. Melissa Ellamil, Dr. Joshua A. Grant, and Dr. Matthew L. Dixon for their kind permission to reproduce portions of figures from their original research throughout this chapter. This work was supported, in part, by Natural Sciences and Engineering Research Council (NSERC) Vanier Canada Graduate Scholarships awarded to K. C. R. F and M. L., and research grants from the Canadian Institutes of Health Research (CIHR) and NSERC awarded to K. C.

References

Addis, D. R., Pan, L., Vu, M. A., Laiser, N., & Schacter, D. L. (2009). Constructive episodic simulation of the future and the past: distinct subsystems of a core brain network mediate imagining and remembering. *Neuropsychologia*, **47**(11), 2222–2238. doi: 10.1016/j.neuropsychologia.2008.10.026

Andrews-Hanna, J. R., Reidler, J. S., Huang, C., & Buckner, R. L. (2010). Evidence for the default network's role in spontaneous cognition. *Journal of Neurophysiology*, **104**(1), 322–335. doi: 10.1152/jn.00830.2009

Andrews-Hanna, J. R., Reidler, J. S., Sepulcre, J., Poulin, R., & Buckner, R. L. (2010). Functional-anatomic fractionation of the brain's default network. *Neuron*, **65**(4), 550–562. doi: 10.1016/j.neuron.2010.02.005

Andrews-Hanna, J. R., Smallwood, J., & Spreng, R. N. (2014). The default network and self-generated thought: component processes and dynamic control. *Annals of the New York Academy of Sciences*, **1316**(1), 29–52.

Augustinova, M., & Ferrand, L. (2012). Suggestion does not de-automatize word reading: evidence from the semantically based Stroop task. *Psychonomic Bulletin and Review*, **19**(3), 521–527.

Bargh, J. A. (1989). Conditional automaticity: varieties of automatic influence in social perception and cognition. *Unintended Thought*, **3**, 51–69.

Bargh, J. A., & Chartrand, T. L. (1999). The unbearable automaticity of being. *American Psychologist*, **54**(7), 462.

Beck, A. T. (1967). *Depression: clinical, experimental, and theoretical aspects (Vol. 32)*. Philadelphia: University of Pennsylvania Press.

Brefczynski-Lewis, J. A., Lutz, A., Schaefer, H. S., Levinson, D. B., & Davidson, R. J. (2007). Neural correlates of attentional expertise in long-term meditation practitioners. *Proceedings of the National Academy of Sciences (USA)*, **104**(27), 11483–11488. doi: 10.1073/pnas.0606552104

Brewer, J. A., Worhunsky, P. D., Gray, J. R., Tang, Y., Weber, J., & Kober, H. (2011). Meditation experience is associated with differences in default mode network activity and connectivity. *Proceedings of the National Academy of Sciences (USA)*, **108**(50), 20254–20259.

Buckner, R. L., Andrews-Hanna, J. R., & Schacter, D. L. (2008). The brain's default network: anatomy, function, and relevance to disease. *Annals of the New York Academy of Sciences*, **1124**, 1–38. doi: 10.1196/annals.1440.011

Buckner, R. L., Krienen, F. M., & Yeo, B. T. T. (2013). Opportunities and limitations of intrinsic functional connectivity MRI. *Nature Neuroscience*, **16**(7), 832–837.

Casiglia, E., Schiff, S., Facco, E., Gabbana, A., Tikhonoff, V., Schiavon, L., . . . Rossi, A. M. (2010). Neurophysiological correlates of post-hypnotic alexia: a controlled study with Stroop test. *American Journal of Clinical Hypnosis*, **52**(3), 219–233.

Chorpita, B. F., & Barlow, D. H. (1998). The development of anxiety: the role of control in the early environment. *Psychological Bulletin*, **124**(1), 3.

Christoff, K. (2012). Undirected thought: neural determinants and correlates. [Review]. *Brain Research*, **1428**, 51–59. doi: 10.1016/j.brainres.2011.09.060

Christoff, K. (2013). Thinking. In K. Ochsner & S. M. Kosslyn (Eds.), *The Oxford handbook of cognitive neuroscience. Vol. 2: The cutting edges* (pp. 318–333). Oxford: Oxford University Press.

Christoff, K., & Gabrieli, J. D. E. (2000). The frontopolar cortex and human cognition: evidence for a rostrocaudal hierarchical organization within the human prefrontal cortex. *Psychobiology*, **28**(2), 168–186.

Christoff, K., Gordon, A. M., Smallwood, J., Smith, R., & Schooler, J. W. (2009). Experience sampling during fMRI reveals default network and executive system contributions to mind wandering. *Proceedings of the National Academy of Sciences (USA)*, **106**(21), 8719–8724. doi: 10.1073/pnas.0900234106

Christoff, K., Ream, J. M., & Gabrieli, J. D. E. (2004). Cognitive and neural basis of spontaneous thought processes. *Cortex*, **40**, 623–630.

Christoff, K., Ream, J. M., Geddes, L., & Gabrieli, J. D. (2003). Evaluating self-generated information: anterior prefrontal contributions to human cognition. *Behavioral Neuroscience*, **117**(6), 1161.

Condon, P., Desbordes, G., Miller, W., & DeSteno, D. (2013). Meditation increases compassionate responses to suffering. *Psychological Science*, **24**(10), 2125–2127.

Craig, A. (2004). Human feelings: why are some more aware than others? *Trends in Cognitive Sciences*, **8**(6), 239–241.

Craig, A. (2009). How do you feel—now? The anterior insula and human awareness. *Nature Reviews Neuroscience*, **10**(1), 59–70.

Critchley, H. D., Wiens, S., Rotshtein, P., Öhman, A., & Dolan, R. J. (2004). Neural systems supporting interoceptive awareness. *Nature Neuroscience*, **7**(2), 189–195.

D'Argembeau, A., Ruby, P., Collette, F., Degueldre, C., Balteau, E., Luxen, A., . . . Salmon, E. (2007). Distinct regions of the medial prefrontal cortex are associated with self-referential processing and per-spective taking. *Journal of Cognitive Neuroscience*, **19**(6), 935–944.

Dasgupta, N., & Greenwald, A. G. (2001). On the malleability of automatic attitudes: combating automatic prejudice with images of admired and disliked individuals. *Journal of Personality and Social Psychology*, **81**(5), 800.

Deeley, Q., Oakley, D. A., Toone, B., Giampietro, V., Brammer, M. J., Williams, S. C., & Halligan, P. W. (2012). Modulating the default mode network using hypnosis. *International Journal of Clinical and Experimental Hypnosis*, **60**(2), 206–228.

Déry, C., Campbell, N. K., Lifshitz, M., & Raz, A. (2014). Suggestion overrides automatic audiovisual inte-gration. *Consciousness and Cognition*, **24**, 33–37.

Devine, P. G. (1989). Stereotypes and prejudice: their automatic and controlled components. *Journal of Personality and Social Psychology*, **56**(1), 5.

Dixon, M. L., Fox, K. C. R., & Christoff, K. (2014). A framework for understanding the relationship between externally and internally directed cognition. *Neuropsychologia*, **62**, 321–330.

Domhoff, G. W., & Fox, K. C. R. (2015). Dreaming and the default network: a review, synthesis, and coun-terintuitive research proposal. *Consciousness and Cognition*, **33**, 342–353.

Draganski, B., & May, A. (2008). Training-induced structural changes in the adult human brain. [Review]. *Behavioural Brain Research*, **192**(1), 137–142. doi: 10.1016/j.bbr.2008.02.015

Duvarci, S., & Nader, K. (2004). Characterization of fear memory reconsolidation. *Journal of Neuroscience*, **24**(42), 9269–9275.

Duvarci, S., Nader, K., & LeDoux, J. E. (2005). Activation of extracellular signal-regulated kinase–mitogen-activated protein kinase cascade in the amygdala is required for memory reconsolidation of auditory fear conditioning. *European Journal of Neuroscience*, **21**(1), 283–289.

Duvarci, S., Nader, K., & LeDoux, J. E. (2008). De novo mRNA synthesis is required for both con-solidation and reconsolidation of fear memories in the amygdala. *Learning and Memory*, **15**(10), 747–755.

Ellamil, M., Dobson, C., Beeman, M., & Christoff, K. (2012). Evaluative and generative modes of thought during the creative process. *Neuroimage*, **59**(2), 1783–1794. doi: 10.1016/j.neuroimage.2011.08.008

Ellamil, M., Fox, K. C. R., Dixon, M. L., Todd, R. M., Thompson, E., & Christoff, K. (in preparation). Neural activity related to the specific content and chaining together of spontaneous thoughts.

Farb, N. A. S., Segal, Z. V., & Anderson, A. K. (2013a). Attentional modulation of primary interoceptive and exteroceptive cortices. *Cerebral Cortex*, **23**(1), 114–126.

Farb, N. A. S., Segal, Z. V., & Anderson, A. K. (2013b). Mindfulness meditation training alters cortical representations of interoceptive attention. *Social Cognitive and Affective Neuroscience*, **8**(1), 15–26. doi: 10.1093/scan/nss066

Farb, N. A. S., Segal, Z. V., Mayberg, H., Bean, J., McKeon, D., Fatima, Z., & Anderson, A. K. (2007). Attending to the present: mindfulness meditation reveals distinct neural modes of self-reference. *Social Cognitive and Affective Neuroscience*, **2**(4), 313–322. doi: 10.1093/scan/nsm030

Feldman, G., Greeson, J., & Senville, J. (2010). Differential effects of mindful breathing, progressive muscle relaxation, and loving-kindness meditation on decentering and negative reactions to repetitive thoughts. *Behaviour Research and Therapy*, **48**(10), 1002–1011.

Finnie, P. S., & Nader, K. (2012). The role of metaplasticity mechanisms in regulating memory destabilization and reconsolidation. *Neuroscience and Biobehavioral Reviews*, **36**(7), 1667–1707.

Fiske, S. T., Cuddy, A. J., & Glick, P. (2007). Universal dimensions of social cognition: warmth and competence. *Trends in Cognitive Sciences*, **11**(2), 77–83.

Fleming, S. M., & Dolan, R. J. (2012). The neural basis of metacognitive ability. *Philosophical Transactions of the Royal Society London B: Biological Sciences*, **367**(1594), 1338–1349. doi: 10.1098/rstb.2011.0417

Fleming, S. M., Dolan, R. J., & Frith, C. D. (2012). Metacognition: computation, biology and function. [Introductory]. *Philosophical Transactions of the Royal Society London B: Biological Sciences*, **367**(1594), 1280–1286. doi: 10.1098/rstb.2012.0021

Fleming, S. M., Weil, R. S., Nagy, Z., Dolan, R. J., & Rees, G. (2010). Relating introspective accuracy to individual differences in brain structure. *Science*, **329**(5998), 1541–1543. doi: 10.1126/science.1191883

Forsyth, J. P., Parker, J. D., & Finlay, C. G. (2003). Anxiety sensitivity, controllability, and experiential avoidance and their relation to drug of choice and addiction severity in a residential sample of substance-abusing veterans. *Addictive Behaviors*, **28**(5), 851–870.

Fox, K. C. R., & Christoff, K. (2014). Metacognitive facilitation of spontaneous thought processes: when metacognition helps the wandering mind find its way. In S. M. Fleming & C. D. Frith (Eds.), *The cognitive neuroscience of metacognition* (pp. 293–319). Berlin, Heidelberg: Springer.

Fox, K. C. R., & Christoff, K. (2015). Transcranial direct current stimulation to lateral prefrontal cortex could increase meta-awareness of mind wandering. *Proceedings of the National Academy of Sciences*. 201504686. doi: 10.1073/pnas.1504686112

Fox, K. C. R., Nijeboer, S., Dixon, M. L., Floman, J. L., Ellamil, M., Rumak, S. P., . . . Christoff, K. (2014). Is meditation associated with altered brain structure? A systematic review and meta-analysis of morphometric neuroimaging in meditation practitioners. *Neuroscience and Biobehavioral Reviews*, **43**, 48–73.

Fox, K. C. R., Nijeboer, S., Solomonova, E., Domhoff, G. W., & Christoff, K. (2013). Dreaming as mind wandering: evidence from functional neuroimaging and first-person content reports. *Frontiers in Human Neuroscience*, **7**, 412. doi: 10.3389/fnhum.2013.00412

Fox, K. C. R., Spreng, R. N., Ellamil, M., Andrews-Hanna, J. R., & Christoff, K. (2015). The wandering brain: meta-analysis of functional neuroimaging studies of mind-wandering and related spontaneous thought processes. *NeuroImage*, **111**, 611–621.

Fox, K. C. R., Thompson, E., Andrews-Hanna, J. R., & Christoff, K. (2014). Is thinking really aversive? A commentary on Wilson et al.'s "Just think: the challenges of the disengaged mind." *Frontiers in Psychology: Cognition*, **5**(1427), 1–4.

Fox, K. C. R., Zakarauskas, P., Dixon, M. L., Ellamil, M., Thompson, E., & Christoff, K. (2012). Meditation experience predicts introspective accuracy. *PLoS ONE*, **7**(9), e45370. doi: 10.1371/journal.pone.0045370.t001

Gaertner, S. L., & Dovidio, J. F. (2008). Addressing contemporary racism: the common ingroup identity model. In C. Willis-Esqueda (Ed.), *Motivational aspects of prejudice and racism* (pp. 111–133). New York: Springer.

Gelbard-Sagiv, H., Mukamel, R., Harel, M., Malach, R., & Fried, I. (2008). Internally generated reactivation of single neurons in human hippocampus during free recall. *Science*, **322**(5898), 96–101.

Grant, J. A. (2014). Meditative analgesia: the current state of the field. *Annals of the New York Academy of Sciences*, **1307**(1), 55–63.

Grant, J. A., Courtemanche, J., Duerden, E. G., Duncan, G. H., & Rainville, P. (2010). Cortical thickness and pain sensitivity in Zen meditators. *Emotion*, **10**(1), 43–53. doi: 10.1037/a0018334

Grant, J. A., Courtemanche, J., & Rainville, P. (2011). A non-elaborative mental stance and decoupling of executive and pain-related cortices predicts low pain sensitivity in Zen meditators. *Pain*, **152**(1), 150–156. doi: 10.1016/j.pain.2010.10.006

Grant, J. A., & Rainville, P. (2009). Pain sensitivity and analgesic effects of mindful states in Zen meditators: a cross-sectional study. *Psychosomatic Medicine*, **71**(1), 106–114.

Greenwald, A. G., Poehlman, T. A., Uhlmann, E. L., & Banaji, M. R. (2009). Understanding and using the Implicit Association Test: III. Meta-analysis of predictive validity. *Journal of Personality and Social Psychology*, **97**(1), 17.

Gunaratana, B. H. (2011). *Mindfulness in plain English*. Somerville, MA: Wisdom Publications.

Holzel, B. K., Ott, U., Gard, T., Hempel, H., Weygandt, M., Morgen, K., & Vaitl, D. (2008). Investigation of mindfulness meditation practitioners with voxel-based morphometry. *Social Cognitive and Affective Neuroscience*, **3**(1), 55–61. doi: 10.1093/scan/nsm038

Horton, J. E., Crawford, H. J., Harrington, G., & Downs, J. H. (2004). Increased anterior corpus callosum size associated positively with hypnotizability and the ability to control pain. *Brain*, **127**(8), 1741–1747.

Huber, A., Lui, F., Duzzi, D., Pagnoni, G., & Porro, C. A. (2014). Structural and functional cerebral correlates of hypnotic suggestibility. *PLoS ONE*, **9**(3), e93187.

Iani, C., Ricci, F., Baroni, G., & Rubichi, S. (2009). Attention control and susceptibility to hypnosis. *Consciousness and Cognition*, **18**(4), 856–863.

Iani, C., Ricci, F., Gherri, E., & Rubichi, S. (2006). Hypnotic suggestion modulates cognitive conflict: the case of the Flanker compatibility effect. *Psychological Science*, **17**(8), 721–727.

Iyengar, B. K. S. (2005). *Light on the Yoga Sutras of Patanjali*. New York: Harper Collins.

Kabat-Zinn, J. (1982). An outpatient program in behavioral medicine for chronic pain patients based on the practice of mindfulness meditation: theoretical considerations and preliminary results. *General Hospital Psychiatry*, **4**(1), 33–47.

Kabat-Zinn, J., Lipworth, L., & Burney, R. (1985). The clinical use of mindfulness meditation for the self-regulation of chronic pain. *Journal of Behavioral Medicine*, **8**(2), 163–190.

Kadosh, R. C., Henik, A., Catena, A., Walsh, V., & Fuentes, L. J. (2009). Induced cross-modal synaesthetic experience without abnormal neuronal connections. *Psychological Science*, **20**(2), 258–265.

Kang, Y., Gray, J. R., & Dovidio, J. F. (2013). The nondiscriminating heart: lovingkindness meditation training decreases implicit intergroup bias. *Journal of Experimental Psychology: General*, **143**(3), 1306.

Kang, Y., Gruber, J., & Gray, J. R. (2013). Mindfulness and de-automatization. *Emotion Review*, **5**(2), 192–201.

Kerr, C. E., Sacchet, M. D., Lazar, S. W., Moore, C. I., & Jones, S. R. (2013). Mindfulness starts with the body: somatosensory attention and top-down modulation of cortical alpha rhythms in mindfulness meditation. *Frontiers in Human Neuroscience*, **7**(12), 1–15.

Killingsworth, M. A., & Gilbert, D. T. (2010). A wandering mind is an unhappy mind. *Science*, **330**, 932.

Kindt, M., Soeter, M., & Vervliet, B. (2009). Beyond extinction: erasing human fear responses and preventing the return of fear. *Nature Neuroscience*, **12**(3), 256–258.

Klinger, E. (1990). *Daydreaming*. Los Angeles: Tarcher.

Klinger, E. (2008). Daydreaming and fantasizing: thought flow and motivation. In K. D. Markman, W. M. P. Klein, & J. A. Suhr (Eds.), *Handbook of imagination and mental simulation* (pp. 225–239). New York: Psychology Press.

Klinger, E. (2013). Goal commitments and the content of thoughts and dreams: basic principles. *Frontiers in Psychology*, **4**, 415. doi: 10.3389/fpsyg.2013.00415

LaBerge, D., & Samuels, S. J. (1974). Toward a theory of automatic information processing in reading. *Cognitive Psychology*, **6**(2), 293–323.

Lazar, S. W., Kerr, C. E., Wasserman, R. H., Gray, J. R., Greve, D. N., Treadway, M. T., . . . Benson, H. (2005). Meditation experience is associated with increased cortical thickness. *Neuroreport*, **16**(17), 1893.

Lifshitz, M., Aubert Bonn, N., Fischer, A., Kashem, I. F., & Raz, A. (2013). Using suggestion to modulate automatic processes: from Stroop to McGurk and beyond. *Cortex*, **49**(2), 463–473.

Lutz, A., Brefczynski-Lewis, J., Johnstone, T., & Davidson, R. J. (2008). Regulation of the neural circuitry of emotion by compassion meditation: effects of meditative expertise. *PLoS One*, **3**(3), e1897. doi: 10.1371/journal.pone.0001897

Markovic, J., Anderson, A. K., & Todd, R. M. (2014). Tuning to the significant: neural and genetic processes underlying affective enhancement of visual perception and memory. *Behavioural Brain Research*, **259**, 229–241.

May, A., & Gaser, C. (2006). Magnetic resonance-based morphometry: a window into structural plasticity of the brain. *Current Opinion in Neurology*, **19**(4), 407–411.

Mazzoni, G., Venneri, A., McGeown, W. J., & Kirsch, I. (2013). Neuroimaging resolution of the altered state hypothesis. *Cortex*, **49**(2), 400–410.

McCaig, R. G., Dixon, M., Keramatian, K., Liu, I., & Christoff, K. (2011). Improved modulation of rostrolateral prefrontal cortex using real-time fMRI training and meta-cognitive awareness. *Neuroimage*, **55**(3), 1298–1305. doi: 10.1016/j.neuroimage.2010.12.016

McGeown, W. J., Mazzoni, G., Venneri, A., & Kirsch, I. (2009). Hypnotic induction decreases anterior default mode activity. *Consciousness and Cognition*, **18**(4), 848–855.

McGurk, H., & MacDonald, J. (1976). Hearing lips and seeing voices. *Nature*, **264**, 746–748.

McMillan, R. L., Kaufman, S. B., & Singer, J. L. (2013). Ode to positive constructive daydreaming. [Review]. *Frontiers in Psychology*, **4**, 626. doi: 10.3389/fpsyg.2013.00626

Menon, V., & Uddin, L. Q. (2010). Saliency, switching, attention and control: a network model of insula function. *Brain Structure and Function*, **214**(5–6), 655–667.

Monteith, M. J., Zuwerink, J. R., & Devine, P. G. (1994). *Prejudice and prejudice reduction: classic challenges, contemporary approaches*. San Diego, CA: Academic Press.

Moors, A., & De Houwer, J. (2006). Automaticity: a theoretical and conceptual analysis. *Psychological Bulletin*, **132**(2), 297.

Morone, N. E., Greco, C. M., & Weiner, D. K. (2008). Mindfulness meditation for the treatment of chronic low back pain in older adults: a randomized controlled pilot study. *Pain*, **134**(3), 310–319.

Moskowitz, G. B., & Li, P. (2011). Egalitarian goals trigger stereotype inhibition: a proactive form of stereotype control. *Journal of Experimental Social Psychology*, **47**(1), 103–116.

Mrazek, M. D., Franklin, M. S., Phillips, D. T., Baird, B., & Schooler, J. W. (2013). Mindfulness training improves working memory capacity and GRE performance while reducing mind wandering. *Psychological Science*, **24**(5), 776–781. doi: 10.1177/0956797612459659

Nader, K., Schafe, G. E., & Le Doux, J. E. (2000). Fear memories require protein synthesis in the amygdala for reconsolidation after retrieval. *Nature*, **406**(6797), 722–726.

Nolen-Hoeksema, S. (1991). Responses to depression and their effects on the duration of depressive episodes. *Journal of Abnormal Psychology*, **100**(4), 569.

Northoff, G., Heinzel, A., de Greck, M., Bermpohl, F., Dobrowolny, H., & Panksepp, J. (2006). Self-referential processing in our brain—a meta-analysis of imaging studies on the self. *Neuroimage*, **31**(1), 440–457.

Olesen, J., Bousser, M. G., Diener, H. C., Dodick, D., First, M., Goadsby, P., . . . Lipton, R. (2006). New appendix criteria open for a broader concept of chronic migraine. *Cephalalgia*, **26**(6), 742–746.

Ouspensky, P. D. (1957). *The fourth way*. London: Routledge & Kegan Paul.

Pagnoni, G., & Cekic, M. (2007). Age effects on gray matter volume and attentional performance in Zen meditation. [Research Support, NIH, Extramural]. *Neurobiology of Aging*, **28**(10), 1623–1627. doi: 10.1016/j.neurobiolaging.2007.06.008

Parris, B. A., Dienes, Z., Bate, S., & Gothard, S. (2013). Oxytocin impedes the effect of the word blindness post-hypnotic suggestion on Stroop task performance. *Social Cognitive and Affective Neuroscience*, **9**(7), 895–899.

Parris, B. A., Dienes, Z., & Hodgson, T. L. (2012). Temporal constraints of the word blindness posthypnotic suggestion on Stroop task performance. *Journal of Experimental Psychology*, **38**(4), 833.

Parris, B. A., Dienes, Z., & Hodgson, T. L. (2013). Application of the ex-Gaussian function to the effect of the word blindness suggestion on Stroop task performance suggests no word blindness. *Frontiers in Psychology*, **4**(647), 1–8.

Rainville, P., Duncan, G. H., Price, D. D., Carrier, B., & Bushnell, M. C. (1997). Pain affect encoded in human anterior cingulate but not somatosensory cortex. *Science*, **277**(5328), 968–971.

Ramon y Cajal, S. (2004). *Advice for a young investigator*. Cambridge, MA: MIT Press.

Raz, A., & Campbell, N. K. (2011). Can suggestion obviate reading? Supplementing primary Stroop evidence with exploratory negative priming analyses. *Consciousness and Cognition*, **20**(2), 312–320.

Raz, A., Fan, J., & Posner, M. I. (2005). Hypnotic suggestion reduces conflict in the human brain. *Proceedings of the National Academy of Sciences (USA)*, **102**(28), 9978–9983.

Raz, A., Kirsch, I., Pollard, J., & Nitkin-Kaner, Y. (2006). Suggestion reduces the Stroop effect. *Psychological Science*, **17**(2), 91–95.

Raz, A., Moreno-Íniguez, M., Martin, L., & Zhu, H. (2007). Suggestion overrides the Stroop effect in highly hypnotizable individuals. *Consciousness and Cognition*, **16**(2), 331–338.

Raz, A., Shapiro, T., Fan, J., & Posner, M. I. (2002). Hypnotic suggestion and the modulation of Stroop interference. *Archives of General Psychiatry*, **59**(12), 1155–1161.

Salzberg, S. (2004). *Lovingkindness: the revolutionary art of happiness*. Boulder, CO: Shambhala Publications.

Sassenberg, K., & Moskowitz, G. B. (2005). Don't stereotype, think different! Overcoming automatic stereotype activation by mindset priming. *Journal of Experimental Social Psychology*, **41**(5), 506–514.

Sawamoto, N., Honda, M., Okada, T., Hanakawa, T., Kanda, M., Fukuyama, H., . . . Shibasaki, H. (2000). Expectation of pain enhances responses to nonpainful somatosensory stimulation in the anterior cingulate cortex and parietal operculum/posterior insula: an event-related functional magnetic resonance imaging study. *Journal of Neuroscience*, **20**(19), 7438–7445.

Schacter, D. L., Addis, D. R., & Buckner, R. L. (2007). Remembering the past to imagine the future: the prospective brain. *Nature Reviews Neuroscience*, **8**(9), 657–661.

Schooler, J. W., Smallwood, J., Christoff, K., Handy, T. C., Reichle, E. D., & Sayette, M. A. (2011). Meta-awareness, perceptual decoupling and the wandering mind. *Trends in Cognitive Sciences*, **15**(7), 319–326. doi: 10.1016/j.tics.2011.05.006

Schwabe, L., Nader, K., Wolf, O. T., Beaudry, T., & Pruessner, J. C. (2012). Neural signature of reconsolidation impairments by propranolol in humans. *Biological Psychiatry*, **71**(4), 380–386.

Singer, J. L. (1966). *Daydreaming: an introduction to the experimental study of inner experience*. New York: Crown Publishing Group/Random House.

Singer, J. L., & McCraven, V. (1961). Some characteristics of adult daydreaming. *Journal of Psychology*, **51**, 151–164.

Singer, T., Critchley, H. D., & Preuschoff, K. (2009). A common role of insula in feelings, empathy and uncertainty. *Trends in Cognitive Sciences*, **13**(8), 334–340.

Smallwood, J., & Andrews-Hanna, J. R.(2013). Not all minds that wander are lost: the importance of a balanced perspective on the mind-wandering state. *Frontiers in Psychology*, **4**(441), 1–6. doi: 10.3389/fpsyg.2013.00441

Smallwood, J., McSpadden, M., Luus, B., & Schooler, J. W. (2008). Segmenting the stream of consciousness: the psychological correlates of temporal structures in the time series data of a continuous performance task. *Brain and Cognition*, **66**(1), 50–56.

Smallwood, J., McSpadden, M., & Schooler, J. W. (2007). The lights are on but no one's home: Meta-awareness and the decoupling of attention when the mind wanders. *Psychonomic Bulletin and Review*, **14**(3), 527–533.

Solms, M. (1997). *The neuropsychology of dreams: a clinico-anatomical study*. Mahwah, NJ, USA: Lawrence Erlbaum Associates Publishers.

Squire, L. R. (2004). Memory systems of the brain: a brief history and current perspective. *Neurobiology of Learning and Memory*, **82**(3), 171–177.

Squire, L. R. (2009). The legacy of patient HM for neuroscience. *Neuron*, **61**(1), 6–9.

Squire, L. R., Stark, C. E., & Clark, R. E. (2004). The medial temporal lobe. *Annual Review of Neuroscience*, **27**, 279–306.

Summerfield, Q., & McGrath, M. (1984). Detection and resolution of audio-visual incompatibility in the perception of vowels. *Quarterly Journal of Experimental Psychology*, **36**(1), 51–74.

Svoboda, E., McKinnon, M. C., & Levine, B. (2006). The functional neuroanatomy of autobiographical memory: a meta-analysis. *Neuropsychologia*, **44**(12), 2189–2208.

Terhune, D. B., Cardeña, E., & Lindgren, M. (2010). Disruption of synaesthesia by posthypnotic suggestion: an ERP study. *Neuropsychologia*, **48**(11), 3360–3364.

Van Dijk, K. R., Hedden, T., Venkataraman, A., Evans, K. C., Lazar, S. W., & Buckner, R. L. (2010). Intrinsic functional connectivity as a tool for human connectomics: theory, properties, and optimization. *Journal of Neurophysiology*, **103**(1), 297.

Völlm, B. A., Taylor, A. N., Richardson, P., Corcoran, R., Stirling, J., McKie, S., . . . Elliott, R. (2006). Neuronal correlates of theory of mind and empathy: a functional magnetic resonance imaging study in a nonverbal task. *Neuroimage*, **29**(1), 90–98.

Walsh, R. (1977). Initial meditative experiences: Part I. *Journal of Transpersonal Psychology*, **9**, 151–192.

Weng, H. Y., Fox, A. S., Shackman, A. J., Stodola, D. E., Caldwell, J. Z., Olson, M. C., . . . Davidson, R.J. (2013). Compassion training alters altruism and neural responses to suffering. *Psychological Science*, **24**(7), 1171–1180.

Woolf, C. J., & Mannion, R. J. (1999). Neuropathic pain: aetiology, symptoms, mechanisms, and management. *The Lancet*, **353**(9168), 1959–1964.

Yapko, M. D. (2013). *Hypnosis and treating depression: applications in clinical practice*. New York: Routledge.

Zatorre, R. J., Fields, R. D., & Johansen-Berg, H. (2012). Plasticity in gray and white: neuroimaging changes in brain structure during learning. *Nature Neuroscience*, **15**(4), 528–536. doi: 10.1038/nn.3045

Chapter 12

Mind wandering and meta-awareness in hypnosis and meditation
Relating executive function across states of consciousness

Benjamin W. Mooneyham and Jonathan W. Schooler

Abstract

Hypnosis and meditation are two of many techniques for altering individuals' cognitive and psychological states (i.e., states of consciousness). Recent investigations have demonstrated that hypnosis and meditation may both produce changes in executive processes (e.g., cognitive control, monitoring), although the precise effects of each on the sub-processes of the executive system are not fully understood, particularly for hypnosis. Drawing from the research domains of attention and meta-awareness, the authors propose an approach that may allow the characterization of the specific functional changes that occur within the executive system during various states of consciousness. As an example of the utility of this approach, the chapter offers an overview of how their empirical protocol may be utilized to examine the similarities and differences between hypnosis, mindfulness meditation, and/or other atypical states of consciousness, and provides a preliminary discussion of the implications of this proposed research.

Introduction

Recently, researchers have become increasingly interested in the ability of intervention programs, targeted to induce alternative or atypical states of consciousness, to alter cognitive abilities, particularly those that are domain-general: for instance, abilities associated with cognitive control (e.g., Colcombe & Kramer, 2003; Erickson et al., 2007; Hillman, Erickson, & Kramer, 2008; Kramer & Erickson, 2007; Morrison & Chein, 2010; Mrazek, Franklin, Phillips, Baird, & Schooler, 2013; Slagter, Davidson, & Lutz, 2011). In this chapter, we propose a method for examining the specific effect(s) of various states of consciousness (such as those induced by popular intervention programs) on executive functions such as executive control and executive monitoring and describe, as an example of this procedure, how our proposed method may inform the understanding of two practices that have each been investigated in the context of their ability to modulate executive functioning: *hypnosis* and *meditation*.

We begin by briefly considering what is already known about the relationship between hypnosis and meditation. This analysis reveals that while these two psychological interventions share some striking similarities, they also diverge in ways that have not yet been fully characterized, warranting further empirical investigation aimed at assessing the functional similarities and differences in executive functioning resulting from hypnosis and meditation. Toward this end, we propose an experimental methodology that may permit both the assessment of the particular changes in executive functioning that are associated with hypnosis, mindfulness meditation, or other atypical state of consciousness, and the direct comparison of the effects of each state within a common experimental design. Our proposed approach, adapted from the research domains of mind wandering and meta-awareness, may offer important insights regarding the relationship between executive processes and various states of consciousness. In this chapter, we employ hypnosis and mindfulness meditation as examples of atypical states of consciousness, and explore how our proposed approach may shed light upon three unresolved research issues related to these particular states: the specific dissociative effects of hypnosis, the effects of meditation practice on executive functioning, and the relationship between hypnosis and meditation.

Hypnosis versus meditation

What is the relationship between meditation and hypnosis? This question has garnered significant interest recently (see Part 3 of this volume). At the surface, meditation and hypnosis share several basic similarities, but upon closer examination it becomes clear that we do not yet fully understand either practice or the precise mechanisms by which they differ from each other.

Characteristics shared by hypnosis and (mindfulness) meditation

Hypnosis and meditation are practices associated with several common principles.

Relaxation

Both hypnosis and meditation participants often report feeling relaxed (Benson, Greenwood, & Klemchuk, 1975; Lynn, Brentar, Carlson, Kurzhals, & Green, 1992; Lynn, Malaktaris, Maxwell, Mellinger, & van der Kloet, 2012; Wallace, Benson, Wilson, 1984). However, relaxation is not required in order for hypnotic responding to occur. Moreover, meditative states can also be distinguished from relaxation states (such as with electroencephalography (EEG); Dunn, Hartigan, & Mikulas, 1999), suggesting that while relaxation may typically occur during hypnosis and meditation alike, neither state's effects can be reduced to the effects of the relaxation that occurs within the state.

Absorption

Both hypnosis and meditation are absorptive practices (see Chapter 14). Absorption can be measured at the trait level, where it indicates a dispositional tendency to experience episodes in which one's "total" attention fully engages one's representational (i.e., perceptual, enactive, imaginative, ideational) resources (Tellegen & Atkinson, 1974). Assessments of absorption have been made in relation to both hypnosis and meditation; absorption correlates positively with hypnotizability (Tellegen & Atkinson, 1974), while long-term meditators indicate higher levels of absorption than do novice meditators (Davidson, Goleman, & Schwartz, 1976). While the particular absorption that occurs during hypnosis and meditation may differ (see Semmens-Wheeler & Dienes, 2012, for a discussion of four modes of mental processing that may each be associated with different "types" of absorption), it is nonetheless reasonable to assert that both practices are associated with some form of attentional absorption.

Characteristic distinctions between hypnosis and meditation

Despite the commonalities shared between hypnosis and meditation, several key differences between these two practices have made it difficult to precisely determine the relationship between them.

Attentional regulation/control

In hypnosis, attention is typically directed toward some external object or behavior, and this direction of attention results from a command or suggestion given by the hypnotist to the individual undergoing hypnosis. As such, attentional control is, in a manner, relegated to the hypnotist and the locus of attention determined through the specific suggestions given to the hypnotized individual. Interestingly, meditation practice often begins in a similar fashion, in which an instructor provides suggestions for the student regarding toward where and what to direct their attention (see Chapter 19). However, over the course of practice, experienced meditators come to control their attention internally (likely by training their meta-cognitive abilities; see Semmens-Wheeler & Dienes, 2012) and, in contrast to what occurs during hypnosis, learn to focus their attention not on some external action or object, but on their own internal states and experiences.

There is ample evidence that meditation practice leads to attentional improvements. For instance, experienced meditators exhibit less Stroop interference than controls during the Stroop task (Moore & Malinowski, 2009; Wenk-Sormaz, 2005), indicating improved attentional control and an ability to override a supposedly automatic process (see Chapter 16). While meditation practice has been shown to improve attentional abilities in a variety of studies, the effect of hypnosis on attention is much less straightforward. Without a hypnotic induction or a task-relevant suggestion, most studies have shown that high-hypnotizable individuals do not demonstrate improved attentional abilities, as measured by Stroop interference (e.g., Egner, Jamieson, &Gruzelier, 2005; Jamieson & Sheehan, 2004; Kaiser, Barker, Haenschel, Baldeweg, & Gruzelier, 1997; Kallio, Revonsuo, Hamalainen, Markela, & Gruzelier, 2001; Nordby, Jasiukaitis, & Spiegel, 1999).

Effect of suggestion

While high-hypnotizable individuals do not possess improved attentional abilities in the absence of a hypnotic induction or task-relevant suggestion, the story changes once a suggestion is given. When given a suggestion to view words presented in a Stroop task as meaningless, high-hypnotizable individuals actually show improved Stroop performance (Parris, Dienes, & Hodgson, 2012; Raz, Shapiro, Fan, & Posner, 2002; Raz et al., 2003). This points to the importance of suggestion within hypnotic responding, and demonstrates that high-hypnotizable individuals that have been given a specific suggestion may indeed have superior attentional abilities in comparison to low-hypnotizable individuals (even when the low hypnotizables also receive a suggestion) who show no improvements in Stroop performance when given the same suggestion.

Hypnotizability is measured through suggestibility, such that individuals who are more likely to respond in accordance with external suggestions are deemed more hypnotizable. As such, the internal state of high hypnotizables may be more malleable than it is for others, which may allow these individuals to respond to suggestions in ways that improve their attentional performance. However, while individuals with meditation practice also show improved attentional performance, they are generally less suggestible; Semmens-Wheeler and Dienes (2012) report that an examination of 12 expert meditators revealed that they were less suggestible than average (passing 3 out of 12 suggestions, compared to an average of 5.5 suggestions passed). Additionally, across over 500 participants, hypnotizability negatively correlated with mindfulness ($r = -0.38$; Semmens-Wheeler & Dienes, 2012).

These results lead to a seemingly paradoxical conclusion: instructing high-hypnotizable individuals to respond less mindfully (i.e., hypnotically, as in the Stroop studies with task-relevant suggestions) leads them to perform better on the same attention tasks upon which meditation training improves performance (Semmens-Wheeler & Dienes, 2012; for an updated account of this research, including more recent findings, see Chapter 7). Additionally, while meditators may be less suggestible as a result of their meditation practice, it is suggestion that enables the improvement in attentional performance in high hypnotizables to occur.

The need to examine attention and executive processing in both hypnosis and meditation

Despite the similarities between hypnosis and meditation, a closer examination of the effects of each practice reveals that the distinction between the two may not be made simply. In order to more fully understand the relationship between hypnosis and meditation, it may be necessary to investigate the effects of each practice at a more fine-grained level by independently examining the component sub-processes of attention and executive processing. We propose an empirical framework in which to examine the effects of each practice on these sub-processes of executive functioning within a single experimental design, and we will outline our proposed approach in the sections to come. First, we discuss current and competing theories of hypnosis, as our protocol may disambiguate a variety of hypnosis-related findings and possibly provide evidence in favor of one theory of hypnosis or another.

Dissociation theories of hypnosis

Various theories of hypnosis exist that posit that some form of dissociation occurs during hypnosis (e.g., Bowers, 1992; Bowers & Davidson, 1991; Hilgard, 1977; Jamieson & Woody, 2007; Janet, 1901, 1907). However, the type of dissociations proposed within the various theories differ, and a distinction can be made between theories that posit a dissociation *of experience* versus a dissociation *of control*.

Dissociation of experience

Theories of dissociated experience within hypnosis have been around for some time (Janet, 1901, 1907), perhaps reflecting the extent to which these theories capture the central feature of hypnosis: the lack of experienced volition. The most prominent of these theories is Hilgard's (1977) "neo-dissociation" theory. This theory proposes that the lack of consciously perceived volition that coincides with the hypnotic state is the result of an *amnesia-like barrier*, which blocks some mental activity from the conscious access it would have in a non-hypnotic circumstance. As such, while a hypnotized individual may have no "conscious" awareness of the volition that accompanies their actions under hypnosis, it is not because volition is lacking, but, rather, because the hypnotized individual becomes dissociated from their own experience of volition. Thus, one may be fully capable of exerting volitional control of one's actions while under hypnosis, but hypnosis may produce a barrier between conscious experience and its subsequent reportability. Additionally, through investigation, Hilgard claimed that, with appropriate suggestions employed, one could access a *hidden observer*, a conscious entity capable of reporting mental activity that had otherwise been blocked from awareness (Hilgard, 1991, 1994; Hilgard, 1977). This led to the conclusion that hypnosis may produce parallel streams of consciousness (through the amnesia-like barrier) that are largely unintegrated.

Given researchers' largely unsuccessful attempts to verify the hidden observer (Green, Page, Handley, & Rasekhy, 2005; Spanos, 1983; Spanos & Hewitt, 1980; Spanos, de Groot, Tiller, Weekes, & Bertrand, 1985), Hilgard's (1977) "neo-dissociation" theory of hypnosis has been met with skepticism. However, Hilgard also argued that hypnotic responses might appear to lack volition (from the perspective of the one hypnotically responding) through a different mechanism (instead of the proposed amnesia-like barrier): circumvention around executive control processes. If hypnotic suggestions are able to bypass the "executive control" system, they may act directly on lower "subsystems of control," thereby initiating the acts demanded by the suggestion without executive initiative. Such a process would produce a similar feeling of a lack of conscious volition, but this feeling would result from an actual dissociation of *control*, in that the suggestion would take effect regardless of the "intent" of the executive control system. With this in mind, Bowers (1992) proposed that neo-dissociation theory should be divided into two separate theories: theories of *dissociated experience* and theories of *dissociated control*.

Dissociation of control

Originally stemming from neo-dissociation theory itself, Bowers (1992) first formalized the *dissociated control theory* of hypnosis. This theory postulates that hypnosis alters control processes themselves rather than merely altering perceived control. In its most basic form, the idea is simple: in hypnosis, the lower "subsystems of control" (such as those involved in coordinating motor movements, lexical processing, etc.) may be directly influenced by suggestion. Such direct access may permit these subsystems of control to produce behaviors that are not directed, initiated, or governed by the higher-level executive control system. Thus, actions performed under hypnosis will lack the usual amount of intervention from executive control processes, and will therefore be perceived to have occurred without volitional control (Sadler & Woody, 2010).

Investigations of executive control processes during hypnosis have lent support to the idea that hypnosis involves some form of dissociated control. Many of these studies have utilized classic "frontal lobe" tasks, such as the Stroop task, to demonstrate that high-susceptible individuals tend to make more errors and suffer greater interference (as measured by reaction time) on the Stroop task than low-susceptible individuals (either while under hypnosis or after a de-induction that was preceded by a hypnotic suggestion) (Jamieson & Sheehan, 2004; Kaiser et al., 1997; Nordby et al., 1999; Sheehan, Donovan, & MacLeod, 1988). *Dissociated control* accounts of hypnosis are bolstered by neuroimaging and electroencephalographic reports of increased activation in conflict-monitoring areas of the brain (specifically, the dorsal anterior cingulate cortex; dACC) for high-susceptible individuals while performing the Stroop task under hypnosis, as well as the finding that the functional connectivity between this conflict-detection region and another "cognitive-control" region, the lateral prefrontal cortex (lPFC), is decreased during the Stroop for high-susceptible individuals while under hypnosis (Egner et al., 2005), a finding which suggests that hypnosis limits the degree to which control processes are able to adjust in response to detected conflict.

Inferring the role of "control" itself in hypnosis from Stroop-like tasks is difficult, however, as it is often unclear whether performance decrements in the Stroop task are due to deficits in conflict monitoring, signaling between conflict monitoring and cognitive-control systems, maintaining and implementing appropriate task set variables within the cognitive-control system, or other processes (Egner & Raz, 2007). Although recent studies have attempted to further clarify the origin of poor Stroop performance under hypnosis, with some success, isolating the changes that occur within particular component processes (and their interactions) during hypnosis will be important to fully explain hypnosis; it is also a central aim of our proposed study.

A variant, and more specific, form of dissociated control theory, the *second-order theory of dissociated control* (a term coined by Woody & Sadler, 1998), also posits that the effect of hypnosis is exerted through dissociated control, but with different locus of dissociation. (This theory shares substantial overlap with the ideas put forth by Jamieson and colleagues in their recent work; Egner et al., 2005; Jamieson & Sheehan, 2004; Jamieson & Woody, 2007). Rather than having the dissociation occur between the higher-level executive control system and the lower subsystems of control, the second-order theory of dissociated control states that the dissociation occurs, instead, between the higher-level *executive control system* and the *executive monitoring system*, such that the executive monitoring system is unable to modulate any directive imposed by the executive control system once the directive has been initiated. This idea is supported by findings that suggest that it may not be a lack of executive processing per se that is responsible for the relationship between hypnosis and poor performance in tasks like the Stroop but, rather, a disconnect between executive monitoring and cognitive control systems: Egner et al. (2005) showed that, while a conflict-detection region of the brain (dACC) showed increased activity for high-susceptible individuals performing the Stroop task under hypnosis, no corresponding increase was observed in a key cognitive-control region (the lPFC), suggesting that there may be a disconnect in communication between these monitoring and control regions during hypnosis. Furthermore, these regions showed decreased functional connectivity during the Stroop task for the high-susceptible individuals, providing direct evidence in support of the notion of *second-order dissociated control*.

Woody & Sadler's integrative model

In response to the propagation of various dissociative theories of hypnosis, Woody and Sadler (Sadler & Woody, 2010; Woody & Sadler, 2008) presented an "integrative model" in which the dissociations predicted by alternative theories could each be depicted within a single framework (see Figure 12.1).

In this model, separate functional modules are depicted for executive control, executive monitoring, and the subsystems of control, with suggestion serving as the input and behavior serving as the output. As such, the model depicts two levels of control: the higher level consists of executive control and executive monitoring, while the lower level is more diverse and consists of various "system-specific" control processes; these "subsystems of control" within the lower level are variegated in nature, comprising constituent and domain-specific processes (such as visual search, word recognition, or motor function) underlying more complex behaviors. Furthermore, the model posits two feedback loops: one loop going from executive control to the subsystems of control, to executive monitoring, and then repeating; the other going reciprocally between executive control and executive monitoring.

Each of these loops are enacted via functional connections between the modules within the model (labeled paths A–E in Figure 12.1) and, according to dissociative theories of hypnosis, it is the relative strengths of these connections that are predicted to change within the hypnotic state. However, the prediction of which particular paths change in strength during hypnosis is determined by the theory being considered. For instance, the theory of dissociated experience predicts that the dissociative effect of hypnosis occurs through a dampening of paths C and E, where information regarding executive control is prevented from reaching awareness in the executive

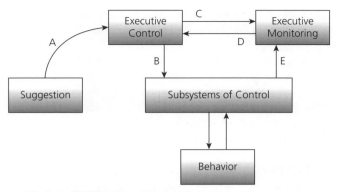

Fig. 12.1 Woody and Sadler's (2008) integrative model.

monitor (path C); such an inhibition may therefore explain why individuals lack awareness of their executive control efforts (i.e., it may simply be because this effort does not get monitored sufficiently enough to reach awareness). Additionally, a more pronounced dissociation of experience (like the form originally proposed by Hilgard) would also involve dampening the outputs from the subsystems of control to the executive monitoring system (path E), thus producing "amnesia" for one's actions altogether.

The theory of dissociated control, on the other hand, posits a reduction in the strength of path B, where the subsystems of control operate without "normal" amounts of executive control being imposed upon them. Thus, the dissociation does not involve a misperception of experience but, rather, a real inability to executively control one's actions under hypnosis.

Finally, the second-order theory of dissociated control predicts a weakening of path D, where the executive monitoring system is therefore unable to modulate the operation of the executive control system, leading to more rigid and less flexible behaviors under hypnosis.

A study proposal: testing the locus of hypnotic dissociation and comparing hypnotic versus meditative effects

Despite a rapid accumulation of findings from empirical investigations into hypnosis and meditation, we have yet to reach a clear understanding of the particular functional changes induced by either activity. We have, as of yet, been unable to reach strong conclusions about how the dissociative effects of hypnosis ought to be characterized, while at the same time, the relationship between the effects of hypnosis and meditation remains largely speculative. We propose that, in order to better resolve this issue, researchers must consider the effects of each activity within a common and comprehensive model of executive functioning. Furthermore, an investigation aimed at distilling the particular functional effects of either meditation or hypnosis (or both) must be able to simultaneously examine each individual functional "connection" within the comprehensive model. If a method can be established to measure each functional connection independently within a single experimental design, then we may be able to specify the particular functional connections that are targeted by hypnotic inductions, meditation practice, or other experiences which produce atypical states of consciousness (such as drug use, brain injury, or the experience of "flow").

We now present a design for a possible approach, rooted in Woody & Sadler's (2008) integrative functional model, that would attempt to separately measure the effects of hypnosis and meditation (or any other atypical state of consciousness) on each individual component "connection" within the model, thereby allowing for a more rich understanding of both the particular functional effects of each activity, as they pertain to executive functioning, and also the functional relationship between the practices/states under investigation.

One design, every path?

Is it possible to characterize the functional changes associated with hypnosis and/or meditation within Woody and Sadler's integrative model, and can changes along each path be quantified within a single study? In order to do so, several requirements must be met:

1 Measure the effect of suggestion alone (compared to suggestion plus hypnosis or suggestion plus meditation; path A)

2 Measure executive control exerted upon "subsystems of control" (path B)

3 Measure executive control exerted upon executive monitoring (path C)

4 Measure the effect of executive monitoring (e.g., meta-awareness) on executive control (path D)

5 Measure awareness of output from subsystems of control (path E).

To meet these requirements, a study needs to combine methodologies. First and foremost, the study must assess cognitive control (such as in the context of sustained attention or response inhibition); this enables a measure of path B. Secondly, the study must assess individuals' awareness of not only their performance but of their fluctuations in cognitive control; this allows paths E and C, respectively. Thirdly, the dependent measure related to the effect of the imposed suggestion must be independent of other influences, permitting a measurement of path A. Finally, the study must measure individuals' propensity/ability to adjust their cognitive control in the face of performance-related cues that reach awareness, in order to assess path D.

A proposed study

What follows is a description of a study design that represents one possible approach toward isolating the specific effects of hypnosis and meditation on cognitive control and awareness within the framework of an integrative model of hypnosis. Such an approach should be able to assess changes in the "strength" of each of the various paths within the model (e.g., paths A through E in the aforementioned integrative model; see Figure 12.1) that occur during either hypnosis or meditation. The approach that we outline here is largely borrowed from a methodology with which the present authors are familiar: to combine a task requiring sustained attention to external stimuli with assessments of on-line meta-awareness. This is a common procedure in the domain of mind wandering (e.g., Christoff, Gordon, Smallwood, Smith, & Schooler, 2009; Levinson, Smallwood, & Davidson, 2012; Smallwood et al., 2008; Smallwood & Schooler, 2006). We believe that this procedure has the capacity to isolate changes along each functional path within Woody and Sadler's integrative model, thus potentially providing useful insights into the nature of hypnosis and meditation.

Basic design

The basic concept of the study is to compare the effects of a hypnotic induction *plus* suggestion or a meditation practice session *plus* suggestion to the effects of suggestion alone, within a task design that allows for each path within the integrative model to be separately tested. As such, we envision this study to have three between-subject conditions:

1 Hypnotic induction *plus* task-based suggestion

2 Meditation practice *plus* task-based suggestion

3 Task-based suggestion *only*.

By employing these three conditions, this study would allow for the effect(s) of hypnosis to be isolated from the effect of suggestion (by comparing the hypnotic-induction (with suggestion) group to the suggestion-only group). The effect(s) of meditation may be similarly isolated by comparing the meditation (with suggestion) group to the suggestion-only group. Finally, this design may also allow for the effect(s) of hypnosis plus suggestion to be compared to the effect(s) of meditation plus suggestion, a comparison that may shed light on the fundamental relationship between these two practices.

Because the integrative model includes paths directly related to aspects of executive control and awareness, the task must garner measurements separately related to each of these. As such, the study should include a task that can be used to measure cognitive control, and also assessments of individuals' awareness (and meta-awareness). We believe that the Sustained Attention to Response Task (SART; Robertson et al., 1997) combined with "thought probes" would be well suited to assess the changes along each path of the integrative model that are uniquely attributable to hypnosis and meditation practice. In brief, this is because the SART provides several dependent measures that reflect aspects of either "lower-level" task performance or cognitive control, while thought probes provide an avenue to examine conscious awareness of these variables (i.e., task performance and cognitive control). The rationale for this particular design will become clearer when we explore how each path could be assessed. First, however, let us divest the rest of the proposed study's design.

Hypnotic induction

Isolating the effect(s) of hypnosis will involve comparing the response characteristics of two groups of individuals: one group who receive a task-related suggestion only, and another group who receive a hypnotic induction prior to being given the same task-related suggestion. As such, this study should only recruit participants who score highly on hypnotic susceptibility in order to ensure that the hypnotic induction will actually have an effect.

Meditation practice

In order to isolate the effect of meditation practice on executive functions such as executive control and meta-awareness, it will be necessary to compare performance on the SART between a group of individuals who receive the "control" treatment, which is a suggestion only, and a group who perform meditation practice and also receive the same suggestion as the control group. However, because it is likely that the effects of meditation and suggestion are not merely additive, but rather more complex, this method of comparing the effects of suggestion only to meditation plus suggestion may not isolate the "pure" effect of meditation on executive functioning. It will, on the other hand, allow an assessment of the cognitive effects of pairing suggestions with meditative practice, rather than in using suggestions in isolation.

Our own laboratory has previously demonstrated that an effect of meditation practice can be observed after a practice session of as little as 8 minutes: a period in which participants are asked to continuously attend to their breath (Mrazek, Smallwood, & Schooler, 2012). This mindful breathing was able to induce changes in SART response behavior in a previous study conducted in our laboratory (Mrazek et al., 2012). As such, the meditation practice plus suggestion group should perform a similar mindfulness practice routine before receiving the task-based suggestion and performing the SART.

The Sustained Attention to Response Task

The Sustained Attention to Response Task, or SART, is a task that is often employed to assess individuals' propensity to exhibit lapses in sustained attention (Cheyne, Carriere, & Smilek, 2006; Cheyne, Carriere, Solman, & Smilek, 2011; Cheyne, Solman, Carriere, & Smilek, 2009; Christoff et al., 2009; McVay & Kane, 2009; Mrazek et al., 2012; Robertson, Manly, Andrade, Baddeley, & Yiend, 1997; Smallwood et al., 2008; Smallwood, Fitzgerald, Miles, & Phillips, 2009). The SART is a variant of the common Go/No-Go procedure, but features a switching of the response demands such that participants are asked to respond to frequent non-target stimuli while withholding responses to infrequent target stimuli.

From the SART, several performance markers are often used as dependent measures. First, the number or proportion of No-Go presentations producing "SART errors" (i.e., errors of commission)—a failure to withhold a response to the target stimulus—is of principle interest, as this measure reflects "strong" lapses in sustained attention or disengagement from the task (Cheyne et al., 2009; Seli, Cheyne, & Smilek, 2012; Smallwood et al., 2008). Additionally, reaction time (RT) measures, such as average RT, may be assessed but, more commonly, the response time coefficient of variability (RT CV)—equal to the standard deviation of an individual's RT, divided by their mean RT—is used as a more subtle measure of failures in sustained attention.

Greater RT CV is posited to reflect less focused sustained attention, as modest attentional disengagements (states described by Cheyne et al. (2009) as *focal task inattention* and *global task inattention*) tend to produce a speeding of RTs, while more pronounced disengagements (*response disengagement*) produce larger RTs; these inattention/disengagement effects, when combined, produce an overall increase in RT CV. As a general conclusion, RT CV appears to most accurately reflect trial-by-trial fluctuations in sustained attention (indicating concomitant fluctuations in cognitive control) to the task (Cheyne et al., 2009, 2011).

SART framing When carrying out the SART, participants are usually instructed to perform the task as quickly and accurately as possible (Robertson et al., 1997). This proposed study would employ a slight variation on the instructions in order to produce dependent measures that capture the strength of each path separately. The instructions for this study's SART should, instead, stress that participants try to perform the task *as accurately as possible* (as in typical versions of the SART), and also *as steadily as possible*. The reason for this modification in the framing of the SART is to allow the estimation of individuals' awareness of the degree of executive control that they have been exerting during the task. By asking individuals to gauge their current pace at moments throughout the task, such as by asking whether it is faster or slower than their average pace up to that point, we can determine the extent to which modulations in executive control (reflected by changes in pacing) reach conscious awareness; this extent will provide an avenue to assess the strength of path C in the aforementioned model (see Figure 12.1).

SART suggestion In order to isolate the effects of hypnosis and meditation from the effect of suggestion, each of the three groups of participants should receive an identical suggestion. Providing a suggestion will allow for comparing the strength of the integrative model's path "A" under hypnosis or after meditation to its strength in the absence of either intervention. In order to isolate this "A" path, we propose the following suggestion: "You may make fewer errors if you go slowly." Thus, the suggestion would be to go slowly; our rationale for this will be explained in detail shortly. It is worth noting, however, that this suggestion may also help overcome methodological issues within standard SART versions, as there is evidence that speed–accuracy trade-offs occur within the SART (Seli et al., 2012). As such, in standard SART versions, the number of SART errors produced is contaminated by this trade-off, where up to half of SART errors may result solely from attempts at speeded responding; instructing participants to go more slowly reduces SART errors overall (presumably reducing the number of errors due to this trade-off), and thus the number of SART errors in a "slow" SART may provide a better pure measure of lapses in sustained attention (Seli et al., 2012).

SART probes Two types of "thought probes" should be presented to the participant during the SART: a "performance" probe and a "pacing" probe. The probes should be presented together following No-Go targets, ideally in counterbalanced order.

Performance probes. To probe their awareness of their performance, participants should be asked: "Did you make an error withholding a response to the last target?" They should then be required to respond either "yes" or "no."

Pacing probes. To probe their awareness of their pacing, participants should also be asked: "Were your reaction times since the most recent probe *more variable* or *less variable* than your average variability in reaction time so far during this task?" They should then be required to respond either "more variable" or "less variable."

Using dependent measures to test each path in the integrative model

The design strategies likely elicit questions regarding why they have been specified, as such, and how they may be used to test particular paths within the model presented earlier. We will now attempt to describe how the paths in the integrative model can be related to dependent measures associated with this study.

Path A: the effect of suggestion on executive control

Path A indicates the degree to which an external suggestion has an effect on executive control. Given that the suggestion provided in this study is to *go slowly* in order to make fewer errors, the suggestion's effect on executive control can be measured by the average RT to non-targets (across the entire task), where relatively slower RTs indicate a greater effect of suggestion. By then comparing the RTs of either the hypnotic-induction or meditation-practice group to the control (suggestion-only) group, we can identify the effect of each of these cognitive interventions on path A[1]:

| Effect of hypnosis/ meditation on path A | = | [Average RT to non-targets (hypnosis/meditation group)] | – | [Average RT to non-targets (control group)] |

---

[1] As mentioned, it is possible that meditation and suggestion do not combine in a purely additive manner. Within path A, we may be able to directly assess this possibility, as a result in which suggestion has a smaller effect within the meditation-plus-suggestion condition than in the suggestion-only condition would demonstrate a reduction in the effect of suggestion as a result of meditation practice, and thus a non-additive effect of combining the two manipulations.

Path B: executive control over "subsystems of control"

Because the SART is a task that requires cognitive control in order to correctly withhold responses to the rare target stimuli, SART errors (in which a participant fails to withhold a response to the target) represent a direct measure of the extent to which individuals' "subsystems of control" are being modulated by executive control. As such, the effects of hypnosis and meditation on path B can be determined by comparing the number of SART errors between participants in each induction-receiving group and the suggestion-only group:

$$\begin{array}{l} \text{Effect of hypnosis/} \\ \text{meditation on path B} \end{array} = \begin{array}{l} [\text{Average number of SART} \\ \text{errors (hypnosis/meditation} \\ \text{group)}] \end{array} - \begin{array}{l} [\text{Average number of SART} \\ \text{errors (control group)}] \end{array}$$

Path C: awareness of executive control

Whether modulations of executive control reach awareness (through executive monitoring mechanisms) determines the strength of path C in the integrative model. With this in mind, note that while SART errors can be seen as an indication of the amount of executive control being directed toward the task, so too can the *pacing* of participants' responses. (Remember that a key alteration of the standard SART protocol in this study is to stress that participants should try to be both *accurate* and *steady*.) Moreover, if a SART error reaches awareness, this must take a route "through the model" that goes via paths B and E. However, the *pacing* of participants' responses should be directed in a top-down manner from the system of executive control, and if information regarding pace reaches awareness directly, then this would be done through path C. As such, measuring the strength of path C requires determining the extent to which participants are aware of variations in the pace at which they are performing the SART. This can be readily measured given knowledge of participants' RTs to each non-target and their responses to the *pacing probes*. For instance, if participants' predictions regarding their individual-trial RT variability are more accurate within the hypnosis group than within the control group, then this would indicate that the strength of path C is increased under hypnosis; if the opposite trend is found, this supports the notion that path C is weakened during hypnosis (a prediction consistent with theories of dissociated experience). This same logic can be applied to examine the effect of meditation practice by comparing the meditation-practice and control groups:

$$\begin{array}{l} \text{Effect of hypnosis/} \\ \text{meditation on path C} \end{array} = \begin{array}{l} [\text{Percent of pacing probes} \\ \text{with correct response} \\ \text{(hypnosis/meditation} \\ \text{group)}] \end{array} - \begin{array}{l} [\text{Percent of pacing probes} \\ \text{with correct response (control} \\ \text{group)}] \end{array}$$

Path D: effect of executive monitoring on subsequent executive control

Path D measures the extent to which the executive monitoring system is able to produce modulations in executive control. The primary, and most obvious, way in which this would occur within the SART would be for the executive monitoring system to signal the executive control system *if it detects an error* (via signals from the subsystems of control), in order to improve subsequent performance. This study has been designed to obtain measurements of when participants are (or are not) aware of whether they have made an error: the performance probes. As such, a method for measuring the strength of path D would consist of examining performance on trials that occur *immediately following a noticed error in the SART*, seeing whether subsequent performance improves. If hypnosis or meditation were to strengthen path D, then we should see that participants in that particular induction-receiving group perform better on the SART following noticed errors than the control group:

Effect of hypnosis/ meditation on path D	=	[Number of SART errors made in trials immediately following performance probes indicating a noticed error (control group)]	−	[Number of SART errors made in trials following performance probes indicating a noticed error (hypnosis/ meditation group)]

Notice that, while this formulation is similar to those of paths A–C, the directionality has been reversed, such that the induction-receiving group's value is subtracted from the control group's value. This is simply for the sake of consistency, such that, were either induction to be associated with an increase in the strength of path D, then the value of this effect would take a positive valence.

Path E: awareness of "subsystem"-produced activity

Path E measures the extent to which signals from the "subsystems of control" are able to reach awareness through executive monitoring of the subsystems. Given that the subsystems of control employed within the SART include both the systems responsible for the visual processing of the stimuli and the systems responsible for responding to the stimuli, path E can be measured by assessing the extent to which participants' performance on the SART reaches awareness (through executive monitoring). Since the study design includes frequent probes regarding their awareness of their performance within the task (the performance probes), we can measure the extent to which participants' awareness of their performance accurately reflects their actual performance. That is, if participants show the ability to make veridical (i.e., accurate) assessments of their performance, then it can be concluded that the response-related activity of the subsystems of control is available to, and being accessed by, the executive monitoring system. If participants' judgments of their performance are non-veridical (i.e., inaccurate), then this is likely due to information not being sufficiently monitored by the executive monitoring system:

Effect of hypnosis/ meditation on path E	=	[Percent of performance probes with correct response (hypnosis/ meditation group)]	−	[Percent of performance probes with correct response (control group)]

As formulated here (and also with regard to path C), this effect would be measurable in terms of a difference in percentages. If hypnosis or meditation were to increase the strength of path E, then this effect would take on a positive value, whereas if either induction were to decrease the strength of path E, then this effect would take a negative value.

Path-related predictions from dissociation theories of hypnosis

In contrasting the strength of these functional "connections" between a hypnosis-plus-suggestion condition and a suggestion-only condition, the set of path(s) that exhibit differences between the two conditions would ultimately be one of many possible outcome sets. The particular set of changes observed may promote one dissociative view of hypnosis over another, as different dissociative accounts make contrasting predictions regarding which paths should be affected by hypnosis. Alternatively, the results of a study such as this may provide compelling evidence against any of the dissociative accounts of hypnosis as they are currently formulated, and/or the results may provide the basis for a new, more comprehensive dissociative theory of hypnosis.

Dissociation of control

Theories which posit that hypnosis induces a *dissociation of control* make relatively straightforward predictions regarding the effect of hypnosis on each of the functional paths included in Woody and Sadler's integrative model (see Figure 12.1). If hypnosis primarily involves a dissociation between cognitive control systems/processes and the lower subsystems that are necessarily recruited during task performance, then the prediction would be that the hypnosis-plus-suggestion group should exhibit a relative (i.e., compared to the suggestion-only group) decrease in the strength of path B in the model. As such, this group should demonstrate a relative increase in SART errors during the task.

Control may, however, be dissociated via another functional change within the model. The theory of *second-order dissociation of control*, for instance, makes a separate prediction from the former control dissociation theory, as it predicts that the dissociation occurs through a weakening of path D, rather than path B. This weakening of path D would impair one's ability to adjust the amount of cognitive control being directed toward the task in situations in which executive monitoring processes reveal the need to do so. In the case of our study design, this would appear as an inability to improve performance subsequent to errors that have been consciously noticed.

Dissociation of experience

The theory of *dissociated experience* during hypnosis makes a prediction that stands in contrast to both of the aforementioned control-related dissociation theories. This theory predicts that the executive monitoring system, being crucial for awareness, should become decoupled from the executive processes that are being initiated, maintained, and adjusted while performing a task under hypnosis. Moreover, the monitoring system may additionally be blinded to the actual performance of the lower "subsystems of control" in the case of a more pronounced dissociation from experience. Thus, within the framework of the integrative model, the theory of *dissociated experience* predicts that the hypnosis-plus-suggestion group should exhibit a relative decrease in the strength of path C, and possibly also in the strength of path E.

In the context of task-related dependent measures, a (relative) reduction in the strength of path C would be modeled by individuals in the hypnosis-plus-suggestion group exhibiting worse accuracy on the *pacing probes* than individuals in the suggestion-only group; because the pacing probes have been specified to measure the extent to which individuals are aware of variations in the degree of executive control that they are exerting, poor performance on this probe item would indicate that information about fluctuations in executive control is not being registered by executive monitoring processes. If the *dissociation of experience* is driven instead by a reduction in the strength of path E, then this should be reflected in the relative performance of the two groups of individuals on the *performance probes*. The performance probes have been specified to measure individuals' conscious awareness of whether or not they have recently made an error on the SART, and so if the hypnosis-plus-suggestion group performs relatively worse on these judgments, this would indicate that the hypnotized individuals lacked awareness of their own performance, implicating deficient appropriate input from the lower subsystems to the executive monitor.

Path-related predictions for meditation practice

The effect of a brief mindfulness meditation training session on SART performance has already been characterized (Mrazek et al., 2012), therefore providing a few clear predictions regarding the path-specific changes that may appear when comparing the meditation-practice group to the control group in our proposed study. In Mrazek et al.'s (2012) study, they found that an 8-minute mindfulness meditation practice session improved two SART-related dependent measures— SART errors and RT CV—when the SART was performed immediately following the meditation session. Both measures decreased (i.e., improved) as a result of meditation practice (Mrazek et al., 2012). As such, this leads us to predict that the proposed study should reveal that meditation (plus suggestion) leads to an increase in the strength of path B, as this is directly measured by the frequency of SART errors.

The predictions regarding the other paths in the model lack such direct empirical support, though this does not prevent us from predicting that meditation practice may increase the strength of paths C, D, and E as well, as meditation practice has often been employed as a means of improving attentional, and therefore executive, functioning overall. However, despite evidence that meditation training improves various aspects of executive functioning (e.g., Chambers et al., 2008; Chiesa, Calati, & Serretti, 2011; Lutz, Slagter, Dunne, & Davidson, 2008; Moore & Malinowski, 2009; Tang et al., 2007; Teper & Inzlicht, 2013; Zeidan, Johnson, Diamond, David, & Goolkasian, 2010), the supposedly altered functional relationships between each of the modules in the model (resulting from meditation training) have not yet been assessed simultaneously in a single study.

Theoretical implications of the proposed study

While it is difficult to forecast the particular outcomes of this proposed study, the results would likely have implications for several points of contention regarding both hypnosis and meditation.

Hypnosis: control versus experience

Given that this study has been proposed as a method for testing the strength of pathways within a model that was originally conceived as a way to integrate pre-existing, yet different, dissociative accounts of hypnosis, it should be unsurprising that the outcome of this study may ultimately weigh in favor of one dissociative account over another. Of central importance here is the debate regarding whether hypnosis involves a dissociation of *experience* or *control*. It is also possible that the idea of a specific, "local" dissociation being responsible for hypnotic effects does not fully account for the hypnotic phenomena which we are able to observe; hypnosis may require a more holistic perspective, one which takes into account each of the dynamic functional relationships between cognitive and psychological component systems/processes, and a study such as this may aid our willingness to adopt and formulate such a conclusion if it is warranted by the data.

Meditation

While Woody and Sadler's (2008) model was originally proposed as a way of integrating various dissociative perspectives of hypnosis into a single framework, it may nonetheless provide a foundation upon which several points regarding the effects of mindfulness meditation may be clarified. For instance, while it is known that mindfulness meditation practitioners have heightened sustained attention abilities and are less susceptible to distractions in tasks of cognitive control (Brefczynski-Lewis, Lutz, Schaefer, Levinson, & Davidson, 2007; Carter et al., 2005), it has not been determined whether this is solely a result of greater executive control per se, or if these characteristics result from a change in communication or cooperation between the executive control system and the executive monitoring system. Working with our proposed framework, this study may be capable of elucidating any change in dynamics that occurs between these functional subsystems.

Summary

Borrowing from methodologies commonly employed to assess lapses in attention (i.e., mind wandering) and meta-awareness, and utilizing a framework that holds different aspects of executive functioning within a single model, we have proposed an experimental protocol that may elucidate our understanding of the particular functional changes that occur with respect to executive functioning as a result of either hypnosis or meditation practice, but which could be applied equally well toward examining the changes in executive functioning that occur alongside other states of consciousness. By formulating various dependent variables so that they correspond to individual and particular functional "connections" within an integrative model of executive functioning, each "connection" may be assessed separately and independently.

The study design that we have proposed and outlined in this chapter, which focuses on the states of consciousness associated with hypnosis and mindfulness meditation, provides an opportunity to simultaneously address three separate research questions related to these practices:

1 Can the dissociation(s) associated with hypnosis be precisely specified?

2 Can a similar specification be made regarding the functional changes associated with mindfulness meditation practice?

3 What is the relationship between the effects of hypnosis and meditation on executive processes?

In addition to the general utility of our combination of model and design in assessing the effects of particular states of consciousness on executive functioning, we believe that the debate regarding the type of dissociation(s) that may occur during hypnosis warrants an empirical investigation that is capable of testing and comparing the various dissociative theories of hypnosis. The potential results from this proposed study would likely bolster pre-existing dissociative theories of hypnosis, but they may also provide an impetus to refocus theories of hypnosis—either toward any "local" dissociations (i.e., along a single path in the model) that may be revealed by this proposed study, or toward a more holistic "conglomeration" of dissociative effects if the results were to suggest that a single-dissociation account is insufficient.

Similarly, the effects of meditation training on executive functioning (although currently better understood than the effects of hypnosis) require better specification, for the relative impact of short meditation practice sessions on executive sub-processes such as control and monitoring has not been fully characterized. Finally, given the natural comparisons drawn between hypnosis and meditation, we believe it is a worthwhile endeavor to directly compare the functional effects of each; in doing so, we may resolve some debates or incite others, but surely the data will speak for itself.

References

Benson, H., Greenwood, M. M., & Klemchuk, H. (1975). The relaxation response: psychophysiologic aspects and clinical applications. *International Journal of Psychiatry in Medicine*, **6**, 87–98.

Bowers, K. S. (1992). Imagination and dissociation in hypnotic responding. *International Journal of Clinical and Experimental Hypnosis*, **40**(4), 253–275. doi:10.1080/00207149208409661

Bowers, K. S., & Davidson, T. M. (1991). A neodissociative critique of Spanos's social-psychological model of hypnosis. In S. J. Lynn & J. W. Rhue (Eds.), *Theories of hypnosis: current models and perspectives (The Guilford clinical and experimental hypnosis series)* (pp. 105–143). New York, NY: Guilford Press.

Brefczynski-Lewis, J. A., Lutz, A., Schaefer, H. S., Levinson, D. B., & Davidson, R. J. (2007). Neural correlates of attentional expertise in long-term meditation practitioners. *Proceedings of the National Academy of Sciences*, **104**(27), 11483–11488. doi:10.1073/pnas.0606552104

Carter, O. L., Presti, D. E., Callistemon, C., Ungerer, Y., Liu, G. B., & Pettigrew, J. D. (2005). Meditation alters perceptual rivalry in Tibetan Buddhist monks. *Current Biology*, **15**(11), R412–R413.

Chambers, R., Lo, B., & Allen, N. (2008). The impact of intensive mindfulness training on attentional control, cognitive style, and affect. *Cognitive Therapy and Research*, **32**(3), 303–322. doi:10.1007/s10608-007-9119-0

Cheyne, J. A., Carriere, J. S. A., & Smilek, D. (2006). Absent-mindedness: lapses of conscious awareness and everyday cognitive failures. *Consciousness and Cognition*, **15**(3), 578–592. doi:10.1016/j.concog.2005.11.009

Cheyne, J. A., Carriere, J. S. A., Solman, G. J. F., & Smilek, D. (2011). Challenge and error: critical events and attention-related errors. *Cognition*, **121**(3), 437–446. doi:10.1016/j.cognition.2011.07.010

Cheyne, J.A., Solman, G. J. F., Carriere, J. S. A., & Smilek, D. (2009). Anatomy of an error: a bidirectional state model of task engagement/disengagement and attention-related errors. *Cognition*, **111**(1), 98–113. doi:10.1016/j.cognition.2008.12.009

Chiesa, A., Calati, R., & Serretti, A. (2011). Does mindfulness training improve cognitive abilities? A systematic review of neuropsychological findings. *Clinical Psychology Review*, **31**(3), 449–464. doi:10.1016/j.cpr.2010.11.003

Christoff, K., Gordon, A. M., Smallwood, J., Smith, R., & Schooler, J. W. (2009). Experience sampling during fMRI reveals default network and executive system contributions to mind wandering. *Proceedings of the National Academy of Sciences*, **106**(21), 8719–8724. doi:10.1073/pnas.0900234106

Colcombe, S., & Kramer, A. F. (2003). Fitness effects on the cognitive function of older adults: a meta-analytic study. *Psychological Science*, **14**(2), 125–130. doi:10.1111/1467-9280.t01-1-01430

Davidson, R. J., Goleman, D. J., & Schwartz, G. E. (1976). Attentional and affective concomitants of meditation: a cross-sectional study. *Journal of Abnormal Psychology*, **85**(2), 235–238. doi:10.1037/0021-843X.85.2.235

Dunn, B. R., Hartigan, J. A., & Mikulas, W. L. (1999). Concentration and mindfulness meditations: unique forms of consciousness? *Applied Psychophysiology and Biofeedback*, **24**(3), 147–165. doi:10.1023/A:1023498629385

Egner, T., Jamieson, G., & Gruzelier, J. (2005). Hypnosis decouples cognitive control from conflict monitoring processes of the frontal lobe. *NeuroImage*, **27**(4), 969–978. doi:10.1016/j.neuroimage.2005.05.002

Egner, T., & Raz, A. (2007). Cognitive control processes and hypnosis. In G.A. Jamieson (Ed.), *Hypnosis and conscious states: the cognitive-neuroscience perspective* (pp. 29–50). Oxford, England: Oxford University Press.

Erickson, K. I., Colcombe, S. J., Wadhwa, R., Bherer, L., Peterson, M. S., Scalf, P. E., . . . Kramer, A. F. (2007). Training-induced functional activation changes in dual-task processing: an fMRI study. *Cerebral Cortex*, **17**(1), 192–204. doi:10.1093/cercor/bhj137

Green, J. P., Page, R. A., Handley, G. W., & Rasekhy, R. (2005). The "hidden observer" and ideomotor responding: a real–simulator comparison. *Contemporary Hypnosis*, **22**(3), 123–137. doi:10.1002/ch.8

Hilgard, E. R. (1977). *Divided consciousness: multiple controls in human thought and action*. Hoboken, NJ: Wiley.

Hilgard, E. R. (1991). A neodissociation interpretation of hypnosis. In S. J. Lynn & J. W. Rhue (Eds.), *Theories of hypnosis: current models and perspectives (The Guilford clinical and experimental hypnosis series)* (pp. 83–104). New York, NY: Guilford Press.

Hilgard, E. R. (1994). Neodissociation theory. In S. J. Lynn & J. W. Rhue (Eds.), *Dissociation: clinical and theoretical perspectives* (pp. 32–51). New York, NY: Guilford Press.

Hillman, C. H., Erickson, K. I., & Kramer, A. F. (2008). Be smart, exercise your heart: exercise effects on brain and cognition. *Nature Reviews Neuroscience*, **9**(1), 58–65. doi:10.1038/nrn2298

Jamieson, G. A., & Sheehan, P. W. (2004). An empirical test of Woody and Bowers's dissociated-control theory of hypnosis. *International Journal of Clinical and Experimental Hypnosis*, **52**(3), 232–249. doi:10.1080/0020714049052349

Jamieson, G.A., & Woody, E.Z. (2007). Dissociated control as a paradigm for cognitive-neuroscience research and theorising in hypnosis. In G.A. Jamieson (Ed.), *Hypnosis and conscious states: the cognitive-neuroscience perspective* (pp. 111–129). Oxford, England: Oxford University Press.

Janet, P. (1901). *The mental state of hystericals: a study of mental stigmata and mental accidents.* New York, NY: G. P. Putnam & Sons.

Janet, P. (1907). *The major symptoms of hysteria (vol. X).* New York, NY: Macmillan Publishing.

Kaiser, J., Barker, R., Haenschel, C., Baldeweg, T., & Gruzelier, J. H. (1997). Hypnosis and event-related potential correlates of error processing in a Stroop-type paradigm: a test of the frontal hypothesis. *International Journal of Psychophysiology*, **27**(3), 215–222. doi:10.1016/S0167-8760(97)00055-X

Kallio, S., Revonsuo, A., Hamalainen, H., Markela, J., & Gruzelier, J. (2001). Anterior brain functions and hypnosis: a test of the frontal hypothesis. *International Journal of Clinical and Experimental Hypnosis*, **49**, 95–108.

Kramer, A. F., & Erickson, K. I. (2007). Capitalizing on cortical plasticity: influence of physical activity on cognition and brain function. *Trends in Cognitive Sciences*, **11**(8), 342–348. doi:10.1016/j.tics.2007.06.009

Levinson, D. B., Smallwood, J., & Davidson, R. J. (2012). The persistence of thought: evidence for a role of working memory in the maintenance of task-unrelated thinking. *Psychological Science*, **23**(4), 375–380. doi:10.1177/0956797611431465

Lutz, A., Slagter, H. A., Dunne, J. D., & Davidson, R. J. (2008). Attention regulation and monitoring in meditation. *Trends in Cognitive Sciences*, **12**(4), 163–169. doi:10.1016/j.tics.2008.01.005

Lynn, S. J., Brentar, J., Carlson, B., Kurzhals, R., & Green, J. (1992). Posthypnotic experiences: a controlled investigation. In W. Bongartz (Ed.) *Hypnosis theory and research*. Konstanz, Germany: University of Konstanz Press.

Lynn, S., Malaktaris, A., Maxwell, R., Mellinger, D., & van der Kloet, D. (2012). Do hypnosis and mindfulness practices inhabit a common domain? Implications for research, clinical practice, and forensic science. *Journal of Mind–Body Regulation*, 2(1), 12–26.

McVay, J. C., & Kane, M. J. (2009). Conducting the train of thought: working memory capacity, goal neglect, and mind wandering in an executive-control task. *Journal of Experimental Psychology: Learning, Memory, and Cognition*, **35**(1), 196–204. doi:10.1037/a0014104

Moore, A., & Malinowski, P. (2009). Meditation, mindfulness and cognitive flexibility. *Consciousness and Cognition*, **18**(1), 176–186. doi:10.1016/j.concog.2008.12.008

Morrison, A. B., & Chein, J. M. (2010). Does working memory training work? The promise and challenges of enhancing cognition by training working memory. *Psychonomic Bulletin and Review*, **18**(1), 46–60. doi:10.3758/s13423-010-0034-0

Mrazek, M. D., Franklin, M. S., Phillips, D. T., Baird, B., & Schooler, J. W. (2013). Mindfulness training improves working memory capacity and GRE performance while reducing mind wandering. *Psychological Science*, **24**(5), 776–781. doi:10.1177/0956797612459659

Mrazek, M. D., Smallwood, J., & Schooler, J. W. (2012). Mindfulness and mind-wandering: finding convergence through opposing constructs. *Emotion*, **12**(3), 442–448. doi:10.1037/a0026678

Nordby, H., Jasiukaitis, K. H. P., & Spiegel, D. (1999). Effects of hypnotizability on performance of a Stroop task and event-related potentials. *Perceptual and Motor Skills*, **88**(3), 819–830. doi:10.2466/pms.1999.88.3.819

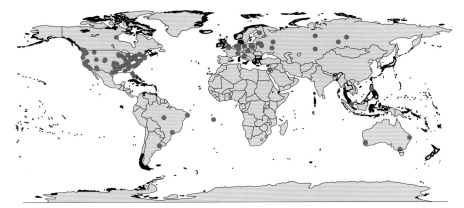

Plate 1 The geographic location of 163 tulpamancers according to a survey conducted in September 2014. (see also Fig. 5.1.)

Tulpamancers

Non-tulpamancers

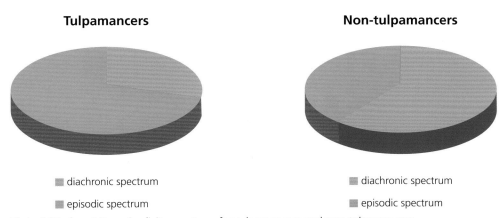

diachronic spectrum

episodic spectrum

diachronic spectrum

episodic spectrum

Plate 2 Diachronicity–episodicity spectrum for tulpamancers and non-tulpamancers. (see also Fig. 5.2.)

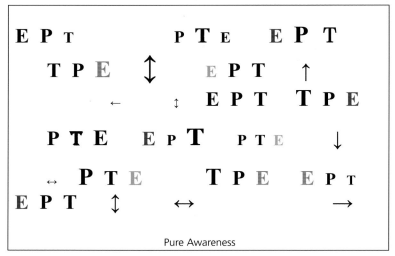

T = Thoughts;   P = Perceptions;   E = Emotions

Plate 3 The busy state of ordinary consensus consciousness. (see also Fig. 9.4.)

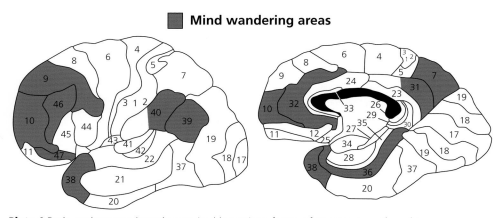

Plate 4 Brain regions consistently recruited by various forms of spontaneous thought. (see also Fig. 11.1.)

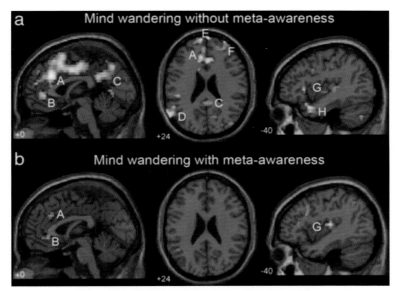

Plate 5 Differences in brain activity between mind wandering with and without meta-awareness. (see also Fig. 11.3.)

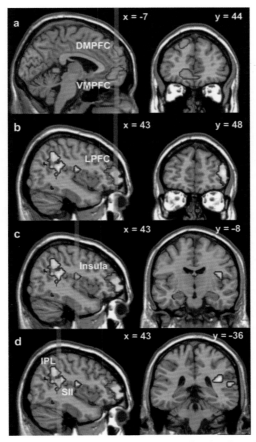

Plate 6 Neural correlates of a non-elaborative mental stance after brief meditation training. (see also Fig. 11.5.)

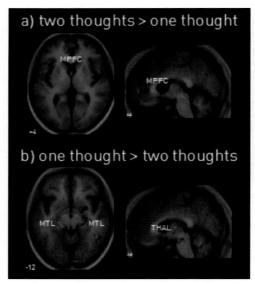

Plate 7 Neural correlates of single transient thoughts versus further elaboration of thoughts. (see also Fig. 11.6.)

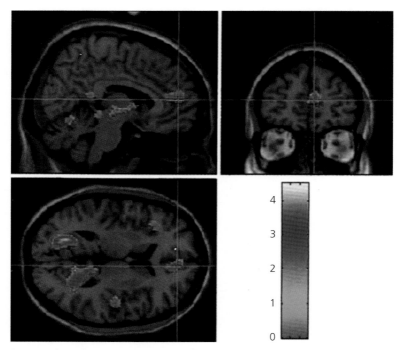

Plate 8 Brain activations during Stroop task conflict are reduced by hypnotic suggestion. (see also Fig. 11.7.)

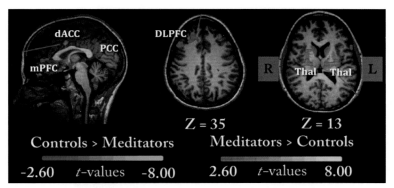

Plate 9 Meditators show less affective-elaborative brain activation in response to pain. (see also Fig. 11.8.)

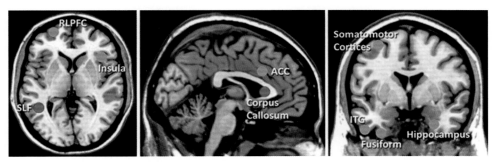

Plate 10 Brain regions showing consistent structural differences in meditation practitioners. (see also Fig. 11.9.)

Green Red Blue Purple
[congruent trials]

Blue Purple Red Green
[incongruent trials]

Plate 11 The Stroop effect: naming the color of the first set of words (congruent trials—name and actual color of type matches) is easier and quicker than the second (incongruent trials—mismatch of name and actual color of type). (see also Fig. 16.1.)

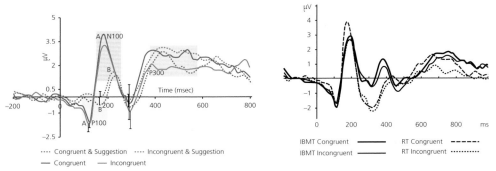

Plate 12 ERPs from hypnosis suggestion and meditation training. Left and right panel show hypnosis suggestion and IBMT effects at frontal midline region, respectively. (see also Fig. 16.2.)

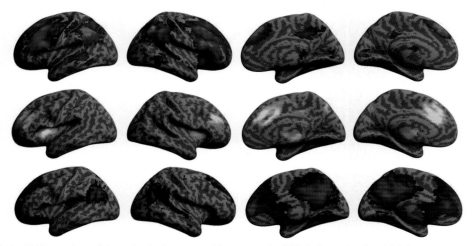

Plate 13 Illustration of three intrinsic connectivity networks (ICNs). (see also Fig. 18.1.)

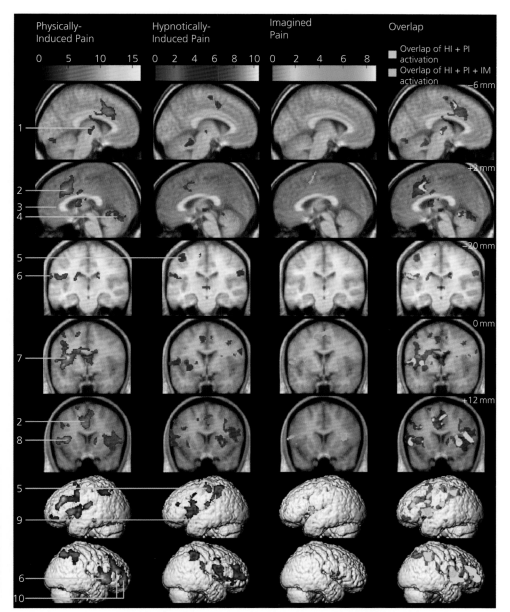

Plate 14 Activated voxels during physically induced pain (left, red–yellow scale); hypnotically induced pain (middle, blue–purple scale); and imagined pain (right, yellow–green scale). (see also Fig. 21.1.)

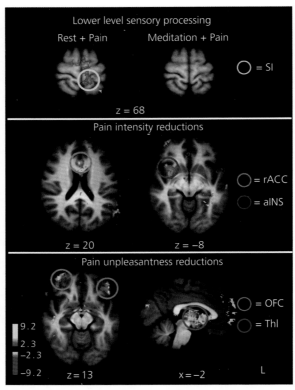

Plate 15 Mindfulness meditation significantly reduced pain through a number of brain mechanisms in beginner meditators. (see also Fig. 21.2.)

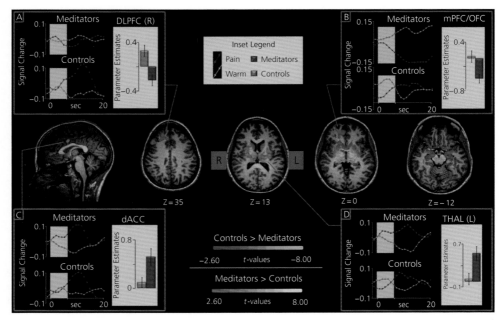

Plate 16 Differences in pain-related activation between meditators and controls. (see also Fig. 21.3.)

Parris, B. A., Dienes, Z., & Hodgson, T. L. (2012). Temporal constraints of the word blindness posthypnotic suggestion on Stroop task performance. *Journal of Experimental Psychology: Human Perception and Performance*, **38**(4), 833–837. doi:10.1037/a0028131

Raz, A., Landzberg, K. S., Schweizer, H. R., Zephrani, Z. R., Shapiro, T., Fan, J., & Posner, M. I. (2003). Posthypnotic suggestion and the modulation of Stroop interference under cycloplegia. *Consciousness and Cognition*, **12**(3), 332–346. doi:10.1016/S1053-8100(03)00024-2

Raz, A., Shapiro, T., Fan, J., & Posner, M. I. (2002). Hypnotic suggestion and the modulation of Stroop interference. *Archives of General Psychiatry*, **59**(12), 1155–1161. doi:10.1001/archpsyc.59.12.1155

Robertson, I. H., Manly, T., Andrade, J., Baddeley, B. T., & Yiend, J. (1997). "Oops!": performance correlates of everyday attentional failures in traumatic brain injured and normal subjects. *Neuropsychologia*, **35**(6), 747–758. doi:10.1016/S0028-3932(97)00015-8

Sadler, P., & Woody, E. (2010). Dissociation in hypnosis: theoretical frameworks and psychotherapeutic implications. In S. J. Lynn, J. W. Rhue, & I. Kirsch (Eds.), *Handbook of Clinical Hypnosis* (pp. 151–178). Washington, DC: American Psychological Association.

Seli, P., Cheyne, J. A., & Smilek, D. (2012). Attention failures versus misplaced diligence: separating attention lapses from speed–accuracy trade-offs. *Consciousness and Cognition*, **21**(1), 277–291. doi:10.1016/j.concog.2011.09.017

Semmens-Wheeler, R., & Dienes, Z. (2012). The contrasting role of higher order awareness in hypnosis and meditation. *Journal Of Mind–Body Regulation*, **2**(1), 43–57.

Sheehan, P. W., Donovan, P., & MacLeod, C. M. (1988). Strategy manipulation and the Stroop effect in hypnosis. *Journal of Abnormal Psychology*, **97**(4), 455–460. doi:10.1037/0021-843X.97.4.455

Slagter, H. A., Davidson, R. J., & Lutz, A. (2011). Mental training as a tool in the neuroscientific study of brain and cognitive plasticity. *Frontiers in Human Neuroscience*, **5**(17), 1–12. doi:10.3389/fnhum.2011.00017

Smallwood, J., Beach, E., Schooler, J. W., & Handy, T. C. (2008). Going AWOL in the brain: mind wandering reduces cortical analysis of external events. *Journal of Cognitive Neuroscience*, **20**(3), 458–469. doi:10.1162/jocn.2008.20037

Smallwood, J., Fitzgerald, A., Miles, L. K., & Phillips, L. H. (2009). Shifting moods, wandering minds: negative moods lead the mind to wander. *Emotion*, **9**(2), 271–276. doi:10.1037/a0014855

Smallwood, J., & Schooler, J. W. (2006). The restless mind. *Psychological Bulletin*, **132**, 946–958.

Spanos, N. P. (1983). The hidden observer as an experimental creation. *Journal of Personality and Social Psychology*, **44**(1), 170–176. doi:10.1037/0022-3514.44.1.170

Spanos, N. P., de Groot, H. P., Tiller, D. K., Weekes, J. R., & Bertrand, L. D. (1985). Trance logic duality and hidden observer responding in hypnotic, imagination control, and simulating subjects: a social psychological analysis. *Journal of Abnormal Psychology*, **94**(4), 611–623. doi:10.1037/0021-843X.94.4.611

Spanos, N. P., & Hewitt, E. C. (1980). The hidden observer in hypnotic analgesia: discovery or experimental creation? *Journal of Personality and Social Psychology*, **39**(6), 1201–1214. doi:10.1037/h0077730

Tang, Y.-Y., Ma, Y., Wang, J., Fan, Y., Feng, S., Lu, . . . Posner, M. I. (2007). Short-term meditation training improves attention and self-regulation. *Proceedings of the National Academy of Sciences*, **104**(43), 17152–17156. doi:10.1073/pnas.0707678104

Tellegen, A., & Atkinson, G. (1974). Openness to absorbing and self-altering experiences ("absorption"), a trait related to hypnotic susceptibility. *Journal of Abnormal Psychology*, **83**(3), 268–277. doi:10.1037/h0036681

Teper, R., & Inzlicht, M. (2013). Meditation, mindfulness and executive control: the importance of emotional acceptance and brain-based performance monitoring. *Social Cognitive and Affective Neuroscience*, **8**(1), 85–92. doi:10.1093/scan/nss045

Wallace, R. K., Benson, H., & Wilson, A. F. (1984). A wakeful hypometabolic physiologic state. In D. H. Shapiro, Jr., & R. N. Walsh (Eds.), *Meditation: classic and contemporary perspectives* (pp. 417–431). New York, NY: Aldine.

Wenk-Sormaz, H. (2005). Meditation can reduce habitual responding. *Alternative Therapies in Health and Medicine*, **11**(2), 32–58.

Woody, E., & Sadler, P. (1998). On reintegrating dissociated theories: comment on Kirsch and Lynn (1998). *Psychological Bulletin*, **123**(2), 192–197. doi:10.1037/0033-2909.123.2.192

Woody, E., & Sadler, P. (2008). Dissociation theories of hypnosis. In M. R. Nash & A. J. Barnier (Eds.), *Oxford handbook of hypnosis* (pp. 81–110). Oxford, England: Oxford University Press.

Zeidan, F., Johnson, S. K., Diamond, B. J., David, Z., & Goolkasian, P. (2010). Mindfulness meditation improves cognition: evidence of brief mental training. *Consciousness and Cognition*, **19**(2), 597–605. doi:10.1016/j.concog.2010.03.014

Chapter 13

Reformulating the mindfulness construct
The cognitive processes at work in mindfulness, hypnosis, and mystical states

John Vervaeke and Leonardo Ferraro

Abstract

This chapter argues for a conceptual reformulation of the mindfulness construct in order to remove theoretical confusion and afford more precise and penetrating theoretical investigation. This reformulation involves four processes: replacing the standard feature list definitions with a feature schema that explicates causal and constitutive relations between features; replacing the language of mindfulness training with a vocabulary drawn from independently established constructs in cognitive science; providing a developmental account of mindfulness; and providing an account of mindfulness praxis that explains how various mindfulness practices fit together within a developmental context. This reformulation will also facilitate bridging the scientific investigation of hypnosis and some of the mystical states produced within mindfulness practices. Additionally, the authors argue for the central role of ritual in cognitive evolution, with its integration of both mindfulness and hypnotic features. This offers potential for investigating the binding of the study of attention with the science of suggestion.

Introduction

In recent years, there has been an explosion of interest in the concepts of mindfulness and different states of consciousness. More than merely the usual background chatter of New Age pseudomysticism that always persists, this groundswell of interest has been rigorously academic. Noted scholars and thinkers have been tackling hard problems that have eluded the scope of the sciences for many years. There has been a sharp increase in the number of experimental studies of mindfulness, across many more disciplines. Initially only the focus of clinical psychological studies, mindfulness is now being explored by cognitive psychologists, neuroscientists, and cognitive scientists. There has even been the creation of a new peer-reviewed journal dedicated to the study of mindfulness. There is a consistent and convergent effort to bring mindfulness under scientific purview. Additionally, given the work of researchers over the past century, hypnosis has also begun to be empirically tractable. Scientific progress has reached a point that now allows us to investigate and construct meaningful theories about altered states of consciousness.

However, as with all new endeavors, there are problems: the research is faced with significant empirical and theoretical issues that need to be addressed if the science is to advance. Toneatto and Nguyen (2007) reviewed a substantial body of mindfulness research. While the results were largely promising, they found many methodological flaws within the research: lack of proper control groups, lack of longitudinal follow-ups, as well as insufficient controls for confounds and placebo effects. Additionally, in general, there is insufficient operationalization of theoretical constructs. We argue that these flaws arise from a common source, namely, a deep theoretical confusion within the mindfulness construct. Without addressing this set of core theoretical defects, additional empirical work will remain fundamentally ambiguous and unable to answer our questions. We propose to directly engage this theoretical dilemma and construct a framework that will afford more precise and penetrating empirical investigation. Along the way, this reconstruction will allow us to bridge to the scientific investigation of hypnosis. Moreover, this new framework would afford a tractable formulation of mystical experiences that have perennially been reported but have thus far eluded scientific explanation.

Resolving this theoretical conundrum requires that we deal with three main concerns:

1 The inadequacy of feature lists in capturing mindfulness phenomenologically and theoretically.

2 The uncritical importation of the language of training into scientific accounts of mindfulness and cognitive processes. In so doing, the psychological reality of the classical elements of mindfulness are presupposed, as opposed to explored and explained in the context of independently established cognitive science.

3 A failure to account for the developmental aspects of mindfulness: both how mindfulness develops and how mindfulness informs development.

These problems are symptomatic of a theoretical incoherence that plagues the investigation of mindfulness: without a unified framework for discussion, it is too easy to descend into ad hoc hypotheses that are not directly comparable and, thus, result in wasted efforts. On the other hand, with a coherent framework, we can begin to determine the systematic relationship between the various mindfulness practices.

Feature list versus feature schema

On the surface, feature lists seem to be an intuitively satisfying approach, especially when dealing with novel or challenging phenomena. By feature list, we mean a conjunctive list of properties that purport to encapsulate our concept of a phenomenon; for example, a triangle is a three-sided, enclosed figure, composed of straight lines, and containing three angles. Most definitions of mindfulness are just such conjunctive lists of features (e.g., being present, non-judging). They seem to help us arrive at conceptual primitives that are clearly demarcated. Research into the psychology of concepts (e.g., Murphy and Medin 1985) has quite consistently shown that people believe that their conceptual understanding is captured in feature lists. However, this research also shows that feature lists fail to account for people's conceptual understandings. Feature lists lack crucial information about the phenomena that falls under the concept. Specifically, feature lists fail to account for relations between features and, due to this, feature lists face the gestalt problem of not being able to account for the organizational structure of the conceptual referent.

A classic example occurs when people are asked which type of bird is more likely to sing, a large or a small bird; people overwhelmingly (and correctly) select the small bird as more likely. That is to say, they know of the relationship between the features of size and singing. However, this knowledge is not expressed in the feature lists for 'bird' provided by the same subjects. This lack of relations results in the deeper problem that the overall organizational structure that exists between the features is missing; this is known as the gestalt problem for feature list theories of concepts.

Consider again the concept of 'bird', reduced to a feature list: wings, feathers, beak, flies. Suppose now that we had a pile of such features and tossed them into the air. This grotesque shower does not constitute a bird. What is missing are the structural relations between features that allows them to function together such that you have a bird and not a horror show. Note how much of what we consider to be a bird is not a list of features but, rather, its gestalt. What is needed is to distinguish types of features and the types of relations that exist between them. To do so, we can turn to Ryle (1949). Ryle was especially concerned with trying to remove confusion in how we conceive of mental phenomena, caused by our failure to distinguish between types of features and being often misled by language. For example, because we have a verb for "believe" that has a mental referent, we suppose that we are referring to some mental action or process. However, Ryle pointed out that we could make a distinction between words that refer to occurrent processes and those that refer to dispositional conditions.[1]

Occurrent processes are those that it makes sense to map in time: they are said to begin, end, be interrupted, recommence, all at particular times. For example, I can begin walking at a certain time, a walk which can be interrupted at some other time and then recommenced some time thereafter, and then, finally, terminated at some specific time. In contrast, dispositional terms express conditional relations between things. To say that salt is soluble is to say that if put into water, it will dissolve. To say that glass is fragile is to say that if it is hit with a hard object, it will break. Neither solubility nor fragility are things that are either being done or happening; they are, rather, the possibilities for certain things to happen given certain conditions. Similarly, the word "believe" does not point to anything we can do in an occurrent fashion. That is why no matter how much I want it to be raining or how vividly I visualize or imagine it to be raining, I cannot simply, as an act of will, believe it to be raining. Instead, what the word "believe" seems to indicate is that certain conditions will elicit certain behaviors (including mental behaviors): for example, if I see drops on the window, I am likely to believe it is raining and take my umbrella when I go out. So, it is necessary to begin by making a distinction within the mindfulness construct between its dispositional and occurrent features, as outlined in Figure 13.1.

Consider four of the most common attributes associated with mindfulness in the psychological literature, namely, being present, non-judging, insightfulness, as well as reduced reactivity (or increased equanimity). In mindfulness meditation, "being present" is clearly occurrent, because it is something we initiate, that is constantly interrupted by mind wandering and then recommenced, and generally comes to an end at some point. Non-judging is similarly occurrent; we can track when it begins, ends, is interrupted, and when it recommences. In contrast, insightfulness and equanimity are dispositional features, indicating new conditional possibilities for how we will interact with our environment; they represent a tendency to behave in a certain manner (i.e., to manifest the occurrent behaviors of being present and not judging). Notice that once we have

---

[1] It is standard in the psychological literature to talk about a state/trait distinction where "state" usually refers to a process and "trait" refers to a disposition to behave in a certain manner. However, the problem with "state" is that it can also clearly refer to a current process or event, and the word "trait" does not makes explicit the dispositional nature of its referent. Therefore, we prefer "occurent/dispositional" as it avoids these potential confusions.

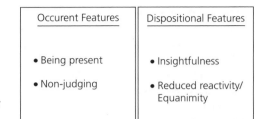

Fig. 13.1 A feature schema for the mindfulness construct.

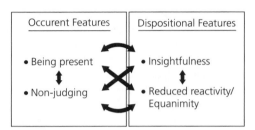

Fig. 13.2 The feature schema, with causal and constitutive arrows.

made this distinction between types of features, we can immediately ask questions about the types of relations between the features; how the occurrent processes cause the dispositional conditions (see Figure 13.2). For example, how does being present make one more insightful?

We can also ask for constitutive relations between occurrent features or between dispositional features: is non-judging a part of being present, or is being present a part of non-judging, or are they both parts of a larger constitutive process? As one provides answers to these causal and constitutive questions, our feature list transforms into a feature schema that allows us to specify the organizational structure of mindfulness. Note that it is these causal and constitutive questions that are the engines of our investigation: this is how a theory not only explains but also directs inquiry. Without that ability to elicit schematic questions, one will misframe a phenomenon and miss essential properties, as feature lists do.

Language of training versus language of explaining

In terms of discussing mindfulness, it has been natural to rely upon the language of practice, which is to say, the language used in the training and instilling of mindfulness. This makes sense, as it has been successful for thousands of years. However, while there is an appealing utility to this uncritical importation of language, the project of making mindfulness scientifically intelligible requires that we challenge this intuition. This is a matter of clarity regarding one's goals and aims, which in turn reflect upon the context of interpretation: in a training situation, the goal is the creation of mindfulness in others in the context of a cooperative joint project, whereas in science, our goal is the rational justification and explanation of truth claims, in the context of a rigorous and vigorous debate. Given the crucial distinction between the language of training and the language of explaining, simply equating them can cause us to seriously misapprehend the phenomenon.

Historically, the classical, tried and true method for training one's memory is the method of loci, which uses the spatial metaphor of walking through a memory palace as a means of remembering large amounts of content. This memory palace has stable locations, with stable objects, to which ideas can be attached, thus allowing classical scholars and orators to walk through their palaces, retrieving those bits of lore placed there. Recitations of long speeches could be performed using this method. Even now, this method can be employed to greatly enhance one's memory.

This might lead one to think that memory must, therefore, itself be spatially organized, functioning in terms of stable objects and locations that are retrieved via a sequential search. However, as Eyesenck and Keane demonstrated (1990), the "spatial metaphor" deeply misrepresents the nature of memory. Things have no stable spatial relation to each other in memory. If one is asked to quickly list colors, one typically responds with red, blue, and green. However, if asked to produce words that rhyme with "blue," one might respond "shoe," "knew," and "grew." Yet, despite this, there is no sense of closeness between "green" and "shoe." Similarly, memory is not searched in a sequential fashion; this is readily apparent when faced with acknowledging that one does not know something. Generally, one is immediately aware of the fact that "splang" is not a word in English, despite no violation of morphological rules. This immediacy contradicts the expected exhaustive, step-by-step search and comparison against one's entire lexicon of English words that the spatial metaphor would predict.

Not only is the space not stable, nor the search sequential, but the "objects" in question are themselves not stable. This is because memory is not primarily reproductive but, rather, largely reconstructive. Memory is not governed by a normativity of accuracy, but by one of adaptivity; we intuitively judge our memory by its accuracy, but in fact, memory is a tool of Darwin, not autobiography. As such, our memory's main function is beneficially informing future behavior, not accurately recalling past events. It is enormously inefficient to try and store all the information that we encounter: far more efficient is to store only the most crucial information and use a standard grammar of reconstruction when needed. The reconstructive process is additionally advantageous in that it can be sensitive to the current context, thus shaping recall to fit the present circumstance. This is a well-established fact in memory research, going back at least as far as 1932, to the work of Carmichael, Hogan, and Walter. Presented in Figure 13.3 are the images from their experiment, in which two groups of subjects were presented the same image, but different words. The images those subjects then recalled, a week later, reflected not the image but, rather, the image informed by the meaning of the word. Memory grabs the gist.

So, we see that the spatial metaphor of memory, so efficacious in training, deeply misrepresents memory and thereby misdirects the attempt to scientifically explain it. Similarly, the language of training mindfulness cannot be uncritically imported into our attempts at constructing a language of explanation.

Let us consider the notion of being present. It cannot mean literal physical presence, as one cannot ever fail to be physically present. Saying it means to pay attention to the present moment is vague. What "present" means is dependent on one's scale of interpretation, and the notion of attention needs to be critically examined. The present is specified by the indexicals "here" and "now," indexicals that are specified by what is relevant to the speaker: "here" can mean this room, this city, this planet, this plane of existence, etc., and similarly for "now." In training situations, this is negotiated pragmatically between teacher and student, but a scientific account cannot rely upon such implicit pragmatic negotiation.

The notion of attention that is uncritically being used employs the "searchlight" metaphor of attention, in which attention is the light of awareness that is shone on an object to make it more salient. One significant problem with the searchlight metaphor is that it represents attention in far too simplistic a manner; it represents attention as a single, simple, basic function. While intuitively appealing, this framing of attention obscures the complex and varied set of functions and

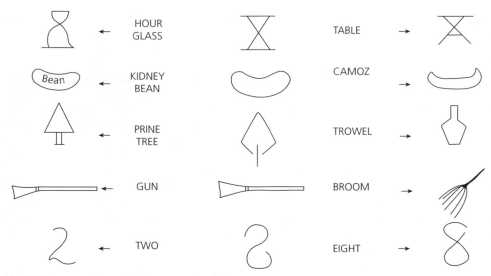

Fig. 13.3 Images demonstrating reconstructive memory.

Reproduced from L. Carmichael, H. P. Hogan, and A. A. Walter, An experimental study of the effect of language on the reproduction of visually perceived form, *Journal of Experimental Psychology*, *15*(1), pp. 73–86. doi:10.1037/h0072671, © 1932, American Psychological Association.

states that constitute this phenomenon, conflating several crucial elements. In fact, Christopher Mole's (2011) work argues that attention is a higher-order function rather than a basic one; it is more about how we perform functions rather than being a function in and of itself. There is no single task being done when we attend: rather, when we are paying attention, we are deploying any number of cognitive functions from a varied set, in a particular manner. That is to say, when we are performing a task, it necessitates some set of cognitive functions—that unison of task-relevant cognitive functions is attention. Attention is like practicing: one does not simply practice, one has to practice something, be it tennis, chess, karate, or kindness. In the context of mindfulness, the searchlight metaphor is actually damaging, in that it misses the crucial integrative function that is constitutive of the nature of attention.

Attentional scaling

Integration is the cornerstone of Polanyi's (1966; Polanyi & Prosch, 1975) theory of attention. He pointed out that attention is inherently relational in nature, in that we are always attending *from* one thing *to* something else. Consider the act of holding a cup: as one does so, sensations are being generated in one's fingers (heat, pressure, etc.). However, one is not typically focally aware of these sensations; instead, one is aware *through* the sensations, of the cup. As Polanyi would put it, we only have a subsidiary awareness of our sensations, but a focal awareness of the cup. To attend to the cup is to *integrate* the subsidiary awareness of these various sensations into that focal awareness of the cup.

Drawing on both Mole and Polanyi, then, attention is thereby the cognitive unison (or integration) of subsidiary awareness into focal awareness. Apter (1982, 1989) and Metzinger (2003) independently arrived at a similar language for the phenomenology of attention that is apropos to

Mole and Polanyi's formulation. Apter and Metzinger each described this cognitive convergence using the terms "transparency" and "opacity." Revisiting the example of holding a cup, the subsidiary sensations are *transparent*: we see through them (in both senses of the word, by means of and to go beyond) to look at the *opaque* cup.

Previously lost or obscured by the searchlight metaphor is how layered the phenomenology of attention truly is. Consider how many ways we can interact with and become focally aware of the cup—we can leave it on the table and tap on it with a pen, thereby determining that it is a cup of a certain size, shape, and location. Notice that in this instance, we are not focally aware of the pen but, rather, we are aware, through the pen, of the cup. We can shift this focal awareness: when tapping the cup, we can choose to be more focally aware of the pen, and the cup disappears from awareness. We can further shift our focus from the pen to our fingertips, allowing the pen to disappear as well. Each one of these shifts is a *transparency/opacity* reversal: in each case, something we were looking through, we are now looking at. This change in focus can move in the opposite direction: we can look through our fingertips into the pen, and then through the pen into the cup. These transformations of awareness are opacity/transparency reversals, in that something we were previously looking at, we come to look through.

In general, our tendency is toward transparency: to integrate sensory information into referential information about objects in the world; opacity/transparency shifts are more prominent, because they enhance our representational scope and power on the world, and the world is generally much more salient to us than our sensations of the world. Opacity to transparency shifts emphasize an awareness of the world at the expense of the awareness of the patterns and processes occurring in the mind. In contrast, a transparency to opacity shift emphasizes an awareness of such patterns and processes, at the expense of an awareness of the world.

Apter (1982) takes this further by pointing out a specific instance of transparency/opacity shifts occurring with respect to representations. He points out that representations have an inherently dual nature. Behold the word *cat*. It has a referential meaning of the small furry mammal that is a popular choice of house pet in North America. However, the word *cat* also has properties in and of itself: it is black on white, largely two-dimensional, and distinctly lacking in mammalian characteristics. In short, the referent and the representational medium have radically different properties. There is what the representation represents, and what the representation is, in and of itself. Normally, we see through the representation to the referent—the representation is cognitively transparent, while the referent is the opaque object of focal awareness. In fact, the transparency of representation is so deeply entrenched that it is largely and strongly automatic, as evidenced by the vast literature on the Stroop effect. Nevertheless, Apter points out that we can do a transparency/opacity reversal and shift our focal awareness from the referent to the properties of the representational medium. When this occurs, the representation stops representing and becomes a thing in itself.

Consider that it is plausible that some level of our cognitive processing is representational in nature; we represent the world to ourselves and these representations are introspectively very salient to us. We have inner monologues and inner pictures. Normally, these cognitive representations are transparent to us: we look through them to the world. However, we can perform a transparency/opacity reversal and become aware of the cognitively representing medium—instead of looking through our mind at the world, we can look at our representing mind. This, we argue, is precisely what is often meant by "being present." "Being present" typically refers to being less representational by engaging in a transparency/opacity reversal that interrupts representation itself. This shift affords awareness of the non-representational aspects of our cognition. This emergent awareness of the non-representational aspects of cognition is the act of "being present." "Being present," in this manner, affords insight into the cognitive medium, the patterns, and processes by which it shapes and frames our experience, which in turn affords new possibilities for intervention and even modification of these patterns and processes. However, "being present" is a complex phenomenon that requires further analysis.

Likewise, as we further critically examine the concept of attention, it becomes clear that it, too, is much more complex than initially appreciated. As we have shown, a simple searchlight metaphor fails to capture the extent of attention. This needs to be replaced with a more nuanced construct that allows for the articulation of distinct dimensions of attention along with different functions. As discussed, one such dimension is bounded by opacity on one end and transparency on the other, with the movement of awareness between them being one such function. This dimension can be called the signification of construal dimension, in that awareness is working through some signifying mental medium, giving priority either to the message (as in transparency) or to the medium (as in opacity). Construal signification (Figure 13.4) indicates how representational the mind is in its functioning.

With all of this, we are not yet finished; the complexity of the higher-order function of attention requires further analysis. Beyond the dimension of signification, there is also the distinct dimension of level of construal. Construal level (Förster & Dannenberg, 2010; Trope & Liberman, 2011) involves moving from the local processing of features level to the global processing of gestalts level, as well as moving from the global/gestalt to the local/featural. For example, we can attend to an entire bookshelf, to a single shelf, or to a single book. In addition to zooming in, we

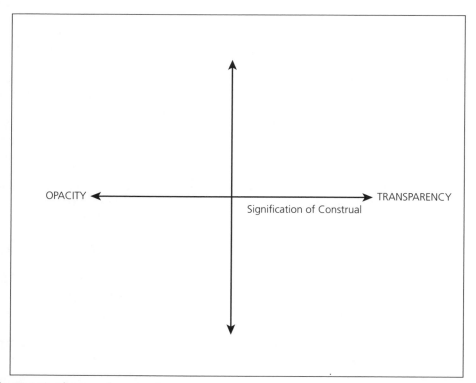

Fig. 13.4 Signification of construal.

can zoom out, moving from the spine of a chosen volume to the entire library. These are simple construal level shifts that do not necessarily involve a transparency to opacity shift. While similar, a construal level shift is not the same as a transparency/opacity shift, in that moving between these levels of construal does not require awareness of one's cognitive/representational medium. These are all still objects in the world for us. In contrast, while undertaking a transparency/opacity shift, the sensations in one's fingers when touching the cup are not features of the cup itself. The construal dimension is quite dynamic, more so than experience might suggest. Consider the interplay between local and gestalt elements when engaged in the act of reading.

Notice the second letter in each word in the top line in Figure 13.5. In the first, level of the letter is read as an "H" and in the second it is read as an "A." While received wisdom tells that we construct words out of letters, this is clearly not the case for "CAT": the gestalt of the word guides the interpretation of the features, rather than simply being composed of letters. Here we see that attention cannot simply be the sequential movement of a searchlight, but rather requires the complex, dynamical, and simultaneous processing of multiple channels. Sequential processing leads to inevitable and computationally intractable chicken-and-egg paradoxes in which you have to read the letters to read the word, but must have already read the word to properly interpret the letters. Instead, as Rumelhart, McClelland, and Group (1986) have shown, there is ongoing, simultaneous

Fig. 13.5 Images demonstrating the parallel top-down and bottom-up nature of visual attention.

Rumelhart, David E., James L. McClelland, and PDP Research Group., Parallel Distributed Processing, Volume 1: Explorations in the Microstructure of Cognition: Foundations, Figure 2, p. 8, © 1986 Massachusetts Institute of Technology, by permission of The MIT Press.

opponent processing at work between the top-down and bottom-up directions of attention (see Figure 13.5).

Analytically, we can distinguish between functions varying exclusively along a single-dimension. In practical terms, attentional functions are often complex and causally interacting, varying along both dimensions simultaneously (see Figure 13.6).

Note that one can do a transparency-to-opacity (TTO) shift while also undergoing a gestalt-to-featural shift (GTF); one is becoming more focally aware of the cognitive medium (TTO) while also becoming more aware of the features of that medium (GTF). One can also do an opacity-to-transparency shift (OTT) while also moving to a more gestalt level of construal (featural-to-gestalt, FTG). This is where objects of awareness are grouped together and, through them, one discerns a deeper pattern of reality—for example, when one considers the movement of light, water, and sound, and views them all as wave phenomena. This is ontological depth perception: just as stereoscopic vision integrates two channels to create visual depth, so we can also cognitively integrate cognitive channels to create ontological depth.

Let us reconsider the cup we have relied upon so much thus far. Suppose you had not yet seen the cup—you have been blindfolded and seated at a table. The cup, unbeknownst to you, is before you. You are given a pencil and told to tap the object in front of you. Initially, all you will sense are vibrations in the pencil, but very rapidly, you cease to be aware of those vibrations. Rather, through them, you become aware of the properties of the cup, such as its shape and weight. The pencil has become a probe: as Polanyi (1967 notes, your sense of identity extends out to include

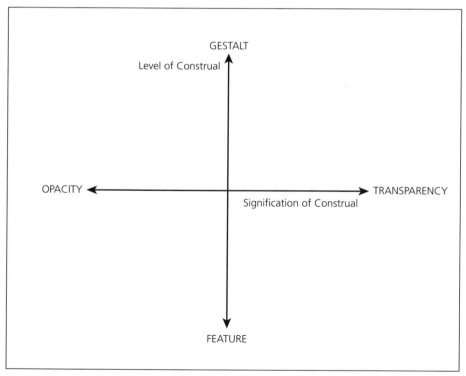

Fig. 13.6 Level of construal.

the pencil. The pencil stops happening to you as the world begins to happen to you through the pencil. Likewise, Polanyi also notes that we can use cognitive probes to allow us to see more deeply into the world. We can nest smaller patterns as features within larger gestalts of patterns, through which we see more deeply into the world. A classic example of this is Einstein's nesting of patterns of acceleration and of gravity into the more encompassing pattern of relativity; Einstein used acceleration and gravity as cognitive probes to see deeper than Newton did into the ontological structure of the universe. These complex shifts can be called attentional scaling—the conjoined functions of TTO and GTF shifts constitute the scaling down of attention, while in contrast, the conjoined OTT and FTG shifts constitute a scaling up of attention (see Figure 13.7).

As such, "being present" can be understood to mean being less transparently representational in one's cognitive processing. One can become less representational by scaling down; the TTO shift reduces the degree of signification, thereby rendering cognition less representational. Additionally, reconstrual from the gestalt to the featural (the GTF shift) removes structural organization. This structural organization serves to afford the transfer of that information in a broad and effective manner (interpolating and extrapolating)—in removing the gestalt, we remove the capacity for such transfer and thereby reduce the capacity for cognition to displace its referent in time and space. Thus, both representational power and inferential power are reduced and the scope of one's cognition is limited to the present. However, there is an enhancement of one's awareness of the patterns and processes within the cognitive medium: attentional, sensory, and interoceptive functions are more accessible and more pronounced.

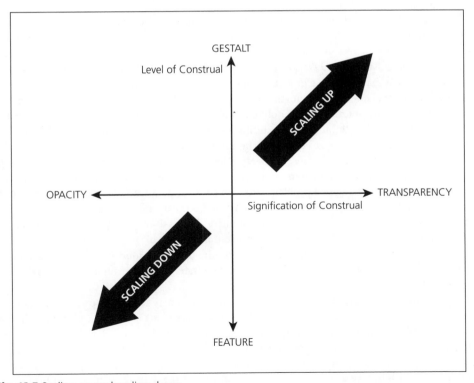

Fig. 13.7 Scaling up and scaling down.

Scaling down and insight

Having operationalized "being present" as scaling down, we can now return to the task of turning the feature list into a feature schema. Under its original, traditional explication, the connection between "being present" and insight is purely promissory: it is unclear what it is about "being present" that facilitates being insightful. There is a potential confusion here that needs to be addressed.

The traditional literature often invokes the notion of insight, specifically, that certain meditative practices will elicit insights into the nature of the mind, the nature of reality, and so on. However, what the traditional literature does not address is precisely how the practice of meditation (including what features or properties of meditative practice) facilitates the *process* and *machinery* of insight. The goal of the traditional texts is to train people to arrive at specific or certain types of insight, not to explain the nature and process of insight itself (these specific insights being the cause, the transformation, or liberation sought by the tradition, such as realizing the impermanence of all things). In formulating "being present" as scaling down, we seek to understand how the attentional processes of meditation (in this case "being present") interact with and enhance the attentional processes that underlie insight. In this manner, we can not only test if they are connected, but also how they are connected. Where the language of training only allows for correlational analyses, a more refined language of explanation allows for causal investigation. Traditions focus on the products of insight and their causal power, while we want to determine the causal processes at work in insight. As such, if the machinery of scaling down is also independently established in the insight literature, then the means of explaining the facilitative effects of "being present" become apparent.

The insight literature presents a series of candidate explanations for how people solve insight problems. Knoblich and colleagues, in a series of studies, build a case for two processes being central to insight problem solving: chunk decomposition and constraint relaxation (Knoblich, Ohlsson, Haider, & Rhenius, 1999; Luo, Niki, & Knoblich, 2006). A "chunk," in this context, is a psychological term that refers to a gestalt. Chunk decomposition is, then, breaking up the gestalt into its component elements (i.e., moving down the axis of level of construal, moving from the gestalt to the featural). Interestingly, Knoblich found that the tighter the chunk, the harder it is to decompose; a chunk is tighter if the resulting elements are less individually meaningful—for example, "strawberry" is easier to break up (because "straw" and "berry" are each individually meaningful words) than either "straw" or "berry." Note how the mind abhors the loss of meaning. Constraint relaxation refers to the removal of implicit assumptions that govern and limit how we see and approach the solving of a problem. How do constraints work? They are automatic filters on our problem formulation. Thus, relaxing a constraint is the de-automatization of the operation of our filters. How does one de-automate an automatic process? One brings one's attention back to the process; one reverses what happens in proceduralization. This is, of course, a transparency-to-opacity shift, along the axis of signification. Thus, the work of Knoblich and other researchers in the field converge upon the claim that one can facilitate insight through scaling down (i.e., combining the GTF and TTO).

This notion of de-automatization has been independently arrived upon by numerous researchers focusing on meditation or insight. Gick and Lockhart (1995), for example, refer to insight as the escape from the "tyranny of automaticity." As far back as 1966, Deikman argued that meditation is a form of de-automatization. Recently, Kang, Gruber, and Gray (2013) have also highlighted the role of de-automatization in mindfulness practices, noting that such practices facilitate insight (see also Chapter 11). McCaffrey (2012) describes an intervention study in which he was able to successfully facilitate insight performance (specifically, a 67% improvement over the control group). The insight problem presented was to connect two metal rings with only the materials at hand, which included a candle and a one-inch metal cube. As part of the instructions, it was noted that the wax would not be useful in holding the rings together. The intervention group received training in two strategies: the first was to mentally break down the objects into component parts, and the second was to re-describe them in as functionally meaningless a manner as possible. For example, the candle was re-described as a cylinder of semi-solid material, containing a wick, which was itself re-described as a string. These strategies afforded the realization that the cube could be used to strip the wax from the wick, which itself, as a string, could be used to tie the rings together, thus solving the problem. What we see here is insight being facilitated by what amounts to attentional scaling down. The objects were subjected both to a gestalt-to-featural shift of attention (i.e., in breaking them down to component parts), as well as to a transparency-to-opacity shift (i.e., in the re-description of the parts in as functionally meaningless a manner as possible). This allowed for the subjects to overcome the common problem of functional fixedness, one of the primary impediments to the solving of insight problems.

DeYoung, Flanders, and Peterson (2008) found evidence that the ability to "break frame" was predictive of insight problem solving. They used an individual differences methodology, in which breaking frame was operationalized via an anomalous card identification task. Participants are flashed a series of cards, each appearing quite briefly; the participant is meant to signal when there is something wrong or different about the card (e.g., a black three of hearts). Success in the detection of anomalous cards was predictive of success in solving insight problems. It is clear that "breaking frame" is an instance of scaling down. The gestalt of the card has to be broken down such that changes in the expected features are noticed, and a transparency-to-opacity shift must de-automatize card identification. Presenting familiar stimuli of this nature generally draws heavily upon automaticity: if one reviews a deck of cards, one tends to see what one expects, and minor anomalies go unnoticed.

In a similar manner, Kaplan and Simon's work on insight (1990; see also Vervaeke & Ferraro 2012, 2013) demonstrated that an ability to notice invariants across problem formulations is predictive of solving the mutilated chessboard insight problem[2]. The "notice invariants" heuristic involves paying attention to what does not change across different, failed formulations of the same problem. By determining what does not vary across failed attempts, one can home in on underlying assumptions or constraints that are hindering success. This is another clear example of a transparency-to opacity shift. However, Kaplan and Simon do not go far enough, because what is crucial to the solution of the mutilated chessboard is the parity cue—noticing that the removed corner pieces are always the same color. In other words, attention has to shift from the gestalt of the board to the individual feature of square color. Thus, we have a complete scaling down facilitating insight: the simultaneous TTO and the GTF shifts.

---

2   The mutilated chessboard problem was first discussed in Kaplan and Simon (1990), in the context of their research on insight problems. The problem is as follows: consider a standard chessboard, consisting of 8 rows and 8 columns, resulting a total of 64 squares. If presented with 32 dominos that each perfectly cover two adjacent squares, then the board can be itself perfectly covered, i.e., the 32 dominos cover the entire surface of the board, without any overhangs, overlaps, or gaps of any sort. If we mutilate the chessboard by removing any two diagonally opposite corners, can we then use 31 of the dominos to perfectly cover the resulting surface?

Before continuing, some clarification of terms is needed. Often, the terms "meditation" and "contemplation" are used synonymously and imprecisely to connote disciplines and practices of concentration and altered states of consciousness. "Meditation" and "contemplative practices" are often used as generic terms. For the purposes of this argument, more precision is required and, thus, we propose to harken to the etymology of the terms in order to specify their meaning more carefully. "Meditate" literally means to move towards the center; for our purposes, this corresponds to practices of scaling down (namely TTO and GTF shifts). "Contemplate" is the translation of the Greek word *theoria*, meaning to see into the divine; for our purposes, this corresponds to practices of scaling up (namely opacity-to-transparency and featural-to-gestalt shifts that enhance ontological depth perception).

In general, scaling up receives less explicit attention, because that is the natural direction of our thoughts, a sort of cognitive Stroop effect.[3] Mindfulness traditions often train both scaling up and scaling down in a larger praxis. Let us contrast Vipassana practice, as a classic example of meditation, with Metta practice, as a classic example of contemplation. A standard practice in Vipassana is following the breath, which means paying attention to the sensations being generated by one's breathing. This is a classic meditative technique for achieving TTO: normally we pay attention through our sensations (to objects in the world), but in following the breath, we pay attention *to* our sensations. Furthermore, in several traditions, one is taught to distinguish between different types, intensities, and even locations of sensations: a clear GTF shift. By contrast, in Metta, one focuses outward, on a particular individual, trying to connect more deeply to that person and see more deeply into them, often through the use of a mantra. For example, one might repeat "may you be free from suffering" as one considers a co-worker. This is a clear example of a OTT shift: one goes from looking at a person to looking into the person, seeking out deeper patterns. Metta starts with being directed towards an individual, then extends to all people, then all beings, and then, ultimately, to the "four corners of the Earth." This is clearly travelling up the level of construal, from the featural to the gestalt. In this way, contemplation, as we have defined it, corresponds with scaling up. So it is plausible to identify meditation, in the sense we have established here, with the phenomenon of scaling down. Thus, if scaling down facilitates insight, as we have shown, it stands to reason that the practice of meditation should likewise enhance one's insight problem-solving abilities.

This hypothesis finds wide support in the literature. To begin with, Ren et al. (2011) found that subjects who were instructed to follow the breath (just as in the Vipassana tradition) were better able to solve insight problems than controls. Ding et al. (2015) found similar results with a shift to right hemispheric activation. Ostafin and Kassman (2012) also used following the breath as their

---

[3] The Stroop effect refers to a robust finding in the psychology literature (Stroop, 1935) that demonstrates the power of automaticity in processing. The effect is often demonstrated as follows: subjects are presented with an array of nonsense words (each word of a different color), followed by an array of proper English words (again, with each word being rendered in a different color), and, lastly, followed by an array of English color words (e.g., red, brown, black, blue, green), also each in a different color and with no word accurately describing its own color (e.g., the word "red" would be in blue or green or yellow font, but never red). The task accompanying each array is to report the color of the letters; subjects find the task trivial in the first array, somewhat challenging in the second, and really challenging in the third, where there is maximal semantic interference. The Stroop effect demonstrates how strongly automatic reading can be—so much so, that it thwarts and overrides color recognition. When we speak of a cognitive Stroop effect, we are speaking of a similarly powerful tendency—the tendency to scale up, to seek transparency and integration.

operationalization of meditation. Like Ren et al., they found that following the breath facilitated the solution of insight problems (although there was no facilitation of non-insight problem solving). Greenberg, Reiner, and Meiran (2012) found that meditation decreased "cognitive rigidity," which was operationalized via the classic three-jar insight problem. Their findings also highlight the connection between meditation and insight problem solving. Additionally, van Leeuwen, Singer, and Melloni (2012) clearly demonstrate both what they refer to as the "global precedence effect" (which is another term for what we have referred to as the cognitive Stroop effect), and how it can be overcome by skilled Buddhist meditators. The evidence strongly indicates that meditative practice enhances insight via scaling down.

Scaling up and insight

Scaling down has been firmly established as an effective enhancer of insight. However, mindfulness has more to offer than just meditation. As specified, contemplative practice exercises scaling up, which has also been shown to enhance insight. Schooler and Melcher (1995) used an individual differences methodology to try and capture what skill best predicts insight problem solving. In their study, the ability to identify the subject of blurred photos was most predictive of successful insight problem solving. This requires an OTT shift, as one must look through the indistinct blotches of color and form to their referent. It also requires a FTG shift since as the incomplete set of features are resolved from the blurred photos, they must be mentally integrated into a coherent image. Hence, scaling up is shown to be importantly predictive of insight. Baker-Sennett and Ceci (1996) also provide evidence of the importance of scaling up. In their experiment, subjects were presented with progressively and incrementally revealed words and figures (see Figure 13.8). The subjects were to try and correctly name the completed item as soon as they were able to. Subjects who could "leap" the furthest (i.e., those who needed the fewest cues to provide the correct response) were the best at solving insight problems. Again, we see the TTO shift, as well as an FTG shift.

Förster, Friedman, and Liberman (2004) were able to generate differences in insight problem solving by manipulating attentional scale: subjects performed differently on insight tasks depending on whether they were primed into a proximal or distal temporal orientation. Förster et al. (2004) provide a comprehensive review showing that inducing a distal temporal orientation produces a shifting of attention to a more abstract level. For example, subjects describing reading a science fiction book tomorrow, as opposed to a year from now, produce radically different formulations of their actions: tomorrow they are "turning pages," but a year from now, they are "broadening their knowledge." They move to a bigger picture orientation, a more gestalt framing of their behavior. In general, when moving from proximal to distal temporal frames, subjects move from highly specific and more superficial descriptions, to higher-level, more abstract ones; this is a FTG shift. Additionally, this also produces an orientation towards deeper, more essential, and more general properties: "why" is highlighted by the distal temporal orientation. This is the OTT shift: they are looking more deeply into things. Förster et al. (2004) found that the distal temporal orientation facilitated insight problem solving. Hunt and Carroll (2008) likewise found that scaling up was facilitative of insight problem solving.

There is now the appearance of a possible contradiction: both scaling up and scaling down appear, counter intuitively, to facilitate insight. As if two seemingly opposite phenomena facilitating the same process were not enough to confuse the issue, it appears that both scaling up and scaling down can also interfere with insight problem solving. This seeming contradiction can be readily resolved by appreciating the complex, dynamical nature of insight. While,

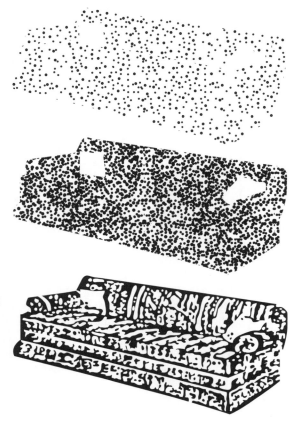

Fig. 13.8 Images demonstrating cognitive leaping.

Reproduced from Clue-Efficiency and Insight: Unveiling the Mystery of Inductive Leaps, Jacquelyn Baker-Sennett and Stephen J. Ceci, *The Journal of Creative Behavior*, 30 (3), pp. 153–172, DOI: 10.1002/j.2162–6057.1996.tb00765.x Copyright © 1996 Creative Education Foundation.

phenomenologically, insight is often tied to the single "Aha!" moment, it is a process with at least two significant phases and two significant functions. In the first phase, we need to break frame, in order to combat poor problem framing. That alone, however, is insufficient; to solve the problem, one must make an appropriate frame. This is the second phase of insight—the construction of an efficacious frame. The function of scaling down enhances breaking frame but impairs making frame, whereas scaling up enhances the making and impairs the breaking of frames. What is needed, then, is a *phase–function fit*; this then explains our apparent contradiction: the very skills that in one phase improve insight, in another phase damage it.

Since we have these two complementary functions, the best way to optimize them for insight is to train them both in a coordinated fashion. The focus of meditation solely on scaling down is insufficient; we want to also cultivate the skills of scaling up, as well as their dynamic coordination. In short, we need both meditative and contemplative practice to optimize mindfulness for insight. This is a plausible explanation for why so many wisdom traditions have a praxis of both meditative and contemplative practices.

Recall our operationalization of "being present" as scaling down; does that imply that we cannot be present while scaling up? In one sense, it would seem so, as contemplative practices seem to rely upon representational states of mind. However, in contemplation, one is practicing a deliberate awareness of the procedural framing of one's representational states. Such procedural framing constitutes the non-representational, and often automatic, processes of constraint formation and chunk composition that go into the creation of representational states. With mindfulness, previously unconscious and automatic processes of framing can now be attended to, to beneficial effect. This strongly suggests that mindfulness is the *cognitive appropriation of the attentional machinery of construal, so as to enhance the awareness of framing, both in breaking frame and making frame.* To the degree to which one maintains an awareness of framing, one can be said to be present, and hence mindful, in whatever activity one is performing. This theoretical extension explains the relevance of mindfulness to many externally oriented behaviors, such as martial arts, calligraphy, or serving tea.

Attentional scaling and self-regulation

Thus far, we have demonstrated the inadequacy of feature lists and shown that the prevalent language of training is ill-suited to rigorous scientific investigation. In so doing, we have been replacing the language of training with a more appropriate language of explanation, and using it to help us replace the old feature list with a feature schema. Continuing in this vein, we will now turn to exploring the causal relationships between attentional scaling and reduced reactivity, with reduced reactivity being understood as the increase of self-regulation. Self-regulation is generally studied as two broad competencies: the delay of gratification and conflict identification. Delay of gratification refers to the ability to forego immediate reward in order to pursue long-term goals, while conflict identification refers to the ability to recognize (and ultimately address) when short-term and long-term goals are in competition. A complicating element here is the notion of hyperbolic discounting (see Figure 13.9), also known as temporal discounting. Essentially, the more distant a stimulus is in time, the less salient it is. This is, of course, strongly adaptive.

As Figure 13.10 illustrates, any given event results in a large branching of possible outcomes and consequences, each with their own implied branchings. As one gets further into the future, the probability of any individual outcome becomes exponentially less likely. It is rational to devote attention to an event in proportion to its likelihood. Therefore, by discounting hyperbolically, attention is rationally constrained in just such a manner. Nevertheless, as with all adaptive machinery, there are circumstances in which it hinders rather than helps. Consider cigarette smoking; it is well understood and widely known to be a bad habit with dire consequences for one's health. Nevertheless, cigarette smoking is one of the (if not *the*) most difficult addictions to overcome. Despite massive media campaigns to shift public perception, giving up cigarettes remains extraordinarily difficult. One way of understanding how and why is hyperbolic discounting: smoking a cigarette has numerous pathways leading to a vast set of catastrophic outcomes. However, each outcome has a low individual probability of occurring. This smoking event might lead to a sequence of events that result in the smoker dying in a specific hospital of cancer in the left lung, or dying in the same hospital but of cancer in the right lung, or dying in another hospital, or dying of emphysema, and so on. Each one of these deaths, each outcome, has a very low chance of occurring and, thus, hyperbolic discounting rationally screens them from attention.

However, in screening off the individual outcomes, it also obscures the larger, cross-contextual invariant, namely, premature death. We are not so much concerned with avoiding death in a particular hospital as we are avoiding death in general. Because premature death is a common feature of many of these outcomes, premature death itself is highly likely, given cigarette smoking. Our basic, uneducated level of hyperbolic discounting, while adaptive, still fails to pick up important cross-contextual facts. Good self-regulation requires that one intelligently intervenes upon one's

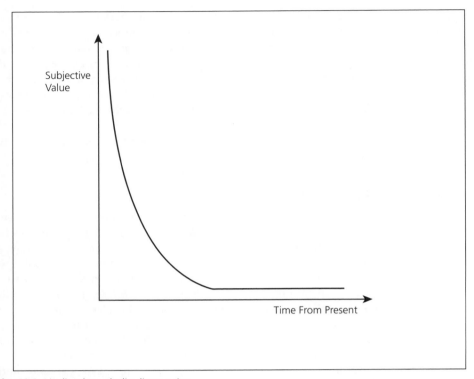

Fig. 13.9 Ainslie's hyperbolic discounting.

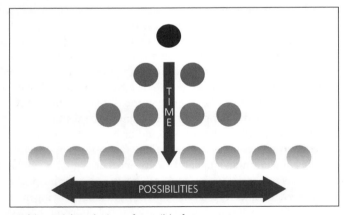

Fig. 13.10 The combinatorial explosion of possible future states.

hyperbolic discounting, so as to enhance its cross-contextual sensitivity, without undermining its adaptive function. This intervention has to be dynamic in nature, as there is no single appreciation of context or contexts that is universally adaptive.

One such intervention is examined in the delay of gratification literature (see Ayduk and Mischel, 2002, for a comprehensive review). In recent years, delay of gratification has come to be seen as developmentally important, similar to IQ in terms of predicting good outcomes in terms of education, occupation, and relationships (see Mischel et al., 2011, for a comprehensive review). The classic experimental design involves presenting a small child with a marshmallow and the following instructions: you can eat the marshmallow whenever you want, but the longer you wait, the more likely it is that you will receive a second marshmallow. The length of time a child can resist consuming the first marshmallow is an index of that child's ability to delay gratification.

 Different approaches have been employed to test this ability. Moore, Mischel, and Zeiss (1976) tested the children under two different conditions. In the first, children were presented with actual rewards (i.e., actual, edible marshmallows), but asked to "put a frame around them," while in the second, children were shown pictures of marshmallows, but asked to pretend that they were real. Note that what is being manipulated here is the significance of construal: the first condition is a transparency-to-opacity shift, while the second is an opacity-to-transparency shift. The results were that the first intervention reliably enhanced delay of gratification, while the second undermined it. As one subject in the first condition famously said: "you can't eat the picture." In 1975, Mischel and Baker also tested two conditions. In the first, children were asked to think of the marshmallows as puffy white clouds—that is, to zero in on shape and color exclusively. In the second, children were asked to think about the sweetness and chewiness of the marshmallows. This is clearly an induction of a gestalt-to-featural shift. Note, however, that simply making this shift is insufficient: the first group had enhanced delay of gratification, but the second group had reduced delay of gratification. It is clear that, in order to be efficacious, a gestalt-to-featural shift needs to be contextually sensitive. In this case, the features chosen need to disrupt the appetitive salience of the marshmallow. This is clear evidence of the utility of scaling down to facilitate delay of gratification.

 However, simply being able to delay gratification more and more is insufficient for good self-regulation and a poor strategy that would undermine the adaptive functionality of hyperbolic discounting. What is needed is a complementary process that calibrates delay of gratification as to when, where, and to what degree it needs to be applied. Myrseth and Fishbach (2009) talk about directing attention in the opposite direction, that is, scaling up. They argue that one needs to engage in "frame widening" and "frame consistency" in order to identify when one's long-term goals are in conflict with one's current goals and to realize that one's current behavior is not isolated and has far-reaching consequences. This is scaling up: frame widening is the shifting to a higher level of construal, while the frame consistency is an opacity-to-transparency shift.

 Myrseth and Fishbach's evidence for the efficacy of scaling up is consistent with Ainslie's evidence of the efficacy of what he calls "symbolic bundling" for overcoming the deleterious effects of hyperbolic discounting. Symbolic bundling involves linking one's current actions meaningfully to future outcomes. Using our cigarette smoking example, the smoker bundles the current act of smoking a cigarette to future instances of smoking, such that transitive inference makes the eventual premature death salient to the current instance. It seems clear that symbolic bundling is the same thing as frame widening and frame consistency, both of which are effective applications of scaling up.

 Once again, we find that both scaling up and scaling down are helpful, in this case, in terms of self-regulation. As before, the optimal praxis, then, is combined practice in both meditation and contemplation. Note that the same machinery of construal management is at work in both insight and self-regulation. This suggests a plausible way of explaining the constitutive relationship between insightfulness and enhanced self-regulation (often labeled "reduced reactivity" or "impulsivity"). This furthers our efforts of transforming the feature list into a feature schema.

Insight, self-regulation, and development

In much the same way that scaling up and scaling down play off each other in both insight and self-regulation, so too are insight and self-regulation themselves similarly organized in a complex opponent process. It is clear that insightfulness opens up cognitive and behavioral possibilities for a person, while self-regulation restricts and limits these possibilities. In this way, our behavioral competence can evolve, with insight introducing variation, and self-regulation exerting selective pressure on which of these possibilities are incorporated into the individual's character. Organized in this manner, we now can see how our feature schema affords an explanation of the developmental role of mindfulness, in that a praxis of mindfulness allows us to intervene upon our development in such a way as to appropriate its evolution, and thus cultivate our character.

Let us see if we can extend this schema to more completely encapsulate the mindfulness phenomenon, by once again considering the occurrent features of "being present" and "non-judging." We have already examined "being present" in depth; "non-judging" runs into the same problem of training language/explanation language confusion. Typically, one is told to pay attention to the meditative focus without making any judgments. However, this standard instruction harbors a potential contradiction, namely, how does one execute these instructions without employing judgment: the breath should be judged more important than the distraction, the meditator should judge the need for correction when their attention has left the meditative focus and onto a distraction, etc.

One way to resolve this contradiction is to make a distinction between propositional judgments, that involve the inferential manipulation of conceptual content, and procedural judgments, that involve the attentional manipulation of salience. Thus, we can now reformulate the instruction to suspend judgment as the instruction to suspend propositional judgment to better afford and enhance procedural judgment. In cognitive terms, the training language serves to trigger a switch from propositional/inferential to procedural/attentional processing. This serves to bring framing into awareness—in this manner, "being present" and "non-judging" are not distinct processes but, rather, two aspects of the same process of the procedural realization of framing.

Thus far, we have met two of the three main requirements for reformulating mindfulness in a manner that affords scientific study, namely, replacing a feature list with a feature schema, and shifting from a language of training to a language of explaining. What remains is to address the developmental questions—how does mindfulness develop and how does mindfulness contribute to cognitive development? One of the few developmental accounts of mindfulness is Siegel's body of work (Siegel 2001 2007). Siegel's theory construes mindfulness as internalized mindsight resonance; mindsight is Siegel's term for people's insight into the mental states of others. Mindsight resonance occurs when people engage in coordinated mindsight activities. Let us consider Bob and Susan having a conversation. Bob's mindsight allows him to pick up on Susan's mental states and affords him some clues as to how to change his own behavior such that Susan is better able to mindsight him. She, in turn, uses this new mindsight in a similar manner, making herself even more mindsightable. This emerging positive feedback loop is *mindsight resonance*. Note how our insights into other people help to drive our own development. In mindfulness practices, we turn that mindsight resonance onto ourselves—this is a clear instance of Vygotskean internalization.

Vygotsky's (1978) primary developmental insight was to move from the individual and to consider development in a social context. Rather than being concerned with any given child in isolation, Vygotsky was interested in how children learned together, among themselves and in the presence of adult teachers and mentors. This results in the situation described by what is widely known in developmental psychology and education circles as Vygotsky's zone of proximal development. Optimal learning occurs when there is a task that is just outside the capabilities of a given individual. However, either through collaboration with peers, or with the coaching of teachers, a person can learn and master the task. Too easy a task means there is nothing to learn, but if the task is too hard, there is no way to relate the actions that solved the problem to one's current complement of abilities.

What is crucial in the zone of proximal development is that the student has not only their own perspective, but also the teacher's, which they can come to imitate. The teacher's perspective includes the student's perspective, and thereby can reveal biases and flaws in that perspective that are not available from within it. Also, the teacher's perspective can inculcate interests and goals that may not be inherent to the student's mindset. In this way, the student can transcend their own perspective by accessing the teacher's perspective. This process of imitation eventually allows the student to work not with the teacher, but with their internal representation of the teacher, speaking to themselves as the teacher would. They begin to engage in mindsight resonance with themselves, and engender a metacognitive awareness of their own cognitive medium.

Siegel argues that mindfulness is a deliberate, sustained practice for enhancing the internalization of mindsight resonance and developing metacognitive abilities. This process of internalization likely plays a significant role in the relationship between the meditation instructor and the meditation student. While there is ample literature covering similar relationships among coaches and athletes, the relationship between meditation instructor and student merits further research.

Note how much Siegel's theory presupposes and relies upon an enhancement of insight abilities. Internalization itself requires a system that travels fluently along the axis of signification of construal; attention has to be directed outwards toward others, and then inwards to the cognitive medium, and so on, in a looping, recursive manner. In short, Siegel's developmental theory requires the cognitive machinery of attentional scaling that we have already outlined as central to mindfulness. This clearly demonstrates a strong theoretical connection between mindfulness and development. Likewise, it lets us see how mindfulness, or at least some mindfulness abilities, develops in people. Notice that this strong connection between mindfulness and development would not be so readily forthcoming if we relied upon the initial language of training and feature list format with which we started. Additionally, our current formulation of mindfulness affords us further theoretical power, allowing us to consider the broader context of altered states of consciousness.

Employing the framework: explaining mystical states

Traditionally, mindfulness practices have been associated with mystical experiences. These mystical experiences are hardly addressed by the recent more scientific and clinical investigations of mindfulness. Moreover, these states are conceived of and addressed in many different ways across numerous traditions, which adds to the conceptual confusion. However, a good theory of mindfulness needs to have some account of these mystical states.

What we propose is to focus on prototypical types of mystical states and apply the framework we have developed in this chapter, in order to explain the cognitive phenomenological features of these states. Forman (1999) has argued for one particular mystical experience, found across many different mindfulness traditions, namely, the pure consciousness event (PCE). In the PCE, one is not conscious of anything, there is no intentional content to one's state, one is not even conscious of one's consciousness. Instead, one is purely conscious, hence the name. One is not blacked out, and one can later remember being in the state. Since there is no propositional content, there must be some significant memory of the procedural processing, in order to afford such a memory. In the context of our feature schema, a PCE is the result of maximal scaling down. Transparency/ opacity and gestalt/featural shifting have gone as far as they can, resulting in a state with neither representational content nor inferential purchase—simply pure consciousness.

Forman and others also discuss a second type of mystical experience, found cross-culturally among mindfulness practitioners, known as the unitive mystical experience (UME), where one feels a deep sense of resonant connection with reality on a profound level. Typically, people describe this as all things being one, or absorbed (or dissolved) into a greater reality. Many of these characteristics are also found in the flow state, described in detail by Csikszentmihalyi (1990). Note that Csikszentmihalyi points out that one of the best predictors of the facility with which one attains flow experiences is previous training in mindfulness practices. This sense of unified connection is, plausibly, a combination of the formation of a massive gestalt, whereas the sense of being connected to what is most real is a case of significant opacity-to-transparency shift. That is to say, the UME is a case of maximal scaling up. This can be seen as the inverse of the PCE, where, instead of grounding out in the most basic scaling down, opacity/transparency and featural/gestalt shifting have gone as far as they can, resulting in a state of maximal ontological depth perception, where often a deep, underlying unifying principle is realized.

There is another mystical state that is referred to throughout various traditions. Where the PCE and UME appear to be almost benchmark states that one encounters as one becomes more skilled in mindfulness practice, this third state is the sought-after goal of many mindfulness traditions. D. T. Suzuki calls this state Prajna. He compares this to Eckhart's Durchbruch (Breakthrough) and cites Eckhart's famous quote that the "eye wherein I see God is the same eye wherein God sees me: my eye and God's eye are one eye, one vision, one knowing, one love" (Eckhart in Suzuki, 1957, p. 35). Notice how Eckhart identifies deep looking out into God with God's deep looking inward into the soul. Suzuki goes on to say about Prajna that the "way of purity opens when the eye sees inwardly as well as outwardly—and this simultaneously" (Suzuki, 1957, p. 35). In a very deft manner, Suzuki draws together the Christian and Buddhist mindfulness traditions to highlight the importance of this prajnic state. Note how Eckhart's famous term, "breakthrough" has unified the senses of both breaking frame and making frame (i.e., breaking (frame) and (seeing) through).

In describing the Zen state of satori, Austin (1999) states that this experience is of sunyata, which is usually translated as emptiness. However, this emptiness "implies no mental constructs," and its foremost meaning is "the deep emptying out from consciousness of every former subjective distinction and personal attachment" (pp. 570–571). The result is what Austin calls a "zero state of the personal psyche," but he goes on to say that the satori mystical experience involves realizing that when "looking out, from inside the zero state, all things will be perceived objectively, just as they really are" (pp. 570–571). This mystical state seems to be a synergy (Apter, 1982, 1989) of the PCE and UME, which would represent the most radical form of insight, which we have argued is a cognitive synergy of breaking frame and making frame. This may be what people have been trying to capture with terms like Prajna, Kensho, Durckbruck, and Vipassana. For the purposes of our schema, we will refer to this state as the synergistic mystical state (SMS).

In speaking of cognitive synergy, Apter (1982) points to a mental state in which we appear to be able to meaningfully hold paradoxes: we can appreciate the metaphor that Sam is a pig, while still appreciating that Sam is actually a persona and that pigs are actually clean animals. In play, a child can treat an object as a sword, and yet still know it is not a sword. Likewise, humor often relies on such paradoxes, in which multiple meanings or senses of words need to be held simultaneously in mind. We are proposing that the SMS is such a cognitive synergy, between scaling down and scaling up, the same sort of cognitive synergy found in insight. This is a rapid cycling between making frame and breaking frame, allowing a fluent moment-to-moment phase/

function fittedness, that self-organizes into a persistent, emergent, metastable state (see Tognoli and Kelso, 2014). This would be to cognition what stereoscopy is to vision: the same way in which we can integrate two different flat channels to produce unified depth perception, so can the brain integrate the two mystical states into this third mystical state that appears to the goal of many mindfulness traditions.

Note that once again, we need to exercise all of our theoretical tools: the reformulated mindfulness construct, the dynamical systems account of insight, and the qualitative nature of growth in cognitive development via Vygotsky and Siegel. This account of the goal of many mindfulness traditions is best explicated by this reformulated construct. The construct is robust enough to allow us to move from everyday mindfulness practice to the extremes of mystical experience. So, let us now turn this model to yet further horizons of altered states of consciousness and see if it affords us a bridge into current work in hypnosis.

Mindfulness, hypnosis, and ritual

Lifshitz and Raz (2012) point out that there is little work on the possible links between mindfulness practices and hypnosis, with what research that is available all being quite recent. As such, while we hope to ground our ideas in rigorous work, of necessity, our discussions around this topic are more tentative and speculative in nature. We hope to propose a theoretical formulation of the linkage that can generate tractable empirical work that will bind (as Lifshitz and Raz, 2012, put it) "the study of attention to the science of suggestion." While many people examining these two phenomena focus on their similarities or differences (see Part 3 of this volume), we propose a third approach. Rather than reducing one to the other, we argue that both hypnosis and mindfulness are components of a larger dynamical process. The development of this dynamic process over human history provides a common ancestry for hypnosis and mindfulness practices (see Chapter 2). This process needs to have the following characteristics: ubiquity, antiquity, and a sharing of important features of both mindfulness and hypnosis. Following the work of Winkelman (2010), Rossano (2007, 2010) McNamara (2009), Rappaport (1999), and Turner (1979), the ritual process meets these criteria.

The ritual process clearly has important mindfulness features. It involves very careful attention paid to one's framing of the ritual context (Turner, 1979), as well as of one's own behavior. McNamara and Rossano point out that ritual involves the training of self-regulation, since it often involves overcoming prepotent impulses in service of long-term symbolic goals. Additionally, ritual involves important frame-breaking and frame-making strategies. This is the case, as Turner emphasizes, because ritual takes place in a liminal state that involves breaking our normal framing of time and space in order to afford a new framing with more ontological depth perception. The machinery being described here echoes many of the details of our theoretical formulation already outlined; namely, scaling down to break frame, scaling up to afford more ontologically perspicacious framing, and the synergestic deployment of these processes. In this way, ritual optimizes the machinery of both insight and self-regulation in a highly coordinated and integrated manner.

Rappaport (1999), in his seminal work on ritual, defines it as "the performance of more or less invariant sequences of formal acts and utterances not encoded by the performers themselves" (p. 24). McNamara (2009, p. 219) elaborates: "[the] fact that participants perform acts in a ritual that were not formulated by themselves suggests that participants temporarily suspend their own identities, including their volitional and intentional states." McNamara (2009, p. 219) then goes on to conclude "that the temporary suspension of ongoing volitional states in favour of performing someone else's action sequences must involve a kind of decentering process." By "decentering,"

McNamara means that one's established self-construct is held in abeyance, in order to afford the appropriation of a more comprehensive self-construct, with enhanced executive powers—one grows the competence of the self. Ritual also involves the internalization of other perspectives and identities; a ritual allows one to speak and to be other than oneself, identifying with or as a deity, an animal, a nation, etc. Rituals are generally comprised of repeated, well-defined patterns, patterns that are often performed rhythmically. This set of features overlaps strongly with those of the induction of hypnosis. Ritual appears to functionally integrate mindfulness practices with hypnosis; it binds the manipulation of attention and suggestion together.

Specifically, just as we have argued that mindfulness is optimally a praxis of meditation and contemplation deployed in a mutually complementary manner, so is ritual a praxis of deploying mindfulness and hypnosis in a mutually complementary manner, enhancing the efficacy of each. To support this thesis, we will examine both the historical/anthropological perspective on the role of ritual in human evolution, as well as apply a cognitive/functional analysis to explain and articulate the mechanics of ritual.

Let us turn our attention back to a critical period in prehistory, namely, the Upper Paleolithic transition. This era, around 50,000 BCE, is the first evidence we have of sophisticated abstract and symbolic thought (accompanied by religious behavior) among human ancestors. From an anatomical and biological perspective, human beings existed for at least 150,000 years before that. What happened during the Upper Paleolithic to so fundamentally change human nature? We see the first cave paintings, representational sculpture, musical instruments, calendrics, the use of bone for tools, and the emergence of sophisticated projectile weapons. This represents a drastic change in cognitive competence—not just a quantitative increase in what humans knew but, rather, a qualitative shift in the kinds of knowledge humans could develop. While there was some evidence of precursor behaviors between 100,000 and 70,000 BCE, Rossano (2007, 2010) argues that true abstract symbolism did not emerge until this Upper Paleolithic transition.

Previous migratory attempts by anatomical humans failed; around 100,000 BCE, they left Africa and attempted to settle in the Levant, but were thwarted by both the cold climate and the Neanderthals. However, when they re-emerged from Africa during the Upper Paleolithic, they not only defeated the Neanderthals and the cold, they swept the planet. The contrast between these two outcomes points to a significant enhancement in cognitive repertoire. Specifically, various scholars (see Rossano 2007, 2010 for a review) have isolated an increase in working memory as the most plausible explanation for such a massive growth in cognitive competence. How did this increase in working memory arise?

While we have historically treated memory as a sort of fixed-capacity resource, like a storage bin which might come in different sizes, more recent work tells a different story. Hasher et al.'s (2007) work on working memory, along with related work by Shanahan and Baars (2005) on global workspace theory, clearly indicate that working memory is better understood as a process, rather than a capacity. Namely, it serves as a higher-order relevance filter, responsible for the framing of experience. The change at the heart of the Upper Paleolithic transition, then, is not a change in working memory capacity, but rather a deep change in the flexibility of framing. Gabora (2013) makes a similar argument, but points to a change in creativity. Her model of creativity is remarkably congruent with our aforementioned model of insight. What is crucial here is that the advantage is cognitive; such an enhancement in working memory would allow for both improved informational integration and differentiation. These emerging humans were better at cross-contextual connections, but also had better context-specific sensitivity.

Rossano (2007, 2010; see also Winkelman, 2010) argues that ritual played a crucial role in this cognitive enhancement. He specifically argues for both the meditative and hypnotic aspects of ritual being responsible for the increase in working memory. He makes two key points: first, he cites current work in neuroscience that establishes both the short- and long-term efficacy of meditation changing the structure and function of cortical areas associated with both working memory and focused attention. Second, he also establishes that hypnotizability (which he describes as "the ability to achieve a ritually-induced, health-enhancing, suggestibility-prone conscious state" [p. 48]) is a fitness-enhancing trait (Rossano, 2007). From this account, we can appreciate that both meditative and hypnotic practices were of significant survival benefit and that ritual was a means of training and enhancing both, via the enhancement of working memory's attentional control of framing. What we see here is that a dynamical praxis of mindfulness functions and hypnotic functions, implemented within ritual processes, played a significant role in the historical transformation and enhancement of human cognition. What is now needed is a more specific analysis of the mechanics of these functions.

A key element and benefit of a hypnotic state is the ability to break automaticity. Lifshitz and colleagues (Lifshitz, Aubert Bonn, Fischer, Kashem, & Raz, 2013) show the powerful effects of hypnosis in thwarting the Stroop effect, the McGurk effect, and automatic processes of visual integration (see also Chapter 11). Considering the potency of these effects, it is clear that hypnosis represents a significant cognitive intervention. A significant challenge to the mastery of various mindfulness practices is the very automaticity of narrative self that pulls one away from the cognitive medium and frame awareness, into the automatic narrative framing of experience (see Chapter 20). It is not difficult to see how the induction of a hypnotic state could then greatly facilitate the development of the skills of mindfulness: the weakening of automaticity via suggestion affords the opportunity for longer and more sustained mindfulness states and experiences, until the initial suggestion is no longer necessary.

Farb (2012) has argued that meditative instruction greatly resembles hypnotic induction (see also Chapter 19). The pedagogical intent is that the student internalizes this instruction and employs it as self-suggestion. If this argument is correct, an important unexplored intersection of meditation and hypnosis has been revealed, namely, the role of self-coaching and self-talk in meditative development. This is an area that calls for empirical investigation. In a ritual context, the hypnotic aspect facilitates the mindful aspects via the de-automatization of the narrative self. This enhances the efficacy of the mindfulness aspect, with more attentional resources being focused upon the framing of the experience, intensifying the involvement with the ritual process much like in the flow state. This, in turn, serves to heighten the suggestive aspects of the ritual, thereby further de-automatizing the self and yet further enhancing the inculcation of mindfulness. While both of these practices have had a largely independent existence and development, it seems clear that, united in the ritual context, they have the potential to mutually support each other in a powerful way.

If this argument is correct, there should be empirical investigation of mindfulness practices that include highly ritualized aspects. In addition to the aforementioned investigation of self-talk and self-coaching in meditation, we can consider the practice of T'ai Ch'i Chu'an, which is both a mindfulness practice that trains attention (Converse, Ahlers, Travers, & Davidson, 2014) and also a highly ritualized system of movements through rhythmic patterns, based on a very careful imitation of an instructor. The goal is *wu wei*, which is a state of spontaneity, where one feels both like one is moving and being moved. This appears to be an ideal candidate for such empirical study: it has features of both the mindfulness and hypnotic aspects present in a ritual context. Additionally, it is widely practiced, with an abundance of potential subjects at all levels of ability.

What we have argued for is the reformulation of the mindfulness construct, so as to improve its theoretical rigor and empirical tractability. In so doing, we have also sought to extend this framework so as to include potential explanations and investigations of other altered states of consciousness. In particular, we argued that this construct affords an explanation of various widely reported mystical states that can occur within mindfulness practices. Additionally, with the support of anthropological and historical evidence, we have tentatively argued for the central role of ritual in cognitive evolution, with its integration of both mindfulness features and hypnotic features, pointing to a possible complementary practice of both. This opens up new avenues for investigating the binding of the study of attention with the science of suggestion.

References

Apter, M. J. (1982). Metaphor as synergy. In D. S. Miall (Ed.), *Metaphor: problems and perspectives* (pp. 55–70). New York, NY, USA: Harvester Press.

Apter, M. J. (1989). *Reversal theory: motivation, emotion and personality (***vol. viii***)*. Florence, KY, USA: Taylor & Frances/Routledge.

Austin, J. H. (1999). *Zen and the brain: toward an understanding of meditation and consciousness.* Cambridge, MA, USA: MIT Press.

Ayduk, O., & Mischel, W. (2002). When smart people behave stupidly: reconciling inconsistencies in social-emotional intelligence. In R. J. Sternberg (Ed.), *Why smart people can be so stupid* (pp. 86–105). New Haven, CT, USA: Yale University Press.

Baker-Sennett, J., & Ceci, S. J. (1996). Clue-efficiency and insight: unveiling the mystery of inductive leaps. *Journal of Creative Behavior*, **30**(3), 153–172. doi:10.1002/j.2162–6057.1996.tb00765.x

Carmichael, L., Hogan, H. P., & Walter, A. A. (1932). An experimental study of the effect of language on the reproduction of visually perceived form. *Journal of Experimental Psychology*, **15**(1), 73–86. doi:10.1037/h0072671

Converse, A. K., Ahlers, E. O., Travers, B. G., & Davidson, R. J. (2014). Tai chi training reduces self-report of inattention in healthy young adults. *Frontiers in Human Neuroscience*, **8**. (pp. 1–7) doi:10.3389/fnhum.2014.00013

Csikszentmihalyi, M. (1990). *Flow: The psychology of optimal experience.* New York, NY, USA: Harper & Row.

Deikman, Arthur J. (1966). "De-automatization and the mystic experience." *Psychiatry* 29.4: 324–338.

DeYoung, C. G., Flanders, J. L., & Peterson, J. B. (2008). Cognitive abilities involved in insight problem solving: an individual differences model. *Creativity Research Journal*, **20**(3), 278–290. doi:10.1080/10400410802278719

Ding, Xiaoqian, et al. (2015). "Short-term meditation modulates brain activity of insight evoked with solution cue." *Social cognitive and affective neuroscience* 10.1: 43–49.

Eysenck, M. W., & Keane, M. T. (1990). *Cognitive psychology: a student's handbook.* New York, NY, USA: Psychology Press.

Farb, N. A. S. (2012). Mind your expectations: exploring the roles of suggestion and intention in mindfulness training. *Journal of Mind–Body Regulation*, **2**(1), 27–42.

Forman, R. K. C. (1999). *Mysticism, mind, consciousness.* Albany, NY, USA: SUNY Press.

Förster, J., & Dannenberg, L. (2010). GLOMOsys: a systems account of global versus local processing. *Psychological Inquiry*, **21**(3), 175–197. doi:10.1080/1047840X.2010.487849

Förster, J., Friedman, R. S., & Liberman, N. (2004). Temporal construal effects on abstract and concrete thinking: consequences for insight and creative cognition. *Journal of Personality and Social Psychology*, **87**(2), 177–189. doi:10.1037/0022–3514.87.2.177

Gabora, L. (2013). Contextual focus: a cognitive explanation for the cultural revolution of the Middle/Upper Paleolithic. *arXiv:1309.2609 [q-Bio]*. Retrieved from http://arxiv.org/abs/1309.2609

Gick, M. L., & Lockhart, R. S. (1995). Cognitive and affective components of insight. In R. J. Sternberg & J. E. Davidson (Eds.), *The nature of insight* (pp. 197–228). Cambridge, MA: MIT Press.

Greenberg, J., Reiner, K., & Meiran, N. (2012). "Mind the trap": mindfulness practice reduces cognitive rigidity. *PLoS ONE*, **7**(5), e36206. doi:10.1371/journal.pone.0036206

Hasher, L., Lustig, C., & Zacks, R. (2007). Inhibitory mechanisms and the control of attention. In C. Jarrold, *Variations in working memory* (pp. 227–249). Oxford, England: Oxford University Press.

Hunt, C., & Carroll, M. (2008). Verbal overshadowing effect: how temporal perspective may exacerbate or alleviate the processing shift. *Applied Cognitive Psychology*, **22**(1), 85–93. doi:10.1002/acp.1352

Kang, Y., Gruber, J., & Gray, J. R. (2013). Mindfulness and de-automatization. *Emotion Review*, **5**(2), 192–201. doi:10.1177/1754073912451629

Kaplan, C. A., & Simon, H. A. (1990). In search of insight. *Cognitive Psychology*, **22**(3), 374–419. doi:10.1016/0010–0285(90)90008-R

Knoblich, G., Ohlsson, S., Haider, H., & Rhenius, D. (1999). Constraint relaxation and chunk decomposition in insight problem solving. *Journal of Experimental Psychology: Learning, Memory, and Cognition*, **25**(6), 1534–1555. doi:10.1037/0278–7393.25.6.1534

Lifshitz, M., Aubert Bonn, N., Fischer, A., Kashem, I. F., & Raz, A. (2013). Using suggestion to modulate automatic processes: from Stroop to McGurk and beyond. *Cortex*, **49**(2), 463–473. doi:10.1016/j.cortex.2012.08.007

Lifshitz, M., & Raz, A. (2012). Hypnosis and meditation: vehicles of attention and suggestion. *Journal of Mind–Body Regulation*, **2**(1), 3–11.

Luo, J., Niki, K., & Knoblich, G. (2006). Perceptual contributions to problem solving: chunk decomposition of Chinese characters. *Brain Research Bulletin*, **70**(4–6), 430–443. doi:10.1016/j.brainresbull.2006.07.005

McCaffrey, T. (2012). Innovation relies on the obscure: a key to overcoming the classic problem of functional fixedness. *Psychological Science*, **23**(3), 215–218. doi:10.1177/0956797611429580

McNamara, P. (2009). *The neuroscience of religious experience*. Cambridge, MA, USA: Cambridge University Press.

Metzinger, T. (2003). Phenomenal transparency and cognitive self-reference. *Phenomenology and the Cognitive Sciences*, **2**(4), 353–393. doi:10.1023/B:PHEN.0000007366.42918.eb

Mischel, W., Ayduk, O., Berman, M. G., Casey, B. J., Gotlib, I. H., Jonides, J.,. . . Shoda, Y. (2011). "Willpower" over the life span: decomposing self-regulation. *Social Cognitive and Affective Neuroscience*, **6**(2), 252–256. doi:10.1093/scan/nsq081

Mischel, W., & Baker, N. (1975). Cognitive appraisals and transformations in delay behavior. *Journal of Personality and Social Psychology*, **31**(2), 254–261. doi:10.1037/h0076272

Mole, C. (2010). *Attention is cognitive unison: an essay in philosophical psychology*. Oxford, England: Oxford University Press.

Moore, B., Mischel, W., & Zeiss, A. (1976). Comparative effects of the reward stimulus and its cognitive representation in voluntary delay. *Journal of Personality and Social Psychology*, **34**(3), 419–424. doi:10.1037/0022–3514.34.3.419

Murphy, G. L., & Medin, D. L. (1985). The role of theories in conceptual coherence. *Psychological Review*, **92**(3), 289–316. doi:10.1037/0033–295X.92.3.289

Myrseth, K. O. R., & Fishbach, A. (2009). Self-control: a function of knowing when and how to exercise restraint. *Current Directions in Psychological Science*, **18**(4), 247–252. doi:10.1111/j.1467–8721.2009.01645.x

Ostafin, B. D., & Kassman, K. T. (2012). Stepping out of history: mindfulness improves insight problem solving. *Consciousness and Cognition*, **21**(2), 1031–1036. doi:10.1016/j.concog.2012.02.014

Polanyi, M. (1967). *The tacit dimension*. Retrieved from http://philpapers.org/rec/POLTTD

Polanyi, M., & Prosch, H. (1975). *Meaning*. Chicago, IL, USA: University of Chicago Press.

Rappaport, R. A. (1999). *Ritual and religion in the making of humanity*. Cambridge, MA, USA: Cambridge University Press.

Ren, J., Huang, Z., Luo, J., Wei, G., Ying, X., Ding, Z.,. . . Luo, F. (2011). Meditation promotes insightful problem-solving by keeping people in a mindful and alert conscious state. *Science China Life Sciences*, **54**(10), 961–965. doi:10.1007/s11427–11011–4233–4233

Rossano, M. J. (2007). Did meditating make us human? *Cambridge Archaeological Journal*, **17**(01), 47–58. doi:10.1017/S0959774307000054

Rossano, M. (2010). *Supernatural selection: how religion evolved*. Oxford, England: Oxford University Press.

Rumelhart, D. E., McClelland, J. L., & Group, P. R. (1986). *Parallel distributed processing: explorations in the microstructure of cognition (Vol. 1: Foundations)*. Cambridge, MA: MIT Press.

Ryle, G. (1949). *The concept of mind*. Florence, KY, USA: Routledge.

Schooler, J. W., & Melcher, J. (1995). The ineffability of insight. In S. M. Smith, T. B. Ward, & R. A. Finke (Eds.), *The creative cognition approach* (pp. 97–133). Cambridge, MA: MIT Press.

Shanahan, M., & Baars, B. (2005). Applying global workspace theory to the frame problem. *Cognition*, **98**(2), 157–176. doi:10.1016/j.cognition.2004.11.007

Siegel, D. J. (2001). Toward an interpersonal biology of the developing mind: attachment relationships, "mindsight," and neural integration. *Infant Mental Health Journal*, **22**(1–2), 67–94.

Siegel, D. J. (2007). *The mindful brain: reflection and attunement in the cultivation of well-being*. New York, NY, USA: W.W. Norton & Company.

Stroop, J. R. (1935). "Studies of interference in serial verbal reactions." *Journal of experimental psychology*, **18**.6: 643.

Suzuki, D. T. (1957). *Mysticism Christian and Buddhist*. London, England: George Allen & Unwin.

Tognoli, E., & Kelso, J. A. S. (2014). The metastable brain. *Neuron*, **81**(1), 35–48. doi:10.1016/j.neuron.2013.12.022

Toneatto, T., & Nguyen, L. (2007). Does mindfulness meditation improve anxiety and mood symptoms? A review of the controlled research. *Canadian Journal of Psychiatry/La Revue Canadienne de Psychiatrie*, **52**(4), 260–266. Retrieved from http://psycnet.apa.org/psycinfo/2007–10109–008

Trope, Y., & Liberman, N. (2011). Construal level theory. In P. A. M. Van Lange, A. W. Kruglanski, & E. T. Higgins (Eds.), *Handbook of theories of social psychology* (pp. 118–134). Thousand Oaks, CA, USA: SAGE Publications.

Turner, V. (1979). Frame, flow and reflection: ritual and drama as public liminality. *Japanese Journal of Religious Studies*, **6**(4), 465–499.

Van Leeuwen, S., Singer, W., & Melloni, L. (2012). Meditation increases the depth of information processing and improves the allocation of attention in space. *Frontiers in Human Neuroscience*, **6**, 1–16. http://doi.org/10.3389/fnhum.2012.00133

Vervaeke, J., & Ferraro, L. (2012). Relevance, meaning and the cognitive science of wisdom. In M. Ferrari, & N. Westrate (Eds.), *The scientific study of personal wisdom* (pp. 21–52). New York, NY, USA: Springer.

Vervaeke, J., & Ferraro, L. (2013). Relevance realization and the neurodynamics and neuroconnectivity of general intelligence. In I. Harvey, A. Cavoukian, G. Tomko, D. Borrett, H. Kwan, & D. Hatzinakos (Eds.), *SmartData privacy meets evolutionary robotics* (pp. 57–68). New York, NY, USA: Springer.

Vygotsky, L. S. (1978). *Mind and society: the development of higher mental processes*. Cambridge, MA: Harvard University Press.

Winkelman, M. (2010). *Shamanism: a biopsychosocial paradigm of consciousness and healing*. Denver, CO, USA: Praeger.

Chapter 14

Absorption in hypnotic trance and meditation

Ulrich Ott

Abstract

If we equate meditation merely with popular conceptions of mindfulness training (i.e., attending non-judgmentally to the present moment), then meditation and hypnosis seem to be diametrically opposed. However, there also exist other types of deeply focused meditation that bear a striking similarity to hypnotic states. The close relationship between deep meditation and hypnotic states is underpinned by the fact that both show a strong correlation with the trait of absorption. The concept of attentional absorption lends a useful tool for characterizing the neurobiological changes brought about via altered planes of awareness. This chapter presents findings of questionnaire, genetic, and neuroimaging studies that elucidate the experiential and neural commonalities between meditative and hypnotic absorption states.

Introduction

In this chapter, hypnosis and meditation are to be compared with regard to absorption. In order to be meaningful, such a comparison requires first a clarification of terms (see Grant, 2012, and Chapter 10). As denoted in the title, this chapter is not concerned with hypnosis as a method (i.e., hypnotic induction procedures) but with the induced state of consciousness (i.e., hypnotic trance or simply the "hypnoidal state,") which will be defined based on a questionnaire score.

In a similar vein, the term "meditation" can be used to designate a meditation method as well as a meditative state, an ambiguity that has led to considerable confusion (Awasthi, 2013; Nash & Newberg, 2013). Again, this chapter is primarily concerned with states of deep meditation and not so much with the methods employed to attain them. The psychological construct of "meditation depth" will be introduced in a separate section.

Finally, the comparison of hypnoidal and meditative states is focused on "absorption," which appears to be a core feature of those states of consciousness, as we will see (for a complementary neurophenomenological comparison see Chapter 6). However, most of the presented empirical findings relate to the "absorption trait" as introduced by Tellegen and Atkinson (1974) and measured with the Tellegen Absorption Scale. In order to avoid misunderstandings, capitalization will be used in this chapter whenever the trait "Absorption" is meant and not a state of (mental or attentional) absorption.

The hypnoidal state—an operational definition

An in-depth analysis of the need and possibilities to define discrete states of consciousness was undertaken nearly forty years ago in a seminal book by Tart (1975), who is still active in the research community (see Chapter 9). Later on, in his "systems approach" to altered states of consciousness, he emphasized that

> ... the presence or absence of a given state of consciousness for a given individual must ultimately be ascertained by an experiential mapping of the dimensions of experience ... Initial selection of mapping dimensions will be crude and 'intuitive,' but techniques such as factor analysis will refine them. (Tart, 1980, p. 252f)

A decade later, the proposal of Tart was realized in an exemplary manner by Pekala (1991), who developed the Phenomenology of Consciousness Inventory (PCI) to enable the comparison of a variety of different states of consciousness by assessing and mapping 12 major and 14 minor dimensions of experience. In one of his studies, participants were asked to describe their experience during a standardized hypnotic induction procedure (Harvard Group Scale of Hypnotic Susceptibility; HGSHS). Afterwards, a regression analysis was performed to predict the actual HGSHS scores based on the dimensions measured by the PCI. The predicted scores were taken by Pekala as indicating a "hypnoidal state." Thus, responsiveness to hypnotic suggestions was taken as an indicator for the depth of the hypnotic state (an assumption that is quite controversial, see Kirsch, 1997). Dimensions significantly correlated with the predicted score for the induced "hypnoidal state" are listed in Table 14.1.

Table 14.1 Dimensions of experience (as measured by the Phenomenology of Consciousness Inventory) that characterize "hypnoidal states," and their correlations (all p < 0.001) with the predicted score of the Harvard Group Scale of Hypnotic Susceptibility

Major and minor dimensions	Correlations
Altered state	0.55
Altered experience	0.50
Body image	0.38
Meaning	0.32
Perception	0.39
Time sense	0.45
Volitional control	−0.52
Self-awareness	−0.49
Attention	0.22
Absorption	0.32
Memory	−0.36
Rationality	−0.32
Internal dialogue	−0.24

Highly significant negative correlations indicate that volitional control and self-awareness are reduced during hypnotic states, supporting the view that hypnotic trance and mindfulness meditation represent diametrically opposed states (see Chapter 7). However, a comparison of the other features leads to mixed results. Internal dialog is reduced in hypnotic trance and also during mindfulness meditation, which strives to inhibit mind wandering (Hasenkamp, 2014). Under hypnosis, the flow of time might speed up, slow down, or even stand still (PCI dimension: altered experience/time sense). During mindfulness meditation, the passing of time seems to slow down too, thereby enhancing perception and memory function (Wittmann & Schmidt, 2014), whereas memory for experiences during hypnotic trance is rather impaired (see negative correlation for memory in Table 14.1).

The most interesting difference in the present context pertains to the dimension of attentional absorption, which is positively correlated with the level of hypnotic trance. A corresponding item of the PCI reads: "I was not distracted, but was able to be completely absorbed in what I was experiencing." Of course, practitioners of mindfulness meditation also wish to overcome distractions, but they do not want to become "completely absorbed" into the object chosen as an anchor for attention—if an anchor is used at all. Mindfulness meditation is characterized by detached observation and insight into the arising and passing away of mental events. Thus, states of complete mental absorption are typically avoided in mindfulness/insight meditation techniques. However, for concentrative meditation techniques, it is a main objective to enter states of deep absorption. Of course, in actual practice, concentrative (Samatha) and insight (Vipassana) meditation techniques are not mutually exclusive, but complement each other. A certain degree of mental stability and focus cultivated by concentrative meditation is often seen as a prerequisite to begin insight meditation practice.

Characteristics of deep meditation states

The experiential qualities of meditation sessions are not always the same, and one attribute widely used by practitioners to describe this variability is the "depth of meditation." Based on the (highly consistent) ratings of 40 longstanding meditation teachers from different traditions (Christian, Taoist, Yoga, and several Buddhist branches), Piron (2001) developed the Meditation Depth Questionnaire (MEDEQ). The 30 items of this questionnaire were found to form five clusters representing stages of meditation with increasing depth (see Table 14.2).

Table 14.2 Five clusters of the Meditation Depth Questionnaire (Piron, 2001), characterized by keywords describing the contents of the respective items

Cluster	Experiences
1. Hindrances	Restlessness, busy mind, laziness, feeling bored
2. Relaxation	Feeling well, smooth breathing, patience, calmness
3. Concentration	Mindfulness, attentive control over the mind, detached from thoughts, emotions, and sensations, energy, centered
4. Essential qualities	Love, surrender, connection, joy, grace, humility, transcending time
5. Non-duality	Rest of thoughts, stillness, no differentiations, unity of all, emptiness, infinity, transcendence of subject and object

Beginners of meditation often have to deal with the difficulties described by the items of the first cluster ("hinderances")—and advanced meditators occasionally as well. Experiences of clusters two ("relaxation") and three ("concentration") are the main target of clinical interventions, whereas from the spiritual perspective, they appear more as a sort of prelude and prerequisite of the stages that follow. The deep positive emotions characterizing the fourth cluster ("essential qualities") have, to some extent, religious connotations and promote a less ego-centered, more selfless stance of devotion.

The deepest stage is characterized by items describing experiences of non-duality, where the subject–object dichotomy of ordinary waking consciousness dissolves and gives way to a mystical experience of all-encompassing unity. At this stage, thought processes might come to a standstill, and the confines of space and time are transcended. In order to reach this stage, for instance, practitioners of concentrative meditation exercise themselves in focusing steadily on a chosen meditation object (e.g., a mantra, picture, or visualization) until they become one with it and with the quality or deity it represents.

Absorption states and the trait of Absorption—empirical findings

The phenomenon of meditative absorption bears a striking similarity to hypnotic states of deep immersion. The yoga tradition especially is famous for states of deep meditative absorption (Sanskrit *samadhi*), which stand in stark contrast to the emphasis on meta-awareness in Buddhist insight meditation (see comparison in Walsh, 1995). In several studies, yogis in meditation were found to be unresponsive to external stimulation, even to severe painful stimuli (e.g., see Peper et al., 2006). In a similar way, hypnotic suggestions have been found to modulate pain processing (for a review, see Chen, 2009 and Faymonville, Boly, & Laureys, 2006; see also the comparisons of pain modulation by hypnosis and meditation in Dumont, Martin, & Broer, 2012 and Chapter 21).

The close relationship between deep meditation and hypnotic states is further underpinned by the fact that both show a strong correlation with the trait of Absorption. In 1974, Tellegen and Atkinson devised the Tellegen Absorption Scale (TAS; consisting of 34 items) in order to assess a disposition "for having episodes of 'total' attention that fully engage one's representational (i.e., perceptual, enactive, imaginative, and ideational) resources" (p. 268). Their intention was to develop a questionnaire that could predict hypnotic susceptibility, and indeed, the TAS score was found to be significantly correlated with hypnotic susceptibility (Jamieson, 2005).

When introducing the construct of Absorption, Tellegen and Atkinson (1974) already noted that

> . . . objects of absorbed attention acquire an importance and intimacy that are normally reserved for the self and may, therefore, acquire a temporary self-like quality. These object identifications have mystical overtones. And, indeed, one would expect high-absorption persons to have an affinity for mystical experience (p. 275).

This expectation was confirmed in a questionnaire study (Hölzel & Ott, 2006) where the TAS and the MEDEQ were administered in a large heterogenous sample of meditators (N = 251). The analysis revealed a significant correlation between Absorption score and the reported depth of meditation sessions during the last week as assessed via the MEDEQ (r = 0.41, p = 0.01).

It is remarkable that TAS scores correlate with both hypnotic susceptibility and depth of meditation experiences because the scale items concern experiences of everyday life like vivid imagination or emotional responsiveness to art and nature. Exploratory and confirmatory factor analyses of an improved version of the TAS by Jamieson (2005) revealed a single higher-order factor and five interrelated primary factors (see Table 14.3).

Table 14.3 The five primary factors of the modified Tellegen Absorption Scale (Jamieson, 2005)

Factor	Exemplary item (highest loading)
1. Synesthesia	I find that different odors have different colors.
2. Altered state of consciousness	I "step outside" my usual self and experience an entirely different state of being.
3. Aesthetic involvement in nature	I am deeply moved by a sunset.
4. Imaginative involvement	I imagine (or daydream) some things so vividly that they hold my attention as a good movie or story does.
5. Extrasensory perception	I know what someone is going to say before he or she says it.

The Absorption trait represents a single higher-order factor underlying these five primary factors that are all highly correlated with each other. Further evidence for a communality between the factors listed in Table 14.3 is provided by other scales containing a set of similar items, namely the scale "self-transcendence" of the Temperament and Character Inventory by Cloninger, Przybeck, Svrakic, and Wetzel (1994) and the Transliminality Scale by Thalbourne (1998) (for a detailed description, see Ott, 2007). The factor "imaginative involvement" has high loadings on the largest number of items (9 of 34); these items address an intense focusing of attention, vivid imagination, and self-forgetfulness, all of which are clearly relevant for both hypnotic trance and deep meditative absorption. Therefore, studies on neurobiological correlates of the Absorption *trait* could provide valuable information about brain mechanisms involved in absorption *states* induced by hypnosis and concentrative meditation.

Neurobiological correlates of Absorption

Absorption represents a general disposition and several studies addressed the question of whether this disposition might be heritable. According to twin studies, approximately 40% of this personality trait is genetically determined (for a detailed review, see Ott, 2007). Data on the involved neural structures are scarce but at least a few findings are available.

A molecular genetic association study (N = 336) found that participants with the T/T genotype of the T102C polymorphism, implying a stronger binding capacity of 5-HT2a receptors, scored significantly higher on the TAS than those with the T/C or C/C genotypes (Ott, Reuter, Hennig, & Vaitl, 2005). This receptor subtype of the serotonin system is known to be the primary target site for some psychedelic drugs. An increased binding potential could lead to stronger responses and, indeed, the TAS score has been found to be the best predictor for responsiveness to psilocybin, surpassed only by drug dose (Studerus, Gamma, Kometer, & Vollenweider, 2012). Thus, genetic polymorphisms affecting neurotransmitter functioning could be, at least in part, responsible for stronger drug-induced alterations of consciousness in people high on Absorption. Interestingly, an interaction of the T102C polymorphism with the VAL158MET polymorphism of the catechol-O-methyltransferase (COMT) gene was found, the latter affecting the dopaminergic neurotransmitter system. Higher Absorption scores were found in carriers of the VAL/VAL (COMT) and T/T (T102C) genotypes. Interactions of this sort could explain why association studies on COMT polymorphism and hypnotic susceptibility have reported equivocal results so far (see a review in Presciuttini et al., 2014).

A recent structural magnetic resonance imaging (MRI) study analyzed cortical thickness related to the Absorption trait in 18 meditators and 18 controls (Grant et al., 2013). Meditators scored moderately but significantly higher than controls on the TAS, and across the entire sample, higher TAS scores were "correlated positively with cortical thickness in several regions corresponding to cingulo-fronto-parietal attention networks. Within these regions the meditation group had greater cortical thickness which was positively related to the extent of prior training." (p. 275) According to the authors, Absorption could be conceived as an attentional skill that might be enhanced by meditation training (for a review of morphometric neuroimaging in meditation practitioners, see Fox et al., 2014). Since the same brain regions show structural deficits in patients suffering from attention deficit and hyperactivity disorder, the authors propose that meditation training could be employed to ameliorate attentional performance in this group of patients.

Two functional imaging studies assessing the subjective intensity of absorption state during hypnosis by participants' ratings reported increased activity in the anterior cingulate cortex (Rainville, Hofbauer, Bushnell, Duncan, & Price, 2002) and in prefrontal attentional systems, while activity in the default-mode network (DMN) was reduced (Deely et al., 2012). These findings are complemented by a recent study on neural correlates of hypnotic suggestibility that included structural neuroimaging and functional connectivity analysis during a resting state (Huber, Lui, Duzzi, Pagnoni, & Porro, 2014). Participants scoring high on hypnotic suggestibility showed higher resting state functional connectivity "in frontal attention networks and in medial posterior areas involved in imagery." (p. 5) By adopting a neurophenomenological approach, Cardeña, Jönsson, Terhune, and Marcusson-Clavertz (2013) found reductions of global (electroencephalographic; EEG) connectivity in medium and high hypnotizable subjects during neutral hypnosis (see also Chapter 15).

Deactivation in core regions of the DMN was also found in meditators across different meditation types (Brewer et al., 2011). Higher connectivity of the DMN and the anterior cingulate cortex during rest and meditation was interpreted as enhanced ability of meditators to detect and prevent mind wandering and daydreaming associated with increased DMN activity. (A detailed comparison of meditation and hypnosis with regard to the DMN can be found in Dumont et al., 2012, as well as in Chapter 18). Sustained focusing of attention during states of meditative or hypnotic absorption requires decreased responsivity to distractions (i.e., engagement of attention networks and inhibition of DMN activity) (Hasenkamp, Wilson-Mendenhall, Duncan, & Barsalou, 2012).

The conceptualization of Absorption as a disposition as well as a skill that can be enhanced by meditation training is in good agreement with the items of the TAS describing situations of deep immersion into a deliberately chosen object of attention. Focused attention during meditation was found to be associated with increased *anti-correlation* between attentional networks and the DMN (Josipovic, 2014). In a similar way, the cultivation of present-centered awareness in mindfulness meditation requires continuous monitoring of mental processes and an inhibition of daydreaming. However, in contrast to object-focused meditation, during mindfulness training, absorption is not intended because it diminishes meta-awareness. According to Lifshitz, Cusumano, and Raz (2014), sometimes one could be "swept up by absorption in particular experiential *contents*" (p. 213; *italics* in the original text). Mindfulness could be easily impeded because "patterns of discursive overlay and absorption in experiential contents are overlearned and highly automatic" (p. 213). Put simply, the ability to become deeply absorbed supports concentrative meditation, while it represents a risk for the preservation of meta-awareness during mindfulness meditation.

With regard to the depth of meditation, experiences of concentration and mindfulness were rated to indicate medium levels only (third cluster; see Table 14.2). Deeper experiences of the next cluster include strong positive emotions, feelings of connection, and affective states characterized by a stance of passivity (surrender, grace, humility). The Absorption scale includes several items that describe enhanced emotional responsiveness (factors 3 and 4; see Table 14.3). To reach these deeper levels, it seems that the cognitive self-regulatory skills developed during effortful meditative training have to be complemented with emotional qualities promoting selflessness and the particular strong "object identifications with mystical overtones" mentioned by Tellegen and Atkinson (1974, p. 275). In view of the profound alterations of consciousness during the deepest level of meditation ("non-duality" cluster; see Table 14.2), its neural correlates are likely to diverge from those of ordinary concentration and mindfulness.

In advanced meditation, deep mental absorption seems to be maintained in an effortless way, as indicated by reduced activation of brain regions involved in sustained attention (Brefczynski-Lewis, Lutz, Schaefer, Levinson, & Davidson, 2007). In the study of Josipovic (2014) with experienced meditators, focused attention was accompanied by increased anti-correlation between attentional networks and the DMN compared to baseline (simple fixation). Yet, when a meditation directed on realizing "non-dual awareness" was practiced, this anti-correlation dropped considerably compared to baseline. Thus, focused attention on an object ("concentration") and non-dual awareness—induced by immersive absorption or other meditation techniques like Vipassana or open presence—differ markedly regarding experiential features, distinctions mirrored also at the neural level.

Future perspectives

As stated at the outset, a meaningful comparison of hypnosis and meditation requires clear-cut definitions of both the investigated methods and resulting consciousness states. For meditation, Nash and Newberg (2013) proposed a set of taxonomical keys that should be used to describe meditation techniques in scientific studies. The proposed specific keys are also contained, without exception, in the comprehensive Meditation Classification System developed and presented recently by Schmidt (2014). In the future, the description of meditation methods, following the proposed standards and using instruments of this kind, will facilitate comparisons across studies.

For a phenomenological mapping of induced states of consciousness, general questionnaires such as the PCI or the questionnaire for the assessment of altered states of consciousness (Aussergewöhnliche Psychische Zustände; APZ) (Dittrich, 1998) have been available for many years, but no common standard has been established across different fields of research, so far. Recently, the successor to the APZ has been psychometrically evaluated and lower-order scales have been proposed which might be better suited to provide ratings of alterations in various dimensions of consciousness (Studerus, Gamma, & Vollenweider, 2010). In neuroimaging studies, the administration of such comprehensive, general questionnaires is often too time-consuming; therefore, a few items, tailored to test specific hypotheses, are presented during or immediately after scanning instead. For instance, Deeley et al. (2012) asked the participants to rate their subjective state regarding the five attributes "relaxed," "absorbed," "distracted," "analytical," and "cluttered" after scanning, using visual analog scales. In addition, semi-structured interviews were conducted to assess the subjective quality of the induced alterations in more detail.

Meditation and hypnosis are objects of study as well as *methods of research* in the new field of neurophenomenology which emphasizes the great importance of the first-person perspective for the investigation of neural correlates of consciousness (Desbordes & Negi, 2013; Lifshitz, Cusumano, & Raz, 2013; Oakley & Halligan, 2013; see Chapters 6 and 15). For a comparison in terms of subjective experience and underlying neural dynamics, future studies should employ within-subject designs that allow the contrast of directly different hypnotic and meditative states (Dumont et al., 2012; Grant, 2012). Of course, this approach requires participants who are highly trained in mind-altering techniques so that they can reliably enter distinct states of consciousness and provide detailed reports retrospectively or during the experiment.

The trait of Absorption and different types of absorption states—ranging from absorbed daydreaming, to focused attention during concentrative meditation and hypnotic trance, and on to deep immersion into mystical experiences of non-duality—represent important facets to consider when characterizing the neurobiological changes brought about via altered planes of consciousness.

References

Awasthi, B. (2013). Issues and perspectives in meditation research: in search for a definition. *Frontiers in Psychology*, **3**, 613. doi: org/10.3389/fpsyg.2012.00613

Brefczynski-Lewis, J. A., Lutz, A., Schaefer, H. S., Levinson, D. B., & Davidson, R. J. (2007). Neural correlates of attentional expertise in long-term meditation practitioners. *Proceedings of the National Academy of Sciences of the United States of America*, **104**(27), 11483–11488. doi: org/10.1073/pnas.0606552104

Brewer, J. A., Worhunsky, P. D., Gray, J. R., Tang, Y.-Y., Weber, J., & Kober, H. (2011). Meditation experience is associated with differences in default mode network activity and connectivity. *Proceedings of the National Academy of Sciences of the United States of America*, **108**(50), 20254–20259. doi: org/10.1073/pnas.1112029108

Cardeña, E., Jönsson, P., Terhune, D. B., & Marcusson-Clavertz, D. (2013). The neurophenomenology of neutral hypnosis. *Cortex*, **49**(2), 375–385. doi: org/10.1016/j.cortex.2012.04.001

Chen, A. C. (2009). Higher cortical modulation of pain perception in the human brain: psychological determinant. *Neuroscience Bulletin*, **25**(5), 267–276. doi: org/10.1007/s12264-009-0918-z

Cloninger, C. R., Przybeck, T. R., Svrakic, D. M., & Wetzel, R. D. (1994). *The Temperament and Character Inventory: a guide to its development and use*. St Louis: Washington University Center for Psychobiology of Personality.

Deeley, Q., Oakley, D. A., Toone, B., Giampietro, V., Brammer, M. J., Williams, S. C. R., & Halligan, P. W. (2012). Modulating the default mode network using hypnosis. *International Journal of Clinical and Experimental Hypnosis*, **60**(2), 206–228. doi: org/10.1080/00207144.2012.648070

Desbordes, G., & Negi, L. T. (2013). A new era for mind studies: training investigators in both scientific and contemplative methods of inquiry. *Frontiers in Human Neuroscience*, **7**, 741. doi: org/10.3389/fnhum.2013.00741

Dittrich, A. (1998). The standardized psychometric assessment of altered states of consciousness (ASCs) in humans. *Pharmacopsychiatry*, **31**(Suppl 2), 80–84. doi: org/10.1055/s-2007-979351

Dumont, L., Martin, C., & Broer, I. (2012). Functional neuroimaging studies of hypnosis and meditation: a comparative perspective. *Journal of Mind–Body Regulation*, **2**(1), 58–70. Retrieved from http://mbr.synergiesprairies.ca/mbr/index.php/mbr/article/view/515/127

Faymonville, M.-E., Boly, M., & Laureys, S. (2006). Functional neuroanatomy of the hypnotic state. *Journal of Physiology (Paris)*, **99**(4–6), 463–469. doi: org/10.1016/j.jphysparis.2006.03.018

Fox, K. C. R., Nijeboer, S., Dixon, M. L., Floman, J. L., Ellamil, M., Rumak, S. P., . . . Christoff, K. (2014). Is meditation associated with altered brain structure? A systematic review and meta-analysis of morphometric neuroimaging in meditation practitioners. *Neuroscience and Biobehavioral Reviews*, **43**, 48–73. http://doi.org/10.1016/j.neubiorev.2014.03.016

Grant, J. (2012). Towards a more meaningful comparison of meditation and hypnosis. *Journal of Mind–Body Regulation*, **2**(1), 71–74. Retrieved from http://mbr.synergiesprairies.ca/mbr/index.php/mbr/article/view/518/124

Grant, J. A., Duerden, E. G., Courtemanche, J., Cherkasova, M., Duncan, G. H., & Rainville, P. (2013). Cortical thickness, mental absorption and meditative practice: possible implications for disorders of attention. *Biological Psychology*, **92**(2), 275–281. doi: org/10.1016/j.biopsycho.2012.09.007

Hasenkamp, W. (2014). Using first-person reports during meditation to investigate basic cognitive experience. In S. Schmidt & H. Walach (Eds.), *Meditation—neuroscientific approaches and philosophical implications* (pp. 75–113). Cham, Switzerland: Springer.

Hasenkamp, W., Wilson-Mendenhall, C. D., Duncan, E., & Barsalou, L. W. (2012). Mind wandering and attention during focused meditation: a fine-grained temporal analysis of fluctuating cognitive states. *NeuroImage*, **59**(1), 750–760. doi: org/10.1016/j.neuroimage.2011.07.008

Hölzel, B., & Ott, U. (2006). Relationships between meditation depth, absorption, meditation practice, and mindfulness: a latent variable approach. *Journal of Transpersonal Psychology*, **28**(2), 179–199.

Huber, A., Lui, F., Duzzi, D., Pagnoni, G., & Porro, C. A. (2014). Structural and functional cerebral correlates of hypnotic suggestibility. *PloS One*, **9**(3), e93187. doi: org/10.1371/journal.pone.0093187

Jamieson, G. A. (2005). The modified Tellegen Absorption Scale: a clearer window on the structure and meaning of absorption. *Australian Journal of Clinical and Experimental Hypnosis*, **33**(2), 119–139.

Josipovic, Z. (2014). Neural correlates of nondual awareness in meditation. *Annals of the New York Academy of Sciences*, **1307**, 9–18. doi: org/10.1111/nyas.12261

Kirsch, I. (1997). Suggestibility or hypnosis: what do our scales really measure? *International Journal of Clinical and Experimental Hypnosis*, **45**(3), 212–225. doi: org/10.1080/00207149708416124

Lifshitz, M., Cusumano, E. P., & Raz, A. (2013). Hypnosis as neurophenomenology. *Frontiers in Human Neuroscience*, **7**, 469. doi: org/10.3389/fnhum.2013.00469

Lifshitz, M., Cusumano, E. P., & Raz, A. (2014). Meditation and hypnosis at the intersection between phenomenology and cognitive science. In S. Schmidt & H. Walach (Eds.), *Meditation—neuroscientific approaches and philosophical implications* (pp. 211–226). Cham, Switzerland: Springer.

Nash, J. D., & Newberg, A. (2013). Toward a unifying taxonomy and definition for meditation. *Frontiers in Psychology*, **4**, 806. doi: org/10.3389/fpsyg.2013.00806

Oakley, D. A., & Halligan, P. W. (2013). Hypnotic suggestion: opportunities for cognitive neuroscience. *Nature Reviews: Neuroscience*, **14**(8), 565–576. doi: org/10.1038/nrn3538

Ott, U. (2007). States of absorption: in search of neurobiological foundations. In G. A. Jamieson (Ed.), *Hypnosis and consciousness states: the cognitive-neuroscience perspective* (pp. 257–270). New York, NY: Oxford University Press.

Ott, U., Reuter, M., Hennig, J., & Vaitl, D. (2005). Evidence for a common biological basis of the Absorption trait, hallucinogen effects, and positive symptoms: epistasis between 5-HT2a and COMT polymorphisms. *American Journal of Medical Genetics. Part B, Neuropsychiatric Genetics*, **137B**(1), 29–32. doi: org/10.1002/ajmg.b.30197

Pekala, R. J. (1991). *Quantifying consciousness. An empirical approach*. New York, NY: Plenum.

Peper, E., Wilson, V. E., Gunkelman, J., Kawakami, M., Sata, M., Barton, W., & Johnston, J. (2006). Tongue piercing by a Yogi: QEEG observations. *Applied Psychophysiology and Biofeedback*, **31**(4), 331–338. doi: org/10.1007/s10484-006-9025-3

Piron, H. (2001). The Meditation Depth Index (MEDI) and the Meditation Depth Questionnaire (MEDEQ). *Journal for Meditation and Meditation Research*, **1**, 69–92. [Available from the author on request]

Presciuttini, S., Gialluisi, A., Barbuti, S., Curcio, M., Scatena, F., Carli, G., & Santarcangelo, E. L. (2014). Hypnotizability and catechol-O-methyltransferase (COMT) polymorphisms in Italians. *Frontiers in Human Neuroscience*, **7**, 929. doi: org/10.3389/fnhum.2013.00929

Rainville, P., Hofbauer, R. K., Bushnell, M. C., Duncan, G. H., & Price, D. D. (2002). Hypnosis modulates activity in brain structures involved in the regulation of consciousness. *Journal of Cognitive Neuroscience*, **14**(6), 887–901. doi: org/10.1162/089892902760191117

Schmidt, S. (2014). Opening up meditation for science: the development of a meditation classification system. In S. Schmidt & H. Walach (Eds.), *Meditation—neuroscientific approaches and philosophical implications* (pp. 137–152). Cham, Switzerland: Springer.

Studerus, E., Gamma, A., Kometer, M., & Vollenweider, F. X. (2012). Prediction of psilocybin response in healthy volunteers. *PloS One*, 7(2), e30800. doi: org/10.1371/journal.pone.0030800

Studerus, E., Gamma, A., & Vollenweider, F. X. (2010). Psychometric evaluation of the altered states of consciousness rating scale (OAV). *PloS One*, 5(8), e12412. doi: org/10.1371/journal.pone.0012412

Tart, C. T. (1975). *States of consciousness*. New York, NY: Dutton.

Tart, C. T. (1980). A systems approach to altered states of consciousness. In J. M. Davidson & R. J. Davidson (Eds.), *The psychobiology of consciousness* (pp. 243–269). New York, NY: Plenum.

Tellegen, A., & Atkinson, G. (1974). Openness to absorbing and self-altering experiences ("absorption"), a trait related to hypnotic susceptibility. *Journal of Abnormal Psychology*, **83**(3), 268–277.

Thalbourne, M. A. (1998). Transliminality: further correlates and a short measure. *Journal of the American Society for Psychical Research*, **92**, 402–419.

Walsh, R. (1995). Phenomenological mapping: a method for describing and comparing states of consciousness. *Journal of Transpersonal Psychology*, **27**(1), 25–56.

Wittmann, M. & Schmidt, S. (2014). Mindfulness meditation and the experience of time. In S. Schmidt & H. Walach (Eds.), *Meditation—neuroscientific approaches and philosophical implications* (pp. 199–209). Cham, Switzerland: Springer.

Part 5

Neural underpinnings

Chapter 15

Toward comprehensive neurophenomenological research in hypnosis and meditation

Etzel Cardeña

Abstract

Research on conscious experience during hypnosis and meditation has been fraught with oversimplifications that have hidden differences across procedures and goals, changes in state, and individual differences. Each of these issues involves complex questions and methodological challenges. A neurophenomenological approach drawing on subjective data in concert with neuroscientific methods can clarify the intricacies of both phenomenological and neurological processes. After reviewing the relevant literature, this chapter presents examples from the author's neurophenomenological research on hypnosis, pointing out various conceptual and methodological issues to be considered. Integrating first-person methods can enrich and guide the analysis of third-person neuroimaging data and vice versa, as long as both approaches are pursued at a similar depth.

Introduction

Research on conscious experience during hypnosis and meditation has been fraught with over-simplifications. This tendency has hidden distinctions between specific procedures and goals, transitions between states of consciousness, short-term consciousness alterations, short- and long-term changes in cognition and personality, and individual differences in the propensity to be affected by meditative or hypnotic procedures. Each of these issues involves complex questions and methodological challenges, which not infrequently are ignored.

If a search for the neurological underpinnings of phenomenal experience is attempted, it is also not infrequent that psychosocial aspects are glossed over while the lion's share of methodological attention is placed on the acquisition and analysis of neural signals. To give but one example from what could be a much longer list, in a functional magnetic resonance imaging (fMRI) and electroencephalography (EEG) study with a "hypnotic virtuoso," the authors failed to report information essential to understanding the hypnotic procedure, including the specific induction used, the nature of the relationship between hypnotizer and participant, how the participant's hypnotic experience was evaluated, the confounding use of post-hypnotic amnesia, and so on (Lipari et al., 2012). In my comment on that paper (Cardeña, 2012), I wrote that the study of conscious experience through brain imaging techniques needs to be a "marriage of equals," requiring conceptual and methodological sophistication in both conscious experiences and the neurosciences. If that is the case, a neurophenomenological approach drawing on subjective data in concert with neuroimaging methods will help clarify the intricacies of both conscious and neurological processes.

The study of conscious experience

Psychology as a systematic and independent discipline began at the end of the nineteenth century (although many of its fundamental ideas and assumptions have, of course, a much longer history; see Robinson, 1995) and had the study of conscious experience as a central problem. Although behaviorism, which came to dominate psychology for most of the twentieth century, sought to invalidate consciousness as a legitimate topic, the situation has changed considerably in the last couple of decades. Consciousness has become a "hot topic" in psychology, the neurosciences, philosophy, and the humanities, although the different concepts and problems of consciousness are often glossed over (see Natsoulas, 1981, 1983). Furthermore, misunderstandings about the limitations of introspective inquiry have made some contemporary scientists wonder whether they can scientifically study conscious experience.

Some common fallacies about the first-person study of conscious experience

The current interest in the study of consciousness has obscured the fact that, despite the dominance of behaviorism in psychology for a number of decades, courageous authors produced relevant and valuable theoretical and empirical works during that period of conceptual "exile" (see, for instance, the reference list in Farthing, 1992). Unfortunately, some of the current discussions on the "new" science of consciousness have ignored the work done between William James and his contemporaries and our days, perhaps because of the nonsensical assumption that conscious experience could not be studied until we developed brain-imaging technology. To name but a few examples, investigators from the Society for Psychical Research were not only concerned with evaluating the possibility of anomalous cognition but also investigated different states of consciousness in mediumship and dissociation (e.g., Troubridge, 1922), the behaviorist Clark L. Hull (1933) studied hypnosis programmatically, and Heinrich Klüver (1928) researched eidetic imagery and perceptual constants produced by mescal consumption. Additionally, of course, in the 1960s there was a plethora of studies on conscious experience in daydreaming, hypnosis, meditation, drug intoxication, and so on (e.g., Singer, 1966; Tart, 1969). Current pronouncements of a "new" science of consciousness show historical naiveté or unjustified disregard of many previous studies in the field. Strawson (2015) makes an even stronger case that philosophical discussions of consciousness have been pursued continuously for centuries and that the topic was not just recently discovered.

One of the main topics discussed in the last few years has been whether and how first-person, introspective reports can be integrated with third-person methods, an idea anchored in the distinction between knowledge by description and by acquaintance, made in 1865 by John Grote and discussed by, among others, William James (1890) and Bertrand Russell (1910–1911). A series of articles (Jack & Roepstorff, 2003–2004) dedicated to the nature and uses of introspection and its possible integration with third-person methods showed that, with few exceptions (such as that of Daniel Dennett), not many authors continue to hold the original or refried versions of radical behaviorism. Nonetheless, some continue to affirm questionable or outright false ideas about the first-person, or introspective, study of phenomenal consciousness. I will now briefly discuss some of them.

There is one form of introspection

By definition, first-person reports involve introspection, which according to the *Oxford English Dictionary* (Soanes, 2001) refers to "the examination or observation of one's thoughts or feelings." Behind this simple idea, there are many types of introspection. One major dimension is whether the person doing the introspection is a naïve or a trained type of introspector. I will describe the type of preparation required in classical phenomenological inquiry, but there have been other types of training, including the analytical handbooks that E. B. Titchener created to teach his participants to analyze experience into its assumed constituents (although he was moving toward a more generally phenomenological stance; see Evans, 1972). More recently, the evaluation and report of perceptual and other experiences according to previously established categories were put to good use by Siegel and West (1975) in their study of experiences associated with ingesting different psychedelic drugs.

In the context of the present chapter, it is interesting to compare how some types of introspective inquiry resemble forms of meditation. Thus, asking participants, as Titchener did, to remain attentive to the sensory qualities of a stimulus is not that dissimilar to focusing meditation, whereas a non-judgmental phenomenological stance to the vagaries of conscious experience is not that dissimilar from the non-judgmental witnessing aspect of mindfulness meditation.

Another option in introspective inquiry is whether to pose open questions to participants about their conscious experiences (e.g., Hurlburt & Schwitzgebel, 2007) or ask them to evaluate them according to specific categories (e.g., Easterlin & Cardeña, 1998/99). A more general issue discussed within anthropology (e.g., Turnbull, 1990) and psychology (Tart, 1972) is whether researchers can even understand some introspective reports if they have not had similar experiences themselves. A counterweight to this argument is that the experimenter may become untowardly biased towards such reports, or may too easily assume that his or her previous experience is equivalent (or not) to that of the participant.

Introspection has been shown to be invalid and unreliable

The "received" (but questionable) wisdom is that psychology abandoned introspection as a research method because it was shown to be invalid and unreliable (Boring, 1953). A later reappraisal by Danziger (1980), however, concluded that the abandonment of introspection was "less a victim of its intrinsic problems than a casualty of historical forces far bigger than itself" (p. 260).

From the beginning, introspection was considered "difficult and fallible . . . [but] the difficulty is simply that of all observation of whatever kind" (James, 1890, p. 191). Unfortunately, this warning about the difficulty of *any type* of observation is often ignored, especially by some laypeople and journalists who hold the notion that neuroimaging is *ipso facto* a more "objective" or "scientific" method than others that do not evaluate brain processes. There is increasing pushback against this notion, with various authors pointing out the "subjectivity" in deciding which neuroscientific data are relevant and what they mean, and how issues of validity, reliability, replicability, and even correct use of statistics haunt brain imaging (Bennett, Baird, Miller, & Wolford, 2010; Tallis, 2011; Vul, Harris, Winkielman, & Pashler, 2009).

Ultimately, the value of any method, whether neuroscientific or introspective, depends on systematic and unbiased research that helps rule out artifacts and reasonable alternative hypotheses, produces verifiable results, and enhances our understanding of the phenomenon investigated.

According to these criteria, one type of introspection has shown to be (imperfectly, as James (1890) had remarked) valid and reliable (Cardeña & Pekala, 2014; Jack & Roepstorff, 2003–2004; Petitmengin & Bitbol, 2009; Singer & Kolligan, 1987). This type refers to reporting of the contents of consciousness, as contrasted with inferences of why we do what we do (Güzeldere, 1995). The latter is a process at which we are very fallible since we are not aware of all the factors that co-determine behavior (Nisbett & Wilson, 1977; but see also Smith & Miller, 1978).

Concerning the validity and reliability of introspective reports about the contents of experience, a couple of examples should suffice. There are *many* neurological cross-validations of hypnotic experience. One that received a lot of attention found that the brain activity of highly hypnotizable participants given the hypnotic suggestion to see a colored pattern in grays (or to see a gray scale pattern as colored) was consistent with the suggestions given and the reported experience of the participants (Kosslyn, Thompson, Costantini-Ferrando, Alpert, & Spiegel, 2000). With regard to reliability, the study by Siegel and West (1975) found that different, trained individuals produced very similar reports about the quality and sequence of experiences during intoxication with specific hallucinogens (I also discuss consistency in the reporting of subjective experiences of highly hypnotizable individuals).

Introspection has not been used in decades

It will probably surprise the reader to read that the creator of an introspective method we will discuss shortly was none other than the behaviorist John Watson (1920). The shock of the surprise should be mitigated by the realization that psychological research very often takes for granted that some type of introspection underlies reports of perception (e.g., conscious recognition of stimuli), memory (what am I aware of remembering?), and personality (what am I conscious of doing in a particular situation?), among other areas (Wilson, 2003). That introspection is assumed rather than underlined in these various areas of research does not mitigate its importance.

Introspection has methodological problems that "objective" methods do not

As mentioned, James (1890) thought that the difficulties with introspection were not of a different kind than those encountered with other types of observations, and here I can list some of the major ones (see Cardeña & Pekala, 2014 for a discussion of how to address these issues systematically):

- Memory problems, including forgetting (especially when the event to be reported is not recent), reconstruction errors/confabulation (which may make an experience more or less "ordinary" than it actually was), and inaccessibility to memories due to state-specific memory and verbal description difficulties.
- Possible distortion of phenomenal experience through observation (see the section "Methods to study conscious experience"), reporting of inferences about observations instead of the observations themselves, and the use of inadequate metrics to evaluate an experience (see Overgaard, Fehl, Mouridsen, Bergholt, & Cleeremans, 2008 for an example of the latter).
- Social factors including censorship of socially awkward material, dissembling because of social desirability, demand characteristics, and experimenter effects.

However, all of these factors can influence not only introspective reports but reports in general (including reports about what a non-human machine has recorded). For instance, it is indeed the case that introspecting on one's mental experience may affect the latter, just the same way as setting up a person in front of a terminal to do an attention experiment will alter the attentional processes that the person had before sitting in front of the computer as part of an experiment, thus the ecological validity of such experiments should be evaluated rather than assumed. Only unobtrusive measures, which are rarely used in psychological research, can claim to not alter the individual.

The one factor that has been singled out as most problematic in introspection is the lack of independent verification or its "subjectivity," but the same thing can be said of reports about "external" events (the reports by others of, for instance, seeing an object could refer to a different object despite using the same word). Ultimately, "objective data" depend on the "subjective" conscious experiences of scientists, which are shared with other conscious experients and are framed according to ontological and epistemological assumptions. Velmans (1993) has elegantly discussed how the boundary between "objective" and "subjective" is one of degree rather than of kind. Also in this regard, Searle (1990) has made a useful distinction between what he calls epistemic and ontological subjectivity; the former depends on value judgments (e.g., Searle is a much better philosopher than Dennett), whereas the latter refers to the conscious experience of an individual. Epistemic subjectivity suffuses all "objective" methods, from the type of questions I believe are worth pursuing using my EEG setup, to evaluating when a trial begins and ends, to which filters I use and which epochs I consider artifactual, to which "outlier" data I think should be removed, to how to interpret numerical differences, and so on. All sources of data, including the most technologically advanced ones, may be misleading, and it is "good scientific practice" (Gallagher, 2003, p. 90) to corroborate them by analyzing all aspects of the report (for instance, its internal consistency) and seeking converging evidence, whether psychophysiological or the report of similar observers in similar circumstances.

Methods to study conscious experience

Before discussing various introspective methods, I should clarify that I do not refer here to the various ways in which conscious experience may be altered, whether by psychological, pharmacological, or other means (for an account of many of these see Cardeña & Winkelman, 2011 a, 2011b), but to first-person or introspective methods to evaluate phenomenal experience, whether spontaneous or following some procedure to alter the state of consciousness. The characteristics of every method subsume strengths and weaknesses. For instance, the advantages implicit in a very controlled context are usually obtained through sacrificing the ecological validity or generalizability of the findings to more naturalistic environments in which many variables interact. In the more specific case of introspective methods, the thoroughness and specificity of a case study usually comes at the price of generalizability, whereas with questionnaires, exactly the opposite is true. In Table 15.1, I compare the general strengths and weaknesses of the methods I describe (see also Cardeña & Pekala, 2014).

I divide the methods here into concurrent and retrospective, but concurrent techniques are not perfectly concurrent insofar as even a fraction of a second will elapse between an experience and its reporting, verbal or otherwise. For most practical purposes, however, such lapses will likely not be of great import, and one of the great advantages of these methods is that they are not as vulnerable to forgetfulness and/or reconstruction as retrospective techniques. Here are some concurrent methods that can be used to study conscious experience:

1. In *thinking out loud*, the participant verbalizes what is going through his/her mind while carrying out a particular task such as solving a problem or being asked to verbalize all mental events during a ganzfeld experiment (e.g., Marcusson-Clavertz & Cardeña, 2011). Although, in general, the only side-effect of the technique is to increase the time to complete a task such as problem

Table 15.1 Comparative characteristics of introspective methods

	Discovery	Quantification	Distortion	Integration	Comprehensive
Phenomenology	+			+	+
Thinking out loud	+			+	
Event recording		+		+	
Experience sampling	+	+		+	
Depth rating		+		+	
Diaries	+		+		+
Case study	+				+
Interview	+			+	
Content analysis	+	+	+	+	
Questionnaires, tests		+	+	+	
Surveys		+	+		

Discovery = likelihood of obtaining new insights. Quantification = ease with which the data can be quantified and analyzed. Distortion = ease with which information may be distorted. Integration = how easily it can be integrated with other methods. Comprehensive = likelihood of obtaining a thorough account.

From Cardeña & Pekala, 2014, p. 26

solution (Fox, Ericsson, & Best, 2011), there are instances in which it may have a more reactive effect (Schooler, 2011), so the experimenter should try to evaluate that possibility first.

2. In *event recording,* the individual marks, through a counter or some other device, every instance of a previously defined event, such as instances of obsessive thoughts (in a clinical context) or mind-wandering episodes during a meditation session (Hasenkamp, Wilson-Mendenhall, Duncan, & Barsalou, 2011; Kubose, 1976).

3. *Experience or thought sampling* requires that the person report what she/he was experiencing just before a pager or a similar device went off. The query may be wide open (Hurlburt & Schwitzgebel, 2007) or address shifts in conscious experience and mind wandering (e.g., Killingsworth & Gilbert, 2010) or specific experiential categories (for an example in meditation, see Easterlin & Cardeña, 1998–1999).

4. *Depth ratings* inquire about the level or "depth" or intensity of a particular experience at a particular time, and can include a definition of experiential landmarks such as claiming that at a certain depth of hypnosis the mind will be completely still (Tart, 1979), or remain undefined as to the characteristics of different depth levels. Depth, whether reported verbally or behaviorally (e.g., McConkey, Barnier, & Szeps, 2001), has been mostly researched in hypnosis but there is no reason it might not be used in other areas (e.g., to measure level or depth of engagement in a particular experience).

Retrospective methods evaluate non-immediate conscious experiences. Although recollection problems are their weakest point, these techniques offer other advantages such as providing a longitudinal account of the long-term effect and possible reinterpretation of an experience. There are a number of reasons why a later reinterpretation may provide more valid information than an instantaneous one. For instance, erotic or ritually induced experiences do not easily allow for a contemporary report (Cardeña, 2009; Cardeña, Van Duijl, Weiner, & Terhune, 2009). Another reason is that later reflexion may illuminate aspects that could not be realized at the moment. To use a familiar example, how many times has a young person sincerely and vehemently expressed that she /he could only love once with such intensity, to find out later that this "once in a lifetime" event actually makes repeated visits and that she/he had misjudged the original experience? Or, in the spiritual realm, a mystical event may seem to the person intense enough to produce a lifelong effect, only to find out that it dissipates after a while without leaving much of a trace. As the extraordinary set of films *7UP* (which follows a group of people every 7 years) reveals, some patterns become clearer when revisited retrospectively. Here are some retrospective methods that can be used to study conscious experience:

1. *Diaries* provide longitudinal narratives of individuals' lives (or a segment of them), focused on specific experiences, as in the dream diaries of a teenager (Bulkeley, 2012), or on the short- and long-term effects of mystical experiences, as in the writings of Santa Teresa de Jesús (see Cangas, Sass, & Pérez-Álvarez, 2008).

2. In *case studies,* various methods such as interviews, experimental techniques, and others target the conscious experience of an individual (but also, potentially, of a group of individuals) across time and circumstances (e. g., Luria, 1968; Sacks, 1995). This focused approach may be extended throughout the person's *life history* (e.g., Hilts, 1996).

3. Although *interviews* are a basic staple in clinical psychology, they do not receive the attention in research that they should. (How often do research psychologists receive training in conducting good interviews, in contrast with just learning to "run subjects"?) There are many options when it comes to interviewing about conscious occurrences, from wide-open, non-directive interviews (e.g., what did you experience during . . . ?) to more or less directive and structured questions (Kvale & Brinkmann, 2008).

4. Common in research is the use of *psychological tests, surveys,* and *questionnaires,* a number of which are geared to the evaluation of conscious experience and have good psychometric characteristics (for reviews of many of these instruments see Cardeña & Pekala, 2014; MacDonald, LeClair, Holland, Alter, & Friedman, 1995). Although they are easy to administer, even to large groups, and are usually free or inexpensive, they may hide important differences in how the respondents interpret the questions and/or response options, and cannot provide a nuanced, specific account of the content of the experience.

5. If there is already a record of introspective reports from interviews, diaries, or other verbal material, qualitative and/or quantitative *content analyses* can help determine semantic or syntactic patterns within a report or across reports (Krippendorff, 2004), and can differentiate across types of experiences (e.g., Oxman, Rosenberg, Schnurr, Tucker, & Gala, 1988).

6. Because each method has strengths and weaknesses, an *integration* of various techniques will likely offer a more comprehensive account of conscious experience (see Table 15.1). Later in this chapter, I describe my rationale in employing various methods and how they supplement each other.

Factors in the study of hypnosis and meditation

There are so many variations within hypnosis and meditation that it is risky to make generalizations about them, but the following factors should be kept in mind to reduce the likelihood of confounds.

Factors regarding hypnosis

Individual differences

Research has shown that there are valid and reliable individual variations in the ability to respond to a hypnotic procedure, also known as hypnotizability or hypnotic suggestibility or susceptibility, which shows remarkable consistency throughout life (Barnier & Council, 2010). People varying in hypnotizability level are typically compared to ascertain whether a hypnotic procedure, rather than a more general factor, produces an effect. If people exhibiting different hypnotizabillity levels react similarly to a specific hypnotic procedure, we have reason to assume that the responsible mechanism is not hypnosis but another factor such as general relaxation or demand characteristics (e.g., Cardeña et al., 2012). The level of hypnotizability is pertinent not only to the use of hypnosis, but also to non-hypnotic suggestions (e.g., McGeown et al., 2012) and the propensity to have anomalous experience (Cardeña, 2014; Cardeña, Lynn, & Krippner, 2014; Pekala, Kumar, & Marcano, 1995).

Within-group differences

Besides the differences *across* levels of hypnotizability, there are also differences *within* levels of hypnotizability. There is growing evidence that within the group of the high hypnotizables there are at least two different types, one exhibiting greater imaginative ability, the other a greater sense of involuntariness (e.g., Terhune & Cardeña, 2010), partly supporting the distinction that T. X. Barber (1999) proposed between the fantasy-prone, the dissociative, and the highly motivated type of high hypnotizable.

Interaction of hypnotizability with other variables

A major thrust of our laboratory has been to evaluate whether dissociativity (the tendency for experiential disconnectedness and/or cognitive/phenomenological compartmentalization; Cardeña, 1994) interacts with hypnotizability. We have found significant differences between high hypnotizables who are or are not also highly dissociative within the hypnotic context, in other laboratory settings, and in everyday experiences (Cardeña & Marcusson-Clavertz, in press; Marcusson-Clavertz, Terhune, & Cardeña, 2012). Of course, other variables that may interact with hypnotizability should also be evaluated depending on the empirical question asked.

Comparison of a hypnotic induction independent of other suggestions

It is not uncommon to find studies in which a putative hypnotic state is assumed while ignoring the potential effects of the specific verbiage used in the induction (Oakley, 2008). For instance, the relaxation so often attributed to hypnotic procedures is an artifact of specific inductions that use relaxation or sleep suggestions and do not manifest in other procedures that do not use relaxation as part of the induction (Cardeña, Alarcón, Capafons, & Bayot, 1998). A good way to evaluate the effect of an induction is to compare groups varying in hypnotizability before and after an induction (De Pascalis & Penna, 1990). An alternative is to use a *neutral* hypnosis condition, trying to avoid as much as possible specific suggestions, although of course just the mention of the word "hypnosis" elicits expectations and assumptions (Gandhi & Oakley, 2005).

Evaluation of specific verbalizations

Both clinical and research hypnosis emphasize that great care must be placed on the phrasing of specific suggestions, although unfortunately, researchers do not report exact wording as often as they should. The importance of this factor is exemplified by the conclusion that contrasting event-related potentials (ERP) results during hypnotically induced hallucinations might be explained by the difference in phrasing between the suggestions used (Spiegel & Barabasz, 1988). Another example is that brain areas correlated with the *pain matrix* respond differently to suggestions related to pain sensation than to those directed to the emotional impact of such sensation (Rainville, Duncan, Price, Carrier, & Bushnell, 1997).

Changes within the hypnotic state

The notion of a hypnotic *depth* level implies that the state of consciousness after a hypnotic procedure is not static but may differ across time. A number of studies going back more than a century have sought to make a cartography of such levels, but clearly this area needs more attention (Cardeña, 2014). In this chapter, I describe changes within the hypnotic state(s) of individuals with high responsivity to hypnosis, along with the correlated brain functions. An area that also deserves more attention is the transitional stages between states, which at least in some cases (e.g., waking–sleep transitions) entail cognitive disorganization (e.g., Foulkes & Vogel, 1965).

The hypnotic relationship

A paradox within hypnosis is that although the social interaction is basic to some definitions of hypnotic procedures (Barnier & Nash, 2008), very little, if anything, is written about it in research reports. Having been on both ends of the hypnotic dyad, I know that my willingness to remain open to suggestions largely depends on how much I like and trust the hypnotist. Treating sentient individuals as *subjects* who just produce data may have a deleterious effect on how much they are willing to engage in the process. This factor should receive far more attention in the training of new researchers and in the actual conduct of experiments.

Factors regarding meditation

Level of training

Meditative practices are often seen as a long-term, if not lifelong, commitment and researchers have found differences between beginners, those with some months or years of experience, and those with many years' practice (e.g., Lutz, Brefczynski-Lewis, Johnstone, & Davidson, 2008). In concordance with some traditional texts, the effects of practice do not seem to be linear, but may show up as sudden developments (e.g., Thomas, Jamieson, & Cohen, 2014).

Evaluation of different meditative practices

Probably even more so than hypnosis, the practice of which can vary (e.g., Ericksonian metaphorical versus more directive approaches), meditation includes a variety of practices (e.g., concentrative, insight, compassion-based, and their mixtures and variations; Goleman, 1988) and goals (e.g., therapeutic, personal growth) that should be distinguished and evaluated accordingly (Grant, 2012). Other potentially important factors such as motivation need to be taken into account (Cardeña, Sjöstedt, & Marcusson-Clavertz, 2015).

Evaluation of social interactions and specific communications

Although suggestion is sometimes considered to be a differentiating aspect between hypnosis and meditation, this may partly result from the lack of research on the specific communications between meditation teachers and their students, along with the ensuing expectations (Lynn, Malaktaris, Maxwell, Mellinger, & Van del Kloet, 2012). The emotional relationship between mentor and meditation student also deserves much more study.

Changes within a state and across time

As with hypnosis, changes in phenomenal experience, even within the same session, should be evaluated, rather than assuming that an overall description suffices for the session (see Hasenkamp et al., 2011). Because there are intensive retreat practices in meditation (e.g., Zen sessions in which many hours of meditation, throughout many days, occur), longitudinal studies could evaluate changes not only over a period of years but also during these intensified events and during the meditation sessions themselves.

Individual differences

Individual differences in the ability to meditate have rarely been investigated systematically (an exception is Maupin, 1965), although practitioners of similar length of practice exhibit phenomenal and neurological differences (Hinterberg, 2014). It would greatly add to our understanding of the response to meditation to investigate the proximal and distal sources of such differences and how they interact with such constructs as absorption, mental boundaries, and self-transcendence, which are related to hypnotizability (Cardeña & Terhune, 2014).

Toward a variegated neurophenomenology

The term *neurophenomenology* was probably coined by Laughlin, McManus, and d'Aquili (1990), who championed the idea in anthropology that behavior and experience are mediated by brain structure and functions, and that considerations of genetic and central nervous system (CNS) function are basic to anthropological discourse (for an alternative view to the traditional model of brain producing mind, see Hoffman, 2008; Kelly et al., 2007). The current use of the term in the neurosciences can be traced to Francisco Varela (1996, p. 330) in his "quest to marry modern cognitive science and a *disciplined approach* to human experience [italics in the original]." Following his phenomenological orientation, he gave primacy to human experience through a "first-person" account, but one based on the development of a set of skills: attitude (the capacity to reflect on automatic assumption), intimacy (the cultivation of alternative forms of apprehension and intuition), a careful description of the contents of consciousness, and sustained training in these endeavors. Another cornerstone of psychological phenomenology is the notion that cognition is embedded within the experience of our embodiedness (Varela, Thompson, & Rosch, 1991).

Although Varela emphasized cognition rather than the neurosciences in his 1996 paper, two of his collaborators gave a succinct but general definition of neurophenomenology as the integration of first-person data about subjective experience with the neurodynamics of consciousness, presenting an example in which varying EEG data could be understood in the light of the person's varying conscious experience (Lutz & Thompson, 2003). In other terms, neurophenomenology can be generally considered as the attempt to synthesize first-person, introspective reports with third-person, neuroimaging, and cognitive data. Without using the term, Bernard Baars (1997) had also called for a similar integration by stating that first- and third-person reports can be functionally related, for instance by comparing the different brain activity in conscious versus non-conscious processes.

Whereas Varela had a very specific philosophical and methodological notion of phenomenology, the term has been also used more broadly. Amedeo Giorgi (1990) described his dialogical, phenomenological approach to interviewing individuals about their conscious experience. His approach shares some of Varela's general principles including the phenomenological *epoché*, or the attempt to "bracket" or suspend automatic assumptions about the nature of the experience and focus instead on how phenomena present themselves to consciousness, and a sensitivity toward and careful description of the contents of consciousness, but places the burden of maintaining this approach on the interviewer/researcher. (For a detailed discussion of how to conduct a phenomenological interview to discern the experienced conscious processes see Petitmengin, 2006.) Even more liberally, the term phenomenology has been used to denote the contents of phenomenal or conscious experience, as in the Phenomenology of Consciousness Inventory or PCI (Pekala, 1991).

In the examples in the following section, I use neurophenomenology in the general sense of attempting to synthesize systematic inquiry using a first-person approach with measures of brain functioning, within diverse experimental protocols. Although Varela et al. (1991) and other authors have championed the use of trained, skilled phenomenologists/meditators, I think it would be as partial and limiting to only use this kind of introspective report as it currently is to obtain information only from convenience samples (i.e., Western undergraduate students; see Henrich, Heine, & Norenzayan, 2010). Not only are meditators skilled in phenomenology a very small segment of the population but there are also some experiences that require full experiential surrender (Naranjo & Ornstein, 1971). To assert that neurophenomenology is applicable to contemplative religious experience, as Thompsons does (2009), while disregarding the ecstatic, Dionysian, uncontrolled aspects of some religious experiences (Cardeña, 2009; Kripal, 2014) falls short of a comprehensive neurophenomenological, cross-cultural, and multi-methodological account of all of human experience, as William James envisioned psychology should be (Taylor, 1998).

Two examples of research on neutral hypnosis

The remainder of this chapter describes two studies in which I integrated diverse introspective and EEG techniques, attempting to clarify the neurophenomenology of spontaneous hypnotic phenomena. Both studies employed what has been called *neutral* hypnosis, purposefully in italics because "neutral" is a relative term since the mere use of the term "hypnosis" affects participants' responses (Gandhi & Oakley, 2005). Nonetheless, this technique helps to disentangle the effects of a hypnotic induction from those of the suggestions that typically follow it. In my studies, I minimized the effect of suggestions by using an induction procedure that consisted just of counting slowly from 1 to 30, with the sole suggestion that, as the count progressed, the participant would go into hypnosis and that she/he would continue to go deeper into hypnosis throughout the session. I should mention, though, that participants had been previously exposed to more traditional hypnotic inductions using relaxation and attention-focusing verbiage.

First study

In Study 1 (Cardeña, 2005; Figure 15.1), I had two main questions: are there patterns of common spontaneous hypnotic experiences among high hypnotizables? And, does type of physical activity affect such experiences? I adopted a 2 (hypnosis versus no hypnosis) × 3 (types of physical activity: quiescence, pedalling a stationary bike, or having a motor pedalling the stationary bike) factorial design. The first factor assumes that whatever effects hypnosis may have on experience, they will be more clearly seen in the group of individuals who are highly responsive to it.

Methodology. I first screened 147 individuals with a group hypnotizability scale and chose those who had scored at least 9 on a scale of 0–12. I then proceeded to administer more stringent individualized hypnosis scales to a subgroup of 23 individuals. I also included a clinical inventory to deselect those with marked psychological problems, for both ethical (i.e., to avoid potential negative reactions to the procedure) and conceptual (i.e., to distinguish purely hypnotic experiences from those related to psychopathology) reasons. Although hypnotic procedures are usually

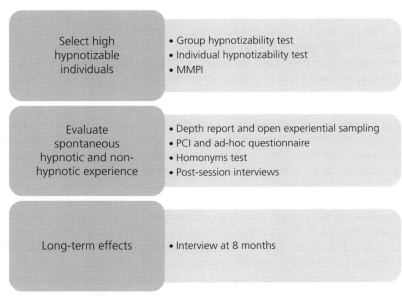

Select high hypnotizable individuals
- Group hypnotizability test
- Individual hypnotizability test
- MMPI

Evaluate spontaneous hypnotic and non-hypnotic experience
- Depth report and open experiential sampling
- PCI and ad-hoc questionnaire
- Homonyms test
- Post-session interviews

Long-term effects
- Interview at 8 months

Fig. 15.1 Design of first study employing neutral hypnosis.

experienced as positive, untoward reactions can occur and a clinically trained person should be part of the research team (Cardeña & Terhune, 2009).

I then proceeded to conduct the study with 12 individuals who continued to fulfill the inclusion criteria (i.e., high hypnotizability and lack of marked psychopathology). Next, I pilot tested the procedure to make sure that my tasks were clearly understandable and to ask the pilot participants for any suggestions on how to improve the procedure. A paradoxical aspect in much research with gifted or experienced participants is that they are not often asked to give their opinion on what research procedures work best for them.

For this chapter, what matters most are the five different methods I used to evaluate the contents of conscious experience. I first made certain during pilot testing that every time I said "state," a number expressing the depth of the hypnotic experience would come automatically to the participants' minds, according to a scale in which 0 = completely alert, 1–10 = feeling slightly different than normal, 11–20 = light hypnosis, and so on. I purposefully did not provide any definition of what constituted light, medium, or deep hypnosis because one of my questions was precisely what people experienced as different levels of hypnosis. During the experimental sessions themselves, I used the neutral induction procedure (counting slowly to 30) and then probed them with "state." Immediately after this probe, I asked participants "what are you experiencing?"—a deliberately open question following phenomenological principles—and recorded what they said and took notes.

I asked for a depth and experience report about 5 minutes after the end of each previous report, although participants had also been invited to initiate contact at any point if they so wanted. I decided against a random interval period to avoid the possibility of one probe quickly following another one and interfering with the experience. Also, pilot testing had shown that 5 minutes seemed an appropriate length of time that would not disrupt the experience too often, nor let it linger so much that aspects of it might be forgotten. Of course, there is nothing sacrosanct about this length of time, and I would expect that other time intervals would be better suited for other tasks and individuals.

I treated participants as co-researchers and pilot tested the procedures and solicited their input throughout the whole research. Edge (2014) has called for an ideal research team to include an expert meditator (hypnotic virtuoso, in my case), and I think that this more general approach gives greater flexibility than assuming that data should be secured only from contemplative, phenomenological practitioners.

The sessions' length was purposefully open, with no time constraints, but at somewhere around 45–75 minutes, participants started reporting less depth, at which point I employed a homonyms test (Secord, 1953). This test uses words with two meanings, one of which is physiological (e.g., organ), and asks for an immediate association. I had hypothesized that the different physical conditions (i.e., quiescent, pedalling, or motorized pedalling) would produce a different sense of embodiment and, thus, the association to the homonym would change according to the condition. However, I found that asking people to provide word associations during hypnosis disrupted their experience considerably. They mentioned that they rapidly started "coming out" of hypnosis while doing this task which, incidentally, did not produce any significant results. This made me realize that there is a limit to what can be inquired about during a hypnotic experience.

Afterwards, I administered a dehypnotization procedure, reversing the original number count. I then interviewed participants and went with them through the notes of what they had said to make sure that I had understood everything and to ask them if there was anything they wanted to add—a process somewhat similar to the video review of a hypnosis session with participants (Sheehan & McConkey, 1982). Finally, I asked volunteers to fill out the PCI for the deepest state during the session, and a list of possible conscious experiences (including no changes from ordinary experiences), rated according to when the participants had experienced these. The PCI (Pekala, 1991) is a psychometrically robust 53-item questionnaire in which the respondent chooses between bipolar statements (e.g., "I felt ecstatic and joyful" versus "I felt no feelings of being ecstatic or joyful") which are grouped in 12 major dimensions (e.g., altered experience, attention, internal dialog, imagery), and has been used in research on hypnosis, meditation, firewalking, and other phenomena (Cardeña & Pekala, 2014).

I also carried out control sessions in which I asked people *not* to do what they ordinarily did to go into hypnosis (the researcher should not assume that easily hypnotizable people may not use their talent when just asked to relax; see Hilgard & Tart, 1966, who also recommended repeated measured designs in this area) but just to be open to their experience. I then counted from 1 to 30, but without a suggestion to go into hypnosis. The control conditions were purposefully time-limited to three reports and lasted about 17 minutes, because pilot testing had shown that participants would get bored or fall asleep if the control condition lasted much longer. I also conducted an 8-month follow-up interview to ask about lingering effects from having participated in the project, which were uniformly positive, extending from greater ability to concentrate to a sense of deeper connectedness with their spirituality.

The procedure included different introspective methods to provide different information. The depth reports, in conjunction with the other methods, gave me an insight of what experiential features were attributed to different levels of hypnosis. It also gave me a sense of the progression of experienced depth. The PCI provided a statistical global assessment of how psychological processes differed across factors (hypnosis/no hypnosis, three levels of physical activity). What the PCI could not provide was information on the specific meaning of what, for example, an altered body sense meant, and here the experiential sampling and the ad hoc questionnaire elucidated the necessary content. Finally, the post-session interviews revealed if I had missed or misinterpreted any important information and helped me to clarify and expand the experiential accounts and other events that did not occur shortly before the probes and had therefore not been reported.

Results. The pattern that emerged after integrating the data from these complementary approaches was of a sequence of phenomenal events that corresponded to levels of self-assessed hypnotic depth. During light hypnosis, phenomenal consciousness was primarily concerned with alterations of body sensations and image; as depth increased, participants experienced floating or flying out of their physical bodies, with ensuing greater affect and imagery, culminating in deep hypnosis with experiences of "being in a different reality" as if in a dream or having various trans-personal experiences such as a sense of "being one with everything," "merging with a light," "a void," and so on. Overall, participants reported various alterations of consciousness and a sense of decreased rationality, control, self-awareness, and memory during deep hypnosis. The convergent validity of the results are supported by the strikingly similar descriptions of the stages in alterations of consciousness derived from the literature on mysticism and hallucinogenic transcendent experiences (cf. Shaw, 2015).

Second study

The second study (Cardeña, Jönsson, Terhune, & Marcusson-Clavertz, 2013) sought to advance the first one by using the whole spectrum of hypnotizability and evaluating the cortical under-pinnings of the spontaneous hypnotic experiences through spectral analysis and global functional connectivity.

Methodology. As with the first study, I evaluated hypnotizability at the group and individual level, and included a measure of psychological distress (see Figure 15.2). In the experimental session, the first step was to set up the EEG electrocap and then, before hypnosis but after a 2-minute eyes-closed rest period (asking participants not to meditate or go into hypnosis but just rest), the participant filled out the PCI for what they had experienced during those 2 minutes. The hypnosis sessions followed the same general structure as in the first study: a 1 to 30 count followed by probes for depth and experience approximately every 5 minutes. For pragmatic reasons, the sessions were limited to about 40 minutes. Last, participants filled out a PCI for the "deepest state" during the session and an interview was conducted. It is worth mentioning, in the context of my previous admonition to have a clinically competent individual present as part of the research staff, that there were two people, out of the dozens tested, who began to feel distressed during the sessions. Since I have training as a clinical psychologist and hypnotist, I stopped the research protocol and could help calm those participants and make sure that they felt fine, then and after the session. Although generally, hypnotic procedures elicit positive emotions, there is one type of high hypnotizable who is more likely to have had traumatic experiences and to experience less control and more negative emotions than the other highs (Terhune, Cardeña, & Lindgren, 2011 a, 2011b).

Results. As with Study 1, there were enough quantitative (depth reports and the PCI) and quali-tative (experiential reports) data to obtain a comprehensive, longitudinal account of individual experiences throughout the sessions. Because each depth and experiential report was timed, it could be related to the specific EEG activity occurring before the probe. We grouped the data by level of hypnotizability, and interesting patterns emerged. The low hypnotizables' experiences were mostly about the ongoing experiment (including the discomfort of the electrode cap) and their everyday concerns; the medium hypnotizables' reports were characterized by a sense of changes in body sensations and image (similar to the experiences reported during light/medium hypnosis by the highs in the first experiment); whereas the highs' reports were characterized by

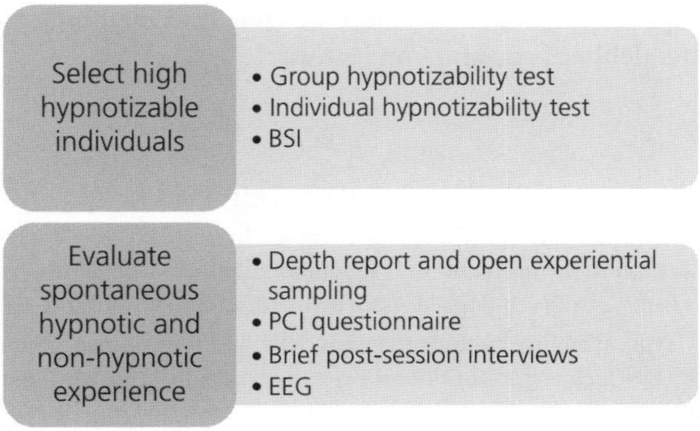

Select high hypnotizable individuals	• Group hypnotizability test • Individual hypnotizability test • BSI
Evaluate spontaneous hypnotic and non-hypnotic experience	• Depth report and open experiential sampling • PCI questionnaire • Brief post-session interviews • EEG

Fig. 15.2 Design of second study employing neutral hypnosis.

imagery and positive affect/transcendent experiences (similar to the reports of the highs during deep hypnosis in the first experiment).

The transcendent experiences in the second study were not as intense as those in the first, and a number of factors might explain this difference. Foremost, the unavoidable discomfort of an EEG cap was distracting and not as conducive to fully surrendering to the experience. Other factors include my not having spent as much time with the participants in the second experiment as with those in the first, there being more light and sound in the laboratory in which the second experiment was conducted, and, perhaps, a cultural difference in expressiveness between inhabitants of southern Sweden (second experiment) and Northern California (first experiment).

With regard to brain dynamics, hypnotic depth correlated with beta2, beta3, and gamma EEG frequencies power. Lower global functional connectivity was associated with the experiences characteristic of highs (imagery and positive affect/transcendent experiences) and, marginally, with hypnotizability. It was notable that, overall, the patterns of correlations with EEG power for highs and for lows were of opposite signs, suggesting non-linear differences in brain processes across hypnotizability. The matching of neurological and experiential processes helped illuminate each other. For instance, the difference in direction of correlations between high and low hypnotizability suggests that the hypnotic procedure not only affects highs more than it affects lows, but it affects them differently. By way of illustration, in unpublished data on this study, we observed that hypnosis tended to make cortical activity more frontal for lows, but more central and dorsal for highs, consistent with the more analytical reports of the lows versus the more imaginative reports of the highs. The result concerning the lower global functional connectivity related to imaginary and transcendent experiences is in general agreement with the decreased connectivity found after ingestion of psilocybin (Carhart-Harris et al., 2012), which can also produce strong imagery and transcendent experiences. The results of our study suggest that this type of "unrestrained cognition" is not artifactual to the ingestion of a drug, but characteristic of transcendent experiences.

Concluding thoughts

I have gone to some length to describe these two studies to illustrate how the use of different introspective methods and their integration with a neurophenomenological approach can provide a comprehensive view of alterations of consciousness. Both studies were very labor- and time-consuming, and the second one required collaboration with EEG experts. A thorough integration of first- and third-person approaches within a neurophenomenological frame cannot be done on the cheap, but it will provide more insights into hypnosis, meditation, and consciousness at large than either procedure on its own.

References

Baars, B. (1997). *In the theater of consciousness*. New York, NY: Oxford University Press.

Barber, T. X. (1999). A comprehensive three-dimensional theory of hypnosis. In I. Kirsch, A. Capafons, E. Cardeña-Buelna, & S. Amigo (Eds.), *Clinical hypnosis and self-regulation: cognitive-behavioral perspectives* (pp. 21–48). Washington, DC: American Psychological Association. doi:10.1037/10282–10001

Barnier, A. J., & Council, J. R. (2010). Hypnotizability matters: the what, why, and how of measurement. In S. J. Lynn, J. W. Rhue, & I. Kirsch (Eds.), *Handbook of clinical hypnosis* (2nd edn.) (pp. 47–77). Washington, DC: American Psychological Association.

Barnier, A., & Nash, M. R. (2008). Introduction: a roadmap for explanation, a working definition. In M. R. Nash & A. J. Barnier (Eds.), *The Oxford handbook of hypnosis* (pp. 1–18). Oxford, UK: Oxford University Press.

Bennett, C. M., Baird, A. A., Miller, M. B., & Wolford, G. L. (2010). Neural correlates of interspecies taking in the post-mortem Atlantic salmon: an argument for proper multiple comparisons correction. *Journal of Serendipitous and Unexpected Results*, **1**(1), 1–5.

Boring, E. G. (1953). A history of introspection. *Psychological Bulletin*, **50**, 176–189.

Bulkeley, K. (2012). Dreaming in adolescence: a "blind" word search of a teenage girl's dream series. *Dreaming*, **22**, 240–252.

Cangas, A. J., Sass, L. A., & Pérez-Álvarez, M. (2008). From the visions of Saint Teresa of Jesus to voices of schizophrenia. *Philosophy, Psychiatry, & Psychology*, **15**, 239–250.

Cardeña, E. (1994). The domain of dissociation. In S. J. Lynn & J. W. Rhue (Eds.), *Dissociation: clinical and theoretical perspectives* (pp. 15–31). New York, NY: Guilford Press.

Cardeña, E. (2005). The phenomenology of deep hypnosis: quiescent and physically active. *International Journal of Clinical & Experimental Hypnosis*, **53**, 37–59.

Cardeña, E. (2009). Beyond Plato? Toward a science of alterations of consciousness. In C. A. Roe, W. Kramer, & L. Coly (Eds.), *Utrecht II: charting the future of parapsychology* (pp. 305–322). New York, NY: Parapsychology Foundation.

Cardeña, E. (2012). Commentary on altered and asymmetric default mode network activity in a "hypnotic virtuoso"? An fMRI and EEG study. *Consciousness and Cognition*, **21**, 1575–1576.

Cardeña, E. (2014). Hypnos and psyche, or how hypnosis has contributed to the study of consciousness. *Psychology of Consciousness: Theory, Research and Practice*, **1**, 123–138.

Cardeña, E., Alarcón, A., Capafons, A., & Bayot, A. (1998). Effects on suggestibility of a new method of active-alert hypnosis. *International Journal of Clinical and Experimental Hypnosis*, **46**, 280–294.

Cardeña, E., Jönsson, P., Terhune, D. B., & Marcusson-Clavertz, D. (2013). The neurophenomenology of neutral hypnosis. *Cortex*, **49**, 375–385. http://dx.doi.org/10.1016/j.cortex.2012.04.001

Cardeña, E., Lehmann, D., Faber, P. L., Jönsson, P., Milz, P., Pascual-Marqui, R. D., & Kochi, K. (2012). EEG sLORETA functional imaging during hypnotic arm levitation and voluntary arm lifting. *International Journal of Clinical and Experimental Hypnosis*, **60**, 31–53. doi 10.1080/00207144.2011.622184

Cardeña, E., Lynn, S. J., & Krippner, S. (Eds.). (2014). *Varieties of anomalous experience: examining the scientific evidence* (2nd edn.). Washington, DC: American Psychological Association.

Cardeña, E., & Marcusson-Clavertz, D. (in press). The influence of hypnotizability and dissociation on everyday mentation: an experience sampling study. *Psychology of Consciousness*.

Cardeña, E., & Pekala, R. J. (2014). Methodological issues in the study of altering consciousness and anomalous experience. In E. Cardeña, S. J., Lynn, & S. Krippner (Eds.), *Varieties of anomalous experience:*

examining the scientific evidence (2nd edn.) (pp. 21–56). Washington, DC: American Psychological Association.

Cardeña, E., Sjöstedt, J. O., & Marcusson-Clavertz, D. (2015). Sustained attention and motivation in Zen meditators and non-meditators. *Mindfulness*, **57**, 1082–1087.

Cardeña, E., & Terhune, D. (2009). A note of caution on the Waterloo Stanford Group Scale of Hypnotic Susceptibility: a brief communication. *International Journal of Clinical and Experimental Hypnosis*, **57**, 222–226.

Cardeña, E., & Terhune, D. B. (2014). Hypnotizability, personality traits, and the propensity to experience alterations of consciousness. *Psychology of Consciousness: Theory, Research, and Practice*, **1**, 292–307.

Cardeña, E., Van Duijl, M., Weiner, L., & Terhune, D. (2009). Possession/trance phenomena. In P. F. Dell & J. A. O'Neil (Eds.), *Dissociation and the dissociative disorders: DSM-V and beyond* (pp. 171–181). New York: Routledge.

Cardeña, E., & Winkelman, M. (2011a). *Altering consciousness. Multidisciplinary perspectives. Volume I: History, culture, and the humanities*. Santa Barbara, CA: Praeger.

Cardeña, E., & Winkelman, M. (2011b). *Altering consciousness. Multidisciplinary perspectives. Volume II: Biological and psychological perspectives*. Santa Barbara, CA: Praeger.

Carhart-Harris, R. L., Erritzoe, D., Williams, T., Stone, J. M., Reed, L. J., Colasanti, A., . . . Nutt, D. J. (2012). Neural correlates of the psychedelic state as determined by fMRI studies with psilocybin. *Proceedings of the National Academy of Science*, **109**, 2138–2143.

Danziger, K. (1980). The history of introspection reconsidered. *Journal of the History of the Behavioral Sciences*, **16**, 241–262.

De Pascalis, V., & Penna, P. M. (1990). 40-Hz EEG activity during hypnotic induction and hypnotic testing. *International Journal of Clinical and Experimental Hypnosis*, **38**, 125–138.

Easterlin, B., & Cardeña, E. (1998–1999). Perceived stress, cognitive and emotional differences between short- and long-term Vipassana meditators. *Imagination, Cognition and Personality*, **18**, 69–82.

Edge, H. L. (2014). Does meditation give us insight into ultimate reality? The ethical aim of Buddhism. In S. Schmidt & H. Wallach (Eds.), *Meditation: neuroscientific approaches and philosophical implications* (pp. 271–295). Cham, Switzerland: Springer.

Evans, R. B. (1972). E. B. Titchener and his lost system. *Journal of the History of the Behavioral Sciences*, **8**, 168–180.

Farthing, G. W. (1992). *The psychology of consciousness*. Englewood Cliffs, NJ: Prentice Hall.

Foulkes, D., & Vogel, G. (1965). Mental activity at sleep onset. *Journal of Abnormal Psychology*, **70**, 231–243.

Fox, M. C., Ericsson, K. A., & Best, R. (2011). Do procedures for verbal reporting of thinking have to be reactive? A meta-analysis and recommendations for best reporting methods. *Psychological Bulletin*, **137**, 316–344.

Gallagher, S. (2003). Phenomenology and experimental design: toward a phenomenologically enlightened experimental science. In A. Jack & A. Roepstorff (Eds.), *Trusting the subject* (Vol 1, pp. 85–99). Exeter, UK: Imprint.

Gandhi, B., & Oakley, D. A. (2005). Does "hypnosis" by any other name smell as sweet? The efficacy of "hypnotic" inductions depends on the label "hypnosis." *Consciousness and Cognition*, **14**, 304–315.

Giorgi, A. (1990). Towards an integrated approach to the study of human problems: the parameters of human science. *Saybrook Review*, **8**, 111–126.

Goleman, D. (1988). *The meditative mind. The varieties of meditative experience*. New York, NY: Tracher/ Putnam.

Grant, J. A. (2012). Towards a more meaningful comparison of meditation and hypnosis. *Journal of Mind–Body Regulation*, **2**, 71–74.

Güzeldere, G. (1995). Consciousness: what it is, how to study it, what to learn from its history. *Journal of Consciousness Studies*, **2**, 30–51.

Hasenkamp, W., Wilson-Mendenhall, C. D., Duncan, E., & Barsalou, L. W. (2011). Mind wandering and attention during focused meditation: a fine-grained temporal analysis of fluctuating cognitive states. *NeuroImage*, 59, 750–760.

Henrich, J., Heine, S. J., & Norenzayan, A. (2010). The weirdest people in the world? *Brain and Behavioral Sciences*, **33**, 61–135.

Hilgard, E. R., & Tart, C. T. (1966). Responsiveness to suggestions following waking and imagination instructions and following induction of hypnosis. *Journal of Abnormal Psychology*, **71**, 196–208.

Hilts, P. J. (1996). *Memory's ghost*. New York, NY: Simon & Schuster.

Hinterberg, T. (2014). I am I from moment to moment: methods and results of grasping intersubjective and intertemporal neurophysiological differences during meditation states. In S. Schmidt & H. Wallach (Eds.), *Meditaton—neuroscientific approaches and philosophical implications* (pp. 95–113). Cham, Switzerland: Springer.

Hoffman, D. (2008).Conscious realism and the mind–body problem. *Mind & Matter*, **6**, 87–121.

Hull, C. L. (1933). *Hypnosis and suggestibility: an experimental approach*. New York, NY: Appleton-Century Crofts.

Hurlburt, R. T., & Schwitzgebel, E. (2007). *Describing inner experience? Proponent meets skeptic*. Cambridge, MA: MIT Press.

Jack, A., & Roepstorff, A. (Eds.) (2003–2004). *Trusting the subject. Volumes 1 and 2*. Exeter, UK: Imprint Academic.

James, W. (1890). *The principles of psychology*. New York, NY: Henry Holt and Company.

Kelly, E. F., Kelly, E. W., Crabtree, A., Gauld, A., Grosso, M., & Greyson, B. (2007). *Irreducible mind: toward a psychology for the 21st century*. Lanham, MD: Rowan & Littlefield.

Killingsworth, M. A., & Gilbert, D. T. (2010). A wandering mind is an unhappy mind. *Science*, **330**, 932.

Klüver, H. (1928). *Mescal: the "divine plant" and its psychological effects*. London, UK: Kegan Paul, Trench, Trubner, and Co.

Kosslyn, S. M., Thompson, W. L., Costantini-Ferrando, M. F., Alpert, N. M., & Spiegel, D. (2000). Hypnotic visual illusion alters color processing in the brain. *American Journal of Psychiatry* **157**, 1279–1284.

Kripal, J. J. (2014). *Comparing religions*. West Sussex, UK: Wiley.

Krippendorf, K. (2004). *Content analysis: an introduction to its methodology* (2nd edn.). Thousand Oaks, CA: Sage.

Kubose, S. K. (1976). An experimental investigation of psychological aspects of meditation. *Psychologia*, **19**, 1–10.

Kvale, S., & Brinkmann, S. (2008). *Interviews: learning the craft of qualitative research interviewing*. Thousand Oaks, CA: Sage.

Laughlin, C., McManus, J., & d'Aquili, E. (1990). *Brain, symbol and experience: toward a neurophenomenology of consciousness*. New York, NY: Columbia University Press.

Lipari, S., Baglio, F., Griffanti, L., Mendozzi, L., Garegnani, M., Motta, A., Cecconi, P., & Pugnetti, L. (2012). Altered and asymmetric default mode network activity in a "hypnotic virtuoso": an fMRI and EEG study. *Consciousness and Cognition*, **21**, 393–400.

Luria, A. R. (1968). *The mind of a mnemonist*. New York, NY: Basic Books.

Lutz, A., Brefczynski-Lewis, J., Johnstone, T., & Davidson, R. J. (2008). Regulation of the neural circuitry of emotion by compassion meditation: effects of meditative expertise. *PLoS ONE*, **3**, e1897. doi: 10.1371/journal.pone.0001897

Lutz, A., & Thompson, E. (2003). Neurophenomenology: integrating subjective experience and brain dynamics in the neuroscience of consciousness. In A. Jack & A. Roepstorff (Eds.), *Trusting the subject. Vol. 1* (pp. 31–52). Exeter, UK: Imprint Press.

Lynn, S. J., Malaktaris, A., Maxwell, R., Mellinger, D. J., & Van der Kloet, D. (2012). Do hypnosis and mindfulness practices inhabit a common domain? Implications for research, clinical practice, and forensic science. *Journal of Mind–Body Regulation*, **2**, 12–26.

MacDonald, D. A., LeClair, L., Holland, C. J., Alter, A., & Friedman, H. L. (1995). A survey of measures of transpersonal constructs. *Journal of Transpersonal Psychology*, **27**, 171–235.

Marcusson-Clavertz, D., & Cardeña, E., (2011). Hypnotizability, alterations in consciousness, and other variables as predictors of performance in a ganzfeld psi task. *Journal of Parapsychology*, **75**, 235–259.

Marcusson-Clavertz, D., Terhune, D. B., & Cardeña, E., (2012). Individual differences and state effects on mind wandering: hypnotizability, dissociation, and sensory homogenization. *Consciousness and Cognition*, **21**, 1097–1108.

Maupin, E. W. (1965). Individual differences in response to a Zen meditation exercise. *Journal of Consulting Psychology*, **29**, 139–145. doi: 10.1037/h0021754

McConkey, K. M., Barnier, A., & Szeps, A. (2001). Indexing the experience of sex change in hypnosis and imagination. *International Journal of Clinical and Experimental Hypnosis*, **49**, 123–138. doi: 10.1080/00207140108410063

McGeown, W. J., Venneri, A., Kirsch, I., Nocetti, L., Roberts, K., Foan, L., Mazzoni, G. (2012). Suggested visual hallucination without hypnosis enhances activity in visual areas of the brain. *Consciousness and Cognition*, **21**, 100–116.

Naranjo, C., & Ornstein, R. E. (1971). *On the psychology of meditation*. New York, NY: Viking Press.

Natsoulas, T. (1981). Basic problems of consciousness. *Journal of Personality and Social Psychology*, **41**, 132–178.

Natsoulas, T. (1983). Concepts of consciousness. *Journal of Mind and Behavior*, **4**, 13–59.

Nisbett, R. E., & Wilson, T. D. (1977). Telling more than we can know: verbal reports on mental processes. *Psychological Review*, **84**, 231–259.

Oakley DA. (2008). Hypnosis, trance and suggestion: evidence from neuroimaging. In M. R. Nash & A. Barnier (Eds.), *The Oxford handbook of hypnosis: theory, research and practice* (pp. 365–392). Oxford, UK: Oxford University Press.

Overgaard, M., Fehl, K., Mouridsen, K., Bergholt, B., & Cleeremans, A. (2008). Seeing without seeing? Degraded conscious vision in a blindsight patient. *PLoS ONE*, **3**(8), e3028. doi:10.1371/journal.pone.0003028

Oxman, T. E., Rosenberg, S. D., Schnurr, P. P., Tucker, G. J., & Gala, G. (1988). The language of altered states. *Journal of Nervous and Mental Disease*, **176**, 401–408.

Pekala, R. J. (1991). *Quantifying consciousness: an empirical approach*. New York, NY: Plenum Press.

Pekala, R. J., Kumar, V. K., & Marcano, G. (1995). Anomalous/paranormal experiences, hypnotic susceptibility, and dissociation. *Journal of the American Society for Psychical Research*, **89**, 313–332.

Petitmengin, C. (2006). Describing one's subjective experience in the second person. An interview method for a science of consciousness. *Phenomenology and the Cognitive Sciences*, **5**, 229–269.

Petitmengin, C., & Bitbol, M. (2009). The validity of first-person descriptions as authenticity and coherence. *Journal of Consciousness Studies*, **16**, 363–404.

Rainville, P., Duncan, G. H., Price, D. D., Carrier, B., & Bushnell, M. C. (1997). Pain affect encoded in human anterior cingulate but not somatosensory cortex. *Science*, **15**, 968–971.

Robinson, D. N. (1995). *An intellectual history of psychology* (3rd edn.). Madison, WI: University of Wisconsin Press.

Russell, B. (1910–1911). Knowledge by acquaintance and knowledge by description. *Proceedings of the Aristotelian Society*, **16**, 108–128.

Sacks, O. (1995). *An anthropologist on Mars*. New York, NY: Alfred A Knopf.

Schooler, J. W. (2011). Introspecting in the spirit of William James: comment on Fox, Ericsson, and Best (2011). *Psychological Bulletin*, **137**, 345–350.

Searle, J. (1990). *The mystery of consciousness*. New York, NY: The New York Review of Books.

Secord, S. M. (1953). The appraisal of body-cathexis: body-cathexis and the self. *Journal of Consulting Psychology*, **17**, 343–347. doi: 10.1037/h0060689

Shaw, P. (2015). Mystical experiences as windows on reality. In E. F. Kelly, A. Crabtree, & P. Marshall (Eds.), *Beyond physicalism: toward reconciliation of science and spirituality* (pp. 39–76). London, UK: Rowan & Littlefield.

Sheehan, P. W., & McConkey, K. M. (1982). *Hypnosis and experience*. New York, NY: Brunner/Mazel.

Siegel, R. K., & West, J. L. (Eds.). (1975). *Hallucination: behavior, experience, and theory*. New York, NY: Wiley.

Singer, J. L. (1966). *Daydreaming: an introduction to the experimental study of inner experience*. New York, NY: Random House.

Singer, J. L., & Kolligan, J. Jr. (1987). Personality: developments in the study of private experience. *Annual Review of Psychology*, **38**, 533–574.

Smith, E., & Miller, F. (1978). Limits on perception of cognitive processes: a reply to Nisbett and Wilson. *Psychological Review*, **85**, 355–362.

Soanes, C. (Ed.) (2001). *Paperback Oxford English dictionary*. Oxford, UK: Oxford University Press.

Spiegel, D., & Barabasz, A. F. (1988). Effects of hypnotic instructions on P300 event-related potential amplitudes: research and clinical implications. *American Journal of Clinical Hypnosis*, **31**, 11–17.

Strawson, G. (2015, February 27). The consciousness myth. *The Times Literary Supplement*, **5839**, 14–15.

Tallis, R. (2011). *Aping mankind: neuromania, Darwinitis and the misrepresentation of humanity*. Durham, UK: Acumen.

Tart, C. T. (Ed.) (1969). *Altered states of consciousness*. New York, NY: Wiley.

Tart, C. T. (1972). States of consciousness and state-specific sciences. *Science*, **176**, 1203–1210.

Tart, C. T. (1979). Measuring the depth of an altered state of consciousness, with particular reference to self-report scales of hypnotic depth. In E. Fromm & R. E. Shor (Eds.), *Hypnosis: developments in research and new perspectives* (2nd edn.) (pp. 567–601). New York, NY: Aldine.

Taylor, E. (1998). William James and the historical influence of hypnosis in the rise of experimental psychopathology. *Psychological Hypnosis*, **7**(1), 9–12.

Terhune, D. B., & Cardeña, E. (2010). Differential patterns of spontaneous experiential response to a hypnotic induction: a latent profile analysis. *Consciousness and Cognition*, **19**, 1140–1150. doi:10.1016/j.concog.2010.03.006

Terhune, D. B., Cardeña, E., & Lindgren, M. (2011a). Dissociative tendencies and individual differences in high hypnotic suggestibility. *Cognitive Neuropsychiatry*, **16**, 113–135.

Terhune, D. B., Cardeña, E., & Lindgren, M. (2011b). Dissociated control as a signature of typological variability in high hypnotic suggestibility. *Consciousness and Cognition*, **20**, 727–736.

Thomas, J., Jamieson, G., & Cohen, M. (2014). Low and then high frequency oscillations of distinct right cortical networks are progressively enhanced by medium and long term Satyananda Yoga meditation practice. *Frontiers in Human Neuroscience*, **10**(8). doi: 10.3389/fnhum.2014.00197

Thompson, E. (2009). Neurophenomenology and contemplative experience. In P. Clayton (Ed.), *The Oxford handbook of religion and science*. Oxford, UK: Oxford University Press. doi: 10.1093/oxfordhb/9780199543656.003.0015

Troubridge, U. L. (1922). The *modus operandi* in so-called mediumistic trance. *Proceedings of the Society for Psychical Research*, **32**, 344–378.

Turnbull, C. (1990). Liminality: a synthesis of subjective and objective experience. In R. Schechner & W. Appel (Eds.), *By means of performance*. Cambridge, UK: Cambridge University Press.

Varela, F. J. (1996). Neurophenomenology: a methodological remedy for the hard problem. *Journal of Consciousness Studies*, **3**, 330–349.

Varela, F. J., Thompson, E., & Rosch, E. (1991). *The embodied mind*. Cambridge, MA: University of Massachusetts Press.

Velmans, M. M. (1993). A reflexive science of consciousness. In Ciba Foundation Symposium 174. *Experimental and theoretical studies of consciousness* (pp. 81–99). Chichester, UK: Wiley.

Vul, E., Harris, C., Winkielman, P., Pashler, H. (2009). Puzzlingly high correlations in fMRI studies of emotion, personality, and social cognition. *Perspectives in Psychological Science*, **4**, 319–324.

Watson, J. B. (1920). Is thinking merely the action of language mechanisms? *British Journal of Psychology*, **11**, 87–104.

Wilson, T. D. (2003). Knowing when to ask: introspection and the adaptive unconscious. In A. Jack & A. Roepstorff (Eds.), *Trusting the subject. Vol. 1* (pp. 131–140). Exeter, UK: Imprint Press.

Chapter 16

Influencing conflict in the human brain by changing brain states

Yi-Yuan Tang and Michael I. Posner

Abstract

This chapter attempts to provide an account of similarities and differences in modifying the ability to resolve conflict between brain states induced by meditation and hypnosis. The authors do not review the massive literature in each field but, instead, confine their discussion to conflict-related cognitive tasks such as the Stroop and flanker. They argue that both hypnotism and meditation change brain states. Meditation increases resting state activity within the anterior cingulate node of the executive attention network, while it appears that increasing depth of hypnosis reduces activity within the anterior cingulate cortex. Hypnotic states may work to prevent internal goals from activating the executive attention network leading to control by external input and prior instruction. Instead, meditation training may work to enhance executive attention leading generally to improved self-control.

Introduction

Lifshitz et al. (2013) argued that although meditation is not the same as hypnosis, comparing the ability of the two to resolve conflict may help illuminate the neural basis of cognitive control. In this chapter, we compare studies dealing with the resolution of conflict following meditation and hypnotic suggestion in order to provide a theoretical account of how the brain states they induce might work. We do not attempt to review the full literature, but instead provide the background for a hypothesis concerning the origin of the control of conflict found in studies of the meditation and hypnotic states.

The Stroop and flanker tasks are among the most common ways to study the resolution of conflict. Stroop interference refers to the response time (RT) difference between congruent and incongruent trials when participants are required to respond with the ink color of a color word (e.g., the word "BLUE" in the incongruent color "RED"; Stroop, 1935). Although there are many ways to administer the Stroop task, they are all based on a comparison between congruent and incongruent trials (see Figure 16.1 and Plate 11). Longer RTs and higher error rates on incongruent trials are a reliable feature of the task, at least for people skilled in reading (McLeod, 1991). A second way to examine brain responses to conflict involves the flanker effect, in which the RT to a target surrounded by congruent flankers is compared to RTs when the flankers are incongruent (Eriksen & Eriksen, 1974).

Green Red **Blue Purple**
[congruent trials]

Blue **Purple** Red **Green**
[incongruent trials]

Fig. 16.1 The Stroop effect: naming the color of the first set of words (congruent trials—name and actual color of type matches) is easier and quicker than the second (incongruent trials—mismatch of name and actual color of type) (see also Plate 11).

It is well known that many features of conflict-related tasks such as the Stroop or flanker can influence the amount of interference. For example, the second of two successive incongruent trials shows less conflict than the first of the series (Lorist & Jolij, 2012). Similarly, the conflict found in a low-probability incongruent trial is larger than when incongruent trials are common within the series (Kane & Engle, 2003). These effects are thought to be instances of priming of the operations involved in resolving conflict. Another way to improve overall performance is to practice the task; interference effects decline with practice.

This chapter is concerned with how post-hypnotic suggestion and meditation training might improve performance of the Stroop and other conflict-related tasks. We first discuss behavioral evidence showing that both hypnotic suggestion and meditation training can influence behavioral performance in conflict tasks by reducing the time to resolve conflict. Next, we examine the brain mechanisms thought to be involved in reduced interference following post-hypnotic suggestion and meditation training. Finally, we speculate on the brain states that support the changes observed following meditation and hypnosis.

Training methods

We have recently distinguished between two methods of training that can be used to improve performance in executive attention tasks. One method is network training, and this basically involves practice of the network involved in the task (Tang & Posner, 2009, 2014). In the case of the Stroop task, this involves prefrontal areas and the anterior cingulate cortex (ACC) in connection to color and word form areas of the posterior brain.

Previous work using the Stroop task has shown that the interference score can be influenced by many specific aspects of the task such as extensive practice, separating the location of the word name from the ink color, viewing the stimulus in peripheral vision, using word names that cannot be read because they are in a foreign language, or providing hypnotic suggestion to perceive the words as nonsense strings (McLeod, 1991; Raz, Fan, & Posne, 2005). All of these methods influence specific elements of the task either by temporarily making the word meaning less accessible or strengthening the color name through practice or priming (Raz, Fan, & Posner, 2005; West and Alain, 2000).

Practice can improve performance in the Stroop and other conflict tasks (McLeod, 1991; MacLeod et al., 2010). For example, Ishigami and Klein (2010) practiced the Attention Network Test (ANT) over ten sessions of training (this task uses the flanker task as the target). They found improvement in executive attention, measured by conflict scores, from 120 to 60 msecs, mainly over the first six sessions. These practice effects may be due in part to changes in connectivity between nodes of the network that improve RT overall and may also reduce conflict since this score is often correlated with overall RT. It is possible that practice in the ANT will generalize to improvements in Stroop performance, but these are unlikely to exceed those obtained by directly practicing the Stroop.

Hypnosis

Hypnosis is generally not a training method. Rather, it is a "highly focused absorbed attentional state that minimizes competing thoughts and sensation" (Oakley & Halligan, 2013). This state can result in stronger control of behavior from an outside force (hypnotist). The use of post-hypnotic suggestion allows the hypnotist to alter the behavior of a person even when they are not in the hypnotic state (Oakley & Halligan, 2013).

It has proven possible to influence the degree of conflict by use of a post-hypnotic suggestion. The Stroop effect can be greatly reduced or abolished by inducing a hypnotic state in highly suggestible people and giving the suggestion that the word is a meaningless string. In one study (Raz et al., 2005), it was found that the Stroop effect, in RT, declined from 91 to 9 msecs when highly hypnotizable participants were given the suggestion. Without the suggestion, there was no significant change in the effect (see Table 16.1). The virtual elimination of conflict with the suggestion among highly hypnotizables was an impressive demonstration of how effective a suggestion can be. However, for less hypnotizable people, the suggestion reduces Stroop interference only slightly. For unselected people, performance on the flanker task was reduced, but not eliminated, following meditation training, and the reduction was less than was reported with substantial practice. While it was found that highly suggestible people showed dramatic reduction in Stroop interference when not in the hypnotic state, using a post-hypnotic suggestion (Raz et al., 2005), it has also been shown that suggestion while in the hypnotic state produces reduced Stroop interference (Cojan et al., 2009). Moreover, for highly suggestible people, it is possible to reduce conflict by a suggestion even without inducing the hypnotic state (see Lifshitz, Bonn, Fischer, Kashem, & Raz, 2013).

Meditation

Brain states refer to reliable patterns of brain activity that involve the co-activation and/or connectivity of multiple large-scale brain networks (Tang, Rothbart, & Posner, 2012). State training uses practice to develop a brain state that may influence the operations of many networks. State training certainly involves networks, but it is not designed to train networks using a cognitive

Table 16.1 Comparing conflict (msec of difference between incongruent–congruent conditions) following post-hypnotic suggestion meditation training and practice

	Highly hypnotizable	**Unselected**
Prior to hypnosis[1]	90 msecs	72 msecs
Following suggestion	9 msecs	61 msecs
Prior to IBMT training[2]		101 msecs
After IBMT training		71 msecs
Low practice[3]		120 msecs
High practice	.	60 msecs

[1] Data from A. Raz, J. Fan, and M. I. Posner (2005) Hypnotic suggestion reduces conflict in the human brain, *Proceedings of the National Academy of Sciences of the United States of America*, 102, 9978–9983.

[2] Data from Y. Fan, Y. Y. Tang, Y. Ma, and M. I. Posner (in press) Brain state modulates conflict processing in Stroop effect.

[3] Data from Y. Ishigami and R.M. Klein (2001) Repeated measurement of the components of attention using two versions of the Attention Network Test (ANT): stability, isolability, robustness, and reliability, *Journal of Neuroscience Methods*, 190(1), 117–128.

task. Research has shown that brain-state training such as physical exercise or mindfulness medi- tation can significantly improve executive attention, emotion regulation, and neuroplasticity through the modulation of self-control networks (Hillman, Erickson, & Kramer, 2008; Tang & Posner, 2009). One example of brain-state training is integrative body–mind training (IBMT), a form of mindfulness meditation adapted mainly from traditional Chinese medicine and Zen practice. IBMT includes elements of body relaxation, mental imagery, and mindfulness train- ing. A qualified trainer is used to ensure that naïve learners achieve the state of restful alertness without strong effort to control thoughts (Tang et al., 2007; Tang & Posner, 2014; Tang, Hölzel, & Posner, 2015; Tang, Rothbart, & Posner, 2012).

Mindfulness meditation involves a systematic training of attention and self-control with an attitude of acceptance and openness to internal and external experiences (Holzel et al., 2011; Tang & Posner, 2013). IBMT has been tested in a number of randomized controlled trials that indi- cate IBMT leads to a very rapid change in brain state, including both the central and autonomic nervous system (Tang et al., 2007; Tang & Posner, 2009; Tang, Rothbart, & Posner, 2012; Tang & Posner, 2013). The rapid effectiveness of IBMT allows studies involving random assignment of persons to experimental and control groups. The control group was given relaxation training popular in the West as a part of cognitive behavioral therapy. In relaxation training, individuals are instructed to relax different muscle groups in turn.

In one study, only 5 days of practice, with 30 minutes per session, was used. The IBMT and RT control groups were given a battery of tests before and after training sessions (Tang et al., 2007). The Attention Network Test, the Profile of Mood States, and a stress challenge of a mental arithmetic task followed by measures of cortisol and secretory immunoglobulin A (sIgA) were given before and after training. All of these are standard assays scored objectively by raters blind to the experimental condition. The expectation was that IBMT would improve functioning of the executive attention network by changing the brain state. The IBMT group showed significantly greater improvement than the RT group in the executive attention network, in mood where posi- tive moods were increased and negative moods reduced, in improved stress reduction (measured by salivary cortisol), and in greater immune reactivity (measured by sIgA) (Tang et al., 2007). The improvements appear to involve a change of state, with increased brain activity in areas related to the parasympathetic portion of the autonomic nervous system producing a quiet alert state con- ducive to focused attention. Also indicative of a change of brain state by IBMT was its alteration of resting-state functional brain networks (Tang et al., 2009, 2012; Xue, Tang, & Posner, 2011; Xue, Tang, Tang, & Posner, 2014).

The improvement of performance on conflict resolution in the ANT led us to expect a similar influence on the Stroop test. To determine the time course of conflict resolution before and after, 35 Chinese undergraduates were randomly assigned to an IBMT or to a relaxation training group and given ten sessions of training, each session lasting 30 minutes. Prior to and following training, all subjects performed the Stroop task while their brain activity was registered using event-related potential (ERPs). We hypothesized that after 5 hours of training, IBMT would reduce the Stroop interference effect in RT more than relaxation training (Fan, Tang, Ma, & Posner, 2015).

The results of this study showed a highly significant improvement in Stroop interference in the IBMT group of 30 msecs versus a non-significant improvement of 6 msecs in the relax- ation control group (see Table 16.1). A similar result was obtained for accuracy. However, even after the training, there remained a significant time to resolve conflict. This contrasted with the non-significant time for conflict resolution after post-hypnotic suggestion of the group of highly hypnotizable participants run under the same conditions. However, since the meditators were not selected for personality characteristics, it is probably better to compare their performance with less highly hypnotizable selected participants in the Stroop who still showed 61 msecs of conflict following post-hypnotic suggestion.

Brain changes

Combining functional magnetic resonance imaging (fMRI) and ERP gives a picture of the time course and localization of changes in the brain following suggestion or training with IBMT. Post-hypnotic suggestion greatly reduced the MRI BOLD response and ERP from posterior brain areas, including the P1 and N1 visual responses (Raz et al., 2005). This effect was stronger in the left hemisphere. It also virtually eliminated the usual increased negativity for incongruent trials (N2) over frontal midline electrodes that has been taken as conflict-related activity of the ACC (Rueda, Rothbart, McCandliss, Saccomanno, & Posner, 2005; van Veen & Carter, 2002) and greatly increased the latency of this difference in the subsequent positivity (P3) reflective of cognitive effort.

The interpretation of this pattern of results suggested that the visually presented word produced less activity in the visual word form area either because information failed to reach this area or because of a lack of attention to that brain region. Subsequently, other researchers have confirmed the reduced conflict produced by post-hypnotic suggestions in both Stroop (Augestinova & Ferrand, 2012; Parris, Dienes, & Hodgson, 2013) and flanker tasks (Iani, Ricci, Gherri, & Ribichi, 2006). In the Stroop study however, it was shown that words semantically related to a color (e.g., apple) produced the same amount of Stroop interference regardless of suggestion (Augustinova & Ferrand, 2012) and, in another study, the major influence of suggestion was on the conflict components of the distribution of interference-related RTs (Parris, Dienes, & Hodgson, 2013). It should be kept in mind that multiple routes can lead from a word to its meaning, thus it would be possible for a semantic effect to continue even if the word form route was completely abolished. Thus, it remains somewhat uncertain whether post-hypnotic suggestion works by abolishing input or by improving conflict resolution or both.

In a recent Stroop study following IBMT, posterior brain potentials did not differ between the IBMT and relaxation control groups but the frontal N2, which has often been related to the effort to resolve conflict, was greatly reduced following IBMT. In addition, the subsequent late positive wave (P3) recorded over frontal electrodes was reduced in latency by IBMT. This combination

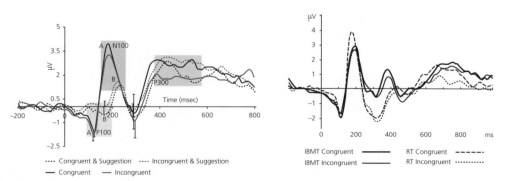

Fig. 16.2 ERPs from hypnosis suggestion and meditation training (see also Plate 12).

Left and right panel show hypnosis suggestion and IBMT effects at frontal midline region, respectively.

suggests that conflict was resolved with less effort and more quickly following IBMT (Fan et al., 2015). See Figure 16.2 (and Plate 12) for comparison of ERPs during performance of the Stroop task induced by hypnotic suggestion and meditation.

While there are strong similarities between Stroop performance following IBMT and with a hypnotic suggestion, the underlying state may be different. Resting-state fMRI studies have shown reduced activation in the ACC during the hypnotic state (Deeley et al., 2012), while following IBMT, resting-state studies reveal a more highly active ventral ACC (Tang et al 2009). A possible interpretation of these findings is that the hypnotic state tends to reduce the mechanisms by which internal goals control behavior though the executive attention network, while leaving intact the ability of external input or working memory to control behavior. Thus performance in the Stroop may be enhanced while the loss of effective internal goals allows the hypnotist stronger control of behavior. Meditation training seems to work by increasing self control though strengthening activation and connectivity of the executive network. Thus meditation enhances the ability of the control of behavior either through external or internal sources.

Mechanisms of state induction

Although both hypnosis and meditation can be used to modify the ability of the brain to handle conflict in the Stroop effect, they may do so using different underlying brain states. In this section, we describe these states and speculate on how these differences arise.

In our work, we have argued for two somewhat separate brain networks related to attention (Petersen & Posner, 2012; Posner, Rothbart, Sheese, & Voelker, 2014). One of them, the orienting network, arises very early in development and works closely in conjunction with sensory systems. Orienting provides a means for sensory information to control behavior. The orienting network can amplify and inhibit input signals and allows the infant and young child to learn the features of their sensory world. The executive network involved in the resolution of conflict is present even in infancy (Gao, Zhu, & Giovanello, 2009; Posner, Rothbart, Sheese, & Voelker, 2014), but the executive network is not sufficiently connected to other brain areas to provide efficient behavioral control. The executive network is the primary way in which adults are able to control their behavior voluntarily in accordance with their own motivations and goals. It is the gateway for voluntary control.

Hypnosis

We have speculated that hypnotism generally blocks the connectivity between frontal areas related to goals and the ACC; thus preventing the usual goal-directed behavior found in adults (Posner & Rothbart, 2011). This blockage allows the orienting network, elements of which are increased in activity in the hypnotic state (Deeley et al., 2012), to foster control by sensory information that currently or previously had been presented by an external authority. This idea has some support from an fMRI study during a hypnotic state in which the participant is instructed that he/she is unable to move a hand when a particular visual signal is presented (Cojan et al., 2009). The authors found a specific disconnection between the motor cortex and the normal areas reflecting motor intention. Instead, the motor system seemed to be related to sensory memories of the hypnotic suggestion. Additional support comes from a combined fMRI and EEG study showing, under hypnotism, a disconnection between the ACC and other brain areas related to cognitive processes (Egner, Jamieson, & Gruzelier, 2005).

Thus, in our view, the hypnotic state returns connectivity to what is dominant early in life. This may help to explain the stronger effect of hypnotic suggestion in children and the association of hypnotic susceptibility with polymorphisms in the COMT gene (Raz, 2008), that is also closely related to the executive attention network (Voelker, Sheese, Rothbart, & Posner, 2009).

Meditation

On the other hand, meditation seems to strengthen the executive network by improving activation and connectivity with the striatum and parasympathetic nervous system (Tang et al., 2015). We used diffusion tensor imaging (DTI) before and after 4 weeks of training with IBMT and relaxation training (Tang et al., 2010). We found significantly greater increase in fractional anisotropy (FA) following IBMT than after the relaxation control. The training effect was in white matter pathways connecting the ACC to other brain areas (Tang et al., 2010). We also found that after 2 weeks, the FA change was entirely due to axial diffusivity, which was discovered to decline significantly more following IBMT than relaxation (Tang, Lu, Fan, Yang, & Posner, 2012). Axial diffusivity (AD) is thought to relate to changes in axonal density (Kumar, Macey, Woo, & Haper, 2010; Kumar, Nguyen, Macey, Woo, & Harper, 2012). After 4 weeks, FA involved changes in both axial and radial diffusivity. Radial diffusivity is thought to reflect myelination (Song et al., 2002, 2003). This evidence suggests that meditation can influence brain areas known to be involved in self-control among children and adults (Posner, Rothbart, Sheese, & Tang, 2007). The earlier growth of axonal density (after 2 weeks), later combined with myelination, resembles what is found in development.

We are currently working on elucidating the mechanisms by which white matter can be changed by either practice or state changes within so short a period (Posner, Tang, & Lynch, 2014). This work may lead to further understanding of the similarities and differences in the pattern of connectivity that seems to be involved in both hypnotic state induction and meditation training. The study of brain states may be fundamental to our understanding of the role of meditation and hypnosis on the resolution of conflict in the Stroop.

As we understand more about brain states, applications can be more fully directed toward achieving benefits. These include application to clinical populations—for example, those suffering from attention deficit hyperactivity disorder (ADHD), stress, mood disorders, or other syndromes related to self-control deficits (Tang et al., 2015). Training brain states may also be applied to a wider population in the educational system to improve the development of attention and self-control, now widely thought to be crucial to success in school and beyond.

Acknowledgments

This work was supported by the Office of Naval Research and NICHD (National Institute of Child Health and Human Development) grant HD060563. We would like to thank Rongxiang Tang for assistance with manuscript preparation.

References

Augustinova, M., & Ferrand, L. (2012). Suggestion does not de-automatize word reading: evidence from the semantically based Stroop task. *Psychonomic Bulletin and Review*, **19**(3), 521–527.

Cojan, Y., Waber, L., Schwartz, S., Rossier, L., Forster, A., & Vuilleumier, P. (2009). The brain under self-control: modulation of inhibitory and monitoring cortical networks during hypnotic paralysis. *Neuron*, **62**, 862–875.

Deeley, Q., Oakley, D. A., Toone, B., Giampietro, V., Brammer, M. J., & Williams, S. C. R. (2012). Modulating the default mode network using hypnosis. *International Journal of Clinical and Experimental Hypnosis*, **60**(2), 206–228, 2012.

Egner, T., Jamieson, G., & Gruzelier, J. (2005). Hypnosis decouples cognitive control from conflict monitoring processes of the frontal lobe. *NeuroImage*, **27**(4), 969–978.

Eriksen, B. A., & Eriksen, C. W. (1974). Effects of noise letters upon the identification of a target letter in a nonsearch task. *Perception and Psychophysics*, **16**, 143–149.

Fan, Y., Tang, Y. Y., Tang, R., & Posner, M. I. (2015). Time course of conflict processing modulated by brief meditation training. *Frontiers in Psychology* **6**, 911.

Gao, W., Zhu, H., Giovanello, K. S., Smith, J. K., Shen, D., Gilmore, J. H., ... Lin,W. (2009). Evidence on the emergence of the brain's default network from 2-week-old to 2-year-old healthy pediatric subjects. *Proceedings of the National Academy of Sciences*, **106**, 6790–6795.

Hillman, C.H., Erickson, K.I. & Kramer, A.F. (2008). Be smart, exercise your heart: exercise effects on brain and cognition Nature Reviews Neuroscience **9**(1), 58–65.

Holzel, B. K., Lazar, S. W., Gard, T., Schuman-Olivier, Z., Vago, D. R., & Ott, U. (2011). How does mindfulness meditation work? Proposing mechanisms of action from a conceptual and neural perspective. *Perspectives on Psychological Science*, **6**, 537–559.

Iani, C., Ricci, F., Gherri, E., & Rubichi, S. (2006). Hypnotic suggestion modulates cognitive conflict: the case of the flanker compatibility effect. *Psychological Science*, **17**(8), 721–727.

Ishigami, Y., & Klein, R. M. (2010). Repeated measurement of the components of attention using two versions of the Attention Network Test (ANT): stability, isolability, robustness, and reliability. *Journal of Neuroscience Methods*, **190**(1), 117–128.

Kane, M. J., & Engle, R. W. (2003). Working-memory capacity and the control of attention: the contributions of goal neglect, response competition, and task set to Stroop interference. *Journal of Experimental Psychology: General*, **132**(1), 47–70.

Kumar, R., Macey, P. M., Woo, M. A., & Harper, R. M. (2010). Rostral brain axonal injury in congenital central hypoventilation syndrome. *Journal of Neuroscience Research*, **88**, 2146–2154.

Kumar, R., Nguyen, H. D., Macey, P. M., Woo, M. A., & Harper, R. M. (2012). Regional brain axial and radial diffusivity changes during development. *Journal of Neuroscience Research*, **90**, 346–355.

Lifshitz, M., Bonn, N. A., Fischer, A., Kashem, I. F., & Raz, A. (2013). Using suggestions to modulate automatic processes: from Stroop to McGurk and beyond. *Cortex*, **49**, 463–473.

Lorist, M. M., & Jolij, J. (2012). Trial history effects in Stroop task performance are independent of top-down control. *PLoS ONE*, **7**(6), e39802.

MacLeod, J. W., Lawrence, M. A., McConnell, M. M., Eskes, G. A., Klein, R. M., & Shore, D. I. (2010) Appraising the ANT: psychometric and theoretical considerations of the Attention Network Test. *Neuropsychology*, **24**(5), 637–651.

McLeod, C. M. (1991). Half a century of research on the Stroop effect: an integrative review. *Psychological Bulletin*, **109**(2), 163–203.

Oakley, D. A., & Halligan, P. W. (2013). Hypnotic suggestion: opportunities for cognitive neuroscience. *Nature Reviews Neuroscience*, **14**(8), 565–576.

Parris, B. A., Dienes, Z., & Hodgson, T. L. (2013). Application of the ex-Gaussian function to the effect of the word blindness suggestion on Stroop task performance suggests no word blindness. *Frontiers in Psychology*, **4**, 647.

Petersen, S. E., & Posner, M. I. (2012). The attention system of the human brain: 20 years after. *Annual Reviews in Neuroscience*, **35**, 73–89.

Posner, M. I., & Rothbart, M. K. (2011). Brain states and hypnosis research. *Consciousness and Cognition*, **20**, 325–327.

Posner, M. I., Rothbart, M. K., Sheese, B. E., & Tang, Y. (2007). The anterior cingulate gyrus and the mechanism of self-regulation. *Cognitive Affective and Behavioral Neuroscience*, **7**, 391–395.

Posner, M. I., Rothbart, M. K., Sheese, B. E., & Voelker, P. (2014). Attention and development: behavioral and brain mechanisms. *Advances in Neuroscience*, Article ID **405094**, 9 pages. doi: org/10.1155/2014/405094

Posner, M. I., Tang, Y. Y., & Lynch, G. (2014). Mechanisms of white matter change induced by meditation. *Frontiers in Psychology*, **5**, 1220. doi: 10.3389/fpsyg.2014.01220

Raz, A. (2008). Genetics and neuroimaging of attention and hypnotizability may elucidate placebo. *International Journal of Clinical and Experimental Hypnosis*, **56**(1), 99–116.

Raz, A., Fan, J., & Posner, M. I. (2005). Hypnotic suggestion reduces conflict in the human brain. *Proceedings of the National Academy of Sciences (USA)*, **102**, 9978–9983.

Rueda, M. R., Rothbart, M. K., McCandliss, B. D., Saccomanno, L., & Posner, M. I. (2005). Training, maturation, and genetic influences on the development of executive attention. *Proceedings of the National Academy of Sciences (USA)*, **102**, 14931–14936.

Song, S. K., Sun, S. W., Ramsbottom, M. J., Chang, C., Russell, J., & Cross, A. H. (2002). Dysmyelination revealed through MRI as increased radial (but unchanged axial) diffusion of water. *Neuroimage*, **17**, 1429–1436.

Song, S. K., Sun, S. W., Ju, W. K., Lin, S. J., Cross, A. H., & Neufeld, A. H. (2003). Diffusion tensor imaging detects and differentiates axon and myelin degeneration in mouse optic nerve after retinal ischemia. *Neuroimage*, **20**, 1714–1722.

Stroop, J. R. (1935). Studies of interference in serial verbal reactions. *Journal of Experimental Psychology*, **18**, 643–661.

Tang, Y. Y., Hölzel, B. K., & Posner, M. I. (2015). The neuroscience of mindfulness meditation. *Nature Reviews Neuroscience*, **6**(4), 213–225.

Tang, Y. Y., Lu, Q., Fan, M., Yang, Y., & Posner, M. I. (2012). Mechanisms of white matter changes induced by meditation. *Proceedings of the National Academy of Sciences (USA)*, **109**(26), 10570–10574.

Tang, Y. Y., Lu, Q., Geng, X., Stein, E. A., Yang, Y., Posner, M. I. (2010). Short-term meditation induces white matter changes in the anterior cingulate. *Proceedings of the National Academy of Sciences (USA)*, **107** (35), 15649–15652.

Tang, Y.Y., Ma, Y., Fan, Y., Feng, H., Wang, J., Feng, S., ... Fan, M. (2009). Central and autonomic nervous system interaction is altered by short term meditation. *Proc. Natl. Acad. Sci. U.S.A.* **106**, 8865–8870.

Tang, Y. Y., Ma, Y., Wang, J., Fan, Y., Feng, S., Lu, Q., . . . Posner, M. I. (2007). Short-term meditation training improves attention and self-regulation. *Proceedings of the National Academy of Sciences (USA)*, **104**(43), 17152–17156.

Tang, Y. Y., & Posner, M. I. (2009). Attention training and attention state training. *Trends in Cognitive Science*, **13**(5), 222–227.

Tang, Y. Y., & Posner, M. I. (2013). Theory and method in mindfulness neuroscience. *Social Cognitive and Affective Neuroscience*, **8**, 118–20.

Tang, Y. Y., & Posner, M. I. (2014). Training brain networks and states. *Trends in Cognitive Science*, **18**(7), 345–350.

Tang, Y. Y., Rothbart, M. K., & Posner, M. I. (2012). Neural correlates of establishing, maintaining and switching brain states. *Trends in Cognitive Science*, **16**(6), 330–337.

Tang, Y. Y., Yang, L., Leve, L. D., & Harold, G. T. (2012). Improving executive function and its neurobiological mechanisms through a mindfulness-based intervention: advances within the field of developmental neuroscience. *Child Development Perspectives*, **6**, 361–366.

van Veen, V., & Carter, C. S. (2002). The timing of action-monitoring processes in the anterior cingulate cortex. *Journal of Cognitive Neuroscience*, **14**, 593–602.

Voelker, P. Sheese, B. E., Rothbart, M. K., & Posner, M. I. (2009). Variations in COMT gene interact with parenting to influence attention in early development. *Neuroscience*, **164** (1), 121–130.

West, R., & Alain, C. (2000). Effects of task context and fluctuations of attention on neural activity supporting performance of the Stroop task. *Brain Research*, **873**(1), 102–111.

Xue, S., Tang, Y. Y., & Posner, M. I. (2011). Short-term meditation increases network efficiency of the anterior cingulate cortex. *NeuroReport*, **22**(12), 570–574.

Xue, S., Tang, Y. Y., Tang, R., & Posner, M. I. (2014). Short-term meditation induces changes in brain resting EEG theta networks. *Brain and Cognition*, **87**, 1–6.

Chapter 17

A unified theory of hypnosis and meditation states: the interoceptive predictive coding approach

Graham A. Jamieson

Abstract

The relationship between the states of awareness that emerge in hypnosis and meditation and within diverging meditation practices (e.g. mindfulness and yoga) is of fundamental importance to understanding the range and potentials of human consciousness. Cognitive neuroscience provides a powerful set of tools for researchers to probe both the effects of specific conscious states and the underlying causal dynamics of their operation. Within cognitive neuroscience the Bayesian framework of predictive coding has generated deep insights into the fundamental unity of the ordinary psychological processes of perception, learning, attention, memory, and action. In what follows key concepts from predictive coding: active inference, generative models, and interoceptive predictive coding (focusing on the role of the insula) are applied to our understanding of hypnosis and meditation states to provide a unified theory of these diverse states with clear implications for researchers and clinicians alike.

Introduction

The terms "hypnosis" and "meditation" are used to refer to a bewildering array of practices across different cultural settings and in different historical epochs. They almost always point to some socially recognized pathway to out-of-the-ordinary experiences which are sought in the hope of some personal transformation. The transformations sought are as diverse as the practices themselves, but all involve some valued alteration in the unity of experience–behavior–body. This chapter seeks to reach beyond the diversity to identify the evolved neurobiological core at the heart of these methods. That core is the unified framework which regulates the moment-by-moment transformation of the mind–brain–body system. Our scientific understanding of this framework, known as *predictive coding*, has emerged only recently as a unifying principle of cognitive, affective and social neuroscience.

Predictive coding is based on the simple insight that the brain seeks to minimize discrepancies between top-down predictions, or *generative models*, and bottom-up inputs across each level of a multi-level processing system. Predictive coding promises to be the grand unifying theory of psychological neuroscience; this chapter seeks to show how that promise is made good in the science of hypnosis and meditation.

Starting from the sense of involuntariness when responding to hypnotic ideomotor suggestions, this chapter examines recent brain imaging studies and links them to developments in the neuroscience of motor control. Predictive coding is then applied to provide a unified account of brain imaging results from both ideomotor and motor paralysis suggestions by means of the unique mechanism of *active inference*, in which predictions bring about the actions needed to confirm them. The sense of reality at the core of hypnotic delusions is explained by an extension of predictive coding from the regulation of action to feeling states of the body. *Interoceptive predictive coding* provides a mechanism by which brain states corresponding to suggested experiences may bring about somatic changes. The critical role of the insula cortex in interoceptive predictive coding is explained here. Next, the interoceptive predictive coding framework is shown to account for the psychological process of aversion and attachment as it is revealed in opening-up (or mindfulness) meditation and for how those practices may effectively intervene to terminate this process.

Finally, this chapter examines concentrative (in particular, yoga) meditation practices to show how the interoceptive predictive coding mechanism enables the emergence of a series of increasingly global cortical states of synchronized gamma-band activity. Such brain states correspond to the integration of cortical representations across the highest levels of the predictive coding hierarchy into a single conscious state; literally, an expanded state of consciousness.

The shared roots of hypnosis and meditation

Hypnosis and meditation refer to families of psychological procedures that appear to have widely divergent contents, each with its own history of development in separate cultures, continents, and historical epochs. Hypnosis traces its source to the practices of ritual suggestion developed by Mesmer and his followers in Western Europe just over 200 years ago, while meditation most clearly refers to a collection of psychological practices cultivated by those religious traditions with historical sources in (Yoga) or in reaction against (Buddhism) the Vedic culture of the Indus valley in the pre-Christian era (Laumakis, 2008). Perhaps what most obviously unites hypnosis and meditation procedures today is that they have both been influential in the development of a wide range of innovative and, in many cases, highly effective psychotherapeutic and behavioral medicine interventions by practitioners in what may be called Western European cultures. In conjunction, the mechanisms by which these methods achieve their effectiveness have come under increasing scientific scrutiny, especially in the rapidly developing field of cognitive, affective and social neuroscience.

Hypnosis and meditation procedures appear to engage quite distinct psychological mechanisms (see Part 3 of this volume). In hypnosis, specific suggestions are utilized to rapidly elicit corresponding changes in experience, behavior, and physiology. The effectiveness of hypnotic suggestions in bringing about psychological state changes is largely dependent upon a readily measurable and highly stable characteristic of the person—their hypnotic susceptibility. That is, the power of hypnosis to effect change is closely related to the attributes (hypnotic susceptibility) that the hypnotized person brings to the hypnotic context.

By contrast, meditation practices may be considered forms of mental training that aim to bring about trait-like alterations in the operation of targeted psychological processes (experience, behavior, and physiology). In traditional contexts, the timescale for the complete unfolding of these training effects may be decades (or indeed lifetimes), although specific changes may be observed in months, if not weeks. At this point, it is not known if there are specific traits prior to meditation training that contribute to the effects of such training or the rate at which these effects develop (or if hypnotic susceptibility itself may be one such trait; see Chapter 7).

Despite apparent (and undoubtedly real) differences between hypnosis and meditation procedures, there are good reasons to consider the possibility of deeper underlying connections. Both appear to emerge as systematic developments of similar methods which the historical record describes in the collective religious rituals of the settled human civilizations that emerged following the development of agriculture in the Middle and Far East. Both methods are widely perceived as individual practices but remain linked to recognizable social goals. Both induce not only reports of remarkable transformations of self–world experience (indeed, such transformation is part of their very aim) but have been repeatedly demonstrated to alter diverse aspects of somatic physiology widely considered to lie outside of volitional control. In these respects, both appear to have a family similarity to the socially cultivated manifestations of altered states of consciousness widely reported in the shamanic practices of hunter-gatherer societies which preceded settled agricultural societies (Lewis-Williams & Pearce, 2005; Winkelman, 2000). These practices, in turn, appear to be the direct antecedents of the collective rituals of antiquity that ultimately gave rise to the methods of both hypnosis and meditation as they are known today. (For an in-depth examination of historical issues surrounding the investigation of these practices, see Chapter 2.)

Although it cannot be known with certainty, the archeological record suggests that a collection of associated practices eliciting apparently extraordinary transformations of experience and somatic physiology have co-evolved with humanity for an extended period. If it is true that both hypnosis and meditation have developed from these practices then, despite their important differences, it is likely that some core mechanism/s at a central nervous system level are implicated in these diverse sets of phenomena. If this hypothesized parallel exists, then it is cognitive, affective, and social (systems-level) neuroscience that must provide the framework in which the mechanisms engaged by different hypnosis suggestions and meditation practices may be investigated, described, and compared, and any deeper relationship identified.

The cognitive neuroscience of hypnosis

Operationally, hypnosis refers to a set of procedures that takes place in a clearly defined social situation between two people with mutually understood and complementary social roles—the hypnotist and the hypnotic subject. Hypnosis is further marked off from other social interactions by the administration of an induction ritual at the start and a de-induction ritual at the close. In this situation, the hypnotist, a trusted authority figure, verbally administers a series of suggestions to the hypnotic subject for experiences that contradict their ordinary experience of inner and outer reality. A "good" hypnotic subject is expected to experience these suggestions as if they are real. To the extent that their susceptibility allows, the willing hypnotic subject responds with changes in experience, behavior, and (though often overlooked) somatic physiology congruent with the suggestions of the hypnotist.

While psychophysiological studies of hypnosis extend to (at least) the early decades of the twentieth century, studies employing a systems-level neuroscience framework began to appear only in the last two decades. At the same time, the leading international centers for hypnosis research within experimental psychology were unraveling. Today, there is little research activity engaging with their sophisticated research agendas or the conflicting theoretical paradigms which drove them (see Sheehan & Perry, 1976). The new wave of hypnosis research began to apply the tools of systems-level neuroscience to understand the psychological effects of specific hypnotic suggestions but largely ignored the fundamental issues that had defined the previous generation.

These studies have focused on the brain mechanisms underlying the perceived involuntariness of response to direct (ideo)motor suggestions (Blakemore, Oakley, & Frith, 2003; Deeley, Walsh, et al., 2013) and paralysis suggestions for motor inhibition (Cojan et al., 2009; Deeley, Oakley, et al., 2013). Hypnotic analgesia suggestions have been intensively studied (Derbyshire, Whalley, & Oakley, 2009; Faymonville et al., 2003; Miltner & Weiss, 2007; Rainville, Carrier, Hofbauer, Bushnell, & Duncan, 1999), as well as a range of other changes in experience due to perceptual cognitive suggestions including alexia (to reduce response conflict) in the Stroop task (Lifshitz, Aubert Bonn, Fischer, Kashem, & Raz, 2013; Raz, Fan, & Posner, 2005), color blindness (Kosslyn, Thompson, Costantini-Ferrando, Alpert, & Spiegel, 2000; McGeown et al., 2012), and auditory hallucination (Szechtman, Woody, Bowers, & Nahmias, 1998). Collectively, these studies have made important contributions to systems-level neuroscience of volition, motor control, attention, and pain perception, and are poised to make further contributions in the areas of memory, delusion, and related clinical conditions. Oakley and Halligan (2013) provide a useful summary of much of this research in a recent *Nature Reviews Neuroscience* article.

While much has been learned about the proximal neural systems modulated by specific types of suggestion, it is apparent that in each case discrete mechanisms underlie the generation of responses to different types of hypnotic suggestion (direct motor suggestion, motor inhibition, hypnotic analgesia, etc.). Outlines of a common mechanism (supporting distinct suggestion-specific mechanisms) have not, so far, been identified in the course of these studies. Hierarchical factor modeling of behavioral response to hypnotic suggestions across a range of hypnotic susceptibility scales reveals four primary content areas (direct motor suggestion, motor inhibition, direct perceptual cognitive suggestion, and hypnotic amnesia suggestion) nested within a single higher-order factor of hypnotic susceptibility (Woody, Barnier, & McConkey, 2005). These results suggest that whatever the discrete mechanisms involved in responding to the demands of particular types of suggestion, there remains a wider integrating framework that has yet to be explained by hypnosis researchers.

In what has become widely recognized as a defining summary of the key findings from decades of hypnosis research, Kihlstrom (1997, p. 1727) described the core manifestations of the altered patterns of experience elicited in susceptible individuals by hypnotic suggestions as "subjective conviction bordering on delusion, and an experience of involuntariness bordering on compulsion." Weitzenhoffer (1980), a co-developer of the classic Stanford Scales of Hypnotic Susceptibility, considered the experienced involuntariness when responding to hypnotic suggestions as an essential feature of the classic suggestion effect, so much so that any scale of hypnotic susceptibility which failed to index this feature of hypnotic experience could not be considered as a valid measure. In fact, both the higher-order factor and each of the four primary factors identified by Woody et al. (2005) have been shown to be related to perceived involuntariness during response to the relevant hypnotic suggestions (Polito, Barnier, & Woody, 2013; see also Chapter 10).

Conviction bordering on delusion refers to the highly susceptible subject's sense of the reality of the events suggested by the hypnotist, despite their often complex awareness of contradicting aspects of reality (McConkey, 1991; Sheehan, 1991). The depth of this sense of the reality of the hypnotic suggestion is brought home by an exchange related by Amanda Barnier between a hypnotist and a highly susceptible male subject given a hypnotic sex-change suggestion. When confronted with their actual reflection in a mirror, the subject acknowledged it was them but then added "I'm not as pretty as I thought" (Barnier, Dienes, & Mitchell, 2008; Noble & McConkey, 1995).

These deep commonalities among successful experiences of diverse hypnotic suggestions likewise point beyond the acknowledged diversity of hypnotic experience (Sheehan & McConkey,

1982) to the existence of core generating processes. Following this lead, let us consider studies of hypnosis, together with conceptual frameworks within systems neuroscience, that directly address the phenomena of perceived involuntariness and perceived reality (cf. the neurophenomenology of Cardeña, Chapter 15). This comparison will provide pointers to the identity of core neural mechanisms engaged in the generation of response to hypnotic suggestions. We will then consider what relevance such mechanisms may have for the understanding of mindfulness and concentrative meditation practices.

Perceived involuntariness

While perceived involuntariness is a feature of all major types of hypnotic suggestion, it is most apparent and most readily studied in the case of ideomotor suggestions where an external force of some kind is suggested to be moving the hypnotic subject's limb. When the corresponding movement occurs, it is experienced as alien and not under the subject's control. In one relevant study, hypnosis was not the direct focus of study but, rather, ideomotor suggestions were utilized as a condition to enable the testing of hypotheses drawn from a specific neuropsychological model of motor control and motor awareness (Blakemore et al., 2003). Before considering the study itself, it will be necessary to present the underlying model.

The central component of this model is a mechanism that allows the distinction between self-generated and other-generated movement (Frith, Blakemore, & Wolpert, 2000). In this computational model, the generation of motor commands is accompanied by a corollary discharge, referred to as an "efference copy," which is issued by high-level motor control regions in parallel with the actual motor commands responsible for bringing about a specific action. The information contained in the efference copy is utilized separately by specialized motor sensory networks (in conjunction with information available from current models of the body in space and its states of motion) to generate what is referred to as a "forward model." The forward model is a prediction of the expected consequences (sensory and, in particular, proprioceptive feedback) of the current motor commands (Miall & Wolpert, 1996; Wolpert, Ghahramani, & Jordan, 1995).

Prior to arrival at the primary and secondary somatosensory cortex (parietal operculum—the parietal cortex overlaying the posterior insula), early processing of proprioceptive signals is believed to occur in the cerebellum. Here, a comparator process between incoming proprioceptive signals and current forward models acts to cancel the matching information in the bottom-up proprioceptive sensory stream. This process functions to highlight the mismatch or error signal (the difference between the predicted consequences of an action by the current forward model and the actual sensory feedback from that action) which is the information that is then passed onwards to the somatosensory cortex, leading to higher-level perceptual processing of the unpredicted component of sensory signals (Blakemore, Wolpert, & Frith, 1998). In normal operation, this system provides the basis for our capacity to discriminate between sensations originating from self-initiated actions and those originating independently of our self-agency, with the latter being experienced with greater intensity or vividness and a sense of being non-volitional or alien (see Figure 17.1). In conditions with delusions of control, such as schizophrenia, it is hypothesized that a malfunctioning of this mechanism is directly responsible for these symptoms (Frith et al., 2000).

In the experiment reported by Blakemore et al. (2003), a hypnotic ideomotor suggestion was used to elicit a left arm raising response from subjects which was experienced as passive movement caused by a (real) motor device to which the arm was attached. A PET (positron emission tomography) scanner was used to compare brain activation during the left arm raising movement

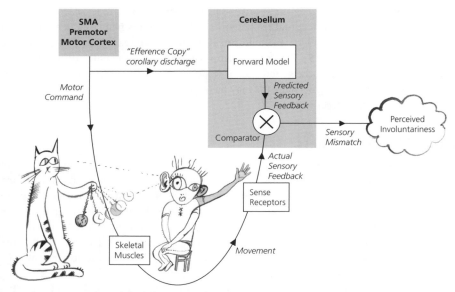

Fig. 17.1 Motor control model of the sense of agency (SMA: supplementary motor area; Premotor: premotor cortex).

when it was experienced as a volitional response (made in cooperation with an ordinary instruction) to when it was (incorrectly) experienced as being due to the movement of the attached mechanical device. It was found that activation in the (ipsilateral) cerebellum and the (contralateral) parietal operculum was increased during the response to the ideomotor suggestion (experience of non-volition) than the response to the ordinary request (experience of volition). While these results confirmed the predictions of the motor control theory under test and lent support to the proposed mechanism for delusions of alien control in various psychiatric and neuropsychological conditions, their relevance to hypnosis, beyond demonstrating the specific effects of ideomotor suggestion, has not yet been recognized.

The overlooked relevance of these findings lies in two points. Firstly, according to the motor control model, the discrepancy between forward models and proprioceptive feedback, which corresponds to the brain activations observed during deluded passive movement, is due to the failure of corollary discharges to generate accurate forward models. Now, corollary discharges may be disrupted either at their source (in the mechanism producing the action), during their transmission, or at their terminus. However, the latter two mechanisms would disrupt the sense of volition of any action made in the hypnotic context, while sense of non-volition during hypnosis is reported only for responses made to hypnotic suggestions. Consider, for example, the difference in volition experienced when responding to the hypnotist's instruction "please place your right hand straight out in front of you" with that in responding to the hypnotist's suggestion "your right hand is floating up into the air." Only the former neural mechanism limits alterations in the sense of volition to responses generated by the hypnotic suggestion itself. As the corollary discharges are presumed to be a consequence of collateral axonal projections from neurons in the motor (and/or premotor and supplementary motor) cortex, the failure to generate them implies that something other than the normal mechanism of motor control is responsible for generating these movements.

Secondly, the computational architecture of forward model generation, top-down comparison with and cancellation of bottom-up information flow to gate-predicted inputs and to feed forward mismatch or error (difference) signals for higher-level processing, corresponds closely to essential features of Karl Friston's development of predictive coding as a general theory of functional information processing in the neocortex.[1] Predictive coding, and its later development in the free energy principle (Friston, 2009), provides a unified account of perception, learning, and action in the human brain that is computationally detailed, physiologically realistic, and experimentally plausible. As such, it is potentially comparable to achievements such as Maxwell's unification of electricity and magnetism in the history of physics. Precisely because it is currently undergoing a period of rapid growth in application and critical evaluation across a range of disciplines, it cannot be predicted what directions this theory will take or what its status will be 10 years from now. What is known, however, is that this is now the most fruitful theoretical framework in systems neuroscience (Clark, 2013) and, as we shall see, it is also able to provide a single explanatory framework for the generation of both the perceived involuntariness and the sense of reality experienced when responding to hypnotic suggestions.

Predictive coding

The theory of predictive coding can be traced to Hermann von Helmholtz, the great nineteenth-century physiologist and physicist who also made fundamental contributions to the developing science of psychology. Helmholtz (1866) argued that the intrinsic ambiguity of the information registered by sense receptors required that perception could proceed only on the basis of some form of underlying inference utilizing prior expectations or knowledge gained from experience. That is, the act of perception corresponds to a process for arriving at a hypothesis as to the most likely cause of the current stimulation given prior knowledge or expectations (Gregory, 1997).

In the 1990s, Geoffrey Hinton and co-workers developed a class of neural network models called Helmholtz machines, which are designed to uncover hidden structures in their data inputs by learning to create *generative models* that best predict these inputs (Dayan, Hinton, Neal, & Zemel, 1995). These networks are comprised of a hierarchy of layers (beginning with the input layer), with bottom-up (feed forward) and top-down (feedback) connections between the elements in adjacent layers (see Figure 17.2).

Each layer within a Helmholtz machine contains elements of two distinctive types: those that represent predictions of the bottom-up inputs being received by the layer below (labeled as R or representation units in the schematic diagram shown in Figure 17.2) and those that represent the error (in effect, the difference) between the predicted inputs of that layer and its actual inputs (labeled E or error units in Figure 17.2). Aside from the bottom-most level of "perceptual input," *feed-forward* connections in these models transmit the *prediction error* from the error units in each layer to representation units in the layer above, thereby constituting the current input to that layer. *Feedback* connections transmit *predictions* of the expected inputs from the representation units of the current layer to the error units of the layer below (which, in turn, enables these error units to make current prediction error calculations).

In operation, each layer in these networks is organized so as to minimize the activity in the layer below—that is, to minimize prediction error. Successive relays of updated predictions and prediction errors are passed up and down the hierarchy of layers until information-processing activity

---

[1] There are important differences in how these concepts are implemented in current motor control and predictive coding approaches (Friston, 2011) but this is not critical for the current argument.

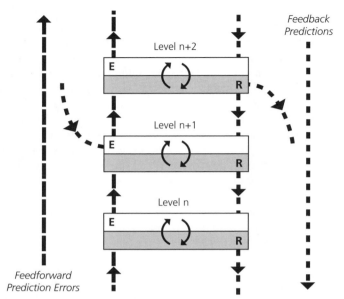

Fig. 17.2 Hierarchical predictive coding model of perception and learning (E: error units; R: prediction units).

in the system rapidly converges to a minimum in which the state of activity in the representation units across the different layers of the system maximally explains or predicts the initial inputs to the system. A useful metaphor is to think of rolling a marble into a basin, the marble will roll around rapidly moving up and down the sides of the basin until it settles at that point where free (in this case, kinetic) energy is at a minimum, the bottom point of the basin. At such minima, the sum state of the representational units constitutes the generative model or best prediction by the system of the causes of its current input. In the case of incoming sensory signals, the corresponding generative model is none other than the momentary contents of perception (Friston, 2009).

Motor suggestions as active inferences

It is remarkable that so many of the specific elements of the motor control model, which provides a compelling account of the experienced involuntariness of responses to hypnotic ideomotor suggestion, should correspond so closely with the operational principles of predictive coding, a model developed to explain not how the brain is able to control its actions in the world but how it is able to perceive that world. The wider relevance of predictive coding to understanding the generation of hypnotic responses becomes even more apparent when one considers how it has been extended in order to account for the generation and control of motor actions.

In predictive coding, the functional activity of the brain develops out of the need to minimize the prediction errors arising from the moment-by-moment collision, across multiple levels, between the incessant flow of bottom-up inputs and the top-down predictions generated by continually forming and reforming models of the sources of those inputs. In the case of exteroception, where sensory inputs are driven by external sources, prediction errors are typically minimized by updating generative models to match predictions with inputs. However, in the case of proprioception, where sensory inputs are derived from the activity of the muscles themselves, another option is open, and that is to change the movement of the muscles, through motor commands, to conform to the predictions of the generative model—a process described by Friston (2010) as *active inference* (see Figure 17.3).

In the active inference model of motor control, cortical representations send proprioceptive predictions, rather than motor commands, through descending spinal pathways that then trigger spinal motor arcs into action to minimize proprioceptive prediction errors by bringing about the necessary movements of the skeletal muscles (Adams, Shipp, & Friston, 2013). An example which illustrates this process, when we are aware of it, would be "feeling our way" through our house in the dark; we reach out, anticipating the touch that we seek to confirm through our movements (Friston, 2010).

Using predictive coding to interpret Blakemore et al's (2003) hypnotic arm raising study, it may be considered that immediate top-down predictions have failed to adequately cancel unexpected proprioceptive signals, resulting in enhanced proprioceptive prediction errors during the suggested ideomotor action. This, in turn, leads to the updating of generative models at higher levels to include a representation of the action as non-volitional. Although this account goes some way to explaining the subjective experience of the hypnotized participant, it does not adequately explain how the action is generated without triggering proprioceptive representations and their associated feedback predictions.

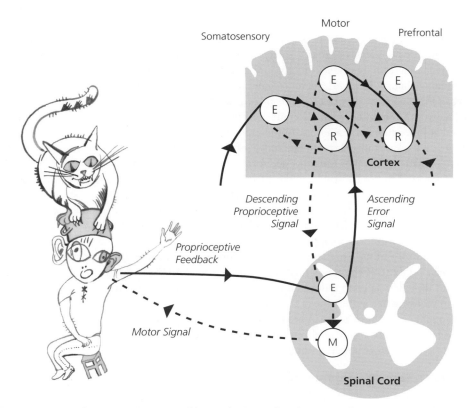

Fig. 17.3 Active inference: motor control by predictive coding (E: error units; M: motor neuron; R: prediction units).

Another hypnosis experiment may provide the clue. Cojan et al. (2009) investigated hypnotic motor paralysis (traditionally referred to as "challenge" suggestions), where it is suggested that some ordinary action has become impossible (due to an illusory scenario) and then subjects are challenged to make that movement. Those who can experience this suggestion not only fail to make the requested motor response but give every appearance of trying actively to make the response. Cojan et al. (2009) found that the right motor cortex became active when subjects were apparently trying to respond during a suggestion for left arm paralysis. This was interpreted as confirming that real motor intentions were being formed. However, they also found that activity increased in the precuneus (medial parietal association cortex), a region with a key role in generating the contents of multimodal imagery, episodic recall (self-representation in memory), and other self-related representations. The more active region of the precuneus showed greater functional connectivity with the right motor cortex during the paralysis suggestion, whereas the right premotor cortex (which is usually responsible for orchestration of the commands executed by the motor cortex) showed decreased functional connectivity with the right motor cortex. It appears that (medial parietal) self-representations generated by suggestions, in conjunction with the reduced influence of the premotor cortex and frontal regions involved in executive control, are responsible for hypnotic motor paralysis.

Generative models are hierarchically integrated networks which span across many levels of cortical representation enabling them to provide context-sensitive guidance to both perceptual and motor processes. In this way, ongoing perception and action are open to modification by the influence of multimodal, higher-level representation units. Thus, the scope of generative models can potentially extend beyond perceptions (exteroception) and action intentions (proprioception) to include high-level constructs such as self-representations and abstract social concepts.

It appears that in hypnotic ideomotor and challenge suggestions, the words of the hypnotist are inducing changes in high-level representational units within generative models (in this case, physical-self models incorporated in the precuneus) which predict the inputs to and receive prediction errors from a variety of different perceptual and proprioceptive representational units situated at lower hierarchical levels. In the predictive coding account of motor control (Adams et al., 2013), the latter are able to initiate active inference in the motor system to produce either the suggested forms of action or the suggested forms of paralysis (see Figure 17.3).

The sources of motor control in active inference are distinct from the action intentions, which engage representational units in the premotor cortex and normally generate the post-motor command feedback predictions which are compared to actual feedback to compute the prediction errors which amplify or attenuate the sensations which underlie the sense of volition. The contrasting role of premotor and supplementary motor areas predicted by an active inference account of motor control and the experience of non-volition in hypnosis receives support in the findings of Deeley et al. (2013) who report that loss of perceived control during hypnotic motor suggestions was directly related to reduced functional connectivity between the supplementary motor area and motor cortex at the time of the response.

Through the process of active inference, predictive coding goes beyond the earlier motor control model to provide a unified account of suggested ideomotor actions and motor paralysis in hypnosis and the sense of non-volition which accompanies these responses.

Hypnotic responses as generative models

Predictive coding provides a mechanism whereby high-level representations of the meaning of hypnotic suggestions are able to effect changes in experience and behavior. Recent proposals, which include the operation of active inference in the self-regulation of the autonomic nervous system (Seth, 2013), provide a single integrated mechanism by which hypnotic suggestions may also regulate peripheral physiology. Generative models of the meaning of suggestions may themselves remain close to a literal interpretation of the words of the hypnotist or may range widely to include idiosyncratic representations related to personal identity, motivations, expectations, and beliefs (Sheehan & McConkey, 1982). Likewise, many aspects of the wider cultural context and cues from the social situation and interpersonal interaction with the hypnotist (Barber, 2000; Orne, 1977) may themselves become incorporated into the generative models which represent the personal meaning of the unfolding hypnotic suggestion.

Insofar as it is legitimate to construe the predictions by representational units of lower-level inputs as "expectancies" and the lower-level inputs predicted as "responses," then such generative models may be considered to be the neural implementation of the "response expectancies," anticipations of involuntary responses to suggestion, proposed by Kirsch (1991, 1999, 2000) as the proximal causes of both hypnotic and placebo responses. At any rate, in the predictive coding framework, hypnotic response expectancies must be considered to be a subset of the generative models elicited by hypnotic suggestions.

There is, however, one major problem for the identification of the hierarchically organized multi-level, multi-domain generative models as the locus for the experiential, behavioral, and physiological responses to hypnotic suggestions, and this is a problem shared by all forms of active inference. By the very nature of hypnotic suggestions, the corresponding generative models do not predict current exteroceptive, proprioceptive, and interoceptive inputs. That is, they inherently drive lower-level prediction errors rather than prediction matches. Unless this process is modulated in some way, it will rapidly destabilize the (suggested) generative model and a hypnotic response will not unfold.

Bottom-up prediction errors continually destabilize each level of the current generative model. This is a special problem for the emergence and stability of generative models derived from hypnotic suggestions as it is of the essence of hypnosis that these suggestions (McConkey, 1991; Orne, 1959) describe states of affairs within and without the hypnotized person that are *not objectively real*. So, for example, in the case of an arm levitation suggestion, there is not actually a helium balloon tied to the subject's wrist gently pulling it slowly but surely up into the air. Any generative models corresponding to the experiential or behavioral response to such a suggestion would produce a surge of predictive error signals across all levels of the model, quickly correcting it with a model more attuned to reality. In fact, this scenario corresponds closely to the experience of low susceptible subjects who, although willing, are unable to respond to hypnotic suggestions. The generation of prediction errors and their subsequent effect on the updating of representation units must be temporarily constrained to allow generative models corresponding to hypnotic suggestions to develop and persist (cf. Shor, 1959, on hypnosis and the loss of generalized reality orientation).

However, prediction errors and their updating of representation units cannot be totally suspended in hypnosis as they constitute the very processes by which the spoken suggestion is itself understood. In order to be attuned to the changing demands of the hypnotist's suggestions, the subject must be able to process and incorporate key aspects of their actual reality in the generative models that correspond to their hypnotic response. Consider the actual example of an age-regressed French-Canadian subject described by Peter Sheehan who, when it was suggested he was a little boy, five years of age, began responding to the English questions of the (monolingual) Australian hypnotist in French (the only language he could speak at that age), but when it was suggested (again in English) that he grow up again and come back to the present, immediately resumed speaking in English. Or consider the following suggestion, "you will not be able to hear anything until I tell you that you are able to do so." If the subject becomes literally unable to hear, they will be unable to respond to the verbal termination of the suggestion. *In order to respond successfully, they must both respond and not respond at the same time.* This dual reality requirement is implicit in all hypnotic suggestions. Therefore, hypnotic responding would be impossible if there were a total suppression of prediction errors by the suggested generative models.

Predictive coding and the sense of reality

Szechtman et al. (1998) conducted a PET study of highly susceptible participants *during hypnosis* as they experienced a hypnotically suggested voice (hallucination), listened to a real voice, imagined a voice speaking to them, or were at rest (hypnotic baseline condition). Comparisons of real and hallucinated voices on the one hand (shared sense of reality) with imagined and baseline (absent sense of reality) on the other revealed that the only region consistently activated across these comparisons was the right rostral anterior cingulate cortex (rACC). In addition, ratings of perceived externality (reality) of the voice during hypnotic hallucination correlated extremely highly ($r = 0.95$) with the degree of blood flow in this region. Note that in this correlation, the region of interest was *identified independently* of the experiential ratings (see Kriegeskorte, Lindquist, Nichols, Poldrack, & Vul, 2010; Vul & Pashler, 2012). Szechtman et al. concluded that activity in the right rACC played a critical role in generating the same subjective sense of reality irrespective of whether the stimulus was real or a hypnotically suggested hallucination. This finding suggests that personal experience of reality is more important to understanding the behavior of an individual than the objective existence of that reality and has profound treatment implications for persons experiencing verbal hallucinations regardless of their underlying cause.

By extension, Szechtman et al. (1998) interpreted rACC activation in their study as indicating that the sense of reality experienced in hypnotic hallucinations is also closely tied to the processes of emotional regulation. This surprising interpretation is supported by neuroanatomical studies of the network of descending projections from the rACC responsible for the arousal of the autonomic nervous system (Craig, 2002). Functional neuroimaging reports of autonomic nervous system regulation during biofeedback also identified that the dorsal regions of the ACC are the cortical source of phasic increases in sympathetic nervous system activity, whereas the rostral region of the ACC is the cortical source of phasic increases in parasympathetic nervous system (Critchley, Nagai, Gray, & Mathias, 2011) activity. Etkin, Egner, Peraza, Kandel, and Hirsch (2006) also identified the rACC as the source of control of affective interference in an emotional Stroop paradigm. Taken together, such findings help to explain the effectiveness of clinical hypnosis as a treatment for anxiety and emotional eating disorders.

Woody and Szechtman (2000) coined the term "yedasentience" for the sense of reality or "feeling of knowing" that acts as an internal safety signal to turn off both threat-related sympathetic arousal and cognitive-perceptual threat evaluations (reality orientation). Rather than arising from an apparently seamless fit of the hypnotic hallucination with ordinary experience, the sense of reality experienced during hypnotic suggestion is understood as a feeling state which "may then serve as the kernel around which plausible content is readily elaborated" (Woody & Szechtman, 2011, p.7). The sense of reality in hypnotic hallucinations also appears to have much in common with the concept of "presence," the sense of "being there" in the virtual reality created by some technological application (Sanchez-Vives & Slater, 2005). Recently, Seth, Suzuki, and Critchley (2011) have proposed an interoceptive predictive coding model of presence (see Figure 17.4), focused on the anterior insula, which provides important insights into how generative models are able to emerge in response to hypnotic suggestions. It is this process, in turn, which provides a common mechanism for the development of experience in a variety of meditative practices.

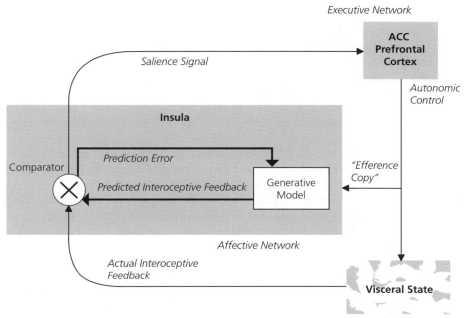

Fig. 17.4 Interoceptive predictive coding of presence, the sense of reality (ACC: anterior cingulate cortex).

Sensory inputs to the brain may be classified according to the sources of sensory information and the anatomical features of the neural pathways that convey those inputs to the brain (Craig, 2002). For present purposes, we will consider three major divisions: exteroception (defined here as conveying signals derived from the external world), proprioception (position and motion of the limbs), and interoception (which conveys inputs from throughout the entire body, concerning the full range of physiological states regulated through homeostasis).

Predictive coding of exteroceptive inputs leads to generative models of the external world (perceptual contents), while predictive coding of proprioceptive inputs leads to generative models of bodily actions and, in particular, allows for the control of action through the process of active inference. In the case of interoceptive inputs, which project to the posterior region of the insula cortex, it has been proposed that feeling states are the result of predictions concerning the physiological state of the body (Singer, Critchley, & Preuschoff, 2009). For example, Paulus and Stein (2006) propose that the feeling state of anxiety results from a mismatch between predicted and actual bodily arousal inputs to the right insula. In the predictive coding account, the generation of a sense of agency is derived from the successful prediction (and thus cancellation) of proprioceptive inputs.

In a parallel account, Seth et al. (2011) propose that the sense of presence develops from the successful prediction of changes in interoceptive inputs resulting from sympathetic and parasympathetic control signals (arising from the dorsal and rostral ACC respectively) and from motor responses to exteroceptive inputs. In this chapter, it will be argued that interoceptive predictive coding plays a pivotal role in the generation of hypnotic responses and provides the essential link between hypnosis and meditation in the emergence of new states of awareness.

The role of the insula

The insula plays the central role in the interoceptive predictive coding model of presence and in the extension of that model to the sense of reality, to hypnotic suggestion, and onwards to meditative consciousness, which we will consider shortly. Beforehand, however, a brief overview of relevant aspects of the functional anatomy of the insula is necessary.

The functional roles of the insula are highly diverse, a feature intrinsically reflected in its structure and connectivity (Klein, Ullsperger, & Danielmeier, 2013). *Reference to the insula as an undifferentiated structure with a single function is highly misleading.* Processing of interoceptive inputs in the insula appears to progress internally along a posterior to anterior gradient (Cerliani et al., 2012). The posterior insula (PI) receives interoceptive signals from viscera throughout the body, many of which are projected onto a somatotopic representation (Craig, 2002, 2009) of the various physical feeling states of different locations within the body (including feelings associated with movements). Outward projections then extend externally to many areas associated with motor control, such as the posterior parietal and lateral motor cortices (Cerliani et al., 2012).

In addition to the representation of interoceptive inputs as the physiological state of the body in posterior and mid insula, numerous functional imaging studies have implicated the anterior insula (AI) in the generation of a wide range of emotional experiences, including empathy and other social emotions (Craig, 2009; Gu, Hof, Friston, & Fan, 2013). A recent meta-analysis of 1768 functional imaging studies reveals another important distinction between the dorsal and ventral anterior insula (dAI and vAI), with cognitive and attentional processes linked to the former and emotional-social processes linked to the latter (Kurth, Zilles, Fox, Laird, & Eickhoff, 2010).

This division is further supported by resting-state functional connectivity analyses (Deen, Pitskel, & Pelphrey, 2011) which identified three distinct regions within the insula—the PI, dAI, and vAI (see Figure 17.5)—on the basis of their distinct networks of intrinsic connectivity. The PI was most closely connected with the motor and somatosensory cortex, while the dAI was most closely connected with the more dorsal (sympathetic efferent) regions of the ACC, and the vAI was most strongly connected with the more rostral (parasympathetic efferent) regions of the ACC. However, all three regions within the insula were strongly interconnected, indicating that one does not function independently of the others. Recently, a meta-analysis of over 4400 imaging studies confirmed essentially the same tripartite division of PI, dAI, and vAI, based separately on an analysis of functional connectivity and functional co-activations (Chang, Yarkoni, Khaw, & Sanfey, 2013).

Menon and Uddin (2010) identified the AI, together with the ACC, as the central hub in a "saliency network" which distinguishes motivationally relevant information (e.g., the fruit seen through the leaves or the snake lying in the grass) for the immediate attention of cognitive and behavioral control systems (see also Corbetta & Schulman, 2002; Dorsenbach et al., 2007). The role of the AI in this network is to detect salient events in a bottom-up fashion, thereby triggering a switch in attention from ongoing self-referential mental activity mediated by the default mode network (DMN; with its major hubs in the rostral-most and posterior divisions of the cingulate cortex) to goal-directed responses controlled by the central executive network (CEN; with major hubs in the left and right dorsolateral prefrontal cortex and posterior parietal cortex) (see also Chapter 18). In terms of predictive coding, a salient stimulus/event is one that brings about a high discrepancy between predicted/expected homeostatic states and current interoceptive inputs. The resulting bottom-up interoceptive prediction error triggers the representation of stimulus salience by the anterior insula which then (through the salience network; SN) initiates corresponding switches in attentional focus, goal-directed executive control, and autonomic nervous system activity in order to resolve the discrepancy.

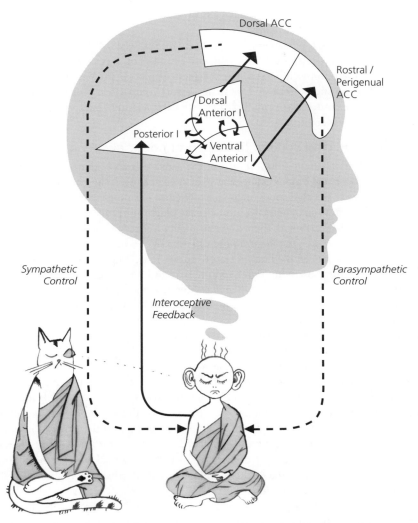

Fig. 17.5 Interoceptive inference: insula and ACC networks of homeostatic control (ACC: anterior cingulate cortex; I: insula).

The dAI and vAI appear to play distinct roles in representing and responding to aspects of stimulus/event salience through their unique connectivity networks. In a study which systematically manipulated both attention tasks and affective experiences, Touroutoglou, Hollenbeck, Dickerson, and Feldman Barrett (2012) were able to demonstrate that the strength of intrinsic (right) vAI connectivity with the perigenual ACC (the rostral-most region of the ACC which overlaps with the region identified by Szechtman et al. (1998) as activated by the sense of reality in hypnotic hallucination) correlated only with the emotional intensity experienced when viewing negative images. In the same study, the strength of intrinsic (right) dAI connectivity with the dACC was correlated only with performance on the Trail Making Test measures of visual attention, processing speed, and set switching.

In the predictive coding model of emotion (Seth, 2013; Seth et al., 2011), specific emotions are generated through the process of updating generative models of the causes of changes in the felt state of the body (interoceptive inputs). Current evidence points to the vAI as the likely site of the top-down (prediction) and bottom-up (prediction error) comparison processes which establish integrative generative models across multiple hierarchical levels and, thus, provide the contents of particular emotional experiences.

Interoceptive predictive coding: the origin of noetic awareness

Woody and Szechtman (2000, 2007) interpret the sense of reality that is experienced when responding to hypnotic suggestions as a feeling state, specifically, a feeling of knowing, rather than as a cognitive inference or belief about ongoing experience. It is noteworthy then that across both Buddhist and Yoga traditions, meditation practice is taught to result in transformative or self-altering experiences that carry with them a noetic quality, a sense of knowing, as a core experiential feature (Goleman, 1984). Despite profound differences in other aspects of their content, this noetic dimension of advanced meditation states appears to overlap the core phenomenology of hypnotic experience for those with high hypnotic susceptibility. In recent technological developments, the experience of "presence," which has emerged as a central feature of the psychology of virtual reality simulations, appears to be another example of this sense of noetic awareness or feeling of knowing (Seth et al., 2011).

By extending the recently developed predictive coding model of conscious presence to the feeling of knowing in hypnosis, a unified predictive coding model of hypnosis emerges that is able to account for the critical problem faced by the active inference model of hypnotic involuntariness. From a predictive coding perspective, this is the problem caused by the disruptive effects of bottom-up prediction errors on the emergence and stability of generative models incorporating hypnotic suggestions. From a phenomenological perspective, this is the problem of setting aside reality awareness in order to experience the hypnotic suggestion. If the generation of the self-transforming experiences found within the practices of hypnosis and meditation do share a common root, then a correct understanding of that process will be essential both for the neuroscience of (human) conscious states and the further development of effective interventions based on the principles of meditation and suggestion.

In the present interoceptive predictive coding account, the "sense of reality" or "feeling of knowing" that arises in the context of hypnosis is considered to develop in the same way as the sense of "presence," that is, as a consequence of successful matching between top-down predictions and interoceptive inputs leading to a cancellation of bottom-up prediction error signals within the vAI. These accurately predicted interoceptive inputs are presumed to develop from the bodily effects of parasympathetic efferents arising from the rostral-perigenual regions of the ACC, as reported by Szechtman et al. (1998). Put another way, the sense of reality in hypnosis arises as a form of *interoceptive inference* (Gu et al., 2013; Seth, 2013).

Interoceptive predictions in the vAI provide set points that drive the response of the parasympathetic nervous system through that region's intrinsic network connections in a manner that directly parallels the role of proprioceptive predictions in the predictive coding model of motor control (Adams et al., 2013). The reduction in proprioceptive prediction errors leads to reduced pressure for updating of current predictive representations, which in turn allows for extended periods of stability to emerge in the activity of the multi-level networks comprising the generative models evoked by a hypnotic suggestion. In this theory, the experienced sense of reality (see

Figure 17.4) is a necessary condition which facilitates the coherent synchronization of the wider network hierarchies that correspond to the experience of the hypnotic suggestion.

Now, recall that bottom-up interoceptive prediction errors are the key inputs driving the detection of salient stimulus events by the dAI and its role in recruiting stimulus-focused attention and goal-directed executive control networks. In predictive coding, the effect of prediction errors on the updating of representational models is weighted in proportion to the precision of those errors, quantified as the inverse of the signal variance (Friston, 2009). In this way, neuromodulators such as noradrenalin (NA), which enhance the signal-to-noise ratio, act to amplify the effect (or gain) of prediction error units upon the prediction units comprising the current generative model, a process that is directly equated with the psychological construct of attention (Friston, 2010).

A critical component of EEG event-related potentials linked to the salience-driven orienting of attention is the P3, a widespread positive waveform emerging 300–600 milliseconds following the stimulus event. The P3 has been interpreted as the cortical information-processing effect of the response of the locus coeruleus (LC), the brainstem source of cortical noradrenergic inputs, to the identification of a salient stimulus event (Nieuwenhuis, Aston-Jones, & Cohen, 2005). Precisely such experimental paradigms elicit activation of the dAI as distinct from other regions of the insula (Harsay, Spaan, Wijnen, & Ridderinkhof, 2011). Moreover, the AI itself is richly connected with the LC (Aston-Jones & Cohen, 2005).

Taken together, these observations support the proposal that a major effect of the error signals indicating a mismatch between interoceptive predictions and inputs in the dAI is to trigger attention to the stimulus event in order to sharpen the precision of prediction errors that drive the rapid and accurate updating of generative models related to the experience of the external event. In fact, the dAI is almost always found to be activated when an experimental paradigm requires goal-directed executive control (Yarkoni, Poldrack, Nichols, Van Essen, & Wager, 2011). It is proposed here that it is the activity of the dAI that drives both reality awareness and the engagement of goal-directed executive control, and that this process must be temporarily suspended (or at least greatly diminished) in order for hypnotic responses to be generated and sustained (see Chapter 12).

If this interpretation is true, then in the rapidly shifting internal and external environments that the brain has evolved to model and respond to, the accuracy of generative models will be closely tied to rapid and precise updating of any incongruence with proprioceptive and interoceptive inputs. That is, the "reality orientation" or fidelity of multi-level generative models to the actual causes of the nervous system's sensory inputs will be closely linked to the activity of the dAI and its corresponding networks. In the model proposed here, interoceptive prediction error is a major source of this dAI SN output. By contrast, the sense of reality is generated by cancellation of interoceptive prediction error in the vAI. Therefore:

1 the ability to quickly generate the felt sense of reality by active interoceptive inference in the vAI simultaneously brings about a reduction in the dAI support for reality orientation and goal-directed executive control;

2 transiently diminishing the impact of bottom-up prediction errors on representational updating throughout the remainder of the cognitive system;

3 and permitting, for a time, the proliferation of generative models incorporating, to varying extents, the perceived meaning of the hypnotist's suggestions throughout representations at various levels of their hierarchy.

In this way, the sense of reality provides the kernel of feeling around which the contents of the hypnotic suggestion manifest, much as Woody and Szechtman (2000, 2007) have proposed.

A recent study investigating the relationship between interoceptive accuracy and susceptibility to the induction of the rubber hand illusion (RHI) provides support for this model. The RHI is induced when the participant observes a rubber hand being touched in synchrony with touch being applied (outside the field of vision) to their own hand. In such conditions, participants report experiencing the rubber hand as if it were their own hand. Tsakiris, Tajadura-Jiménez, and Costantini (2011) found that participants' susceptibility to this profound alteration in the experience of body ownership was inversely related to their ability to accurately perceive their own heartbeat. The beat-to-beat interval of the heart is not constant, even at rest, and accurate perception of one's own heartbeat over a period of time can be considered to reflect the accuracy of continually updated interoceptive predictive models and, hence, the sensitivity of these models to correction by prediction errors (reality orientation). Consistent with the theory developed here, the emergence and maintenance of this profound alteration in the experience of the self is associated with less, rather than more, sensitivity to interoceptive prediction errors by their corresponding generative models.

The proposed role of active interoceptive inference in generating responses to hypnotic suggestions implies that the core effects of hypnosis must include changes in somatic physiology in addition to the intensively studied behavioral and experiential effects. For example, both hypnotic induction and hypnotic susceptibility have been shown to modulate stress-induced endothelial dysfunction (Jambrik, Sebastiani, Picano, Ghelarducci, & Santarcangel0, 2005), heart rate variability (Diamond, Davis, & Howe, 2007, and ventricular arrhythmia (Taggart et al., 2005). The present theory has the further implication that vAI predictive representations may act as set points to bring about the psychophysiological effects of individual hypnotic suggestions (and placebo effects; Kirsch, 1999, 2000) by a process of interoceptive inference. It directly supports the investigation and development of clinical applications of hypnotic techniques based on these principles. It may also provide a framework that can guide similar investigations of the clinical applications of the somatic and emotion-regulation effects of various meditation practices.

Opening-up and concentrative meditation

Building upon a distinction found in the Abhidhamma—a collection of early (but by no means universally accepted) Buddhist texts containing systematic reflections on the teachings and (meditation) practices of its historical community—psychological studies of meditation (Goleman, 1977; Naranjo & Ornstein, 1971) have adopted the terms "opening-up" and "concentrative" meditation (understood as describing the object of attention) to classify a wide range of meditation practices across different traditions. The former was intended to include all forms of mindfulness meditation, a fundamental practice in most schools of Buddhism, while the latter was intended to include most Yoga meditation practices (including mantra meditation) as well as the preliminary meditation exercises upon which Buddhist mindfulness practice is developed. In reality, however, major Buddhist and Yoga schools teach a variety of meditation practices which appear to include both "opening-up" and "concentrative" methods. Although these two categories do not exhaust the diversity of existing meditation traditions, the current model is specifically directed to understanding the major paradigms of Buddhist mindfulness and Yoga concentrative meditation practice and teaching.

Opening-up—mindfulness meditation

Which practices constitute mindfulness and how it should be defined are strenuously contested within the current meditation research literature (Chiesa, 2013; Dorjee, 2010)—and perhaps it has always been so. For present purposes, it can be said that during mindfulness meditation, practitioners seek to be aware of whatever experiences arise, without approval or rejection (and, by implication, any mental response arising from such evaluations) but, rather, maintaining a state of simple observation of whatever is currently present in awareness. Concentrative or focused-attention meditations direct awareness to some specific focus (content) and seek to maintain that awareness continually, without disruption. When the meditator notices that their awareness has drifted, they simply return it to the object of their practice.

The most basic practice within Theravada Buddhism and many (but not all) forms of Mahayana Buddhism starts from maintaining awareness on the (interoceptive) sensations of breathing, held to be a concentrative practice, which then subtly shifts to awareness of the flow of these sensations, a practice which is now mindfulness proper. In this way, the development of an adequate capacity for maintaining focused awareness is seen as a prerequisite for mindfulness practice to begin. From this point, mindfulness can be extended to many circumstances, including daily life—an approach that has recently been adopted with great success in a growing number of psychotherapeutic interventions.

Interoceptive predictive coding appears to play a major role in both concentrative and mindfulness practices. In Buddhist psychology, the origin of suffering lies in our attachment and aversion to the feelings evoked by the events we experience, which in turn gives rise to a flood of mental activity seeking to cling to or flee from ongoing experiences (Grabovac, Lau, & Willett, 2011). The aim of mindfulness, in its Buddhist context, is to cut off the process which generates suffering at its root, by ending the habitual psychological response of attachment and aversion. When this is achieved, knowledge or insight into the true nature of things arises, and it is this state that is the ultimate goal of the practice (Dorjee, 2010; MacKenzie, 2013).

The feeling states of the body arise through a series of interoceptive processing steps extending from the posterior to mid insula (Craig, 2002, 2009). The generation of emotional experience requires a further step: the process of comparing these feeling states with predicted states in the vAI. The generative models (the contents of our emotions) that emerge from this process are in a state of constant change, driven by the flow of prediction errors in a self-perpetuating cycle. In this way, the contents of our everyday emotions (both pleasant and unpleasant) may be considered as experiences of the "unsatisfactoriness" of the felt moment which, by providing the next set of predictions, propel the experienced unsatisfactoriness of the following moment.

The process by which the salience of a stimulus event captures attention and drives the response of higher cognitive systems (memories, thoughts, plans, and expectations) appears to correspond closely with the dynamics of attachment/aversion and mental proliferation described in Buddhist psychologies of mindfulness. If this correspondence is valid, then the non-reactivity or non-attachment to the contents of awareness that is cultivated in mindfulness must correspond to a heightened level of matching between interoceptive predictions and the felt state of the body, as well as to a reduction in the salience response of the dAI (as does the sense of reality in the case of hypnosis). On this account, a suitable awareness of bodily sensations, such as breathing, acts as a gateway to unfolding states of mindfulness.

An important consequence of the process described here will be the longer duration of current generative models (with perceived slowing of time; Naish, 2007; Ott, 2013) due to reduced destabilization by prediction error signals. Thus, it is expected that time dilation will form an essential part of the cognitive phenomenology accompanying the interoceptive representations, within the insula and across the highest available levels of model representation hierarchies, which are now released from the ordinary disruption by the salience and central executive networks.

Concentrative meditation

Paradoxically, the outcomes of maintaining a single focus of awareness without disruption for extended periods during concentrative meditation may be explained in a similar way. The static postures, rhythmic breathing (pranayama), and repetitive mantras found in Yoga meditation may all be expected to establish a continuous predictable pattern of interoceptive inputs, while practices such as body scan meditation focus awareness specifically on interoceptive inputs, the felt state of the body. These practices may be expected to diminish interoceptive prediction mismatch in the dAI and vAI. In turn, this will result in diminished salience system activity and reduced constraints by bottom-up prediction errors from sensory and motor inputs, as well as reduced activity within the executive control system. This allows the emergence of active, integrated networks of high-level multimodal or amodal representations prohibited by everyday modes of brain activity.

Progress in Yoga meditation has been traditionally described as similar to a process of peeling the successive layers or skins of an onion to reach its innermost core (Maheswarananda, 2005). In a predictive coding framework, the outermost layers will correspond to generative self-models, dominated by prediction errors derived firstly from exteroception, then from somatosensory and proprioceptive inputs, then from the activity of the central executive (e.g., thoughts and memories). This process requires not only the frequency but also the influence (the signal gain or attentional amplification) of these bottom-up prediction errors to be attenuated, which itself requires reduced activity/reactivity in the dAI and associated SN. Growing out of this process of external withdrawal, the practitioners' experience of meditation is said to undergo a series of changes. The first is undisturbed concentration on the meditation practice, then complete absorption in the meditation practice, and, finally, the emergence of a form of awareness described as self-realization (samadhi) that is the final goal of the practice.

Placed in this sequence, "concentration" in meditation cannot be seen as focused attention elicited either by the SN or the central executive network, although it has been habitually interpreted in this way by generations of experimental psychologists. Longer periods of undisturbed awareness of meditation practice do correspond to reduced mind wandering and, thus, reduced activity in the DMN (Brewer et al., 2011; Farb, Segal, Mayberg, Bean, McKeon, Fatima, & Anderson, 2007; Hölzel et al., 2007), but this appears to be an effect rather than a cause of changes in meditative experience. Rather, longer periods of synchronized activity across the representational elements of generative models, particularly at the higher multimodal and amodal levels of such representational hierarchies, will spontaneously occur due to the *absence* of the influence of the bottom-up prediction error signals that focused attention and executive control facilitate. This account directly parallels the explanation given for the same phenomena in hypnosis by dissociated control theory (Jamieson & Sheehan, 2004; Woody & Sadler, 2008).

Absorption

Absorption is a quality of experience that emerges in hypnosis, meditation, and episodes of daily life (Jamieson, 2005; Ott, 2007; Tellegen & Atkinson, 1974; see also Chapters 6 and 14). During absorption one becomes oblivious to other concerns (loss of generalized reality orientation; Shor, 1959) and becomes so immersed in the current experience that it acquires a sense of hyper-reality (cf. the sense of presence). During absorption, the sense of being an observing self, separate from what is being experienced, vanishes (Pekala, 1991).

Absorption may occur in periods of imaginative involvement, religious contemplation, listening to music, experiencing beauty in art or in nature, and in many other daily-life contexts (Hilgard,

1970). This quality of experience is also characterized by a sense of effortlessness (Bowers, 1978), which further separates it from everyday goal-directed striving.

In the theory proposed here, states of absorption during hypnosis and meditation (as elsewhere) can be understood as an extension of the same processes that lead from external withdrawal to concentration. As the time periods during which high-level generative models (which provide the contents of consciousness in moments of absorption) can be maintained is extended, it is reasonable to predict that the scope (i.e., the number, diversity, and levels) of the representational units that may be incorporated in these integrated hierarchical models is also expanded. As it is, not only the sense of reality of that moment but also the scope of the reality able to be encompassed in the experience itself may be greatly expanded beyond that which is possible within the constraints imposed by the ordinary operation of the SN and CEN. If so, it is to be expected that these states will be accompanied by a qualitatively unique "cognitive phenomenology" (see Bayne & Montague, 2011), which may well correspond to descriptions in the analytic discourse which has grown up among observers within related traditions.

There is now a wide body of evidence that synchronization in fast frequencies of the EEG (gamma band >30 Hz) plays an essential role in the temporal binding of separated cell assemblies throughout the cortex, coding for diverse representational features, into unified representational states (Engel & Singer, 2001; Singer & Gray, 1995). While initial research identified gamma synchronization as a determinant of perceptual feature binding, this role has since been extended to include the binding of representational elements in a wide range of cognitive processes (Senkowski, Schneider, Foxe, & Engel, 2008; Uhlhaas et al., 2009). Therefore, it is expected that the expanded generative models predicted in episodes of absorption will be accompanied by extensive and intense patterns of EEG gamma-band synchronization which support them.

There is now evidence from a number of studies of Buddhist meditation in advanced practitioners that such techniques elicit specific patterns of synchronized gamma activity (Berkovich-Ohana, Glicksohn, & Goldstein, 2012; Cahn, Delorme, & Polich, 2010; Lehmann et al., 2001; Lutz, Greischar, Rawlings, Ricard, & Davidson, 2004). In particular, Lutz et al. (2004) reported levels of synchronized gamma activity during meditation in advanced Buddhist meditators that were the highest known to be recorded in the absence of pathology. Modulation of gamma-band activity has been repeatedly observed in response to hypnotic suggestion (De Pascalis, 2007). Likewise in the case of hypnotic suggestion, the topography of observed gamma-band activity has been directly linked to the specific content of the experiences being suggested in the case of both positive suggestions, such as hypnotic recollection of emotional experiences (DePascalis, Marucci, & Penna, 1989) and hypnotic dream (DePascalis, 1993), and negative suggestions, such as hypnotic analgesia (Croft, Williams, Haenschel, & Gruzelier, 2002; De Pascalis, Cacace, & Massicolle, 2004). Furthermore, the magnitude of these effects is directly related to the person's level of hypnotic susceptibility.

Samadhi

Ott (2013) has proposed that the state of samadhi, variously described in both Yoga and Buddhist traditions, and perhaps the "enlightenment" experiences found in other contemplative traditions as well as spontaneously occurring mystical experiences, share a common neurophysiological basis in events of massively synchronized gamma activity throughout the entire cortex, effectively sweeping up into one conscious moment all available representational units within the brain as a single unified whole. Such a state would be fundamentally different from the much more limited freely flowing multisensory representations elicited by hypnotic suggestions. It would also diverge from many of the states associated with specific Buddhist meditations. Yet, perhaps the massive cortical synchronization required to generate some of the gamma levels observed by Lutz et al. during non-referential compassion practice (2004) may not be far removed. Unfortunately, Lutz et al. (2004) do not report estimations of the cortical sources engaged in generating this effect.

One recent study of EEG source activity differences between intermediate (4 years' practice) and advanced (30 years' practice) yoga practitioners, within a single tradition, reported significantly greater gamma-band activity in the advanced group across all conditions (Thomas, Jamieson, & Cohen, 2014). During mantra meditation, significant increases were found in 2092 out of a possible 6239 cortical gray matter voxels, with the maximal difference located in the right insula. In addition to the insula, increased gamma-band activity was found principally in the anterior temporal lobe, inferior frontal gyrus, and orbitofrontal and frontopolar cortical regions. Significant gamma differences in the occipital, parietal, somatosensory, and motor cortex were conspicuously absent. In addition to the insula, the large volume of cortex (one third) engaged in synchronized gamma activity lay at the anterior terminus of two extensive regions of secondary association cortex, the temporal lobe and the inferior frontal lobe. Both regions implement a posterior to anterior hierarchy of progressively more abstract and amodal self-other-world representations. Whereas there is no evidence of a global state of cortical gamma synchronization, there is evidence, at the highest levels of meditation expertise, for the emergence of a conscious state corresponding to a generative model which integrates the highest levels of representation found in the brain orchestrated around the (right) insula.

Critical questions

In the present model, the characteristic experiences of hypnosis and meditation reflect a switch in the dynamics governing the formation, persistence, and updating of generative models under a predictive coding framework. Changes in interoceptive prediction within and between the PI, dAI, and vAI play a fundamental role, both in initiating these states and in the unfolding of generative models during these episodes, through alterations in the wider network dynamics which they regulate. There are numerous issues that this model raises for those who research and practice in the fundamentally linked areas of hypnosis and meditation.

Hypnosis is initiated in an interpersonal context in which the spoken word plays a fundamental role. Trust in the hypnotist (a sense of safety) and attention to the hypnotist's voice are the most essential elements of any hypnotic suggestion. Both features play an essential role in the activation of rapid changes in parasympathetic regulation, particularly the cardiovascular system, via the myelinated branch of the vagus nerve (Porges, 2001). The engagement of the mammalian myelinated vagus acts as a brake on the sympathetic arousal elicited by active attention and environmental threat (Porges, 2007) and likely plays a fundamental role in generating the predictable interoceptive feedback that this model requires for hypnotic responses to form (a hypothesis which has received support from a study just completed by Fraser and Jamieson).

The error-related positivity (Pe), a P3-like response closely linked with awareness of error commission and the recruitment of compensatory cognitive resources (Ullsperger, Harsay, Wessel, & Ridderinkhof, 2010), has been found to be reduced in hypnosis for high, but not for low, hypnotically susceptible individuals (Cleary, Jamieson, Croft, Findlay, & Hammond, 2012; Kaiser, Barker, Haenschel, Baldeweg, & Gruzelier, 1997). This finding is an expected outcome of diminished attentional responses to prediction errors, which is a core prediction of the present model. However, while salient stimulus detection (which evokes the P3) activates the dAI, conscious error detection appears to activate the vAI (Harsay et al., 2012). Therefore, development of the interoceptive predictive coding model of (at least) hypnosis requires a more nuanced account of the intersecting (and perhaps multiple) roles of the dAI and vAI than is presented here. Finally, the current model does not yet offer a developed account of negative hypnotic hallucinations, including hypnotic amnesia, which appear to require targeted inhibition of perceptual and cognitive processing in addition to the positive formation of generative models of the suggested response (cf. Austin, 2013).

While numerous studies of Buddhist meditation methods (in particular mindfulness) support the key role of insula regions (e.g., Lutz, Brefczynski-Lewis, Johnstone, & Davidson, 2008; Lutz, McFarlin, Perlman, Salomons, & Davidson, 2013), few of these studies bear directly on the specific mechanisms proposed in the present model. Studies are required which combine effective parcellation of at least the three major functional anatomical divisions of the PI, dAI, and vAI (e.g., Farb et al., 2013) *and* multi-regional functional connectivity (e.g., Froeliger et al., 2012). Careful construction of experimental designs will be required in order to tease apart the relative contribution, within any region, of activity due to predictive representations and that due to prediction errors.

Lazar et al. (2005) reported increased cortical thickness in the right dAI associated with long-term mindfulness meditation and Hölzel et al. (2008) reported a parallel result for gray matter density (but see Luders, Toga, Lepore, & Gaser, 2009), while Luders et al. (2012) reported increased gyrification in the right dAI associated with years of meditation (mixed traditions). It is evident that changes in the right dAI play a central role in skilled meditation practice, consistent with the present model. However, such changes are likely to be driven by interaction with other subregions of the insula and several high-level cortical regions (Gu et al., 2013). It is probable that predictive coding in this region plays some further role in the generative models of meditation experience beyond modulating the gain of wider prediction errors (Farb et al., 2013). Likewise, the current model makes no functional distinction between the role of right and left insula regions and networks (see e.g., Lutz et al., 2013). Such nuances remain to be determined by future data and ongoing theoretical developments.

Finally, this interoceptive predictive coding model of non-ordinary conscious states directs investigators to examine the dynamics and structure of the generative models underlying such states, whether in hypnosis, creative insight, reveries, or contemplative practices. Electrophysiology and correctly chosen measures (see Jamieson & Burgess, 2014) of gamma-band functional connectivity will play a major role here.

Conclusion

The states of awareness that emerge in hypnosis and meditation are of fundamental importance to our understanding of the range of potentials open to human consciousness. Cognitive neuroscience has provided researchers with a powerful set of tools to probe not only the effects of these conscious states but the actual causal dynamics of their operation (Jamieson, 2007). Within cognitive neuroscience, the Bayesian framework of predictive coding has generated deep insights into the fundamental unity of the ordinary psychological processes of perception, learning, attention, memory, and action. This chapter has sought to demonstrate how the framework of predictive coding, through the core concepts of generative models, active inference, and interoceptive predictive coding also provides a unified understanding of the diverse practices of hypnosis and meditation.

Interoceptive predictive coding, the process of matching *top-down* and *bottom-up predictions* of internal bodily states, acting through network hubs in the dorsal anterior insula, provides the basis for suppressing the *gain of prediction errors* from lower levels of cortical processing. This is expressed at a phenomenological level as a "feeling of knowing" or sense of noetic awareness. At a cognitive level, this is expressed as reduced activity and responsiveness in salience and executive attention networks. In turn, this allows for the emergence and persistence of multi-level *generative models*, including the highest representational levels. In the case of hypnosis, these generative models are shaped both by the suggestions of the hypnotist and by the expectations of the subject; they are able to elicit corresponding behavioral, experiential, and physiological responses through the process of *active inference*.

The interoceptive predictive coding analysis of mindfulness (opening-up) meditation practices provides a clear account of key components of the Buddhist psychological models by which these practices are explained within their originating traditions. The role of attachment and aversion in triggering the cascade of mental events that generate suffering, and the actual mechanism by which mindfulness practice is able to bring release from this suffering, are directly accounted for within this cognitive neuroscience framework. A consequence of this model is that suitable forms of interoceptive awareness must play an essential role in initiating states of mindfulness. This common feature of actual mindfulness practice is not explained in alternative models.

Concentrative meditation practices enable the match between interoceptive inputs and interoceptive predictions to be maintained within critical bounds for a sufficient period to allow the emergence and stabilization of large-scale generative models integrating the most abstract and high-level neural representations into a unified conscious state. Such states are normally prohibited by the effects of sensory prediction errors in everyday interactions with the external world—although they may arise in more fragmentary form in episodes of absorption. In the current model, they emerge as a potential form of noetic awareness latent within the normal operation of the Bayesian brain.

Dedication

I dedicate this chapter to the memory of Matthew Raymond Doyle (1995–2014), the bravest man I ever knew.

Acknowledgments

I am grateful to many colleagues, including several authors in this volume, who provided their intellectual encouragement and support during the development of this chapter. However, I must particularly thank Tobias Egner, Michael Lifshitz, Warwick Olphert, Amir Raz, and Hans Receveur for their detailed critical comments. Thank you all.

Illustrations are by Australian artist and designer Anna Terentieva. Special thanks to *Kot Bajun* ("La-la Puss"), the hypnotic cat from the Russian folk tale "Ivan the Idiot."

References

Adams, R. A., Shipp, S., & Friston, K. J. (2013). Predictions not commands: active inference in the motor system. *Brain Structure and Function*, **218**(3), 611–643.

Aston-Jones, G., & Cohen, J. D. (2005). Adaptive gain and the role of the locus coeruleus–norepinephrine system in optimal performance. *Journal of Comparative Neurology*, **493**(1), 99–110.

Austin, J. H. (2013). Zen and the brain: mutually illuminating topics. *Frontiers in Psychology*, 4, 784.

Barber, T. X. (2000). A deeper understanding of hypnosis: its secrets, its nature, its essence. *American Journal of Clinical Hypnosis*, **42**(3–4), 208–272.

Barnier, A. J., Dienes, Z., & Mitchell, C. J. (2008). How hypnosis happens: new cognitive theories of hypnotic responding. In M. Nash & A. Barnier (Eds.), *The Oxford handbook of hypnosis: theory, research, and practice* (pp. 141–178). Oxford: Oxford University Press.

Bayne, T., & Montague, M. (Eds.). (2011). *Cognitive Phenomenology*. Oxford University Press.

Berkovich-Ohana, A., Glicksohn, J., & Goldstein, A. (2012). Mindfulness-induced changes in gamma band activity—implications for the default mode network, self-reference and attention. *Clinical Neurophysiology*, **123**(4), 700–710.

Blakemore, S-J., Oakley, D. A., & Frith C. D. (2003). Delusions of alien control in the normal brain. *Neuropsychologia*, **41**(8), 1058–1067.

Blakemore, S-J., Wolpert, D. M., & Frith, C. D. (1998). Central cancellation of self-produced tickle sensation. *Nature Neuroscience*, **1**(7), 635–640.

Bowers, P. (1978). Hypnotizability, creativity and the role of effortless experiencing. *International Journal of Clinical and Experimental Hypnosis*, **26**(3), 184–202.

Brewer, J. A., Worhunsky, P. D., Gray, J. R., Tang, Y. Y., Weber, J., & Kober, H. (2011). Meditation experience is associated with differences in default mode network activity and connectivity. *Proceedings of the National Academy of Sciences*, **108**(50), 20254–20259.

Cahn, B. R., Delorme, A., & Polich, J. (2010). Occipital gamma activation during Vipassana meditation. *Cognitive Processing*, **11**(1), 39–56.

Cerliani, L., Thomas, R. M., Jbabdi, S., Siero, J. C., Nanetti, L., Crippa, A., . . . & Keysers, C. (2012). Probabilistic tractography recovers a rostrocaudal trajectory of connectivity variability in the human insular cortex. *Human brain mapping*, **33**(9), 2005–2034.

Chang, L. J., Yarkoni, T., Khaw, M. W., & Sanfey, A. G. (2013). Decoding the role of the insula in human cognition: Functional parcellation and large-scale reverse inference. *Cerebral Cortex*, **23**, 739–749.

Chiesa, A. (2013). The difficulty of defining mindfulness: current thought and critical issues. *Mindfulness*, **4**(3), 255–268.

Clark, A. (2013). Whatever next? Predictive brains, situated agents, and the future of cognitive science. *Behavioral and Brain Sciences*, **36**(3), 181–204.

Cleary, J., Jamieson, G., Croft, R., Findlay, B., & Hammond, S. (2012). Hypnosis and the Dissociation of Cognitive Control. *Frontiers in Human Neuroscience Conference Abstract: ACNS-2012 Australasian Cognitive Neuroscience Conference.*

Cojan, Y., Waber, L., Schwartz, S., Rossier, L., Forster, A., & Vuilleumier, P. (2009). The brain under self-control: modulation of inhibitory and monitoring cortical networks during hypnotic paralysis. *Neuron*, **62**(6), 862–875.

Corbetta, M., & Shulman, G. L. (2002). Control of goal-directed and stimulus-driven attention in the brain. *Nature Reviews Neuroscience*, **3**(3), 201–215.

Craig, A. D. (2002). How do you feel? Interoception: the sense of the physiological condition of the body. *Nature Reviews Neuroscience*, **3**(8), 655–666.

Craig AD. (2009). How do you feel–now? The anterior insula and human awareness. Nature Reviews. *Neuroscience*, **10**(1), 59–70.

Critchley, H. D., Nagai, Y., Gray, M. A., & Mathias, C. J. (2011). Dissecting axes of autonomic control in humans: insights from neuroimaging. *Autonomic Neuroscience*, **161**(1), 34–42.

Croft, R. J., Williams, J. D., Haenschel, C., & Gruzelier, J. H. (2002). Pain perception, hypnosis and 40 Hz oscillations. *International journal of psychophysiology*, **46**(2), 101–108.

Dayan, P., Hinton, G. E., Neal, R. M., & Zemel, R. S. (1995). The Helmholtz machine. *Neural Computation*, **7**(5), 889–904.

Deeley, Q., Oakley, D. A., Toone, B., Bell, V., Walsh, E., Marquand, A. F., . . . Halligan, P. W. (2013). The functional anatomy of suggested limb paralysis. *Cortex*, **49**(2), 411–422.

Deeley, Q., Walsh, E., Oakley, D. A., Bell, V., Koppel, C., Mehta, M. A., & Halligan, P. W. (2013). Using hypnotic suggestion to model loss of control and awareness of movements: an exploratory fMRI study. *PloS One*, **8**(10), e78324.

Deen, B., Pitskel, N. B., & Pelphrey, K. A. (2011). Three systems of insular functional connectivity identified with cluster analysis. *Cerebral Cortex*, **21**(7), 1498–1506.

Derbyshire, S. W., Whalley, M. G., & Oakley, D. A. (2009). Fibromyalgia pain and its modulation by hypnotic and non-hypnotic suggestion: an fMRI analysis. *European Journal of Pain*, **13**(5), 542–550.

De Pascalis, V. (1993). EEG spectral analysis during hypnotic induction, hypnotic dream and age regression. *International journal of psychophysiology*, **15**(2), 153–166.

De Pascalis, V. D. (2007). Phase-ordered gamma oscillations and the modulation of hypnotic experience. In G. A. Jamieson (Ed.), *Hypnosis and conscious states: The cognitive neuroscience perspective* (pp. 67–89). Oxford, England: Oxford University Press.

De Pascalis, V., Cacace, I., & Massicolle, F. (2004). Perception and modulation of pain in waking and hypnosis: functional significance of phase-ordered gamma oscillations. *Pain*, **112**(1), 27–36.

De Pascalis, V., Marucci, F. S., & Penna, P. M. (1989). 40-Hz EEG asymmetry during recall of emotional events in waking and hypnosis: Differences between low and high hypnotizables. *International Journal of Psychophysiology*, **7**(1), 85–96.

Diamond, S. G., Davis, O. C., & Howe, R. D. (2007). Heart-rate variability as a quantitative measure of hypnotic depth. *International Journal of Clinical and Experimental Hypnosis*, **56**(1), 1–18.

Dorjee, D. (2010). Kinds and dimensions of mindfulness: why it is important to distinguish them. *Mindfulness*, **1**(3), 152–160.

Dosenbach, N. U., Fair, D. A., Miezin, F. M., Cohen, A. L., Wenger, K. K., Dosenbach, R. A., ... Petersen, S. E. (2007). Distinct brain networks for adaptive and stable task control in humans. *Proceedings of the National Academy of Sciences*, **104**(26), 11073–11078.

Engel, A. K., & Singer, W. (2001). Temporal binding and the neural correlates of sensory awareness. *Trends in cognitive sciences*, **5**(1), 16–25.

Etkin, A., Egner, T., Peraza, D. M., Kandel, E. R., & Hirsch, J. (2006). Resolving emotional conflict: a role for the rostral anterior cingulate cortex in modulating activity in the amygdala. *Neuron*, **51**(6), 871–882.

Farb, N. A., Segal, Z. V., Mayberg, H., Bean, J., McKeon, D., Fatima, Z., & Anderson, A. K. (2007). Attending to the present: mindfulness meditation reveals distinct neural modes of self-reference. *Social cognitive and affective neuroscience*, **2**(4), 313–322.

Farb, N. A., Segal, Z. V., & Anderson, A. K. (2013). Mindfulness meditation training alters cortical representations of interoceptive attention. *Social Cognitive and Affective Neuroscience*, **8**, 15–26.

Faymonville, M. E., Roediger, L., Del Fiore, G., Delgueldre, C., Phillips, C., Lamy, M., ... Laureys, S. (2003). Increased cerebral functional connectivity underlying the antinociceptive effects of hypnosis. *Cognitive Brain Research*, **17**(2), 255–262.

Friston, K. J. (2009). The free-energy principle: a rough guide to the brain? *Trends in Cognitive Sciences*, **13**(7), 293–301.

Friston, K. J. (2010). The free-energy principle: a unified brain theory? *Nature Reviews Neuroscience*, **11**(2), 127–138.

Friston K. J. (2011). What is optimal about motor control? *Neuron*, **72**(3), 488–498.

Frith, C. D., Blakemore, S-J., & Wolpert, D. M. (2000). Abnormalities in the awareness and control of action. *Philosophical Transactions of the Royal Society of London. Series B: Biological Sciences*, **355**(1404), 1771–1788.

Froeliger, B., Garland, E. L., Kozink, R. V., Modlin, L. A., Chen, N. K., McClernon, F. J., ... & Sobin, P. (2012). Meditation-state functional connectivity (msFC): strengthening of the dorsal attention network and beyond. *Evidence-based Complementary and Alternative Medicine*, 1–9.

Goleman, D. (1977). *The varieties of the meditative experience*. New York: Dutton.

Goleman, D. (1984). The Buddha on meditation and states of consciousness. In D. H. Shapiro & R. N. Walsh (Eds.), *Meditation: classic and contemporary perspectives* (pp. 317–360). New York: Aldine.

Grabovac, A. D., Lau, M. A., & Willett, B. R. (2011). Mechanisms of mindfulness: a Buddhist psychological model. *Mindfulness*, **2**(3), 154–166.

Gregory, R. L. (1997). Knowledge in perception and illusion. *Philosophical Transactions of the Royal Society of London. Series B: Biological Sciences*, **352**(1358), 1121–1128.

Gu, X., Hof, P. R., Friston, K. J., & Fan, J. (2013). Anterior insular cortex and emotional awareness. *Journal of Comparative Neurology*, **521**(15), 3371–3388.

Harsay, H. A., Spaan, M., Wijnen, J. G., & Ridderinkhof, K. R. (2012). Error awareness and salience processing in the oddball task: shared neural mechanisms. *Frontiers in Human Neuroscience*, **6**, 246.

Helmholtz, H. von (1866). Concerning the perceptions in general. In *Treatise on physiological optics*, vol. III (3rd edn.) (translated by J. P. C. Southall, 1925, *Journal of the Optical Society of America*, Section 26; reprinted 1962, New York: Dover).

Hilgard, J. R. (1970). *Personality and hypnosis:a study of imaginative involvement*. Chicago: University of Chicago Press.

Hölzel, B. K., Ott, U., Gard, T., Hempel, H., Weygandt, M., Morgen, K., & Vaitl, D. (2008). Investigation of mindfulness meditation practitioners with voxel-based morphometry. *Social Cognitive and Affective Neuroscience*, **3**(1), 55–61.

Hölzel, B. K., Ott, U., Hempel, H., Hackl, A., Wolf, K., Stark, R., & Vaitl, D. (2007). Differential engagement of anterior cingulate and adjacent medial frontal cortex in adept meditators and non-meditators. *Neuroscience Letters*, **421**(1), 16–21.

Jambrik, Z., Sebastiani, L., Picano, E., Ghelarducci, B., & Santarcangelo, E. L. (2005). Hypnotic modulation of flow-mediated endothelial response to mental stress. *International Journal of Psychophysiology*, **55**(2), 221–227.

Jamieson, G. A. (2005). The modified Tellegen Absorption Scale: a clearer window on the structure and meaning of absorption. *Australian Journal of Clinical and Experimental Hypnosis*, **33**, 119–139.

Jamieson, G. A. (Ed.). (2007). *Hypnosis and conscious states: the cognitive neuroscience perspective*. Oxford: Oxford University Press.

Jamieson, G. A., & Burgess, A. P. (2014). Hypnotic induction is followed by state-like changes in the organization of EEG functional connectivity in the theta and beta frequency bands in high-hypnotically susceptible individuals. *Frontiers in Human Neuroscience*, **8**, 528.

Jamieson, G. A., & Sheehan, P. W. (2004). An empirical test of Woody and Bowers's dissociated-control theory of hypnosis. *International Journal of Clinical and Experimental Hypnosis*, **52**(3), 232–249.

Kaiser, J., Barker, R., Haenschel, C., Baldeweg, T., & Gruzelier, J. H. (1997). Hypnosis and event-related potential correlates of error processing in a Stroop-type paradigm: a test of the frontal hypothesis. *International Journal of Psychophysiology*, **27**(3), 215–222.

Kihlstrom, J. F. (1997). Hypnosis, memory and amnesia. *Philosophical Transactions of the Royal Society of London. Series B: Biological Sciences*, **352**(1362), 1727–1732.

Kirsch, I. (1991). The social learning theory of hypnosis. In S. J. Lynn & J. Rhue (Eds.), *Theories of hypnosis: current models and perspectives* (pp. 439–466). New York: Guilford Press.

Kirsch, I. (1999). Hypnosis and placebos: response expectancy as a mediator of suggestion effects. *Anales de Psicologia*, **15**(1), 99–110.

Kirsch, I. (2000). The response set theory of hypnosis. *American Journal of Clinical Hypnosis*, **42**, 274–292.

Klein, T. A., Ullsperger, M., & Danielmeier, C. (2013). Error awareness and the insula: links to neurological and psychiatric diseases. *Frontiers in Human Neuroscience*, **7**, 14.

Kosslyn, S. M., Thompson, W. L., Costantini-Ferrando, M. F., Alpert, N. M., & Spiegel, D. (2000). Hypnotic visual illusion alters color processing in the brain. *American Journal of Psychiatry*, **157**(8), 1279–1284.

Kriegeskorte, N., Lindquist, M. A., Nichols, T. E., Poldrack, R. A., & Vul, E. (2010). Everything you never wanted to know about circular analysis, but were afraid to ask. *Journal of Cerebral Blood Flow & Metabolism*, **30**(9), 1551–1557.

Kurth, F., Zilles, K., Fox, P. T., Laird, A. R., & Eickhoff, S. B. (2010). A link between the systems: functional differentiation and integration within the human insula revealed by meta-analysis. *Brain Structure and Function*, **214**(5–6), 519–534.

Laumakis, S. J. (2008). *An introduction to Buddhist philosophy*. Cambridge: Cambridge University Press.

Lazar, S. W., Kerr, C. E., Wasserman, R. H., Gray, J. R., Greve, D. N., Treadway, M. T., . . . & Fischl, B. (2005). Meditation experience is associated with increased cortical thickness. *NeuroReport*, **16**(17), 1893–1897.

Lehmann, D., Faber, P. L., Achermann, P., Jeanmonod, D., Gianotti, L. R., & Pizzagalli, D. (2001). Brain sources of EEG gamma frequency during volitionally meditation-induced, altered states of consciousness, and experience of the self. *Psychiatry Research: Neuroimaging*, **108**(2), 111–121.

Lewis-Williams, J. D., & Pearce, D. G. (2005). *Inside the neolithic mind: consciousness, cosmos and the realm of the gods*. London: Thames & Hudson.

Lifshitz, M., Aubert Bonn, N., Fischer, A., Kashem, I. F., & Raz, A. (2013). Using suggestion to modulate automatic processes: from Stroop to McGurk and beyond. *Cortex*, **49**(2), 463–473.

Luders, E., Kurth, F., Mayer, E. A., Toga, A. W., Narr, K. L., & Gaser, C. (2012). The unique brain anatomy of meditation practitioners: alterations in cortical gyrification. *Frontiers in Human Neuroscience*, **6**, 34.

Luders, E., Toga, A. W., Lepore, N., & Gaser, C. (2009). The underlying anatomical correlates of long-term meditation: larger hippocampal and frontal volumes of gray matter. *NeuroImage*, **45**(3), 672–678.

Lutz, A., Brefczynski-Lewis, J., Johnstone, T., & Davidson, R. J. (2008). Regulation of the neural circuitry of emotion by compassion meditation: effects of meditative expertise. *PloS One*, **3**(3), e1897.

Lutz, A., Greischar, L. L., Rawlings, N. B., Ricard, M., & Davidson, R. J. (2004). Long-term meditators self-induce high-amplitude gamma synchrony during mental practice. *Proceedings of the National Academy of Sciences of the United States of America*, **101**(46), 16369–16373.

Lutz, A., McFarlin, D. R., Perlman, D. M., Salomons, T. V., & Davidson, R. J. (2013). Altered anterior insula activation during anticipation and experience of painful stimuli in expert meditators. *Neuroimage*, **64**, 538–546.

MacKenzie, M. (2013). Enacting selves, enacting worlds: on the Buddhist theory of karma. *Philosophy East and West*, **63**(2), 194–212.

Maheshwarananda, P. (2005). *The system "yoga in daily life."* Vienna: European University Press.

McConkey, K. M. (1991). The construction and resolution of experience and behavior in hypnosis. In S.J. Lynn & J.W. Rhue (Eds.), *Theories of hypnosis: Current Models and perspectives* (pp. 542–563).New York: Guilford Press.

McGeown, W. J., Venneri, A., Kirsch, I., Nocetti, L., Roberts, K., Foan, L., & Mazzoni, G. (2012). Suggested visual hallucination without hypnosis enhances activity in visual areas of the brain. *Consciousness and Cognition*, **21**(1), 100–116.

Menon, V., & Uddin, L. Q. (2010). Saliency, switching, attention and control: a network model of insula function. *Brain Structure and Function*, **214**(5–6), 655–667.

Miall, R. C., & Wolpert, D. M. (1996). Forward models for physiological motor control. *Neural Networks*, **9**(8), 1265–1279.

Miltner, W. H. R., & Weiss, T. (2007). Cortical mechanisms of hypnotic pain control. In G. A. Jamieson (Ed.), *Hypnosis and conscious states: the cognitive-neuroscience perspective* (pp. 51–66). Oxford: Oxford University Press.

Naish, P. L. (2007). Time distortion, and the nature of hypnosis and consciousness. *Hypnosis and conscious states: the cognitive-neuroscience perspective* (pp. 271–292). Oxford: Oxford University Press.

Naranjo, C., & Ornstein, R. E. (1971). *On the psychology of meditation*. New York: Viking Press.

Nieuwenhuis, S., Aston-Jones, G., & Cohen, J. D. (2005). Decision making, the P3, and the locus coeruleus—norepinephrine system. *Psychological Bulletin*, **131**(4), 510–532.

Noble, J., & McConkey, K. M. (1995). Hypnotic sex change: creating and challenging a delusion in the laboratory. *Journal of Abnormal Psychology*, **104**(1), 69–74.

Oakley, D. A., & Halligan, P. W. (2013). Hypnotic suggestion: opportunities for cognitive neuroscience. *Nature Reviews Neuroscience*, **14**(8), 565–576.

Orne, M. T. (1959). The nature of hypnosis: artifact and essence. *Journal of Abnormal Psychology*, **58**(3), 277–299.

Orne, M. T. (1977). The construct of hypnosis: implications of the definition for research and practice. *Annals of the New York Academy of Sciences*, **296**(1), 14–33.

Ott, U. (2007). States of absorption: in search of neurobiological foundations. In G. A. Jamieson (Ed.), *Hypnosis and consciousness states: the cognitive-neuroscience perspective* (pp. 257–270). Oxford: Oxford University Press.

Ott, U. (2013). Time experience during mystical states. In A. Nicolaidis & W. Achtner (Eds.), *The evolution of time: studies of time in science, anthropology, theology* (pp. 104–116). Bentham Science Publishers.

Paulus, M. P., & Stein, M. B. (2006). An insular view of anxiety. *Biological Psychiatry*, **60**(4), 383–387.

Pekala, R. J. (1991). *Quantifying consciousness: an empirical approach*. New York: Plenum Press.

Polito, V., Barnier, A. J., & Woody, E. Z. (2013). Developing the sSense of Agency Rating Scale (SOARS): an empirical measure of agency disruption in hypnosis. *Consciousness and Cognition*, **22**(3), 684–696.

Porges, S. W. (2001). The polyvagal theory: phylogenetic substrates of a social nervous system. *International Journal of Psychophysiology*, **42**(2), 123–146.

Porges, S. W. (2007). The polyvagal perspective. *Biological Psychology*, **74**(2), 116–143.

Rainville, P., Carrier, B., Hofbauer, R. K., Bushnell, M. C., & Duncan, G. H. (1999). Dissociation of sensory and affective dimensions of pain using hypnotic modulation. *Pain*, **82**(2), 159–171.

Raz, A., Fan, J., & Posner, M. I. (2005). Hypnotic suggestion reduces conflict in the human brain. *Proceedings of the National Academy of Sciences of the United States of America*, **102**(28), 9978–9983.

Sanchez-Vives, M. V., & Slater, M. (2005). From presence to consciousness through virtual reality. *Nature Reviews Neuroscience*, **6**(4), 332–339.

Senkowski, D., Schneider, T. R., Foxe, J. J., & Engel, A. K. (2008). Crossmodal binding through neural coherence: implications for multisensory processing. *Trends in Neurosciences*, **31**(8), 401–409.

Seth, A. K. (2013). Interoceptive inference, emotion, and the embodied self. *Trends in Cognitive Sciences*, **17**(11), 565–573.

Seth, A. K., Suzuki, K., & Critchley, H. D. (2011). An interoceptive predictive coding model of conscious presence. *Frontiers in Psychology*, **2**, 395. doi: 10.3389/fpsyg.2011.00395

Sheehan, P.W. (1991). Hypnosis, context, and commitment. In S.J. Lynn & J.W. Rhue (Eds.), *Theories of hypnosis: Current models and perspectives* (pp. 520–541). New York: Guilford Press.

Sheehan, P. W., & Perry, C. W. (1976). *Methodologies of hypnosis*. Hillsdale, NJ: Erlbaum.

Shor, R. E. (1959). Hypnosis and the concept of the generalized reality-orientation. *American Journal of Psychotherapy*, **12**, 582–602.

Singer, T., Critchley, H. D., & Preuschoff, K. (2009). A common role of insula in feelings, empathy and uncertainty. *Trends in Cognitive Sciences*, **13**(8), 334–340.

Singer, W., & Gray, C. M. (1995). Visual feature integration and the temporal correlation hypothesis. *Annual review of neuroscience*, **18**(1), 555–586.

Szechtman, H., Woody, E., Bowers, K. S., & Nahmias, C. (1998). Where the imaginal appears real: a positron emission tomography study of auditory hallucinations. *Proceedings of the National Academy of Sciences*, **95**(4), 1956–1960.

Taggart, P., Sutton, P., Redfern, C., Batchvarov, V. N., Hnatkova, K., Malik, M., . . . Joseph, A. (2005). The effect of mental stress on the non-dipolar components of the T wave: modulation by hypnosis. *Psychosomatic Medicine*, **67**(3), 376–383.

Tellegen, A., & Atkinson, G. (1974). Openness to absorbing and self-altering experiences ("absorption"), a trait related to hypnotic susceptibility. *Journal of Abnormal Psychology*, **83**(3), 268–277.

Thomas, J., Jamieson, G. A., & Cohen, M. (2014). Low and then high frequency oscillations of distinct right cortical networks are progressively enhanced by medium and long term Satyananda Yoga meditation practice. *Frontiers in Human Neuroscience*, **8**, 197.

Touroutoglou, A., Hollenbeck, M., Dickerson, B. C., & Feldman Barrett, L. (2012). Dissociable large-scale networks anchored in the right anterior insula subserve affective experience and attention. *Neuroimage*, **60**(4), 1947–1958.

Tsakiris, M., Tajadura-Jiménez, A., & Costantini, M. (2011). Just a heartbeat away from one's body: interoceptive sensitivity predicts malleability of body-representations. *Proceedings of the Royal Society B: Biological Sciences*, **278**(1717), 2470–2476.

Uhlhaas, P., Pipa, G., Lima, B., Melloni, L., Neuenschwander, S., Nikolić, D., & Singer, W. (2009). Neural synchrony in cortical networks: history, concept and current status. *Frontiers in Integrative Neuroscience*, **3**, 17.

Ullsperger, M., Harsay, H. A., Wessel, J. R., & Ridderinkhof, K. R. (2010). Conscious perception of errors and its relation to the anterior insula. *Brain Structure and Function*, **214**(5–6), 629–643.

Vul, E., & Pashler, H. (2012). Voodoo and circularity errors. *Neuroimage*, **62**(2), 945–948.

Weitzenhoffer, A. M. (1980) Hypnotic susceptibility revisited. *American Journal of Clinical Hypnosis*, **22**, 130–146.

Winkelman, M. (2000). *Shamanism: the neural ecology of consciousness and healing*. Westport CN: Bergin and Garvey.

Wolpert, D. M., Ghahramani, Z., & Jordan, M. I. (1995). An internal model for sensorimotor integration. *Science*, **269**(5232), 1880–1882.

Woody, E. Z., Barnier, A. J., & McConkey, K. M. (2005). Multiple hypnotizabilities: differentiating the building blocks of hypnotic response. *Psychological Assessment*, **17**(2), 200—211.

Woody, E. Z., & Sadler, P. (2008). Dissociation theories of hypnosis. In M. R. Nash & A. J. Barnier (Eds.), *The Oxford handbook of hypnosis* (pp. 81–110). Oxford, UK: Oxford University Press.

Woody, E., & Szechtman, H. (2000). Hypnotic hallucinations and yedasentience. *Contemporary Hypnosis*, **17**(1), 26–31.

Woody, E., & Szechtman, H. (2007). To see feelingly: emotion, motivation and hypnosis. In G. A. Jamieson (Ed.), *Hypnosis and conscious states: the cognitive-neuroscience perspective* (pp. 241–255). Oxford, UK: Oxford University Press.

Woody, E., & Szechtman, H. (2011). Using hypnosis to develop and test models of psychopathology. *Journal of Mind–Body Regulation*, **1**, 4–16.

Yarkoni, T., Poldrack, R. A., Nichols, T. E., Van Essen, D. C., & Wager, T. D. (2011). Large-scale automated synthesis of human functional neuroimaging data. *Nature Methods*, **8**(8), 665–670.

Chapter 18

Hypnosis, hypnotic suggestibility, and meditation: an integrative review of the associated brain regions and networks

William Jonathan McGeown

Abstract

The number of neuroimaging studies on hypnosis and meditation has multiplied rapidly in recent years. The methods and analytic techniques that are being applied are becoming increasingly sophisticated and approaches focusing on connectomics have offered novel ways to investigate the practices, enabling brain function to be investigated like never before. This chapter provides a review of the literature on the effects of hypnosis and meditation on brain network functional connectivity. Numerous cross-sectional as well as longitudinal studies have also reported enduring transformations in brain structure and function in practitioners of meditation, while evidence is mounting which demonstrates a relationship between hypnotic suggestibility and variations in neuroanatomy/functional connectivity that may facilitate hypnosis. The similarities (and differences) between the brain regions and networks associated with each type of practice are highlighted, while links are tentatively made between these and the reported phenomenology.

Introduction

This chapter focuses on functional and structural neuroimaging studies of hypnotic suggestibility, hypnosis, and meditation. The content emphasizes functional magnetic resonance imaging (fMRI) studies, and draws reference to positron emission tomography (PET) and single photon emission tomography (SPECT), whereas the literature on temporal dynamics using electroencephalography and magnetoencephalography has not been included.

The studies detailed are not intended to be an exhaustive review of the literature, but should nonetheless provide a comprehensive and up-to-date overview of those that appear relevant when comparing the practices of hypnosis and meditation. A number of functional neuroimaging studies with traditional designs (e.g., block design) are described, often as a preface to those which have applied functional connectivity (FC) analyses. Readers should note that the FC studies that are included predominantly focus on the assessment of baseline (resting) states in those that are hypnotically suggestible and in meditators, and on the changes associated with hypnosis and meditation themselves, as opposed to the effects that those states might have on the brain networks which underpin particular tasks (e.g., how FC in the pain matrix may be modulated). Three brain networks in particular are discussed within the chapter: the executive control network (Seeley et al., 2007), the salience network (Seeley et al., 2007), and the default mode network (DMN; Greicius, Krasnow, Reiss, & Menon, 2003; Raichle et al., 2001) (see Figure 18.1 and Plate 13).

Structural neuroimaging research is reviewed which reports neuroanatomical variations in high suggestible people (highs), as are studies which appear to demonstrate structural differences linked to meditative practice. Within this review, readers will also be exposed to the wide range of neuroimaging methods that are employed within these fields of research.

As a preview to the chapter, activity within brain regions such as the anterior cingulate cortex (ACC) and the dorsolateral prefrontal cortex (DLPFC), which are components of the salience and executive control networks, is frequently modulated as people engage in hypnosis and meditation. These are structures that have been linked to attentional and executive function, absorption, and metacognitive processes. Hypnosis and meditation also both tend to lead to alterations in FC and deactivation of the DMN, which is associated with mind wandering and spontaneous thought. Expansion of FC within the salience and executive control networks may underpin hypnotic suggestibility and reflect long-term changes due to meditation. In terms of brain structure, variations within the ACC, DLPFC, and insular cortices are associated with hypnotic suggestibility/response to hypnosis and meditative practice.

These findings paint a small part of a greater picture that is certainly not so simplistic however. A range of methodological differences, which appeared to especially impact the more numerous meditation studies (e.g., the type of meditation, length of practice, task, analysis technique), often

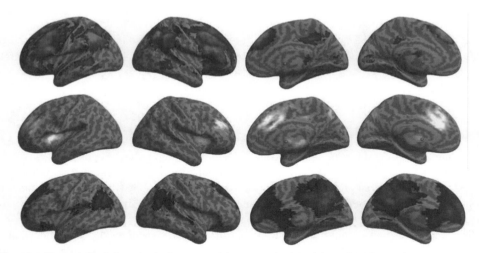

Fig. 18.1 Illustration of three intrinsic connectivity networks (ICNs) (see also Plate 13).
Top row: left and right executive control networks (combined); middle row: salience network; bottom row: default mode network (DMN).

The figure shows the results from an independent components analysis on 29 people. Note that the brain regions shown to comprise each ICN might differ slightly across research studies.

severely limited the conclusions that could be drawn from between-study comparisons. The same problems can be seen in studies of hypnosis, with different suggestibility scales, tasks, and analytic methods likely impacting the results. While attempting to interpret the neuroimaging findings, many authors (including me and my colleagues) have suggested potential links between phenomenology/cognition/behavior and associated brain function/structure. Throughout the chapter, the worthwhile endeavor of performing contemporary confirmatory assessments of these relationships in the same study samples is highlighted (see also Chapter 15).

Phenomenology of hypnosis and meditation

The phenomenology associated with hypnosis and various kinds of meditation will be addressed in richer detail within other chapters of this volume. A brief description is however provided here so that these qualitative aspects can be explored in relation to the neuroimaging results. During hypnosis, people may experience a range of phenomena. These include increased absorption, dissociation, decreased self-agency and self-monitoring, mental relaxation, reduced spontaneous thought, and a suspension of orientation toward time and place (Cardeña, 2005; Grant & Rainville, 2005; Rainville, Hofbauer, Bushnell, Duncan, & Price, 2002; Rainville & Price, 2003; Tart, 1970). Experiential accounts of hypnotic phenomena also relate to the level of suggestibility of the participant (Cardeña, Jonsson, Terhune, & Marcusson-Clavertz, 2013).

The term "meditation" is used to refer to a wide range of mental training practices with varied goals and techniques. Lutz, Slagter, Dunne, and Davidson (2008), in relation to Buddhist traditions, describe two main styles of meditation: focused attention (FA) and open monitoring (OM). FA refers to the maintenance of attention (sustained attention, narrow field) on a chosen internal or external object (e.g., a thought, a mantra, breathing). This type of meditation also involves identifying distractors, disengaging attention from them, and redirecting attention back to the object of focus. OM, on the other hand, captures the practice of passive monitoring (wide field of attention) of the self or environment (acknowledging, but not evaluating extensively or responding) and of emotional and internal bodily awareness. Combinations of these meditative styles can be found in Zen, Tibetan Buddhism, Vipassana, and mindfulness-based stress reduction (Lutz, Slagter, et al., 2008). These attention-oriented practices were chosen for review, as opposed to, for example, compassion-based meditation, because attentional modulation is often theorized as central to hypnosis and hypnotic suggestibility (e.g., Gruzelier, 1998; Raz, Kirsch, Pollard, & Nitkin-Kaner, 2006).

Brain networks

Many functional neuroimaging studies on hypnosis and meditation, especially those carried out prior to approximately 2010, tended to employ traditional designs and methods of data analysis which enabled brain regions to be identified that were more (or less) active during the states of hypnosis and meditation. The results of these studies provided important contributions to the literature and a number of key findings will be detailed during the course of this chapter.

Revealing how different brain regions communicate with each other, however, provides another level of understanding about the effects of meditation and hypnosis, and interest in the networks of the brain has grown steadily over recent years. This shift toward networks is necessary to further understand how discrete sets of functional units within the brain result in the emergence of higher-level cognition and states of consciousness. A number of multi-region brain networks can be isolated from fMRI data through FC analyses. This is possible due to low-frequency oscillations in the blood oxygenation level dependent signal, which have a physiological basis (Biswal, Yetkin, Haughton, & Hyde, 1995). Methods such as independent components analysis (ICA) or setting of seed regions and subsequent correlation assessment enable the extraction of these networks (which are comprised of brain regions activated in a coordinated fashion).

A major benefit of these types of analysis is that participants need not complete a task in the scanner and the networks can be isolated from data acquired during periods while participants do nothing but rest. It should be noted that FC analysis of data collected during tasks is also commonplace. For networks isolated through FC analysis, the term "resting-state networks" has often been applied. The term "intrinsic connectivity networks" (ICNs; Seeley et al., 2007) will instead be used in this chapter as it is applicable to networks extracted during rest or during the period in which a participant completes a task.

Questions to consider throughout the chapter are:

1   Which brain regions are jointly activated (and deactivated) during hypnosis and in different types of meditation?

2   In terms of networks, are there similarities or differences between the effects of hypnosis and meditation on FC within and between ICNs?

3   Is ICN FC associated with hypnotic suggestibility or meditative practice, and if so, do network alterations correspond?

4   Can neuroanatomical variations be seen in association with hypnotic suggestibility or as a consequence of meditative practice?

5   What are the likely implications of any variation in activity/FC/brain structure?

Executive control network and salience network

The brain regions that comprise the executive control network are commonly activated during tasks that require focused and sustained attention (see e.g., Corbetta, Patel, & Shulman, 2008). The executive control network incorporates the left and right lateral fronto-parietal cortices and the dorsomedial PFC (Seeley et al., 2007). The salience network is involved with sensory filtering and integration, pain, interoception, autonomic functioning, and emotional processing, and includes brain regions such as the dorsal ACC (dACC) and fronto-insular cortices (Critchley, 2005; Critchley, Wiens, Rotshtein, Ohman, & Dolan, 2004; Seeley et al., 2007). The salience network has also been proposed as an interface that enables switching between the more task-relevant executive control network and the more introspective DMN (Sridharan, Levitin, & Menon, 2008), which has been linked to internal processes such as mind wandering and thinking about the past and present (Buckner, Andrews-Hanna, & Schacter, 2008).

It should be noted that the neuroimaging literature also refers to "extrinsic" (or task- positive) systems and "intrinsic" (or task-negative) systems. These systems typically correspond, on the one hand, to combinations of the salience and executive control networks in addition to task-relevant sensory networks (extrinsic/task-positive) and, on the other hand, to the DMN (intrinsic/task-negative) (Fox et al., 2005; Tian et al., 2007). Anti-correlation has been demonstrated between those systems (Fox et al., 2005).

Hypnosis and hypnotic suggestibility

Hypnosis-related activation has been observed within components of both the executive control and salience networks. For example, activity has been detected within the ACC (Maquet et al., 1999; Rainville et al., 2002; Rainville, Hofbauer, et al., 1999), the lateral frontal cortical regions (Deeley et al., 2012; Maquet et al., 1999; Rainville et al., 2002; Rainville, Hofbauer, et al., 1999), and the insular cortex (Rainville et al., 2002; Rainville, Hofbauer, et al., 1999). The involvement of the ACC and PFC presumably reflects processes such as focused/sustained attention and executive functions (Grahn & Manly, 2012; Posner & Rothbart, 2007), whereas activation of the insular cortex is more unclear and may be related to the perceived salience of the object of attention, or to processes such as interoception, and the modulation of sensory integrative processes (Critchley, 2005; Critchley et al., 2004; Menon & Uddin, 2010; Seeley et al., 2007).

Discrepancies between study designs are likely to be of major importance to the results obtained. For example, whether hypnosis leads to activation of the fronto-parietal network may depend on the content of the induction and/or the task requirements. A simple visual display such as that used by Deeley et al. (2012) may promote focused and sustained attention (even if participants are instructed only to look at the screen), which could explain their findings of greater activity in fronto-parietal regions in relation to hypnotic depth, whereas decreased activity in the parietal cortices found by Rainville et al. (2002, 1999) might relate to their induction which included "specific instructions for decreased orientation to, and interest in, irrelevant external sources of stimulation" (p. 897). These are of course speculations as to the sources of activation and deactivation, but these subtle distinctions in experimental design are likely to be extremely important. Variations such as these are also expected to contribute to the FC modulations in relation to hypnosis and meditation. For interpretation, the devil is likely to be in the detail.

Demertzi and colleagues (2011) compared FC during hypnosis to a mental imagery condition in highs. An informative feature of their study was the use of participant self-report data on level of dissociation (from the environment), absorption, and external thoughts. During hypnosis, participants reported greater dissociation and FC mirrored these reports, revealing a reduction in lateral cortical regions associated with executive control and external processing (Demertzi et al., 2011). This association appears to be appropriate as the hypnotic induction required revivication of autobiographical memories, which would require an internal rather than external focus. In another FC study, which instead used a regression approach, McGeown, Mazzoni, Vannucci, and Venneri (2015) found that reports of greater hypnotic depth were linked to decreased FC within portions of the salience and executive control networks, such as the left insula and right DLPFC (but increased FC within the ACC). Clearly, additional research with larger sample sizes is needed to further refine the complex changes in FC that may occur during hypnosis.

Turning now from the features of the hypnotic state to the trait of hypnotic suggestibility, Hoeft et al. (2012) found that highs (during rest, without the use of hypnosis) had greater FC between the dorsal ACC and DLPFC bilaterally, but particularly within the left hemisphere. This pattern of FC illustrates an expansion of the salience network in highs to incorporate part of the executive control network. The authors suggest that this association may underpin hypnotizability (Hoeft et al., 2012).

A recently published study by Huber, Lui, Duzzi, Pagnoni, and Porro (2014) did not replicate the findings of Hoeft et al. (2012) exactly, but showed that people higher in suggestibility also had an expansion of the salience network (described differently in their article as the "executive control network," but similarly comprised of the ACC and bilateral insula), this time in connection with the right inferior parietal lobule (IPL) and postcentral gyrus. Higher suggestibility was also associated with higher FC between the left fronto-parietal network and the precuneus and posterior cingulate cortex (PCC) (and lower FC between the right fronto-parietal network and the right thalamus and caudate). Huber et al. suggest that the pattern of results may reflect greater absorption, use of self-monitoring and imagery, and less distractibility at rest, in those that are more suggestible.

While neither set of authors studied the effects of hypnosis on FC in highs, the findings of Demertzi et al. (2011), already described, demonstrate a reduction of FC within these networks (which it would appear are expanded at baseline), following a hypnotic induction.

A related point is that activity within the DLPFC has been shown to be suppressed during hypnosis, when no external focus is required (McGeown, Mazzoni, Venneri, & Kirsch, 2009). Moreover, interventions, such as with transcranial magnetic stimulation, which have targeted neural activity within the PFC/left DLPFC, have been shown to increase response to suggestion (e.g., Dienes & Hutton, 2013; Semmens-Wheeler, Dienes, & Duka, 2013). These results suggest that disruption of the expanded network may underpin hypnotic response.

Meditation

Across various studies on meditation (involving FA, OM, or a combination) either the dACC, the DLFPC, or, more generally both, are activated (Baron Short et al., 2010; Brefczynski-Lewis, Lutz, Schaefer, Levinson, & Davidson, 2007; Farb et al., 2007; Hasenkamp, Wilson-Mendenhall, Duncan, & Barsalou, 2012; Lazar et al., 2000; Manna et al., 2010; Newberg et al., 2001). Activation of the fronto-parietal networks (that underpin the executive control network) has been observed (Brefczynski-Lewis et al., 2007; Hasenkamp et al., 2012; Lou et al., 1999). The insular cortices have also been a common site of activation (Brefczynski-Lewis et al., 2007; Farb et al., 2007; Hasenkamp et al., 2012).

Careful consideration of the processes involved during focused (and sustained) attention can shed more light on the underlying neural systems that are utilized. Using fMRI on experienced meditators who practiced FA, Hasenkamp and colleagues (2012) showed that focused attention activated the right DLPFC; mind wandering, the DMN; becoming aware of a distraction, the dACC and anterior insula bilaterally; and shifting attention away from the distraction and back to the object of attention, the right DLPFC and bilateral inferior parietal cortex (see Hasenkamp et al., 2012, for full details). These findings fit closely with research unrelated to meditation, which has described the neuroanatomical correlates of sustained attention, alerting, and orienting (e.g., Corbetta et al., 2008; Fan, McCandliss, Fossella, Flombaum, & Posner, 2005; Posner & Rothbart, 2007). Hasenkamp et al. (2012) demonstrate that FA meditation involves a complex interplay between attentional sub-systems. A certain degree of overlap with the neural systems recruited by OM meditation is likely, although different demands may be placed on the attentional sub-systems, with Lutz et al. (2008) instead indicating for OM, reliance on monitoring, vigilance, and attentional disengagement.

In the sub-section "Hypnosis and hypnotic suggestibility," (within the section "Executive control network and salience network") evidence was presented for trait-related expansion of ICNs in high suggestible people. Research has also shown expansion of ICNs in meditators both while meditating and during rest. We will turn first to the studies that have demonstrated expansions of ICNs in meditators engaged in practice (Froeliger et al., 2012; Kilpatrick et al., 2011). Kilpatrick et al. (2011) found that when instructed to be mindfully aware and to pay attention to the noise of the scanning environment, compared to waiting-list controls, a meditation group trained for 8 weeks on mindfulness-based stress reduction (MBSR; involves FA and OM) had greater FC within a merged network that the authors refer to as the "auditory/salience" network; named as such due to its inclusion of brain regions from other ICNs that have been documented (Seeley et al., 2007; Smith et al., 2009).

Froeliger et al. (2012) instead examined the dorsal attention network (DAN), which is comprised bilaterally of the frontal eye fields (FEFs), intraparietal sulcus and middle temporal area (MT) (Corbetta et al., 2008; Fox, Corbetta, Snyder, Vincent, & Raichle, 2006; Raichle, 2011), and overlaps with the executive control network. Meditation (in experienced practitioners of Hatha yoga) versus rest was associated with increased FC between the DAN (right FEF) and DMN nodes; and multiple nodes of the DAN and the salience network (right anterior PFC).

Both of these studies suggest that increased FC may reflect a shift toward a more functionally integrated network, which incorporates attentional, self-referential, and salience processing (but additional decreases in FC reported in the latter study suggests that this interpretation is incomplete).

Expanding on these meditation state-related changes, there is evidence of greater anti-correlation between the extrinsic and intrinsic systems during FA (versus rest), in Tibetan Buddhist meditators (Josipovic, Dinstein, Weber, & Heeger, 2011). Alternatively, as the participants practiced non-dual awareness (NDA) meditation (which operates through the integration of external and internal experience), weaker anti-correlation was observed between the networks. The results highlight the importance of the type of meditation and the malleability of the organization of FC within ICNs.

Taking all of these findings together, they suggest that greater integration of ICNs is possible if the meditation task requires it (e.g., Froeliger et al., 2012; Josipovic et al., 2011; Kilpatrick et al., 2011) and that greater separation may also occur during meditative styles that predominantly require activation and coordination of the extrinsic network (Josipovic et al., 2011).

As already alluded to, repeated activation of the brain networks utilized during meditation may lead to long-term trait-related changes during rest (when participants have not been directed to meditate). Hasenkamp and Barsalou (2012) showed that FC defined from a seed region within the right DLPFC, the area previously found to be associated with focused attention (Hasenkamp et al., 2012), was observed to be higher in more experienced meditators (mixed styles), in relation to the mid-cingulate gyrus, the left DLPFC, and three regions within the right insula. The authors suggest that this pattern of increased FC might explain the reports of superior attentional skills in meditators (including both short-term trainees and more experienced practitioners) versus controls (e.g., Chan & Woollacott, 2007; Hodgins & Adair, 2010; Jha, Krompinger, & Baime, 2007). Furthermore, they propose that the increased FC to the insula might afford experienced meditators additional access to present-moment awareness and the perception of internal states when engaging executive functions, or provide the ability to more efficiently switch between the executive control network and the DMN. Yet, without assessing the mental activities of participants during rest or their attentional skills outside of these periods, there are major difficulties in interpreting the meaning of ICN modifications (and it remains unclear whether these alterations persist while meditators are performing the same mental tasks as controls).

A further point that should be taken from these studies is that meditation appears to decouple visual cortical areas from those associated with the salience network, both as a short-term state feature during meditation and as a trait change observable at rest in long-term practitioners (Hasenkamp & Barsalou, 2012; Kilpatrick et al., 2011). This could reflect a decrease in the attentional resources allocated to unnecessary visual processing or may indicate capacity for better cross-modal inhibition (Hasenkamp & Barsalou, 2012; Kilpatrick et al., 2011).

Providing stronger evidence for long-term causal effects of meditation on ICNs, Xue, Tang, and Posner (2011) demonstrated, with a randomized longitudinal design (with an active control group), that engaging a meditation regimen labeled integrative body–mind training (IBMT) for 11 hours, over a period of one month, increased network efficiency and connectivity degree in the left ACC (assessed with graph theory) during rest. IBMT aims to develop relaxation, FA, and mindfulness (Tang et al., 2007). The increased network efficiency could reflect the capacity of the ACC to integrate information from across brain regions, whereas the increase in connectivity degree demonstrates that the ACC had more direct connections to other nodes (Xue et al., 2011).

Summary

As already described, key regions of the executive control and salience networks, such as the ACC, DLPFC, and insular cortices, are consistently activated in studies both on hypnosis (Deeley et al., 2012; Maquet et al., 1999; Rainville et al., 2002; Rainville, Hofbauer, et al., 1999) and meditation (Baron Short et al., 2010; Brefczynski-Lewis et al., 2007; Farb et al., 2007; Hasenkamp et al., 2012; Lazar et al., 2000; Manna et al., 2010; Newberg et al., 2001). The activity in these brain regions may reflect processes such as attentional and affective regulation and saliency processing (Menon & Uddin, 2010; Posner & Rothbart, 2007). Where discrepancies between studies occur, careful examination of the content of the hypnotic induction (and the requirements during the hypnotic period) and the type of meditation practiced is likely to help explain the patterns of activation and deactivation, and may generate testable hypotheses for future studies.

On the whole, higher suggestibility appears to be associated with an expansion of the salience network (Hoeft et al., 2012; Huber et al., 2014), although the regions that have higher FC vary between studies. Enhanced FC within the salience network and the executive control network can also often be seen in meditators (Froeliger et al., 2012; Hasenkamp & Barsalou, 2012; Xue et al., 2011). These functional organizations may reflect more unitary and integrated networks that provide additional control over attentional and affective processing, assist the goals of the meditative practices, and confer on highs the ability to substantially modulate attention. The effect of hypnosis on FC was a decrease within brain regions that underpin the extrinsic system; a finding that fits closely with reported phenomenology such as dissociation (Demertzi et al., 2011). Meditation, on the other hand, was associated with increased FC within components of this system (Froeliger et al., 2012; Kilpatrick et al., 2011), which probably reflects task requirements (e.g., paying attention to the scanner noise in the study by Kilpatrick et al., 2011). Further evidence indicating that the flexibility of ICNs depends on the type of meditation was provided by Josipovic et al. (2011).

Finally, meditation led to decreased interaction between brain regions associated with attention and visual areas (Hasenkamp & Barsalou, 2012; Kilpatrick et al., 2011). Hypnotic suggestibility, on the other hand, was associated with increased FC to visual regions, which may underpin reports of mental imagery in hypnosis (Maquet et al., 1999; Rainville, Hofbauer, et al., 1999). Previous research has also shown that during hypnosis, spontaneous mental imagery (even when not requested) has occurred in participants, in addition to corresponding brain activity in relevant regions (Rainville, Hofbauer, et al., 1999).

Default mode network

The DMN has featured frequently in FC studies on hypnosis and meditation. It is composed of brain regions such as the ACC and PCC, the ventral and dorsal medial frontal cortex, the hippocampal formation, lateral temporal cortex, lateral parietal cortex, and precuneus (Buckner et al., 2008). As previously described, this network is usually active during self-referential thought, autobiographical memory, future planning, daydreaming, and social cognition (Buckner & Carroll, 2007; Gusnard, Akbudak, Shulman, & Raichle, 2001; Mason et al., 2007).

Hypnosis and hypnotic suggestibility

McGeown et al. (2015) demonstrated that after a hypnotic induction, greater levels of self-reported hypnotic depth were associated with reduced FC within the anterior DMN in a group of participants who varied from high to low in hypnotic suggestibility. Further evidence for a decrease in DMN connectivity due to hypnosis comes from Lipari et al. (2012) who examined the effects of hypnosis in a single hypnotic virtuoso using regional homogeneity (ReHo) analysis. ReHo provides a measure of the similarity of the time series in adjacent voxels and, as opposed to FC which examines inter-regional relationships, it offers a measure of coherence among voxels in localized regions (Zang, Jiang, Lu, He, & Tian, 2004). Decreased ReHo was apparent within the medial PFC and middle PFC (with increased ReHo in the occipital cortex).

The findings across both studies appear to support previous observations of suppressed DMN activity during hypnosis (Deeley et al., 2012; McGeown et al., 2009), and the occipital ReHo increases may reflect the use of visual imagery as reported in other previous hypnosis studies (Maquet et al., 1999; Rainville et al., 2002). Some degree of caution must be applied to ReHo findings however, given the single-case approach and the fixed order, single repetition, of the conditions of no hypnosis and hypnosis.

In the aforementioned study by Demertzi et al. (2011), a complex picture emerges in which hypnosis-related decreases in DMN FC were seen within the left parahippocampal gyrus and PCC, whereas increases occurred within the medial prefrontal cortex and angular gyrus, bilaterally. The apparent discrepancy between the increased anterior DMN connectivity observed in the study by Demertzi et al. (2011) and the reported decreased FC/ReHo (Lipari et al., 2012; McGeown et al., 2015) could result from Demertzi and colleagues' comparison of hypnosis to a mental imagery control condition as opposed to rest. Although the direct statistical comparison of hypnosis versus rest was not reported in the Demertzi et al. study (despite the networks being displayed individually), examination of the supplied figure (Demertzi et al., 2011, Figure 2, p. 316) suggests that hypnosis reduced both the anterior and posterior DMN substantially in relation to the rest condition. During hypnosis, participants also reported significantly less external thoughts (mind wandering), which suggests suppression of the DMN. An explanation for higher FC in some elements of the DMN in the Demertzi et al. study, during hypnosis versus mental imagery, might relate to the requirements of the hypnosis condition. This involved revivication of autobiographical memories, which is a task requirement that is likely to depend upon the DMN (Andreasen et al., 1995). Neuroimaging research on autobiographical memory retrieval has indeed indicated involvement of the medial PFC (Buckner et al., 2008; Cabeza & St. Jacques, 2007).

Focusing now on hypnotic suggestibility, and the FC differences that might facilitate the experience of hypnosis, Hoeft et al. (2012) and McGeown et al. (2015) did not find any significant relationship between hypnotic suggestibility and DMN FC. Huber et al. (2014), on the other hand, found a number of interactions between the DMN and regions that comprise other ICNs. For example, people higher in suggestibility had increased FC between the lateral visual network and the cuneus, precuneus, and PCC. The authors interpreted the increased FC to cortical regions relating to vision as congruent with reports that high suggestibility is associated with vivid imagery and fantasy proneness (e.g., Lynn & Rhue, 1986).

The differences between the FC studies could relate to a range of factors, including the scales used to measure hypnotic suggestibility. These were inconsistent across the three studies. As item composition differs across scales (e.g., in the number relating to motor challenge, perceptual alteration), this is likely to impact the number of suggestions people respond to in each class, and due to the relationship with neuroanatomy that each type of suggestion has, this might result in the identification of slightly different brain/behavior relationships. Another factor contributing to discrepancies in the findings could be the composition of the participant samples (in distribution of suggestibility, gender, etc.).

Meditation

A study by Brewer and colleagues (2011) offers insight into the effects of meditation on DMN FC both during meditative practice and in relation to the putative long-term changes observed during rest. Concentration (FA), loving-kindness, and mindfulness (involving FA and OM) in experienced mindfulness/insight meditators led to less self-reported mind wandering and lower activity within anterior and posterior areas of the DMN (collapsed across all three types of meditation) versus the controls. The findings parallel others which have demonstrated lower levels of activity within the DMN during meditation, more effective inhibition of the network in meditators compared to controls, and that capacity to inhibit correlates with attentional performance outside of the scanner (e.g., Farb et al., 2007; Garrison et al., 2013; Pagnoni, 2012). The FC analyses added to this picture, showing expansion of the DMN to the dACC (during meditation and rest) and left posterior insula (during meditation). Providing additional evidence for trait-related changes during rest, meditators were found to have increased FC between the posterior DMN and the DLPFC, bilaterally. The increased FC between the DMN and the other brain regions may reflect greater cognitive control over the DMN, which may reduce interference (Brewer et al., 2011). Despite being consistent with the theory that meditation leads to long-term changes in resting-state FC, practitioners might have assumed a state of meditation during rest (spontaneously, with or without awareness), even when it was not required.

The study by Hasenkamp et al. (2012) described previously adds to the findings of enhanced connectivity between the DMN and other brain regions at baseline. During rest, increased FC was detected between the DMN and the orbito-frontal cortex/ventromedial PFC (and a decoupling was observed between anterior and posterior DMN regions of the experienced meditators). Jang et al. (2011) also investigated FC in the DMN at baseline in meditators (who practiced brain-wave vibration meditation, the goals of which are to quiet the mind and reduce negative emotions through FA). Greater FC was found within the ventromedial PFC in meditators compared to controls. The higher connectivity involving the ventromedial PFC may reflect greater control over the regulation of emotional processing, inhibition of emotional response (Carretie, Lopez-Martin, & Albert, 2010; Winecoff et al., 2013), and/or the internalization of attention (Jang et al., 2011).

Providing further support that DMN FC appears to undergo long-term modulation in relation to sustained meditative practice, Taylor et al. (2013) examined FC between particular nodes of the DMN, during rest, comparing a group of Zen meditators who were experienced in mindfulness (which involves both FA and OM) to beginner meditators. The experienced group had less connectivity between the dorsomedial PFC (dmPFC) and ventromedial PFC (vmPFC), and between the dmPFC and left IPL. The authors point out the role that these anterior components of the DMN play in analytic self-referential processing and emotional judgment (Buckner et al., 2008; Taylor et al., 2013). The experienced meditators also had instances of increased FC, for example, between the dmPFC and the right IPL, and between the right IPL and the PCC and left IPL. The results of this study alone can highlight the complexity of ICN interactions and the associated interpretative difficulties.

The wide range of neuroimaging studies reported throughout this chapter are provided to highlight the similarities across studies where possible (e.g., expansion of ICNs), but the results of these studies have been provided in sufficient detail to raise awareness that the findings are often complex and that both increases and decreases in FC between elements of different ICNs often occurs. Attempting to map the patterns of FC across brain regions to the abilities of meditators or those who are hypnotized often leads only to speculative interpretations of the meaning of the patterns, that may have theoretical support from a wide range of scientific literature, but the proposed relationships are rarely assessed directly.

In the future, the inclusion of subjective measures could be extremely useful in understanding FC findings (Taylor et al., 2013), as could data collection pertaining to the abilities that are assumed to be superior in the participant (e.g., in regulating aspects of their emotions or cognition). Collection of this type of data would also aid interpretation of putative long-term changes to the resting state. To reinforce a point I made earlier, when meditators are asked to rest in a scanner, given the context of the study, they might partially engage in meditative practices (despite being instructed not to), meaning that their mental content is not representative of their resting cognitive state in everyday life. The possibility is also there that during rest periods (in a scanner or elsewhere), people highly experienced in meditation spontaneously engage in meditative processes (rest becomes more meditation- like). A third alternative is that the mental processes utilized during rest might not differ from controls, while FC patterns in the ICNs have undergone long-term changes.

Summary

Brain activity appears to be reduced within the DMN during meditation (e.g., Brewer et al., 2011; Farb et al., 2007) and hypnosis (Deeley et al., 2012; McGeown et al., 2009). Suppression of DMN activity in both may reflect reduced elaboration during the processing of self-referential thoughts (should they occur) and less mind wandering (Buckner et al., 2008).

A complicated pattern of DMN FC emerges in experienced meditators during rest, which may be characterized by an expansion of the DMN (Brewer et al., 2011; Taylor et al., 2013) to include areas associated with attention and executive control. Other findings include increased FC within the anterior DMN (Jang et al., 2011), but others instead report a reduction (Taylor et al., 2013). Divergent findings such as these may relate to the different requirements of the meditation under study. Further to this, as the studies on meditation tend to focus on many different styles (with little convergence on a particular type), this may present particular problems for the interpretation of FC analyses, where multiple relationships between nodes (positive and negative) may exist. Interpretative errors may well occur, especially without more insight into the mental state of practitioners (during the meditation and rest periods). Other factors that differ among studies and which may restrict interpretation include the level of experience of meditators and the analytic techniques that are applied.

Hypnosis, compared to rest, led to reduced FC (and ReHo) within the DMN (Demertzi et al., 2011; Lipari et al., 2012), and increased depth of hypnosis was associated with greater decreases within the anterior DMN (McGeown et al., 2015). Taken together, these alterations to the DMN may be interpreted as reduced spontaneous thought and mind wandering during hypnosis, but again, the conclusions remain speculative. Of the aforementioned studies on hypnotic suggestibility, neither the findings of Hoeft et al. (2012), nor of Huber et al. (2014) or McGeown et al. (2015) appear to parallel the DMN FC findings in meditators. Associations between the DMN and the visual cortices may assist in imagery (Huber et al., 2014) but, to date, hypnotic suggestibility appears to be more strongly linked to the salience and executive control networks (Hoeft et al., 2012; Huber et al., 2014).

Structural analyses

Investigations of regional gray matter (GM) have steadily multiplied over recent years. Cross-sectional and longitudinal studies in this area suggest the occurrence of plasticity related changes across a host of activities. To name but a few examples, variation in GM corresponds to navigation skills (Maguire et al., 2000), musical abilities (Gaser & Schlaug, 2003), learning to juggle (Draganski et al., 2004), picking up a second language (Mechelli et al., 2004), and extensive learning (Draganski et al., 2006). Interestingly, macroscopic changes to regional GM can occur over very brief time periods, such as a number of days (May et al., 2007). Given the short time period over which GM changes can occur, the underlying neural changes are more likely associated with dendritic branching or synaptic plasticity, as opposed to glial or neuro-genesis (May et al., 2007).

Typically, greater skill acquisition is related to greater GM volume/density/concentration/cortical thickness in associated brain regions, but this does not always appear to be the case. For example, decreased GM in brain regions could reflect higher automaticity (see Granert, Peller, Jabusch, Altenmuller, & Siebner, 2011; Hanggi, Koeneke, Bezzola, & Jancke, 2010; James et al., 2014). Another point to note is that GM cannot indefinitely expand with the acquisition of each new skill or with prolonged practice, and an inverse u-shaped curve relating to GM volume changes in association with skill learning over time has been demonstrated (Driemeyer, Boyke, Gaser, Buchel, & May, 2008).

Hypnotic suggestibility and hypnosis

The degree of susceptibility to suggestions provided in hypnosis appears relatively stable throughout one's life. For example, a study by Piccione, Hilgard, and Zimbardo (1989) showed that susceptibility scores between a test and retest period had a correlation of 0.82 after a 15-year retest, and 0.71 after 25 years. Additional studies also suggest a role for genetics (Morgan, 1973) and have highlighted an association between polymorphisms in the catechol-O-methyltransferase (COMT) gene and hypnotizability (Lichtenberg, Bachner-Melman, Gritsenko, & Ebstein, 2000; Raz, 2005; Szekely et al., 2010). Given these findings that high and low suggestible participants appear to vary in their behavioral capabilities and genetic profile, it might be that individual differences in response to hypnosis or suggestions are associated with variance in the neuroanatomy/neurobiology of brain structures (McGeown et al., 2015).

ACC and PFC

Two studies have assessed the relationship between hypnotic suggestibility and regional GM volume using regression (Huber et al., 2014; McGeown et al., 2015). Huber et al. found that those higher in suggestibility had greater GM volume in the left superior and medial frontal gyrus. The authors interpreted the frontal correlations mainly in terms of the overlap with the supplementary motor area (SMA)/pre-SMA and cited the roles of these regions in the control of movement, postural stability, and in sensory-motor association (pointing out that highs have been shown to have more effective sensory-motor integration; Menzocchi et al., 2010).

The findings of McGeown et al. (2015) did not replicate these results precisely, but did however find that greater self-reported depth of hypnosis was associated with more GM in the ACC, superior frontal gyrus, and medial PFC, bilaterally. As already shown, these brain regions have been implicated in attentional and affective regulation, and there is also overlap with the DMN. The larger volume of these cortical regions may facilitate hypnosis by enabling the suspension of spontaneous thought/self-referential processing. Interactions between the ACC and superior frontal gyrus may also perhaps enable the modulation of metacognition during hypnosis (refer to the cold control theory of hypnosis—Dienes & Perner, 2007; Semmens-Wheeler & Dienes, 2012; see also Chapter 7).

Insular cortices

Huber et al. (2014) found that suggestibility correlated negatively with GM volume within the left posterior insula and superior temporal gyrus. The role of the insula in interoception and in integrating external information was flagged, as were the associations between insular and temporal GM abnormalities in people with schizophrenia, who have symptoms such as hallucinations and difficulties determining whether stimuli are self-generated (e.g., Menon et al., 1995; Wylie & Tregellas, 2010). McGeown et al. (2015) instead identified a *positive* correlation between suggestibility and volume within the left superior temporal gyrus, and at a less conservative statistical threshold, the left insula. It is unclear why this discrepancy has arisen and further research is required. Despite controversy as to the direction of the relationship, both sets of authors pointed out the roles that one or both of these brain regions appear to play in the formation of hallucinations and in determining agency. A positive relationship was also observed between reports of hypnotic depth and insular volume, but again only when a more liberal threshold was adopted (McGeown et al., 2015).

Future studies should consider much larger sample sizes to increase statistical power, gather convergent evidence using different suggestibility scales, and could assess the neuroanatomical variation between sub-types of highs (such as those reported by, for example, Terhune & Cardeña, 2010).

White matter

The first study to address the potential relationship between suggestibility and neuroanatomy focused on white matter (WM) and was provided by Horton, Crawford, Harrington, and Downs (2004). By manually measuring the subdivisions of the corpus callosum, highs were found to have greater volume within the rostrum when compared to lows. Higher volume within this WM tract that provides inter-hemispheric information transfer might facilitate hypnosis and increase attentional and inhibitory capabilities (Horton et al., 2004). In the first whole brain analysis, Hoeft et al. (2012) detected structural differences (WM/GM) between highs and lows within parietal, temporal, and cerebellar brain regions, but the differences did not satisfy the primary statistical threshold set by the researchers and no further information was supplied on these within the publication. WM microstructure was also assessed with diffusion tensor imaging (DTI) but no between-group differences were detected.

Meditation

Compared to the dearth of neuroanatomical analyses concerning hypnotic suggestibility, there is an extensive literature on meditation. A very comprehensive systematic review and meta-analysis on this topic has been recently published by Fox et al. (2014) and readers may want to refer to this. Given the extent of the literature in this area, reporting the full set of brain regions that appear to undergo meditation-related change is beyond the scope of this chapter and, instead, the focus will be placed on those studies and sets of brain regions that appear also to be relevant to hypnosis and/or suggestibility.

ACC and PFC

As the ACC and lateral aspects of the PFC have been shown to be consistently activated during meditation (see e.g., Hasenkamp et al., 2012; Manna et al., 2010), these brain regions (which are central to attentional and executive processing) might be anticipated to undergo long-term neuroanatomical change in meditators.

The first assessment of structural neuroanatomy in relation to meditation by Lazar et al. (2005) revealed significantly greater cortical thickness in the right middle and superior frontal sulci and insula of Buddhist insight meditators (who practice FA and OM) compared to controls. Similarly, Vestergaard-Poulsen et al. (2009) found that meditators who practiced Tibetan Buddhism (Dzogchen) had higher GM density in the left superior frontal gyrus, compared to controls. Later studies identified increased cortical thickness in the superior frontal, ventromedial, and orbitofrontal cortices in those who practice brain-wave vibration meditation, which involves FA on bodily sensations and emotions (Kang et al., 2013), and in the right dACC in Zen meditators, who practice mindfulness (Grant, Courtemanche, Duerden, Duncan, & Rainville, 2010).

The findings of these studies support the assumption that repeated meditative practice (e.g., involving FA) leads to modulation of structure in brain regions such as the ACC and DLPFC, which play key roles in attentional regulation (Corbetta et al., 2008; Fan et al., 2005). As already mentioned, the ACC and DLPFC also seem to have increased volume in those who are higher in hypnotic suggestibility (Huber et al., 2014) and who report deeper levels of hypnosis (McGeown et al., 2015), findings which appear to highlight the similarities across practices in their utilization of these brain regions.

In a further analysis (which illustrates the utility of collecting additional information on participants that may be incorporated into the designs of future neuroimaging studies), Grant et al. (2013) showed that participant scores on the Tellegen Absorption Scale (Tellegen & Atkinson, 1974) were higher in meditators, were associated with the number of days of practice per week, and were positively related to cortical thickness in regions which included the left ACC, superior frontal gyrus, and the middle frontal gyrus, bilaterally. Note that a PET study on hypnosis by Rainville et al. (2002) complements these results closely, showing a positive relationship between regional cerebral blood flow in the ACC and ratings of absorption, and that other functional neuroimaging studies demonstrate high levels of absorption during hypnosis (Deeley et al., 2012; Demertzi et al., 2011). For an in-depth discussion of how absorption is related to both practices, see Chapter 14.

Activation of the dACC has also been reported during pain perception (Rainville et al., 1999), and Grant et al. (2010) suggest that greater cortical thickness in the dACC might enhance attentional control over pain and/or decrease emotional reactivity to pain. This is an interesting point as both hypnosis and meditation can be effective at modulating perceptions of pain (Grant et al., 2010; Grant & Rainville, 2009; Horton et al., 2004).

An alternative explanation for the enlargement of the left superior PFC in meditators might reflect a goal of certain types of meditation, namely, the development of mindfulness or metacognition. Semmens-Wheeler and Dienes (2012) argue that hypnosis involves a disruption of metacognition (or higher-order thoughts), whereas meditation attempts to promote metacognition. While meditative practice might be expected to lead to greater development of the left DLPFC, the theory that hypnosis disrupts metacognition does not necessarily translate into an expectation for decreased cortical thickness in the left DLPFC in highs. It might instead be that greater development of the DLPFC, such as in the finding mentioned by Huber et al. (2014) who found greater GM volume in the left DLPFC in association with suggestibility, or by McGeown et al. (2015) who reported larger GM volume in the PFC in association with reports of deeper levels of hypnosis, may enable fractionation of metacognition. A functional explanation for the modulation would also be sufficient, possibly in terms of decreased activation (McGeown et al., 2009) or decreased FC (Demertzi et al., 2011; McGeown et al., 2015). For more information on the contrast between hypnosis and meditation in terms of metacognition and the links to the left DLPFC, see Chapter 7.

Insular cortices

Many functional neuroimaging studies of meditation have highlighted the involvement of the insular cortices (e.g., Brefczynski-Lewis et al., 2007; Hasenkamp et al., 2012; Lutz, Brefczynski-Lewis, Johnstone, & Davidson, 2008). In meditators, FC also appears to be altered between the insular cortex and the executive control and/or DMN regions during meditation (Froeliger et al., 2012; Kilpatrick et al., 2011) and during rest (Froeliger et al., 2012).

The study described by Lazar et al. (2005) showed that meditators had greater cortical thickness in the right insula, when compared to controls. Additional support for meditation-related adaptations to the insular cortex is provided by Holzel et al. (2008) who found that Vipassana (involving OM) meditators had greater GM concentration in regions that included the right anterior insula (compared to controls). In association with experience, a cluster within the right anterior insula also approached significance.

Adopting a different methodological approach, Luders, Kurth, et al. (2012) demonstrated that meditators had greater cortical gyrification (the degree of cortical folding, in which a higher index equates to more surface area) in the insula, bilaterally (with years of meditation experience correlating with gyrification in the right insula). Activities practiced during meditation, such as FA on interoceptive stimuli and awareness of emotion, cognition, and external stimuli are likely causes of insular cortical development (Holzel et al., 2008; Lazar et al., 2005).

Not all studies have provided evidence for adaptation of the insular cortex due to meditation however. For example, a short-term training course (8 weeks) on MBSR meditation (which involves both FA and OM), and a subsequent region of interest (ROI) analysis focused on the insular cortices (and hippocampus), did not detect adaptations in gray matter concentration in either the left or right insula, but did detect change within the hippocampus (Holzel et al., 2011). Findings such as these may reveal the temporal dynamics of plasticity in some brain regions over others (or alternatively, may highlight differential effects of contrasting meditative practices).

The insular cortex seems to be relevant to both meditation (Holzel et al., 2008; Luders, Kurth, et al., 2012) and suggestibility/depth of hypnosis (Huber et al., 2014; McGeown et al., 2015). Posterior portions of the insula have been linked to interoceptive processes; anterior aspects to exteroceptive processes (Farb, Segal, & Anderson, 2013); and middle portions have been suggested to provide sites for the integration of each input and a more unified experience of present-moment awareness (Craig, 2009; Farb et al., 2013). Insular function also differs between hemispheres (e.g., in emotional processing and autonomic control—Craig, 2005, 2009). Of note, Critchley et al. (2004) demonstrate the role of the right insula in awareness of interoceptive processes, which appears to be particularly relevant to meditation.

In future studies of meditation and hypnosis, more detailed analysis of insular function should be illuminating, both for our understanding of the practices and for higher- order brain functions themselves.

White matter

Cross-sectional studies, using DTI, have revealed higher fractional anisotropy (DTI-FA) in many of the major fiber tracts in the brains of meditators. For example, Luders, Clark, Narr, and Toga (2011) found differences within the superior longitudinal fasciculus temporal component, superior longitudinal fasciculus, uncinate fasciculus, corticospinal tract, and forceps minor of meditators of mixed practices versus controls.

Higher DTI-FA values usually reflect enhanced connectivity, presumably due to greater numbers of fibers, changes in axonal structure, or increases in myelination (Luders et al., 2011). Additional studies have demonstrated higher DTI-FA in meditators in regions such as the ventromedial PFC (Kang et al., 2013) and the anterior portion of the corpus callosum (Luders, Phillips, et al., 2012).

Others have shown that very short periods of practice can influence DTI measures. For example, Tang, Lu, Fan, Yang, and Posner (2012) showed that only 5 hours of IBMT training led to a reduction in DTI axial diffusivity (which reflects axonal morphological changes), whereas a longer training regimen of 11 hours had a similar effect but, in addition, showed a reduction in radial diffusivity (which reflects increased myelination) and an increase in DTI-FA within multiple fiber pathways including the genu and body of the corpus callosum (Tang et al., 2012, 2010).

The higher DTI-FA values in experienced meditators (and those that have undergone short-term training), for example, in the corpus callosum, may reflect superior inter-hemispheric transfer capabilities (Luders, Phillips, et al., 2012; Tang et al., 2010). These findings appear to be congruent with the findings and interpretations of Horton et al. (2004), who found that highs had greater WM volume in the rostrum of the corpus callosum than lows. Differences such as these may underpin the enhanced emotional regulation and attentional skills that have been reported in meditators (e.g., Hodgins & Adair, 2010; Jha et al., 2007), and the attentional skills in highs (e.g., Castellani, D'Alessandro, & Sebastiani, 2007).

The meditation studies appear to be paving the way in this area and a much wider investigation of how WM varies macroscopically and in terms of microarchitecture in relation to hypnotic suggestibility and the capacity to experience hypnotic phenomena is necessary.

Overall summary and future directions

This chapter has included a range of neuroimaging studies that relate to meditation, hypnotic suggestibility, and hypnosis. The most salient similarities between the practices have been highlighted, as have to a lesser extent, the differences.

The studies on meditation have included participants of many types of practices (sometimes even within the same study) and of varying levels of experience, different requirements during the scanning period, and various analytic techniques. The diversity of results, not always conveyed in their entirety in this chapter, appears to reflect these changeable factors, and although discovering the neural underpinnings of each particular style of meditation may be informative, well-designed studies to replicate and build upon previous findings are necessary. Similar considerations should be made in relation to hypnosis studies. For example, various screening scales for hypnotic suggestibility are adopted, different analytic approaches used, and baseline comparison periods may vary (e.g., resting state, mental imagery). Even subtle changes in methodology can lead to substantially different findings, and sometimes it can be difficult to pool results. A number of key findings have, however, emerged from the literature and these will now be explored.

Drawing upon the functional neuroimaging literature on meditation, the ACC and the PFC were repeatedly activated (Baron Short et al., 2010; Brefczynski-Lewis et al., 2007; Farb et al., 2007; Hasenkamp et al., 2012; Lazar et al., 2000; Manna et al., 2010; Newberg et al., 2001), which may reflect processes such as focused attention, attentional control, conflict resolution, and absorption (Egner, Jamieson, & Gruzelier, 2005; Fan et al., 2005; Grant et al., 2013). As a possible consequence of the repeated application of processes such as these, meditation appears to be linked to greater GM density/cortical thickness in these brain regions (Grant et al., 2010, 2013; Kang et al., 2013; Lazar et al., 2005; Vestergaard-Poulsen et al., 2009). On a related point, FC studies illustrate increased connectivity between the cingulate cortex and DLPFC, and their connectivity to ICNs such as the DMN and executive control network, both during meditation and rest (Brewer et al., 2011; Hasenkamp & Barsalou, 2012), which may reflect more integration of brain networks, with coordination possibly leading to greater attentional control. Note, however, that most evidence comes from cross-sectional comparison rather than well-controlled, randomized, longitudinal designs, and future investigations should take this into account to more firmly establish the causal effects of meditation.

Interestingly, there are reports of ACC and PFC activity during hypnosis as well (Deeley et al., 2012; Maquet et al., 1999; Rainville et al., 2002; Rainville, Hofbauer, et al., 1999), and studies that have used different hypnotic inductions and different experimental designs have led to similar reports of phenomenology (e.g., increased absorption and reduced spontaneous thought; Deeley et al., 2012; Demertzi et al., 2011; Rainville et al., 2002). As in meditation, the activity within the ACC and the PFC may relate to attentional regulation and phenomena such as absorption, and neuroanatomical variations within these brain structures may underpin hypnotic suggestibility and facilitate hypnosis (Huber et al., 2014; McGeown et al., 2015). In sum, the interaction between the ACC and PFC appears to be highly relevant to both practices and, as already mentioned, structural adaptations within the left DLPFC, in particular, may be associated with improved metacognition in meditators and/or enhanced flexibility to modulate that system in those that are suggestible and capable of deep levels of hypnosis (for additional discussion, see Chapter 7).

In many of the studies, reverse inference is used in an attempt to back-translate activity or link an alteration in FC to a cognitive process that is assumed to take place, but which has not been explicitly tested. Careful measurement of the phenomenology of hypnosis and meditation within future neuroimaging studies, and of the characteristics of people that vary in hypnotic suggestibility/meditative experience (e.g., attentional abilities) may help to avoid this problem, as it would allow relationships between these variables and neurophysiology/neuroanatomy to be explored (see Chapter 15).

The insular cortex is another brain region of interest for meditation and hypnosis. Activation of the insular cortices has been reported in both practices (Brefczynski-Lewis et al., 2007; Farb et al., 2007; Hasenkamp et al., 2012; Rainville et al., 2002; Rainville, Hofbauer, et al., 1999). Greater GM concentration/cortical thickness/gyrification of the insular cortices have been reported in those that meditate, with the extent of the differences relating to experience (Holzel et al., 2008; Lazar et al., 2005; Luders, Kurth, et al., 2012), and associations have been shown with hypnotic suggestibility and those who report deeper levels of hypnosis (Huber et al., 2014; McGeown et al., 2015).

Studies on meditation (Froeliger et al., 2012; Kilpatrick et al., 2011) and hypnotic suggestibility (Hoeft et al., 2012) show alterations in FC between the salience network, which includes the insular cortices, and regions underpinning executive control and/or the DMN. The neuroanatomical variance and modified FC within the insular cortices may contribute to alterations in the perceived salience of environmental or internal stimuli, sensory integration, or interoception (Craig, 2009, 2011; Critchley, 2005; Critchley et al., 2004; Seeley et al., 2007).

The insular cortex also appears to play a crucial role in supporting a sense of embodied presence (Craig, 2009, 2011), which may have significance for both practices, and has been linked to feelings of agency (Farrer et al., 2003; Farrer & Frith, 2002), which may be especially important for hypnosis and hypnotic suggestibility. Given the anatomical and functional connections between the insula and the ACC (Medford & Critchley, 2010), the coordination of activity within these brain regions (each heterogeneous in function) is likely to be a large contributor to the effects and phenomenology of both hypnosis and meditation. The relationship between the ACC and insula may also assist the effective modulation of pain perception that has been reported both in meditators (Grant et al., 2010; Grant & Rainville, 2009) and in high suggestible people (Derbyshire, Whalley, & Oakley, 2009; Horton et al., 2004). For more information on the effects of meditation and hypnosis on pain perception, see Chapter 21.

Investigations of WM suggest that meditation-related modifications are widespread and are especially prominent within anterior brain regions. Higher suggestibility has also been linked to increased WM volume in the corpus callosum (Horton et al., 2004). These findings may explain reports of superior attentional skills in meditators (e.g., Hodgins & Adair, 2010; Jha et al., 2007) and in highs (e.g., Castellani et al., 2007; Raz et al., 2006; Raz, Shapiro, Fan, & Posner, 2002). Future neuroimaging studies should further investigate associations between WM microstructure and hypnotic suggestibility, as well as the capacity to experience certain hypnotic phenomena.

Alterations in activity and FC are present within the DMN during both hypnosis (Demertzi et al., 2011; Lipari et al., 2012; McGeown et al., 2015, 2009) and meditation (Brewer et al., 2011; Froeliger et al., 2012), as well as in experienced meditators during rest (Brewer et al., 2011; Hasenkamp & Barsalou, 2012; Jang et al., 2011; Taylor et al., 2013). Decreased activity tends to be seen during both practices, which may reflect a decrease in mind wandering or a reduction in the further processing of spontaneous or self-referential thoughts should they have occurred. With hypnosis, decreased FC/ReHo has been recorded within the anterior DMN (Demertzi et al., 2011; Lipari et al., 2012; McGeown et al., 2015), which again may relate to decreased mind wandering and spontaneous self-referential thought. Within the meditation literature, however, there are discrepant reports both of increased (Jang et al., 2011) and decreased FC (Taylor et al., 2013) within the anterior DMN in meditators during rest, the reasons behind which remain highly speculative, especially in the absence of information relating to the mental activities of the meditators.

FC within the extrinsic system (which involves salience/executive control regions such as the lateral fronto-parietal cortices) decreases during hypnosis (Demertzi et al., 2011), whereas it has been shown to increase during meditation (Froeliger et al., 2012). These differences are likely to reflect what is required from participants in each study; for example, dissociation from the environment in hypnosis, and attentional focus (FA) and monitoring of the environment or internal sensations in meditation (mindfulness).

Conclusion

Studies exploring the neural basis of meditation with FC and structural neuroimaging methods have multiplied faster than those focusing on the effects of hypnosis and the potential underpinnings of hypnotic suggestibility. However, analytic techniques such as ICA, seed-based analyses, and DTI-FA are beginning to be applied more frequently to the study of hypnosis and suggestibility, and future studies will further elucidate the commonalities and differences between the practices.

Components of the salience and executive control networks—the ACC, DLPFC, and insula—often undergo functional modulation in both practices. Alteration in brain structure within these regions can also often be seen in meditators, and variations in these structures may likewise be associated with hypnotic suggestibility, and the ability to experience deep levels of hypnosis and phenomena such as absorption. The DMN is affected during meditative practice and hypnosis, and its activity appears to be suppressed in both cases. In terms of FC, the majority of evidence seems to suggest that this network is expanded at rest in meditators, but it does not appear to be as strongly linked to suggestibility.

Finally, many studies apply reverse inference to their findings and future neuroimaging studies which apply phenomenological measures, and cognitive/behavioral/affective/physiological assessments, are likely to be hugely informative in our understanding of both practices and of brain function in general.

References

Andreasen, N. C., O'Leary, D. S., Cizadlo, T., Arndt, S., Rezai, K., Watkins, G. L., . . . Hichwa, R. D. (1995). Remembering the past: two facets of episodic memory explored with positron emission tomography. *Am J Psychiat*, **152**(11), 1576–1585.

Baron Short, E., Kose, S., Mu, Q., Borckardt, J., Newberg, A., George, M. S., & Kozel, F. A. (2010). Regional brain activation during meditation shows time and practice effects: an exploratory FMRI study. *Evid Based Complement Alternat Med*, **7**(1), 121–127. doi: 10.1093/ecam/nem163

Biswal, B., Yetkin, F. Z., Haughton, V. M., & Hyde, J. S. (1995). Functional connectivity in the motor cortex of resting human brain using echo-planar MRI. *Magn Reson Med*, **34**(4), 537–541.

Brefczynski-Lewis, J. A., Lutz, A., Schaefer, H. S., Levinson, D. B., & Davidson, R. J. (2007). Neural correlates of attentional expertise in long-term meditation practitioners. *Proc Natl Acad Sci USA*, **104**(27), 11483–11488. doi: 10.1073/pnas.0606552104

Brewer, J. A., Worhunsky, P. D., Gray, J. R., Tang, Y. Y., Weber, J., & Kober, H. (2011). Meditation experience is associated with differences in default mode network activity and connectivity. *Proc Natl Acad Sci USA*, **108**(50), 20254–20259. doi: 10.1073/pnas.1112029108

Buckner, R. L., Andrews-Hanna, J. R., & Schacter, D. L. (2008). The brain's default network: anatomy, function, and relevance to disease. *Ann NY Acad Sci*, **1124**, 1–38.

Buckner, R. L., & Carroll, D. C. (2007). Self-projection and the brain. *Trends Cogn Sci*, **11**(2), 49–57. doi: 10.1016/j.tics.2006.11.004

Cabeza, R., & St. Jacques, P. (2007). Functional neuroimaging of autobiographical memory. *Trends Cogn Sci*, **11**(5), 219–227. doi: 10.1016/j.tics.2007.02.005

Cardeña, E. (2005). The phenomenology of deep hypnosis: quiescent and physically active. *Int J Clin Exp Hypn*, **53**(1), 37–59. doi: 10.1080/00207140490914234

Cardeña, E., Jonsson, P., Terhune, D. B., & Marcusson-Clavertz, D. (2013). The neurophenomenology of neutral hypnosis. *Cortex*, **49**(2), 375–385. doi: 10.1016/j.cortex.2012.04.001

Carretie, L., Lopez-Martin, S., & Albert, J. (2010). The role of the ventromedial prefrontal cortex in the response to negative emotional events. *Rev Neurol*, **50**(4), 245–252.

Castellani, E., D'Alessandro, L., & Sebastiani, L. (2007). Hypnotizability and spatial attentional functions. *Arch Ital Biol*, **145**(1), 23–37.

Chan, D., & Woollacott, M. (2007). Effects of level of meditation experience on attentional focus: is the efficiency of executive or orientation networks improved? *J Altern Complement Med*, **13**(6), 651–657. doi: 10.1089/acm.2007.7022

Corbetta, M., Patel, G., & Shulman, G. L. (2008). The reorienting system of the human brain: from environment to theory of mind. *Neuron*, **58**(3), 306–324. doi: 10.1016/j.neuron.2008.04.017

Craig, A. D. (2005). Forebrain emotional asymmetry: a neuroanatomical basis? *Trends Cogn Sci*, **9**(12), 566–571. doi: 10.1016/j.tics.2005.10.005

Craig, A. D. (2009). How do you feel—now? The anterior insula and human awareness. *Nat Rev Neurosci*, **10**(1), 59–70. doi: 10.1038/nrn2555

Craig, A. D. (2011). Significance of the insula for the evolution of human awareness of feelings from the body. *Ann NY Acad Sci*, **1225**, 72–82. doi: 10.1111/j.1749-6632.2011.05990.x

Critchley, H. D. (2005). Neural mechanisms of autonomic, affective, and cognitive integration. *J Comp Neurol*, **493**(1), 154–166. doi: 10.1002/cne.20749

Critchley, H. D., Wiens, S., Rotshtein, P., Ohman, A., & Dolan, R. J. (2004). Neural systems supporting interoceptive awareness. *Nat Neurosci*, **7**(2), 189–195. doi: 10.1038/nn1176

Deeley, Q., Oakley, D. A., Toone, B., Giampietro, V., Brammer, M. J., Williams, S. C., & Halligan, P. W. (2012). Modulating the default mode network using hypnosis. *Int J Clin Exp Hypn*, **60**(2), 206–228. doi: 10.1080/00207144.2012.648070

Demertzi, A., Soddu, A., Faymonville, M. E., Bahri, M. A., Gosseries, O., Vanhaudenhuyse, A., . . . Laureys, S. (2011). Hypnotic modulation of resting state fMRI default mode and extrinsic network connectivity. *Prog Brain Res*, **193**, 309–322. doi: 10.1016/B978-0-444-53839-0.00020-X

Derbyshire, S. W. G., Whalley, M. G., & Oakley, D. A. (2009). Fibromyalgia pain and its modulation by hypnotic and non-hypnotic suggestion: an fMRI analysis. *Eur J Pain*, **13**(5), 542–550. doi: 10.1016/j.ejpain.2008.06.010

Dienes, Z., & Hutton, S. (2013). Understanding hypnosis metacognitively: rTMS applied to left DLPFC increases hypnotic suggestibility. *Cortex*, **49**(2), 386–392. doi: 10.1016/j.cortex.2012.07.009

Dienes, Z., & Perner, J. (2007). The cold control theory of hypnosis. In G. Jamieson (Ed.), *Hypnosis and conscious states: the cognitive neuroscience perspective* (pp. 293–314). Oxford, England: Oxford University Press.

Draganski, B., Gaser, C., Busch, V., Schuierer, G., Bogdahn, U., & May, A. (2004). Neuroplasticity: changes in grey matter induced by training. *Nature*, **427**(6972), 311–312. doi: 10.1038/427311a

Draganski, B., Gaser, C., Kempermann, G., Kuhn, H. G., Winkler, J., Buchel, C., & May, A. (2006). Temporal and spatial dynamics of brain structure changes during extensive learning. *J Neurosci*, **26**(23), 6314–6317. doi: 26/23/6314 [pii] 10.1523/JNEUROSCI.4628-05.2006

Driemeyer, J., Boyke, J., Gaser, C., Buchel, C., & May, A. (2008). Changes in gray matter induced by learning—revisited. *PLoS One*, **3**(7), e2669. doi: 10.1371/journal.pone.0002669

Egner, T., Jamieson, G., & Gruzelier, J. (2005). Hypnosis decouples cognitive control from conflict monitoring processes of the frontal lobe. *Neuroimage*, **27**(4), 969–978.

Fan, J., McCandliss, B. D., Fossella, J., Flombaum, J. I., & Posner, M. I. (2005). The activation of attentional networks. *Neuroimage*, **26**(2), 471–479. doi: 10.1016/j.neuroimage.2005.02.004

Farb, N. A., Segal, Z. V., & Anderson, A. K. (2013). Attentional modulation of primary interoceptive and exteroceptive cortices. *Cereb Cortex*, **23**(1), 114–126. doi: 10.1093/cercor/bhr385

Farb, N. A., Segal, Z. V., Mayberg, H., Bean, J., McKeon, D., Fatima, Z., & Anderson, A. K. (2007). Attending to the present: mindfulness meditation reveals distinct neural modes of self-reference. *Soc Cogn Affect Neurosci*, **2**(4), 313–322. doi: 10.1093/scan/nsm030

Farrer, C., Franck, N., Georgieff, N., Frith, C. D., Decety, J., & Jeannerod, A. (2003). Modulating the experience of agency: a positron emission tomography study. *Neuroimage*, **18**(2), 324–333. doi: 10.1016/S1053-8119(02)00041-1

Farrer, C., & Frith, C. D. (2002). Experiencing oneself vs another person as being the cause of an action: the neural correlates of the experience of agency. *Neuroimage*, **15**(3), 596–603. doi: 10.1006/nimg.2001.1009

Fox, M. D., Corbetta, M., Snyder, A. Z., Vincent, J. L., & Raichle, M. E. (2006). Spontaneous neuronal activity distinguishes human dorsal and ventral attention systems. *Proc Natl Acad Sci USA*, **103**(26), 10046–10051.

Fox, M. D., Snyder, A. Z., Vincent, J. L., Corbetta, M., Van Essen, D. C., & Raichle, M. E. (2005). The human brain is intrinsically organized into dynamic, anticorrelated functional networks. *Proc Natl Acad Sci USA*, **102**(27), 9673–9678.

Fox, K. C., Nijeboer, S., Dixon, M. L., Floman, J. L., Ellamil, M., Rumak, S. P., . . . Christoff, K. (2014). Is meditation associated with altered brain structure? A systematic review and meta-analysis of morphometric neuroimaging in meditation practitioners. *Neurosci Biobehav Rev*, **43**, 48–73. doi: 10.1016/j.neubiorev.2014.03.016

Froeliger, B., Garland, E. L., Kozink, R. V., Modlin, L. A., Chen, N. K., McClernon, F. J., . . . Sobin, P. (2012). Meditation-state functional connectivity (msFC): strengthening of the dorsal attention network and beyond. *Evid Based Complement Alternat Med, e-pub, article ID 680407, 1–9*. doi: 10.1155/2012/680407

Garrison, K. A., Scheinost, D., Worhunsky, P. D., Elwafi, H. M., Thornhill, T. A. IV, Thompson, E., . . . Brewer, J. A. (2013). Real-time fMRI links subjective experience with brain activity during focused attention. *Neuroimage, 81*, 110–118. doi: 10.1016/j.neuroimage.2013.05.030

Gaser, C., & Schlaug, G. (2003). Gray matter differences between musicians and nonmusicians. *Ann NY Acad Sci, 999*, 514–517.

Grahn, J. A., & Manly, T. (2012). Common neural recruitment across diverse sustained attention tasks. *PLoS One, 7*(11), e49556. doi: 10.1371/journal.pone.0049556

Granert, O., Peller, M., Jabusch, H. C., Altenmuller, E., & Siebner, H. R. (2011). Sensorimotor skills and focal dystonia are linked to putaminal grey-matter volume in pianists. *J Neurol Neurosurg Psychiatry, 82*(11), 1225–1231. doi: 10.1136/jnnp.2011.245811

Grant, J. A., Courtemanche, J., Duerden, E. G., Duncan, G. H., & Rainville, P. (2010). Cortical thickness and pain sensitivity in Zen meditators. *Emotion, 10*(1), 43–53. doi: 10.1037/a0018334

Grant, J. A., Duerden, E. G., Courtemanche, J., Cherkasova, M., Duncan, G. H., & Rainville, P. (2013). Cortical thickness, mental absorption and meditative practice: possible implications for disorders of attention. *Biol Psychol, 92*(2), 275–281. doi: 10.1016/j.biopsycho.2012.09.007

Grant, J. A., & Rainville, P. (2005). Hypnosis and meditation: similar experiential changes and shared brain mechanisms. *Med Hypotheses, 65*(3), 625–626. doi: 10.1016/j.mehy.2005.04.013

Grant, J. A., & Rainville, P. (2009). Pain sensitivity and analgesic effects of mindful states in Zen meditators: a cross-sectional study. *Psychosom Med, 71*(1), 106–114. doi: 10.1097/PSY.0b013e31818f52ee

Greicius, M. D., Krasnow, B., Reiss, A. L., & Menon, V. (2003). Functional connectivity in the resting brain: a network analysis of the default mode hypothesis. *Proc Natl Acad Sci USA, 100*(1), 253–258. doi: 10.1073/pnas.0135058100

Gruzelier, J. (1998). A working model of the neurophysiology of hypnosis: a review of evidence. *Contemp Hypn, 15*(1), 3–21.

Gusnard, D. A., Akbudak, E., Shulman, G. L., & Raichle, M. E. (2001). Medial prefrontal cortex and self-referential mental activity: relation to a default mode of brain function. *Proc Natl Acad Sci USA, 98*(7), 4259–4264. doi: 10.1073/pnas.071043098

Hanggi, J., Koeneke, S., Bezzola, L., & Jancke, L. (2010). Structural neuroplasticity in the sensorimotor network of professional female ballet dancers. *Hum Brain Mapp, 31*(8), 1196–1206. doi: 10.1002/hbm.20928

Hasenkamp, W., & Barsalou, L. W. (2012). Effects of meditation experience on functional connectivity of distributed brain networks. *Front Hum Neurosci, 6*, 38. doi: 10.3389/fnhum.2012.00038

Hasenkamp, W., Wilson-Mendenhall, C. D., Duncan, E., & Barsalou, L. W. (2012). Mind wandering and attention during focused meditation: a fine-grained temporal analysis of fluctuating cognitive states. *Neuroimage, 59*(1), 750–760. doi: 10.1016/j.neuroimage.2011.07.008

Hodgins, H. S., & Adair, K. C. (2010). Attentional processes and meditation. *Conscious Cogn, 19*(4), 872–878. doi: 10.1016/j.concog.2010.04.002

Hoeft, F., Gabrieli, J. D., Whitfield-Gabrieli, S., Haas, B. W., Bammer, R., Menon, V., & Spiegel, D. (2012). Functional brain basis of hypnotizability. *Arch Gen Psychiatry, 69*(10), 1064–1072. doi: 10.1001/archgenpsychiatry.2011.2190

Holzel, B. K., Carmody, J., Vangel, M., Congleton, C., Yerramsetti, S. M., Gard, T., & Lazar, S. W. (2011). Mindfulness practice leads to increases in regional brain gray matter density. *Psychiatry Res, 191*(1), 36–43. doi: 10.1016/j.pscychresns.2010.08.006

Holzel, B. K., Ott, U., Gard, T., Hempel, H., Weygandt, M., Morgen, K., & Vaitl, D. (2008). Investigation of mindfulness meditation practitioners with voxel-based morphometry. *Soc Cogn Affect Neurosci*, **3**(1), 55–61. doi: 10.1093/scan/nsm038

Horton, J. E., Crawford, H. J., Harrington, G., & Downs, J. H., III. (2004). Increased anterior corpus callosum size associated positively with hypnotizability and the ability to control pain. *Brain*, **127**(Pt 8), 1741–1747. doi: 10.1093/brain/awh196

Huber, A., Lui, F., Duzzi, D., Pagnoni, G., & Porro, C. A. (2014). Structural and functional cerebral correlates of hypnotic suggestibility. *PLoS One*, **9**(3), e93187. doi: 10.1371/journal.pone.0093187

James, C. E., Oechslin, M. S., Van De Ville, D., Hauert, C. A., Descloux, C., & Lazeyras, F. (2014). Musical training intensity yields opposite effects on grey matter density in cognitive versus sensorimotor networks. *Brain Struct Funct*, **219**(1), 353–366. doi: 10.1007/s00429-013-0504-z

Jang, J. H., Jung, W. H., Kang, D. H., Byun, M. S., Kwon, S. J., Choi, C. H., & Kwon, J. S. (2011). Increased default mode network connectivity associated with meditation. *Neurosci Lett*, **487**(3), 358–362. doi: 10.1016/j.neulet.2010.10.056

Jha, A. P., Krompinger, J., & Baime, M. J. (2007). Mindfulness training modifies subsystems of attention. *Cogn Affect Behav Neurosci*, **7**(2), 109–119.

Josipovic, Z., Dinstein, I., Weber, J., & Heeger, D. J. (2011). Influence of meditation on anti-correlated networks in the brain. *Front Hum Neurosci*, **5**, 183. doi: 10.3389/fnhum.2011.00183

Kang, D. H., Jo, H. J., Jung, W. H., Kim, S. H., Jung, Y. H., Choi, C. H., . . . Kwon, J. S. (2013). The effect of meditation on brain structure: cortical thickness mapping and diffusion tensor imaging. *Soc Cogn Affect Neurosci*, **8**(1), 27–33. doi: 10.1093/scan/nss056

Kilpatrick, L. A., Suyenobu, B. Y., Smith, S. R., Bueller, J. A., Goodman, T., Creswell, J. D., . . . Naliboff, B. D. (2011). Impact of mindfulness-based stress reduction training on intrinsic brain connectivity. *Neuroimage*, **56**(1), 290–298. doi: 10.1016/j.neuroimage.2011.02.034

Lazar, S. W., Bush, G., Gollub, R. L., Fricchione, G. L., Khalsa, G., & Benson, H. (2000). Functional brain mapping of the relaxation response and meditation. *Neuroreport*, **11**(7), 1581–1585.

Lazar, S. W., Kerr, C. E., Wasserman, R. H., Gray, J. R., Greve, D. N., Treadway, M. T., . . . Fischl, B. (2005). Meditation experience is associated with increased cortical thickness. *Neuroreport*, **16**(17), 1893–1897.

Lichtenberg, P., Bachner-Melman, R., Gritsenko, I., & Ebstein, R. P. (2000). Exploratory association study between catechol-O-methyltransferase (COMT) high/low enzyme activity polymorphism and hypnotizability. *Am J Med Genet*, **96**(6), 771–774. doi: 10.1002/1096–8628(20001204)96:6<771::AID-AJMG14>3.0.CO;2-T [pii]

Lipari, S., Baglio, F., Griffanti, L., Mendozzi, L., Garegnani, M., Motta, A., . . . Pugnetti, L. (2012). Altered and asymmetric default mode network activity in a "hypnotic virtuoso": an fMRI and EEG study. *Conscious Cogn*, **21**(1), 393–400. doi: 10.1016/j.concog.2011.11.006

Lou, H. C., Kjaer, T. W., Friberg, L., Wildschiodtz, G., Holm, S., & Nowak, M. (1999). A 15O-H2O PET study of meditation and the resting state of normal consciousness. *Hum Brain Mapp*, **7**(2), 98–105.

Luders, E., Clark, K., Narr, K. L., & Toga, A. W. (2011). Enhanced brain connectivity in long-term meditation practitioners. *Neuroimage*, **57**(4), 1308–1316. doi: 10.1016/j.neuroimage.2011.05.075

Luders, E., Kurth, F., Mayer, E. A., Toga, A. W., Narr, K. L., & Gaser, C. (2012). The unique brain anatomy of meditation practitioners: alterations in cortical gyrification. *Front Hum Neurosci*, **6**, 34. doi: 10.3389/fnhum.2012.00034

Luders, E., Phillips, O. R., Clark, K., Kurth, F., Toga, A. W., & Narr, K. L. (2012). Bridging the hemispheres in meditation: thicker callosal regions and enhanced fractional anisotropy (FA) in long-term practitioners. *Neuroimage*, **61**(1), 181–187. doi: 10.1016/j.neuroimage.2012.02.026

Lutz, A., Brefczynski-Lewis, J., Johnstone, T., & Davidson, R. J. (2008). Regulation of the neural circuitry of emotion by compassion meditation: effects of meditative expertise. *PLoS One*, **3**(3), e1897. doi: 10.1371/journal.pone.0001897

Lutz, A., Slagter, H. A., Dunne, J. D., & Davidson, R. J. (2008). Attention regulation and monitoring in meditation. *Trends Cogn Sci*, **12**(4), 163–169. doi: 10.1016/j.tics.2008.01.005

Lynn, S. J., & Rhue, J. W. (1986). The fantasy-prone person: hypnosis, imagination, and creativity. *J Pers Soc Psychol*, **51**(2), 404–408.

Maguire, E. A., Gadian, D. G., Johnsrude, I. S., Good, C. D., Ashburner, J., Frackowiak, R. S., & Frith, C. D. (2000). Navigation-related structural change in the hippocampi of taxi drivers. *Proc Natl Acad Sci USA*, **97**(8), 4398–4403. doi: 10.1073/pnas.070039597

Manna, A., Raffone, A., Perrucci, M. G., Nardo, D., Ferretti, A., Tartaro, A., . . . Romani, G. L. (2010). Neural correlates of focused attention and cognitive monitoring in meditation. *Brain Res Bull*, **82**(1–2), 46–56. doi: 10.1016/j.brainresbull.2010.03.001

Maquet, P., Faymonville, M. E., Degueldre, C., Delfiore, G., Franck, G., Luxen, A., & Lamy, M. (1999). Functional neuroanatomy of hypnotic state. *Biol Psychiatry*, **45**(3), 327–333.

Mason, M. F., Norton, M. I., Van Horn, J. D., Wegner, D. M., Grafton, S. T., & Macrae, C. N. (2007). Wandering minds: the default network and stimulus-independent thought. *Science*, **315**(5810), 393–395.

May, A., Hajak, G., Ganssbauer, S., Steffens, T., Langguth, B., Kleinjung, T., & Eichhammer, P. (2007). Structural brain alterations following 5 days of intervention: dynamic aspects of neuroplasticity. *Cereb Cortex*, **17**(1), 205–210. doi: 10.1093/cercor/bhj138

McGeown, W. J., Mazzoni, G., Vannucci, M., & Venneri, A. (2015). Structural and functional correlates of hypnotic depth and suggestibility. *Psychiatry Res*, **231**(2), 151–159. doi: 10.1016/j.pscychresns.2014.11.015

McGeown, W. J., Mazzoni, G., Venneri, A., & Kirsch, I. (2009). Hypnotic induction decreases anterior default mode activity. *Conscious Cogn*, **18**(4), 848–855. doi: 10.1016/j.concog.2009.09.001

Mechelli, A., Crinion, J. T., Noppeney, U., O'Doherty, J., Ashburner, J., Frackowiak, R. S., & Price, C. J. (2004). Neurolinguistics: structural plasticity in the bilingual brain. *Nature*, **431**(7010), 757. doi: 10.1038/431757a

Medford, N., & Critchley, H. D. (2010). Conjoint activity of anterior insular and anterior cingulate cortex: awareness and response. *Brain Struct Funct*, **214**(5–6), 535–549. doi: 10.1007/s00429-010-0265-x

Menon, R. R., Barta, P. E., Aylward, E. H., Richards, S. S., Vaughn, D. D., Tien, A. Y., . . . Pearlson, G. D. (1995). Posterior superior temporal gyrus in schizophrenia: grey matter changes and clinical correlates. *Schizophr Res*, **16**(2), 127–135.

Menon, V., & Uddin, L. Q. (2010). Saliency, switching, attention and control: a network model of insula function. *Brain Struct Funct*, **214**(5–6), 655–667. doi: 10.1007/s00429-010-02622-0

Menzocchi, M., Paoletti, G., Huber, A., Carli, G., Cavallaro, F. I., Manzoni, D., & Santarcangelo, E. L. (2010). Hypnotizability and sensorimotor integration: an Italian Space Agency project. *Int J Clin Exp Hypn*, **58**(1), 122–135. doi: 10.1080/00207140903316169

Morgan, A. H. (1973). The heritability of hypnotic susceptibility in twins. *J Abnorm Psychol*, **82**(1), 55–61.

Newberg, A. B., Alavi, A., Baime, M., Pourdehnad, M., Santanna, J., & d'Aquili, E. (2001). The measurement of regional cerebral blood flow during the complex cognitive task of meditation: a preliminary SPECT study. *Psychiatry Res*, **106**(2), 113–122.

Pagnoni, G. (2012). Dynamical properties of BOLD activity from the ventral posteromedial cortex associated with meditation and attentional skills. *J Neurosci*, **32**(15), 5242–5249. doi: 10.1523/JNEUROSCI.4135–11.2012

Piccione, C., Hilgard, E. R., & Zimbardo, P. G. (1989). On the degree of stability of measured hypnotizability over a 25-year period. *J Pers Soc Psychol*, **56**(2), 289–295.

Posner, M. I., & Rothbart, M. K. (2007). Research on attention networks as a model for the integration of psychological science. *Ann Rev Psychol*, **58**, 1–23. doi: 10.1146/annurev.psych.58.110405.085516

Raichle, M. E. (2011). The restless brain. *Brain Connect*, **1**(1), 3–12. doi: 10.1089/brain.2011.0019

Raichle, M. E., MacLeod, A. M., Snyder, A. Z., Powers, W. J., Gusnard, D. A., & Shulman, G. L. (2001). A default mode of brain function. *Proc Natl Acad Sci USA*, **98**(2), 676–682.

Rainville, P., Carrier, B., Hofbauer, R. K., Bushnell, C. M., & Duncan, G. H. (1999). Dissociation of sensory and affective dimensions of pain using hypnotic modulation. *Pain*, **82**, 159–171.

Rainville, P., Hofbauer, R. K., Bushnell, M. C., Duncan, G. H., & Price, D. D. (2002). Hypnosis modulates activity in brain structures involved in the regulation of consciousness. *J Cogn Neurosci*, **14**(6), 887–901. doi: 10.1162/089892902760191117

Rainville, P., Hofbauer, R. K., Paus, T., Duncan, G. H., Bushnell, M. C., & Price, D. D. (1999). Cerebral mechanisms of hypnotic induction and suggestion. *J Cogn Neurosci*, **11**(1), 110–125.

Rainville, P., & Price, D. D. (2003). Hypnosis phenomenology and the neurobiology of consciousness. *Int J Clin Exp Hypn*, **51**(2), 105–129. doi: 10.1076/iceh.51.2.105.14613

Raz, A. (2005). Attention and hypnosis: neural substrates and genetic associations of two converging processes. *Int J Clin Exp Hypn*, **53**(3), 237–258. doi: 10.1080/00207140590961295

Raz, A., Kirsch, I., Pollard, J., & Nitkin-Kaner, Y. (2006). Suggestion reduces the stroop effect. *Psychol Sci*, **17**(2), 91–95. doi: 10.1111/j.1467–9280.2006.01669.x

Raz, A., Shapiro, T., Fan, J., & Posner, M. I. (2002). Hypnotic suggestion and the modulation of Stroop interference. *Arch Gen Psychiatry*, **59**(12), 1155–1161. doi: yoa10206 [pii]

Seeley, W. W., Menon, V., Schatzberg, A. F., Keller, J., Glover, G. H., Kenna, H., . . . Greicius, M. D. (2007). Dissociable intrinsic connectivity networks for salience processing and executive control. *J Neurosci*, **27**(9), 2349–2356. doi: 10.1523/JNEUROSCI.5587–06.2007

Semmens-Wheeler, R., & Dienes, Z. (2012). The contrasting role of higher order awareness in hypnosis and meditation. *J Mind-Body Reg*, **2**(1), 43–57.

Semmens-Wheeler, R., Dienes, Z., & Duka, T. (2013). Alcohol increases hypnotic susceptibility. *Conscious Cogn*, **22**(3), 1082–1091. doi: 10.1016/j.concog.2013.07.001

Smith, S. M., Fox, P. T., Miller, K. L., Glahn, D. C., Fox, P. M., Mackay, C. E., . . . Beckmann, C. F. (2009). Correspondence of the brain's functional architecture during activation and rest. *Proc Natl Acad Sci USA*, **106**(31), 13040–13045. doi: 10.1073/pnas.0905267106

Sridharan, D., Levitin, D. J., & Menon, V. (2008). A critical role for the right fronto-insular cortex in switching between central-executive and default-mode networks. *Proc Natl Acad Sci USA*, **105**(34), 12569–12574. doi: 10.1073/pnas.0800005105

Szekely, A., Kovacs-Nagy, R., Banyai, E. I., Gosi-Greguss, A. C., Varga, K., Halmai, Z., . . . Sasvari-Szekely, M. (2010). Association between hypnotizability and the catechol-O-methyltransferase (COMT) polymorphism. *Int J Clin Exp Hypn*, **58**(3), 301–315. doi: 10.1080/00207141003760827

Tang, Y. Y., Lu, Q., Fan, M., Yang, Y., & Posner, M. I. (2012). Mechanisms of white matter changes induced by meditation. *Proc Natl Acad Sci USA*, **109**(26), 10570–10574. doi: 10.1073/pnas.1207817109

Tang, Y. Y., Lu, Q., Geng, X., Stein, E. A., Yang, Y., & Posner, M. I. (2010). Short-term meditation induces white matter changes in the anterior cingulate. *Proc Natl Acad Sci USA*, **107**(35), 15649–15652. doi: 10.1073/pnas.1011043107

Tang, Y. Y., Ma, Y., Wang, J., Fan, Y., Feng, S., Lu, Q., . . . Posner, M. I. (2007). Short-term meditation training improves attention and self-regulation. *Proc Natl Acad Sci USA*, **104**(43), 17152–17156. doi: 10.1073/pnas.0707678104

Tart, C. T. (1970). Transpersonal potentialities of deep hypnosis. *J Transpers Psychol*, **2**, 27–40.

Taylor, V. A., Daneault, V., Grant, J., Scavone, G., Breton, E., Roffe-Vidal, S., . . . Beauregard, M. (2013). Impact of meditation training on the default mode network during a restful state. *Soc Cogn Affect Neurosci*, **8**(1), 4–14. doi: 10.1093/scan/nsr087

Tellegen, A., & Atkinson, G. (1974). Openness to absorbing and self-altering experiences ("absorption"), a trait related to hypnotic susceptibility. *J Abnorm Psychol*, **83**(3), 268–277.

Terhune, D. B., & Cardeña, E. (2010). Differential patterns of spontaneous experiential response to a hypnotic induction: a latent profile analysis. *Conscious Cogn*, **19**(4), 1140–1150. doi: 10.1016/j.concog.2010.03.006

Tian, L., Jiang, T., Liu, Y., Yu, C., Wang, K., Zhou, Y., . . . Li, K. (2007). The relationship within and between the extrinsic and intrinsic systems indicated by resting state correlational patterns of sensory cortices. *Neuroimage*, **36**(3), 684–690. doi: 10.1016/j.neuroimage.2007.03.044

Vestergaard-Poulsen, P., van Beek, M., Skewes, J., Bjarkam, C. R., Stubberup, M., Bertelsen, J., & Roepstorff, A. (2009). Long-term meditation is associated with increased gray matter density in the brain stem. *Neuroreport*, **20**(2), 170–174. doi: 10.1097/WNR.0b013e328320012a

Winecoff, A., Clithero, J. A., Carter, R. M., Bergman, S. R., Wang, L., & Huettel, S. A. (2013). Ventromedial prefrontal cortex encodes emotional value. *J Neurosci*, **33**(27), 11032–11039. doi: 10.1523/JNEUROSCI.4317–12.2013

Wylie, K. P., & Tregellas, J. R. (2010). The role of the insula in schizophrenia. *Schizophr Res*, **123**(2–3), 93–104. doi: 10.1016/j.schres.2010.08.027

Xue, S., Tang, Y. Y., & Posner, M. I. (2011). Short-term meditation increases network efficiency of the anterior cingulate cortex. *Neuroreport*, **22**(12), 570–574. doi: 10.1097/WNR.0b013e328348c750

Zang, Y., Jiang, T., Lu, Y., He, Y., & Tian, L. (2004). Regional homogeneity approach to fMRI data analysis. *Neuroimage*, **22**(1), 394–400. doi: 10.1016/j.neuroimage.2003.12.030

Part 6

Clinical applications

Chapter 19

Suggesting mindfulness: reflections on the uneasy relationship between mindfulness and hypnosis

Michael D. Yapko

Abstract

Now that mindfulness meditation has expanded from its roots as an exclusively spiritual practice to also being used as a clinical tool for its therapeutic benefits, new questions arise regarding the possible mechanisms underlying its effectiveness. We know mindfulness works, but *how*? For whom does it work, and in what contexts? In this brief reflection chapter, the differences between spiritual practice and clinical applications are viewed through the lens of hypnosis as they apply to the shared methods and aims of mindfulness and hypnosis. These overlaps include the role of focus, dissociation, and the inevitable utilization of suggestion embedded within such experiential approaches. Given the unique requirements of clinical applications, the author urges a careful consideration of the dynamics of mindful meditation as a therapeutic intervention, since these may differ substantially from using such methods for personal or spiritual growth.

Introduction

Interest in mindful meditation has continued to grow rapidly and steadily. Much of the focus has been in the realm of neuroscience, studying the brains and cognitive functions of meditators, but at least as much attention has been paid to the clinical merits of meditation as a therapeutic intervention in diverse healthcare contexts. The use of focusing strategies, as taught in mindful meditation programs, has strong parallels to the well-established field of clinical hypnosis, an intervention tool which also relies on focusing as its foundation. *Mindfulness and hypnosis: the power of suggestion to transform experience* (Yapko, 2011) was the first book to directly consider the relationship between the practice of clinical hypnosis and the utilization of guided meditation processes as they are conducted in the course of psychotherapy.

In this short reflection chapter, I will share some of my observations about the relationship between hypnosis and guided mindful meditations *as applied in clinical practice*. These observations may or may not be applicable in other contexts in which these methods are used. I hope to highlight some of what I consider to be the key ingredients that tie both approaches together and make them clinically valuable. I also want to comment on the direction much of the research seems to be taking that may limit its practical value for clinicians.

Treatment is a social process

Rather than exploring neurological or epigenetic changes that arise from meditative practices, my focus has exclusively been on analyzing the interpersonal relationship between clinician and client, particularly the suggestive language shared by guided meditations and hypnosis as tools of clinical intervention. The use of suggestive language that facilitates qualities of focus in the client is the foundation for both hypnosis and meditation methods taught and practiced in clinical contexts.

Mindful meditation in clinical usage is nearly always introduced by a clinician to an inexperienced client. Since the clinician typically provides the first meditative experiences through structured guided experiences, the goals and methods of meditation arise in an interpersonal, rather than independent, context. Furthermore, there is inevitably a goal-oriented, purposeful framework that is provided by the clinician as an introduction to meditation that is designed to educate and motivate the novice client to fully participate in such experiences. The wide array of social factors that influence the client's response to meditation, such as the quality of rapport with the clinician or the prestige of the sponsoring institution, have not yet been explored in depth to know what degree of inevitable influence they have on individual outcomes.

The field of clinical hypnosis has explored the social aspects of focusing methods to a far greater extent, but has yet to resolve a basic question both approaches ask: is the use of either hypnosis or meditation to be considered a solitary endeavor or a special type of social interaction? It may seem obvious to some, myself included, that if there is more than one person in the room it should be regarded as a social process and, therefore, subject to social influences. However, as neuroscientists study the brains of people in meditation or hypnosis, the unit of study is decidedly individual and, even more reductionistically, the individual brain. Thus, people test for hypnotizability as if it is an innate characteristic unaffected by social and contextual forces, and even advance global perspectives such as the familiar creed, "all hypnosis is self-hypnosis." As a clear parallel, in researching my book and interviewing well-known meditation experts, many proclaimed that their guidance during the meditative process was irrelevant and only the "awakening" of an individual's consciousness mattered. The perspective offered was that even in *guided* meditations, obviously an interpersonal process, the guide's influence was deemed negligible and only the experience of the client mattered.

To guide someone's subjective experience, but take no responsibility for what emerges as a result of that guidance by maintaining a philosophy that precludes taking such responsibility, seems a remarkable self-deception. Treatment occurs in an interpersonal context, and the guide, whether conducting a hypnosis session or a guided mindful meditation, is inevitably half the interaction. Both processes use the clinician's relationship with the client to introduce focus. *What* they focus the client on and *what* they encourage the client to focus on represent some of the key content differences between them.

Making the jump from spiritual to clinical

I have been interested in the rising rate of guided meditations utilized by psychotherapists in the context of psychotherapy and by other healthcare practitioners in the domain of behavioral medicine. The popularity of these approaches was captured in the *TIME* magazine cover story, "The mindful revolution: the science of finding focus in a stressed-out, multitasking culture" (Pickert, 2014). More specifically, I have been interested in how healthcare practitioners first introduce meditation into the therapeutic relationship and then how they deliver it as a healthcare intervention. As I described in *Mindfulness and hypnosis* (Yapko, 2011), how and under what circumstances meditation is introduced to the client can have a profound impact on its eventual effects. What began long ago and far away as a spiritual practice to enhance one's sense of well-being and raise consciousness has now become a mainstream clinical practice.

In January 2014, a highly publicized comprehensive and lengthy report entitled "Meditation programs for psychological stress and well-being" (Goyal et al., 2014a) was released by the Agency for Healthcare Research and Quality (AHRQ) (part of the American Department of Health and Human Services). (An abbreviated version by the same authors was published in *JAMA Online*; see Goyal et al., 2014b.) The authors wrote: "Meditation, a mind-body method, employs a variety of techniques designed to facilitate the mind's capacity to affect bodily function and symptoms" (p. viii). This first sentence of their paper could just as easily and correctly have begun with the word "hypnosis" instead of "meditation." They continued,

> We aimed to determine the efficacy and safety of meditation programs on stress-related outcomes . . . after a review of 17,801 citations, we included 41 trials with 2993 participants . . . Mindfulness and meditation programs had moderate SOE (strength of evidence) for improvement in anxiety . . . depression . . . and pain . . . We found either low SOE of no effect or insufficient SOE of an effect of meditation programs on positive mood, attention, substance abuse, eating, sleep, and weight. In our comparative effectiveness analyses, we did not find evidence to suggest that these meditation programs were superior to any specific therapies they were compared with . . . Stronger study designs are needed to determine the effects of meditation programs in improving the positive dimensions of mental health as well as stress-related behavioral outcomes." (Goyal et al., 2014, p. viii)

Despite the popularity of meditation and the frequent enthusiastic reports of its near-miraculous effectiveness in popular magazines and even some journals, it seems reasonable to say that yes, meditation has some therapeutic merit. However, only further and more multi-dimensional analysis will say how much, in what areas, in which clinical populations, and by what mechanisms. Yet, thus far, I have seen little interest by others in asking the questions I think need to be asked, including:

- How does paying attention—focusing—translate into non-volitional yet meaningful clinical responses?
- Why do some people respond so dramatically to experiential processes such as mindfulness or hypnosis, finding them "transformative," while others find them tepid and uninspiring?
- What general factors determine one's capacity to respond meaningfully to such experiential, subjective approaches?
- What role do specific factors such as expectancy, suggestibility, and dissociation play in client responsiveness?
- Can an individual's quality of responsiveness to such methods be increased?

These questions are critically important: suggesting acceptance, for example, or forgiveness, can be a great therapeutic objective; but *how* and under what specific conditions do the *suggestions* for acceptance or forgiveness translate into the *felt experiences*?

To answer such questions, one would have to consider the interpersonal and suggestive nature of guided meditations in the clinical arena (to be sharply contrasted with the independent or solo practice of meditation). One would have to acknowledge that one is being suggestive in using such methods with clients. Obvious as that seems, to me at least, I had more than one of the experts I interviewed for my book emphatically state, "I don't use suggestions in my work." *Really*? Do they really think they can say, "close your eyes" or "focus on the breath" *without* it being suggestive?

The fact that some authors and teachers in the field—even at least one contributor to this volume—think "hypnosis involves self-deception" but meditation is about "truth" is both shocking and frightening to me. It perpetuates the negative myths about mind control and hypnosis, while also perpetuating the myth that meditation is pure and can only help, never harm, as if there is *any* treatment that cannot be iatrogenic. It is a profound misrepresentation of hypnosis to advance the idea that it is programmed in the individual by someone else and robs one of choice, while portraying meditation as about self-discovery and "awakening to the truth." Such perspectives seem to miss the point that hypnosis or meditation is structured by the facilitator, clinician, or teacher, and what emerges within the individual depends a great deal on what is encouraged. Hypnosis is just as capable of being used to stimulate growthful self-reflection or greater compassion as meditation, if it is similarly structured to do so.

Suggestion is inevitable in both mindfulness and hypnosis

There is often a huge difference between what someone is doing, what they *think* they are doing, and the way they *describe* what they are doing. Nowhere is this more evident than in how suggestions are structured and delivered in guided meditations. Consider the following typical suggestions for some of the rituals of mindfulness and especially focus on what the suggestion catalyzes as a therapeutic response (described in italics, in parentheses):

◆ You can expect this experience/method to be helpful to you (*thereby building expectancy*).

◆ You can stop focusing on problems and just focus on breathing (*thereby curtailing rumination*).

◆ You can trust your breath to always be there (*thereby providing stabilizing, empowering self-regulation and utilization of the inevitable*).

◆ You can notice your experience without judging it (*thereby curtailing negative self-evaluation*).

◆ You can be present in the moment (*thereby detaching from the painful past or anxiety-provoking future*).

Does either hypnosis or mindfulness cure people? No! It is what happens *during* these experiences—the new and beneficial *associations* the client forms through the shift in focus and absorption in new possibilities—that holds the potential to be therapeutic. Also, this is why studies of meditation's effectiveness, such as the AHRQ meta-analysis reported in the section "Making the jump from spiritual to clinical," will predictably show what research about every other clinical technique shows: it helps some people, but does not help others. The field of hypnosis has studied this phenomenon in depth. The field of meditation is just beginning to ask the key question: who is more or less likely to benefit from these approaches? For whom might it actually make them feel *worse*? Or, should it be assumed that all people can derive equal benefit if they just believe in it and practice it enough?

Not everyone is equally responsive to suggestions, not everyone is capable of meaningful focus, and not everyone is capable of learning and forming new associations through directed or spontaneous experiences of absorption. This is what has troubled hypnosis researchers and clinicians for over a century: why are some people so responsive to hypnosis and why are others so much less so? For those who teach and practice guided meditations with their clients, I had hoped my book would stimulate their curiosity about what the hypnosis research has had to say about this all-important topic, given how much attention has been paid to the question of determinants and measurement of hypnotic responsiveness. To the contrary, the attitude I have personally encountered, if not the actual verbiage, has been, "Don't get that icky hypnosis all over my nice mindfulness." By viewing them as opposites, by portraying hypnosis negatively and in direct conflict with the purity and good of meditation, the therapists applying meditation see no reason to study hypnosis, which is a terrible shame, in my opinion.

Confusing the spiritual with the clinical

As a clinician, my focus is on the clinical applications of the methods of mindful meditation. However, going from a spiritual practice to a clinical intervention strategy is a new evolutionary step for meditation, one with uncertain implications. It seems clear, though, that changing the context in which such methods are used must have some consequences, and these need to be studied. As Lama Surya Das, a leading teacher, author, and one of the foremost American lamas in the Buddhist tradition, said in his Foreword to my book:

> Throughout the 2,500 years that mindfulness has been a part of the Buddhist contemplative tradition, it was never intended to strictly be an awareness or attention-regulation exercise. Rather, it was always cultivated while concomitantly evoking the heartful, soulful quality of attunement, including tenderness, care, loving-kindness, wishing well for others and oneself, unselfish love, and compassion. (Yapko, 2011, p. xii)

To highlight a key difference between the clinical and the spiritual, consider the following well-known Zen parable:

> *Muddy road*
>   Tanzan and Ekido were once traveling together down a muddy road. A heavy rain was still falling. Coming around a bend, they met a lovely girl in a silk komono and sash, unable to cross the intersection.
>   "Come on, girl," said Tanzan at once. Lifting her in his arms, he carried her over the mud.
>   Ekido did not speak again until that night when they reached a lodging temple. Then he could no longer restrain himself. "We monks don't go near females," he told Tanzan, "especially not young lovely ones. It is dangerous. Why did you do that?"
>   "I left the girl there," said Tanzan. "Are you still carrying her?"
>
> (Reps & Senzaki, 1998, p. 33)

This classic story has been handed down in Buddhist teachings over the centuries because of its simplicity in addressing an issue that is anything but simple. The important teaching embedded in the story is about "letting go" rather than "holding on" to that which is worrisome or troubling. It teaches the importance of action over contemplation, it models the ability to bend the rules flexibly when circumstances may warrant doing so, and it illustrates the merits of decisiveness over second-guessing.

However, let us shift viewpoints for a moment and consider the story of Tanzan and Ekido from a psychotherapeutic perspective. As monks, both Tanzan and Ekido have taken a sacred vow of celibacy. They are taught to avoid any situations where they may be tempted to violate their vows. To assist the young woman, Tanzan seemingly harmlessly engages with her in a way that might well have crossed the line of what was deemed appropriate behavior for a monk, and Ekido dares to question him about it. Tanzan's response to Ekido's questioning is, in essence, "let it go." *Instead of offering some insight* into his reasoning process regarding his decision to cross the line in this exceptional instance, he simply says, "let it go." *Instead of using it as a teaching opportunity* to educate Ekido about when to follow rules strictly and when to bend them based on varying circumstances, he simply says, "let it go." *Instead of compassionately acknowledging that Ekido has a valid point* (i.e., a legitimate basis for wondering about the protocol violation) or perhaps even *praising Ekido for his thoughtfulness* in contemplating the episode rather than just impulsively attacking him for what he did, Tanzan's reply suggests he is above questioning and it is therefore Ekido's problem for still thinking about the episode.

Imagine that Tanzan and Ekido agree to come for psychotherapy to resolve their differences about this episode with the young woman. How many therapists would listen to the story of what happened and then join Tanzan in telling Ekido to "just let it go" rather than sort through the details and implications of what happened? As a reasonable parallel, imagine a couple come in for therapy because one partner did something that crossed a previously agreed-upon line and then refused to discuss it when the other partner questioned him or her about it. Is there any therapist *anywhere* that would simply tell the concerned partner to "let it go" without trying to talk it through toward some constructive resolution that would well serve the relationship? From this clinician's vantage point, Tanzan's reply to Ekido is not enlightening—it is *avoidant*.

There are differences we must acknowledge between a spiritual philosophy and a clinical context, and between what is metaphorically elegant and pragmatically valuable. When someone cannot recognize those differences and respond to them meaningfully, they can too easily place abstract concepts (e.g., discovering "truth") ahead of concrete realities (e.g., if you are human, your view of the world is inevitably filtered and distorted by personal limitations ranging from neurological to social, contextual, and historical, and thus, on a spiritual level, you *cannot* know "the truth" beyond what *you yourself* define as "the truth"). The "big picture" of meditation as a means of discovering the truth is attractive, but in the clinical realm, one's problem-solving ability is found in the details of what one *actually says and does* in response to the challenges one faces.

Dissociation as a driving force in mindfulness and hypnosis

When people close their eyes and focus, something extraordinary happens to both the brain and the mind. The rigid boundaries of perception that have held the person in place begin to soften. "Reality" becomes less real and more negotiable. People discover, through direct subjective experience, that their *perceptions are malleable*, whether it is their perceptions of time, space, their body, the meanings ascribed to life experiences, self-awareness, or other perceptions. What the neuroscience shows us is that these malleable perceptions of the mind also have consequences in the brain.

What makes suggested shifts in awareness and perception translate into "felt" experiences? In part, the answer lies in the phenomenon of dissociation. Dissociation is one, perhaps *the*, key component of the experience of hypnosis and mindfulness. Dissociation is evident in an ability to compartmentalize experience, the capacity to break global experiences into their component parts and focus on one aspect to the exclusion or near exclusion of the other parts. It is the force that makes focus possible, as well as the automatic (i.e., non-volitional) responses derived from narrowed attention. Unfortunately, too many clinicians only know of dissociation as a basis for pathology (e.g., dissociative identity disorder) and not as a basis for meaningful clinical intervention (e.g., pain management).

The ability to detach from your own thoughts and other aspects of your internal experience is essential to transforming it: every therapeutic intervention, to one degree or another, involves some combination of dissociation and association—moving away or *separating from* (dissociation) or *moving closer to* (association) some element of experience (e.g., physical sensation or an emotion). Dissociation is evident in suggestions for mindfulness, as in the following common examples:

- *"Focus on acceptance"* suggests separating what one either wishes for or strives to deny from what is present in the moment.

- *"Focus on breathing"* suggests separating one's attention on breathing from other elements of experience.

- *"Focus on compassion"* suggests separating one's attention from the usual self (or other) criticism or harsh judgment.

- *"See your thoughts as if clouds floating across the sky"* suggests separating one's thoughts from the self.

If dissociation is so critically important in mediating hypnotic and mindful responses, then how is it understood, defined, and measured in mindfulness meditation? What means is there for measuring the client's potential response to such dissociative procedures in order for the clinician to better tailor their approaches to the client's capacities?

If you consider the aims of guided mindful meditations and structured hypnosis sessions, you can appreciate that the psychotherapist is attempting to redirect the client's attention in presumably positive directions. To suggest to a troubled client that they can begin to focus more on breathing right now, than on trying to solve all of their problems today, requires that individual to be able to *separate a focus on the breath right now from everything else*. To suggest to a highly self-critical perfectionist that they focus on a message of loving kindness toward themselves requires the ability to *set aside the usual focus on self criticisms* and *instead focus on the message of compassion* toward the self.

Can *anyone* do this? Under what conditions and to what degree? Is the capacity to dissociate a learnable skill that all people can acquire with a good teacher and lots of practice? Or, is the capacity for dissociation a stable trait that changes little over time no matter how much you practice, as some hypnosis literature suggests (Yapko, 2012)?

It is a well-established fact in the hypnosis literature that people differ substantially in their capacities to experience the dissociation of hypnosis meaningfully. Simply put, people differ in their hypnotic responsiveness, including their responsiveness to suggestions for dissociation. There is virtually unanimous agreement about this fact among hypnosis experts. Where the experts differ, however, is in their interpretations of what the differences across individuals means. Is hypnotic responsiveness a genetically or biologically determined phenomenon as some suggest? Is it something that is determined by the context in which hypnosis is applied? Or, is it a combination of these two and perhaps other variables as well? The same questions are immediately relevant in striving to understand people's responses to guided meditations.

The content and process of hypnosis and mindfulness

When someone is encouraged to focus on their breathing, as the basis for building a deeper experience of absorption, the content of the approach is the breath. The client may become aware of the sensory details associated with breathing, such as the rate of inhaling and exhaling, the volume of breath taken in and released, the location of the breath (whether at the nostrils or in the chest or diaphragm), the temperature of the breath, and so forth. These sensory details can easily occupy the person's awareness as it flitters from one sensory experience to another, all a part of "being in the moment."

At the process level, though, the person is encouraged to focus attention on an internal experience. The content is what you focus on and this naturally varies from technique to technique: one can focus internally on the taste and texture of food in one's mouth if one wants to learn to "eat mindfully;" one can focus internally on emotions that surface in response to different images or thoughts that pass through awareness if one wants to become more "emotionally present;" or one can focus internally on sensations changing in location or intensity if one strives to better "manage pain mindfully." What one focuses on is vitally important, for it is unquestionably true that *what you focus on defines the quality of your experience.*

Is it the *content*, such as the suggestion to "focus on the breath" that matters, or is it the *process* of focusing that matters? I would suggest that while the content certainly matters, it is the process that matters even more. A parallel example is the process of "developing a personal code to live by." What does it matter if your code is defined by the Hippocratic oath or the oath of citizenship when the greater goal is to live a meaningful and humane life, which one can do from within either framework? Yet, consider the hostility engendered when someone else's code does not match your own, when one is sure one is right and, therefore, everyone else must be wrong. People, including researchers and clinicians, get far too attached to the content of their methods and think the power is only to be found there. For example, at one meeting I attended, a neuroscientist told a roomful of clinicians, none of whom by definition could (or would *want*) to meet the challenge, "If you don't have brain scans, you've got *nothing* [to demonstrate the effects of your use of hypnosis]." One can promote the merits of an approach or code to live by without negating the merits of another. Mindful meditation is one code for focusing, hypnosis another. Each has merit, each uses the same structural process, but each differs in the content of its language when describing goals, philosophies, and methods.

This is also why the neuroscience is at least a little misleading. Looking for the differences in brain signatures between mindfulness and hypnosis is a common approach to trying to distinguish them. Yet, it is well established that brain signatures vary with the nature of the task being undertaken. The suggestions given to someone in a guided meditation for focusing on the breath or feeling compassion are different both in content and process than the kinds of suggestions a clinician is likely to give in hypnosis to help someone solve a specific problem. The focus of mindfulness and hypnosis overlap in process terms, but the kinds of things one would suggest to focus upon are going to be quite different in terms of content. Thus, it is no surprise when the brain signatures differ. Is there a way to suggest mindfulness and suggest hypnosis that is the same in terms of content and process?

If we are going to focus people on developing a mindful orientation, and I think we *should*, we need to be explicit about the nature of the process of mindfulness, providing a greater insight into its methods so we do not foster rigidity in either ourselves or our clients. For example, we need to be clear that if and when you ring a Tibetan meditation bell to encourage "a sense of arriving" or to signal the start (or end) of a meditative period, the bell is meant to be an associative cue that signals something is expected of the client or student. Thus, *the bell is only the content.* You could just as easily substitute a finger-snap, a Led Zeppelin riff, or any other auditory stimulus that *the client accepts as a valid signal* for shifting and engaging attention. It is not the bell that is significant; rather, what *is* significant is that there is a signal established that suggests to the listener that something important is about to occur. The signal further suggests that they should pay attention in the manner of the others present or in the manner modeled by the therapist as the "right" or ideal way to respond. The bell offers what is called, in hypnotic terms, an "implied directive," an indirect suggestion about what you should do if you are to respond appropriately.

In this respect, mindfulness is like every other intervention: a client has to be instructed in the concepts, terminology, rituals, and methods of whatever therapy they subscribe to. Whether it is the willingness to lie down on a couch with the analyst sitting behind you while you describe your dreams, or whether it is keeping a daily thought record and catching your cognitive distortions, therapy is a process of absorbing the client in the rules and rituals of a perspective that is promised to help. Clients comply because they want the help they are promised. The more invested someone is in following those rules and rituals, the more likely they are to benefit from them: there is evidence that the more demands you make on the client, the better the client's results (Kirsch, 2010).

Conclusion

This short reflection chapter was simply intended to share some of my observations and concerns about the fields of hypnosis and mindfulness. As a long-time practitioner of clinical hypnosis and a student of the research into the phenomena related to hypnosis, such as suggestion structures and cognitive processing, placebo and nocebo effects, expectations and treatment response, human suggestibility and social demand characteristics, situational specificity, and so much more, I find the attention now being paid to attention very encouraging. Yet, I am also concerned that clinicians and researchers are so loyal to a meditation doctrine, so invested in adhering to a traditional Buddhist perspective and even using its ancient terminology, so attached to spiritual interpretations of the meaning of such experiences, so narrow in their thinking that neuroscientific evidence is what gives justification to such approaches, and so rigid in their applications of focusing that they too easily dismiss an invaluable source of information and perspective—hypnosis—because it is defined as "icky" compared to the "purity" of mindful meditation. I find these troublesome perspectives lacking in both scientific curiosity and humanistic compassion.

In writing this, I am making an undisguised effort to encourage a greater ease and comfort in the relationship between advocates of meditation and hypnosis, for clinical purposes. Each has much to offer the other in sharing the dynamics of meaningful focus.

Deep questions remain: how do we create the conditions that encourage knowing and growing the best parts of ourselves and others? How can we make the merits of mindfulness, hypnosis, and other such opportunities for experiential learning more understandable, usable, and available to the clients we serve? How can we selflessly share knowledge that makes the whole greater than the sum of the parts? I think Buddha's answer to such questions is perfect: "Mind comes first. Before deed and words comes thought or intention."

References

Goyal, M., Singh, S., Sibinga, E., Gould, N., Rowland-Seymour, A., Sharma, R., Haythornthwaite, J. (2014a). *Meditation programs for psychological stress and well-being. Comparative effectiveness review no. 124*. Rockville, MD: Agency for Healthcare Research and Quality (AHRQ). AHRQ publication no. 13(14)-EHC116-EF, January 2014. Retrieved from www.effectivehealthcare.ahrq.gov/reports/final.cfm

Goyal, M., Singh, S, Sibinga, E., Gould, N., Rowland-Seymour, A., Sharma, R., Haythornthwaite, J. (2014b). Meditation programs for psychological stress and well-being: a systematic review and meta-analysis. *JAMA Internal Medicine* [online], January 6, 2014. doi:10.1001/jamainternmed.2013.13018

Kirsch, I. (2010). *The emperor's new drugs: exploding the antidepressant myth*. New York: Perseus.

Pickert, K. (2014, February 3). The art of being mindful. *TIME*, **183**(4), 40–46.

Reps, P., & Senzaki, N. (1998). *Zen flesh, Zen bones: a collection of Zen and pre-Zen writings*. Boston: Tuttle Publishing.

Yapko, M. (2011). *Mindfulness and hypnosis: the power of suggestion to transform experience*. New York: Norton.

Yapko, M. (2012). *Trancework: an introduction to the practice of clinical hypnosis* (4th edn.). New York: Routledge.

Chapter 20

Self-transformation through hypnosis and mindfulness meditation
What exactly is being transformed?

Norman A. S. Farb

Abstract

This chapter explores how hypnosis and mindfulness training alter a person's sense of self to create cognitive and behavioral change. Optimally, self-serving biases promote an individual's interests, but sometimes they may also entrench maladaptive patterns of cognition and behavior. From this perspective, hypnosis and mindfulness training can be viewed as potential moderators of self-serving habits, with related but distinct mechanisms of action. To support this claim, the chapter reviews cognitive and neural mechanisms underlying hypnosis and mindfulness traditions, illustrating distinct effects on personal identity that promote different forms of transformation. Both traditions reduce reliance on prior self-knowledge, freeing cognition and behavior to operate in novel ways. However, while mindfulness reduces reliance on habitual self-appraisals, enabling open-ended inquiry and exploration, hypnosis is concentrative, directing perception and/or action toward a particular specified end. These twin processes of exploratory and focal attention may thereby serve complementary purposes in establishing trajectories of personal transformation.

Introduction

From the Dalai Lama's keynote address at the 2005 of the Society for Neuroscience, to meditation on the cover of *Time* magazine, mainstream culture seems increasingly willing to explore non-traditional avenues to understanding the mind. For many, this desire is motivated by practical rather than metaphysical concerns: awareness-modifying techniques such as meditation or hypnosis are increasingly linked to a variety of health benefits. Given the frenetic pace and increasing complexity of modern lifestyles, the promise of safe and effective self-improvement is enticing.

To understand how shaping awareness promotes well-being, we must confront a new set of mysteries. We no longer question that physical exercise benefits the body, but the science behind improving the mind is far less established. The enigmatic efficacy of attentional practices such as meditation and hypnosis may add to their allure, but understanding how and why they work would allow us to make better use of these practices. Such understanding is particularly important when we consider that different techniques may have very different mental targets and effects, and knowledge of these practice-outcome relationships may be critical for generating positive trans-formations (for thoughtful reflections on this topic from a seasoned clinician, see Chapter 19).

One may object that it does not matter why hypnosis or mindfulness training (MT) work; it is enough that they do. Yet, an example of why efficacy alone is not sufficient knowledge can be made by way of analogy to physical exercise. While exercise is generally beneficial, certain types of exercise are better suited for a given set of goals than others. For example, a person seeking to improve their ability to run long distances would do better to undertake cardiovascular train-ing than heavy weight training, the latter of which is likely to build muscle, improving explosive strength but reducing long-distance running efficiency. Similarly, it is likely that different contem-plative or hypnotic practices, while commonly promoting self-transformation, also differ in the specific targets of such transformation. Thus, just as the marathon runner does not wish to unin-tentionally add 40 pounds of muscle, an individual who feels isolated from emotional experience does not necessarily need to change emotional response habits—the training that would be most beneficial for such an individual would be one that increases awareness of experience rather than altering regulatory responses.

In this chapter, I discuss how hypnosis and MT practices operate to alter a person's sense of self to create cognitive and behavioral change. The discussion begins with a conceptualization of the self as a construct for describing a hierarchical set of heuristics to direct an organism's perception and action. Critically, this view of the self is agnostic with respect to a given habit's adaptive value. Optimally, self-serving biases promote an individual's interests, but sometimes they may also entrench maladaptive patterns of cognition and behavior. From this perspective, hypnosis and MT can be viewed as potential moderators of self-serving habits, with related but distinct mech-anisms of action. To support this claim, the chapter will review cognitive and neural mechanisms underlying hypnosis and mindfulness traditions, illustrating distinct effects on personal identity that promote different forms of transformation.

Both traditions reduce reliance on prior self-knowledge, freeing cognition and behavior to operate in novel ways. However, while mindfulness reduces reliance on habitual self-appraisals to enable open-ended inquiry and exploration, hypnosis is concentrative, aiming to direct per-ception and/or action toward a particular specified end. These twin processes of exploration and direction may thereby serve complementary purposes in establishing trajectories of personal transformation.

What do we mean by "self"?

Without minimizing their potential impacts, both mindfulness and hypnosis can be considered forms of "self-help." Through a series of attentional exercises, practitioners expect to realize sub-stantial personal growth, change that would not otherwise be afforded through simple intentions to think or act differently. Yet what is this sense of self that we are trying to change? Why does such self-modification require dedicated therapy or practice?

From the outset, it is important to acknowledge that the self is a psychological construct and has been defined in many different ways. For instance, in Chapter 22, Toneatto and Courtice pro-vide a different, more psychoanalytic perspective on how hypnosis and meditation alter the sense of self. It is through examination of these definitions, in particular, the distinction between the *self-as-subject* and *self-as-object*, that we may begin to understand what exactly is being targeted

WHAT DO WE MEAN BY "SELF"? | **383**

through meditation and hypnosis. The *self-as-subject* denotes the experience of agency, of having some volition and control over one's perception and action, as experience unfolds from moment to moment. The *self-as-object* denotes the conceptual descriptions that explain one's actions, infer motivation, and situate behavior in a narrative context that links momentary experiences across time. To simplify these terms, we may benefit from seminal social psychologist George Herbert Mead's distinction between the "I" (self-as-subject) and the "Me" (self-as-object) (Mead, 1913), which uses our instinctive understanding of grammar to clarify how the subjective and objective senses of identity may interrelate.

The distinction between subjective and objective accounts of the self is a perennial distinction in the social sciences. James William, widely considered to be a founding father of psychology, made use of this distinction, partitioning the Me into physical, social, and spiritual knowledge representations distinct from I (William, 1890). In James' words, the I is described as "the pure ego," founded on the idea that "a continuum of feelings (especially bodily feelings) experienced along with things widely different in all other regards, thus constitutes the real and verifiable 'personal identity' which we feel" (p. 207). In other words, while we attend to many things that we identify as belonging to, or excluded from, the self, underneath all experience is the I, a consistent undercurrent of familiarity, a sense that we are somehow doing the experiencing. The French phenomenologist Maurice Merleau-Ponty described the I in this way:

> My body is geared to the world when my perception offers me a spectacle as varied and as clearly articulated as possible, and when my motor intentions, as they unfold, receive from the world the responses they anticipate. This maximum distinctness in perception and action defines a perceptual ground, a basis of my life, a general milieu for the coexistence of my body and the world. (Merleau-Ponty, 1996, p. 250)

While there are important distinctions between the contents of self-reference (the Me), such as physical, social, and spiritual traits, the description of the self as subject (the I) is of a fundamentally different kind. It describes the momentary experience of situating one's body in the world, and a realization of potential operations on the world through the body.

The distinction between I and Me has not been lost on the scientific community. Cross-species researchers have remarked on the idea that animals must have some sort of basic, agentic identity that is distinct from human conceptual self-reference, a sense that we as human beings share, and known as the "core" as opposed to "higher order" self (Panksepp & Northoff, 2009). Neuroscientists such as Antonio Damasio have made parallel distinctions between "core" and "extended" forms of consciousness (Damasio, 1998), in which core consciousness is "incessantly generated relative to any object" whereas extended consciousness requires the aggregation of conceptual memories about one's actions and intentions. Philosophers have echoed this distinction: Shaun Gallager offered a distinction between the "minimal" self, which amounts to sensory input and cognitive-behavioral responses in the present moment, as opposed to a "narrative" self that unites experiences across time, serving to integrate experience into a coherent historical framework (Gallagher, 2000). Memory researchers have grappled with the problem of primary and reflected experience, using the term "noetic" for the act of knowing in the moment, whereas "auto-noetic" refers to remembering, linking, or projecting experiences across time (Tulving, 1985). Social psychologists have used this distinction in research on first- versus third-person perspective taking (Libby, Eibach, & Gilovich, 2005).

The integration of this dynamic, present-centered I across time then allows for the ongoing updating of the temporally extended Me. In turn, the Me may inform the momentary movements of the I. To understand how the I and the Me interrelate, the concept of "affordances" may be helpful. The term was introduced by psychologist J. J. Gibson in 1977 (Gibson, 1977) to situate the study of human behavior in an ecological context. Affordances describe all of the potential perceptual, cognitive, and behavioral acts that an organism is capable of given its surroundings. From this perspective, the I operates within a contextual field of affordances at each moment, a sea of possible actions from which only a few possibilities may be consciously realized at any given time. There are almost always hugely more affordances available to us in a given moment—even now, I could sing, recall what I had for dinner last night, wander in search of coffee, or type another line of this chapter—and this is just the tip of the iceberg. There are seemingly limitless potential affordances in any moment, which would be paralyzing and perhaps impossible to consider at once. Yet, we move through most of our day effortlessly, intuitively acting within the world. Thus, it would seem that there must be some way that affordances are organized to meet a person's cognitive capacity. The Me has the potential to serve this organizational role.

Evidence for the Me as a psychological construct

It can be argued that a theorized psychological construct such as the Me is of little use unless it can be shown to perform some sort of psychological "work," accounting for patterns of biology and behavior. Indeed, emerging evidence supports the notion that human experience is organized in terms of its relevance to this objective self. In this section, I will briefly review such evidence, as the neural and cognitive mechanics of the objectified Me may prove useful in later discussions about self-transformation.

Initial evidence for the Me as a psychological construct came from Rogers' 1977 demonstration of the self-reference effect on memory (Rogers, Kuiper, & Kirker, 1977). The experiment was an extension of the levels of processing model, which illustrated that deeper, more elaborative forms of cognition during stimulus encoding leads to better subsequent recall (Craik & Lockhart, 1972). For example, if I am asked to judge whether the word "book" is presented in upper-case rather than lower-case letters (structural judgment), this is a shallower form of encoding than judging whether the word rhymes with "hook" (phonemic judgment), which is, in turn, shallower than judging whether the word fits in a bread box (semantic judgment). The levels of processing model demonstrated that deeper judgments yield deeper memory, suggesting privileged encoding for stimuli at deeper levels of cognitive engagement, perhaps because such encoding situates experience within a pre-existing representational milieu.

In the demonstration of the self-reference effect, Rogers et al. extended levels of processing theory by including judgments of self-relevance to the paradigm; for example, "am I 'happy'?" led to superior word recall compared to structural (upper or lower case?), phonemic (does it rhyme with "sappy"?), or even semantic (is it a positive or negative word?) types of judgments (Craik & Lockhart, 1972). These results were indicative of a privileged form of cognitive engagement reserved for attributions of self-relevance, suggesting that consideration of experience in relation to a latent self-concept is situated within a deeper conceptual milieu than other forms of semantic judgment. Such organizational precedence forms the basis for the idea that the Me serves to guide perception and behavior, providing relative salience among affordances accessible to the I.

Over the past few decades, our understanding of the Me has expanded with the advent and popularization of cognitive neuroscience research methods. The same self-reference paradigm has been fruitfully applied, numerous times, to identify neural correlates of the Me, implicating a set of cortical midline regions and, in particular, the medial prefrontal cortex (MPFC) in self-referential evaluation (Fossati et al., 2003; Kelley et al., 2002). This same region, along with another cortical midline structure known as the posterior cingulate, overlap with the brain's default mode network, the pattern of brain activity that is observed when people are not focused on a particular attention-demanding task (Whitfield-Gabrieli et al., 2011). Furthermore, MPFC activity is graduated when considering other people, such that people closer to the self (e.g., a mother or close friend) activate the MPFC more than more distant acquaintances (Mitchell, Macrae, & Banaji, 2006). Taken together, this research suggests a role for the MPFC in the organization of experience with reference to a temporally extended, objective self—the Me.

How the Me constrains the I

Based upon the behavioral and neuroscience evidence, it would seem as though the consideration of self-relevance, the ascription of traits, relationships, and experiences as belonging to a stable self, is an automatic and universal property of human cognition. However, it is important to note that the types of information afforded self-relevance may vary between individuals and between cultures. For example, in collectivist cultures, respected authority figures activate the MFPC more than the self (Chiao et al., 2009), suggesting that the most deeply processed concepts need not relate to the individual but, rather, to one's esteemed leaders. A speculative but reasonable implication of this finding is that the affordances an individual experiences in a collectivist culture are determined more by the interests and history of the group and relatively less by the individual's idiosyncratic preferences or habits.

A second consideration is that an individual's self-referential processing heuristics may change over time. For example, individuals from collectivist cultures who migrate to the West appear more like individualistic Westerners if they also possess a strong commitment towards cultural assimilation, responding more to individual self-reference over respected others and authority figures (Chen, Wagner, Kelley, Powers, & Heatherton, 2013). Of course, in such cross-sectional research, it is difficult to infer individual change—it is possible that immigrants who are likely to endorse assimilation values always possessed Western-style self-reference. The findings are, nevertheless, provocative in demonstrating the variety of self-referential modes, even if further research is needed to demonstrate the mutability of such modes.

A further implication of this research is that the types of information that one attends to, the types of sensations and attributes that are considered self-relevant, importantly constrain the interpretive and behavioral affordances, and do so in different ways between individuals. These differences are particularly important when considering psychopathologies such as affective disorders. For example, following a negative event, individuals with a history of depression are more likely to endorse negative self-trait adjectives than healthy individuals (Miranda & Persons, 1988; Miranda, Persons, & Byers, 1990). In addition, the tendency to endorse negative self-traits predicts failure to recover from depression (Williams, Healy, Teasdale, White, & Paykel, 1990), and is predictive of depressive relapse in patients remitted from depression at the time of testing (Segal, Gemar, & Williams, 1999). In this way, the interpretive options afforded to the I following a negative event appear to be highly constrained toward dysphoric rumination rather than empowering positive responses. The I, while seemingly agnostic to life history and static traits, is nonetheless shaped in its perceptual and behavioral affordances by the Me.

While depression research provides a useful example of the self-as-object constraining the movements of the self-as-subject, it is important to remember that depression refers to an abnormal tendency to veer towards dysphoric self-ideation, perhaps an elevated level of constraints on the I in the face of a rigidly and negatively defined Me. Optimally, the interplay between the two forms of self-reference is more nuanced and bi-directional. In the context of mental health, Watkins and Teasdale proposed a theory of distinct self-referential modes in depression, distinguishing between experiential and analytic forms of self-focus (Watkins & Teasdale, 2004). Experiential focus involves attending to momentary sensation, thoughts, and feelings, in contrast to analytic focus, which turns attention toward elaboration on the implications of such sensations for the self-as-object. According to the interacting cognitive subsystems (ICS) approach, adaptive human behavior comes from symbiotic interactions between concrete/experiential and holistic/analytic levels of meaning; when flexibility between these levels is lost, one can experience a confusing loss of broader meaning, or, perhaps more insidiously, one can become locked into a particular set of meanings, which forms the basis for a cognitive model of depression (Teasdale, 1993).

When flexible transitions between the I and Me are realized, their dynamic interplay allows for more nuanced consideration of one's relationship to one's environment. When choosing a course of action, adaptive choice requires reflection on what is afforded to the I in a given moment, rather than simply doing what is familiar. This is true of our relationship with the physical environment, lest we neglect signs of wet paint or an open manhole, and also of our social milieu—our way of interacting with others ought to importantly consider their changing moods and goals. The flexibility cuts both ways, as each choice we make should optimally also modify the Me: a persistent view of myself as physically fit is not very helpful when I am halfway through a bag of potato chips—an updated view of how our actions may be impacting our temporally extended self concept should lead to better self-regulation. Thus, we neglect either facet of our identity at our peril. If, for example, I act only in service of my immediate impulses and perceptions, I should have great difficulty following social conventions or living up to past promises. On the other hand, if I feel as though my actions are unalterably constrained by my knowledge of how "a person like me" must act in a given situation, I limit my ability to notice unexpected affordances.

Automaticity at the heart of self-constraint

If adaptive function requires flexibility between the I and the Me, how is it that we find ourselves over-determined in our perception and action? We might consider that the role of the Me is not simply to organize descriptive information about the self for introspective interpretation and elaboration, but also to heuristically organize procedural information to regulate perception and behavior. By this logic, each time the I's perception or action is restructured with reference to the self-as-object, it increases the likelihood of similar restructuring in the future. In doing so, habits of perception and action are formed. The consequence of such habit formation is that the process of restructuring perception and action may become increasingly automatic; the calculation of how to attend or respond to a given situation occurs with greater and greater efficiency, reducing situational ambiguity, and thus minimizing the role of the I in determining how to interpret the now-familiar situation (for an in-depth analysis of the de-automatization of habitual thought patterns, see Chapter 11).

To offer a concrete example of this automation process, we may consider a hypothetical niece speaking to a cantankerous uncle, who constantly supplies unwanted advice. In early interactions, the niece might attempt multiple methods for resolving the conflict, ranging from passive silence to confronting the relative for his aggressive tutelage. Over time however, one may learn that arguing with the uncle simply agitates him and prolongs the discussion, whereas feigning agreement and changing the topic successfully redirects the conversation with little acrimony. With each subsequent conversation and emotional challenge, the act of avoiding conflict and redirecting attention becomes an overlearned regulatory response to a stressful situation. Years later, our fictitious niece may realize that she exhibits habitual conflict-avoidance tendencies, and wonder how this came to pass. Over time, the learned behavior has become informationally encapsulated, unfolding without volition or even awareness.

The idea of encapsulation is perhaps most prominently introduced into psychological discourse by Jerry Fodor, who contributed important ideas about the modularity of the mind (Fodor, 1983). Specifically, the modularity hypothesis states that there are particular units in our brains that take only certain types of input, but given the correct input, automatically and surreptitiously transform this information into a particular fixed type of output. In this way, cognitive operations are streamlined through encapsulation into particular functional modules.

While we now understand information processing in the brain to occur in more flexible, distributed ways, the idea that some information processing occurs automatically and subconsciously still holds considerable merit: our modern world is full of examples of such encapsulation, which may be more directly observed in cases of observable behavior. The research literature on touch-typing is a rich resource in this regard; skilled typing is a concrete example in which momentary typing intentions form an "outer loop" of executive control, but the details of how the hands translate thoughts into keystrokes forms an "inner loop" of behavioral execution that is overlearned and not particularly amenable to conscious control (Logan & Crump, 2011). Indeed, momentary attention to the particular keystrokes during typing appears to interfere with the typing process (Logan & Crump, 2009), reducing the efficiency of the overlearned typing procedure.

While examinations of learned behaviors such as typing are particularly amenable for demonstrating the power of automaticity in learning, there is reason to believe that cognitive attributions and decision making follow these same rules of habit reliance. The tendency toward dysphoric rumination in depression, for example, may be one instance of an overlearned interpretive style that overrides momentary intentions. A classic example of this is the phenomenon of overgeneral memory in depression (Williams & Scott, 1988). In this paradigm, participants are asked to report on a specific instance of a past event (e.g., "Tell me about the last time you went to the beach?"). A correct response would involve episodic recall, naming particular details about a particular day at the beach. However, participants with ongoing or former depression tend to respond at the semantic or implicational level, describing things that always happen at the beach rather than reporting on a specific event. It is as though these depressed individuals have overlearned operating at an abstract/holistic level (Barnhofer, Jong-Meyer, Kleinpaß, & Nikesch, 2002), consistent with the implicational/analytic mode discussed in Barnard and Teasdale's ICS model (Teasdale, 1993).

Critically, depressed individuals retain the capacity to engage in episodic recall if they are reminded of the task instructions throughout the recall paradigm (Yanes, Roberts, & Carlos, 2008), and training interventions aimed at redeveloping a concrete cognitive style appear to be effective in reducing this bias, and related depressive symptoms (Watkins, Baeyens, & Read, 2009).

So, while there are numerous ways of understanding overgeneral memory in depression, the tendency for an emotional stressor to automatically capture attention and trigger an overgeneral, ruminative style is a likely contributing factor (Williams, 2006). Furthermore, in our work, engagement of rumination has been directly linked to activation of the MPFC, our neural correlate of self-as-object processing, in response to an emotional challenge (Farb, Anderson, Bloch, & Segal, 2011). In Farb et al.'s study, viewing sad film clips provoked MPFC engagement without any additional processing instructions, and the magnitude of MPFC activation was correlated both with current rumination tendencies and also with future relapse into depression. In this way, an interpretive bias in the face of a stressor constrains interpretive responses toward dysphoric elaboration, resulting in detrimental longitudinal impact on well-being. In the parlance of this chapter, depression vulnerability can be construed as the dominance of a well-entrenched, negative Me over the I in structuring the interpretive response to adverse life events.

How mindfulness meditation and hypnosis impact the self

In the preceding sections, I attempted to outline a theory of two self-referential modes: the I which acts as agent within a given context, and the Me which organizes experience and supplies this context to the I. From this perspective, it may be possible to gain insight into how practices such as mindfulness meditation and hypnosis attempt to achieve positive personal transformations. In particular, I present a theory that mindfulness and hypnosis seek to shape cognition and behavior in two distinct ways: while MT focuses on strengthening engagement with the I (self-as-subject), hypnosis attempts to modify the affordance constraints placed upon the I, directly interfacing with the implicit Me (self-as-subject). Before either of these mechanisms can be realized, a prior mechanism may be required to engender change: understanding the nature of one's own conditioned state.

Mechanism 1: awareness of how the Me constrains the I

When one considers changing longstanding personal habits, several obstacles are readily apparent. The first obstacle is epistemological: one must have some knowledge of habits before one can change them. Of course, change can and does occur without conscious awareness—we are all constantly conditioned by life experiences and past choices. However, in the context of self-improvement, it is fair to say that change is desired and intentionally pursued. One technique for dealing with the epistemological problem of self-transformation is to introduce direct, experiential knowledge of maladaptive habits, creating a context in which the need for change becomes concrete and salient. People sign up for MT courses or hypnotherapy for many reasons, but, barring idle curiosity, most are dissatisfied with their lives in some way. Despite this general malaise, a client may not understand the specific reasons why they feel dissatisfied or upset—Freud's classic theories on repression make this case in detail (Freud, 1922)—but even today, when therapeutic techniques extend beyond classical psychoanalysis, understanding the sources of one's suffering is a critical step in moving toward positive change.

While it may be tempting to blame one's dissatisfaction on others, traditions of both hypnosis and meditation place the locus of change squarely within the individual. A client may expect their therapist or intervention facilitator to help "fix" their problems in some way. Rather than seeking to change interpersonal or environmental stressors, the meditation or hypnosis instructor aims to alter the client's relationship to these stressors, improving their capacity to act adaptively. Ultimately, these practices are designed to engender in clients a sense of responsibility for one's own happiness, to realize that it is one's internal appraisal of events that determines well-being. For example, mindfulness communication courses reduce the tendency to blame others for communication difficulties (Huston, Garland, & Farb, 2011), and MT interventions in cancer-care contexts increase feelings of self-control despite the progression of an insidious illness (Tacón, Caldera, & Ronaghan, 2004). Similarly, hypnotherapy promoting positive self-appraisal increased feelings of internal control relative to a control group that only discussed the importance of feelings of personal responsibility (Stanton, 1979).

In any therapeutic relationship, there is a risk of a participant becoming dependent on a "guru" or "healer." However, the goal of these practices is to empower the client to make their own life choices, so we ought not to confuse the risks of fostering dependence with such interventions with their intended function. The 8-week format of many MT interventions, which sets an end point to the therapeutic relationship, and the progression towards self-hypnosis in hypnotherapy, which obviates the need for therapist instruction, both support the movement towards client independence rather than dependence.

One consequence of promoting personal responsibility and an internal locus of control is that participants are asked to rigorously attend to and evaluate personal choices and behaviors. In other words, they are asked to document the I's choices throughout the day, as well as the experience of afforded choices or the lack thereof (i.e., the Me underlying such choices). For example, the introspective exercises early in MT courses focus on noticing patterns of positive and negative experiences each day (Kabat-Zinn & Hanh, 2009). From such diarizing of daily experience, participants may begin to become aware of biases inherent to integrating daily events into self-appraisals of well-being. In other words, mindfulness practices aim first to generate an understanding that the I's movements are deeply conditioned, with an occasional propensity to fixate on, and sometimes exacerbate, stressful events and interpretations. The French existentialist Jean-Paul Sartre described this process of coming to realize the limits to the I's movements as *facticity* (Sartre, 1943); it is through insight into the facticity surrounding the I's movements that barriers to freedom are revealed. MT interventions seek to engender awareness of this facticity as a first step toward the realization of personal change.

In hypnotherapy, insight into personal habits is usually a prerequisite rather than a focus of the therapeutic process. Clients may have particular behavioral complaints, such as addictions, compulsions, or other maladaptive habits, that they have already identified and wish to target through hypnotherapy. Alternatively, clients may have non-specific feelings of dissatisfaction or inadequacy that they wish to explore with a therapist. In the former case, hypnosis may attempt to operate directly upon the habits, the affordances given by the Me, without requiring any deeper insight into the nature of the self and the I/Me relationship. In the latter case, hypnosis may be used to help foster insight into self-referential habits before attempting to modify them. In fact, Freud's use of hypnotherapy, a century ago, was intended to reduce defensive reactions to self-inquiry, with the idea that understanding one's maladaptive reactive patterns is central to improving one's lot in life (Hatcher, 1973, p. 378). While Freud later abandoned hypnosis in favor of free association techniques, hypnosis still relies upon inquiry during hypnotic states as a means of generating insight around distressing ideas or habits (Anbar, 2008; Astor, 1973).

Despite the potential for using hypnotic states to promote spontaneous insight, it is fair to say that hypnosis interventions are more often employed with a particular goal in mind. Mindfulness techniques, on the other hand, explicitly eschew creating such suggestions in the pursuit of insight experiences (Farb, 2012; Holroyd, 2003). These different emphases may have very important implications for understanding how these traditions impact the self. While awareness of one's self-defeating habits is perhaps necessary for achieving positive change, such awareness alone may not be sufficient. Further explanatory work is needed to determine what other elements, if any, are needed to bolster transformation following personal insight.

Mechanism 2: changing the Me

Given some insight into one's undesired cognitive habits, a second major obstacle to self-transformation is one of implementation: awareness of one's own habits may be insufficient to overcome such habits. The junkie who wishes to kick their drug addiction, the late-night snacker seeking to lose a few pounds, and the parent who wishes they did not react as angrily to their children, all face the same dilemma: they wish to act differently but find their behavior bound to the tracks of past conditioning. In other words, the I is willing, but unable to overcome the Me.

Mindfulness and hypnosis interventions rely upon many of the same principles to effect change: they both contain elements of suggestion and/or expectation, a ritualized set of exercises that are promised to help realize these expectations, and a therapeutic alliance between client and instructor (Farb, 2012). In the present discussion, all of these elements can be seen as restructuring the Me to afford the I with more adaptive options for perception and action. Despite these similarities, how the Me is modified, and its ideal post-modified state, may be very different between these traditions.

Changing the Me through acceptance-based deconditioning

In mindfulness, there is a strong caveat against holding expectations during meditation. A meditation practitioner can and should hold strong conviction that their practice has the potential to effect positive change (Kabat-Zinn, 1982). On the other hand, most forms of modern mindfulness meditation involve bringing attention to immediate, present-moment experience, without transitioning into judgment or conceptual elaboration. In other words, the immediate goal during mindfulness meditation is to stage engaged-with awareness of the I, without slipping into activation of the Me. It should be noted that not all meditation practices aim for realization of this agentic state: for a discussion of other forms of meditation involving explicit cultivation of specific thoughts and perceptions, see Chapters 3 and 4.

As an example of how cultivation of the agentic I is achieved, consider that a practitioner may experience discomfort after sitting in meditation for an extended period of time. The inclinations of the body to move, changes in the sensation itself, the arising of thoughts around whether the discomfort is too much to bear, and immediate positive and negative evaluations of the physical sensations are all constitutive of experiencing the I in the present moment, and, as such, are consistent with the meditative focus. However, worrying about how moving will reflect one's reputation or success as a meditator, lapsing into memories or worry about the future, appraising movement as a "failure" or stoically enduring discomfort as "success," or other cognitive elaborations are seen as undesired states, requiring the redirection of attention back to the present moment.

When we consider this distinction between desired and undesired objects of attention during meditation, we can see evidence that attention is being repeatedly redirected toward the I at the expense of inferences that activate or modify the Me. The tendency to jump from the I into the Me is seen as the primary obstacle to freedom, the sense of worldly conditioning whose traces are strengthened with every habit-driven response to the I (Goenka, 1982). By repeatedly switching from the Me back to an I form of self-reference, mindfulness practice may serve to weaken the conditioned association between the two modes, freeing the I from its traditional affordances and allowing novel, spontaneous, and situation-specific patterns of action that will, in theory, be more adaptive and satisfying.

In my group's neuroimaging research, participants completing an 8-week MT course showed a greater ability to transition from prefrontal activity associated with the Me and visceral sensory representations associated with the I (Farb et al., 2007). This ability is important, as the tendency to enter conceptual self-elaboration typical of the Me mode of processing was apparent in a community sample of participants exposed to sadness-inducing film clips, to the exclusion of momentary I representations (Farb et al., 2010). In this same study, greater biases toward the Me over the I following mood challenge predicted depression symptoms, whereas MT was associated with more balanced recruitment of the Me and I brain networks, and reductions in such symptoms in the MT completers.

While further steps may be needed to introduce long-term change and stress resilience, one early mechanism by which MT alters the self is by extinguishing the seemingly obligatory association between the self-as-subject's immediate sensation and the self-as-object's channeling of experience into well-rehearsed response patterns. Longitudinally, continued mindfulness practice may serve to reduce reliance on the Me more generally (Goenka, 1982). I have heard experienced meditators discuss an experience of "flipping a switch" in which the balance shifts and the I becomes the default way of knowing, instead of the Me.

The extent to which extinction of the Me is a goal of most Western practitioners is debatable, and not well-characterized by the research literature. Nevertheless, the strengthening of sensory over conceptual representations seems to be a consistent finding in the emerging neuroscience of mindfulness (Farb, Segal, & Anderson, 2013; Kilpatrick et al., 2011), and so this idea of weakening self-appraisal habits through radical acceptance of the I may be what it means to transform oneself through MT.

Changing the Me through hypnotic suggestion

Hypnosis takes a different tack in endeavoring to alter the self, attempting to directly modify the Me's constituent reactive habits rather than extinguishing them through extended deconditioning practice. In MT, reactive habits are cast into sharp relief relative to a baseline awareness of body sensation. The practitioner is expected to notice these habits as being constitutive of the Me, and reflect on other potential ways of being—other Mes—in the face of gradually extinguished reactive habits. Hypnosis, by contrast, is characterized by "absorption," the ability to maintain engagement with the hypnotic state (Tellegen & Atkinson, 1974). While not all people are hypnotizable, those high in this capacity show the ability to powerfully modify cognitive and behavioral habits; tellingly, the modification of even deeply conditioned habits often occurs in the absence of volitional experience, as though the Me is being transformed without need for the momentary agent's involvement. In this way, hypnosis may radically alter the Me through bypassing the I, rather than empowering the I as a transformative presence.

For example, highly hypnotizable individuals can override the highly automatic habit of word reading, reducing conflict on a Stroop task, which measures the interference associated with reading a color-word (e.g., the word "red" printed in a color that is not red) (Raz, Moreno-Íniguez, Martin, & Zhu, 2007). Hypnotic suggestion seems to reduce reliance on a perceptual processing heuristic (i.e., reading) without resorting to extinction through mindful awareness and reactivity. Instead, perceptual biases appear to be altered through explicit instruction that does not rely on the slow extinction of conditioned habits (for a detailed analysis of how meditation and hypnosis influence Stroop-like phenomena, see Chapter 16).

The ability to block word reading using hypnosis provides a parallel to our earlier discussion of touch-typing, except operating in the perceptual rather than action domain. Recalling the characterization of automated habits as contributing to the Me, hypnotic suggestion seems to modulate the Me's longstanding affordances to the I (i.e., the ability to shape letters into words, phonemes, and meanings). The ability of hypnotic suggestion to rapidly modify even low-level perceptual processes has been replicated across several other domains, most notably hypnotic analgesia, with powerful reductions in pain perception through suggestion (Montgomery, DuHamel, & Redd, 2000). Hypnosis also appears to operate on other low-level perceptual processes, such as vision–sound binding in speech perception (the McGurk effect), introducing a visual mask to identify the direction of rotating geometric figures (the masked diamond paradigm), and creating a target "pop-out" effect in a visual search paradigm (Lifshitz, Cusumano, & Raz, 2013). Once again, these experiments demonstrate that hypnotic suggestion can both introduce and remove automatic processing, without trials of practice through which to shape implicit processing biases.

Neurally, placebo-based expectations of reduced pain do indeed seem to reduce sensory processing, particularly in "affective" rather than "sensory" aspects of the brain's pain processing network such as the anterior insula and anterior cingulate cortex (Wager et al., 2004). In a neuroimaging study of hypnotic suggestion reducing Stroop conflict, researchers observed that suggestions that block word reading appeared to reduce conflict monitoring in prefrontal regions of the brain, while simultaneously reducing activation in visual representation regions (Raz, Fan, & Posner, 2005). These patterns are consistent with enhancement of sensory processing filters, and a commensurate reduction in higher cortical regions linked to cognitive control and conflict monitoring. It is unclear whether reduced cortical activation causes filter enhancement, or whether it is a consequence of reduced conflict due to improved feature selection.

Despite increased interest in understanding the mechanisms by which suggestion can modulate highly automated perceptual and affective processes, how suggestion operating at an abstract, verbal level of representation translates into changes to early perceptual systems is unknown. However, regardless of such nuances, it seems that processing heuristics can be rapidly and powerfully altered through suggestion, changing the characteristics by which the Me constrains the I.

The nature of the self-transformation

The preceding review and discussion has been an attempt to place hypnosis and meditation within a common lexical framework for discussing personal transformation. The I has been defined as the actor in the present moment, the source of agency and connection to the world. The Me has been construed as the set of learned facts and modes of interpretation and behavior that act as heuristics by which the I's perceptions and actions are organized. In most cases, there is a free and dynamic interplay between these two self-referential systems, in which the I's choices serve to reinforce or extinguish affordances or meanings derived from the Me, even as the Me helps to regulate the I. However, in other situations, overlearned modes of perceiving or responding may run counter to one's intentions and/or values, leading to suffering. It is in these situations that we seek to change ourselves.

It is my hope that this chapter has begun to address the question of what exactly we hope to change when we engage in these self-transformative projects. In his story within a story entitled "The grand inquisitor," the great Russian existentialist write Fyodor Dostoyevsky once proposed the idea that absolute freedom was too great a burden to bear (Dostoyevsky, 1967), a theory of existential suffering predicated upon the perception of the I's absolute freedom. My sense is that the suffering that most people wish to correct is not of this kind. Instead, it is the frustration that the movements of this seemingly unbound I could be so effectively and completely stymied by the affordances provided by the Me, the feeling of absolute freedom running aground on the shoals of facticity.

Mindfulness meditation and hypnosis offer effective but distinct ways to overcome the Me, the forces of habit that both inform who we are and limit who we might become. While mindfulness interventions seek to bring clarity to the nature of the Me and its impact on the world, hypnosis presupposes at least a modicum of this understanding. Hypnosis, on the other hand, is more directly applied toward modification of the Me, targeting and modifying specific perceptions or responses, whereas mindfulness meditation avoids a fixation on achieving particular states or behaviors. Certainly, hypnosis can be used to reduce fear or resistance during introspection, and mindfulness can be used to tolerate distress in pursuit of one's goals, so perhaps the differences between these practices are due to the traditions surrounding their application rather than a sign of their unique mechanisms of action.

Despite their shared efficacy, there is evidence that supports the notion that mindfulness and hypnosis have very different ways of transforming the self. In its current Western incarnation, mindfulness is very much a disciple of deconditioning experience, reducing the power of the Me in favor of empowering and liberating the I. Hypnosis also seeks to empower the I, but by over-writing "Me-enshrined" habits rather than non-judgmentally reviewing them. Hypnosis appears to be far more rapid and pervasive in its effects than mindfulness, at least in the short term. However, in the pursuit of lasting change, we have little data on the relative long-term efficacies of these two traditions.

Although more comparative research is warranted, it seems that mindfulness and hypnosis may be best suited for different life circumstances. In cases where either the cause of distress is diffi-cult to perceive, or the solution to a problem seems elusive in its framing rather than execution, MT may be better suited than hypnosis. In other cases, where a person possesses clarity about an unwanted habit, or wishes to act in a specified manner but requires extra support, hypnosis may be a better choice. In other words, the relative utility of these traditions depends upon whether self-transformation seeks to uncover and liberate the I from the Me, which supports the use of mindfulness, or whether one wishes to rewrite the terms of that relationship in a particular man-ner, which supports the use of hypnotic suggestion instead.

It is my hope that this discussion has introduced some plausible ideas on the mechanisms of mindfulness meditation and hypnosis, but also that it has provided insight into the nature of the self in general. A satisfying life requires some balance between the freedom of the I, which in its extreme would lead to a random and anxious existence, and the consistency of the Me, which in its extreme leads to a form of determinism and helplessness. Given these two extremes, adaptive projects of self-transformation ought to seek a middle path that addresses the nature of the self-imbalance. Forging this middle path, however, requires some ability to assess the nature of the I/Me relationship to detect imbalances. Such a diagnostic process is not well-specified in contemporary psychological or clinical theory. Developing practical methods for assessing identity imbalance may be an important step to learning to walk this middle path, to integrating two promising thera-peutic traditions in attempting to improve our lives and the lives of those around us.

References

Anbar, R. D. (2008). Subconscious guided therapy with hypnosis. *American Journal of Clinical Hypnosis*, **50**(4), 323–334.

Astor, M. H. (1973). Hypnosis and behavior modification combined with psychoanalytic psychotherapy. *International Journal of Clinical and Experimental Hypnosis*, **21**(1), 18–24.

Barnhofer, T., Jong-Meyer, R., Kleinpaß, A., & Nikesch, S. (2002). Specificity of autobiographical mem-ories in depression: an analysis of retrieval processes in a think-aloud task. *British Journal of Clinical Psychology*, **41**(4), 411–416.

Chen, P.-H. A., Wagner, D. D., Kelley, W. M., Powers, K. E., & Heatherton, T. F. (2013). Medial prefront-al cortex differentiates self from mother in Chinese: evidence from self-motivated immigrants. *Culture and Brain*, **1**(1), 3–15.

Chiao, J. Y., Harada, T., Komeda, H., Li, Z., Mano, Y., Saito, D., . . . Iidaka, T. (2009). Neural basis of individualistic and collectivistic views of self. *Human Brain Mapping*, **30**(9), 2813–2820.

Craik, F. I., & Lockhart, R. S. (1972). Levels of processing: a framework for memory research. *Journal of Verbal Learning and Verbal Behavior*, **11**(6), 671–684.

Damasio, A. R. (1998). Investigating the biology of consciousness. *Philosophical Transactions of the Royal Society of London. Series B: Biological Sciences*, **353**(1377), 1879–1882.

Dostoyevsky, F. (1967). *The brothers Karamazov (vol. 1)*. http://Retrieved from eBookEden.com.

Farb, N. A. (2012). Mind your expectations: exploring the roles of suggestion and intention in mindfulness training. *Journal of Mind–Body Regulation*, **2**(1), 27–42.

Farb, N. A., Anderson, A. K., Bloch, R. T., & Segal, Z. V. (2011). Mood-linked responses in medial prefrontal cortex predict relapse in patients with recurrent unipolar depression. *Biological Psychiatry*, **70**(4), 366–372.

Farb, N. A., Anderson, A. K., Mayberg, H., Bean, J., McKeon, D., & Segal, Z. V. (2010). Minding one's emotions: mindfulness training alters the neural expression of sadness. *Emotion*, **10**(1), 25–33.

Farb, N. A., Segal, Z. V., & Anderson, A. K. (2013). Mindfulness meditation training alters cortical representations of interoceptive attention. *Social Cognitive and Affective Neuroscience*, **8**(1), 15–26.

Farb, N. A., Segal, Z. V., Mayberg, H., Bean, J., McKeon, D., Fatima, Z., & Anderson, A. K. (2007). Attending to the present: mindfulness meditation reveals distinct neural modes of self-reference. *Social Cognitive and Affective Neuroscience*, **2**(4), 313–322.

Fodor, J. A. (1983). *The modularity of mind: an essay on faculty psychology*. Cambridge, MA: MIT press.

Fossati, P., Hevenor, S. J., Graham, S. J., Grady, C., Keightley, M. L., Craik, F., & Mayberg, H. (2003). In search of the emotional self: an fMRI study using positive and negative emotional words. *American Journal of Psychiatry*, **160**(11), 1938–1945.

Freud, S. (1922). The unconscious. *Journal of Nervous and Mental Disease*, **56**(3), 291–294.

Gallagher, S. (2000). Philosophical conceptions of the self: implications for cognitive science. *Trends in Cognitive Sciences*, **4**(1), 14–21.

Gibson, J. (1977). The concept of affordances. In R. Shaw & J. Bransford (Eds.), *Perceiving, acting, and knowing* (pp. 67–82). Hoboken, NJ: John Wiley and Sons.

Goenka, S. (1982). *Vipassana meditation*. New York: Harper and Row.

Hatcher, R. L. (1973). Insight and self-observation. *Journal of the American Psychoanalytic Association*, **21**(2), 377–398.

Holroyd, J. (2003). The science of meditation and the state of hypnosis. *American Journal of Clinical Hypnosis*, **46**(2), 109–128.

Huston, D. C., Garland, E. L., & Farb, N. A. (2011). Mechanisms of mindfulness in communication training. *Journal of Applied Communication Research*, **39**(4), 406–421.

Kabat-Zinn, J. (1982). An outpatient program in behavioral medicine for chronic pain patients based on the practice of mindfulness meditation: theoretical considerations and preliminary results. *General Hospital Psychiatry*, **4**(1), 33–47.

Kabat-Zinn, J., & Hanh, T. N. (2009). *Full catastrophe living: using the wisdom of your body and mind to face stress, pain, and illness*. New York: Random House LLC.

Kelley, W. M., Macrae, C. N., Wyland, C. L., Caglar, S., Inati, S., & Heatherton, T. F. (2002). Finding the self? An event-related fMRI study. *Journal of Cognitive Neuroscience*, **14**(5), 785–794.

Kilpatrick, L. A., Suyenobu, B. Y., Smith, S. R., Bueller, J. A., Goodman, T., Creswell, J. D., . . . Naliboff, B. D. (2011). Impact of mindfulness-based stress reduction training on intrinsic brain connectivity. *Neuroimage*, **56**(1), 290–298.

Libby, L. K., Eibach, R. P., & Gilovich, T. (2005). Here's looking at me: the effect of memory perspective on assessments of personal change. *Journal of Personality and Social Psychology*, **88**(1), 50.

Lifshitz, M., Cusumano, E. P., & Raz, A. (2013). Hypnosis as neurophenomenology. *Frontiers in Human Neuroscience*, **7**(469), 1–7.

Logan, G. D., & Crump, M. J. (2009). The left hand doesn't know what the right hand is doing: the disruptive effects of attention to the hands in skilled typewriting. *Psychological Science*, **20**(10), 1296–1300.

Logan, G. D., & Crump, M. J. (2011). Hierarchical control of cognitive processes: the case for skilled type-writing. *Psychology of Learning and Motivation—Advances in Research and Theory*, **54**, 1.

Mead, G. H. (1913). The social self. *Journal of Philosophy, Psychology and Scientific Methods*, **10**, 374–380.

Merleau-Ponty, M. (1945). *Phenomenology of perception*. New York: Gallimard.

Miranda, J., & Persons, J. B. (1988). Dysfunctional attitudes are mood-state dependent. *Journal of Abnormal Psychology*, **97**(1), 76–79.

Miranda, J., Persons, J. B., & Byers, C. N. (1990). Endorsement of dysfunctional beliefs depends on current mood state. *Journal of Abnormal Psychology*, **99**(3), 237–241.

Mitchell, J. P., Macrae, C. N., & Banaji, M. R. (2006). Dissociable medial prefrontal contributions to judgments of similar and dissimilar others. *Neuron*, **50**(4), 655–663.

Montgomery, G. H., DuHamel, K. N., & Redd, W. H. (2000). A meta-analysis of hypnotically induced analgesia: how effective is hypnosis? *International Journal of Clinical and Experimental Hypnosis*, **48**(2), 138–153.

Panksepp, J., & Northoff, G. (2009). The trans-species core SELF: the emergence of active cultural and neuro-ecological agents through self-related processing within subcortical-cortical midline networks. *Consciousness and Cognition*, **18**(1), 193–215.

Raz, A., Fan, J., & Posner, M. I. (2005). Hypnotic suggestion reduces conflict in the human brain. *Proceedings of the National Academy of Sciences of the United States of America*, **102**(28), 9978–9983.

Raz, A., Moreno-Íniguez, M., Martin, L., & Zhu, H. (2007). Suggestion overrides the Stroop effect in highly hypnotizable individuals. *Consciousness and Cognition*, **16**(2), 331–338.

Rogers, T. B., Kuiper, N. A., & Kirker, W. S. (1977). Self-reference and the encoding of personal information. *Journal of Personality and Social Psychology*, **35**(9), 677.

Sartre, J.-P. (1943). *Being and nothingness*. New York: Gallimard.

Segal, Z. V., Gemar, M., & Williams, S. (1999). Differential cognitive response to a mood challenge following successful cognitive therapy or pharmacotherapy for unipolar depression. *Journal of Abnormal Psychology*, **108**(1), 3–10.

Stanton, H. (1979). Increasing internal control through hypnotic ego-enhancement. *Australian Journal of Clinical & Experimental Hypnosis, 7*(3), 219–223.

Tacón, A. M., Caldera, Y. M., & Ronaghan, C. (2004). Mindfulness-based stress reduction in women with breast cancer. *Families, Systems, and Health*, **22**(2), 193.

Teasdale, J. D. (1993). Emotion and two kinds of meaning: cognitive therapy and applied cognitive science. *Behaviour Research and Therapy*, **31**(4), 339–354.

Tellegen, A., & Atkinson, G. (1974). Openness to absorbing and self-altering experiences ("absorption"), a trait related to hypnotic susceptibility. *Journal of Abnormal Psychology*, **83**(3), 268.

Tulving, E. (1985). Memory and consciousness. *Canadian Psychology/Psychologie Canadienne*, **26**(1), 1.

Wager, T. D., Rilling, J. K., Smith, E. E., Sokolik, A., Casey, K. L., Davidson, R. J., . . . Cohen, J. D. (2004). Placebo-induced changes in FMRI in the anticipation and experience of pain. *Science*, **303**(5661), 1162–1167.

Watkins, E. R., Baeyens, C. B., & Read, R. (2009). Concreteness training reduces dysphoria: proof-of-principle for repeated cognitive bias modification in depression. *Journal of Abnormal Psychology*, **118**(1), 55.

Watkins, E., & Teasdale, J. D. (2004). Adaptive and maladaptive self-focus in depression. *Journal of Affective Disorders*, **82**(1), 1–8.

Whitfield-Gabrieli, S., Moran, J. M., Nieto-Castañón, A., Triantafyllou, C., Saxe, R., & Gabrieli, J. D. (2011). Associations and dissociations between default and self-reference networks in the human brain. *Neuroimage*, **55**(1), 225–232.

James, W. (1890). *The principles of psychology*. Cambridge, MA: Harvard University Press.

Williams, J. M. G. (2006). Capture and rumination, functional avoidance, and executive control (CaRFAX): three processes that underlie overgeneral memory. *Cognition and Emotion*, **20**(3–4), 548–568.

Williams, J. M., Healy, D., Teasdale, J. D., White, W., & Paykel, E. S. (1990). Dysfunctional attitudes and vulnerability to persistent depression. *Psychological Medicine*, **20**(2), 375–381.

Williams, J., & Scott, J. (1988). Autobiographical memory in depression. *Psychological Medicine*, **18**(3), 689–695.

Yanes, P. K., Roberts, J. E., & Carlos, E. L. (2008). Does overgeneral autobiographical memory result from poor memory for task instructions? *Memory*, **16**(7), 669–677.

Chapter 21

Meditative and hypnotic analgesia
Different directions, same road?

Fadel Zeidan and Joshua A. Grant

Abstract

Meditation and hypnosis have both been found to reliably attenuate behavioral and neural responses to pain, rendering them important options for treatment of chronic and acute pain in clinical settings. Despite a fair amount of research on the topic, exactly how these potentially related cognitive states influence pain is still debated. Converging lines of evidence suggest that hypnotic and meditative states reduce pain through overlapping but unique mechanisms involving attention and cognitive control, appraisal processes, and suggestibility. This chapter provides a comprehensive overview of the mechanisms supporting the modulation of pain by meditation and hypnosis, with an emphasis on more recent brain imaging studies. The chapter begins with brief primers on meditation, hypnosis, pain, and pain modulation. Hypnotic and meditative analgesia are then reviewed separately.

Introduction

Meditation and hypnosis have both been found to reliably attenuate behavioral and neural responses to pain, rendering them important treatment options for acute and/or clinical pain. The exact mechanisms underlying these modulation strategies are still unknown. However, it has been postulated that the two cognitive states may share common mechanisms (Grant & Rainville, 2005). Indeed, this volume is dedicated to examining the relationship between hypnosis and meditation. This chapter deals specifically with how the two phenomena relate, in terms of the subjective experience of pain and the brain regions supporting the construction and modulation of pain.

The chapter will begin with brief primers on meditation, hypnosis, pain, and pain modulation. Hypnotic and meditative analgesia will then be reviewed separately. Meditative analgesia will be split into practices primarily involved with focusing and sustaining attention (i.e., shamatha) and techniques aimed at cultivating a more open, non-judgmental mental stance (i.e., vipassana). These terms are used as categories, which both involve mindfulness, rather than to the specific techniques by the same names. While such a division (Lutz, Slagter, Dunne, & Davidson, 2008) is far from perfect, it does seem useful in terms of examining the influence of meditation on pain (Grant, 2014). Finally, parallels will be drawn between hypnotic and meditative analgesia. We focus nearly exclusively on experimental pain studies. Studies assessing the role of hypnosis and/or meditation on clinical pain are limited and are complicated by the comorbid nature of chronic pain (Jensen et al., 2012). Therefore, clinical studies of meditation and hypnosis will be excluded from the present chapter.

Primers on meditation, hypnosis, pain, and pain modulation

What is meditation?

Meditation is not a single construct but a host of mental training exercises originating from different schools of thought and for different purposes, which purportedly shape the brain/mind in highly specific ways, just as more typical skills are now known to do. Thus, the type of meditation studied will certainly influence the result of a comparison with hypnosis. Traditionally, practitioners are taught a number of techniques, dependent on the lineage, which more or less proceed sequentially across many years.

Mindfulness-based practices can be approximately divided into the preliminary techniques which involve restricting the focus of attention and deploying it for sustained periods (focused attention or shamatha) and more advanced techniques which can broaden the scope of attention and simultaneously de-emphasize the elaborative and narrative nature of the mind (vipassana). Shamatha practices aim to stabilize the mind and can be viewed scientifically as attention training, whereas vipassana practices are said to promote wisdom and more objective perception of one's experiences. The variability that arises from a myriad of meditation practices, levels of proficiency, and, presumably, brain networks which underlie the attained skills, greatly complicates the task of unraveling the influence on pain or any other mental construct.

What is hypnosis?

Hypnosis is described by the American Psychological Association as a cooperative interaction wherein a hypnotist gives a participant suggestions after hypnotic induction. Hypnosis is typically defined in terms of the induction of the hypnotic state, while hypnotizability is defined as responsiveness to suggestion following a hypnotic induction, measured via a standardized test. The hypnotic state itself has well-defined characteristics including increased relaxation, absorption, an altered sense of space, time, agency, and contextual evaluation of the subjective and sensory environment (Rainville & Price, 2003). Interestingly, responsiveness to suggestion does not actually require a hypnotic state and hypnotizability scales have been suggested to measure sensitivity to suggestion, rather than the effects of hypnosis per se (Kirsch et al., 2011; Weitzenhoffer, 1980). This has led to a debate in the field as to how to define hypnosis (Kirsch et al., 2011).

Behavioral and neural dimensions of pain

The subjective experience of pain is constructed and modulated by interactions between sensory, cognitive, and affective factors. Noxious stimulation leads to a subjectively available experience of pain as localized primary afferent information enters sensory discriminative processing streams. The affective dimension of pain reflects the emotional and motivational evaluation of the state/stimulus, while cognitive factors correspond to the relation of pain to one's ongoing experience.

A large number of brain regions have been implicated in processing nociceptive afferent signals and the experience of pain. The primary and secondary somatosensory cortices (SI, SII), thalamus (Thal), and posterior insula (pINS) are believed to underlie the sensory-discriminative dimension of pain where brain activity commonly corresponds to participants' pain intensity ratings as well as stimulus strength (Coghill, McHaffie, & Yen, 2003; Coghill, Sang, Maisog, & Iadarola, 1999). The affective-motivational dimension of pain is thought to be processed in the dorsal anterior cingulate cortex (dACC) and the anterior insula (aINS), where ratings of pain unpleasantness are often found to correspond with brain activity levels (Coghill et al., 1999; Rainville, Duncan, Price, Carrier, & Bushnell, 1997). It is important to note that the distinction between sensory and affective pain ratings, or anatomy, is not absolute and that these brain regions are not pain-specific. Finally, in terms of pain perception, portions of the prefrontal cortex (PFC) are thought to underlie evaluation, appraisal, or memory related to the event and/or stimulus (Coghill et al., 1999; Lorenz, Minoshima, & Casey, 2003; Strigo, Duncan, Boivin, & Bushnell, 2003).

Non-pharmacological modulation of pain

Pain can be modulated, non-pharmacologically, through numerous means including, but not limited to, distraction, placebo, hypnosis, and meditation (Bushnell, Ceko, & Low, 2013). Divided attention-mediated reductions in pain are associated with attenuated pain-related brain activation involving regions implicated in cognitive control, including the rostral ACC and orbitofrontal cortex (OFC) (Bantick et al., 2002). Similarly, positive mood induction also reduces pain-related behavioral and neural responses through activation of the PFC (Villemure & Bushnell, 2009).

Placebo analgesia operates via multiple mechanisms including the so-called "descending modulatory system." In the context of the cognitive modulation of pain, this system is postulated to reduce pain through top-down regulation (i.e., via PFC activation) of the opioid-rich periaqueductal gray (PAG) and rostroventral medulla (RVM) (Eippert et al., 2009). Similar to divided attention, placebo reduces pain-related neural processing (Wager et al., 2004) through activation of the dorsolateral PFC (DLPFC) (Krummenacher, Candia, Folkers, Schedlowski, & Schonbachler, 2010). Non-opioid, cortico-cortical processes are also involved (Bandura, O'Leary, Taylor, Gauthier, & Gossard, 1987; Petrovic et al., 2010) along with attenuation of expectations (De Pascalis, Chiaradia, & Carotenuto, 2002; Fields, 2000; Koyama, McHaffie, Laurienti, & Coghill, 2005). Interestingly, DLPFC activation has also been implicated in the effects of suggestibility (Raij, Numminen, Narvanen, Hiltunen, & Hari, 2009).

Taken as a whole, cognitive manipulations of pain seem to attenuate pain-related neural processing, and pain, by activating higher-order brain regions (i.e., the PFC).

Hypnotic analgesia

It has long been recognized that hypnosis/suggestibility can have a profound impact on pain perception. A meta-analysis of 18 studies using hypnosis for analgesia, either experimentally or clinically, found moderate to large effect sizes for hypnotic analgesia (Montgomery, DuHamel, & Redd, 2000). The first important study to examine hypnotic analgesia with brain imaging gave participants suggestions, following hypnotic induction, for a selective decrease of pain unpleasantness, but not pain intensity (Rainville et al., 1997). Behavioral results confirmed that unpleasantness could be modulated in both directions, with pain intensity remaining unchanged. This study was instrumental in demonstrating that activity in the ACC, but not the somatosensory cortices (SI, SII), is involved in the coding of pain affect. The result typically cited from that work is activation of the ACC correlating positively with pain unpleasantness ratings, when looking at conditions with suggestions for unpleasantness increases and decreases combined. That is, as activation in the ACC increases/decreases, so does pain unpleasantness. Often overlooked is that ACC activation during pain (as well as INS and SI) was reportedly greater for both suggestion conditions (i.e., pain increases and decreases) compared to pain during the hypnotic state alone (i.e., without suggestion).

In a second report (Rainville et al., 1999) and a second study by the same group (Rainville, Hofbauer, Bushnell, Duncan, & Price, 2002), it was reported that the hypnotic state itself involves activation of ACC and INS (among other regions) but does not influence pain perception (Rainville et al., 2002; 1999). Hypnosis-mediated and pain regulation-related ACC peaks were adjacent but non-overlapping and were inversely correlated with visual activation thought to underlie increased mental imagery. Relaxation, as well as absorption, also had significant correlations with the ACC (Rainville et al., 2002). The putative increase in the ability or clarity of mental imagery during the hypnotic state may explain why studies have shown activation of nearly all pain-related brain regions during hypnotic suggestion to "construct" pain, compared to mental imagery of pain without hypnosis (Figure 21.1 and Plate 14) (Derbyshire, Whalley, Stenger, & Oakley, 2004; Raij, Numminen, Narvanen, Hiltunen, & Hari, 2005).

The same group also reversed the suggestion specification to focus on a selective modulation of pain intensity (Hofbauer, Rainville, Duncan, & Bushnell, 2001; Rainville et al., 2002). Here, decreased activity in the SI cortex was observed, paralleling changes in pain intensity. Interestingly, pain experience was not dissociable when specifically regulating intensity, as it was for unpleasantness. That is, pain unpleasantness tracked the successful modulation of intensity. This last point is important as it suggests multiple pathways by which the affective component of pain can be modulated. Directly targeting the affective dimension of pain, with suggestion, involves the ACC. However, unpleasantness can also be modulated indirectly, through intensity-based suggestion, which the ACC does not appear to be involved in.

Work happening concurrently in other groups was largely consistent with the aforementioned studies, with a few exceptions. Faymonville et al. (2000) found that pain was reduced during a hypnotic state (without explicit suggestions) compared to a mental imagery and resting baseline condition. Both pain intensity and unpleasantness were reduced, resembling more the study of Hofbauer et al. (2001) where intensity and unpleasantness were modulated in synchrony, as opposed to Rainville et al. (1997) where a selective change in unpleasantness was achieved. However, contrary to Faymonville et al. (2000), the hypnotic state in both Hofbauer et al. (2001) and Rainville et al. (1999) was reported to have no influence on pain. This discrepancy may be explained by the fact that the induction procedure of Faymonville et al. (2000) involved the reliving of a positive personal experience. It is known that positive emotion can attenuate both dimensions of pain experience (Roy, Peretz, & Rainville, 2008; Villemure & Bushnell, 2009). This indicates that hypnotic states are highly variable and the effects dependent not only on what (if anything) is suggested, but also upon the content of the induction itself, not to mention individual difference in suggestibility (see Chapters 10 and 15).

One commonality between the studies of hypnosis discussed thus far is the activation of the ACC during the hypnotic state itself, whether related to pain (Faymonville et al., 2000) or not (Hofbauer et al., 2001; Rainville et al., 1997, 1999, 2002). In addition to the ACC, Faymonville et al. (2000) also observed involvement of the bilateral caudate; Rainville et al. (1997), the left posterior INS and SI; and Hofbauer et al. (2001) and Rainville et al. (2002), a more extensive ACC activation and bilaterally, and more anterior INS. Studies in other research domains corroborate the involvement of the ACC as well as the INS in the hypnotic state (Burgmer et al., 2013; Deeley et al., 2013). Thus, in terms of neurophysiology, the hypnotic state appears to overlap with that of pain perception; particularly, the affective dimension of pain (ACC, INS).

In an attempt to get closer to an actual mechanism of hypnotic analgesia, Faymonville et al. (2003) reanalyzed their original data (Faymonville et al., 2000), this time using a psychophysiological

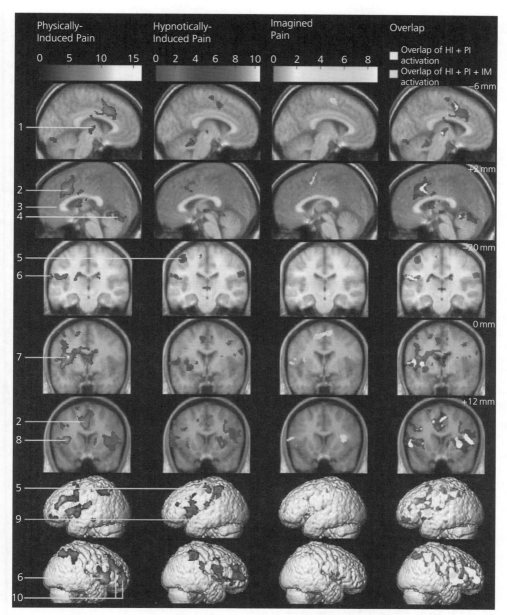

Fig. 21.1 Activated voxels during physically induced pain (left, red–yellow scale); hypnotically induced pain (middle, blue–purple scale); and imagined pain (right, yellow–green scale) (see Plate 14).

Regions: 1 = thalamus; 2 = anterior cingulate; 3 = posterior anterior cingulate; 4 = cerebellum; 5 = primary somatosensory cortex; 6 = secondary somatosensory cortex, insula; 7 = insula, putamen; 8 = anterior insula; 9 = inferior parietal cortex; 10 = prefrontal cortex.

Reprinted with permission from "Cerebral activation during hypnotically induced and imagined pain," by Derbyshire, S. W., Whalley, M. G., Stenger, V. A., & Oakley, D. A., 2004, *NeuroImage*, 23(1), p. 394. Copyright 2004 Elsevier Inc.

interaction analysis (PPI) with the ACC as the seed region. In the hypnosis condition, during pain, and compared to rest and mental imagery, increased functional connectivity was observed between the ACC and the bilateral INS, perigenual ACC, pre-supplementary motor area (SMA), right PFC, striatum, thalamus, and brainstem. Thus, it would seem the hypnotic state, at least in that study, recruits a much more unified pain-related network when compared to the control conditions, with the apparent absence of the somatosensory cortices (SI, SII). What also seems noteworthy is that decreased connectivity between the ACC and occipital cortex was observed (Faymonville et al., 2003), paralleling Rainville et al. (1999) where EEG (electroencephalographic) delta power and occipital brain activity was inversely correlated with the ACC pain-related peak but positively correlated with the ACC hypnosis-related peak.

A final contribution to the hypnosis/pain literature will be discussed before turning to the meditation literature. Spurred by previous findings demonstrating large, predominantly frontal, networks underlying hypnotic suggestion (Rainville et al., 1999) and altered functional connectivity between the DLPFC and ACC during hypnosis (Faymonville et al., 2003), Raij et al. (2009) specifically tested whether frontal activation during hypnotic suggestion predicts subsequent painful experience and pain-related brain activity. They found that DLPFC activation during the suggestion for initiation of hypnotic pain (i.e., no actual pain stimulus) predicted subsequent perceived intensity of the hypnotically induced pain as well as activation of SII. Importantly, a similar result has been reported for placebo, where DLPFC activation predicted greater analgesia (Benedetti, Mayberg, Wager, Stohler, & Zubieta, 2005; Wager, Atlas, Leotti, & Rilling, 2011; Wager et al., 2004). These findings suggest that hypnosis and placebo engage similar psychological (modulations of expectations; suggestibility) and neural (DLPFC; also OFC) mechanisms in the reduction of pain.

Summary of hypnosis–pain neuroimaging studies

1   Outside of any involvement in pain, hypnosis is associated with increased ACC as well as INS activation.

2   Hypnosis is capable of modulating pain, in both directions, through greater ACC activation and alternative pathways, depending on the suggestion and content of the induction.

3   Hypnosis is associated with increased occipital activation, possibly reflecting increased mental imagery, which predicts greater reductions in pain and pain-related responses in the ACC.

4   During hypnosis, greater occipital activation is associated with greater hypnosis-specific ACC activation and reports of relaxation.

5   Hypnotic suggestion is associated with widespread frontal activation predictive of subsequent painful experience and brain activation.

Mindfulness meditation and pain

Mindfulness meditation practice is associated with improving mood (Carlson, Speca, Patel, & Goodey, 2003; Zeidan, Johnson, Gordon, & Goolkasian, 2010), reducing expectations of impending stimuli (Brown & Jones, 2010), uniquely engaging (or disengaging) cognitive appraisal processes (Garland, Gaylord, & Park, 2009; Grant, Courtemanche, & Rainville, 2011; Zeidan, Martucci, Kraft, McHaffie, & Coghill, 2013), and enhancing acceptance-based coping (Kabat-Zinn, 1982), cognitive control, and emotion regulation strategies (Allen et al., 2012; Farb et al., 2010; Kilpatrick et al., 2011; Zeidan, Johnson, Diamond, David, & Goolkasian, 2010). Importantly, these are the same mechanisms involved in the cognitive modulation of pain. However, it is important to note that the analgesic components of mindfulness meditation likely vary across level of training/ expertise and the specific brand of mindfulness meditation being practiced (Zeidan, Grant, Brown, McHaffie, & Coghill, 2012). To this extent, we will delineate the mechanisms supporting meditation-related pain relief attempting to take into consideration two basic classes of mindfulness practice (i.e., shamatha and vipassana).

The aim of shamatha or breath awareness practices (also called focused attention practices) is to stabilize the practitioner's attention by engaging exclusively with a chosen object for long periods of time. Shamatha techniques are perhaps the most basic forms of meditation and can be viewed as a prerequisite of more advanced meditative practices. Prerequisite in the sense that the ability to wield one's attention effectively and efficiently makes the challenging states of more advanced practices easier to achieve and sustain. Experientially, shamatha practices are said to still the mind and increase attentional stability. In terms of the relation to known pain modulators, shamatha could be described primarily as an attention-altering technique that *should* most closely resemble effects of attention and distraction. This would depend of course on whether the focus of attention is placed on the pain itself, where one might expect increases in pain, or away from the stimulus (distraction), where pain reductions could be expected (Bantick et al., 2002; Bushnell et al., 1999; Tracey et al., 2002; Valet et al., 2004). Unfortunately, there are few studies dealing exclusively with shamatha techniques as they are rarely practiced in isolation; meaning practitioners likely also have the skill sets associated with other forms of meditation, particularly vipassana-related techniques.

The aim of vipassana-related practices (also called open monitoring) is the development of wisdom and equanimity by deliberate, non-elaborated, and non-judgmental observation of one's experience or a predetermined subset (e.g., thoughts) of one's experience. Experientially, vipassana-related practices are associated with fully experiencing sensory events as they arise without self-directed appraisals of those respective experiences. In terms of known pain modulators, these techniques are unique. While in some senses similar to the emotion regulation strategy of reappraisal, vipassana techniques could be more appropriately described as non-appraisal strategies. Applying a vipassana-related mindset when experiencing a noxious stimulus is not an attempt to reduce pain per se but an attempt to more objectively experience the stimulus (i.e., without undue thought attached). One might expect reductions in brain regions supporting evaluation or appraisal and perhaps, secondarily, emotion, but not necessarily reductions in pain-related areas, as the noxious stimulus itself would be the attended percept.

Behavioral effects of mindfulness meditation-related pain relief

Following an initial report that brief training in mindfulness meditation, primarily rooted in vipassana, leads to increased cold pain tolerance (Kingston, Chadwick, Meron, & Skinner, 2007), Grant and Rainville (2009) found that Zen practitioners, a tradition with features of both shamatha and vipassana, were less sensitive to noxious heat than controls. In an attempt to dissociate the influences of shamatha- and vipassana-related traits on pain, the study had participants attend to painful heat but not formally meditate. When instructed to sustain their attention on the stimulation (i.e., shamatha-like), control subjects reported pain increases of approximately 15%, in line with results in healthy individuals (Miron, Duncan, & Bushnell, 1989; Villemure, Slotnick, & Bushnell, 2003). Meditators, on the other hand, showed no difference from their own baseline. When instructed to sustain attention on the stimulation but in a moment to moment, non-judgmental manner (vipassana-like), control subjects reported no difference in pain compared to their baseline ratings, while Zen practitioners reported significantly reduced sensory (18%) and affective (23%) pain ratings.

The most experienced meditators exhibited the largest reductions in pain. Meditators also scored higher on several dimensions of a mindfulness questionnaire and had lower respiration rates that paralleled their pain ratings across conditions. Interestingly, one might have expected meditators who practice sustaining attention to have larger increases when directing their focus toward pain. This was not the case, but pain was also not decreased, suggesting that the pain-reducing properties of Zen stem more from the vipassana-related components and/or the induction of a calm, parasympathetic dominant state.

Work with other meditative traditions revealed similar results. Perlman, Salomons, Davidson, and Lutz (2010) found no significant differences in pain intensity between novice meditators (1 week of training) and long-term vipassana practitioners (more than 10,000 hours' experience) during shamatha practice. However, adept meditators had significantly reduced affective pain ratings when compared to novices when practicing vipassana-based meditation. These data were later replicated in a study that found that long-term vipassana practitioners (910–20,855 hours' experience) exhibited no differences in pain intensity, but significant reductions in pain unpleasantness (Gard et al., 2011). As a whole, these studies with well-trained practitioners are encouraging, in showing that meditation may be effective in controlling pain. However, they are also discouraging from a clinical perspective, suggesting that many thousands of hours of practice may be needed. Studies by Zeidan and colleagues (Zeidan, Gordon, Merchant, & Goolkasian, 2010; Zeidan et al., 2011) have largely turned that notion upside down.

The initial pain study from Zeidan et al. (2010) demonstrated that brief mindfulness meditation practice (3 days) is more effective at reducing pain than distraction-based cognitive approaches. For instance, practicing mindfulness meditation (a blend of shamatha and vipassana) in the presence of noxious electrical stimulation was significantly more effective at reducing pain than a well-validated math distraction task (Zeidan, Gordon, et al., 2010). In a follow-up study (discussed more in the section "Neural correlates and mechanisms of meditation-related pain relief") subjects were instructed to "focus on the changing sensations of the breath" during noxious heat. Before their respective mindfulness meditation interventions, no significant change in pain intensity or unpleasantness ratings was observed (Zeidan et al., 2011). In contrast, after successfully completing a brief mindfulness-based meditation training regimen, the same sample of participants exhibited 40% and 57% reductions in pain intensity and pain unpleasantness ratings, respectively, in response to the same experimental instructions/procedures. These data illustrate that mindfulness meditation reduces pain more effectively than divided attention.

Taken together, the meditation studies discussed so far have repeatedly demonstrated that mindfulness meditation significantly attenuates the subjective experience of pain. Given that mindful-based attention involves monitoring of the experience itself, it is unlikely that the results can be explained through simple distraction, as tested and confirmed by Zeidan and colleagues. The multifaceted descriptions of mindfulness in the literature suggest there are likely multiple mechanisms at play when it comes to pain modulation (Grant, 2014; Zeidan et al., 2012, 2011). We turn now to brain imaging studies, which offer more insight into these mechanisms.

Neural correlates and mechanisms of meditation-related pain relief

The use of functional imaging methods have, to some extent, validated Buddhist monks' reports (Bohdi, 2005) of meditation-induced improvements in cognition, awareness, and health. Concerning pain, the meditation-related imaging studies that have been published to date are quite consistent with one another, as well as with the behavioral findings and certain Buddhist claims. This section will begin with an important longitudinal imaging study of newly trained meditators and, subsequently, move to studies in more advanced practitioners.

The second study by Zeidan et al. (2011), employing arterial spin labeling fMRI (functional magnetic resonance imaging), trained previously meditation-naïve participants over 4 days in shamatha- and vipassana-based meditation skills. Prior to training, meditating during noxious thermal stimulation did not reduce pain compared to a control condition. However, following training, meditation dramatically reduced both intensity and unpleasantness pain ratings. Furthermore, mindfulness meditation significantly reduced left primary somatosensory cortical activation corresponding to the stimulation site (i.e., the right calf) (Figure 21.2 and Plate 15).

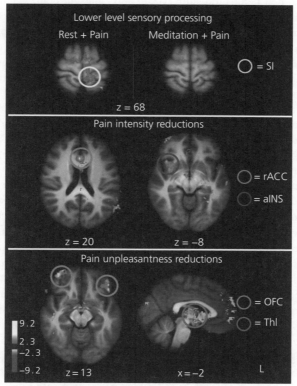

Fig. 21.2 Mindfulness meditation significantly reduced pain through a number of brain mechanisms in beginner meditators (see Plate 15). In the presence of noxious heat, meditation reduced activation of the primary somatosensory cortex (SI) corresponding to the stimulation site (top). Regression analyses revealed that meditation-related pain-intensity reductions were associated with greater activity in the rostral ACC (middle). Greater right anterior INS activity also predicted pain-intensity reductions during meditation (middle). Greater OFC activity was associated with greater decreases in pain unpleasantness ratings (bottom). Thalamic (Thl) deactivation was associated with reductions in pain unpleasantness (bottom).

Adapted with permission from "Brain mechanisms supporting the modulation of pain by mindfulness meditation," by Zeidan, F., Martucci, K. T., Kraft, R. A., Gordon, N. S., McHaffie, J. G., & Coghill, R. C., 2011, *J NeuroSci*, 31(14), p. 5545.

Regression analyses revealed that greater activation in higher-order brain regions such as the rostral ACC and OFC predicted reductions of pain during meditation (Figure 21.2). The authors postulated that meditation-induced activation of the OFC was associated with altering the contextual evaluation of the nociceptive sensory environment (Zeidan et al., 2011). Greater activation in higher-order sensory evaluation areas (i.e., right anterior insula) also predicted reductions in pain. Finally, greater deactivation of the thalamus, a brain region critical for transmitting nociceptive information, was associated with meditation-related pain relief.

These findings demonstrate that in newly trained individuals, meditation reduces pain not through one avenue, but through multiple mechanisms associated with cognitive control, emotion regulation, sensory evaluation, and a significant reduction of lower-level sensory processes. Studies with long-term meditators show remarkable congruence with these effects and together offer a picture of how meditative analgesia may evolve with expertise.

In a follow up to their behavioral study, Grant and colleagues (2011) conducted an experiment with Zen practitioners, employing fMRI to measure the brain activity during pain induced by noxious thermal stimulation. In a normal waking state (i.e., non-meditative baseline), stronger brain activation was observed for meditators compared to controls, in several pain-related areas (dACC, aINS, Thal) (Figure 21.3 and Plate 16), despite having matched the groups in terms of painful experience. These results are consistent with those in novices reported by Zeidan et al (2011) and remained after statistically controlling for the higher input level of meditators. Interestingly, numerous brain regions exhibited reduced activity for the meditators during pain, which were not observed for controls, including the amygdala, hippocampus, and OFC, medial-prefrontal cortex (mPFC), and DLPFC (Figure 21.3). This particular pattern of brain activation, while unique at the time, has since been largely replicated by two groups.

Studying vipassana practitioners, Gard et al. (2011) found reductions in the affective dimension of pain during meditation for practitioners compared to controls. These reductions were associated with increased activation of pain-related areas (pINS) and decreased lateral frontal activity. Studying highly experienced Tibetan meditation practitioners performing a vipassana practice, Lutz, McFarlin, Perlman, Salomons, and Davidson (2013) recently reported greater aINS and dACC activity during pain for meditators compared to controls. During the meditation/anticipation phase, meditators also showed lower activation of the ACC, INS, and the amygdala (brain regions that likely influence the subsequent experience of pain). These studies of experienced meditators show an impressive correspondence and, in many ways, also correlate with the results in novices (Zeidan et al., 2011), particularly given clear differences in methodologies, designs, and meditation traditions being studied.

The results suggest that vipassana-based techniques lead to pain reduction, not through decreases in pain-related areas but through enhancement, particularly of the dACC and INS, along with reduced activation of frontal and limbic regions. It should be noted that novices did, however, show attenuation of SI (Zeidan et al., 2011). Examining the functional roles, particularly of the "deactivated" brain areas, allows a more fine-grained view and leads to the conclusion that certain Buddhist claims may in fact be accurate.

In terms of the positively activated brain regions (dACC, aINS), these areas are thought to underlie, and modulate, pain and other bodily states, but have also been termed key nodes of a salience network (Seeley et al., 2007). For the deactivated brain regions: the OFC receives input from all sensory modalities and is believed to incorporate the relative value or contextual importance of the stimulus for the individual (Rolls, 2008). The amygdala, often activated in pain studies (Fernando, Murray, & Milton, 2013), is classically associated with emotional salience

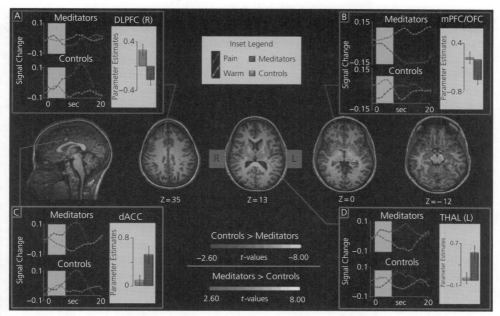

Fig. 21.3 Differences in pain-related activation between meditators and controls (see Plate 16). Central MRI images illustrate brain regions with statistically significant group differences in pain-related responses (orange–yellow: meditators > controls) (blue–green: controls > meditators). Corner insets show mean pain-related parameter estimates for each group (right side of each box) (error bars = SEM, standard error of the mean) as well as the time courses of activation (left side) for pain (red) and warmth (blue) for each group separately. Gray bars represent stimulus presentation.

Top left corner: right DLPFC; top right corner: right med-PFC/OFC; bottom right corner: left THAL; bottom left corner: dACC spanning the midline. X, Y, Z are in Talairach space. R = right, L = left, N = 26.

Reprinted with permission from "A non-elaborative mental stance and decoupling of executive and pain-related cortices predicts low pain sensitivity in Zen meditators," by Grant, J. A., Courtemanche, J., & Rainville, P., 2011, *Pain*, 152(1), p. 153. Copyright 2010 International Association for the Study of Pain.

and memory, whereas the hippocampus is a more general memory-related structure which has been suggested to work in concert with the DLPFC in retrieval processes (Bechara, Damasio, & Damasio, 2003; Suzuki, 2008). Lastly, the mPFC has been implicated in self-referential processing (Mitchell, 2009). Reduced activity in these regions corresponds very well to descriptions of mindfulness.

Speculatively, the activation increases in dACC and aINS could very well correspond to increased stimulus saliency due to intentional monitoring of the experience (Seeley et al., 2007). DLPFC and hippocampal activity reductions may reflect the inverse of increased monitoring, that is, less retrieval-related processing as one engages less in elaborate mental narratives. OFC and amygdala reductions may reflect the non-judgmental and non-reactive aspects of mindfulness, respectively. While the aforementioned account is elaborate, speculative, and biased by the framework in which these studies were conducted (mindfulness), there are several additional findings that offer some support.

The imaging study of Zen practitioners also reported that during pain, meditators (but not controls) reduced the functional connectivity between the DLPFC and the dACC (Grant et al., 2011). The degree to which these regions were decoupled predicted the baseline pain sensitivity of the individual. That is, meditators with the highest pain tolerance showed the greatest decoupling, suggesting that this may be the means by which they are able to withstand such high temperatures. The second important finding was present in two of the three imaging studies already discussed. Brain activity in pain-related areas was not correlated with pain ratings in meditators (intensity and unpleasantness—Grant et al., 2011 and unpleasantness controlling for intensity—Lutz et al., 2013), whereas it was for control subjects, as is typical. For Zen practitioners, pain ratings were, rather, correlated with DLPFC activation, such that greater reductions in DLPFC activity were associated with lower pain reports. This provides evidence that the decay of activity in this brain region is in some way related to the perception of pain in meditators. Taken together, these results suggest that meditators have learned to decouple the monitoring of aversive stimulation from the processes that lead to it being labeled as pain.

Lastly, as we suggested in an earlier review (Zeidan et al., 2012), the primary difference between findings in advanced practitioners and novices was deactivation and activation of the OFC, respectively. Consistent with the concept of mindfulness, it may be the case that beginners cannot inhibit the automatic appraisal of their experience and must actively reappraise it within the framework of mindfulness, whereas advanced practitioners may be more proficient and actually achieve something closer to "no appraisal." However, these claims will certainly require more work to validate or invalidate. As already mentioned, novices also exhibited SI activity decreases, whereas similar findings have not been observed for advanced practitioners. The reason for this is unclear.

Summary of meditation-related pain studies

1 Meditation is associated with decreases in pain unpleasantness in all studies and also with intensity in some studies.

2 While some studies find baseline tolerance/sensitivity differences between practitioners and controls, others do not.

3 Across disciplines and expertise level, activation of pain-related regions (ACC, INS), during pain, is increased during meditation and decoupled from pain ratings in experts.

4 Advanced practitioners have widespread activity reductions during pain, most frequently in frontal areas.

5 Activation of OFC is increased in novices meditating during pain and associated with pain reductions, whereas it is decreased in advanced practitioners.

6 Pain reduction in novices during meditation is associated with appropriate SI activity reductions, whereas this does not appear to be true for advanced practitioners.

7 Connectivity between the DLPFC and ACC is decreased in meditators, which predicts baseline pain sensitivity.

Integration of meditative and hypnotic analgesia

Contrary to a recent review concluding that there is little evidence for shared mechanisms of pain modulation between hypnosis and meditation (Dumont, Martin, & Broer, 2012), in our reading of the literature there are clear points of convergence, as well as divergence. Most obvious is the involvement of the dACC in both phenomena. In hypnosis, there appear to be discrete but adjacent regions of the dACC which activate during the state itself and during pain modulation (in either direction), whether with (Rainville et al., 1997, 1999, 2002) or without suggestion (Faymonville et al., 2000). When pain is experienced/modulated in meditation, dACC activation also increases compared to either control subjects or control conditions (Gard et al., 2011; Grant et al., 2011; Lutz et al., 2013; Zeidan et al., 2011). Thus, both phenomena seem to influence pain through at least one common pathway, dACC activation. While the INS has not been centrally implicated in hypnotic analgesia, it was active during the state itself as well as for pain during hypnosis compared to control conditions (Rainville et al., 1997, 1999, 2002), as it was in all four imaging studies of meditation/pain.

In relation to pain, both phenomena also involve the PFC, where activation levels are increased during hypnosis but decreased during meditation. Evidence suggests hypnosis-related prefrontal increases result from the suggestion, which subsequently influence pain-related brain activity and experience (Raij et al., 2009). By definition, a hypnotic suggestion involves changing or reappraising a percept and presumably must require *active* regulation, whether conscious or not. Mindfulness meditation, on the other hand, involves an attempt to refrain from cognitive appraisal and elaborative/mnemonic processes. As already suggested (e.g., Grant, 2014), it is consistent with traditional descriptions of mindfulness that such practices would deactivate a similar set of frontal brain regions during pain. This suggests the two phenomena involve similar mental processes but differentially engaged; invoked during hypnosis and withdrawn during mindfulness meditation.

Consistent with this, opposing functional connectivity changes, between the same brain regions, have also been observed for the two phenomena. During hypnosis, connectivity between the DLPFC and dACC was increased, while in meditators, connectivity between these same regions was decreased, the degree to which predicted baseline pain sensitivity. These connectivity effects are paralleled by differences in the relation between dACC activation and pain reports. Whereas dACC activation is positively correlated with pain ratings during hypnosis (Faymonville et al., 2000; Rainville et al., 1997), it is decoupled in meditators, where pain ratings correspond to DLPFC activation (Grant et al., 2011; Lutz et al., 2013). This suggests appropriate input from the DLPFC may be necessary for dACC activation to reflect experienced pain.

Taken together, this integration of several of the more prominent findings from the two fields suggests that while there are certainly overlapping brain networks involved (dACC, INS, and DLPFC), the nature of the effects seems different. Both phenomena have been suggested to involve frontal modulation of pain-related areas and experience. Our reading of the literature suggests hypnosis accomplishes this through active implementation of a suggestion, whereas meditation appears to involve a retraction of the same processes.

Many questions remain however. For example, if modulation involves frontal areas influencing the ACC, how can we reconcile a positively activated dACC in both meditation and hypnosis, despite DLPFC reductions and increases, respectively? One suggestion is that DLPFC effects are secondary to intense sensory monitoring, and dACC activation, in meditators, with DLPFC activity ultimately decaying as elaborative processes give way to the monitoring (Grant, 2014). Also unanswered is the role of the INS and OFC in these techniques, the latter of which shows differential activation during pain for expert meditators and novices. Might novice meditators show an activation pattern halfway between hypnotic analgesia and mindfulness mediation due to the inability to fully invoke mindful attention? Future work will undoubtedly bring us closer to a full understanding of the mechanisms involved in meditative and hypnotic analgesia. Until that time, we would conclude that they are the same . . . yet different.

References

Allen, M., Dietz, M., Blair, K. S., van Beek, M., Rees, G., Vestergaard-Poulsen, P., . . . Roepstorff, A. (2012). Cognitive-affective neural plasticity following active-controlled mindfulness intervention. *J Neurosci*, **32**(44), 15601–15610.

Bandura, A., O'Leary, A., Taylor, C. B., Gauthier, J., & Gossard, D. (1987). Perceived self-efficacy and pain control: opioid and nonopioid mechanisms. *J Pers Soc Psychol*, **53**(3), 563–571.

Bantick, S. J., Wise, R. G., Ploghaus, A., Clare, S., Smith, S. M., & Tracey, I. (2002). Imaging: how attention modulates pain in humans using functional MRI. *Brain*, **125**(Pt 2), 310–319.

Bechara, A., Damasio, H., & Damasio, A. R. (2003). Role of the amygdala in decision-making. *Ann NY Acad Sci*, **985**, 356–369.

Benedetti, F., Mayberg, H. S., Wager, T. D., Stohler, C. S., & Zubieta, J. K. (2005). Neurobiological mechanisms of the placebo effect. *J Neurosci*, **25**(45), 10390–10402.

Bohdi, B. (2005). *In the Buddha's words: an anthology of discourses from the Pali canon.* Boston, MA: Wisdom Publications.

Brown, C. A., & Jones, A. K. (2010). Meditation experience predicts less negative appraisal of pain: electrophysiological evidence for the involvement of anticipatory neural responses. *Pain*, **150**(3), 428–438.

Burgmer, M., Kugel, H., Pfleiderer, B., Ewert, A., Lenzen, T., Pioch, R., . . . Konrad, C. (2013). The mirror neuron system under hypnosis—brain substrates of voluntary and involuntary motor activation in hypnotic paralysis. *Cortex*, **49**(2), 437–445.

Bushnell, M. C., Ceko, M., & Low, L. A. (2013). Cognitive and emotional control of pain and its disruption in chronic pain. *Nat Rev Neurosci*, **14**(7), 502–511.

Bushnell, M. C., Duncan, G. H., Hofbauer, R. K., Ha, B., Chen, J. I., & Carrier, B. (1999). Pain perception: is there a role for primary somatosensory cortex? *Proc Natl Acad Sci USA*, **96**(14), 7705–7709.

Carlson, L. E., Speca, M., Patel, K. D., & Goodey, E. (2003). Mindfulness-based stress reduction in relation to quality of life, mood, symptoms of stress, and immune parameters in breast and prostate cancer outpatients. *Psychosom Med*, **65**(4), 571–581.

Coghill, R. C., McHaffie, J. G., & Yen, Y. F. (2003). Neural correlates of interindividual differences in the subjective experience of pain. *Proc Natl Acad Sci USA*, **100**(14), 8538–8542.

Coghill, R. C., Sang, C. N., Maisog, J. M., & Iadarola, M. J. (1999). Pain intensity processing within the human brain: a bilateral, distributed mechanism. *J Neurophysiol*, **82**(4), 1934–1943.

De Pascalis, V., Chiaradia, C., & Carotenuto, E. (2002). The contribution of suggestibility and expectation to placebo analgesia phenomenon in an experimental setting. *Pain*, **96**(3), 393–402.

Deeley, Q., Oakley, D. A., Toone, B., Bell, V., Walsh, E., Marquand, A. F., . . . Halligan, P. W. (2013). The functional anatomy of suggested limb paralysis. *Cortex*, **49**(2), 411–422.

Derbyshire, S. W., Whalley, M. G., Stenger, V. A., & Oakley, D. A. (2004). Cerebral activation during hypnotically induced and imagined pain. *Neuroimage*, **23**(1), 392–401.

Dumont, L., Martin, C., & Broer, I. (2012). Functional neuroimaging studies of hypnosis and meditation: a comparative perspective *J Mind–Body Reg*, **2**(1), 58–70.

Eippert, F., Bingel, U., Schoell, E. D., Yacubian, J., Klinger, R., Lorenz, J., & Buchel, C. (2009). Activation of the opioidergic descending pain control system underlies placebo analgesia. *Neuron*, **63**(4), 533–543.

Farb, N. A., Anderson, A. K., Mayberg, H., Bean, J., McKeon, D., & Segal, Z. V. (2010). Minding one's emotions: mindfulness training alters the neural expression of sadness. *Emotion*, **10**(1), 25–33.

Faymonville, M. E., Laureys, S., Degueldre, C., DelFiore, G., Luxen, A., Franck, G., . . . Maquet, P. (2000). Neural mechanisms of antinociceptive effects of hypnosis. *Anesthesiology*, **92**(5), 1257–1267.

Faymonville, M. E., Roediger, L., Del Fiore, G., Delgueldre, C., Phillips, C., Lamy, M., . . . Laureys, S. (2003). Increased cerebral functional connectivity underlying the antinociceptive effects of hypnosis. *Brain Res Cogn Brain Res*, **17**(2), 255–262.

Fernando, A. B., Murray, J. E., & Milton, A. L. (2013). The amygdala: securing pleasure and avoiding pain. *Front Behav Neurosci*, **7**, 190.

Fields, H. L. (2000). Pain modulation: expectation, opioid analgesia and virtual pain. *Prog Brain Res*, **122**, 245–253.

Gard, T., Holzel, B. K., Sack, A. T., Hempel, H., Vaitl, D., & Ott, U. (2011). Pain attenuation through mindfulness is associated with decreased cognitive control and increased sensory processing in the brain. *Cereb Cor*, **191**(1), 36–43.

Garland, E., Gaylord, S., & Park, J. (2009). The role of mindfulness in positive reappraisal. *Explore (NY)*, **5**(1), 37–44.

Grant, J. A. (2014). Meditative analgesia: the current state of the field. *Ann NY Acad Sci*, **1307**, 55–63.

Grant, J. A., Courtemanche, J., & Rainville, P. (2011). A non-elaborative mental stance and decoupling of executive and pain-related cortices predicts low pain sensitivity in Zen meditators. *Pain*, **152**(1), 150–156.

Grant, J. A., & Rainville, P. (2005). Hypnosis and meditation: similar experiential changes and shared brain mechanisms. *Med Hypotheses*, **65**(3), 625–626.

Grant, J. A., & Rainville, P. (2009). Pain sensitivity and analgesic effects of mindful states in Zen meditators: a cross-sectional study. *Psychosom Med*, **71**(1), 106–114.

Hofbauer, R. K., Rainville, P., Duncan, G. H., & Bushnell, M. C. (2001). Cortical representation of the sensory dimension of pain. *J Neurophysiol*, **86**(1), 402–411.

Jensen, K. B., Berna, C., Loggia, M. L., Wasan, A. D., Edwards, R. R., & Gollub, R. L. (2012). The use of functional neuroimaging to evaluate psychological and other non-pharmacological treatments for clinical pain. *Neurosci Lett*, **520**(2), 156–164.

Kabat-Zinn, J. (1982). An outpatient program in behavioral medicine for chronic pain patients based on the practice of mindfulness meditation: theoretical considerations and preliminary results. *Gen Hosp Psychiat*, **4**(1), 33–47.

Kilpatrick, L. A., Suyenobu, B. Y., Smith, S. R., Bueller, J. A., Goodman, T., Creswell, J. D., . . . Naliboff, B. D. (2011). Impact of mindfulness-based stress reduction training on intrinsic brain connectivity. *Neuroimage*, **56**(1), 290–298.

Kingston, J., Chadwick, P., Meron, D., & Skinner, T. C. (2007). A pilot randomized control trial investigating the effect of mindfulness practice on pain tolerance, psychological well-being, and physiological activity. *J Psychosom Res*, **62**(3), 297–300.

Kirsch, I., Cardena, E., Derbyshire, S., Dienes, Z., Heap, M., Kallio, S., . . . Whalley, M. (2011). Definitions of hypnosis and nypnotizability and their relation to suggestion and suggestibility: a consensus statement. *Contemp Hypn*, **28**(2), 107–115.

Koyama, T., McHaffie, J. G., Laurienti, P. J., & Coghill, R. C. (2005). The subjective experience of pain: where expectations become reality. *Proc Natl Acad Sci USA*, **102**(36), 12950–12955.

Krummenacher, P., Candia, V., Folkers, G., Schedlowski, M., & Schonbachler, G. (2010). Prefrontal cortex modulates placebo analgesia. *Pain*, **148**(3), 368–374.

Lorenz, J., Minoshima, S., & Casey, K. L. (2003). Keeping pain out of mind: the role of the dorsolateral prefrontal cortex in pain modulation. *Brain*, **126**(5), 1079–1091.

Lutz, A., McFarlin, D. R., Perlman, D. M., Salomons, T. V., & Davidson, R. J. (2013). Altered anterior insula activation during anticipation and experience of painful stimuli in expert meditators. *Neuroimage*, **64**, 538–546.

Lutz, A., Slagter, H. A., Dunne, J. D., & Davidson, R. J. (2008). Attention regulation and monitoring in meditation. *Trends Cogn Sci*, **12**(4), 163–169.

Miron, D., Duncan, G. H., & Bushnell, M. C. (1989). Effects of attention on the intensity and unpleasantness of thermal pain. *Pain*, **39**(3), 345–352.

Mitchell, J. P. (2009). Inferences about mental states. *Philos Trans R Soc Lond B Biol Sci*, **364**(1521), 1309–1316.

Montgomery, G. H., DuHamel, K. N., & Redd, W. H. (2000). A meta-analysis of hypnotically induced analgesia: how effective is hypnosis? *Int J Clin Exp Hypn*, **48**(2), 138–153.

Perlman, D. M., Salomons, T. V., Davidson, R. J., & Lutz, A. (2010). Differential effects on pain intensity and unpleasantness of two meditation practices. *Emotion*, **10**(1), 65–71.

Petrovic, P., Kalso, E., Petersson, K. M., Andersson, J., Fransson, P., & Ingvar, M. (2010). A prefrontal non-opioid mechanism in placebo analgesia. *Pain*, **150**(1), 59–65.

Raij, T. T., Numminen, J., Narvanen, S., Hiltunen, J., & Hari, R. (2005). Brain correlates of subjective reality of physically and psychologically induced pain. *Proc Natl Acad Sci USA*, **102**(6), 2147–2151.

Raij, T. T., Numminen, J., Narvanen, S., Hiltunen, J., & Hari, R. (2009). Strength of prefrontal activation predicts intensity of suggestion-induced pain. *Hum Brain Mapp*, **30**(9), 2890–2897.

Rainville, P., Duncan, G. H., Price, D. D., Carrier, B., & Bushnell, M. C. (1997). Pain affect encoded in human anterior cingulate but not somatosensory cortex. *Science*, **277**(5328), 968–971.

Rainville, P., Hofbauer, R. K., Bushnell, M. C., Duncan, G. H., & Price, D. D. (2002). Hypnosis modulates activity in brain structures involved in the regulation of consciousness. *J Cogn Neurosci*, **14**(6), 887–901.

Rainville, P., Hofbauer, R. K., Paus, T., Duncan, G. H., Bushnell, M. C., & Price, D. D. (1999). Cerebral mechanisms of hypnotic induction and suggestion. *J Cogn Neurosci*, **11**(1), 110–125.

Rainville, P., & Price, D. D. (2003). Hypnosis phenomenology and the neurobiology of consciousness. *Int J Clin Exp Hypn*, **51**(2), 105–129.

Rolls, E. T. (2008). Functions of the orbitofrontal and pregenual cingulate cortex in taste, olfaction, appetite and emotion. *Acta Physiol Hung*, **95**(2), 131–164.

Roy, M., Peretz, I., & Rainville, P. (2008). Emotional valence contributes to music-induced analgesia. *Pain*, **134**(1–2), 140–147.

Seeley, W. W., Menon, V., Schatzberg, A. F., Keller, J., Glover, G. H., Kenna, H., . . . Greicius, M. D. (2007). Dissociable intrinsic connectivity networks for salience processing and executive control. *J Neurosci*, **27**(9), 2349–2356.

Strigo, I. A., Duncan, G. H., Boivin, M., & Bushnell, M. C. (2003). Differentiation of visceral and cutaneous pain in the human brain. *J Neurophysiol*, **89**(6), 3294–3303.

Suzuki, W. A. (2008). Associative learning signals in the brain. *Prog Brain Res*, **169**, 305–320.

Tracey, I., Ploghaus, A., Gati, J. S., Clare, S., Smith, S., Menon, R. S., & Matthews, P. M. (2002). Imaging attentional modulation of pain in the periaqueductal gray in humans. *J Neurosci*, **22**(7), 2748–2752.

Valet, M., Sprenger, T., Boecker, H., Willoch, F., Rummeny, E., Conrad, B., . . . Tolle, T. R. (2004). Distraction modulates connectivity of the cingulo-frontal cortex and the midbrain during pain—an fMRI analysis. *Pain*, **109**(3), 399–408.

Villemure, C., & Bushnell, M. C. (2009). Mood influences supraspinal pain processing separately from attention. *J Neurosci*, **29**(3), 705–715.

Villemure, C., Slotnick, B. M., & Bushnell, M. C. (2003). Effects of odors on pain perception: deciphering the roles of emotion and attention. *Pain*, **106**(1–2), 101–108.

Wager, T. D., Atlas, L. Y., Leotti, L. A., & Rilling, J. K. (2011). Predicting individual differences in placebo analgesia: contributions of brain activity during anticipation and pain experience. *J Neurosci*, **31**(2), 439–452.

Wager, T. D., Rilling, J. K., Smith, E. E., Sokolik, A., Casey, K. L., Davidson, R. J., . . . Cohen, J. D. (2004). Placebo-induced changes in FMRI in the anticipation and experience of pain. *Science*, **303**(5661), 1162–1167.

Weitzenhoffer, A. M. (1980). Hypnotic susceptibility revisited. *Am J Clin Hypn*, **22**(3), 130–146.

Zeidan, F., Gordon, N. S., Merchant, J., & Goolkasian, P. (2010). The effects of brief mindfulness meditation training on experimentally induced pain. *J Pain*, **11**(3), 199–209.

Zeidan, F., Grant, J. A., Brown, C. A., McHaffie, J. G., & Coghill, R. C. (2012). Mindfulness meditation-related pain relief: evidence for unique brain mechanisms in the regulation of pain. *Neurosci Lett*, **520**(2), 165–173.

Zeidan, F., Johnson, S. K., Diamond, B. J., David, Z., & Goolkasian, P. (2010). Mindfulness meditation improves cognition: evidence of brief mental training. *Conscious Cogn*, **19**(2), 597–605.

Zeidan, F., Johnson, S. K., Gordon, N. S., & Goolkasian, P. (2010). Effects of brief and sham mindfulness meditation on mood and cardiovascular variables. *J Altern Complement Med*, **16**(8), 867–873.

Zeidan, F., Martucci, K. T., Kraft, R. A., Gordon, N. S., McHaffie, J. G., & Coghill, R. C. (2011). Brain mechanisms supporting the modulation of pain by mindfulness meditation. *J Neurosci*, **31**(14), 5540–5548.

Zeidan, F., Martucci, K. T., Kraft, R. A., McHaffie, J. G., & Coghill, R. C. (2013). Neural correlates of mindfulness meditation-related anxiety relief. *Soc Cogn Affect Neurosci*, **9**(6), 751–9.

Chapter 22

Hypnosis and mindfulness meditation: a psychoanalytic perspective

Tony Toneatto and Erin Courtice

Abstract

While the biological and psychological substrates underlying the clinical and therapeutic efficacy of mindfulness meditation and hypnosis has attracted the bulk of scientific study, mindfulness meditation was historically directed also toward the optimization of human functioning through a transformative series of insights into the nature of subjectivity. The achievement of such personal growth, however, remains unstable unless it rests on the ability to sustain and maintain focused attention (as described in hypnosis) which serves as an "anchor" for these initially disturbing insights. Hypnosis grounds the sense of self that may transiently become destabilized by the Buddhist insights of impermanence, dissatisfaction, and conditionality that accompany sustained mindfulness of mental processes. This chapter describes a psychoanalytic model of optimal human functioning. It examines how mindfulness meditation and hypnosis interact to facilitate a reorganization of the personality through the dissolution of narcissistic ego functioning as described in the Buddhist soteriological literature.

Introduction

Recent years have witnessed a surging scientific interest in mindfulness meditation and hypnosis as effective treatments for a wide range of medical and emotional disorders (e.g., see reviews by Brown, 2007; Chiesa & Serretti, 2011; Flammer & Bogartz, 2003; Shapiro & Carlson, 2009). Until recently, however, the empirical literatures on hypnosis and mindfulness have coexisted separately and interacted very little despite similarities in phenomenology, therapeutic benefits, neural substrates, and cognitive mechanisms (Lifshitz & Raz, 2012; Lifshitz, Campbell, & Raz, 2012).

Interest continues to grow toward understanding how hypnosis and meditation may complement and contribute to each other. Indeed, a burgeoning wealth of literature has been developing on this very topic, particularly focusing on the processes by which these two practices converge and deviate, as well as how they might be integrated in treating medical and psychological symptoms (Lifshitz & Raz, 2012; Farb, 2012).

Theoretical models to account for the clinical benefits of hypnosis and mindfulness meditation have tended to focus on biological and cognitive processes as key mediating variables. While these clinical and process-oriented approaches are certainly important and needed, they are for, the most part, reductionistic in their focus and do not reflect the phenomenological, integrative, and experiential impact of mindfulness and hypnosis. Largely absent from the scientific literature is an examination of the ways in which mindfulness meditation and hypnosis may optimize the psychological development of the whole individual beyond attenuating symptoms, improving cognitive processing, enhancing brain functioning, or regulating attention.

The focus of this chapter is to describe a model of optimal human functioning that addresses the question of how mindfulness meditation and hypnosis may promote a profound reorganization of the personality as described in the Buddhist soteriological literature (Brahm, 2006). This analysis will rely on a psychoanalytic conceptual framework. Psychoanalysis remains the most comprehensive description of human development, normal personality, psychopathology, and treatment despite its increasing marginalization within academic psychology, psychiatry, and clinical psychology (Mitchell & Black, 1995).

The breadth and depth of psychoanalytic theorizing are unparalleled and provide a starting point to investigate the effects of mindfulness meditation and hypnosis on adult personality development. Indeed, the past few years have also witnessed an explosive growth in psychoanalytic writings on meditation, contemplative science, and Buddhist psychology (Cooper, 2010; Engler, 2003; Epstein, 1986, 1995; Rubin, 2003; Safran, 2003). Unfortunately, this literature is not well known by those who investigate the cognitive, behavioral, and biological processes mediating the therapeutic benefits of mindfulness meditation and hypnosis.

This chapter will introduce the reader to a psychoanalytic perspective that may contribute to a more complete understanding of how hypnosis and mindfulness meditation may cultivate optimal personality functioning.

Major types of meditative practice

Within the Buddhist religious tradition at least two distinct types of mindfulness meditative practice have been described: concentration meditation and insight meditation (Brahm, 2006; Goleman 1988). However, not all meditative practices fit neatly into these categories (Goleman, 1988; see also Chapters 3 and 4).

Concentration meditation (samatha-bhavana; samadhi-bhavana), a core practice found within Buddhism and Hinduism but also part of many other spiritual traditions practice, is characterized by sustained, restricted, focused, and narrowed attention on a meditative object such as the breath. The aim of concentration meditation is to train the mind to maintain one-pointed focus on the meditative object. Repeated practice of concentration meditation culminates in deep states of calm, serenity, and relaxation (Brahm, 2006; Wallace, 1999). When attention strays from the object of meditation, it is gently but firmly returned to the object. With sustained practice, attentional stability can be achieved (Rapgay & Bystrisky, 2009; Wallace, 1999). When consistently placed on an object for a prolonged period of time, attention can be fully and vividly experienced and the qualities of that experience can be examined and investigated (Wallace, 1999; Anälayo, 2006).

In the traditional spiritual literature, such focused attentional placement can elicit very deep states of merger and absorption (termed jhanas in the Buddhist sutras and, in its most superficial states, approximates the state of flow), and can produce progressively more subtle states of calm, relaxation, and serenity, often accompanied by deep bliss. The Buddha claimed that skill in maintaining attentional equipoise is a necessary element in achieving a stable understanding of subjectivity devoid of the mental projections, reifications, and associations that automatically

veil our everyday contact with subjective reality and subsequently contribute to emotional suffering (Thera, 1973; for an in-depth discussion of how the trait of absorption impacts hypnotic and
meditative experiences, see Chapter 14).

Insight meditation (vipassana-bhavana; prajnha-bhavana), a uniquely Buddhist meditative
practice, is broad, open, and non-specific, characterized by detached, non-judgmental awareness
of all cognitive events as they arise within awareness. In contrast to concentration meditation,
insight meditation cultivates observation of all sensory and mental phenomena as they appear to
awareness, rather than restricting attention to the meditative object. Insight meditation makes the
moment-to-moment flow of present experience the focus of attention. Here, one is not focused on
an attentional object as in concentration meditation. Instead, one maintains a heightened awareness of the ongoing stream of cognition (Rapgay & Bystrisky, 2009; Wallace, 1999).

Sustained insight meditation practice culminates in wisdom defined within the Buddhist tradition by three key insights or realizations that regard mental phenomena as:

 (i) constructed, composite, and conditioned, and thus lacking inherent ontological existence
      (i.e., empty or *anatta*);

 (ii) constantly changing, transient processes (i.e., impermanent or *anicca*);

(iii) incapable of producing durable happiness and satisfaction (i.e., suffering or *dukkha*).

In other words, mindfulness meditation culminates in direct, perceptual (i.e., non-conceptual,
non-cognitive) discernment of the constructed and conditioned, transient and ultimately unsat-
isfying nature of subjective experience (Goleman, 1988; Grabovac, Lau, & Willett, 2011). These
insights are believed to be the foundation for the development of authentic wisdom and understanding of the mind and what distinguishes Buddhist meditation from secular meditation as
described within mindfulness-based interventions (Rapgay & Bystrisky, 2009).

While concentration and insight meditation are distinct practices, they are typically utilized in
tandem (Anälayo, 2006; Wallace, 1999). When skilfully integrated, the cultivation of sustained
periods of attention on an object fosters attentional stability that, when followed by introspective
insight awareness, yields a deeper understanding of the nature of subjectivity (Rapgay & Bystrisky,
2009). Such mindfulness practice also facilitates perceptual and cognitive regulation, the repeated switching between attention to, and introspective awareness of, subjective experience (Thera,
1973). Such cognitive and perceptual fluidity helps increase mental flexibility through an attitude
of non-identification with, or decentering from, cognitive experience—a feature characteristic of
optimal mental health (Shapiro & Carlson, 2009).

Psychological processes mediating effects of hypnosis and mindfulness meditation

Psychological models of mindfulness meditation tend to emphasize learning and cognitive processes. Segal, Williams, and Teasdale (2002) have described mindfulness as a metacognitive state
of detached awareness of one's thoughts. Fox, Kang, Lifshitz, and Christoff (Chapter 11) propose
a neurocognitive model whereby mindful awareness allows individuals to notice and override
habitual thought processes. Shapiro and Carlson (2009) conceptualize mindfulness as a form of
emotion-focused coping that modifies the response to stress or change, rather than reflexively
reacting to it, allowing the individual to disrupt automatic, conditioned, or impulsive response to
such cognitions (Breslin, Zack, & McMain, 2002). Shapiro, Carlson, Astin, and Freedman (2006),
as well as Vervaeke and Ferraro (Chapter 13), have suggested that mindfulness meditation may
exert its beneficial effects by producing a fundamental shift in perspective. Learning processes

such as habituation and desensitization have also been suggested as mechanisms of mindfulness (Ivanovski & Malhi, 2007). Hypnotic phenomena have been accounted for by a number of cognitive mechanisms, neurochemical and neural substrates, and attentional allocations (Lifshitz & Raz, 2012).

Conceptual explanations of the hypnotic process and its benefits tend to fall within two categories. The first views the hypnotic state as a condition of altered consciousness, characterized by absorption, concentration, and focused attention (Green, Barabasz, Barrett, & Montgomery, 2005). A second interpretation considers hypnosis as a cooperative interaction, whereby one individual (the hypnotist) guides another (the subject) to become highly focused on, and receptive to, suggestions for alterations in subjective experience (i.e., perception, thought, emotion, or behavior; Dumont, Martin, & Broer, 2012). Both of these categories of hypnotic induction closely resemble the instructions traditionally provided by the meditation teacher to induce concentration meditative states (e.g., what to attend to, what not to attend to, how to attend). Within the meditative tradition, the specific instructions and guidelines transmitted by the meditation teacher are considered indispensable in successfully mastering mindfulness (Yapko, 2011). Of course, for both hypnosis and meditation, the perception of the teacher or instructor as competent and trustworthy is critical, highlighting the intersubjective component that is necessary for benefitting from these practices.

Very little attention has been paid to mechanisms underlying the impact of hypnotic and meditative practices on personality integration, the major goal of Buddhist psychology and practice (cf. Fromm, 1970; Watts, 1975 for efforts in this direction). While Western approaches to mindfulness meditation stress the alleviation of clinical symptoms or the regulation of attention, the traditional aim of such practice was intended to enhance human functioning through the discernment of, or insight into, the nature of subjectivity as already described (Bodhi, 2005). Understanding how these two traditions may synergistically interact to produce the kinds of personality development attributed to long-term meditative practice and hypnosis (although not always an explicit goal of hypnosis) is lacking.

In the remainder of this chapter, a model for understanding how hypnosis and mindfulness meditation can be integrated and promote optimal personality functioning will be elucidated within a psychoanalytic framework.

A psychoanalytic mechanism for the efficacy of mindfulness and hypnotic meditative states as regression

Psychoanalysts of the early twentieth century were among the first to study meditation-related mystical experiences (Parsons, 1999). The interest in the nature of such psychological states was part of an "oriental renaissance" that began in the mid nineteenth century, through contact with Eastern religious, primarily Hindu, texts. As such, it is important to not confuse this early understanding of meditation with the uniquely Buddhist contribution of insight meditation that became the focus of psychoanalytic thinking much later.

Freud (1930/2005) provided one of the first psychoanalytical efforts to understand the mystical states associated with concentration meditation. He identified the core, common feature of mystical experiences as a state of oneness, or limitless merger with the universe or divinity and a concomitant loss of ego boundary or separateness which he termed the "oceanic feeling." Meditators continue to seek this experience—the feeling of oneness, merger, loss of individual identity/ego, union with God, etc.—and some believe it to be the core of spiritual "enlightenment" (Goleman, 1988; Watts, 1975; Wilber, 2007). Freud (1930/2005) further argued that the allure of the "oceanic feeling" lies in its ability to revive, in the individual, a time in their lives (i.e., early infancy) when they indeed did not have a distinct sense of self/ego or a concept of the "other" (i.e., primary narcissism). Concepts of "otherness" or of an individuated sense of self is a later developmental achievement (Mitchell & Black, 1995). Thus, this pre-egoic, undifferentiated phase of infant mental development can be likened to a narcissistic state, insofar as all subjective experience is an aspect of the infant's primitive self. Without a sense of separateness or individuality there is neither a corresponding sense of a self nor an awareness of an "other" that is distinct and separate.

According to Freud (1930/2005), concentration meditation can temporarily reinstate this primitive pre-egoic feeling and restore the limitless narcissism of infancy (e.g., loss of boundaries, omnipotence, non-differentiated self, grandiosity) in the adult. Meditation-induced mystical experiences, thus, hearken to an earlier developmental phase. In effect, the adult meditator is attempting to reinstate a pre-natal, pre-verbal, pre-cognitive state of constancy, a feeling of completion or wholeness that no longer exists. Freud (1930/2005) tended to dismiss such experiences as a regressive pursuit of narcissistic merger that was no longer possible and, thus, psychopathological. In his view, such experiences may feel "mystical" precisely because they are pre-verbal, pre-conceptual, and pre-symbolic. However, they are not necessarily indicative of any profound wisdom or spiritual attainment. Rather, one is simply avoiding adult reality.

In addition to meditation, such mystical experiences, including states of merger and fusion, may rise during states of intoxication, florid psychosis, mania, orgasm, flow, trance, and spirit possession in which the temporary loss of ego boundaries (i.e., primary ego feeling) is accompanied by feelings of deep satisfaction, stillness, and wholeness. It may be argued that hypnotic states can also produce states of merger or fusion and, like concentration meditation, elicit feelings of calm, relaxation, and peace and resemble pre-egoic, pre-symbolic mental states. While concentration meditation and hypnosis are not equivalent practices, with sufficient training, both appear to produce comparable mental states based on the ability to regulate and allocate attention (e.g., Otani, 2003; Holroyd, 2003, Epstein, 1995).

Freud (1930/2005) was not alone in interpreting mystical experiences as regressive and potentially harmful because they represented a pathological avoidance of reality. Alexander (1931), for example, one of the first classical psychoanalysts to write specifically about Buddhist meditation, wrote that meditative practices culminate in "Nirvana," which he argued was a deep regression that reversed personality development to its origins in intrauterine life. In general, the first generation of psychoanalysts viewed concentration meditative states as a defensive regression in response to unbearable emotional conflict—a retreat to a "mythical" time when one experienced a sense of safety, security, and wholeness.

It is important to note that, historically, psychoanalysis and hypnosis were closely tied. Freud was strongly influenced by Charcot, a renowned French professor of neurology, who discovered that symptoms of hysteria could be relieved by hypnotic suggestion, indicating a non-physiological basis to this disorder. Freud also collaborated with Breuer, who employed hypnosis to discover the unconscious causes of hysteria. Eventually, Freud came to abandon hypnosis (in favor of free association) for a number of reasons. He observed that the benefits of hypnosis were sometimes short-lived, that some patients might become addicted to hypnosis, that its applicability was limited primarily to hysteriform disorders, that many patients could not be easily hypnotized, and that hypnosis did not necessarily afford insight into the psychodynamics underlying symptoms (Bachner-Melman & Lichtenberg, 2001). Freud, however, maintained an interest in hypnosis throughout his career and admitted the debt of psychoanalysis to hypnosis, though it is less widely perceived that he largely repaid this debt with his prescient observations about the nature of hypnosis and the hypnotic process . . . His approach to hypnosis as comprising psychological states and social expectations, attentional processes and role playing, essentially anticipated the major agendas of hypnosis research to this day. (Bachner-Melman & Lichtenberg, 2001, p. 45)

Meditative states and narcissism

While the early psychoanalysts viewed meditation-associated mental states with suspicion, later psychoanalytic writers have argued that mystical states could be healthy and adaptive. Federn (1952) considered concentration meditation as potentially ego-enhancing rather than simply regressive. Bion (1963) identified "O," the unknowable, ineffable, ultimate reality, or truth of existence which may approximate the stillness, equanimity, and presence found within concentration meditation but can only be experienced in mental states characterized by neither "memory nor desire" (Grotstein, 1981). Bion's "O" intimates that a sense of coherence and completeness cannot be known by the physical senses except through intuitive perception.

Consistent with the early psychoanalytic suspicion of meditation states, some writers have also argued that meditation is most beneficial and salutary for those who have first established a healthy sense of self or ego (Engler, 2003; Preece, 2006). More recently, Rubin (2003), and especially the integrative writings of Epstein (1986), from which many of the following points are drawn, have articulated how insight and concentration meditation can diminish pathological narcissism and enhance interpersonal functioning in ways consistent with the highest aspirations described within Buddhism.

For those in whom the sense of self is fragmented, prone to dissociation, or traumatized, meditation may not only lack benefit but may even be harmful, by reinforcing the avoidance of difficult emotions and strengthening narcissistic, schizoid, or paranoid states of mind (e.g., Suler, 1993; Welwood, 2000). Only a self or ego that is resilient and capable of forming satisfying social relationships and tolerating negative affect can benefit maximally from meditation. Paradoxically, however, many people attracted to meditative practices may be emotionally unstable and display signs of neurotic symptomatology (e.g., trauma, obsessions, anxiety, depression) (Epstein, 1986). This, in and of itself, is not unusual as most psychospiritual paths promise authentic and durable happiness. It is also not unusual that narcissistic pathology (e.g., grandiosity, feeling of superiority, self-centered, magical thinking, feeling of omnipotence or omniscience, specialness) characterizes spiritual seekers who are attracted to the mystical and the esoteric practices that have often been associated with Buddhism (e.g., Mahayana, Tantric) in which there is an element of magic, contact with divinities, and potential for supranormal powers (Suler, 1993; Welwood, 2000). Indeed, Buddhist soteriological doctrines may encourage narcissistic pathology through their promotion of extremely high ideals of human potential (such as the attainment of perfect Buddhahood in which one repeatedly incarnates in order to facilitate the enlightenment of other sentient beings and to acquire miraculous supranormal powers) which, to an outsider, may appear impossible and grandiose. In some Buddhist traditions, it is explicitly taught that everyone possesses inherent Buddhahood and that the goals of meditative practices are to actually become a Buddha (Bodhi, 2005).

While normal narcissism is the basis of healthy self-esteem and a sense of personal contentment, pathological residues of extreme narcissism can persist throughout the life span and may be aroused and nurtured by certain types of meditative practices. As already described, within the psychoanalytic tradition such narcissistic residues are considered to be an archaic memory of the infant's initial blissful symbiotic union with their mother/caretaker. If normal infant development is interrupted by significant trauma, neglect, or deprivation, the initial state of primary narcissism is replaced by pathological narcissistic ideals rather than evolving into a more adaptive sense of self. Such pathological states would need to be transformed and overcome if the individual is to benefit from meditative practices. Otherwise, the meditative path may only serve to strengthen, inflate, and protect the sense of self and ego rather than facilitate a realization of its ontological nature (i.e., emptiness). Realizing that the self lacks inherent existence or essence is the apex of Buddhist wisdom and incompatible with pathological narcissism which overly values and privileges the self at the expense of healthy relations with others.

To understand how mindfulness meditation can transform the narcissistic self/ego into the wisdom self/ego associated with sustained meditation in which the self is experienced as a fluid, conditioned process, one must first understand the typical developmental outcome of the primary, archaic narcissism of infancy (i.e., the undifferentiated symbiotic fusion with mother that exists prior to conceptual cognition). Over the course of the first year or two of life, through repeated encounters with reality (e.g., hunger, thirst, cold, pain), mediated by an adequate, care-giving environment that is never perfect (i.e., parents can never be perfectly attentive to the infant's needs), the infant comes to realize the severe limits to their primary narcissism. In response, the infant learns to cope by adapting to their physical and social environment, realistically rather than narcissistically. The infant becomes increasingly aware of the limits of their efficacy, attentive to the presence of others who are independent and separate beings, and attuned to the boundaries that separate them from their surrounding environment. In the best-case scenario, the developing child continues to transform narcissism into healthy ego functioning and self-esteem characterized by mutuality and inter-subjectivity. However, if the care-giving environment is not ideal, narcissistic residues may persist beyond infancy and influence a myriad of life choices, impact relations with others, and distort personality functioning. Specifically, narcissistic residues may find expression in the distortions of two developmental pathways: ideal ego and ego ideal (Hanly, 1984).

The ideal ego and the ego ideal

The ideal ego is the idealized image of our ego as solid, permanent, immortal, complete, eternal, real, and perfect. This image is, of course, completely illusory and is the vestige of the vague memory of the infant's primary narcissism (Epstein, 1986). The ideal ego defines a core self-image which may even feel more real than the limited, ordinary ego that we actually are. Within the worldview of the ideal ego, the reality of ego as it really is (limited, imperfect, finite, etc.) is denied (Hanly, 1984). For example, one may exaggerate one's attributes or be unaware of one's personal limitations, believe that one's essence is immortal, claim to possess special powers, feel entitled to special treatment or attention, etc. One can observe a similarity between the experience of the ideal ego (and the loss of ego boundaries) and states of merger, fusion, and non-differentiation found in concentration and hypnotic practices.

Conversely, the ego ideal is what the maturing ego yearns to become, fuse, unite, and merge with. The ego ideal is also based on an archaic memory of the perfect (infantile) world in which there was no distinction between self and other. This is a perfection still to be realized, drawing on one's unrealized potential. One can observe an association between the ego ideal and the Buddhist ideal personality of the perfected Buddha, Arhat (i.e., one who has realized the true nature of reality within Theravada Buddhism) or Bodhisattva.[1] Instead of looking *backward* to a perfect

---

[1] Within the Mahayana Buddhist tradition, enlightened beings are known as Bodhisattvas who, upon attaining Nirvana, out of absolute compassion work toward the spiritual evolution of all sentient beings. What begins as a realization of the ego ideal moves beyond, free of any narcissistic residue or self-interest, solely focused on the welfare of other beings who remain mired in samsara, the ordinary world of cyclic existence.

state that one once was (which is what the ideal ego is), the ego ideal looks *forward* to a state of becoming perfect, which is projected and reflected in one's life choices. The specific form of the ego ideal will be strongly influenced by familial, cultural, and societal models of potentiality and is often considered an aspect of the superego (Epstein, 1986; Hanly, 1984).

Thus, the ideal ego assures the self of its own intrinsic completeness, wholeness, and perfection (i.e., "you *are* perfect"). On the other hand, the ego ideal assures the self that one will become complete, whole, perfect (i.e., "you *will be* perfect") (Hanly, 1984). Both of these residual expressions of primary narcissism are nevertheless based on an illusory subjective world of perfection, happiness, and bliss that existed (albeit briefly) at the beginning of life (i.e., in the womb and shortly after birth). While the ego ideal is realistic (i.e., strives after goals set out by society, parents, the superego through career, etc.), the ideal ego is idealistic (i.e., strives after goals that are impossible to attain, except in fantasy of a perfect self, superhero, a Buddha, all-powerful, etc.). Individuals with such archaic narcissistic residues may be drawn to spiritual practices that actually satisfy the ideal ego (i.e., samadhi, bliss, sense of oneness) and/or the ego ideal (i.e., enlightenment, Buddha nature, supranormal powers) and thus reinforce and inflate the narcissistic ego.

Mindfulness meditation as a means of transforming narcissism

How can meditation dissolve these residues of primary narcissism and contribute to the development of a healthier personality? To understand this process, recall that during both hypnosis and concentration meditation one develops the ability to one-pointedly fix attention on a meditative object, promoting stability and equanimity, and evoking a deep state of well-being, presence, and stillness. Both procedures involve a specific instructional set delivered by a recognized expert or teacher and which specifically guides the individual's attentional allocation. Both of these practices gratify the ego ideal by inducing states of merger, unity, and oneness—what Federn (1952) called a "mental orgasm." If one seeks such states for their own sake, the resulting bliss/pleasure/calm can become "addictive," in the sense that meditation or hypnotic practices are engaged in primarily, or solely, to experience these unitive states. While initially salutary, these experiences can become obstacles to a veridical understanding of mental events, as already described.

Unlike concentration meditation or hypnotic absorption, insight meditation leads to an understanding of subjective experience as impermanent, conditioned, and only conditionally satisfying. Thus, the outcome of insight meditation directly challenges the ideal ego by directly confronting the illusory nature of the self/ego (i.e., the mistaken view that the self is real, essential, substantial, and eternal) (Epstein, 1986; Grabovac, Lau, & Willett, 2011). If one is unprepared for this insight (e.g., insufficient practice of concentration meditation, absence of a suitable context for such perceptions) or is emotionally or psychologically unstable, these insights may evoke discomfort, anxiety, fragmentation, terror, and existential anxiety (e.g., Do I exist? Who am I? Am I falling apart? Am I real?). The basis for this terror is the threat that insight meditation poses to the grandiose "false view" of the self (i.e., the compelling belief that we truly exist, are eternal, real, powerful, separate, etc., rather than the Buddhist insight that the ego is a process and empty of inherent existence). These insights threaten the sense of the self/ego as permanent, real, and eternal (Epstein, 1986).

However, the insights of mindfulness meditation can be tolerated, processed, and properly integrated within the personality if the practitioner continues with active concentration meditation practice which helps to ground the self in present-focused awareness, the here and now (Brahm, 2006; Epstein, 1995; Goleman, 1988). In other words, in order to avoid intense anxiety, psychic dread, dissociation, or depersonalization, it is important that the practitioner has access to an experience that is stabilizing and sensory-based, such as concentration meditation or hypnotic inductions. The stillness and calm associated with these practices serve as an anchor for psychological stability should insight meditation produce emotional distress. With this safeguard in place, the insights of mindfulness meditation can be integrated into the personality without seriously threatening the coherence of the self/ego. As a result, the residual, infantile illusion of primary narcissism, as embodied in the ideal ego, is slowly weakened (Hanly, 1984). The idealized image that the ego had held of itself as real, permanent, perfect, since infancy, is pierced. Once emptiness of the self is realized and stabilized, the psychic energy invested in ego-aggrandizing narcissism of the ideal ego may be released. Not uncommonly, feelings of joy, equanimity, and peace are experienced as a result (Epstein, 1986).

However, these insights into the nature of the self are not a threat to the ego ideal (which is activated through concentration meditation/hypnotic induction) since the ego ideal fosters a feeling of calm and stillness that arises from the fusion with the meditative object and, by definition, temporarily eliminates the subjective sense of a separate self. Thus, sustained practice of meditation affects the ego ideal and ideal ego in different ways. The ego ideal is initially strengthened (during concentration practice or hypnotic induction) and the ideal ego (the view of self as real) is weakened during insight meditation. As Epstein (1986) has argued, the ego ideal must *first* be strengthened by concentration/hypnotic practice in order to be able to tolerate the release of the narcissistic ideal ego and its illusion of a real substantial self. The ego ideal is required during this radical and transformative process as it fosters a feeling of stability, serenity, and wholeness while the threat to one's primary narcissism and the accompanying anxiety, terror, and discomfort of realizing the nature of the self that arises during insight meditation is processed. Having access to attentional and emotional stability provides a safe psychic space in which to process and integrate the trauma to one's own narcissistic grandiosity.

However, once the ideal ego has been transformed through insight meditation and the insight into the emptiness of the self has been stabilized, which can take years of dedicated practice, the bliss and pleasure that accompanies concentration practices (i.e., the ego ideal) can now be examined and its nature also investigated. If the nature of the bliss is misinterpreted (i.e., taken as permanent and substantial), there is a danger that the ego ideal will remain intact and even strengthened as the pleasurable feelings of merger and "oneness" with the "world" become the focus of meditation practice. If the ego ideal, reinforced through concentration or hypnotic practices, is not subjected to the same clear comprehension that accompanies insight meditation, there is a danger of developing an excessive reliance or pursuit of these merger states and strengthening the grandiose delusion that one may be omnipotent, omniscient, or otherwise unique or special (Epstein, 1986). However, when the practice of insight meditation is also applied to the bliss and merger experiences associated with concentration meditation, they too are understood as empty, impermanent, and conditional.

Implications for practice

Traditionally, concentration meditation practices precede insight meditation (Goleman, 1988). Until one can stabilize attention, insight meditation is discouraged. This advice can be understood psychoanalytically given the analysis here. Without a firm basis in concentration meditation, insight meditation can be destabilizing to a coherent sense of self. Contemporary mindfulness practices often provide very minimal training in concentration meditation and may privilege insight meditation (Chiesa & Serretti, 2011). Premature practice of insight meditation, without first experiencing the stabilization associated with concentration practices (through the transitional strengthening function of the ego ideal), may make the practitioner prone to feeling anxious, threatened, dissociated, and depressed, since their (narcissistic) (i.e., self-centered, grandiose, entitled) view of the self is undermined too quickly or prematurely. In other words, if one lets go of the belief in an abiding, inherent self (the ideal ego) too early, without the grounding presence of the ego ideal, one can feel dissociated and disturbed, lost and alienated, unreal, depersonalized. Even long-term practitioners may abandon their meditative practice or be at risk of developing serious psychological symptoms (Engler, 2003; Preece, 2006; Suler, 1993; Welwood, 2000).

Insight and concentration meditation/hypnotic practices are thus both necessary to realize the psychospiritual benefits of meditation safely. In skillful combination, they can be viewed as a vehicle for freeing oneself from unhealthy narcissism and egoism and approaching the Buddhist ideals of human potential.

A psychoanalytic perspective of mindfulness meditation and hypnosis has practical implications. Based on the interplay between the grounding effects of concentration practices and the liberating wisdom of insight meditation, optimal progress along the path of enlightenment may be facilitated by repeated oscillations between episodes of concentration/hypnotic inductions and insight meditative practices.

In most meditation programs, concentration meditation may be used initially to establish a period of calm and serenity, which is then followed by the penetrative awareness of insight meditation. It is not uncommon for concentration meditation, however, to be practiced only briefly, with emphasis placed on insight meditation, even with novice meditators. The analysis elucidated here suggests that this approach to meditation may be harmful because a premature insight into the nature of the self can evoke a number of reactions that may diminish the practitioner's resolve to continue practicing, including intense boredom, anxiety attacks, emotional volatility, and dread. The individual may simply abandon their practice or drop out of a clinical intervention. Only when an individual can reliably fix their attention on the meditative object through concentration meditation, for increasingly longer periods of time, should they proceed to extend periods of insight meditation.

Hypnosis can play an important role in creating a conducive environment for sustained attentional placement. In the early phases of practice, concentration meditation and hypnosis may appear quite similar as they rely on instructions and suggestions to deepen relaxation, maintain attention on a meditative object, and return the attention to this object (Yapko, 2011). Oscillating between brief periods of both types of meditative practice can diminish the harmful effects of either type of meditation.

Psychoanalytic understanding goes beyond the relatively limited analyses of mindfulness meditation and hypnotic practice that focus on cognitive processes, neural substrates, or biological mechanisms. Our perspective elucidates how these practices can gradually and synergistically transform the structure of the meditator's character, shifting from narcissistic, ego-centered relationships to healthier social bonds based on mutuality and symmetry.

References

Alexander, F. (1931). Buddhistic training as an artificial catatonia. *Psychoanalytic Review*, **19**(2), 129–141.

Anälayo, V. (2006). Mindfulness in the Pali Nikayas. In D. K. Nauriyal, M. S. Drummond, & Y. B. Lal (Eds.), *Buddhist thought and applied psychological research: transcending the boundaries* (pp. 229–249). London: Taylor and Francis.

Bachner-Melman, R., & Lichtenberg, P. (2001). Freud's relevance to hypnosis: a reevaluation. *American Journal of Clinical Hypnosis*, **44**, 37–50.

Bion, W. R. (1963). *Elements of psychoanalysis*. London: Heinemann.

Bodhi, B. (2005). *In the Buddha's words: an anthology of discourses from the Pali canon*. Boston: Wisdom Publications.

Brahm, A. (2006). *Mindfulness, bliss and beyond: a meditator's handbook*. Boston: Wisdom Publications.

Breslin, F. C., Zack, M., & McMain, S. (2002). An information-processing analysis of mindfulness: implications for relapse prevention in the treatment of substance abuse. *Clinical Psychology and Science Practice*, **9**, 275–299.

Brown, D. (2007). Evidence-based hypnotherapy for asthma: a critical review. *International Journal of Clinical and Experimental Hypnosis*, **55**, 220–247.

Chiesa, A., & Serretti, A. (2011). Mindfulness based cognitive therapy for psychiatric disorders: a systematic review and meta-analysis. *Psychiatry Research*, **187**(3), 441–453.

Cooper, P. C. (2010). *The Zen impulse and the psychoanalytic encounter*. New York: Routledge.

Dumont, L., Martin, C., & Broer, I. (2012). Functional neuroimaging studies of hypnosis and meditation: a comparative perspective. *Journal of Mind–Body Regulation*, **2**(1), 58–70.

Engler, J. (2003). Being somebody and being nobody: a re-examination of the understanding of self in psychoanalysis and Buddhism. In J. D. Safran (Ed.), *Psychoanalysis and Buddhism: an unfolding dialogue* (pp. 35–79). Boston: Wisdom Publications.

Epstein, M. (1986). Meditative transformations of narcissism. *Journal of Transpersonal Psychology*, *18*, 143–158.

Epstein, M. (1995). Thoughts without a thinker: Buddhism and psychoanalysis. *Psychoanalytic Inquiry*, *82*, 391–406.

Farb, N. A. (2012). Mind your expectations: exploring the roles of suggestion and intention in mindfulness raining. *Journal of Mind–Body Regulation*, **2**(1), 27–42.

Federn, P. (1952). *Ego psychology and the psychoses*. New York: Basic Books.

Flammer, E., & Bogartz, W. (2003). On the efficacy of hypnosis: a meta-analytic study. *Contemporary Hypnosis*, **20**, 179–197.

Freud, S. (2005). *Civilization and its discontents* (Standard Edition). New York: W. W. Norton & Co. (Original work published in 1930.)

Fromm, E. (1970). *Zen Buddhism and psychoanalysis*. Canada: Harper-Collins.

Goleman, D. (1988). *The meditative mind: the varieties of meditative experience*. New York: G. P. Putnam & Sons.

Grabovac, A. D., Lau, M. A., & Willett, B. R. (2011). Mechanisms of mindfulness: a Buddhist psychological model. *Mindfulness*, **2**, 154–166. doi:10.1007/s12671–12011–0054–5

Green, J. P., Barabasz, A. F., Barrett, D., &, Montgomery, G. (2005). Forging ahead: the 2003 APA Division 30 definition of hypnosis. *International Journal of Clinical and Experimental Hypnosis*, *53*(3), 259–264.

Grotstein, J. (1981). Bion the man, the psychoanalyst, and the mystic: a perspective on his life and work. In J. S. Grotstein (Ed.), *Do I dare disturb the universe? A memorial to Wilfred R. Bion*. Beverly Hills: Caesura Press.

Hanly, C. (1984). Ego ideal and ideal ego. *International Journal of Psychoanalysis*, **65**, 253–260.

Holroyd, J. (2003). The science of meditation and the state of hypnosis. *American Journal of Clinical Hypnosis*, **46**, 109–128.

Ivanovski, B., & Malhi, G. S. (2007). The psychological and neurophysiological concomitants of mindfulness forms of meditation. *Acta Neuropsychiatrica*, **19**, 76–91.

Lifshitz, M., Campbell, N. K. J., &, Raz, A. (2012). Varieties of attention in hypnosis and mindfulness. *Consciousness and Cognition*, **21**, 1582–1585.

Lifshitz, M., & Raz, A. (2012). Hypnosis and meditation: vehicles of attention and suggestion. *Journal of Mind–Body Regulation*, **2**(1), 3–11.

Mitchell, S. A., & Black, M. J. (1995). *Freud and beyond: a history of modern psychoanalytic thought*. New York: Basic Books.

Otani, A. (2003). Eastern meditative techniques and hypnosis: a new synthesis. *American Journal of Clinical Hypnosis, 46*, 97–108.

Parsons, W. B. (1999). *The enigma of the oceanic feeling: re-visioning the psychoanalytic theory of mysticism.* New York: Oxford University Press.

Preece, R. (2006). *The wisdom of imperfection.* Ithaca: Snow Lion Publications.

Rapgay, L., & Bystrisky, A. (2009). Classical mindfulness: an introduction to its theory and practice for clinical application. *Annals of the NY Academy of Science, 1172*, 148–162.

Rubin, J. B. (2003). Close encounters of a new kind: toward an integration of psychoanalysis and Buddhism. In S. R. Segall (Ed.), *Encountering Buddhism: Western psychology and Buddhist teachings* (pp. 31–60). Albany: State University of New York Press.

Safran, J. D. (2003). *Psychoanalysis and Buddhism: an unfolding dialogue.* Boston: Wisdom Publications.

Segal, Z., Williams, & Teasdale, J., (2002). *Mindfulness-based cognitive therapy for depression.* New York: Guilford Press.

Shapiro, S. L., & Carlson, L. E. (2009). *The art and science of mindfulness.* Washington DC: American Psychological Association.

Shapiro, S. L., Carlson, L. E., Astin, J. A., & Freedman, B. (2006). Mechanisms of mindfulness. *Journal of Clinical Psychology, 62*, 373–386.

Suler, J. R. (1993). *Contemporary psychoanalysis and Eastern thought.* Albany: SUNY Press.

Thera, N. (1973). *The heart of Buddhist meditation.* New York: Samuel Weiser.

Wallace, B. A. (1999). The Buddhist tradition of shamatha: methods for refining and examining consciousness. *Journal of Consciousness Studies, 6*(2–3), 175–187.

Watts, A. (1975). *Psychotherapy East and West.* New York: Vintage.

Welwood, J. (2000). Realisation and embodiment: psychological work in the service of spiritual development. In G. Watson, S. Batchelor, & G. Claxton (Eds.), *The psychology of awakening: Buddhism, science, and our day-to-day lives* (pp. 137–166). Boston: Weiser.

Wilber, K. (2007). *The integral vision.* Boston: Shambhala Publications.

Yapko, M. D. (2011). *Mindfulness and hypnosis: the power of suggestion to transform experience.* New York, NY: W. W. Norton & Co.

Chapter 23

When worlds combine: synthesizing hypnosis, mindfulness, and acceptance-based approaches to psychotherapy and smoking cessation

Steven Jay Lynn, Joseph P. Green, Victor Elinoff, Jessica Baltman, and Reed Maxwell

Abstract

The authors of this chapter contend that hypnosis, mindfulness, and acceptance-based approaches can be combined in a multifaceted smoking cessation intervention to take advantage of the unique characteristics of each approach in a comprehensive, empirically grounded, cognitive behavioral treatment. The authors review the theoretical and empirical literature that supports the combination of these approaches in a more encompassing intervention. The chapter highlights the potential benefits of a synergistic approach to treatment. It also provides readers with clinical strategies and excerpts of scripts derived from the intervention that the authors have developed and refined over the course of more than 25 years. The chapter concludes with a discussion of the complementary nature of hypnosis and mindfulness and avenues that researchers can pursue to further explore the integration of hypnosis, meditation, and acceptance-based strategies.

Introduction

In this chapter, we discuss how hypnosis, mindfulness, and acceptance-based approaches can be combined to capitalize on the unique characteristics of each approach in a comprehensive cognitive behavioral treatment. Our contribution extends previous publications that discussed how hypnosis, mindfulness, and acceptance-based approaches could be integrated in the treatment of depression (Lynn, Barnes, Deming, & Accardi, 2010) and post-traumatic stress disorder (Lynn, Malaktaris, Condon, Maxwell, & Cleere, 2012). Here, we consider a smoking cessation program we initially developed more than 25 years ago and have revised recently to include strategies that meld hypnosis and mindfulness in an empirically grounded, cognitive-behavioral intervention.

We begin with a discussion of hypnosis, followed by a consideration of meditation and acceptance-based approaches, and then summarize our efforts to integrate these disparate methods in a brief, cost-effective treatment to achieve smoking cessation. We conclude with a consideration of avenues that researchers can pursue to validate the components of our program and to explore the influence of attitudes, beliefs, and expectancies in relation to treatment dropout and retention.

An Introduction to Hypnosis

In the past three decades, and arguably longer, hypnosis has merged into the fast lane of psychological science and proved to be a unique crucible for examining psychological processes and mechanisms that encompass

(a) the influence of expectancies, beliefs, and attitudes on human behavior;

(b) suggestibility;

(c) attention, fantasy, and imagination;

(d) the role of rapport in relationships; and

(e) memory, automaticity, and spontaneous versus goal-directed thought (see Lynn, Rhue, & Kirsch, 2010; Nash & Barnier, 2008).

Concurrently, clinicians have increasingly incorporated hypnosis into empirically supported psychotherapies (e.g., Alladin, 2008; Green, Laurence, & Lynn, 2014; Kroger & Yapko, 2007), while researchers have dispelled treatment-interfering myths and misconceptions regarding hypnosis and conducted studies that document the promise of hypnosis to catalyze a wide assortment of psychotherapies and modify consciousness in often profound ways. Qualitative reviews and meta-analytic studies consistently report the effectiveness or promise of hypnosis in treating a wide variety of psychological and medical conditions ranging from acute and chronic pain to obesity and irritable bowel syndrome (Covino & Pinnell, 2010; Elkins, Jensen, & Patterson, 2007; Flammer & Alladin, 2007; Flammer & Bongartz, 2003; Flory, Martinez Salazar, & Lang, 2007; Lynn, Kirsch, Barabasz, Cardena, & Patterson, 2000; Lynn, Rhue, & Kirsch, 2010; Neron & Stephenson, 2007), and meta-analyses have shown that hypnosis enhances the effectiveness of both psychodynamic and cognitive behavioral psychotherapies (Kirsch, 1990; Kirsch, Montgomery, & Sapirstein,1995).

Although hypnosis is not typically used as a stand-alone therapy, a suggestive approach has immense potential to facilitate therapeutic interventions for many reasons. Hypnosis affords clinicians vast opportunities to channel spontaneous, involuntary thoughts (Smallwood & Schooler, 2006) that characterize much of our waking (and sleeping) consciousness in useful directions, and to challenge maladaptive schemas and reinforce adaptive schemas that relate to the self and others, past events, and future possibilities. Hypnotic suggestions are a potent means to create positive response expectancies and response sets that influence our sense of what we are capable of accomplishing in line with valued goals and activities (Kirsch & Lynn, 1999; Lynn & Kirsch, 2006). As our self-image, ideas of what is possible or impossible for ourselves, and our reactions to social stimuli often become automatized, we cease to believe that "things can be any different than the way they are." As Erickson, Rossi, and Rossi (1976) state so cogently, therapeutic hypnosis occurs when

> the limitations of one's usual conscious sets and belief systems are temporarily altered so that one can be receptive to an experience of other patterns of association and modes of mental functioning . . . that are usually experienced as involuntary by the patient (p. 20).

Hypnosis may be useful in either automatizing or de-automatizing behaviors, depending on the suggestions delivered (see Chapter 11). As we have suggested elsewhere (Lynn, Das, Hallquist, & Williams, 2006), hypnotic suggestions may not only interrupt or de-automatize unhealthy habits of thought and automatic response sets (e.g., rumination), they also may create positive response sets that prepare cognitive and behavioral schemas or scripts for efficient (automatic) activation when triggered or activated by internal (e.g., sensations or moods) or external stimuli (Kirsch & Lynn, 1997, 1998). For example, suggestions can be provided for individuals to observe and interrupt and, thereby, de-automatize their habitual negative behaviors by becoming cognizant of the first sign of an urge to smoke, and engaging in distracting, urge-interfering behaviors. Alternately, suggestions can be provided for individuals to automatically experience relaxation when they feel an urge to smoke. Whether it is easier to automatize or de-automatize an ongoing chain of behavior has yet to be determined on an experimental basis.

The long-debated question of whether one must be in an altered or special state of consciousness to achieve the benefits of hypnotherapy becomes moot to the extent that we acknowledge that ordinary consciousness reflects perpetual changes in our mental state: shifts of awareness, emotions, thoughts, sensations, and action tendencies are the rule, rather than the exception (Lynn, Kirsch, Knox, & Lilienfeld, 2006). Hypnosis can thus be a potent way to steer the constant flux of mental associations and response tendencies toward targeted therapeutic ends in a goal-directed, planned manner.

Therapeutic hypnosis proceeds on the optimistic assumption that human consciousness is pliable and that suggestions can be used both to structure (or restructure) our imaginings, experiences, and personal narratives, and to access and make salient our latent or dormant personal resources to solve problems and better one's life. To provide a few examples, therapists can marshal personal resources by restructuring

(a) current experiences by transforming tension into relaxation and providing graded exposure to anxiety-provoking experiences,

(b) past experiences through reframing of negative memories and selective focus on positive memories and mastery experiences, and

(c) future experiences by way of imaginative rehearsal, goal setting, and imagining alternative actions in target situations.

Because much psychopathology can be conceptualized in terms of negative self-suggestions (e.g., catastrophic thoughts about the future in anxiety disorders and negative views of the self and the past in depression; Aladdin & Alibhai, 2007; Lynn & Kirsch, 2006), a suggestive approach that identifies and targets negative self-suggestions, and replaces them with positive self-talk, can be valuable (Yapko, 2011, 2013). Hypnotic suggestions can also be useful in regulating emotions, as situational triggers of maladaptive or excessive reactions (i.e., stressors) in everyday life can be identified, and suggestions can be provided for alternative ways of reacting to such stressors. For example, patients can first engage in *response modulation* (Ritschel & Ramirez, 2015) in the face of stressors by learning to relax (e.g., release tension) via suggestion and then associating such relaxation with a cue word or phrase (e.g., calm and at ease, let it go) or physical gesture, such as touching two fingers together or forming a circle with the thumb and forefinger (so-called anchoring). These cognitive and behavioral strategies can then be enacted in the face of the stressor, along with suggestions for reappraising the stressor to downregulate negative emotions (see Butler, Chapman, Forman, & Beck, 2006). People who are able to reappraise negative situations report greater self-esteem, optimism, and life satisfaction (Gross & John, 2003). Hypnosis practitioners can implement strategies that minimize negative emotion and maximize positive emotion (i.e., hedonically oriented), along with strategies that move people toward their goals (i.e., goal-oriented; Koole, 2009).

Fortunately, most suggestions that are used in a therapeutic context, such as for relaxation or imaginative rehearsal, are relatively easy for patients to experience (Barber, 1985), so most individuals are able to achieve quick and sometimes dramatic success, even upon their first exposure to hypnosis. This simple fact can have enormous treatment implications: if one can experience "new things" and clear-cut alterations in the perception of "reality" during hypnosis, why not outside the consulting room? If patients are prisoners of negative self-suggestions and habitualized ways of responding to life's challenges, then perhaps they can rewrite stagnant and unworkable narratives and develop a scaffolding of more healthy suggestions for a better life. In short, a suggestive approach can provide a sense of reality-based optimism about the possibility of change and provide a means to formulate and actively engage with a network of suggestions that facilitates experiential learning and attaining valued goals.

The use of hypnosis in cognitive behavioral therapy (CBT) interventions can be traced to the early pioneers of CBT (Goldfried & Davison, 1976; Lazarus, 1973; Wolpe, 1958) who recognized the power of the hypnotic context to enhance treatment expectancies and promote relaxation (Lazarus, 1999). The mere description of treatment procedures as "hypnotic" conveys favorable expectations of treatment success based on widespread positive beliefs regarding the ability of hypnosis to produce impressive changes in consciousness (Barber, 1985). Additionally, the hypnotic context provides opportunities to detach from mundane concerns and tasks and focus, instead, on therapeutic images, thoughts, and suggestions. Indeed, a marriage between hypnosis and CBT is eminently sensible insofar as hypnotic interventions are well suited to engender the very sorts of changes CBT is designed to produce—alterations in cognitions, behaviors, and emotions (see also Alladin, 2008; Chapman, 2005; Lynn et al., 2012). The expectancy-enhancing ability of hypnosis also implies that it would be of potential benefit in multi-component treatment packages and would be amenable to integration with an eclectic assortment of methods, which brings us to the topic of implementing hypnosis, mindfulness, and acceptance-based approaches in a single psychotherapy.

Meditation, Mindfulness, and Hypnosis

As hypnosis has moved more centrally into the scientific mainstream than ever before, meditation, mindfulness, and acceptance-based practices have captured the public and the scientific imagination. Over the past five years, meditation has mushroomed in popularity: in a 2007 national survey, 9.4% of 23,393 adults sampled reported that they had meditated in the past 12 months, compared with 7.6% in a similar survey conducted in 2002 (Barnes, Bloom, & Nahin, 2008). Those surveyed reported that they meditated to ameliorate pain, anxiety, depression, stress, insomnia, and symptoms associated with chronic illnesses. Scientific evidence supports these anecdotal accounts. Over the past decade or so, a sizable corpus of data has amassed showing that meditation can be successfully applied to promote psychological health, enhance coping and resilience, alleviate pain, and reduce stress (see Malaktaris, Lemons, Lynn, & Condon, 2015 for a review).

Like hypnosis, meditation involves an array of practices. In the case of hypnosis, the diversity of suggestive methods that can be used is virtually limitless, yet they all qualify as "hypnotic" when they are presented to patients as "hypnotic" in nature (e.g., a relaxation protocol is introduced as "hypnosis"), thereby accessing relevant socio-cognitive beliefs, attitudes, and expectancies regarding hypnosis. Meditation, too, encompasses diverse practices, and most can be described as "an effort to train the mind through the cultivation of mindful awareness and attention to the present moment" (Das, 1997, p. 260). Like hypnosis, meditation is a self-regulation practice that

(a) accesses and focuses attentional resources;

(b) invites non-judgmental acceptance of the contents of consciousness (suggested or not) and absorption in the world of experience; and

(c) implicitly or explicitly discourages focusing attention on extraneous stimuli that compete with task demands (Lynn, Das, Hallquist, & Williams, 2006; Shapiro, 2008).

Notably, some degree of attentional flexibility is involved in successful response to hypnotic suggestions and meditation (Davidson & Goleman, 1977; Gruzelier, Gray, & Horn, 2002; MacLeod, 2011), and meditation may, in turn, enhance cognitive flexibility and attentional functions (Moore & Malinoski, 2009).

In mindfulness-based meditation and other mindfulness approaches, which is our focus in this chapter, the prime directive is to attend to (be mindful of) the ebb and flow of consciousness; that is, to let thoughts, sensations, memories, images, and feelings pass through awareness without judgment, avoidance, or active suppression. In Vipassana, or insight meditation, the contents of consciousness may be labeled and ascribed to categories such as sensations, thoughts, and memories to acquire greater objectivity and distance from what spontaneously bubbles up in the stream of consciousness. Other meditative traditions (e.g., transcendental meditation; Barnes & Orme-Johnson, 2012) use a mantra (word, phrase, sound repeated silently) to minimize distracting thoughts, or suggest to practitioners that they focus on unconditional compassion and kindness to all beings, often extending to wishing for the peace, happiness, health, and well-being of strangers and even enemies (i.e., loving- kindness/compassion meditation; Fredrickson, Cohn, Coffey, Pek, & Finkel, 2008).

Each of these traditions is grounded in suggestions that guide the practice (Yapko, 2011; see also Chapter 19). So in this sense, hypnosis and meditation both fall under the broad domain of suggestive approaches, although in meditation the suggestions for practice are, naturally, not administered in a hypnotic context (Lynn, Malaktaris, Maxwell, Mellinger, & van der Kloet, 2012). The subjective effects of hypnosis and meditation will thus likely vary with the specific suggestions/instructions administered, as well as individuals' willingness and ability to respond to task demands (Lynn et al., 2006).

This similarity aside, mindfulness meditation and hypnosis diverge not only in the context established, but also in their aims. In the case of hypnosis, the aim is to think, imagine, and feel, along with whatever the hypnotist suggests (or self-administered suggestions); and in the case of mindfulness meditation, the aim is to simply be aware of whatever passes through the field of awareness, with an attitude of patience, tolerance, and willingness to experience whatever arises in an open, accepting, curious, and non-judgmental manner. In the latter case, there is no imperative to think, feel, or act in any particular way, merely to "observe and accept" without steering the course of conscious experience (Kerr, Josyula, & Littenberg, 2011). Thus, in mindfulness practice, attention is self-directed, whereas in traditional hypnosis it is typically directed externally by the hypnotist/hypnotic suggestions (Lynn, Malaktaris, Maxwell, et al., 2012). In self-hypnosis, however, suggestions are self-generated and attention is typically directed internally.

Moreover, suggestions to experience mindfulness are geared to facilitate meta or observational awareness—being aware of being aware—which, ideally, is accomplished in a conscious, self-directed, deliberate manner. In contrast, the passive wording of hypnotic suggestions and the hypnotic context collaborate to dampen awareness of the fact that responding to suggestions is often self-initiated; in hypnosis, participants often (mistakenly) attribute the influence of suggestions to the hypnotist and experience suggested effects as arising automatically or involuntarily (see Lynn, Rhue, & Weekes, 1990; Lynn, Snodgrass, Rhue, Nash, & Frauman, 1987). As Semmens-Wheeler and Dienes (2012) have argued, "hypnosis is a form of self-deception, whereas meditation is a way of getting to know your mind" (p. 43; see also Chapter 7).

The differences between hypnosis and mindfulness we have alluded to may well account for the fact that practice in meditation does not appear to increase hypnotic responsiveness, nor do hypnotic suggestibility and meditation appear to be related substantially (see Lynn et al., 2006). In fact, in one study, individuals who were highly suggestible were less likely to be compliant with mantra meditation practice, three months following training, than their less suggestible counterparts (Delmonte, 1988). Accordingly, by combining hypnosis and meditation in treatment, it may be possible for a broader clientele to benefit from one, if not both, of the methods (e.g., a low hypnotizable person may, nevertheless, benefit from meditation). Moreover, when hypnosis is used as a context for providing mindfulness instructions as suggestions, as is the case in our smoking cessation program described here, hypnosis may potentially enhance the effectiveness of mindfulness instructions, just as the hypnotic context has been shown to enhance the effectiveness of CBT when instructions are worded as hypnotic suggestions (see Kirsch et al., 1995).

One advantage of mindfulness meditation, with its prescription for acceptance and nonjudgment, is that it can mitigate experiential avoidance—the often reflexive tendency to avoid thoughts and feelings related to aversive internal or external experiences (Chawla & Ostafin, 2007). Much psychopathology is rooted in experiential avoidance. Indeed, according to the DSM-5 diagnostic criteria for mental disorders, some form of avoidance is implicated in avoidant personality disorder, obsessive compulsive disorder, phobia, post-traumatic stress disorder, and substance dependence (Williams & Lynn, 2010). As B. F. Skinner (1972) keenly observed, the "time and energy consumed in the avoidance of punishment" could be freed up for "more reinforcing activities" (p. 76). More perniciously, attempts to suppress unwanted thoughts and emotions often paradoxically increase their frequency and attendant distress (Beevers, Wenzlaff, Hayes, & Scott, 1999; Gross & Levenson, 1993; Wegner, 1989, 2011) and can increase aversive physiological arousal (Campbell-Sills, Barlow, Brown, & Hofmann, 2006).

Relatedly, emotional non-acceptance—the tendency to evaluate emotions as bad or wrong (Gratz, Bomovalova, Delaney-Brumsey, Nick, & Lejuez, 2007, p. 257)—is associated with excessive feelings of guilt, shame, and anxiety (Salters-Pedneault, Tull, & Roemer, 2004). Mindfulness practice suggestions promote emotional acceptance and encourage individuals to detach or decenter from the implication that a particular thought carries with it the demand to act on it or to be embraced unquestionably as a defining measure of the self (e.g., because a person thinks he is unlovable, does not signify the person is in fact unlovable). In mindfulness terms, "a thought is just a thought" and "a feeling is just a feeling" to be aware of, and need be nothing more. In other words, internal events such as thoughts and feelings are merely events that occur within the self; they are not the self (Williams, Hallquist, Cole, Barnes, & Lynn, 2010). Of course, certain thoughts and feelings may demand attention at some time when they pertain to a situation that requires problem solving and/or implementing immediate coping measures in everyday life.

Given the potential benefits of mindfulness meditation, which encompass enhanced positive emotions, decreased reactivity to thoughts and emotions, diminished rumination and negative affect, and increased response flexibility (Davis & Hayes, 2011), it is not surprising that it is now a part of an expanding number of cognitive behavioral techniques that include acceptance and commitment therapy (ACT; Hayes, Strosahl, & Wilson, 1999), dialectical behavior therapy (DBT; Linehan, 1993), mindfulness-based stress reduction (MBSR; Kabat-Zinn, 2003), mindfulness-based cognitive therapy (MBCT; Segal, Williams, & Teasdale, 2002), and integrative behavioral couple therapy (IBCT; Christensen, Jacobson, & Babcock, 1995).

Integrating hypnosis, mindfulness, and acceptance: the Winning Edge Program

We can see that in many respects, mindfulness meditation is distinct from hypnosis. Yet we will see, in the following sections, that hypnosis and mindfulness meditation can be complementary. To this end, we turn our attention to our hypnosis and smoking cessation program that illustrates how a suite of cognitive behavioral interventions can be integrated with suggestions for mindfulness and acceptance.

Tobacco smoking is the leading preventable cause of premature mortality and morbidity. Each year, in the USA alone, approximately 440,000 people die of a smoking-attributable illness. Smoking accounts for 89% of all lung cancer mortalities, and also contributes significantly to mortality rates for other cancers and illnesses such as pulmonary and cardiovascular disease (CDC, 2001). Smoking cessation, in turn, is associated with decreased mortality and morbidity—for example, ex-smokers reduce their excess lung cancer risk by up to 50% within ten years of quitting. With close to a billion people worldwide still smoking, it is imperative to develop cost-effective treatments that promote long-term abstinence.

One advantage of using hypnosis is that it is a popular method that may overcome resistance to partake in smoking cessation treatment. In one survey (Sood, Ebbert, Sood, & Stevens, 2006) of 1117 patients at an outpatient tobacco treatment specialty clinic, 27% reported that they used complementary and alternative medicine techniques such as hypnosis, relaxation, and acupuncture. Respondents indicated that the treatment of greatest interest for use in the future was hypnosis.

The two-session program we present has its roots in a single-session program for smoking cessation developed by the senior author (SJL) with Victor Neufeld. The program was devised at the invitation of the American Lung Association of Ohio and designed to present material from the "Freedom from Smoking" program in a single-session format with an added component of self-hypnosis. The initial treatment was effective in achieving self-reported continuous abstinence of 18.5% at 6-month follow-up (Neufeld & Lynn, 1988). Beginning in 1992, Lynn and Green expanded the protocol into a two-session cognitive behavioral treatment. A recent randomized trial (Carmody et al., 2008) that recruited a larger sample (N = 286) of current smokers at the San Francisco Veterans' Affairs Medical Center, and used biochemical confirmation, evaluated the effects of hypnosis based on a protocol we developed some time ago (Green, 1996, 1999; Lynn, Neufeld, Rhue, & Matorin, 1993). The researchers compared hypnosis with standard behavioral counseling when both interventions were combined with nicotine patches.

At 6 months, 29% of the hypnosis group reported 7-day point-prevalence abstinence, compared with 23% of the behavioral counseling group. Based on biochemical or proxy confirmation, 26% of the individuals in the hypnosis group were abstinent at 6 months, compared with 18% of the behavioral group. At 12 months, the self-reported 7-day point-prevalence quit rate was 24% for the hypnosis group and 16% for the behavioral group, with proxy or biochemical confirmation of 20% of the hypnosis participants compared with 14% of the behavioral group. Interestingly, participants with depression exhibited higher (statistically significant) validated point-prevalence quit rates at 6- and 12-month follow-up in the hypnosis versus counseling group, and the number of dropouts was lower in the hypnosis group.

Since the Carmody et al. (2008) research, our program has been revised numerous times. We have restructured our protocol in significant respects, aligning interventions more closely with the current literature on CBT and hypnosis, and, most recently, incorporating mindfulness-based and acceptance strategies.

The Winning Edge Program: session 1

Session 1 provides participants with an introduction to the program, educational information, cognitive behavioral strategies for smoking cessation, brief mindfulness training, and a self-hypnosis exercise. We review the history of the program, its basis in empirical research, and explain why our program will give participants the "winning edge" in achieving smoking cessation for life. We then play a video clip in which a physician conveys accurate information regarding health risks of smoking with encouragement to not smoke. A Cochrane Review (Lancaster & Stead, 2004) concluded that even brief physician advice produces a small (2.5%) yet meaningful increase in the odds of quitting. A recent meta-analysis (Lai, Cahill, Qin, & Tang, 2010) revealed that motivational enhancement techniques produce gains in smoking cessation when delivered by a physician.

We emphasize the importance of motivation, self-efficacy, visualizing success, and obtaining social support, and we debunk the myth that people universally experience severe withdrawal. Participants complete a "*strength of the habit*" worksheet and calculate the number of times that they have raised a cigarette to their mouth. They also complete a "*reasons to stop smoking*" worksheet and create wallet-sized reminder cards of why they wish to stop smoking and initiate a behavioral contract during the first session to signify their intention to stop smoking. Participants learn cue-controlled relaxation and how to anchor (i.e., with a cue word or touching their thumb and fore-finger together) feelings of empowerment, determination, and success. We discuss the importance of identifying triggers associated with smoking, and provide participants with cognitive behavioral strategies that include stimulus-control procedures, stress management, relapse prevention (e.g., identifying and avoiding high-risk situations), and countering irrational thinking, cognitive distortions, and widespread erroneous beliefs regarding smoking cessation (e.g., emotional reasoning— "because I feel like I am a failure, I am a failure"; black/white thinking; inevitable weight gain).

Mindfulness and acceptance play a pivotal role in managing urges and negative mood in our program, the latter being essential to quit smoking endeavors (Sayette, 2004). Recently, we modified our program to reflect innovations in CBT, with an emphasis on experiential acceptance, and share with participants that attempts to suppress negative feelings are not as effective as accepting that they will arise and pass, and acting in keeping with needs and values—in this case, refraining from smoking and becoming "a non-smoker for life." We noted that a smoking cessation program based on urge management and acceptance produced better outcomes at 1-year follow-up than nicotine replacement therapy (Gifford, Kohlenberg, Hayes, Antonuccio, & Piasecki, 2004; see also Marlatt, 1994).

We introduce participants to mindfulness practice by inviting them to close their eyes for 5 minutes and be mindful of the changing thoughts and feelings they experience, while letting them come and go in awareness without judgment. We state that our experience of life comes largely from the wellspring of spontaneous, involuntary thoughts that course through our minds, and that we need not react to the changing contents of consciousness. Further, we can decouple our thoughts, feelings, and actions and make decisions about what to do, or not do, based on our values and goals (i.e., to stop smoking). We further inform participants that should they encounter discouraging and self-deprecating thoughts regarding their efforts to stop smoking, they can observe them and watch them pass out of awareness; it is best to view such typically transient phenomena as "merely thoughts" that need have no bearing on their behavior. We point out that even brief mindfulness training (1 hour total) can result in reductions in heart rate, depression, fatigue, and negative mood (Zeidan, Johnson, Gordon, & Goolkasian, 2010) and ask participants to practice mindful, non-judgmental awareness of their experience for 10–20 minutes each day, either sitting quietly or in the midst of everyday life, in the week between session 1 and 2.

We also introduce urge management in this session. We use the metaphor of a person in a tug of war with a monster (in this case, the urge to smoke) holding onto a rope that spans a deep pit. Rather than continue the struggle and risk a rather unpleasant encounter with the bottom of the pit, so the story goes, the best solution is to let the rope drop (accept the urge) and go on with life. To the extent that participants are prepared for urges to well up, they need not view them as a threat to curtail their stop smoking efforts. Rather, urges are to be accepted as a part of the quitting process and not to be feared or perceived as intimidating. We suggest that participants be mindful of their thoughts and feelings, including their intention to cease smoking, and that should an urge arise, they are to observe it carefully as it changes in intensity and eventually passes out of awareness. We describe this process as "surfing the urge," riding its wave and seeing the wave blend into the expanse of the ocean, no longer distinguishable from the ever-changing sea (see Marlatt, 2002; Ostafin & Marlatt, 2008). As participants surf the urge, they also focus on their reasons to stop smoking.

We then review the benefits of nicotine replacement therapy (NRT) and provide summary sheets about NRT products. We inform participants that the combination of CBT and pharmacotherapy produces abstinence rates that are up to double those of either approach alone (Fiore, 2008; Hughes, 1995).

Participants complete a "*rewards worksheet*" listing their short- and long-term rewards for successfully achieving their goal. The session proceeds with a video "testimonial" of a coping model who describes the successful use of CBT.

At the close of the first session, participants learn more about self-hypnosis and discuss myths associated with hypnosis. They are informed that they are always in control and can choose to respond or not to respond to any suggestion. In another video clip, the same coping model briefly describes her success using self-hypnosis.

We then present a short 12–15 minute self-hypnosis exercise. The hypnosis script guides the client through several visualization exercises focusing on empowerment, serenity, and self-efficacy. In sessions 1 and 2, we use hypnosis to suggest that participants "breathe in" acceptance, self-compassion, and breathe out judgment, self-criticism, and negative emotions. Themes of self-preservation, health, and longevity are interspersed with suggestions to prioritize behaviors and goals in an attempt to live a life consistent with personal values. Participants also receive suggestions to reinforce mindfulness practice.

We suggest a "one step at a time" approach in which stopping smoking is the highest priority, so as not to inflate demands for self-control (Baumeister, Heatherton, & Tice, 1994). We also discuss behavioral strategies to minimize weight gain during smoking cessation.

We provide participants with a CD (or home access to an online audio file) for home practice of hypnosis and mindfulness. Additionally, we provide a DVD recapitulating the first session, virtually word for word, and encourage participants to review the DVD at home, with a significant other, to both consolidate their knowledge about the program and also to invite social support from someone who will encourage them to complete the program.

The Winning Edge Program: session 2

The second session begins with a review of the previous week (e.g., review of self-reward sheets; plan to avoid trigger situations and substitute smoking with more healthy behaviors; discuss mindfulness, self-hypnosis experiences). We provide time for personal reflection and explore what circumstances may have provided the impetus to smoke in the first place. We briefly review key components identified in the first session, with additional attention paid to stress management and relapse prevention.

The centerpiece of the second session is an expanded self-hypnosis session (lasting approximately 25–30 minutes). We use hypnosis to:

(a) crystallize reasons for stopping smoking;

(b) enhance self-efficacy;

(c) facilitate acceptance, mindfulness, and urge management;

(d) imaginatively rehearse resisting smoking in high-risk situations;

(e) imagine scenes where one successfully resists the urge to smoke and instead chooses an alternative, more healthy behavior;

(f) suggest sensory awakening of taste and smell following smoking cessation;

(g) teach cue-controlled relaxation (anchoring) in stressful situations;

(h) redefine image of self from a "smoker" to a "non-smoker," and visualize self as a non-smoker in a variety of situations, with people complimenting one for being a non-smoker;

(i) suggest mindful eating and enjoyment of eating in moderation;

(j) review plans for action;

(k) increase motivation to take valued action pertaining to one's health; and

(l) give examples of how to deal with counterproductive and self-defeating thoughts.

Throughout the session, participants are instructed to go "just as deep" as they would like to go in their experience of hypnosis.

An important element of this session builds on mindfulness/acceptance-based urge management strategies introduced in session 1. The following is an excerpt of suggestions provided during hypnosis:

> Now we'll focus on how to manage any urges to smoke that may come up and practice self-compassion. Get in touch with your kindness . . . your caring . . . and direct this kindness and caring inward, toward yourself. Practice self-compassion. Smoking urges are normal when you make the commitment to stop smoking. Get in touch with a deep sense of compassion that you can direct toward yourself, a kindness toward yourself, a caring directed toward yourself. And in this framework of kindness and caring allow yourself to be kind and caring even if an occasional urge should arise. And if you feel an urge to smoke, flow with it . . . notice how it can come and can go. Ride any urge out . . . observe it . . . breathe it out. Let it exit your body with each breath, more and more, more and more, notice it happen. Let it leave your body, just as it came. Leave your mind. Let it go. Breathe it out. Take a breath; breathe it out. Ride it like a wave . . . surf it . . . notice how it may change in intensity and how it passes . . . it just leaves, it just goes, as you go on with your life with the knowledge that you don't have to smoke . . . no need to do so. Go on with your life . . . without smoking. Live your life. Live it with compassion, kindness, acceptance, and caring for yourself . . . for your body. If an urge comes, breathe it out of your body . . . observe it, and let it go . . . it will pass . . . it will pass . . . trust that it will pass . . . no need to act on it, no need at all . . . it will pass . . . remember your commitment to respect your body . . . to take care of yourself . . . the urge will pass, surf it, ride it out, and it will pass. Keep in mind that you are your body's keeper . . . and you can do so many things besides smoking . . . any urge will pass. You ride the urge like a wave . . . a wave that flows into the water and exists no more once it leaves you . . . just let it flow away . . . fade away . . . go away . . . you can ride it out . . . you can choose not to smoke as you focus on your reasons to stop smoking. If an urge should arise after our session, watch the urge fade, let it come and feel it go. And with each urge that comes up and you mindfully watch, let pass in and out of your awareness, the pull of the urge becomes less strong, as your mind learns that you need not react to the urge. Learning more and more . . . more and more . . . you know that you need not smoke just because you have an urge to do so, more and more learning, more and more caring for yourself, preserving your health, your well-being, mindful of who you are in the moment, accepting, letting thoughts come and go, accepting the negative with the positive, the positive with the negative, all just a part of your thought stream, as you focus more and more on your values, what is truly important, being, becoming, being a non-smoker for life, with each urge you resist . . . more and more as you go deeper and deeper with a commitment to preserve your health and well-being as your experiences come and go.

At the close of the program, we hold a "*goal achievement ceremony*" in which clients are invited to throw away old cigarettes or some other smoking-related paraphernalia and announce that they are a "*non-smoker, forever!*" Finally, participants receive a CD that recapitulates the script of the second session and are encouraged to use the tools they acquired to achieve their goal of becoming a non-smoker.

When worlds combine: hypnosis and mindfulness

Our program illustrates just a few of the ways that hypnosis and mindfulness can be combined. Elsewhere, we have provided illustrations of how mindfulness practices can be used to orient focus on moment-to-moment experiences to break the grip of rumination in depression (Lynn et al., 2010) and counter flashback experiences in post-traumatic stress disorder (Lynn, Malaktaris, Condon, et al., 2012). Hypnosis, in turn, can be used to reinforce mindfulness practice, an attitude of compassion, acceptance of self and others, and tolerance both for when the mind wanders during practice and for troubling feelings regarding situations that cannot be changed (Lynn, Das, Hallquist, & Williams, 2006).

We have seen here how hypnosis can also be used to facilitate cognitive behavioral strategies through establishing a positive expectational context, reinforcing and repeating key elements of treatment, and encouraging both the use of imagination (where appropriate) and feelings of self-efficacy. Whereas hypnosis encourages experiential engagement with suggestions, meditation trains participants in metacognition or what is called cognitive defusion (Hayes & Wilson, 2003)—witnessing yet distancing and detaching from thoughts and feelings that pass through consciousness while maintaining a present focus that is often lacking or degraded in psychological disorders and conditions. Accordingly, hypnosis and mindfulness methods are highly complementary and convenient for practitioners to include in cognitive behavioral treatment packages. Whether their inclusion in comprehensive interventions makes a difference in treatment outcome can be determined only by research that dismantles the full treatment and examines the separate and interactive effects of individual components (i.e., mindfulness and hypnosis).

Preliminary studies suggest that, as we have taken care to do in our smoking cessation program, engendering positive expectations and positive beliefs regarding meditation can contribute to enhanced treatment outcomes (Delmonte, 1985) and perhaps minimize dropout (Delmonte, 1981), which can be as high as 54% after 2 years of meditation practice (Delmonte, 1988). Studies that examine particular beliefs that are associated with persistence in meditating, including doubts (i.e., cognitive and physical challenges; Sears, Kraus, Carlough, & Treat, 2011) and ignorance regarding the benefits of meditation (Gryffin, Chen, & Erengue, 2014), preexisting psychopathology (Frewen, Lundberg, MacKinley, & Wrath, 2011; Smith, 1978), and personality traits (Beaubouef, 2011; Delmonte, 1988; Rivers & Spanos, 1981), will be important to conduct. It will also be worthwhile to compare dropout rates in mindfulness meditation practices versus hypnosis/self-hypnosis and to determine whether different or similar variables predict dropout across both practices.

There is certainly much to learn about hypnosis and mindfulness and how they can be combined skillfully in the context of empirically supported interventions. Nevertheless, we believe that there exists sufficient reason for clinicians to incorporate both methods in psychotherapy, as the potential benefits outweigh the relatively small costs of integrating these brief and highly portable interventions into more comprehensive treatments.

References

Aladdin, A., & Alibhai, A. (2007). Cognitive hypnotherapy for depression: an empirical investigation. *International Journal of Clinical and Experimental Hypnosis*, **55**(2), 147–166.

Alladin, A. (2008). *Cognitive hypnotherapy: an integrated approach to the treatment of emotional disorders.* Chichester, UK: John Wiley.

Barber, T. X. (1985). Hypnosuggestive procedures as catalysts for psychotherapies. In S. J. Lynn & J. P. Garske (Eds.), *Contemporary psychotherapies: models and methods* (pp. 333–376). Columbus, OH: Charles E. Merril.

Barnes, P. M., Bloom, B., & Nahin, R. L. (2008). Complementary and alternative medicine use among adults and children: United States, 2007. *National Health Statistics Reports*, **12**, 1–24.

Barnes, V. A., & Orme-Johnson, D. W. (2012). Prevention and treatment of cardiovascular disease in adolescents and adults through the transcendental meditation® program: a research review update. *Current Hypertension Reviews*, **8**(3), 227.

Baumeister, R. F., Heatherton, T. F., & Tice, D. M. (1994). *Losing control: How and why people fail at self-regulation*. New York: Academic Press.

Beaubouef, M. E. (2011). *Meditation attitudes and the likelihood to meditate*. (Master's thesis). Available from ProQuest Dissertations and Theses database. (UMI No. 1502396).

Beevers, C. G., Wenzlaff, R. M., Hayes, A. M., & Scott, W. D. (1999). Depression and the ironic effects of thought suppression. *Clinical Psychology: Science and Practice*, 6(2), 133–148.

Butler, A. C., Chapman, J. E., Forman, E. M., & Beck, A. T. (2006). The empirical status of cognitive-behavioral therapy: a review of meta-analyses. *Clinical Psychology Review*, **26**(1), 17–31.

Campbell-Sills, L., Barlow, D. H., Brown, T. A., & Hofmann, S. G. (2006). Effects of suppression and acceptance on emotional responses of individuals with anxiety and mood disorders. *Behaviour Research and Therapy*, 44, 1251–1263.

Carmody, T. P., Duncan, C., Simon, J. A., Solkowitz, S., Huggins, J., Lee, S., & Delucchi, K. (2008). Hypnosis for smoking cessation: a randomized trial. *Nicotine and Tobacco Research*, **10**(5), 811–818.

Centers for Disease Control and Prevention (CDC). (2003). Cigarette smoking among adults—United States, 2001. *Morbidity and Mortality Weekly Report*, **52**(40), 953–956.

Chapman, R. A. (2005). The clinical use of hypnosis in cognitive behavior therapy: a practitioner's casebook. New York: Springer Publishing Company.

Chawla, N., & Ostafin, B. (2007). Experiential avoidance as a functional dimensional approach to psychopathology: an empirical review. *Journal of Clinical Psychology*, **63**(9), 871–890.

Christensen, A., Jacobson, N. S., & Babcock, J. C. (1995). *Integrative behavioral couple therapy*. New York: Guilford Press.

Covino, N. A., & Pinnell, C. (2010). Hypnosis and medicine. In S.J. Lynn, J.W. Rhue, & I. Kirsch (Eds.), *Handbook of clinical hypnosis* (pp. 551–574). Washington, DC: American Psychological Association.

Das, L. S. (1997). *Awakening the Buddha within*. New York: Broadway Books.

Davidson, R. J., & Goleman, D. J. (1977). The role of attention in meditation and hypnosis: a psychobiological perspective on transformations of consciousness. International Journal of Clinical and Experimental Hypnosis, 25(4), 291–308.

Davis, D. M., & Hayes, J. A. (2011). What are the benefits of mindfulness? A practice review of psychotherapy-related research. *Psychotherapy*, **48**(2), 198–208.

Delmonte, M. M. (1981). Expectation and meditation. *Psychological Reports*, **49**, 699– 709.

Delmonte, M. M. (1985). Effects of expectancy on physiological responsivity in novice meditators. *Biological Psychiatry*, **21**, 107–121.

Delmonte, M. M. (1988). Personality correlates of meditation practice frequency and dropout in an out-patient population. *Journal of Behavioral Medicine*, **11**(6), 593–597.

Elkins, G., Jensen, M. P., & Patterson, D. R. (2007). Hypnotherapy for the management of chronic pain. *International Journal of Clinical and Experimental Hypnosis*, **55**, 275–287.

Erickson, M. H., Rossi, E. L., & Rossi, S. I. (1976). *Hypnotic realities: the induction of hypnosis and forms of indirect suggestions*. New York: Irvington.

Fiore, M. (2008). *Treating tobacco use and dependence: 2008 update. Clinical practice guideline*. Darby, PA: DIANE Publishing.

Flammer, E., & Alladin, A. (2007). The efficacy of hypnotherapy in the treatment of psychosomatic disorders: meta-analytical evidence. *International Journal of Clinical and Experimental Hypnosis*, **55**(3), 251–274. doi:10.1080/00207140701338696

Flammer, E., & Bongartz, W. (2003). On the efficacy of hypnosis: a meta-analytic study. *Contemporary Hypnosis*, **20**(4),179–197. doi:10.1002/ch.277

Flory, N., Martinez Salazar, G. M., & Lang, E. V. (2007). Hypnosis for acute distress management during medical procedures. *International Journal of Clinical and Experimental Hypnosis*, **55**, 303–371.

Fredrickson, B. L., Cohn, M. A., Coffey, K. A., Pek, J., & Finkel, S. M. (2008). Open hearts build lives: positive emotions, induced through loving-kindness meditation, build consequential personal resources. *Journal of Personality and Social Psychology*, **95**(5), 1045.

Frewen, P., Lundberg, E., MacKinley, J., & Wrath, A. (2011). Assessment of response to mindfulness meditation: meditation breath attention scores in association with subjective measures of state and trait mindfulness and difficulty letting go of depressive cognition. *Mindfulness*, **2**, 254–269.

Gifford, E. V., Kohlenberg, B. S., Hayes, S. C., Antonuccio, D. O., & Piasecki, M. M. (2004). Acceptance-based treatment for smoking cessation. *Behavior Therapy*, **35**, 689–704.

Goldfried, M. R., & Davison, G. C. (1976). *Clinical behavior therapy*. New York: Holt Rinehart & Winston.

Gratz, K. L., Bornovalova, M. A., Delany-Brumsey, A., Nick, B., & Lejuez, C. W. (2007). A laboratory-based study of the relationship between childhood abuse and experiential avoidance among inner-city substance users: the role of emotional nonacceptance. *Behavior Therapy*, **38**(3), 256–268.

Green, J.P. (1996). Cognitive-behavioral hypnotherapy for smoking cessation: a case study in a group setting. In S. J. Lynn, I. Kirsch, & J. W. Rhue (Eds.), *Casebook of clinical hypnosis* (pp. 223–248). Washington, DC: American Psychological Association.

Green, J. P. (1999). Hypnosis and the treatment of smoking cessation and weight loss. In I. Kirsch, A. Capafons, E. Cardena-Buelna, & S. Amigo (Eds.), *Clinical hypnosis and self-regulation: cognitive behavioral perspectives* (pp. 249–276). Washington, DC: American Psychological Association.

Green, J. P., Laurence, J-R., & Lynn, S. J. (2014). Hypnosis and psychotherapy: from mindfulness to Mesmer. *Psychology of Consciousness* **1**(2), 1999–2012.

Gross, J. J., & John, O. P. (2003). Individual differences in two emotion regulation processes: implications for affect, relationships, and well-being. *Journal of Personality and Social Psychology*, **85**(2), 348.

Gross, J. J., & Levenson, R.W. (1993). Emotional suppression: physiology, self-report, and expressive behavior. *Journal of Personality and Social Psychology*, **64**, 970–986.

Gruzelier, J., Gray, M., & Horn, P. (2002). The involvement of frontally modulated attention in hypnosis and hypnotic susceptibility: cortical evoked potential evidence. *Contemporary Hypnosis*, **19**(4), 179–189.

Gryffin, P., Chen, W., & Erengue, N. (2014). Knowledge, attitudes and beliefs of meditation in college students: barrier and opportunities. *American Journal of Educational Research*, **2**, 189–192.

Hayes, S. C., Strosahl, K. D., & Wilson, K. G. (1999). *Acceptance and commitment therapy: an experiential approach to behavior change*. New York: Guilford Press.

Hayes, S. C., & Wilson, K. G. (2003). Mindfulness: method and process. *Clinical Psychology*, **10**(2), 161–165.

Hughes, J. R. (1995). Combining behavioral therapy and pharmacotherapy for smoking cessation: an update. In L. S. Onken, J. D. Blaine, & J. J. Boren (Eds.), *Integrating behavior therapies with medication in the treatment of drug dependence: NIDA Research Monograph* (pp. 92–109). Monograph no. 150. Washington, DC: US Government Printing Office.

Kabat-Zinn, J. (2003). Mindfulness-based interventions in context: past, present, and future. *Clinical psychology: Science and Practice*, **10**(2), 144–156.

Kerr, C. E., Josyula, K., & Littenberg, R. (2011). Developing an observing attitude: an analysis of meditation diaries in an MBSR clinical trial. *Clinical Psychology and Psychotherapy*, **18**(1), 80–93.

Kirsch, I. (1990). Changing expectations: a key to effective psychotherapy. Pacific Grove, CA: Brooks/Cole.

Kirsch, I., & Lynn, S. J. (1997). Hypnotic involuntariness and the automaticity of everyday life. *American Journal of Clinical Hypnosis*, **40**, 329–348.

Kirsch, I., & Lynn, S.J. (1999). The automaticity of behavior and clinical psychology. *American Psychologist*, *54*, 504–515.

Kirsch, I., Montgomery, G., & Sapirstein, G. (1995). Hypnosis as an adjunct to cognitive- behavioral psychotherapy: a meta-analysis. *Journal of Consulting and Clinical Psychology*, **63**(2), 214.

Koole, S. L. (2009). The psychology of emotion regulation: an integrative review. *Cognition and Emotion*, **23**(1), 4–41.

Kroger, W. S., & Yapko, M. D. (2007). *Clinical and experimental hypnosis: in medicine, dentistry, and psychology*. Philadelphia: J.B. Lippincott.

Lai, D. T., Cahill, K., Qin, Y., & Tang, J. L. (2010). Motivational interviewing for smoking cessation. *Cochrane Database Systematic Reviews*, *1*, doi: 10.1002/14651858.CD006936.pub2.

Lancaster, T., & Stead, L. F. (2004). Self-help interventions for smoking cessation. *Cochrane Database of Systematic Reviews*,3, Oct 18; CD000165.

Lazarus, A. A. (1973). "Hypnosis" as a facilitator in behavior therapy. *International Journal of Clinical and Experimental Hypnosis*, **21**(1), 25–31.

Lazarus, A. A. (1999). A multimodal framework for clinical hypnosis. In I. Kirsch, A. Capafons, E. Cardena-Buelna, & S. Amigo (Eds.), *Clinical hypnosis and self-regulation: cognitive-behavioral perspectives* (pp. 181–210).Washington, DC: American Psychological Association.

Linehan, M. M. (1993). *Cognitive-behavioral treatment of borderline personality disorder*. New York: Guilford Press.

Lynn, S., Barnes, S., Deming, A., & Accardi, M. (2010). Hypnosis, rumination, and depression: catalyzing attention and mindfulness-based treatments. *International Journal of Clinical and Experimental Hypnosis*, **58**(2), 202–221.

Lynn, S. J., & Kirsch, I. (2006). *Essentials of clinical hypnosis: an evidence-based approach*. Washington, DC: American Psychological Association.

Lynn, S. J., Das, L. S., Hallquist, M., & Williams, J. (2006). Mindfulness, acceptance, and hypnosis: cognitive and clinical perspectives. *International Journal of Clinical and Experimental Hypnosis*, **54**,143–166.

Lynn, S. J., Kirsch, I., Barabasz, A., Cardena, E., & Patterson, D. (2000). Hypnosis as an empirically supported adjunctive technique: the state of the evidence. *International Journal of Clinical and Experimental Hypnosis*, **48**, 343–361.

Lynn, S. J., Kirsch, I., Knox, J., & Lilienfeld, S. (2006). Hypnosis and neuroscience: implications for the altered state debate. In G. Jamieson (Ed.), *Hypnosis and conscious states: the cognitive-neuroscience perspective* (pp. 145–165). New York/Oxford: Oxford University Press.

Lynn, S. J., Malaktaris, A., Condon, L., Maxwell, R., & Cleere, C. (2012). The treatment of posttraumatic stress disorder: Cognitive hypnotherapy, mindfulness, and acceptance-based approaches. *American Journal of Clinical Hypnosis*, **54**(4), 311–330.

Lynn, S. J., Malaktaris, A., Maxwell, R., Mellinger, D., & van der Kloet, D. (2012). Do hypnosis and mindfulness practices inhabit the same domain? Research, clinical, and forensic implications. *Mind–Behavior Self Regulation*, **12**, 12–26.

Lynn, S. J., Neufeld, V., Rhue, J. W., & Matorin, A. (1993). Hypnosis and smoking cessation: a cognitive-behavioral treatment. In J. W. Rhue, S. J. Lynn, & I. Kirsch (Eds.), *Handbook of clinical hypnosis* (pp. 555–585). Washington, DC: American Psychological Association.

Lynn, S. J., Rhue, J., & Kirsch, I. (2010). *Handbook of clinical hypnosis* (2nd edn.). Washington, DC: American Psychological Association.

Lynn, S. J., Rhue, J., & Weekes, J. R. (1990). Hypnotic involuntariness: a social cognitive analysis. *Psychological Review*, **97**, 169–184.

Lynn, S. J., Snodgrass, M. J., Rhue, J., Nash, M., & Frauman, D. (1987). Attributions, involuntariness, and hypnotic rapport. *American Journal of Clinical Hypnosis*, **30**, 36–34.

MacLeod, C. (2011). Hypnosis and the control of attention: where to from here? *Consciousness and Cognition*, **20**, 321–324.

Malaktaris, A., Lemons, P., Lynn, S. J., & Condon, L. (2015). Chilling out: meditation, relaxation, and yoga. In S. J. Lynn, W. O'Donohue, & S. O. Lilienfeld (Eds.), *Better, stronger, wiser: health, happiness, and well-being. Better living through psychological science* (pp. 142–167). New York: SAGE.

Marlatt, G. A. (1994). Addiction, mindfulness, and acceptance. In S. C. Hayes, N. S.Jacobson, V. M. Follette, & M. J. Dougher (Eds.), *Acceptance and change: content and context in psychotherapy* (pp. 175–197). Reno, NV: Context Press.

Marlatt, G. A. (2002). Buddhist philosophy and the treatment of addictive behavior. *Cognitive and Behavioral Practice*, **9**, 44–49.

Moore, A., & Malinowski, P. (2009). Meditation, mindfulness and cognitive flexibility. *Consciousness and Cognition*, **18**, 176–186.

Nash, M. R., & Barnier, A. J. (Eds.). (2008). *The Oxford handbook of hypnosis: theory, research, and practice*. Oxford, UK: Oxford University Press.

Neron, S., & Stephenson, R. (2007). Effectiveness of hypnotherapy with cancer patient's trajectory: emesis, acute pain, and analgesia and anxiolysis in procedures. *International Journal of Clinical and Experimental Hypnosis*, **55** (3), 336–354.

Neufeld, V., & Lynn, S. J. (1988). A single-session group self-hypnosis smoking cessation: a brief communication. *International Journal of Clinical and Experimental Hypnosis*, **36**, 75–79.

Ostafin, B. D., & Marlatt, G. A. (2008). Surfing the urge: experiential acceptance moderates the relation between automatic alcohol motivation and hazardous drinking. *Journal of Social and Clinical Psychology*, **27**, 404–418.

Ritschel, L. A., & Ramirez, C. L. (2015). Emotional regulation: staying in control. In S. J. Lynn, W. O'Donohue, & S. O. Lilienfeld (Eds.), *Healthier, happier, wiser: better living through psychological science* (pp. 14–40). New York: Wiley-Blackwell.

Rivers, S. M., & Spanos, N. P. (1981). Personal variables predicting voluntary participation in and attrition from a meditation program. *Psychological Reports*, **49**(3), 795–801.

Salters-Pedneault, K., Tull, M. T., & Roemer, L. (2004). The role of avoidance of emotional material in the anxiety disorders. *Applied and Preventive Psychology*, **11**(2), 95–114.

Sayette, M. A. (2004). Self-regulatory failure and addiction. In R. F. Baumeister & K. D. Vohs (Eds.), *Handbook of self-regulation: research, theory, and applications* (pp. 447–465). New York: Guilford Press.

Sears, S. R., Kraus, S., Carlough, K., & Treat, E. (2011). Perceived benefits and doubts of participants in a weekly meditation study. *Mindfulness*, **2**, 167–174.

Segal, Z. V., Williams, S., & Teasdale, J. (2002). *Mindfulness-based cognitive therapy for depression: a new approach to preventing relapse*. New York: Guilford Press.

Semmens-Wheeler, R., & Dienes, Z. (2012). The contrasting role of higher order awareness in hypnosis and meditation. *Journal of Mind–Body Regulation*, **2**(1), 43–57.

Shapiro Jr, D. H. (2008). Meditation: Self-regulation strategy and altered state of consciousness. Piscataway, NJ: Transaction Publishers.

Skinner, B. F. (1972). *Beyond freedom and dignity*. New York: Knopf.

Smallwood, J., & Schooler, J. W. (2006). The restless mind. *Psychological Bulletin*, **132**(6), 946–958.

Smith, J. C. (1978). Personality correlates of continuation and outcome in meditation and erect sitting control treatments. *Journal of Consulting and Clinical Psychology*, **46**, 272–279.

Sood, A., Ebbert, J. O., Sood, R., & Stevens, S. R. (2006). Complementary treatments for tobacco cessation: a survey. *Nicotine and Tobacco Research*, **8**, 767–771.

Wegner, D. M. (1989). White bears and other unwanted thoughts: Suppression, obsession, and the psychology of mental control. New York: Penguin Press.

Wegner, D. (2011). Setting free the bears: escape from thought suppression. *American Psychologist*, **66**(8), 671–680.

Williams, J., Hallquist, M., Cole, A., Barnes, S., & Lynn, S. J. (2010). Mindfulness, acceptance, and hypnosis: artful integration. In S. J. Lynn, I. Kirsch, & J. W. Rhue (Eds.), *Handbook of Clinical Hypnosis* (2nd edn.). Washington, DC: American Psychological Association.

Williams, J., & Lynn, S. J. (2010). Acceptance: an historical and conceptual review. *Imagination, Cognition, and Personality*, **30**, 5–56.

Wolpe, J. (1958). *Psychotherapy by reciprocal inhibition*. Stanford, CA: Stanford University Press.

Yapko, M. D. (2011). *Mindfulness and hypnosis: the power of suggestion to transform experience*. New York, NY: W. W. Norton & Co.

Yapko, M. D. (Ed.). (2013). *Hypnosis and treating depression: applications in clinical practice*. London, UK: Routledge.

Zeidan, F., Johnson, S. K., Gordon, N. S., & Goolkasian, P. (2010). Effects of brief and sham mindfulness meditation on mood and cardiovascular variables. *Journal of Alternative and Complementary Medicine*, **16**(8), 867–873. doi:http://dx.doi.org/10.1089/acm.2009.0321

Part 7

Conclusion

Chapter 24

Hypnosis and meditation as vehicles to elucidate human consciousness

Amir Raz

Abstract

From Jean-Martin Charcot in Europe to the Tantras of East Asia, both hypnosis and meditation seem to index consciousness in some uncommon, atypical fashion and provide a way to study subjective mental states from the first-person perspective. Whereas the anterior cingulate cortex seems to be a key node in both hypnosis and some forms of meditation, the dorsolateral prefrontal cortex appears to engage in hypnosis as a function of suggestion and, in meditation, as a function of proficiency. Studying such special mental phenomena and their underlying neural substrates paves the road to a more scientific understanding of human consciousness.

Introduction

This edited volume is a tribute to my co-editor—student, colleague, and (meditation) mentor, Michael Lifshitz. This writing project came about following a series of nocturnal discussions I held with Michael in the basement of the Institute for Community and Family Psychiatry at the Jewish General Hospital in Montreal. Once I put the bug in his ear, it was easy to facilitate this book through continuing conversations at McGill University and by reading and interacting with multiple experts—both scholars and practitioners. Oxford University Press immediately recognized the value of this contribution, and once the skeletal backbone of the book was in place and we had decided on the contributors we wanted to line up and the direction we wanted to forge, Michael gradually took charge of this production, making the entire transition—from student, to colleague, to mentor—all within the process of compiling this book. He taught me a great deal about the field of meditation and I am grateful to him.

Talking about hypnosis and meditation, especially to a Western audience, often draws on overlapping terminology, using words such as "absorption," "dissociation," and "attention." It also conjures up folklore images of hysterical women under the spell of an authority figure (à la Charcot), movies by Woody Allen, esoteric monks in caves (à la Tantras in East Asia), and the Dalai Lama.

Both hypnosis and meditation seem to index consciousness in some uncommon atypical fashion—away from the bustle of modern life. In this regard, hypnosis and meditation appear similar. However, on many dimensions, hypnosis and meditation seem disparate. For example, we often construe hypnosis through the lens of hypnotherapy as an acute therapeutic intervention for a specific problem, whereas meditation is almost akin to a way of life—a practice that, like exercise or prayer, becomes a part of an entrenched routine. In this regard, meditation seems more closely yoked with religion than with hypnosis, just as a pre-established proclivity towards "suspension of disbelief" seems more deeply entrenched in the lore of hypnosis than in that of meditation.

Automaticity, involuntariness, and the "effortless effort" are phenomena more ubiquitous in the realm of hypnosis than of meditation. Hypnosis, even self-hypnosis, often comes with an operator or a hypnotic coach, whereas meditation is usually a solo experience. With time, meditators get better and more skilled, whereas highly hypnotizable individuals seem biologically wired to act on suggestion of the hypnotic type. Attention is more externally (and internally) mediated in hypnosis and meditation, respectively.

Organization

My training and expertise lie in the field of information processing in the brain, with an emphasis on the cognitive neuroscience of attention. Over time, I have learned about hypnosis and altered consciousness and leveraged empirical paradigms that involved hypnosis to design many unusual experiments, which probed circumscribed questions. My interest in meditation came about naturally and through my interactions with colleagues, students, clinicians, and scholars who educated me about the roots of contemplative practices and the presence of meditative components in nearly every major religion. As I embarked on my quest for a deeper understanding of meditation, I quickly realized that the presence of the word "meditation" in the popular media has given it the designation of a "term of art," entailing multiple meanings. Meditation could refer to a Buddhist-like tradition of compassion and loving kindness, fostering an altruistic perspective toward others; or to mindfulness—open-monitoring meditation—which tries to cultivate a less reactive awareness to affect, thoughts, and sensations to prevent them from spiraling out of control and creating mental distress.

In organizing the framework for this book, we did not make clear distinctions between types and stages of meditation. While we fully acknowledge that meditation is hardly monolithic, we treat meditation, including non-classical forms of meditation, as a large set of different meditation derivatives, although we appreciate that many are uniquely discernible. As a case in point, in classical concentration meditation, one of the principle guiding tenets encourages practitioners to focus continuously on a single target; anything else forms a distraction. The goal is to invest attention uninterruptedly, over time, without breaking the ribbon of concentration. However, in pure awareness meditation, the concept of distraction becomes a moot point because the goal is to train continuous, uninterrupted monitoring and to eliminate inflection points and lapses from the global windshield of awareness. Thus, in this book, we refer broadly to meditation as the overarching cultivation of basic human qualities, such as a more robust and lucid mind and emotional stability. (In this book, we have hardly touched on the development of a sense of caring, compassion, and love, but those too are important components of meditation.) We also construe meditation as a process of familiarization with a more tranquil and supple approach to living and being.

In principle, meditation—like hypnosis—appears straightforward: a routine that can be practiced just about anywhere; requiring neither equipment nor special attire but just a comfortable posture—neither too stiff, nor overly slack—and an attitude accepting of self-change; cogitations over well-being; wishing for the lifting of suffering; and so on. The important point, however, is that practitioners must learn to control their mind, which is often frazzled and races on inner tangents. Honing the mind requires mental clarity and the ability to let go of automatic mental conditioning and internal chatter. These processes are at the heart of a new science of self-regulation and top-down control—a science wherein hypnosis, too, is a partner (Raz, 2011).

The similarities between meditation and hypnosis are striking. Whether hypnotizability is a biological propensity akin to a fingerprint or a learned trait, the highly hypnotizable individual, like the expert meditator, is a special participant that researchers would like to keep in a "gold cage." Scientists can learn a great deal from how these unique individuals process information and from the mental dynamic their brains seem to follow as they perform their extraordinary neural computations.

Both hypnosis and meditation have witnessed a scientific renaissance, at least in the sense that serious scientists have taken an interest in them, both theoretical and applied, to elucidate key questions about cognition, emotion, thought, and action; both hypnosis and meditation are fast becoming important tools in the clinical armamentarium of practitioners. In the field of hypnosis, the conservative medical community has been exposed to cumulative accounts that often triangulate social studies of medicine and psychosocial factors in clinical science (Gauld, 1995; Oakley & Halligan, 2013). In meditation, the trend has been more recent. In the 1980s, the Dalai Lama started a dialogue about science and Buddhism, which led to the study of contemplative science through the establishment of the Mind and Life Institute. The term "contemplative neuroscience," which emerged around 2000, invited scientists to study the brains of expert meditators. Subsequently, monks and other practitioners of Buddhism came to participate in multiple experiments conducted by leading cognitive neuroscientists.

Philosophically and practically, the goals of meditation overlap with many of the objectives of clinical psychology, psychiatry, preventive medicine, and even aspects of education. Research findings now suggest that meditation may be effective in treating depression and chronic pain and in promoting a general sense of well-being. The hypnosis literature is replete with parallel accounts (Landry & Raz, in press). I think that part of the allure of this type of research lies in the comforting realization that the human brain—in this case, the adult brain—is transformable through experience and neuroplasticity. In the same way that a brain region that controls the movement of the fingers of a pianist becomes progressively more robust with mastery of piano performance, a similar process appears to happen when the meditator/hypnotizee modulates brain states to achieve a form of inner self-regulation. In this regard, these processes seem to rewire brain modules to produce substantial effects beyond the mind and brain and into the body.

Consciousness and Brain

Hypnosis and meditation provide a way to study consciousness and subjective mental states from the first-person perspective (Lifshitz, Cusumano, & Raz, 2014). The importance of such phenomenological accounts relate directly to the exceptional performance some of these master meditators/hypnotic virtuosos demonstrate. For example, highly hypnotizable individuals performed on benchmark cognitive tasks with unusual measures (Lifshitz, Aubert Bonn, Fischer, Kashem, & Raz, 2013; Raz, Fan, & Posner, 2005); expert meditators were able to volitionally sustain specific neuroelectrophysiological (EEG) patterns (e.g., high-amplitude gamma-band oscillations) relevant for cognitive and affective functions during learning and conscious perception (Lutz, Greischar, Rawlings, Ricard, & Davidson, 2004; Lutz et al., 2009). More importantly, hypnosis and meditation often instigate experiences reminiscent of epiphanies or mental awakenings—not of a chthonic nature or related to occult experiences but, rather, insightful and grounded in self-reflection. The stability and robustness of such awakenings hold implications for mental health.

Despite some reservations I harbor concerning the popularity of mindfulness even in the face of some seemingly robust clinical findings regarding its therapeutic value in the West, changes in the experience of the self (e.g., as indexed through changes in neural activations at the medial prefrontal cortex and insula) provide important clues to understanding the neurobiological underpinnings of both hypnotic and meditative phenomena (cf. Macdonald & Raz, 2014).

Other changes attributed to hypnosis or meditation seem to depend on the type of hypnotic suggestion and also type of meditation and level of experience, namely, changes in the experience of the self and the use or suspension of metacognitive monitoring. Whereas the anterior cingulate cortex seems to be a key node in both hypnosis and some forms of meditation, the dorsolateral prefrontal cortex appears to engage in hypnosis as a function of suggestion and, in meditation, as a function of proficiency. A variety of meditation styles, including focused attention and loving kindness, link with deactivation of the posterior cingulate cortex (Brewer & Garrison, 2014)—an area we construe as a primary hub of the default mode network. Cumulative findings begin to sketch a landscape wherein concepts such as the "sense of self," "sense of control," and "levels of processing awareness" nest at different recursive layers within our neural core. Unpacking these concepts would pave the road not just to a better scientific understanding of their mechanisms and functional systems, but also to practical applications that would aid mental health and enhance quality of life (Raz & Macdonald, 2015).

References

Brewer, J. A., & Garrison, K. A. (2014). The posterior cingulate cortex as a plausible mechanistic target of meditation: findings from neuroimaging. *Ann NY Acad Sci*, **1307**, 19–27. doi: 10.1111/nyas.12246

Gauld, A. (1995). *A history of hypnotism*. Cambridge, UK: Cambridge University Press.

Landry, M., & Raz, A. (in press). Neurophysiology of hypnosis. In G. Elkins (Ed.), *The clinician's guide to medical and psychological hypnosis: foundations, systems, applications and professional issues*. New York, NY: Springer.

Lifshitz, M., Aubert Bonn, N., Fischer, A., Kashem, I. F., & Raz, A. (2013). Using suggestion to modulate automatic processes: from Stroop to McGurk and beyond. *Cortex*, **49**(2), 463–473. doi: 10.1016/j.cortex.2012.08.007

Lifshitz, M., Cusumano, E. P., & Raz, A. (2014). Meditation and hypnosis at the intersection between phenomenology and cognitive science. In S. Schmidt & H. Walach (Eds.), *Meditation—neuroscientific approaches and philosophical implications. Studies in neuroscience, consciousness and spirituality*: **2**. Switzerland: Springer International Publishing.

Lutz, A., Greischar, L. L., Rawlings, N. B., Ricard, M., & Davidson, R. J. (2004). Long-term meditators self-induce high-amplitude gamma synchrony during mental practice. *Proc Natl Acad Sci USA*, **101**(46), 16369–16373. doi: 10.1073/pnas.0407401101

Lutz, A., Slagter, H. A., Rawlings, N. B., Francis, A. D., Greischar, L. L., & Davidson, R. J. (2009). Mental training enhances attentional stability: neural and behavioral evidence. *J Neurosci*, **29**(42), 13418–13427. doi: 10.1523/JNEUROSCI.1614-09.2009

Macdonald, E. B., & Raz, A. (2014). The marginalization of phenomenological consciousness. *Frontiers in Human Neuroscience*, **8**(306), 1–2.

Oakley, D. A., & Halligan, P. W. (2013). Hypnotic suggestion: opportunities for cognitive neuroscience. *Nat Rev Neurosci*, **14**(8), 565–576. doi: 10.1038/nrn3538

Raz, A. (2011). Hypnosis: a twilight zone of the top-down variety. Few have never heard of hypnosis but most know little about the potential of this mind–body regulation technique for advancing science. *Trends Cogn Sci*, **15**(12), 555–557. doi: 10.1016/j.tics.2011.10.002

Raz, A., Fan, J., & Posner, M. I. (2005). Hypnotic suggestion reduces conflict in the human brain. *Proc Natl Acad Sci USA*, **102**(28), 9978–9983. doi: 10.1073/pnas.0503064102

Raz, A., & Macdonald, E. B. (2015). Paying attention to a field in crisis: psychiatry, neuroscience, and functional systems of the brain. In L. J. Kirmayer, R. Lemelson, & C. A. Cummings (Eds.), *Re-visioning psychiatry: cultural phenomenology, critical neuroscience, and global mental health* (pp. 273–304). Cambridge, UK: Cambridge University Press.

Afterword

Daniel Brown

Introduction

Hypnosis and meditation offers a comprehensive understanding of current scientific research comparing hypnosis and meditation. The chapters present data within useful categories to organize research findings, such as procedure versus outcome; short- versus long-term effects; trait versus state; cognitive and social influences; and contextual influences. The value of these chapters lies in the fact that they provide a relatively consistent view of the similarities and differences between hypnosis and meditation—a line of inquiry we opened many years ago (Brown, Forte, Rich, & Epstein, 1983).

According to the findings in this book, both hypnosis and meditation are states of absorption and directed attention. Both seem to be states of consciousness characterized by shifting out of a normal waking busy condition, thought rumination, and mind wandering. There also are important differences between hypnosis and meditation. Attention control is more externally guided in hypnosis and more internally guided in meditation. Involuntariness and self-deception is more apparent in hypnosis than meditation. Other changes attributed to hypnosis or meditation seem to depend on the type of hypnotic suggestion and also the type of meditation and level of experience, namely, changes in the experience of the self and the use or suspension of metacognitive monitoring. At least some authors (e.g., see Chapters 19 and 23) argue that suggestive effects are also operative in meditation as in hypnosis.

The chapters on neuroimaging (e.g., see Chapters 11 and 18) also point to consistent regions of interest relevant to understanding hypnosis and meditation. First, it is very clear that anterior cingulate cortex (ACC) activation is important in both hypnosis and at least concentration meditation, and that such activation is related to enhanced, effortful, selective attention in both hypnosis and concentration meditation. Second, both hypnosis and meditation are states that are a response to mind-wandering mode (see Chapter 11). The role of the dorsolateral prefrontal cortex (DLPFC) appears to depend, in hypnosis, on the type of suggestion given and, in meditation, on the level of practice. For example, DLPFC deactivation in hypnosis via suggestion may signify a suspension of metacognitive processes as seen, for example, in uncritical acceptance, but other studies report an activation of the DLPFC in hypnosis (e.g., Dienes & Hutton, 2013). In concentration meditation, both novices and experienced meditators activated the ACC, but only experienced meditators activated the right DLPFC, coincident with metacognitive monitoring of instances of becoming distracted (Brefczynski-Lewis, Lutz, Schafer, Levinson, & Davidson, 2007). The role of the medial prefrontal cortex (mPFC) in sense of self also seems to undergo important changes in hypnosis and meditation, also dependent on the type of instruction given and level of practice. At least some studies suggest that embodied awareness associated with insular activation is important in both hypnosis and meditation, but the critical issue is what *level* of awareness the particular type of meditation practice represents.

A limitation across these chapters, reflecting a general tendency in the field, is the failure to make clear distinctions between types and stages of meditation. As Anne Harrington (Chapter 2) suggests, meditation is a heterogeneity of methods. For example, Lutz, Slagter, Dunne, and Davidson (2008) have made an important distinction between focused meditation (classical concentration meditation) and pure awareness meditations. In classical concentration meditation, focus is repeatedly and continuously on a single concentration object, and anything other than that is distraction. The goal is to sustain concentration completely (without apportioning attention to other things) and continuously on the concentration object. There is no concept of distraction in pure awareness meditation. The goal is to train continuous, uninterrupted awareness (or to diminish discontinuities and lapses in awareness) of whatever comes up next in the field of awareness. Pure awareness meditations are associated with deactivation of the posterior cingulate cortex (PCC; Brewer & Garrison, 2014).

The Problem of Using Non-Classical Forms of Meditation in Western Research

The problem with this book comparing hypnosis and meditation, and modern Western studies on meditation in general, is that it relies largely on non-classical forms of meditation. For example, in the Indian Hindu system, the great work on meditation is Patanjali's Yoga Sutras (Mishra, 1973). Maharishi Mahesh Yogi developed a greatly simplified version of this meditation for Westerners, transcendental meditation (TM), and it was the TM version, not the classical Yoga Sutras version that became the main focus of scientific research in the West (Yogi, 1968). Several problems arise here. First, of the four stages (or chapters) in the Yoga Sutras, TM practice is largely restricted to the first two levels only. The more advanced practices, and in my opinion, those most relevant to mental health, are largely eliminated from the version of TM taught in the West. Furthermore, TM de-emphasizes the critical role of posture as a foundation for concentration meditation. Postural practice is the first, and foundational, limb of the eight ingredients of concentration meditation in the classical Yoga Sutras. In his studies of electromyographic (EMG) response in novice and advanced Zen meditators, Akishigi (1970) found that, with respect to the striate musculature, meditation is best seen as an even output and distribution of muscle work over time. The effort to hold a firm meditation posture had two positive effects. First, it guaranteed a certain optimal level of alertness, so that the meditator was less likely to get sleepy or dull. Second, mind wandering was significantly reduced as a result of holding a good meditation posture over time. The simplified TM, as compared to the classical Yoga Sutras, by virtue of eliminating the traditional meditation posture, may confound pure concentration meditation with the default mode of mind wandering and a general relaxation effect.

Similarly, the now very popular Burmese version of mindfulness meditation has become the standard for the majority of the comparative studies on hypnosis and meditation. A specific type of Burmese mindfulness, originated by Mahasi Sayadaw, has become popular in the West. However, most proponents of mindfulness fail to realize that it is a hybrid. The great treatise on the stages of meditation in early Buddhism is the Visuddhimagga (The Path of Purification) (Buddhaghosa, 1976). As part of what anthropologists call a revitalization movement, Mahasi Sayadaw greatly simplified the practices of the Visuddhimagga and created a very accessible form of meditation (Sayadaw, 1965). Addressing changes in the self by means of classical meditation on the five aggregates was eliminated. Furthermore, the new system advocated spending some time concentrating on the breath in order to calm the busy state of ordinary consciousness, and then to use labels to approximate on-going continuous awareness, free of lapses in awareness. The result of the new synthesis is essentially a hybrid—a mixture of concentration and pure awareness practice. Functional magnetic resonance imaging (fMRI) studies on this type of mindfulness tend to show patterns of activation/deactivation characteristic of both concentration and pure awareness meditations (Holzel et al., 2008), but not a strong representation of the effects of either pure type of meditation.

Therefore, given the uncritical acceptance of Burmese mindfulness in the majority of scientific research studies on meditation, I am not at all convinced we have produced a clear picture of the phenomenological and neuroimaging effects of deep concentration meditation or awareness meditation in their pure, classical forms.

Awakening as the Heart of Meditation

Polito and Connors (Chapter 10) make an important distinction between procedure and product (effects). While that distinction has been useful in framing our understanding of hypnosis, it has not been applied adequately to understanding meditation. The explosion of studies on the therapeutic effects of mindfulness makes it very clear that, in the West, we see the product or outcome of meditation mainly in terms of the clinical benefits of mindfulness. This view is unfortunately narrow and reductionistic. Thupten Jinpa (Chapter 3) raises an important point, namely, that "meditation is part of the larger soteriological project of spiritual awakening". Soteriology means a system of liberation (i.e. freedom from suffering).

As a translator, for over 40 years, of meditation texts from Sanskrit, Pali, and mostly Tibetan, and as someone who has taught Indo-Tibetan meditation retreats for over 35 years (as well as being a Western psychologist), I am amazed how rarely awakening and enlightenment are mentioned as end points in meditation in the West. It seems to me that if we were being fair to the great Buddhist meditation systems, we might want to learn about what the texts say about the higher states and outcomes. Furthermore, since the higher states and outcomes, according to the original texts, have far greater implications for mental health than foundational level meditation techniques, we would want to make these states the object of serious scientific inquiry. As is said in Great Completion meditation, since the experience of awakening is the confluence of all the great variety of Buddhist teachings, the fact that awakening is virtually totally ignored in scientific studies on meditation misses the heart of the teachings. With the phenomenological tools and neuroimaging resources now available and described in this book, there is no reason why these same tools could not be used to study the experience of awakening, or even higher meditation attainments.

The Three Turnings of the Wheel of Buddhism

As a scholar of Buddhism for over 40 years, I find the way mindfulness is construed by many of its proponents in the West short-sighted, because it belies crucial developments in the history of Buddhism in the past 2500 years. Within the framework of Tibetan Buddhism, for example, there are three major developments—called the Three Turnings of the Wheel of the Dharma. The First Turning of the Wheel characterizes the teachings of Shakyamuni Buddha as represented in the earliest written canons. The emphasis of these teachings is on the Four Noble Truths, the first being the "truth of suffering," and the Eightfold Path that defines the way out of everyday suffering. The Second Turning of the Wheel characterizes Mahayana Buddhism. Important new discoveries at this level of the Indian and Tibetan Mahayana tradition include a complete revision of the earlier concept of no-self into the self as an empty construction of mind; a revision of dissolution experience in deep meditation (as described in the Vissiddhimagga), into the very different experience of everything being here, all at once, in an inter-connected field via emptiness of time meditation; and based on that direct experience of inter-connectedness, a vision of bodhisattvas acting for the benefit of all beings within that field.

The Third Turning of the Wheel characterizes the Indo-Tibetan essence traditions—Great Gesture (Tibetan *phyag chen*), Great Completion (Tibetan, *rdzogs chen*), and the Buddhist tantras. All these traditions share a similar theory of mind, namely, that awakened awareness is inherent and always right here in the mind stream of each individual, but that layers and layers of constructions of mind cloud over and obscure direct realization of this awakened awareness. Awakened awareness is likened to the sun that always shines but that cannot be seen if covered by clouds. The application of emptiness meditation to all constructions of mind—self, thought, emotions, perceptions, the body, time, duality, and our information-processing system— systematically removes the clouds until recognizing our inherent awakened nature. Then, what shines forth is the inherent positivity of the awakened mind. The Lalitavistara Sutra (Goswami, 2001) is one of the earliest sources on the 80 positive qualities of a realized mind. What followed later in the essence traditions was a very detailed set of methods to achieve this condition of flourishing positivity.

These Three Turnings of the Wheel are best understood much like we in the West construe scientific revolutions in the West (Kuhn, 1962). In science, once enough anomalies are encountered, a major paradigm shift occurs (e.g., like the shift from Newtonian physics to quantum mechanics). In science, we tend to see such major shifts as significant improvements or advances in our scientific knowledge. As Westerners, however, we do not extend this same type of thinking to the Buddhist tradition. For example, we think that the teachings close to the original teachings of the Buddha must be the most authentic. However, this is a fallacy since the type of Buddhist mindfulness largely popularized in the West represents a very conservative reinterpretation of early Buddhist practices, which fails to acknowledge many of the substantial improvements in meditation methods and outcomes in Buddhism in the past 2500 years. This logical fallacy would be like a scientist in this day and age citing Ptolemaic texts proving that the earth is the center of the universe because Ptolemaic texts are older and more authoritative than the evidence that instigated the Copernican Revolution. So, let us see where such logical fallacies about Buddhism lead us.

The Problem of Self

Within the First Turning of the Wheel in Buddhism, there were three insights derived from meditation—suffering, impermanence, and no-self. Suffering pertains to the reactivity inherent in ordinary information processing, by which the mind moves toward what it likes to make more of the experience, or away from what it dislikes to make less of it. The outcome of this moment by moment reactivity is the experience of suffering. Secondly, observing one's own experience leads to the realization that everything changes and is therefore impermanent. Thirdly, systematic concentration reduces thought elaboration and, at some point, the sense of self is temporarily deconstructed. This temporary dropping away of the self as a constructed representation is called *anatta* (literally "no self") in Pali.

The original concept of no-self was problematic. Over the next 500 years in Buddhism, considerable debates and revisions occurred, the outcome of which was a very different idea, namely, the meditations on emptiness in general, and of emptiness of self in particular. The term emptiness is best understood as "merely a construction." The Mahayana Buddhist theory of emptiness is very similar to Western constructivist psychology, that is, that the mind operates by making constructions or representations for experience. With respect to self or personal identity, Western developmental psychology asserts that the psychological sense of self is not present at birth but is constructed, at between 12 and 20 months, as a function of the development of the capacity for representational thinking.

In everyday relative reality, the development of a psychological sense of self is useful in that the self becomes a central organizing principle, offers coherence of mind, and provides constancy across location and time. The Mahayana Buddhist view is that while operating out of a psychological sense of identity may be useful in everyday day, the main negative consequence is the habit of reification (Tibetan *dngos 'dzin*; literally, "take it as real"). Two problems arise from reification: firstly, the self has "grab," (Tibetan *'dzin pa*) (i.e., built-in reactivity that creates suffering); and secondly, the self, as a construction of mind, has the capacity to "obscure" or cloud over (Tibetan *mun pa*) the inherent awakened nature of the mind.

Mahayana emptiness, as a meditation practice, is not designed to get rid of the self. The problem with the "no-self" concept is the risk of developing a nihilistic view that the self is something to eliminate in meditation, or of developing an eternalistic view, that the self is independently existing and something that becomes even more reified in meditation. The Mahayana belief is to view the self for what it is, namely, merely a construction, so as to "see beyond" it (Tibetan *lhag mthong*). From a Mahayana perspective, the problem is that the self or personal identity, like all other constructions of mind, once reified, has the capacity to obscure seeing beyond it into the nature of awareness itself. Emptiness of self practice is an affirming negation of the tendency to experience the self as substantial and reified, or more accurately, as independently existing, so as to support a level of awareness that is cleaned up of the self, as the basis of operation for the meditation. The purpose of emptiness meditation is to shift one's basis of operation from a sense of "self" to a sense of awareness itself.

Moving beyond the self to operate out of a deeper awareness in meditation does not necessitate getting rid of the self. What opens up in the meditation is a pure field of awareness, no longer clouded over by the ordinary convention of the self, or, to use a Tibetan metaphor, like separating the pure yak milk from the solid curds.

Why are the practices of emptiness of self important to mental health in the West? Firstly, because "self grab" is considered the main cause of suffering in Mahayana Buddhism and, secondly, because the direct experience of awakening becomes clouded over by the construction of the self and other constructions of mind. The stability of awakening has major implications for mental health.

One problem with the type of Burmese mindfulness that has become so popular in Western science and psychotherapy is that it may fail to address the issue of the self adequately. Other than an instruction to "notice the mental processes engaged in noticing" (Sayadaw, 1965, p. 6), there is no explicit meditation in that system to handle the problem of the self. Moreover, an early attempt at analyzing the self according to First Turning of the Wheel practice, namely, the very detailed practice of analyzing the five aggregates (Buddhaghosa, 1976), is not mentioned in the revisionist Burmese mindfulness developed by Mahasi Sayadaw. Thus, the version of mindfulness that has become so popular in Western science and psychotherapy is virtually devoid of the basic meditation tools developed in various layers of the Buddhist tradition to handle the problem of the self. Thus, we are at risk of spawning a generation of mindfulness practitioners, teachers, and patients who are indeed practicing mindfulness, but who are either trying unduly to negate the self or to become unduly self important through mindfulness practice. Mindfulness practice, as currently taught, generally fails to accomplish what Toneatto and Courtice (Chapter 22) have correctly called "transforming narcissism into a deconstructed self."

Unfortunately, this version of Burmese mindfulness does not provide us in the West with the basic cultural tools and meditations to handle the issue of the self adequately, as other layers of the Buddhist tradition do.

Levels of Awareness and Realizations

Furthermore, in Burmese mindfulness as now taught in the West, the main goal has become to sustain continuous, non-reactive mindfulness. There is no concept of levels of awareness in this version of Burmese Buddhism, as compared to the Mahayana and essence traditions. In the essence traditions, the levels of awareness include:

1 Ordinary awareness confounded with thinking and other mental content;
2 Ordinary awareness relatively separated from thinking as a confound but still confounded by sense of self;
3 Awareness itself confounded by neither thought nor self;
4 Changeless, boundless, ocean-like awareness not confounded by the construction of conventional time;
5 Non-dual awareness;
6 Awakened awareness;
7 Simultaneous awareness across many fields at once; and
8 Enlightened awareness.

Enlightened awareness is not simply the complete transcendence of thought and emotion, as Tart in Chapter 9 asserts. In fact, an enlightened mind manifests what is called discriminating wisdom, wherein thought returns to its original purity, and the directionality and specificity of what was once thought, now with lightning speed and complete lack of interference, serves the benefit of others by being able to immediately know what each being needs, like an infinite array of rays of light directed in all directions.

According to the essence traditions, each level of awareness represents a distinct and quite noticeable shift in experience. Another way of viewing this path of awareness is from the perspective of removing various constructions of mind that cloud over levels of awareness. For example, concentration meditation calms thought activity sufficiently so that, at some point, it becomes experientially obvious to the meditator that he or she is operating out of pure awareness rather than out of thought ("awareness gone beyond thought"). Yet, nevertheless, the meditator is still operating out of his or her ordinary sense of self at this point. By practicing emptiness of the self, the meditator shifts the basis of operation from the self to a level of "awareness gone beyond the self," called awareness itself. However, the meditation experience still seems, at this point, to fluctuate within ordinary time. By practicing a version of emptiness of time meditation, the meditator shifts the basis of operation to ocean-like changeless, boundless awareness that goes beyond the convention of time. Nevertheless, awareness at this point still seems packaged within the constraints of our moment by moment information-processing system and still seems localized within our seeming individual consciousness. By using special "crossing over" instructions in the essence traditions, like "non-meditation" meditation instructions in Mahamudra or "thoroughly cutting through" instructions in Great Completion meditation, the meditator shifts the basis of operation from its localization within seeming individual consciousness to awakened awareness—a boundless wholeness of lucid, non-localized, awakened awareness/compassion.

These significant shifts in level of awareness are captured in the mantra of *Heart Sutra, gati gati paragati parasamgati bodhi svaha* ("gone; gone; gone way beyond; gone way, way beyond; oh! what a realization"). This pathway of levels of awareness can be unpacked as follows:

♦ awareness gone beyond being clouded over by thought;

♦ awareness itself gone beyond being clouded over by self representation;

♦ ocean-like changeless, boundless awareness gone way beyond being clouded over by the convention of time; and

♦ awakened awareness gone way, way beyond being clouded over by the constraints of our information-processing system and seeming localization in individual consciousness. Oh! What a realization!

The reason why the *Heart Sutra* mantra has been so popular is that is defines the path to awakening by showing how to shift through each level of awareness.

Unfortunately, the kind of Burmese mindfulness that has become popular in the West conveys nothing about these levels of awareness, and mindfulness per se, taken as the end point of practice, misses the main point and shows us very little about the path to awakening. As long as we stay on this track, awakening is unlikely to become valued as a source of inquiry, either in Western science or in Western meditation practice.

Furthermore, the essence traditions representing the Third Turning of the Wheel have shifted the emphasis of mental health from suffering to positivity. Once awakened, there is an entire world of meditation methods; for example, Great Completion meditation is designed to stabilize awakening so that the practitioner has awakened awareness as his or her basis of operation continuously, all the time—on and off the meditation pillow, and throughout the day, deep sleep, and dreaming sleep. Then, the meditator sets up a certain way of viewing unfolding experience so as to no longer form immediate karmic memory traces. When this practice is done correctly, it forces the mind to release the entire storehouse of ripening karmic impressions at a rapidly accelerated rate. This process is called dharmadhatu exhaustion, and if done uninterruptedly, it reaches completion in around 6 years. The outcome is profound. First, the propensities toward negative states of mind have become completely exhausted. Second, there are 80 types of positive states of mind that flourish at this point. The word for a Buddha in Sanskrit is derived from the root *budh* which means "realized one." When the Tibetans translated this term, they used a different compound term in Tibetan, *sang rgyas* ("purification/flourishing"). *Sang ba* means "purified" and *rgyas ba* means "flourishing." The compound term describes a level of realization wherein there is a complete absence of negative states and a flourishing of 80 positive states.

Some years ago, Jack Engler and I gave Rorschach inkblots to practitioners at different levels of practice and realization. The Rorschach protocols at this level of realization were like nothing we had ever seen before. Responses showed a complete absence of any negative emotions or conflicts and were consistent with deep positivity and caring across all ten cards (Brown & Engler, 1984).

There is no concept of flourishing of positive states in the First Turning of the Wheel of Buddhism, and likewise, the teachings about and methods for flourishing of all positive states is virtually absent in the kind of Burmese mindfulness that has become the main focal point of current scientific research in the West. Most proponents of contemporary mindfulness are locked into an early and limited Buddhist view that all life is suffering, and have never considered that the essence traditions within Buddhism move far beyond suffering and offer straightforward meditation methods to achieve flourishing.

Certainly, "purification/flourishing" has major implications for mental health that go far beyond our Western notions of such, and should therefore, in my opinion, become a main emphasis of scientific research. Developing research initiatives around flourishing of positive states is timely, especially since the popularization of Barbara Fredrickson's pioneering work on positive emotions and flourishing. She found that when the ratio of positive to negative emotions in daily life reaches a critical tipping point of greater than 11:1, that such individuals report flourishing in every aspect of their lives (2009). The Buddhist meditation attainment of purification/flourishing is a far more radical claim, and offers the key for lasting well-being in everyday life on all levels.

It is not my intention to be critical about the popularity of mindfulness. As a psychotherapist for over 40 years, I am impressed by the robust outcomes data on the therapeutic benefits of mindfulness. However, the very popularity of this version of mindfulness runs the risk of obscuring some very important issues. In a society where attention deficit disorder has become a cultural metaphor, techniques such as hypnosis and pure concentration, as compared to hybrid Burmese mindfulness, are likely to do a better job with activating the ACC and putting it back on line (see Chapter 16) because the methods more consistently entail sustained concentration (Baker & Brown, 2014). Moreover, some of the neuroimaging evidence discussed in this book suggests that changes in experiences of the self (mediated by the mPFC and insula) and pure awareness (mediated by the insula and likely by areas of the parietal system) are important in understanding hypnosis and meditation. I have tried to introduce to this Western scientific audience how sense of the self and levels of awareness are conceived at different levels in the Tibetan Buddhist tradition and show that these have significant implications for mental health and lasting well-being.

References

Akishige, Y. (1970). *Psychological studies on Zen*. Tokyo, Japan: Zen Institute of Komazawa University.

Baker, R. L., & Brown, D. (2014). On engagement: learning to pay attention. *University of Arkansas Law Review*, **36**, 337–385.

Brefczynski-Lewis, J. A., Lutz, A., Schafer, H. S. Levinson, D. B., & Davidson, R. J. (2007). Neural correlates of attentional expertise in long-term meditation practitioners. *Proceedings of the National Academy of Science USA*, **104** (27), 11483–11488.

Brewer, J. A., & Garrison, K. A. (2014). The posterior cingulate cortex as a plausible mechanistic target of meditation: findings from neuroimaging. *Annals of the New York Academy of Sciences*, **1307**, 19–27.

Brown, D., & Engler, J. (1984). A Rorschach study of the stages of mindfulness meditation. In D. Shapiro & R. Walsh (Eds.), *Meditation: classic and contemporary perspectives* (pp. 232–262). New York: Aldine.

Brown, D., Forte, M., Rich, P., & Epstein, G. (1983). Phenomenological differences among self hypnosis, mindfulness meditation and imagining. *Imagination, Cognition and Personality*, **2**, 291–309.

Buddhaghosa, B. (1976). *Visiddhimagga [The path of purification]*. B. Nyanamoli (Trans.). Berkeley, CA: Shambhala.

Dienes, Z., & Hutton, S. (2013). Understanding hypnosis metacognitively: RTMS applied to left DLPFC increases hypnotic suggestibility. *Cortex*, **49**, 386–392.

Fredrickson, B. (2009). *Positivity: top-notch research on the 3 to 1 ratio that will change your life*. New York: Random House.

Goswami, B. (2001). *Lalitavistara sutra*. B. Goswami (Trans.). Kolkata, India: The Asiatic Society.

Holzel, B. K., Ott, U., Gard, T., Hempel, H., Weygandt, M., Morgan, K., & Vaitl, D. (2008). Investigation of mindfulness meditation practitioners with voxel-based morphometry. *Social, Cognitive and Affective Neuroscience*, **3**(1), 55–61.

Kuhn, T. S. (1962). *The structure of scientific revolutions*. Chicago: University of Chicago Press.

Lutz, A., Slagter, H. A., Dunne, J. D., & Davidson, R. J. (2008). Attention regulation and monitoring in meditation. *Trends in Cognitive Science*, **12** (4), 163–169.

Mishra, R. S. (1973). *Yoga sutras: the textbook of yoga psychology*. New York: Doubleday.

Sayadaw, M. (1965). *The progress of insight through the stages of purification: a modern Pali treatise on Buddhist Satipatthana meditation*. N. Thera (Trans.). Kandy, Ceylon: The Forest Hermitage.

Yogi, M. M. (1968). *Transcendental meditation: serenity without drugs*. New York: Bantam Books.

Index

L

language of invisibility 57–8
lateral frontal cortex (LFC), PNM 94
lateral parietal cortices, PNM networks 90
lateral parietal lobe, spontaneous thought 192
Laurence, Jean-Roch 24
LC (locus coeruleus), noetic awareness 329
learned behaviors 387
levels of attainment, insight meditation *(vipaśyanā/
  lhag mthong)* 154–5, 154t
levels of awareness 454–6
level of training, meditation 289
Levinson, Steven 58
LFC (lateral frontal cortex), PNM 94
lhag mthong see insight meditation *(vipaśyanā/lhag
  mthong)*
lhai naljor see Tibetan deity-yoga *(lhai naljor)*
Libet paradigm, hypnosis 115
linguistic relativity 58
locus coeruleus (LC), noetic awareness 329
locus of hypnotic dissociation studies 227–35, 227f
  basic design 229
  hypnosis implications 235
  hypnotic induction 229
  meditation implications 235–6
  meditation practice 229–30
  Sustained Attention to Response Task 230–1
loneliness, tulpas 59, 61
long-term outcomes, meditation 175
Luhrmann, Tanya 64, 66

M

M 1, hypnosis 47
MAAS (Mindfulness Attention Awareness Scale) 110,
  177
Magic and mystery in Tibet (David-Néel) 58
magnetic resonance imaging (MRI)
  absorption 273–4
  functional *see* fMRI (functional magnetic resonance
    imaging)
Mahayana Buddhism 331
malleability of perceptions 376
mandala 36
maya 155
the Me
  changing of 389–92
    acceptance-based deconditioning 390–1
    hypnotic suggestion 391–2
  constraint by the I 385–6
  constraint of the I 388–9
  partitioning of 383
  as psychological construct 384–5
MEDEQ (Meditation Depth Questionnaire) 271, 271t
media 31–2
medial prefrontal cortex, spontaneous thought 192, 193
medial temporal lobe
  cognitive-emotional flexibility & neural
    plasticity 210–11, 211f
  spontaneous thought 192
meditation
  absorption *see* meditative absorptions *(dhyana)*
  aspiration 34

awakening 451
brain regions 343–67
  insular cortex 357
  posterior cingulate cortex 81
brain wave frequency changes 25
changes within state and across time 290
cognitive enhancement 264–5
conflict resolution 305–6
deep meditational states 271–2
default mode network 349, 352–3
definitions of 32–3, 33–4, 254, 345, 398
depth of 274–5
diverse array of 34
goals of 447
historical aspects 172
hypnosis *vs. see* comparisons between hypnosis and
  meditation
hypnotic responsiveness 431–2
as imagined simulation 34
individual differences 290
intrinsic connectivity networks 349–50
level of training 289
long-term outcomes 175
major types of 416–17
mindfulness *see* mindfulness meditation
motivation 6
neural correlates 175
neurophenomenology 81
non-classical forms 450–1
open monitoring *see* open monitoring (OM/
  receptive) meditation
path-related predictions 235
phenomenology 345
popularity 430
practice evaluation 289
practices (types) 430–1
  absorptive meditation *(jog com)* 34
  calm meditation *see* calm meditation *(śamatha)*
  concentrative *see* concentrative (focused attention/
    quieting/*samādhi*) meditation
  discursive meditation *(che gom)* 34
  focused attention *see* concentrative (focused
    attention/quieting/*samādhi*) meditation
  insight *see* insight meditation *(vipaśyanā/lhag
    mthong)*
  non-dual awareness meditation 349
  quieting *see* concentrative (focused attention/
    quieting/*samādhi*) meditation
  receptive (open monitoring) meditation 134
  visualization meditation 45–6
  Zen meditation 450
psychological processes 417–18
research 174–5
scientific study 34–5
as self-hypnosis 143–69
self-transformation *see* self-transformation
social context 179–80
social interactions 289
specific communications 289
spontaneous thought re-automatization 208–9
stages of 446
state descriptions 88